*Routledge Revivals*

# A History of Europe

First published in 1932, this book looks at a period that has often been thought of as a time of general decline in the most characteristic features of medieval civilisation. While acknowledging decline in many areas during this period — the power of the Church, feudalism, guilds, the Hanseatic League, the autonomy of towns and the end of the two Roman empires — the author argues that there was also signs of development. National consciousness, the power of the bourgeoisie and trade and industry all rose markedly in this period alongside intellectual and artistic achievements outside of Italy. This book asserts that in amongst the failure and decline new forces were creating new substitutes.

# A History of Europe
## From 1378 to 1494

### W.T. Waugh

First published in 1932
by Methuen

This edition first published in 2016 by Routledge
2 Park Square, Milton Park, Abingdon, Oxon, OX14 4RN
and by Routledge
711 Third Avenue, New York, NY 10017

*Routledge is an imprint of the Taylor & Francis Group, an informa business*

© 1932 W.T. Waugh

All rights reserved. No part of this book may be reprinted or reproduced or utilised in any form or by any electronic, mechanical, or other means, now known or hereafter invented, including photocopying and recording, or in any information storage or retrieval system, without permission in writing from the publishers.

**Publisher's Note**
The publisher has gone to great lengths to ensure the quality of this reprint but points out that some imperfections in the original copies may be apparent.

**Disclaimer**
The publisher has made every effort to trace copyright holders and welcomes correspondence from those they have been unable to contact.

A Library of Congress record exists under LC control number: 32031346

ISBN 13: 978-1-138-65897-4 (hbk)
ISBN 13: 978-1-315-62046-6 (ebk)

# A HISTORY OF EUROPE
## FROM 1378 TO 1494

BY

# W. T. WAUGH

LATE KINGSFORD PROFESSOR OF HISTORY IN McGILL UNIVERSITY

WITH FOUR MAPS

**THIRD EDITION**

METHUEN & CO. LTD.
36 ESSEX STREET W.C.
LONDON

*First Published* . . . *September 22nd 1932*
*Second Edition* . . . *November  1943*
*Third Edition* . . . *1949*

CATALOGUE NO. 4353/U

PRINTED IN GREAT BRITAIN

## PREFACE

IN accordance with the general plan of the series to which this volume belongs, I have noticed English affairs only when they had a direct bearing on the fortunes of the European continent. But, since this is, after all, an English book, particular attention has been given to those peoples who have most influenced the English-speaking nations of today.

I owe thanks to many friends for their help—notably to Professor Edward Fiddes, of the University of Manchester, and Mr. V. H. Galbraith, Reader in Diplomatic in the University of Oxford, who read my proofs and offered valuable and welcome criticism. Without the constant aid of my wife, this book would never have been completed.

W. T. W.

MONTREAL
*April, 1932*


## NOTE TO THIRD EDITION

The bibliographies have been revised and brought up to date by Miss Margaret Seymour of the Department of History, University of Manchester.

# CONTENTS

## INTRODUCTION
Traditional view of the fifteenth century (1); decline of medieval institutions (2); political conditions (5); rise of nationalism (6); growing strength of the middle class (7); learning, art, and geographical discovery (8)

## CHAPTER I
**FRANCE, 1380–1407—CHARLES VI AND THE PRINCES OF THE LILIES**    10

Accession of Charles VI; his uncles (10); widespread unrest in France (11); the *Maillotins* (12); suppression of risings (13); rebellion in Flanders; Philip van Artevelde (14); battle of Roosebeke (15); further government reprisals (16); crusade of Bishop Despenser (16); succession of Philip the Bold to Flanders (17); misgovernment in France (18); Charles VI's *coup d'état* (21); his madness (23); rivalry of Burgundy and Orléans (24); France and Pope Benedict XIII (25); further civil dissension (27); death of Philip the Bold; John the Fearless (28); murder of Louis of Orléans (30)

## CHAPTER II
**FRANCE, 1407–1429—TREASON AND INVASION**    31

Burgundians and Armagnacs (31); civil war (33); meeting of the Estates-General (34); the Cabochians (35); their defeat; civil war renewed (38); negotiations with Henry V (39); France invaded (42); battle of Agincourt (44); confusion in France; mediation of King Sigismund (46); France again invaded; Burgundian successes against Armagnacs (48); capture of Rouen by Henry V (50); attempted reconciliation of French parties (51); murder of John the Fearless (52); the Treaty of Troyes (53); Armagnac resistance (54); Normandy under the English (55); battle of Baugé (56); siege of Meaux (58); deaths of Henry V and Charles VI (59); John, Duke of Bedford (59); conditions in Northern France (60); Charles VII and his counsellors (63); battle of Verneuil (66); embarrassments of Bedford; Humphrey Duke of Gloucester (67); siege of Orléans (69)

## CHAPTER III
**FRANCE, 1429–1461—EXPULSION OF THE ENGLISH, AND ESTABLISHMENT OF THE ROYAL AUTHORITY**    71

Early Life of Joan of Arc (71); Joan at Chinon and Poitiers (72); progress of the siege of Orléans (73); Orléans relieved (74); battle of Patay (75); coronation of Charles VII (76); Joan's capture, trial, and death (77); continued confusion in France (79); the Treaty of Arras (81); Paris taken for Charles VII; stubborn resistance of the English (83); plots against Charles VII (84); the *Écorcheurs* (85); increase of royal power (86); truce with

England (87); creation of a standing army (88); conquest of Normandy (89); conquest of Guienne (90); the battle of Castillon (91); Charles VII's mistresses and advisers (92); his methods of government (93); his relations with the Dauphin (94); his foreign and ecclesiastical policy (95); rehabilitation of Joan of Arc (96)

## CHAPTER IV

GERMANY, 1378–1410—WENZEL AND RUPERT . . . . . 99

Political conditions in Germany (99); King Wenzel (105); strife between the princes and the cities (106); Wenzel's unpopularity (108); his troubles and mistakes (109); his deposition (112); King Rupert; his Italian expedition (114); confusion in Germany (116); Rupert and the Council of Pisa (118)

## CHAPTER V

THE GREAT SCHISM, 1378–1413 . . . . . . . 120

Condition of the Church in 1378 (120); election of Urban VI and of Clement VII (125); division of Europe (126); policy of Clement (127); policy of Urban (129); his violence (130); Boniface IX (131); attempts to end the Schism (132); rival schemes in the University of Paris (133); Benedict XIII (134); withdrawal of French obedience from Benedict (136); his obduracy (138); French obedience restored (140); Innocent VII (141); new breach between Benedict and the French (142); Gregory XII; his fruitless negotiations with Benedict (143); neutrality of France declared (145); rebellion of the cardinals (146); General Councils summoned (147); the Council of Perpignan (148); the Council of Pisa (149); Alexander V and John XXIII (153); Council of Rome; the city captured by Ladislas of Naples (155)

## CHAPTER VI

GERMANY, 1410–1437—SIGISMUND . . . . . . . 157

Disputed election to the Crown (157); Sigismund's second election; his character (158); his policy in Germany (160); Sigismund in Italy (161); in France and England (162); his troubles in Germany and Bohemia (162); Sigismund crowned Emperor (168); his last years (169)

## CHAPTER VII

THE COUNCIL OF CONSTANCE . . . . . . . . 171

The Council opened (171); its size and significance (172); attitude towards Hus and the Papacy (173); organization (174); conflict with John XXIII (175); deposition of John and abdication of Gregory XII (176); effect of Sigismund's absence (177); the Capitulation of Narbonne (178); dissensions in the Council (179); deposition of Benedict XIII; dispute concerning the papal election (183); election of Martin V (185); reforms and Concordats (186)

## CHAPTER VIII

THE COUNCILS OF SIENA AND BASEL . . . . . . 188

Aims and policy of Martin V (188); the Council of Pavia transferred to Siena (190); failure of the Council (191); Martin V and the Council of Basel (192); the Council opened; its first conflict with Eugenius IV (193); the Hussites at Basel (197);

# CONTENTS

organization and policy of the Council (198); the Council and the Eastern Church (200); renewed strife between the Council and the Pope; the Council split (201); the Council of Ferrara-Florence (203); Eugenius IV suspended and deposed by the Council of Basel (204); election of Felix V (205); the Council transferred to Lausanne and dissolved (206)

## CHAPTER IX

JOHN HUS AND HIS FOLLOWERS . . . . . . . 208

Bohemia in the fourteenth century (208); advocates of religious reform (211); early life of Hus (213); Hus and Wycliffe (214); religious disputes; secession of Germans from Prague University (216); Hus excommunicated (217); mediation of King Wenzel; dispute over indulgences (218); Hus at the Council of Constance (219); effects of his death in Bohemia (222); Hussite divisions (223); death of King Wenzel (225); opposition to Sigismund (226); the Four Articles of Prague (227); John Zizka (227); battles of Saaz and Kuttenberg (229); civil war in Bohemia (230); Zizka's death (231); Procop the Great (232); Hussite victories at Aussig and Mies; the Hussite offensive (233); a crusade routed at Tauss; the Hussites invited to Basel (235); their negotiations with the Council (236); growing divisions among them; battle of Lipan (237); the Compacts of Prague signed at Iglau (238); Sigismund accepted as King of Bohemia (239)

## CHAPTER X

FRANCE, 1461–1494 . . . . . . . . . 240

Character of Louis XI (240); his early relations with his ministers (242), the Church, the nobility (243), Brittany, and Burgundy (244); the War of the Public Weal (245); renewed civil strife (247); interview of Louis and Charles the Bold at Péronne (248); the King's fortunes retrieved (249); further strife with Burgundy (250); France invaded by Edward IV of England (252); final defeat of Charles the Bold (253); Burgundian territory seized by Louis (254); Louis checked by Maximilian of Austria (255); death of Mary of Burgundy (256); Louis' relations with Spain and with René of Anjou (257); his government of France (258); his death (260); accession of Charles VIII; the Beaujeus (261); the Estates-General of 1484 (263); aristocratic disaffection (266); the Duke of Brittany defeated; treaty of Sablé; marriage of Charles VIII and Anne of Brittany (268); preparations for an expedition to Italy (269)

## CHAPTER XI

THE GREATNESS AND DOWNFALL OF BURGUNDY . . . . 271

Bases of Burgundian power (271); Duke Philip the Good, his early successes (273); his character, policy, and ambitions (274); personality and aims of Charles the Bold (278); his suppression of Liége and Ghent (279); his unpopularity (280); his hatred of France (281); his acquisitions in Alsace and Swabia (282); his annexation of Guelders (283); his relations with the Emperor Frederick III (284); disaffection in Alsace—the Lower Union (285); alliance of the Lower Union, the Swiss, and Sigismund of Habsburg (286); the siege of Neuss (287); Charles at war with the Swiss; his conquest of Lorraine (288); battles of Granson and Morat (289); Lorraine lost (290); battle of Nancy (291)

x        EUROPE FROM 1378 TO 1494

## CHAPTER XII

PAGE

FRANCE—ECONOMIC AND SOCIAL CONDITIONS . . . . . 293
Economic effects of the Hundred Years War: rural life (294), town life (296); rise of capitalism (298); condition of trade (299); Jacques Coeur (300); French society: the nobility (303); the *bourgeoisie* (306); the criminal class (308); the Church (309); the Universities (311); anti-clericalism and witchcraft (312); popular piety (313)

## CHAPTER XIII

GERMANY, 1437–1493—KINGS AND PRINCES . . . . . 314
Albert II (314); election of Frederick III, his character and aims (315); Frederick, the Pope, and the Electors (316); the Concordat of Vienna (318); Frederick crowned Emperor; confusion in Germany (319); futile proposals for reform (321); Frederick driven from Austria (323); election of Maximilian (323); the Swabian League; union of Habsburg lands (324); the *Landtage* (325); disintegration of principalities checked (326); the princes and their vassals, the cities (327), and the Church (330); political reforms of princes (333); the Swiss Confederation (335)

## CHAPTER XIV

GERMANY—SOCIAL AND ECONOMIC CONDITIONS . . . . 341
Germany's weakness in the fifteenth century (341); social influence of the princes (342); the knights (342); the clergy (344); the burghers (345); German trade (347); the Hanseatic League (349); the peasants (359); peasants' risings (361); the *Vehme* (362)

## CHAPTER XV

THE SCANDINAVIAN COUNTRIES . . . . . . . 368
Social and political conditions of the Scandinavian countries (368); the Regent Margaret (369); the Union of Kalmar (370); war of Denmark and Holstein (371); Engelbrekt Engelbrektsson; deposition of King Eric (372); union of Denmark and Norway; King Christian I; union of Slesvig and Holstein (373); Christian I dethroned in Sweden (374); rivalry of Sten Sture and King John; Norway in the fifteenth century (375); condition of Denmark at the end of the century (376)

## CHAPTER XVI

SPAIN . . . . . . . . . . . . 378
General condition of Spain (378); Castile under John I and Henry III; the government of Castile (379); the nobility and clergy of Castile (381); the Castilian towns (382); weakness of the Castilian crown; Moors and Jews (383); reign of John II (384); Henry the Impotent (385); the kingdom of Aragon—its government (386); political history of Aragon from 1378 to 1458 (390); reign of John II (392); marriage of Ferdinand of Aragon and Isabella of Castile (393); union of the two kingdoms; conquest of Granada (395); domestic policy of Ferdinand and Isabella (396); the history of Portugal (398)

# CONTENTS

## CHAPTER XVII

EASTERN EUROPE . . . . . . . . . . 402

Conditions in Eastern Europe in the fourteenth century (402); Poland under Lewis of Hungary (404); union of Poland and Lithuania (405); the Teutonic Order in Prussia (406); war between the Order and Poland—battle of Tannenberg (408); Poland and Lithuania in the days of Ladislas II (409); succession of Sigismund of Luxemburg to Hungary (411); his policy and difficulties (412); Hungary under Albert of Austria, Ladislas of Poland, and Ladislas Postumus (414); Casimir IV of Poland (415); his victory over the Teutonic Order (416); West Prussia annexed by Poland (418); Bohemia after the death of Sigismund (418); George of Podiebrad, King of Bohemia (419); civil war in Bohemia (420); John Hunyadi regent of Hungary (421); confused politics of Eastern Europe towards the end of the fifteenth century (422); the Treaty of Pressburg (424); Ivan III, Grand-duke of Muscovy (424)

## CHAPTER XVIII

THE FALL OF THE BYZANTINE EMPIRE AND THE TURKISH CONQUEST OF THE BALKAN PENINSULA . . . . . . . 427

Deplorable condition of the Byzantine Empire in the fourteenth century; early Ottoman successes in Europe (428); Turkish wars against Serbs and Bulgars—first battle of Kossovo (429); Bajazet I—battle of Nicopolis (430); Bajazet and Timur—battle of Angora; Turkish power restored (433); Murad II (434); John Hunyadi's exploits; battle of Varna (435); second battle of Kossovo; Mohammed II (436); his siege of Constantinople (437); fall of the city (439); relief of Belgrade by John Hunyadi (440); Turkish conquest of Bosnia (441); Scanderbeg (441); the Morea seized by Mohammed II (443); war between the Turks and the Venetians; Turkish invasion of Italy (444)

## CHAPTER XIX

ITALIAN POLITICS . . . . . . . . . . 446

Political state of Italy in the fourteenth century (446); Italian warfare (447); Italy and medieval culture; Italian problems in 1378 (451); Gian Galeazzo Visconti—his ambitions and achievements (453); conflict between Milan and Venice (454); the States of the Church; Naples conquered by Alfonso of Aragon (456); rise of the Medici in Florence (457); Francesco Sforza, Duke of Milan (458); alliance of Milan, Florence, and Naples (460); Lorenzo the Magnificent (461); conspiracies against the Sforza and Medici families (462); Ludovico Sforza (463); rising in Naples; Charles VIII of France invited to Italy (464)

## CHAPTER XX

THE PAPACY AND THE CHURCH IN THE LATTER PART OF THE FIFTEENTH CENTURY . . . . . . . . . . 467

State of European religion (467); Nicolas V and the Italian Renaissance (470); Calixtus III (473); Pius II—the Congress of Mantua (474), the Constitution *Execrabilis* (476), his diplomacy, his crusade and death (477), his character and attainments (478); Paul II (480); his breach with the Humanists; Sixtus IV (481); his place in history (483); Innocent VIII (484)

CHAPTER XXI

THE CLASSICAL RENAISSANCE, AND ITS RELATION TO THOUGHT, LETTERS AND ART IN THE FIFTEENTH CENTURY . . . . . 486

Traditional view of the Renaissance (486); its real character (487); Italian Humanism (488); achievements and defects of the Humanists (490); Humanism outside Italy (492); Renaissance architecture (493); the Renaissance and vernacular literature (494); fifteenth-century sculpture (495) and painting (497); influence of the Humanists and the artists (500)

CHAPTER XXII

SCIENCE, DISCOVERY AND INVENTION IN THE FIFTEENTH CENTURY    503

Science in the fifteenth century (503); exploration before 1400 (504); conquest of the Canaries (505); navigation in the fifteenth century; Prince Henry the Navigator (509); Portuguese exploration after his death; importance of the Portuguese discoveries (511); Christopher Columbus (512); his first voyage to America (513); Vasco da Gama; the Cabots; historical significance of the discoveries (515); the invention of printing (517); its) development in Germany (519); and in other countries (520); effects of the invention (522)

GENEALOGICAL TABLES . . . . . . . . . 525

INDEX . . . . . . . . . . . . 531

## LIST OF MAPS

FRANCE, OCTOBER 1428 . . . . . . . . *Page* 68

TERRITORIES OF THE HOUSE OF BURGUNDY . . . . „ 273

GERMANY IN 1440 . . . . . . . . *Facing page* 316

EAST CENTRAL EUROPE IN 1386 . . . . . „ „ 404

*From drawings by Richard Cribb.*

# A HISTORY OF EUROPE FROM 1378 TO 1494

## INTRODUCTION

THE period of History with which this book is concerned has often been treated slightingly. It was, we are commonly told, a time of general decadence. The Middle Ages were passing away. The most characteristic and attractive features of medieval civilization were disappearing; medieval principles and ideals were ceasing to satisfy. And as yet no adequate substitutes had been found. Men's minds had, as it were, lost their sense of direction. They could see neither stars nor landmarks. Hence the greater part of Europe became a welter of confusion, in which the basest and most sordid motives impelled petty men to paltry actions. One bright patch indeed there was. Italy was illumined by the rays of the Renaissance, which towards the end of the fifteenth century began to shed a faint but increasing light on other lands. It was therefore Italy alone that really repaid the attention of the historian. Other countries might not indeed be ignored; but it seemed reasonable, only a few years ago, for the author of a very well-known history of Europe in the later Middle Ages to devote one quarter of his space to Italian affairs.

One may well dispute the assumption that a period of decadence is less worthy of study than a period of growth. But it must be recognized that for the traditional view of the fifteenth century there was much to be said. Most of the institutions which had moulded the fortunes of medieval Europe were losing their influence. The decline of the Church will be amply illustrated in the following pages. The Papacy, its prestige grievously hurt by the Great Schism, its authority shaken by the Conciliar Movement, failed utterly to recover its old moral ascendancy after these crises, and has rarely sunk into such disrepute as attached to it at the end of our period. In all countries the secular clergy were hated and derided. Monasticism was riddled with abuses and appealed to very few. Crusades aroused little interest, although Catholic Europe was more seriously menaced by Islam than it had been for centuries. In several countries the Church fell under the control of the temporal authority to an extent not known since the eleventh century, while Bohemia offered the unwonted spectacle of a nation in successful revolt against her.

If the Church was in evil case, far worse was the plight of the two Empires which called themselves Roman. On their continued existence the life of medieval Europe had in great measure depended. In the fifteenth century one of them came to its end, an end unworthy of it, yet far less ignominious than the fate in store for the other. That fate was to be deferred for more than three hundred years, but already the Holy Roman Empire had far outlived its dignity and influence. Such authority and renown as still clung to it were inevitably lost during a century in which it had at its head three such men as Wenzel, Rupert, and Frederick III. Perhaps, however, it was the attempt of the Emperor Sigismund to restore its vitality that most clearly displayed its decrepitude.

Feudalism—a phenomenon peculiar to no one age, but perhaps seen at its best in medieval times—was also losing force. It is true that for a while it seemed to have gained a new lease of life. The rise in the power of Burgundy, the civil broils in France, the domestic strife which culminated in the Wars of the Roses, the frequency and ubiquity of " private " war in Germany, the prolonged anarchy in Castile —all these seemed to indicate the decline of royal authority and a corresponding revival of feudal licence. But in the first place it must be remembered that a state may be afflicted with over-mighty subjects even though feudal relationships are quite unknown there; further, a good many of the troublesome elements in France and England owed their strength to conditions which had nothing to do with feudalism; in Germany, much of the internecine strife was virtually public warfare, the feudal bond between the princes and the Emperor having lost its meaning and these same princes being the chief foes of feudalism in their several territories; and lastly, whatever vicissitudes may have occurred during the century, its end saw Burgundy worsted and monarchy in the ascendant in England, France, and Spain, while even in Germany many princes had won against their vassals notable successes which presaged the still more striking victories that were shortly to follow. The economic arrangements to which feudalism gave rise continued, it is true, to hold their ground stubbornly, the amelioration of the peasant's lot in some countries being roughly counterbalanced by its deterioration elsewhere; and feudal ideas and standards still determined social relationships in many parts. But the military value of feudalism had almost vanished before the English long-bows, the Swiss pikes, the Hussite hand-guns, and the artillery of the Bureau brothers and Mohammed II.

Another institution which, having played a great part in medieval life, was beginning to decay in the fifteenth century, was the gild. There were of course many kinds of gilds, and some of them remained almost, if not quite, as flourishing as ever. Thus the religious and philanthropic gilds were still very numerous, very popular, and very active throughout central and western Europe; and the Universities, which were essentially gilds of teachers or students, made up by an increase in their numbers for the loss of influence which they perhaps sustained through a decline in the quality of their work. But the most famous types—the merchant and craft gilds—had manifestly seen their best days. Their power continued to be very great. They still controlled a great deal of trade and most industrial activity. But the erstwhile ascendancy of the merchant gilds had long been impaired in most regions where they existed; and as for the craft-gilds, they had generally become federations of masters, frequently with an hereditary membership, and their influence was being reduced by the agitation of journeymen's unions on the one hand and the competition of the big capitalist on the other. Our period likewise witnessed a decline in the fortunes of one of the most famous of the commercial associations to which the Middle Ages gave birth—the Hanseatic League.

It has been customary to regard the Gothic architecture

of the fifteenth century as decadent; but it is a matter of taste whether one likes the Flamboyant Gothic of the continent or the Perpendicular of England less than the preceding fashion, or whether one prefers the exuberance of the first, or, alternatively, the spacious dignity of the second. And, whatever may be said of ecclesiastical architecture, it can hardly be contended that domestic architecture was declining. On the other hand, when one turns from art to learning, it cannot be denied that the methods of study and speculation commonly summarized as Scholasticism were now yielding much less fruit than they had formerly produced. This was particularly noticeable in the fields of theology and philosophy, where there was little save barren wrangling over trivialities. At the same time the sterility of the Old Learning has often been exaggerated. During our period there was not only a great deal of acute political speculation which was essentially medieval in character, method, and inspiration, but also, as scholars are beginning to realize, a considerable amount of scientific inquiry and research which owed nothing to the Italian Renaissance.

In several medieval countries the towns had enjoyed a measure of independence which had enabled them to exercise a deep and generally wholesome influence on the political life of the time. But during our period their autonomy was being diminished on all hands, notably in Italy, Germany and Spain. Their influence on European culture, though still great, had also begun to wane. Closely associated with the rise of towns had been the rise of representative institutions in politics. They had been one of the most promising features of the life of the Middle Ages, and were destined to prove one of the greatest medieval bequests to modern times. But on the whole they fared ill in the fifteenth century. Everyone with a smattering of English history knows how the English parliament declined in prestige and weight, until it was in danger of extinction. One may see a similar process in several continental lands. In France, the Estates-General, though its power fluctuated during the period which concerns us, was unquestionably weaker at its end than at its beginning. In Castile, the Cortes began to feel the pressure of the new Spanish monarchy. Though they did much useful work and here and there increased in power, the prospects of the Estates of the German principalities were decidedly worse in 1500 than they had been a century earlier. The gains made by representative assemblies in one or two countries—such as Sweden and Bohemia—were far from compensating for the losses suffered elsewhere. It must not be overlooked that the failure of the Conciliar Movement, whether for good or for evil, was a blow to the cause of constitutional government.

If the several states of Europe be regarded merely as political Powers, few will be found to have prospered during the years covered by this volume. Germany, as a political unit, had almost ceased to carry weight in international diplomacy. The relative importance of England had sunk, though just before the end of our period it began to rise again. Events were about to show the feebleness of the political units of Italy. France, which had been in the depths, had made a characteristic recovery, and in 1494 was again the leading state of Europe; yet she was little if any stronger or healthier than she had been at the death of Charles V. In Scandinavia, Norway was apparently decadent, Denmark and Sweden had wasted their strength in the disputes occasioned by the Union of Kalmar. The people of Bohemia, a virtually independent kingdom, had just reason to be proud of their achievements; but they had mostly been accomplished in defiance of the country's rulers, and as a force in international politics Bohemia had somewhat declined. Poland seemed to have grown in power, and had cut a greater figure than in any previous period; but she was suffering from a deadly internal disease which was destined to kill her. Though Hungary had gained much military glory, her rulers had allowed their overweening ambitions to distract them from their proper work of resisting the Moslem, while the Balkan peoples were submerged beneath the Turkish flood, and on the whole deserved their fate. There were, in fact, only three European States whose strength had substantially increased and was still increasing. The Turkish Sultanate was of course one. The others were at the farther end of Europe. The fifteenth century is the most glorious in the annals of Portugal, and at its close she was near the very peak of her fortune. As for the other Christian kingdoms of the Iberian peninsula, they had expelled their ancient enemy and welded themselves into one of the Great Powers of Europe.

If a survey of the political conditions of fifteenth-century Europe is on the whole depressing, it also reminds one that the situation had its brighter side. There was, for instance, a marked increase in the force of national sentiment; and this, whatever harm it may have wrought, was preferable to the parochialism that had afflicted the mind of the average man in medieval Europe. The force of nationalism in the Middle Ages has often been underestimated by modern writers, who, accustomed to its extravagant manifestations, have supposed that, where it was not the dominating influence on men's actions, it did not exist at all. It may be doubted whether anywhere and at any time in the Middle Ages national sentiment would have led people to do things palpably detrimental to their intellectual and economic welfare, as has often happened in our own day. Here and there, nevertheless, the influence of national patriotism was very powerful. In the fifteenth century, the Czechs were filled with it: indeed the enthusiasm of some of their leaders, exhibited in both word and deed, could hardly be surpassed by their living descendants. A national consciousness of course existed in England, and in certain circles of the Scottish people it was very strong indeed. Attempts by Denmark to enforce the Union of Kalmar stimulated nationalist fervour in Sweden; the Poles felt it, though in a lesser degree; and at times it rose high in Hungary. Even the Germans had a national self-consciousness, and though it influenced their actions but little, it was largely responsible for the continued existence of the German crown and the Holy Roman Empire. In France the force of patriotism varied strangely. That the French thought of themselves as a nation, and felt a certain pride therein, is plain from numerous indications, among which may be mentioned their conduct at the Council of Constance. But many of them failed to draw the inference that all Frenchmen should form one united State; and the following pages will show clearly that many who were conscious and proud of being French were far more strongly moved by other considerations, so strongly that on occasion they would join hands with their king's enemies. Nevertheless, we see in Joan of Arc an upholder of the principle of " France for the French," and the cry undoubtedly evoked a widespread response. Had it been otherwise, the expulsion of the English would have taken far longer than it actually did. In the Iberian peninsula, the Portuguese clearly possessed a strong sense of their nationhood; but, notwithstanding the union of Castile and Aragon, there was not, at the close of the fifteenth century, any self-conscious Spanish nation, though the prevalent localism was fast being broken down. It is lamentably evident that where national enthusiasm ran high, it was commonly stimulated by the allied emotions of fear and hatred; it seems rarely to have caused individuals of the same nation to love one another better than before. The patriotic enthusiasm aroused by Henry V was followed in England by the internecine strife which culminated in the Wars of the Roses. Frenchmen continued to fight one another to the end of the period under review. Even the Czechs did the cause of their nation much harm by domestic strife, and Hungarian leaders were compassing one another's deaths at the moment of the nation's greatest triumph over the Turk. But while national zeal might have unworthy origins, and while it might often be worsted by rival motives, the strengthening of a stimulus destined to have such powerful effects on the subsequent fortunes of mankind adds very greatly to the interest of fifteenth-century History.

Everyone knows that the present importance of the middle class is a feature which differentiates modern from medieval society. Notwithstanding the decline in the political influence of towns and in the weight and prosperity of commercial and industrial gilds, the fifteenth century witnessed a marked rise in the status of the bourgeoisie over against the nobility on the one hand and the peasantry on the other. Despite the numerous wars, chronic disorder by land, and piracy at sea, European trade and industry continued to grow; and it was the middle class that reaped most of the fruits. In many countries we find kings and princes favouring it as a counterpoise to the nobility. The successes of Charles VII of France in war and administration were in great measure due to men of bourgeois origin. Louis XI was notoriously anxious to keep the middle class on his side. It was the real source of the strength of Burgundy, however much the dukes might conceal the fact. The Yorkist dynasty in England owed its short-lived success largely to the support which it received from the trading classes. Nor must it be forgotten that a society of merchants —the Hansa—ranked throughout our period as one of the great Powers of northern Europe.

There is no need to expatiate here on the intellectual and artistic activity of Italy during our period. It has commonly been considered the one redeeming feature of the times. But in other countries there was far more mental and aesthetic vigour than has usually been supposed, some of it no doubt inspired by Italy, much of it not. And modern research has gravely discredited the traditional conception of the Renaissance. No sane man would now accept Acton's assertion that the " modern age " (which for him began with the sixteenth century) was " unheralded " and " founded a new order of things, under a law of innovation, sapping the ancient reign of continuity." The more History, medieval or other, is studied, the more it becomes evident that the so-called Italian Renaissance was but a phase in that activity of European thought and art, which, beginning about the year 1000, has continued, with varying effects but scarcely an interruption, from that time to this. But while one may not despise the achievements of earlier times, nobody is likely to deny the immense interest and value of the doings of the fifteenth-century Italians in learning and art, especially the latter. At all events, the age saw no decline in the intellectual and artistic life of Europe. The mere invention of printing would probably have sufficed to prevent that.

It is no doubt natural for a dweller in the New World to feel a special interest in the doings of the fifteenth-century explorers, and some may think that the importance attributed to them below is excessive. It is true, furthermore, that their discoveries were made outside Europe. But these men were Europeans; they sailed in the service of European princes or merchants from European ports, whither, if lucky enough, they returned. And their exploits immediately had a profound effect upon Europe's political and economic life, and were destined to alter the relations and prospects of all her peoples. The work of the explorers—and very various nations shared in it—would in itself be convincing proof that, whatever ideas and institutions might be losing strength, there was no lack of courage, virility, and self-devotion among the Europeans of the time.

Thus while we shall have to record the failure and decadence of old and famous things, we shall also have to notice the forces that were to create substitutes for them. If heroes seem rare and knaves and fools abundant, it is largely because contemporary annals concern themselves mainly with those spheres of life where decay was worst. Many of the artists, explorers, and merchants of those days are mere names to us, some not even so much. But, thanks to them, the fifteenth century is not wanting in those creative achievements which make the study of an age attractive.

## CHAPTER I

## FRANCE, 1380–1407

### CHARLES VI AND THE PRINCES OF THE LILIES

A Regency established

WHEN, on September 16, 1380, Charles V of France died, his elder son, also called Charles, was only eleven years old. The boy had been carefully educated under the direction of Philip of Mézières, who was held in high regard for his knightly prowess, his learning, and his piety. Charles was not, however, brilliant in any respect—being far less clever than the other royal minor of the time, Richard II of England. But he resembled Richard in being cursed with a superfluity of uncles. There were the three brothers of the late King—Louis, Duke of Anjou, Philip, Duke of Burgundy, and John, Duke of Berry—and the brother of the late Queen, Louis, Duke of Bourbon. Of these Anjou and Burgundy had the widest political ambitions; but all could be trusted to put their own interests before any others and to use every opportunity of feathering their own nests. Charles V, with his customary foresight, had made provision for a royal minority with the evident object of mitigating some of the disadvantages to which the new king would be exposed. The Duke of Anjou, the eldest of the three brothers, was to be regent. The King's person was to be in the charge of Burgundy and Bourbon, who were to be advised by a council specially chosen for the purpose. Charles VI, it was also laid down, should be deemed to have come of age on his fourteenth birthday.

These dispositions were never put into complete effect. No sooner was Charles V dead than quarrels of all kinds broke out—between the King's uncles, between the university and the city of Paris, between Charles V's confidential counsellors and their rivals. Louis of Anjou claimed both the regency and the personal charge of the King; but it was decided that until the coronation he should content himself with the former, while Charles VI, as his father had wished, should be under the tutelage of Burgundy and Bourbon. This arrangement lasted but a short while, for the coronation took place at Rheims on November 4. It was ominous that Anjou and Burgundy nearly came to blows over a point of precedence at the very coronation feast. The negotiations that followed are in many respects obscure, but the upshot was that on January 28, 1381, a council of Regency was established. It was composed of twelve members, among whom were the four royal dukes, with the Duke of Anjou as president.

The new Council soon had a chance of proving its mettle. For some years past, France, like England, had been the victim of serious internal unrest. Charles V's success in defeating the English and restoring good government to his subjects had not been inexpensive, and resentment at his exactions was bitter and widespread. Already, both in the far south and in the far north, it had come to open violence. The disorders in the south, where Montpellier had been particularly disturbed, had been put down temporarily and drastically punished by the Duke of Anjou. In Flanders, however, Ghent was in arms against the Count, and the revolt was spreading rapidly among the other towns. *Widespread disorder*

On his death-bed Charles V had renounced the direct taxes called *fouages*, which for years had been a terrible burden on many parts of the country. By many it was understood that all extraordinary taxation had been abolished, and even among those who interpreted Charles's intentions correctly there was a determination to use the opportunity to obtain release from the sales-taxes, commonly called "impositions," and from the still more unpopular salt-tax—the *gabelle*. In November 1380, an assembly containing representatives of the Three Estates met at Paris, and was asked by the chancellor to sanction the levy of a new imposition. This demand, so contrary to expectation, set Paris aflame. Next day a crowd, headed by the *prévôt des marchands* and said to number 20,000 persons, appeared at the *Palais*, and the royal Council, frightened into compliance, ordained the abandonment of all *aides*, a term commonly applied to all revenues save those derived regularly from the King's *domaine*.

The Parisians believed that they had secured freedom

from all except feudal exactions. But the Government interpreted its concession to mean simply that it remitted what was due on taxes already demanded. It had not given any undertaking for the future; the next winter saw several meetings of Estates, provincial and general, in Languedoil, the outcome being that, in March 1381, a new *fouage* was levied in order to raise troops for the English war. The effect of recent events, however, was shown in the elaborate regulations drawn up to prevent misapplication of the money and the government's handsome promises of administrative reform.

**Rising in Rouen, Feb. 1382**

How far the Rising which convulsed England a little later stimulated the malcontents of France to further violence it is hard to say. Its influence was probably slight, for nothing sensational happened in France until the English insurgents had been completely suppressed and their rebellion was a manifest failure. Whatever the cause, however, the year 1382 witnessed disorder in many French towns. In February the news that the *fouage* of the previous year was to be increased caused a rising in Rouen. The participants were mainly people of small estate, but a few rich merchants figured as leaders and still more were believed to be encouraging the movement behind the scenes. The happenings during the three days when Rouen was in the hands of the insurgents remind one of what had occurred in London eight months before. Royal officials, the higher clergy, unsympathetic merchants, Jews, were attacked. The charters of the abbey of St. Ouen were torn up, and the abbot had to renounce its rights and privileges. The prisons were thrown open, and a few great houses plundered. Finally the famous charter of the Normans was solemnly read in the cathedral, and all present swore to observe it. Then disorder ceased, and envoys went to Paris to placate the government.

**The Maillotins in Paris**

Meanwhile, on March 1, a rebellion had broken out in Paris itself, owing to attempts to collect a new sales-tax to which the town had refused its consent. The mob had armed itself with iron mallets which it had found in the arsenal of the *Hôtel de Ville*, and the uprising was consequently remembered as the revolt of the *Maillotins*. Jews, tax-collectors and lawyers were maltreated or killed. Prisons were opened, archives pillaged, wine-cellars plundered. The King was constrained to negotiate with the rebels, who demanded a general amnesty, the abolition of *aides*, and a return to the financial system of Louis IX and Philip the Fair. He might have been compelled to make humiliating promises but that the richer citizens, alarmed by the excesses of the *Maillotins*, now intervened forcibly and soon got the upper hand. In response to their overtures, the government agreed to follow the financial policy of St. Louis (whatever that might be) and to grant an amnesty to everyone but the ringleaders of the *Maillotins*. Paris returned to its obedience, though the executions of rebels, which were unexpectedly numerous, nearly provoked another outbreak.

The King then went to deal with Rouen, where royal officers had already begun reprisals. The city underwent a terrible punishment. The Commune, which dated from the time of Henry II of England, was abolished, and the place put under a royal *bailli*. A heavy indemnity was also exacted. Shortly afterwards the Estates of Normandy consented to the levy of a number of impositions. The first attempt to collect these caused a fresh riot in Rouen; but the royal captain of the town was able to cope with the emergency, the malcontents were harshly punished, and the final result of this series of disturbances was that the people of Normandy were more heavily taxed than they had been at the beginning of the year. Paris, too, found itself threatened with further punishment, but managed to turn aside the wrath of the government by paying a large sum of money.

There were likewise troubles in the south. In the autumn of 1381 the mere announcement that the Duke of Berry had been appointed lieutenant of the King in Languedoc was enough to cause an insurrection in Béziers. Many of the leading men of the place were killed, and there was much plundering of wealthy houses. The disturbances died away without interference from outside; but the Duke executed more than forty artisans, and exacted a heavy indemnity. He then demanded of the Estates of Languedoc a new *fouage*, which he levied notwithstanding protests from many towns. When Carcassonne refused to receive him, the neighbouring countryside was laid waste by his troops.

The greater part of southern France, indeed, had for

some time been disturbed by the so-called *Tuchins*, a name
of uncertain meaning. In the north they would simply
have been called brigands. They were people down on
their luck, ruined by the wars, or good for nothing. In some
regions they subjected themselves to a rough discipline;
and now and then they had an understanding with the
authorities of a town or with an impoverished noble. But,
notwithstanding attempts to prove that the activity of the
Tuchins was part of a great democratic or anti-clerical movement, they seem as a rule to have been mere marauders,
who were driven to crime by hunger and tried to avoid
violence. In 1382 a vigorous effort to suppress them was
initiated, and after a year or two some effect was produced,
though Languedoc remained very restless. This is not
astonishing when one learns the punishment which was
meted out to the whole area in 1383. A not very representative assembly held at Lyons was partly surprised,
partly cajoled, partly terrified into consenting to the re-
establishment of all the *aides* levied in the days of Charles V.
It was further told that to purge its misdeeds Languedoc
must pay a fine of 800,000 francs. Every community, however loyal and orderly it might have been, had to contribute to this sum, though it is true that those deemed
specially culpable had to pay more than the rest. The
amount was mainly raised by crushing *fouages*: and to
gauge the effect on the minds of the people it should be
remembered, first, that they had believed the *fouage* to have
been abolished; secondly, that in 1382 the King and the
Duke of Berry had granted what passed as a general pardon
for recent disturbances.

Philip van Artevelde in Ghent

The harshness of the Government was due largely to
what had been happening in Flanders. There for a year or
two after Charles V's death the country had remained divided
between the Count—Louis de Maele—and the aristocratic party
on the one hand, and the democratic party, headed by Ghent,
on the other. At the beginning of 1382 things were going ill
for the rebels, and in the hope of reviving the morale of their
party the democrats of Ghent chose as their captain-general
Philip van Artevelde, son of the great Jacques, a wealthy,
public-spirited, eloquent, and energetic man. He sternly
suppressed disaffection, introduced very strict disciplinary

measures, arranged for the more equitable distribution of the dwindling food-supply, and placed the government of the city more completely under popular control. Having failed in an attempt to come to terms with the Count, he was obliged by lack of food to take the field against Bruges. On May 3, the citizens of Bruges followed the Count and his knights in a rash assault on the entrenchments of the men of Ghent at Beverhoutsveld. They were ignominiously repulsed; the victors entered Bruges at their heels, the town was pillaged, the members of the aristocratic party were slain by hundreds, and the Count barely escaped to Lille in disguise. Numerous towns forthwith drove out the aristocrats and joined the revolt.

Louis de Maele turned for help to his son-in-law Philip the Bold, who, as his probable successor, had every reason for upholding his authority. For his part, Charles VI was eager to try his hand at fighting, especially against schismatic rebels. Thus, in the summer of 1382, it was decided by the royal Council to organize an expedition against the insurgents of Flanders. Ghent, alarmed, tried to negotiate an agreement, but without success, and had to console itself with the promise of help from England.

The French began their campaign in the November of a rainy Flanders autumn. The strength of their army lay in the men-at-arms, and Artevelde would have been well advised to rely mainly upon mud. As a matter of fact, he showed little military capacity at any stage. The French cleverly secured the passage of the Lys at Comines, and took Ypres. Artevelde then advanced from Bruges and entrenched himself at Roosebeke. There, on November 27, he foolishly took the offensive, his whole army charging in a closely packed triangle, with the men of Ghent at the striking point. The attack, though made with great resolution and temporary success, was on too narrow a front; the wings of the French army swung inwards; the Flemings were helplessly trapped and butchered. Artevelde perished; his body was hung in chains by order of the Count, and burial was denied to the corpses of the other slaughtered Flemings. [Battle of Roosebeke, Nov. 27, 1382]

Bruges at once surrendered, promising to pay an indemnity and to recognize Pope Clement VII. But Ghent rejected the demands of Charles VI, who was tired of the campaign and went back to France.

**Harsh treatment of Paris**

The abrupt departure of the French from Flanders was partly accounted for by the belief of the Regency that it would now be safe to supplement the reprisals already inflicted upon Paris and Rouen. It was said, indeed, that the Parisians had given covert aid to the Flemish rebels, and Charles entered his capital as though it were a conquered town. A number of notable officials and over 300 citizens were arrested. Many executions speedily followed, one victim at least suffering for deeds alleged to have been committed during the troubles of 1358. The Council began to levy new impositions without even a pretence of securing the approval of an assembly of Estates. On January 27, 1383, the King ceremoniously promulgated an enactment withdrawing the city's privileges; the office of *prévôt des marchands* was abolished, his powers being entrusted to the royal *prévôt*; the gilds were to be subject to officers named by the King; no gild or fraternity might meet save to go to church. The executions continued briskly for another month, and when on March 1 the King granted a general pardon, forty persons were excluded from its operation.

**Further reprisals at Rouen**

At Rouen royal commissioners arrested more than 300 citizens. An appeal to the royal pardon of the previous year—even a letter from the King ordering the commissioners to regard it—produced no apparent effect, since it was alleged that disturbances since its issue had cancelled it. Many of the prisoners were executed, more held to ransom. A new fine was levied on the town. As years passed, the Commune began to function again in fact if not in name, and a certain prosperity returned, but Rouen never wholly recovered.

**Bishop Despenser's crusade**

It is gratifying to find that the government had to pay for its eagerness to castigate royal towns; for its failure to crush Ghent after the battle of Roosebeke compelled it to send two further expeditions to Flanders and frustrated enterprises which it wished to undertake elsewhere. Both rival popes were organizing crusades against each other, and Urban VI committed the command of one of these holy expeditions to Henry Despenser, Bishop of Norwich, who had displayed his warlike proclivities in the suppression of the Peasants' Revolt in England. Under the influence of the English government and Parliament it was decided to send the crusaders to Flanders, where they would help Ghent and its allies. It was true that most of the Flemings, whatever their political party, were Urbanists in regard to the Schism in the Church. Still, it might be argued that anything that helped Ghent would harm the King of France, who was the most powerful supporter of Clement VII at Avignon.

The expedition might have been very dangerous to France, but it was grossly mismanaged. The English crusaders, thanks to their archers, won a little battle against an army of the Count's. They took Dunkirk, Bourbourg, Cassel, and other adjacent places, and laid siege to Ypres. Responding to an appeal from the Count, Charles VI came to the rescue in the summer of 1383. On the approach of the French army, Despenser left Ypres, evacuated most of his conquests, and prepared to defend Gravelines. But he soon accepted a sum of money and went home. The English were angry at this ignominious end to the enterprise, but the French made no effort to exploit their success, and Ghent remained unconquered.

Next year the situation in Flanders was profoundly changed by the death of Louis de Maele, and the succession of Philip the Bold of Burgundy. He had no difficulty in securing recognition in the greater part of the county. Ghent, perceiving that only foreign support could enable it to withstand so powerful an enemy, bid high for English aid, placed itself under the protection of King Richard, and flew the English flag. In 1385 it accepted as captain an English knight, John Bourchier, with whose retinue its citizens succeeded in taking Damme. A great French army, which had been assembled for a descent on England, was thereupon diverted to north Flanders; Damme was besieged and recovered, and the surrounding country savagely plundered. But again Charles VI went away without attempting to reduce Ghent itself. *Philip the Bold of Burgundy succeeds to Flanders, 1384*

One reason why the French seldom pushed home their victories in Flanders was that the Counts did not like to see them there except in time of special danger. The Duke of Burgundy was particularly anxious to restore order in his new county without assistance from outside. He let it be known that he was in a conciliatory mood. It was not long before envoys from Ghent and its allies met representatives of the Duke at Tournai. The two sides bargained like equals, and the men of Ghent steadfastly refused to ask for mercy on their knees. In December, 1385, peace was signed, on terms very favourable to the rebels. The privileges of Ghent and its allies were confirmed. Trade was to be as free as heretofore. In Flanders the Duke would appoint only officials of Flemish birth. The men of Ghent might favour either Pope as they pleased. It is not surprising that the Duke was well received when he made his solemn entry into Ghent soon afterwards.

The story of these risings in France is not of great interest. But they have commonly been too lightly passed over by historians. The reign of Charles V is remembered as one of the most successful in the medieval history of France. French arms were victorious, and the government was unusually efficient. Yet it is clear from what followed the change of ruler that there was bitter and widespread discontent, and that, if the French had generally preferred Charles V to Edward III, it was not because they believed his rule to be better. The treatment accorded by the Regency to the malcontents is instructive. Disaffection was treated as unpardonable. If mercy was ever shown, it was only because it would have been impolitic to act otherwise. Unquestioning obedience was assumed to be the duty of all the Crown's subjects. If they demurred or resisted, force or fraud might be used against them to the utmost limit. And the authorities who applied such theories were, as we shall see, conducting public affairs incapably and corruptly. The lack of loyalty with which the French of that generation and the next are often reproached is not at all astonishing and hardly blameworthy. Not that the French people themselves showed much wisdom in their attitude towards misgovernment and oppression. Their demand for the total abolition of all *aides* was unpractical and short-sighted. If a fourteenth-century king was to defend and govern his country properly, he could not live on the resources of his domain. This the French should have recognized, and, instead of crying for the moon, should have insisted that for all extraordinary

*The French government and the French people*

taxation the consent of an assembly of Estates—preferably the Estates-General—should be obtained. That demand, steadily and wisely pressed, might have given the Estates-General the stability which was being acquired by the English Parliament. In England, it is true, one might still hear the foolish cry that "the King should live of his own," but, finding the whole loaf unattainable, the English contented themselves with bringing extraordinary taxation under parliamentary control. It is of course true that the English Parliament had a great advantage over the French Estates-General inasmuch as the Hundred Years War was usually, from the English standpoint, a royal luxury, whereas to the Frenchman it was an unavoidable struggle against invasion. Still, in the early years of Charles VI it was the French rather than the English who were the aggressors, and the French Estates had a real opportunity of making themselves an indispensable element in the French system of government. To all appearance, they were never aware that such an opportunity existed.

For some time after 1385 there was no open rebellion in France, though the country suffered to an abnormal degree from that lawless violence which was endemic in all medieval countries. Of the King's uncles, the Duke of Anjou was dead. In 1382 he had led an army to Italy as champion of Clement VII and heir to Queen Joanna of Naples. His aspirations and exploits are better treated elsewhere; here it is enough to say that before he could achieve anything substantial he died in September 1384, leaving an heir of seven and a claim to the throne of Naples which was to have far-reaching consequences.

The Dukes of Burgundy and Berry remained to afflict France. The latter cared less for politics and power than for his books, jewels, and strange beasts, though his tastes were just as expensive as the more spectacular ambitions of his brother. The two, in fact, were equally rapacious and very jealous of each other. Burgundy's strength was much increased by his inheritance of Flanders and his reconciliation with Ghent. For a year or two he dominated the King, and played the tune to which French policy had to march. Though in 1385 the projected expedition against England had been diverted against Damme in the interests of the Duke, he was really eager for vigorous prosecution of the war. In 1386 John of Gaunt led a so-called crusade to Castile in prosecution of his claim to the crown of that kingdom, and at the instance of Philip the Bold it was resolved in France to take advantage of the situation by launching a very formidable attack on England. An exceptionally large army was assembled on the north coast, with the largest fleet since the Creation. The most careful preparations were made for ensuring the permanence of any military success that might be gained: for instance, a fortified camp of wood was to be transported, all ready to be put together in a few hours. But the undertaking was ruined by an unpunctuality which was abnormal even in medieval France. Summer was almost over when the King reached Sluys, the port of embarkation, and it was not until October that the Duke of Berry, with the troops under his command, made his appearance. If, as men said, it was his deliberate purpose to frustrate the expedition, he was successful. There was a spirit of pessimism abroad, some minor engagements had gone in favour of the English, and the weather had turned stormy. The expedition was postponed to the spring. Before the army could sail, Olivier de Clisson, the Constable, who was to command half the French fleet, was seized and imprisoned by the Duke of Brittany; and by the time that royal intervention brought about a reconciliation, it was too late to invade England that year. In 1388 a truce between the two realms was signed, and the project of a great revenge for Creçy and Poitiers fell to the ground. It had cost a vast amount of money.

France's relations with Germany were likewise determined by Duke Philip. It was to his interest to be on good terms with the Wittelsbachs, for a branch of that house ruled the coveted counties of Holland, Zeeland, and Hainault. Philip sought a marriage alliance between the two families, but Count Albert of Holland proved wary and exacting. Finally, in the spring of 1385, Philip's son John married a daughter of the Count, while Albert's son William of Ostrevant married Philip's daughter Margaret. The policy embodied in these alliances demanded that Charles VI should himself marry a Wittelsbach, and it was owing to the Duke that a match was arranged between him and Isabel, daughter of Duke Stephen of Bavaria. The wedding took place in July 1385. The marriage has been much execrated, and Isabel is one of the traditional objects of patriotic hatred in France. But in 1385 she was a charming girl of fifteen, with whom Charles at once fell and long remained deeply in love.

The overweening ambition of Philip the Bold naturally excited hostility in many quarters, and presently began to irk the King. In 1388 the Duke strained his influence too far. He had taken up a quarrel of the Duchess of Brabant against the Duke of Guelders, and had enlisted the military support of France, notwithstanding the fact that his opponent had been an ally and pensioner of Charles V. The threatened ruler allied himself with England, defied and insulted Charles VI, and only offered a very equivocal submission when a great French army advanced against him in 1388. The dispute had really had nothing to do with the French Crown; Charles's dignity had suffered; the campaign had been inglorious and costly. It must have needed little effort to screw the King to the sticking-point. At a great council held at Rheims in November, the oldest of Charles's councillors, the Cardinal of Laon, urged that, since he was now twenty years old, he should govern the kingdom himself. The King agreed, formally thanked his uncles for their services, and disregarded their protests, warnings, and inordinate requests for reward. They eventually accepted their lot, and for several years little was seen of them at court. There is no doubt that this episode inspired Richard II of England when a few months later he rid himself of the tutelage of his uncles with equal ease.

*Charles VI's coup d'état*

The country had high hopes of the new regime, but it must be confessed that they had little warrant. Charles himself was good-natured, but he lacked both intelligence and force of character. He fell increasingly under the influence of his brother, Louis Duke of Touraine, who was now seventeen. Louis was an active and clever young man, more interested than the King in art and letters, but also much given to pleasure and swayed by restless political ambition. The downfall of the King's uncles was accompanied by the removal from office of many of their creatures and by the revival of the influence of some of Charles V's old counsellors, slightingly called the *Marmousets* by the great nobles, such as Bureau de la Rivière and Jean le Mercier. There was a great parade of reforming the administration, every branch of which was affected by a series of ordinances promulgated in the first months of 1389. In particular, it was laid down that vacancies in the *Parlement* should be filled by co-optation, and that *baillis, sénéchaux*, and officers of justice should be chosen by the *Grand Conseil*. It is very doubtful whether these regulations would have been beneficial, even if they had been strictly enforced. An attempt was made to conciliate the Parisians by appointing an upright young lawyer, Jean Jouvenel of Troyes, to the custody of the *prévôté des marchands*, the office itself being soon restored in practice though not in name. A progress of the King through Languedoc did something to pacify that region, reduced to despair by the grasping administration of the Duke of Berry. One of the Duke's most faithful agents was entrapped into uttering heresy and promptly burned as an earnest of the King's goodwill towards his subjects.

The King's failure

It was only by the exercise of strict economy that the new government could have undone the evil wrought by the old one. And economy was the last thing to be expected from Charles VI and his brother. For three years they lived in a round of extravagant dissipation, the like of which had never been seen in France before. There were ceremonies, spectacles, tournaments, balls, banquets without end, all very splendid and many of them organized with real skill and taste. Even more ruinous was the foreign policy of these years. With England hostilities were suspended by a series of truces, and the eclipse of the Duke of Burgundy saved France from entanglements in Germany. But the ramifications of the Great Schism and the ambitions of the Duke of Touraine involved her in hare-brained projects beyond the Alps. The Duke was married to Valentina Visconti, daughter and heiress of Gian Galeazzo, Lord of Milan. This alliance turned his thoughts towards Italy, and disposed him to accept Clement VII's offer to enfeoff him with a large part of the Papal States, on condition of his driving out the rival Pope and maintaining Clement in

Rome. Simultaneously, Charles VI had taken up the cause of his young cousin, Louis of Anjou, who was pressing his father's claims to Naples and Sicily; so he was easily won over to support the projects of Touraine. In 1390 preparations were made for a great French expedition in the following year. It would be led by Charles VI himself, and would result in the establishment of Clement in Rome, of Louis of Touraine in north Italy, and of Louis of Anjou in the south. Pope Boniface IX and his supporters were much alarmed.

The army never started. A month before the date fixed for its march, an English embassy reached Paris with suggestions for a final peace between England and France and a personal meeting of the two kings. Charles did not dare to turn his back on these proposals; the Italian expedition was postponed, and so, for that matter, was his interview with Richard II. On one pretext or another the English put it off for the whole of that year, and when, in the spring of 1392, there was a conference at Amiens, it was not attended by Richard and consequently ended without definite result. There has been much discussion as to whether the English intervention was deliberately timed so as to frustrate the French plans in Italy or whether it was sincere and happened by accident to occur at a specially critical moment. The former alternative is probably correct. In any case, the French government had again wasted vast sums of money on abortive military preparations.

The most serious element in the situation, however, was the state of the King's health. Charles VI had been leading a fast and harassing life. At the conference of Amiens in the spring of 1392, the discourteous absence of Richard II seems to have annoyed him intensely, and he had what would nowadays be called a nervous breakdown. From this he seemed to have recovered; but a few weeks later he was greatly shocked by an attempt to murder Olivier de Clisson, the Constable, in whom he had much confidence. The author of the crime was Pierre de Craon, a disreputable kinsman of Clisson's enemy the Duke of Brittany. It was generally believed that Craon had been instigated by the Duke, with whom he took refuge. Despite the opposition of the King's uncles, it was resolved to lead a punitive expedition against Brittany.

*The King's mental breakdown*

The King was in a nervous, excitable state, but remained with the army until it had passed Le Mans. Then, one very hot August day, while crossing a bare sandy plain, he suddenly had the delusion that he was being attacked, broke into a frenzy, assailed those nearest him, among them being his brother, wounded several pages—perhaps killed one or two—and, after being disarmed by force, remained silent, with rolling eyes, seeming to recognize none of those around him. Under—or perhaps despite—medical treatment, the violent phase of the malady passed away in a few days, and in a month Charles seemed quite well. But he was never again able to devote himself fully to business of state. Attacks of violent madness recurred, at first every year, afterwards at more frequent intervals and in growing strength. Eventually the King's lucid moments became rare, and when he was sane he was wholly lacking in energy. For France it had been better if the King had died at the time of the first crisis. Nothing could have been worse for the country than the situation created by the character of his disorder.

**Burgundy against Orléans**

The collapse of Charles VI restored to power his two uncles. Adversity had reconciled them, and henceforth the Duke of Berry could generally be relied upon to support his brother. The *Marmousets* were driven from office, and many of them would probably have lost their lives but for the speedy recovery and personal intervention of the King. As for Charles's brother, who had been made Duke of Orléans shortly before the King's illness, he soon became the bitter rival of the Duke of Burgundy. But his arrogant and profligate ways made him unpopular. It is significant that when Charles VI was nearly burned to death at a court revel, public opinion was inclined to condemn his brother, who was supposed to have been careless, if not worse. In 1393 he was named as Regent in the event of the King being incapacitated, but the restrictions imposed on his authority were so great as almost to turn the honour into an insult.

**Truce with England**

As ruler of Flanders, Philip the Bold had now decided that peace with England was desirable. The negotiations begun before the King's collapse were continued, and after the death of Richard II's Queen, Anne of Bohemia, a royal marriage alliance was mooted. In 1395 Richard formally asked for the hand of Charles's little daughter, Isabel, and early in 1396 the two were betrothed. Isabel was to bring with her a dowry of 800,000 francs, and to renounce all claim to the throne of France. The existing truce was prolonged for twenty-eight years. In October the two kings met with great pomp and circumstance between Ardres and Calais. Relations were courteous but formal, and little progress was made towards the conclusion of a definitive peace. After the conference, however, Isabel was left with Richard, who married her at Calais in November. The English king was certainly sincere in his policy of reconciliation, and in 1397, by accepting from the Duke of Brittany 120,000 francs in exchange for Brest, he evacuated one of the few remaining ports still held by the English in France.

Very soon after his marriage Richard embarked on that headlong career of folly which in less than three years brought about his deposition and death. The marriage alliance had failed of its purpose. The relations of the two countries naturally became precarious. The little Queen Isabel was sent home, but there was a long dispute about her dowry, and the Duke of Orléans, by his blustering talk about revenge for Richard's fate, did what he could to stimulate bad feeling. The truce, however, was renewed for several years, and the Duke of Burgundy was still for peace, actually securing from the French Crown permission for the towns of Flanders to conclude a special commercial truce with England, which should hold good even when the two realms were actively at war.

Less successful was the policy favoured by Burgundy in relation to the Great Schism. When the projected expedition of 1391 came to nothing, there was a revulsion of feeling against the use of force to settle the problem. The University of Paris, silenced by the government some years before, made its voice heard again. The progress of the discussion, which of course was not limited to France, is best described elsewhere. In France, however, it should be noted, opinion turned steadily in favour of what was called "the way of cession"—both Popes, that is to say, should resign, leaving the path clear for the election of a successor of unquestioned authority. Benedict XIII, who in 1394 had followed Clement VII at Avignon, had professed himself in favour of this solution. But when called

*Philip the Bold and the Great Schism*

upon to act accordingly he refused. The University of Paris thereupon advocated the refusal of obedience to the Pope until union was achieved. Its views met with a mixed reception in other European countries, but in 1398 a council of the Church in France voted the immediate withdrawal of obedience from Benedict. This policy had the vigorous support of the Duke of Burgundy, who was keenly interested in the affairs of Germany, where, as in Flanders, most people adhered to the Roman Pope; indeed, he probably tampered with the votes cast in the Council which made the momentous decision. The Duke of Orléans, on the other hand, still hankering after an Italian kingdom, would have liked to keep on good terms with Benedict, though for the moment he acquiesced in his country's policy.

*Benedict XIII successfully defies France*

The effects of France's stroke fell short of expectations. The Pope remained obdurate, even when besieged in Avignon by a French force. The sudden withdrawal of papal authority, though hailed by many reformers as restoring to the Church of France her pristine freedom, was found in practice to cause much inconvenience and confusion. There had always been a strong minority loyal to the Pope, and this tended to increase. The Duke of Orléans openly pressed for the restitution of obedience to Benedict. When, in March 1403, the Pope escaped from Avignon and took refuge in Provence, it was widely recognized in France that nothing was to be gained by continuing to disobey him. Pressed by his brother and some of the leading French prelates, Charles VI proclaimed in May that Benedict should again be treated as lawful Pope.

*French activity in various quarters*

Once again the policy of the central government had proved abortive. In Italy, too, French influence had been singularly ineffective. Nothing had come of various projects for carving a principality out of the Papal States for one of the French royal family. In 1399 Louis II of Anjou was driven from Naples. Only in the extreme north had French ambition received any encouragement. Genoa, threatened with revolution at home and defeat abroad, offered itself to the King of France. It thus came about that from 1396 to 1409 Genoa, while remaining an imperial town, was ruled by governors acting in the name of the King of France. Of these the most notable was the Marshal

Boucicaut, one of the models of the chivalry of that time, who gave the city good government, added Monaco and Elba to the possessions of Charles VI, and fought successfully against Cyprus and Venice. Nevertheless France would have been wiser to reserve her strength for enterprises which more intimately concerned her, or for the cure of her own disorders. One cannot, it is true, withhold admiration for the energy of her sons. In crusading zeal, for instance, they far exceeded any other nation. In 1390, it was the Duke of Bourbon and his French followers who had won success for an expedition, initiated by the Genoese, against the Moslem pirates of El-Mahadia in Tunis and Cagliari in Sardinia, and six years later France contributed more than any other country of Western Europe to the campaign against the Turks which ended in the catastrophe of Nicopolis.

In the twenty-five years which followed the death of Charles V, French policy had been almost consistently unsuccessful. No advantage had been taken of the weakness of England, which had lost but little ground in France since 1380. The country was on the whole more impoverished and less orderly than it had been in Charles V's last years. And yet France was not a decadent country. As we have seen, there was no lack of virility and enterprise among her people, who were ready enough to answer appeals to their more generous sentiments. What crippled her was the selfish dissension among the princes of the blood—notably between the Dukes of Orléans and Burgundy. As years passed, and the former gained in confidence and experience, the feud grew steadily more bitter. When the King was sick—and his spells of lunacy tended to become longer and more frequent—the Duke of Burgundy usually had the upper hand. But in his lucid intervals, Charles relied more and more on his brother. The Duke of Burgundy at first possessed far greater resources of his own, and he managed to draw repeatedly and extensively on the royal treasury. In such operations, however, he was excelled by his rival, who in the opening years of the fifteenth century derived huge sums from the *aides*, while he also received from his royal brother fiefs which, taken together, gave him territory in France which in extent, though not in wealth, approached that of Philip. In 1401

*Growth of rivalry between Burgundy and Orléans*

the Duke of Guelders, a thorn in the side of the Duke of Burgundy, did homage to him; and he actually managed to get a footing between the two main centres of Burgundian power, for by cultivating the friendship of the house of Luxemburg, he was recognized in 1402 as governor of that duchy and lord of a part of it. By this time hostility between the two dukes had become a habit. Wherever one had interests, the other tried to frustrate them. They pursued rival policies in Italy and towards England; and the friendship of Orléans for the Luxemburgs was suggested by the alliance between Burgundy and the Wittelsbachs.

Of the two, Orléans was the more attractive man; but he was the more unpopular. He was thoroughly selfish, he was grasping, profligate, and extravagant. Burgundy was no less selfish, but, with his own vast resources, he had less need to plunder the treasury; an older man, he had less temptation to stray from the path of outward respectability; and he was credited—justly indeed—with being a friend of peace. Thus he had the city of Paris on his side, and his ecclesiastical policy won him the approval of the university, a most important consideration.

*Death of Philip the Bold, 1404* — In 1404, at a moment when things were going well for the Duke of Orléans, the death of Philip the Bold seemed to ensure his unshakable ascendancy. The Queen, who had been an ally of Philip, now inclined towards the other side. Orléans had himself made lieutenant and captain-general of Normandy and Picardy. The Princess Isabel, widow of Richard II, was betrothed to his son Charles. The *aides* were under his control. But in the following year he came face to face with the new Duke of Burgundy, John, afterwards called the Fearless, and it was soon evident that his prospects had, if anything, deteriorated.

*John the Fearless* — Duke John was thirty-four, a little older, that is to say, than Duke Louis. He was singularly lacking in physical graces, a poor speaker, shabby in his dress, with a reputation for meanness. But on occasion he could be recklessly brave, as he had shown at Nicopolis, where he had been taken prisoner. He was no fool, he was extremely ambitious, well-informed on everything that concerned his political interests, and wholly unscrupulous. When he first met

Orléans at the royal Council, early in 1405, the latter was particularly unpopular, mainly because of a recent attempt on his part to debase the currency, an attempt frustrated by the *Chambre des Comptes*. John at once assumed an openly hostile attitude towards Louis. A little later, Orléans, as director of *aides*, ordered the levy of a new tax for the resumption of the war against England. Burgundy declared that it should not be paid in his fiefs, and in the summer marched on Paris at the head of an army. He entered the city, got possession of the King and the Dauphin, and presented a long list of grievances to them, the *Parlement*, and the *Chambre des Comptes*. The Duke of Orléans offered a formal and defiant reply, and the authorities to whom appeal was made, not knowing who was going to win, were in a quandary. Both sides, however, were finding it hard to maintain armies in the field, and in the autumn a so-called reconciliation was arranged. Orléans and the Queen returned to Paris; the two dukes swore everlasting fraternity and behaved like dear friends; a stern ordinance forbade anyone in future to raise armed men without the King's order.

France at this time was drifting into a renewal of active warfare with England. In 1405 a French force landed in Wales to help Owen Glendower, but, though it had some initial success and got within a few miles of Worcester, it had in the end to go home without achieving anything decisive. There were vigorous but inconclusive operations in the neighbourhood of Calais, and a good deal of petty fighting at sea. In 1406 the Duke of Burgundy, wishing to prove his zeal, announced that he would capture Calais, but, alleging that the Duke of Orléans had withheld the necessary funds, did nothing. For his part, Orléans organized a great expedition for the conquest of Guienne, but, what with English resistance, disease, and autumn mud, it proved an ignominious failure. Each unsuccessful commander criticized the other, and in the autumn of 1407, when the two met again in Paris, they were as bitter as ever. In November, however, the Duke of Berry cajoled them into a renewed display of mutual affection, which seems really to have imposed upon him and perhaps put Orléans off his guard.

*Growing animosity of French factions*

*Louis of Orléans murdered, Nov. 1407*

In the night of November 23, 1407, Duke Louis was set upon in the streets of Paris by a gang of armed men, who stabbed him to death. The *prévôt* of Paris showed admirable promptitude in discovering the identity of the murderers, and declared that he had good hopes of finding the instigator of the deed. The Duke of Burgundy thereupon confessed to the Dukes of Anjou and Berry that, induced by the devil, he had been the author of the murder. Next day, November 26, before Anjou and Berry had made up their minds what to do, he fled from Paris. Such was the black prologue to one of the blackest periods of French history.

CHAPTER II

FRANCE, 1407-1429

TREASON AND INVASION

PRECISELY what the Duke of Burgundy expected to gain by the murder of the Duke of Orléans is not certain. If he had hoped that his guilt would be undetected, he was absurdly sanguine. He put himself in danger of utter ruin. Yet, from his standpoint, the risk was justified by the event. His position after the removal of Orléans was, all things considered, stronger than it had been before. None of his later enemies was so formidable. *The profits of murder*

It is true that when the widowed duchess, Valentina Visconti, besought Charles, sane for the moment, to take vengeance on the murderer, the King declared that he would execute prompt and complete justice. But no action followed; the culprit mustered troops in Flanders, and, despite the protestations of the Dukes of Anjou and Berry, he entered Paris on February 28, 1408, amid cheering crowds. A week later, in the presence of the Dauphin, Duke John himself, and a large audience of notables, John Petit, one of the most renowned theologians of the University of Paris, delivered his famous " Apology " for the crime. The reading of it took four hours; there was nothing sensational in Petit's presentation of his case, which consisted of closely reasoned argument. Petit's treatise is generally styled a vindication of tyrannicide; but it was rather a defence of the slaying of traitors, Orléans, it was urged, having been guilty of treason towards Charles VI. Petit's arguments of course convinced only those who had already excused Duke John, whose real strength was based partly on his material resources and partly on public opinion. The townsfolk and peasants of northern and central France generally believed, not without reason, that the Duke of Orléans had cared nothing for them and that they had him to thank for the recent heavy taxation. The Duke of Burgundy, on the other hand, was regarded as the friend of the people; if he had the government in his hands, he would restore peace and abolish the taxes.

*Burgundians and Armagnacs*

Most of the great French nobles, it is true, ranged themselves against him. His uncles, the Dukes of Berry and Bourbon, were hostile. So were the Duke of Brittany and the Counts of Alençon and Armagnac. In 1410 Armagnac's daughter was married to Charles, the eldest son of the murdered Duke, a youth of nineteen. The Count was thus a man of weight in the counsels of the party, where his fiery and impetuous temper would in any case have given him a leading place. His importance was signalized by the fact that the opponents of Burgundy soon became known as Armagnacs. The name is a useful reminder that the conflict was in great measure one between the south of France and the north, though this generalization is subject to many qualifications.

Notwithstanding the hatred which each side felt for the other, the actual outbreak of civil war was delayed for over three years. The Duke of Burgundy was usually ready to fight, but his opponents feared his power, and showed boldness only when he was absent. In 1408 he had to spend some time chastising the rebellious subjects of his brother-in-law, the Bishop of Liége, an operation in which he cheaply won his nickname of "the Fearless." In the meantime the King and Queen returned to Paris; the Duchess of Orléans and her young son Charles renewed their demand for justice; and an assembly like the one which had listened to John Petit heard his arguments eloquently confuted by the Abbot of Cerisi. The Council collected troops to coerce the Duke if he should refuse to submit himself to justice. But when in the autumn the criminal, with his victorious army, prepared to return to Paris, the court and the Armagnac princes quickly left the city, which he again entered without opposition. The death of the Dowager Duchess of Orléans opened the way to a hollow reconciliation, which took place at Chartres in the spring of 1409. Next year, however, the enmity of the two factions was as bitter as ever; both had armies in the field, and it was only a lack of money and a certain reluctance to strike the first blow that averted a battle. In the autumn of 1410, another agreement was patched up. All this while the influence of Burgundy was predominant in the Government, thanks largely to his control over the Dauphin Louis, his son-in-law, and to the unwavering support which he received from the Parisians. In regions where his party predominated, there was no security for the lives or goods of Armagnacs.

In 1411 there occurred a most ominous development in the situation. Both sides began to negotiate with Henry IV of England. The Armagnacs, it seems, would have been content with his neutrality; but John the Fearless wanted his active aid. The Burgundians had more to offer than their opponents; the Duke proposed the marriage of one of his daughters to the Prince of Wales, and a small English force was dispatched to his aid. In the autumn there was fighting in Picardy, and the Armagnacs tried to take Paris. But, with the help of the English contingent, which greatly distinguished itself in an action at St. Cloud, the Duke relieved the city. *Civil war begins, 1411*

The Armagnacs now made a great effort to detach Henry IV from his alliance with Duke John and to win him over to their side. They succeeded in negotiating a treaty, signed at Eltham in May 1412, whereby they undertook to aid Henry in conquering the whole of the duchy of Aquitaine, which he was to hold in full sovereignty. In return, Henry was to send 1,000 men-at-arms and 3,000 archers to help them in the campaign that was about to open.

John the Fearless could now pose as a patriot. His army became the army of France; Charles VI took the oriflamme at St. Denis, placed himself at the head of the troops, and laid siege to Bourges, the chief town of the Duke of Berry. It was not long, however, before negotiations between the two sides were begun and hostilities suspended. In August 1412, at an assembly of nobles held at Auxerre, a formal peace was concluded. Both sides renounced their alliances. All confiscated goods and usurped offices were to be restored. Royal castles in the hands of nobles were to be given up. The peace of Auxerre caused great enthusiasm in France, but there was no chance of its being kept by either side. As for the English, the promised troops landed in Normandy just after the agreement was made, but they ravaged far and wide in north-west France, and the Armagnac leaders had to bribe them very heavily before they would depart to *Pacification of 1412*

Guienne. The events of these two years had revealed to the English the bitterness of the hatred between the two French factions and the inefficiency of the leaders on both sides.

**Deplorable condition of France**

Already the rivalry of Armagnacs and Burgundians had crippled the administration in many parts of France. The great nobles of each faction raised troops and kept them under arms; and when hostilities were not in progress or imminent, these men made themselves a terror to the regions where they were quartered. The peasants and small tradesmen were in miserable plight; their lives and property were insecure, and yet the authorities who failed to protect them were continually demanding taxes. The extravagance and corruption of the court and the organs of the central government were notorious. On all sides there was a sullen growl of resentment.

**The Estates-General of 1413**

It was widely believed that the English were about to invade the country. The government needed money to organize resistance, but evidently feared what might follow an increase in taxation. It was probably the Duke of Burgundy who formed the resolve of having recourse to the Estates-General, evidently trusting that his popularity in the towns was still strong enough to render the assembly favourable to his demands. It is significant, however, that the summons merely affected Languedoil: Languedoc, where Armagnac influence was in the ascendant, was ignored.

Even from Languedoil the response was poor. Very few Armagnac nobles appeared in person, and not a few towns failed to send representatives. When, in January 1413, the government demanded from the assembly an aid for raising a large army, those present were told to deliberate, not in the traditional way, but by ecclesiastical provinces, the university and town of Paris being allowed to debate apart. The reason for this singular arrangement was not revealed at the time and has never been discovered. Presumably the Duke of Burgundy expected that it would render the Estates more amenable than they would otherwise have been, though why it should have had that effect is hard to see. Whatever his hopes, the Duke must have been disappointed at the sequel. Rheims, the only province which was adequately represented, demanded the reform of the administration of justice and finance. Rouen advocated the restoration of order and (strange to say) the renewal of war against England, perhaps in the belief that this would unite the hostile factions. The spokesman of the province of Lyons, a member of the Duke of Burgundy's Council, was particularly bold. As for money, let it be taken from the King's careless and fraudulent officials or from the princes, who had received so much from the Crown that surely they would be willing to give some of it back to aid the realm. Afterwards, there must be a drastic reform, beginning at the top and sparing nobody. The other provinces and the university and town of Paris showed equal reluctance to vote new taxes. The government consequently announced that it would forgo an *aide* and that reforms would straightway be initiated.

Then the representatives of the university and town of Paris came forward with an enormous memorandum of grievances and proposals. The royal officials were denounced in unmeasured terms : twenty-two were singled out by name and their offences specified. The Council, the *Parlement*, and other courts of justice were also severely condemned. The document next proposed the dismissal of all officials who had to do with finance. Those who were innocent might be restored later ; but meanwhile the property of all should be confiscated, and what had been acquired by fraud should be applied to the needs of the country. The principal organs of central government should be reconstructed, and a commission should be set up to inquire further into abuses and to organize a thorough reform.

The authorities professed themselves favourable to these demands. Numerous officials were suspended, and a commission of reform began to work. At this point the Paris mob, as has happened so often at similar crises, intervened with disastrous effect. For some years the lesser craftsmen and tradesmen had been growing in power, and more than once they had terrorized the municipal authorities, who had lately been restored by the Crown to their old status and functions. The unruly element in the city seems to have been incited by rich merchants and tradesmen who kept in the background ; it had plenty of weapons and turned to its advantage arrangements recently made for the organization of a civic militia. The lead in its activities was taken by the

*The Cabochians intervene*

powerful gild of butchers, supported by various gilds dependent on it, such as the skinners and the tanners. Simon Caboche, a skinner, had become specially influential, and was treated with much favour by the Duke of Burgundy. For the Paris mob was even more Burgundian in sympathy than the Town Hall or the University.

Soon after the commission of reform began its work Caboche and his associates began to suspect that it was not sincere. The Dauphin, who was now taking a leading part in the government of the realm, showed signs of a desire to escape from the control of the Duke of Burgundy. Favours were bestowed on Armagnacs. The Duke of Orléans was said to be preparing for a renewal of the civil war. The Parisian nose began to smell " traitors."

At the end of April 1413, when the commission of reform had been sitting for two months, the storm broke. The butchers and skinners defied the municipal authorities, besieged and took the Bastille, invaded the Dauphin's palace, seized fifteen " traitors," and committed two or three murders. The Duke of Burgundy tried in vain to restrain them: the best he could do was to protect the lives of their prisoners.

*The Cabochians in control*

The Cabochians, as the rioters were called, now had full control of the town. They opened negotiations with the people of other French towns, urging them to take drastic measures against traitors. In Paris the Dauphin had to submit to further insult and to fill offices according to the wishes of the rebel leaders. The Cabochians went so far as to set up a tribunal to try certain officials whom they had denounced as public enemies. The situation seemed to be improved by the sudden return to sanity of Charles VI, who donned the white hood of the Cabochians and began to mediate between the hostile elements in the city. But on May 22 an immense crowd entered the courts of the palace clamouring for the arrest of the Queen, her brother Lewis of Bavaria, various officials, and a number of ladies of the royal household; and it was with great difficulty that the Duke of Burgundy induced them to be content with the surrender of Lewis. A day or two later, the Cabochian leaders demanded the immediate issue of an ordinance embodying the work of the reform commission. Their request was granted. On

May 26 Charles VI attended a session of the *Parlement*, and held a *lit de justice*. The reading of the measures drafted by the commission took up the whole of one session that day and two the next. Charles solemnly approved them and all present took oath to observe the ordinance.

The Cabochian Ordinance, as the measure was and is commonly called, had as its principal object the reform of the central administration. It consisted very largely of previous enactments which had been abortive or had ceased to be observed. But what particularly distinguished its authors was their conviction that "quiet calm deliberation disentangles every knot." It was laid down that the King and various exalted functionaries must consult the Council, or the *Parlement*, or the *Chambre des Comptes* in numerous specified contingencies. Few officials, central or local, were to take action on anything important without the concurrence of a committee. For the choice of officials and their advisers the reform commission had great faith in " election." Most public offices were to have an electoral committee attached to them. Thus the functionaries in charge of the royal finances were to be chosen by the members of the *Chambre des Comptes*, the chancellor, the members of the Council and the *Parlement*, and certain others. Vacancies in the *Parlement* and the *Chambre des Comptes* themselves were to be filled by committees specially appointed. Great local officers, such as the *baillis*, were to be chosen by the *Parlement* in the presence of the chancellor and some of the Council.

The Cabochian Ordinance throws an interesting light on the political ideas of the professional classes and other elements of the higher bourgeoisie in fifteenth-century France. There is no need to linger over its details, however, because only one or two of its enactments were ever applied at all. Indeed, the arrangements which it prescribed would never have worked satisfactorily even if given a fair chance.

The Cabochian Ordinance utterly failed to satisfy the Cabochians. Its publication was followed by a reign of terror. Several political prisoners were put to death, some without even a pretence of a trial. The Cabochian leaders became more violent and insolent in their behaviour towards the royal family. And they disgusted many of their erstwhile supporters by attempting to collect a tax for the impending war against England.

*The reaction*

Meanwhile the leading Armagnac nobles were collecting troops in Normandy. The Cabochians were not strong enough to prevent the court, the University, or the lawful municipal officers from treating with them, hoping that, as the Duke of Burgundy took part in the negotiations, their interests would be safeguarded. At Pontoise, on July 28, it was agreed that a general amnesty should be granted, all parties should lay aside their arms, and there should be an interview between the royal family and the leaders of the contending factions.

What followed is somewhat mysterious. The middle-classes of Paris plucked up courage, rallied round the Dauphin, and showed their intention of using force against the Cabochians. These, deserted by all the time-servers among the humbler orders, seem to have lost their nerve; at all events, they collapsed without so much as a show of resistance. The government began reprisals and the Parisians donned Armagnac badges. The Duke of Burgundy, threatened with arrest, if not with death, made a vain attempt to kidnap the King, and then fled to Flanders. The Armagnac leaders entered Paris amid great rejoicing. The offices of state were filled with Armagnacs; the Cabochian Ordinance was formally annulled; many Cabochians were executed, and more banished.

*Civil war renewed, 1414*

The Armagnacs soon showed that they did not intend to introduce any reforms in place of those prescribed in the Cabochian Ordinance. They ruled Paris with great severity. The King, when in his right wits, was entirely at their service; as for the Dauphin, he soon found their tutelage so irksome that he begged help from the Duke of Burgundy. Despite a prohibition put into the mouth of the King, John the Fearless advanced with an army to St. Denis in February 1414, but the Parisians dared not rise in his behalf, and he had to withdraw. He was outlawed, the feudal host was called out against him, and Charles VI put himself at the head of the Armagnac army. Soissons was sacked with a brutality conspicuous even in the wars of that time: but the Burgundians held out successfully at Arras, where a peace of the usual insincere character was signed in September.

The next winter was a terrible one for the peasantry of many parts of France. Government was utterly inefficient, and the disbanded soldiery plundered and ravished to their hearts' content. France was well acquainted with military licence before Henry V landed a man on its shores.

The Armagnac lords remained in possession of the offices of State, and showed themselves recklessly improvident. Their diplomacy was not much better than their administration. They were faced with a danger that concerned the whole nation, but instead of trying to meet it with a united front, they acted as though they wished to drive John the Fearless to the side of the enemy.

To understand the diplomatic situation at the beginning of 1415, one must go back to the accession of Henry V to the English throne in March 1413. As Prince of Wales he had been in favour of an alliance with the Burgundians, so that, John the Fearless being at the moment the predominant influence at Paris, relations between the two crowns were for a while friendly. Henry appointed commissioners to treat for peace with Charles VI, alliance with the Duke, and a renewal of the existing truce with France. Before anything could be done, the Duke had fallen from power; but the Duke of York, visiting Paris in the autumn, proposed a marriage between Henry and Charles VI's daughter Catherine. When, however, at the end of the year an embassy from France arrived in London to discuss the suggestion, Henry V's spokesmen asserted his right to the French throne, a subject with which the French naturally had no authority to deal. The best that could be done was to conclude a truce between the two realms which should last until February 2, 1415.

It was a little later that Henry received from the Dauphin or some other great man in France the famous present of a tun of tennis-balls. It was not delivered by a formal embassy; Henry himself took it as a joke, albeit an insolent one which must be turned against the jester. But he was not the man to suffer a childish trick to affect his diplomatic and military schemes. As for the French, while of course denying Henry's right to be their king, they judged correctly that he did not regard his claim very seriously and was ready to bargain

*Negotiations with Henry V*

about it. So negotiations for the marriage continued throughout 1414.

**Attitude of John the Fearless**

All this while, however, Henry was in close touch with the Duke of Burgundy. In May, envoys from the Duke were at Leicester, where they concluded an agreement whereby Henry was to send a military force to aid the Duke to conquer the possessions of the Armagnacs. The spoil was to be shared between the two. At the same time a marriage between Henry and one of the Duke's daughters was again proposed.

Further negotiations followed in Flanders, the outcome being that Duke John promised not to oppose Henry's claim to the French throne, and even to aid him against Charles VI. French historians—and many English ones too—have cried out against the Duke's perfidy. Remembering the murder of the Duke of Orléans, we may condemn him, for that crime led logically to the treachery just described. But it is only fair to bear in mind the Duke's position in the spring and summer of 1414. His King had outlawed him, had taken the oriflamme against him, and, when the last agreement with Henry was signed, had besieged his town of Arras. The feudal bond was broken, and not by the Duke. Why should he not seek succour where he could? As for his undertaking to fight against Charles VI, was not Charles VI already fighting against him? When, in September, peace was signed at Arras, the Duke declared that he had made no compact with the English, or, if he had, it was annulled. This assertion has been denounced as a cynical lie; but John may have meant that since he was now reconciled with the King of France, he did not hold himself bound by his promises to the King of England. At all events, the agreements between him and Henry in the spring and summer of 1414 were never carried out. Equally abortive, it seems, were obscure negotiations which were simultaneously proceeding between Henry and the Duke of Orléans. The fact is that both French parties were tarred with the brush of treason.

**Henry's demands and motives**

On the main issue between the two kingdoms little progress was made until the summer of 1414, when an imposing English mission asked for the hand of the Princess Catherine, whom Henry would marry if the crown of France were yielded to him. The envoys added, however, that Henry might perhaps content himself with the execution of the Treaty of

Brétigny, together with the surrender, in full sovereignty, of Touraine, Anjou, Maine, Normandy, and Flanders. As discussion proceeded the English, among other new demands, asked for a dowry of two million crowns with Catherine. The French offered to hand over the duchy of Aquitaine, according to its ancient limits, as the Armagnac leaders had undertaken to do in 1412, and intimated that they might furnish 600,000 crowns for the dowry: but more they would not concede, and the English embassy went home.

In November an English parliament met, and Henry laid before it his resolve to recover his French " inheritance " and asked for a grant of money so that, if necessary, he might support his rights by force. The Commons were generous, though they urged the King to exhaust the resources of diplomacy before resorting to arms. It has been inferred from this episode that Henry had already decided on war, and it is pointed out that he had been making very elaborate military preparations. It used of course to be believed—and the story is enshrined in Shakespeare—that Henry's renewal of the French war was instigated by the English clergy, who wished to divert his attention from their own shortcomings and from proposals for the confiscation of ecclesiastical property. But besides being quite unsupported by contemporary evidence, this explanation lacks all verisimilitude in view of Henry's character, opinions, and previous relations with the Church and her critics. It is highly probable, however, that Henry, conscious of the weakness of his title to the throne, wished to give his subjects something else to think about. He calculated—correctly, as the event proved—that victory over the French would make him personally popular; while, if he could persuade his subjects to support his right to the crown of France, they could hardly deny his right to the crown of England. In any case, however, Henry was an energetic and ambitious young man: he knew that France was weak and divided; and it is likely that, even if his claim to the English throne had been beyond cavil, he would have tried to suck some advantage out of her misfortunes. His title to the throne of France he was always ready to sell for territorial concessions, and if the French had been willing to pay his exorbitant price they could probably have avoided war. But at this juncture neither the Burgundians nor the

Armagnacs would have dared to yield what he wanted, and there is little doubt that Henry suspected this from the first. So, while he would negotiate until the impossibility of agreement was obvious to all, he meanwhile got ready to strike as soon as diplomacy should break down.

*Failure of the negotiations, July 1415*

The truce between England and France underwent successive prolongations which extended it to August 1, 1415. In February a weighty English embassy visited Paris. It might have been possible to arrange the marriage, if that matter could have been kept separate from Henry's demands for French territory, but on the latter question the two sides remained far asunder. Henry now began to raise men, in addition to amassing munitions, and the troops were ordered to muster at or near Southampton by midsummer. Nevertheless negotiations went on. In June a French mission went to England. The two sides came to terms on the question of the dowry; and Henry appeared willing to content himself with the concessions offered in Aquitaine, on condition that the French would agree to a fifty-years' truce. Possibly the English were not sincere; at all events, they outmanœuvred the French brilliantly, for when it looked as if an agreement was possible, the French began to discover reasons why they could not carry out their own proposals, and Henry was able to allege, with every show of justification, that their offers had never been seriously meant to promote peace. When this stage was reached, war was inevitable. Henry presented an ultimatum declaring that he would prosecute his claim to the French crown by force unless Charles VI yielded to him Aquitaine, Poitou, Touraine, Anjou, Maine, Normandy, and Ponthieu. The French replied defiantly. The final breach occurred on July 6, 1415, an evil day for Europe, for it witnessed also the burning of John Hus at Constance.

*France invaded, Aug. 14, 1415*

The Armagnac lords who were supposed to be governing France must have known for many months that an invasion was almost certain. But their preparations to meet it were derisory. They had no army in the field, and no clear idea of where the English meant to land. Thus Henry's great fleet crossed the Channel unhindered, and his army, numbering some 9,000 fighting men, landed unopposed at the Chef de Caux on August 14, 1415. Three days later the siege of Harfleur began.

Harfleur was strongly fortified, but its garrison, though Fall of reinforced at the last moment and commanded by the Lord of Harfleur, Gaucourt, a very resolute leader, consisted of only five or six Sept. 1415 hundred men. All things considered, the place did well to hold out for five weeks. The English invested the town, and relied mainly on bombardment. The besieged frustrated all their attempts to make a practicable breach in the main defences. But, faced with the prospect of a general assault and its sequel of sack and massacre, the garrison, on September 18, offered to surrender if not relieved within four days. They were allowed to send a message to Rouen, where a French army had been slowly mustering, but the reply was that nothing could be attempted at the moment. Harfleur accordingly passed into Henry's hands. Ecclesiastics and those who would swear allegiance to Henry were allowed to remain in the town; others must leave. Englishmen were invited to settle in the place, which Henry clearly intended to make an English outpost in France, like Calais.

The season for campaigning was nearly over, and the Henry's capture of Harfleur, though a substantial success, was hardly march to enough to satisfy English expectations after the immense Calais preparations that had been made. But what could be done? The casualties of the English had been very heavy, for disease had broken out in the siege-lines. When Henry had buried his dead, sent home his sick, and furnished Harfleur with a garrison, he had fewer than 6,000 men available. Some spectacular exploit, however, was needed for public opinion in England; and Henry resolved to march across northern France to Calais. It was a decision bold to the point of foolhardiness.

Meanwhile the French army at Rouen had become very large. It consisted almost wholly of Armagnacs, for the Duke of Burgundy held aloof, though in palliation of his conduct it should be noted that the government at Paris had indicated that it did not desire him to serve in person and wanted only a small contingent from his lands. The Duke of Brittany also hung back; but even without the aid of these powerful lords, the French army far outnumbered Henry's.

For some time after Henry left Harfleur on October 6 the strategy and tactics of the French were good. Their aim was to delay the English by holding the fords and bridges of the streams which they would have to cross, so that they would either perish of starvation or be compelled to fight at a fatal disadvantage. Thus when the English essayed to cross the Somme estuary by the famous ford of Blanque Taque, they learned that it was strongly guarded. They perforce turned upstream, and in miserable weather toiled into regions where five hundred years later their descendants were to suffer still more grievously, until a lapse in French vigilance enabled them to cross the Somme at Bethencourt and Voyennes, near St. Quentin. But precious time had been lost; the little army had shrunk through disease, and the survivors were weary and hungry. The French, furthermore, had moved a great host eastwards from Rouen, and it was now at Péronne, between the English and their objective. Despite the counsel of some of their most experienced leaders, the French resolved to offer battle. When told of this, Henry answered that he would welcome the opportunity, but that he would not interrupt his march until compelled. It thus came about that the two armies, whose intelligence service seems to have been very bad, marched by parallel routes for some days without encountering each other. But on October 24, the French cut the English line of march near the village of Agincourt in Artois. Henry offered to surrender his prisoners and all that he had gained in France if the French would grant him passage. But the answer was that he must fight.

The battle of Agincourt, Oct. 25, 1415

The battle of Agincourt, which took place next day, is one of the famous fights of history. On the whole, the traditional account of it is not far astray. The English cannot have numbered more than 5,000, of whom about four-fifths were lightly armoured archers. The French were probably five or six times as numerous, perhaps more; their force consisted mainly of fully-equipped men-at-arms.[1] They drew up their array on a short front between the villages of Agincourt and

[1] The late Professor Delbrück, reputed to be a great authority on military history, countenanced a foolish attempt by another and more obscure German writer to prove that the English outnumbered the French (*Geschichte der Kriegskunst*, iii. 477 *sq.*). The real basis for this singular enterprise seems to have been the German conviction, in the years before the Great War, that Englishmen could not fight. Professor Delbrück admitted later that he had been wrong in his general estimate of the military abilities of the English; but as his silly theory about Agincourt may still be read in a work that passes as authoritative, it seemed well to insert a warning against it.

Tramecourt, each of which lay in a wood, and thus forfeited much of their numerical advantage. Their discipline was bad; there was bitter jealousy among the leaders; there was no reasoned plan of battle. The ground between them and the English—ploughed and sodden with rain—was barely passable for heavily weighted men. Yet, when the English, who had to advance or starve, moved towards them, the French refused to remain on the defensive. They sent forward bodies of cavalry, who were promptly shot down. On this they hastily brought into action some of their crossbowmen, but these were utterly outmatched by the English archers. Then the vanguard of knights and men-at-arms essayed to advance on foot. Toiling painfully through the mud, in their oppressive plate-armour, they at last came to close quarters with the main English " battle," consisting also of dismounted knights and men-at-arms in full harness. For a while the sheer weight of the French array thrust the English back, and King Henry was at one moment in peril of his life. But as the front rank of the French was checked and the rear ranks still pressed on, the mass became tightly wedged and almost helpless. Then the English archers, with their knives, axes, and maces, fell upon the struggling throng. Not only was there an enormous slaughter, but very many unwounded Frenchmen were suffocated. Just when the mêlée was over and the English were about to resume their advance, the Duke of Brabant made a belated appearance on the field, and French marauders and camp-followers attacked the English baggage. It was hastily inferred that the French had rallied, and at Henry's reiterated orders, the English slew nearly all their prisoners, sparing only the very greatest. Thus the French losses in dead were much increased; indeed it is probable that in knights and men-at-arms alone they lost as many as the entire English army. The Dukes of Alençon, Brabant, and Bar and the Constable d'Albret were among the slain. Of the surviving prisoners the most notable were the Dukes of Orléans and Bourbon, Arthur Count of Richemont, the Counts of Eu and Vendôme, and Marshal Boucicaut, who thus, as the event proved, ended a long and honourable career in his country's service. In comparison the English casualties were ridiculously small—certainly not more than a hundred or two in dead.

When the fighting was all over, and the broken, though still powerful, French army had withdrawn, the English pursued their way towards Calais, arrived there without further opposition, and then for the most part went home, where the King was received with tumultuous enthusiasm.

*Continued confusion in France*

Notwithstanding the loss of Harfleur and the defeat at Agincourt, the French had no reason to be downcast at the results of the campaign. All Henry's costly preparations had gained him very little. But the French neither learned wisdom from their misfortunes nor exploited their advantages. Several Armagnac leaders being dead or prisoners, the Count of Armagnac became the real as well as the titular head of the party. He was a hot-headed, boastful, and brutal man, likely to inflame rather than to compose domestic animosities, and bitterly hated by the bourgeoisie of Paris and other great towns. His control over the government was rendered the more complete by the death of Louis the Dauphin in December 1415, followed six months later by that of the Duke of Berry, the last of the King's uncles.

The condition of northern France became deplorable. A few weeks after Agincourt, the Duke of Burgundy led an army towards Paris, and though he gained no substantial success, he remained near the capital for some weeks, while his men ravaged far and wide. To resist him, the Count of Armagnac summoned troops from his own country in the south-west; and these afflicted the peasants in the vicinity of Paris even more than the Burgundians. As for the populace of Paris, it was subjected to a regime of terrorism, which kept it quiet, but made it eager to seize the first chance of admitting John the Fearless.

*Failure to recapture Harfleur, 1416*

One great object of the Count of Armagnac was the recapture of Harfleur. During the spring and summer of 1416 the place was beset by land and sea, and the English were hard pressed. But, as usual, slackness and corruption crippled the French; and eventually Harfleur slipped from their grasp through a great naval victory gained by the English at the mouth of the Seine on August 15, 1416, a success which enabled them to reinforce and revictual the garrison.

*King Sigismund's mediation*

Meanwhile, Sigismund, King of the Romans, had visited Paris with the object of mediating between France and

England. His diplomacy had little success. Some of the French leaders, like the Count of Armagnac, did not want peace; and Sigismund made himself much disliked personally by his tactlessness, meanness, and unconcealed licentiousness. On his side there were complaints that the French were inhospitable and uncivil, and when he crossed to England in May 1416, he was in the mood to be profoundly impressed by the magnificence and lavishness of the entertainment which Henry V offered him. Nevertheless, negotiations for peace continued. But, just when it seemed certain that at least a long truce would be arranged, the intervention of the Count of Armagnac undid all the progress that had been made. Bitterly chagrined, Sigismund, by the treaty of Canterbury of August 1416, made an offensive and defensive alliance with Henry. He did not expressly abandon the part of mediator, but a conference at Calais in the autumn resulted only in a short truce between the French and the English, while conversations with the Duke of Burgundy at the same place led to an *entente*, if not a written treaty, between him and Henry, and paved the way for the conclusion of an alliance between him and Sigismund in the following year. Simultaneously the Duke's troops were raiding and plundering in northern France, even to the walls of Paris. *Sigismund's alliance with England and Burgundy*

Expecting help from Sigismund and at least neutrality on the side of Burgundy, Henry now made up his mind to renew his invasion of France. During the winter England was busy with preparations even greater than those of two years before. The French did practically nothing to meet the renewed peril. The Armagnacs remained in control of Paris, increasingly discontented though it was. The death of the Dauphin John in the spring of 1417 rather strengthened their cause, for he had been married to Jacqueline of Hainault, daughter of William Count of Holland, and had thus been within the Burgundian sphere of influence, while the new Dauphin Charles was under Armagnac tutelage. Another important event was the banishment of Queen Isabel to Tours. She had disgusted public opinion by her loose life, and the punishment imposed on her by the King, during an interval of sanity, was generally considered lenient. But it had lamentable results for France. *Situation in France*

**Henry V's second invasion of France, Aug. 1417**

On August 1, 1417, with about 11,000 fighting men, Henry again landed in Normandy without serious opposition, this time at Touques. His narrow escape at Agincourt had taught him caution. He was always willing to fight a pitched battle, but he would not run risks in order to provoke one. If the French would not put their fate to the touch, he would systematically proceed with the reduction of the country. So for two or three years the war consisted of a series of sieges. The old-fashioned raid of the Black Prince's day was for the time given up. Henry advanced steadily from one strong place to the next, never leaving his rear uncovered and always trying to secure his flanks. The first notable success was the capture of Caen, the town being taken by storm with great carnage, while the castle soon afterwards surrendered. Thence Henry sent out a detachment which took Bayeux, thus covering his right flank as he turned southward, to Sées, Argentan, and Alençon, all of which surrendered with but little resistance. A force flung out eastward secured Mortagne and Verneuil, and was in a position to hinder any advance from Paris, while Henry was able to devote the best part of his strength to the siege of the great fortress of Falaise. He was becoming a master of siege warfare, and it was indeed a notable achievement to reduce the town after a month in the depth of winter, the castle, deemed impregnable, sharing the same fate six weeks later.

**Alliance between Queen Isabel and John the Fearless**

That no serious attempt was made to send help to any of the Norman towns captured by Henry was due partly to the miserable inefficiency of the authorities in Paris, but partly also to the doings of the Duke of Burgundy. A few days after the English landed in Normandy he led a great army, probably much larger than Henry's, towards Paris, being welcomed in many important towns on the way. He besieged the capital, hoping to reduce it by hunger or to gain admittance through treachery; but after suffering one or two reverses he had to withdraw baffled. Nevertheless his campaign was not fruitless. Queen Isabel, hitherto an enemy of his, sent word from her exile at Tours offering her alliance if the Duke would rescue her. A sudden and well-executed dash brought the plot to success; the Queen declared herself regent and appointed the Duke governor of the kingdom; they made their headquarters at Troyes, where they established a Council, a *Parlement*, and the whole apparatus of government. Nearly all northern France acknowledged their authority, and a Burgundian force sent into Languedoc won over wide areas and influential towns in that region, where Armagnac influence had hardly been challenged. One or two foreign kings and princes recognized the government of Troyes as the sovereign authority of France.

Such was the situation during the winter. The Duke of Brittany had signed a treaty of neutrality with Henry, so that the English were safe from interruption, and their king was free to lay his plans for the next campaign.

In the spring Henry's brother, Humphrey, Duke of Gloucester, with a small force, overran the Cotentin in a few weeks, only Cherbourg, which stood a siege of more than four months, offering any strenuous resistance. Meanwhile the main English army had been pushing eastward from Caen. Évreux was taken in May, Louviers in June, Pont de l'Arche in July. At the beginning of August Henry was before Rouen. *Conquest of Lower Normandy completed by the English*

Some of the places captured by the English had defended themselves creditably, but there had been no serious attempt to relieve any of them. The attention of most Frenchmen, indeed, was directed towards Paris rather than Normandy. The prospects of the Queen and the Duke of Burgundy were still so uncertain as to dispose them to welcome a chance of coming to terms with their opponents. Thus negotiations were resumed in the spring, and for a while bade fair to be successful. In the end, however, the uncompromising ferocity of the Count of Armagnac reduced the fruits of the discussions to a three-weeks' truce. In their chagrin, some of the Parisians forgot their dread of the Count and plotted to admit a Burgundian force under the Lord of L'Isle Adam. In the night of May 29 the conspirators achieved their purpose. The greater part of the populace rose in support of L'Isle Adam; many Armagnacs were slain, several of their leaders were captured, and the King fell into the hands of the Burgundians. The Dauphin, it is true, was carried off by the Armagnacs in the nick of time; but an Armagnac attempt to retake the city was beaten off, and with the fall of the Bastille of St. Antoine, the whole of Paris passed under Burgundian domination. The Duke of Burgundy was far away in Franche *Paris seized by the Burgundians, May 1418*

Comté, and seemed in no hurry to make for Paris. For some weeks, therefore, the city was without a stable government; the populace was restless and nervous, and after a fortnight, in a fit of panic, broke into the prisons and slaughtered upwards of a thousand Armagnacs, among them the Count himself. It must be confessed, indeed, that when the Duke arrived, he either could not or would not keep in hand the mob, which soon afterwards perpetrated an even more ferocious massacre of captive Armagnacs. Duke John, however, being in possession of the King and the capital, besides having the countenance of Queen Isabel, now assumed the rôle of defender of France against the English invader. He announced that he was about to take the field with a view to the relief of Rouen. Whatever promises he had made to Henry he flung to the winds as soon as the central government was in his hands. In point of patriotism there was nothing to choose between the two French parties, for, after being ousted from Paris, the Armagnacs made little effort to oppose Henry and soon began to treat with him.

Siege and fall of Rouen, Aug. 1418– Jan. 1419

While Henry was always ready to bargain with anyone who had something to offer, he never allowed diplomacy to interfere with the progress of military operations. During the autumn the siege of Rouen was relentlessly pressed, though, the defences being strong and the garrison adequate and resolute, Henry trusted in the main to hunger. For a while the city had confident hopes of relief, which inspired it to endure bitter hardship. But though the Duke of Burgundy raised an army, and left Paris at its head in November, it never got farther than Beauvais. In the last weeks of the year the sufferings of Rouen became intolerable. Several thousand women, children, and old men were thrust out of the city, and lay under the walls perishing of hunger and cold. A despairing appeal to John the Fearless having proved fruitless, the defenders, on New Year's Eve, asked for a parley. The consequent negotiations lasted some time, and more than once were on the verge of breaking down; but on January 19 the city was surrendered to the English. Rouen was to keep her ancient privileges (which theoretically had been suspended ever since the commotions of 1382); but she was to pay a heavy indemnity. While soldiers of the garrison from other provinces were allowed to go away unarmed, Norman inhabitants who would not swear allegiance to Henry were to be held prisoners, and nine persons who had been conspicuous in the defence were to be at Henry's mercy, though only one was put to death. The terms after all were not as hard as they might well have been, and in the event the English had to show some forbearance in the exaction of the ransom, which was never fully paid. Henry made Rouen the headquarters of the civil Government which he was establishing in Normandy as his conquest proceeded, and ere long the city renewed its importance and recovered much of its prosperity.

After the fall of Rouen, Upper Normandy was soon in Henry's hands, very few places offering resolute resistance, and pushing up the Seine the English took Vernon and Mantes without trouble. Then followed a lull, during which one or two isolated fortresses were besieged and there was some raiding and counter-raiding on the frontier of the territory conquered by the English, but major operations came to a standstill. The truth was that Henry realized the magnitude of his task. What with casualties and the provision of garrisons for conquered towns, the field army at his disposal was absurdly small for an attack on Paris; and he was the more disposed to listen to the embassies which both the Dauphin and Duke John were still sending to discuss peace. The Dauphin's offers were attractive, but he failed to appear at a conference which had been arranged for March 1419. The Duke of Burgundy was more businesslike. He agreed to a truce; and in May, amid much pomp and circumstance, Henry met the King and Queen of France, Princess Catherine, and the Duke at Meulan. Diplomatic conversations continued intermittently for a month, and the story went that Henry was conquered by the charms of Catherine; but, as usual, the English asked too much and the French offered too little; Henry learned that the Duke of Burgundy was bargaining with the Dauphin; and after high words between the two the conference came to a barren end. A few days later Duke John concluded with the Dauphin an agreement known as the Treaty of Pouilly: civil strife was to cease, the two parties were to unite in governing France and fighting the English, and a further interview between the two leaders was soon to be held to settle outstanding points.

*Conference of Meulan and Treaty of Pouilly, May–July 1419*

**Fall of Pontoise, July 31, 1419**

Though it looked as if Henry would now have a united France against him, he faced the new situation with a bold front. His truce with the French government expired a week or two later, and two days afterwards, by a brilliant night attack, the English took Pontoise, a town of great strategic importance. The court fled from Paris to Champagne, the city was panic-stricken, and within a few days Henry's brother, the Duke of Clarence, raided to its very walls. Of course, treachery apart, Paris could be taken only after a long siege; but these incidents served to strengthen the awe with which Henry was regarded by the French.

**Murder of John the Fearless at Montereau, Sept. 10, 1419**

It was not long before the friendship between Burgundians and Armagnacs began to wither. Rumours of plots and counter-plots were plentiful. It was only after much hesitation that the Duke of Burgundy consented to fulfil his promise to have a further interview with the Dauphin. The meeting-place was to be the bridge of Montereau-faut-Yonne. Every conceivable precaution was taken and guarantee given to preclude treachery. On September 10, John the Fearless entered the fenced enclosure on the bridge where the Dauphin was awaiting him. Precisely what followed will never be known: but it is certain that the Duke was almost immediately killed by a blow from an axe, several of his attendants being likewise murdered. The crime was undoubtedly premeditated. The Armagnac leaders put about a story that the Duke had offered violence to the Dauphin; but Duke John, who was no fool, must have known that any act of the sort must have fatal results to himself. It is, however, and always will be doubtful whether the Dauphin was privy to the plot, and, if he was, whether he approved of it. In any case, nothing could have done more harm to his cause. The murder flung the new Duke Philip into the arms of the English, and, as Henry was quick to see, rendered possible a triumph which in his heart he had never hoped for. As for Charles VI, he no longer had any will of his own, even in his lucid moments; and Queen Isabel was utterly committed to the Burgundian cause and regarded the Dauphin with bitter hatred.

**The Treaty of Troyes, May 21, 1420**

If Henry held all the winning cards, it must be recognized that he played them with great skill. He kept up his military reputation by completing the reduction of Normandy, till at the end of January 1420, only Mont St. Michel held out against him. He also continued his advance up the Seine, taking Meulan and other places, so that by Christmas his main army was within a few miles of the walls of Paris. More important than these military exploits were the negotiations which he was meanwhile conducting with the French Crown, with Burgundy, and with the city of Paris. The upshot was that in December a truce with the French government was concluded, while with Duke Philip a treaty was signed whereby the English and the Burgundians were to co-operate against the Armagnacs, and the Duke agreed that Henry should marry the Princess Catherine, should be recognized by Charles VI as heir to the French throne, and should act as regent of France during Charles's lifetime. The next few months were mainly occupied by negotiations with the French court on the basis of the terms outlined above; and in May, Henry, at the head of a strong force, marched to Troyes in Champagne, where on the 21st the treaty of peace was solemnly signed. On his side, Henry abandoned his claim to the French crown and promised not to style himself king but only heir and regent of France as long as Charles VI lived. He would employ all his resources for the discomfiture of the Armagnacs; but territory wrested from them should of course be restored to the allegiance of the crown of France, and not subjected to that of England. He undertook to maintain French law and custom, and to uphold all individuals and corporations in the enjoyment of their property, rights, and privileges. As regent he would rule with a Council of Frenchmen. If these conditions were fulfilled, the Treaty proceeds, the French would obey him as regent, and accept him or his heir as king when Charles died. They acquiesced, too, in Henry's demand that until he became king those parts of France which he had conquered before the conclusion of the Treaty should belong to him in full sovereignty. On his accession to the French throne, however, they should again be joined to the kingdom of France. The marriage alliance was of course approved, and the wedding took place at Troyes on June 2. All officials and clergy were to swear to observe the Treaty; and any Frenchman might be required to do so.

It is possible that for a short time Henry thought that opposition to the Treaty would be slight, and that a real peace

*Effect of the Treaty in France*

would soon be attained. That is what the people of England ingenuously expected. But it soon became evident that the Armagnacs or Dauphinists, as they were now frequently called, would resist with all their might. South of the Loire their hold was even firmer than it had been a year or two before. For some time they had been seeking aid from Scotland, and late in 1419 six thousand Scots had reinforced their fighting strength. A naval victory, gained with Castilian assistance off La Rochelle, further encouraged them, and in petty warfare on the borders of the territory held by the English they were giving as much as they were getting. They had throughout asserted that the Dauphin ought to be regent when his father was incapacitated, and that contention they continued to uphold, alleging that no King of France, least of all one who was never fully responsible for his actions, had the right to disinherit his son and bestow the realm on one who, even if the Dauphin were dead, would still have no title to it. What was yet more disturbing to Henry, many Frenchmen who had hitherto supported the Burgundian cause now went over to the other side; while it soon became clear that not a few who remained loyal to Duke Philip nevertheless disliked the Treaty of Troyes and would try to avoid assisting in its enforcement. The signing of the Treaty enabled Henry to draw directly on the resources of a small part of France and placed in his hands a great deal of patronage: but it is possible that the Burgundians would have cooperated with him more effectively if it had never been concluded, and it certainly did not strengthen his position as much as he had hoped or as modern historians have often supposed.

*Henry in Paris, Dec. 1420*

For almost six months after his marriage Henry was occupied in reducing places which hindered communication between Paris and Burgundy. Sens and Montereau did not delay him long; but Melun, though it had but a small garrison, and the besieging force, which included many Burgundians, was very large, held out for four months. It was December before Henry was able to make his formal entry into Paris, where he was received with what seems to have been sincere enthusiasm. Charles VI was with him, but the direction of affairs was entirely in the hands of Henry. He met the three Estates of Languedoil, received their approval of the Treaty of Troyes, heard their advice on the best means of restoring order, announced a reform of the currency, and secured their consent to a levy of silver to provide metal for the new coinage. Judicial proceedings against the murderers of John the Fearless were formally initiated before the King, and judgment was given that they were guilty of treason and incapable of succeeding to any property or holding any office. A little later the Dauphin was solemnly cited to appear, and on his failing to do so the Royal Council and the *Parlement* pronounced him contumacious and declared that he had forfeited his right to the crown. The Parisians soon found that Henry's arrival did not bring with it the prosperity which they had innocently expected to accompany him, and some of them were grieved when at Christmas Henry feasted in great splendour, attended by many nobles, French and English, while Charles celebrated the festival almost alone. *Formal condemnation of the Dauphin*

At the end of the year Henry went to Normandy, where he met the Estates, obtained from them a *taille* of 400,000 *livres*, and inspected the machinery of government. Normandy and adjacent regions conquered by Henry before the Treaty of Troyes were under the administration of a small Council, partly English, partly French, sitting at Rouen. The financial authority, the *Chambre des Comptes*, had its seat at Caen. The principal civil officials—the Chancellor, the seneschal, the treasurer, and the *baillis* (eight in number) —were English, but those of lower rank were almost all French. The military administration of Normandy, on the other hand, was entrusted almost exclusively to Englishmen. The King's lieutenant—the Earl of Salisbury—the Admiral of Normandy, and the captains of the King's castles were, with scarcely an exception, English. At this time, there were some 4,000 English troops in the various garrisons of Normandy; in addition, the Englishmen who had received lands confiscated from defiant Normans were under obligation to furnish contingents amounting in all to about 1,500 men, and Henry might furthermore call out the feudal host, an expedient to which he seldom resorted. There had not been much displacement of the population; the new English landowners were few in comparison with the Normans who took the oath of allegiance to Henry and remained in enjoy- *Normandy under Henry's sovereignty* ment of their property; and while English settlers were encouraged to dwell in three or four towns on or near the coast, there was no persistent attempt to turn these places into English colonies, and the number of immigrants was always small. Private law and custom remained unaltered; and it cannot be questioned that the government tried to avoid giving offence and on the whole kept the English soldiery well in hand. There was, however, a good deal of disorder and distress in Normandy. In some districts "brigandage," as the English called it, was rife, and the extent to which rural life was disturbed is indicated by the fact that wolves had greatly increased in numbers since the English invasion. Every now and then, Normandy was raided by Dauphinist forces from outside, and though these were always soon driven out, they sometimes did much damage and usually, it seems, were regarded with sympathy by the inhabitants. Except in the regions near Rouen and Caen, it was difficult to collect revenue. During Henry's regency of France, Normandy paid for itself, but it contributed only a small sum to the cost of Henry's operations elsewhere.

After his visit to Normandy, Henry went to England, where his presence was eagerly desired. Some well-founded apprehension had been expressed as to the effect of the Treaty of Troyes on English independence; but when Henry met Parliament it ratified the treaty without demur and, so far as we know, without debate.

*The battle of Baugé, March 22, 1421*

During Henry's absence, things went badly for his cause in France. The captain of Le Crotoy in Picardy, Jacques d'Harcourt, a member of a great Norman family, hitherto a staunch Burgundian, was moved by dislike of the Treaty of Troyes to change sides; he began to attack the Burgundians in Picardy, took one or two places in the Somme valley, was joined by a number of local lords, and threatened, by reaching a hand to the Dauphinist garrisons of Guise and Compiègne, to cut the routes from Paris to Flanders. Henry had left his brother Thomas, Duke of Clarence, in command of the English troops in France. Instead of dealing with Harcourt, Clarence, having mustered a force of five or six thousand men, made an old-fashioned and futile raid southward from Normandy through Maine and into Anjou. Deeming Angers too strong to besiege with any hope of speedy success, he turned back, but found his retreat barred by a superior force of Scots and French at Baugé. Clarence heard of their presence while halting at Beaufort-en-Vallée, several miles away. He at once made off to attack them, ordering his men-at-arms, some 1,500 in number, to accompany him, but leaving almost all his archers behind. On reaching Baugé, Clarence, without pausing to array his men (who had become scattered during the long ride), attacked the enemy with headlong impetuosity. Though they fought very valiantly, the English were overwhelmed by numbers; Clarence was slain, together with some notable English leaders, while the Earls of Somerset and Huntingdon, among many others, were captured. The English losses would have been still greater but for the fall of darkness. The honours of the day rested mainly with the Scots, who were commanded by the Earl of Buchan.

The battle of Baugé might have had decisive consequences had the victors used their advantage with vigour and intelligence. But the Earl of Salisbury, who had been left in command at Beaufort, completely outmanœuvred them, and after a brilliant retreat, brought the English archers safely back to Normandy. The Dauphin and his generals spent several weeks in characteristic inactivity, and when they eventually sent a force to lay siege to Alençon, the bold front shown by Salisbury destroyed their resolution, and, turning their backs on the chance of recovering Normandy, they foolishly set their faces towards Paris. After cheaply capturing a number of unimportant strongholds in Maine and Perche, they were held up by Chartres, which they were besieging when they learned that Henry had returned to France with reinforcements amounting to 4,000 men. Meanwhile Salisbury had completely restored the morale of the English troops in Normandy, and had even raided Anjou once more, an enterprise justified by its effect on the spirits of both sides. *The Dauphinists foiled by Salisbury*

Henry had resolved to crush Harcourt, and accordingly landed with his fresh troops at Calais. Hearing, however, of the siege of Chartres, he decided that the loss of so important a city must not be risked, and led his force to its relief. Before he had even crossed the Seine, the Dauphinist army precipitately withdrew beyond the Loire. *Henry's campaign in 1421*

Henry besieged and took Dreux, and then made for the Loire in the belief that the Dauphin, who had collected large reinforcements, was ready to offer battle. But Charles and his generals remained inert, and suffered Henry to take Beaugency, plunder the suburbs of Orléans, and lead his army across Beauce and the Gâtinais. It was a striking assertion of the moral ascendancy which he had established over the enemy, but his army lost heavily from disease and hunger, and though he cannot be blamed for failing to bring the Dauphinists to action, yet the fact remained that their military strength was as great as ever. Henry's energy, however, did not flag. He resolved to capture Meaux, whence *Siege of* a Dauphinist garrison had been giving much trouble to the *Meaux, Oct.* adjacent countryside. Meaux was a place of considerable *1421–May* natural strength, and Henry's besieging force consisted of *1422* only some 3,000 men, almost all English. The siege occupied him all winter, the English casualties were heavy, and if the Dauphinists had shown decent resolution they might easily have relieved the place. Despairing of rescue, however, the garrison in May 1422 surrendered their last defences. By the terms of the capitulation, a number of lesser strongholds in northern France, including Compiègne, were also yielded to Henry. Meanwhile, the Burgundians had been operating against Jacques d'Harcourt; they had recovered nearly all the places which he had taken, and he was soon penned in Le Crotoy. Guise was now the only other notable town in the north held by the Dauphinists.

Henry had planned to dispose of Harcourt once and for all, but a Dauphinist offensive on the upper Loire captured La Charité, and he had to dispatch a large English contingent to join the Burgundian army with which Duke Philip was about to attempt the relief of Cosne, a purpose successfully *Death of* accomplished. Henry, however, had been taken ill in July, *Henry V,* and though he had tried to lead his men to Cosne, he was forced *Aug. 31,* to stop at Corbeil and send the Duke of Bedford in his place. *1422* Early in August he betook himself to Bois de Vincennes, and there, on the 31st, he died. The fatal disorder seems to have been some form of dysentery; how he contracted it is not known; there seems no good reason to ascribe it to the hardships he had undergone, for these were not very great, and his health was apparently fairly good until after the end of the siege of Meaux. On his deathbed he counselled his brother Bedford to offer the regency of France to the Duke of Burgundy and to take it himself if Philip refused. Whatever might betide, Normandy was not to be given up. His younger brother Gloucester he wished to be regent in England for his heir, the infant Henry VI.

The death of Henry was a very grave blow to the English cause. He was unquestionably the greatest Englishman of the time; and the demoralized French believed him to be greater than he really was. No one else had any chance of enforcing the terms of the Treaty of Troyes. It is indeed highly improbable that Henry himself could have done so. The Dauphinist resistance showed no sign of breaking, and the alliance with Burgundy was anything but secure. The personal relations between Henry and the Duke must have become very bad, for Philip never visited him on his deathbed, though he might easily have done so, and he never attended any of the obsequies which took place in France before Henry's body was transported to England. For this estrangement Henry himself was partly to blame, since in 1421 he had welcomed in England, Jacqueline, Countess of Holland, Hainault, and Zeeland, who by leaving her husband the Duke of Brabant, a kinsman of Duke Philip's, had given a severe shock to Burgundian policy. The Duke still needed the English alliance, and English and Burgundians still co-operated; but there was little cordiality between the allies. Henry, it seems, was conscious of the magnitude of his task, and in the last months of his life had tried to renew negotiations with the Dauphinists. *Effects of Henry's death*

The Duke of Bedford, it must be acknowledged, was an able man; he was, too, rather more genial and tactful than Henry, so that for a while friendliness between the English and the Burgundians was restored. He was soon relieved of the presence of Charles VI, who was dead before Henry was buried, the little Henry VI being then proclaimed King of France in Paris and Bedford ruling in his name. But Bedford lacked something of Henry V's personality, he was not so good a general or administrator, and he had not that command of English resources which Henry had of course enjoyed. That he was able to retain and even to extend the territory which the English held at Henry V's death was *John, Duke of Bedford* due far more to the slackness and incapacity of the Dauphinists than to his own power or skill.

**Policy of Bedford**

It is a mistake to suppose, as modern historians have usually done, that the regency of Bedford inaugurated a fundamental change in English policy. It is not true that Henry V, in his capacity of regent of France, treated the area under his control as conquered territory, extorting from it all he could get and ruling it through Englishmen. Henry kept the Treaty of Troyes in spirit as well as in letter. His Council consisted almost entirely of Frenchmen. The *Parlement* and the *Chambre des Comptes* remained wholly French in personnel. So far as we know all civil officers in the parts which acknowledged Henry as regent were French. The garrisons of the towns were as a rule under a French captain, only a very few places outside Normandy being held by English troops under English officers. Henry upheld the law and custom of the districts under his sway. The reforms he made in the central government only touched details, and their purpose was to check the scandalous waste and corruption that had flourished ever since the death of Charles V. Bedford's more conciliatory manner may have led the French to imagine that he was giving them more control than his brother had done; but really he followed very closely in Henry's footsteps. In accordance with the Treaty of Troyes the position of Normandy and the annexed regions was altered. Their financial authority was merged with the *Chambre des Comptes* in Paris, and they were now officially regarded as part of the realm of France. Nevertheless, Bedford, mindful of Henry's dying injunctions, maintained a great part of the special machinery which Henry had set up for Normandy, including the Council at Rouen, composed partly of English and partly of French.

**Condition of the regions under Bedford**

It is easy to draw a very gloomy picture of the regions in which Henry VI was acknowledged as king. They were not very extensive. Apart from the fiefs of Philip the Good, within which the Duke was virtually an independent sovereign, they comprised Normandy, Picardy, the Île de France, the Chartrain, Champagne, and, of course, part of the ancestral lands of the English kings in Guienne.[1] There was scarcely a

---

[1] The Duke of Brittany wavered in his allegiance, and for some years was virtually a neutral.

district where Bedford was able to maintain peace and order. There were still Dauphinist strongholds in Champagne, and both that province and Normandy were exposed to raids from outside. Everywhere, too, there was a great deal of what the officials called brigandage. Peasants, gentry, and even clergy had been driven, partly by restlessness, partly by want, to adopt an outlaw's life. Sometimes they formed great bands, which observed a crude discipline; more often they were mere opportunists, who might associate for a particular enterprise but would separate when it was accomplished. They were hard to suppress. Ten thousand are said to have been executed in Normandy during the English occupation; the number is perhaps exaggerated, but of course far more remained at large than were caught. It must not be overlooked, however, that many of these " brigands" were taken by Normans, and that in some districts the Normans were willing to pay for a police force to put them down.

Agriculture was in evil plight; many villages were destroyed; monasteries were ruined; wild beasts in addition to wild men increased the troubles of rural life. Towns fell into decay. Bedford and his officials—nearly all of them Frenchmen, be it remembered—naturally punished crime and conspiracy when they encountered it; there is no reason to suppose that the administration of justice was any harsher than it had been before the English invasion; indeed, Bedford won great praise even from hostile contemporaries for his reform of the court of the Châtelet at Paris and the prisons under its jurisdiction. Bedford has been blamed for bestowing ecclesiastical appointments on supporters of his own side, as if any sane man would have done otherwise; and he has been denounced for betraying the " Liberties of the Gallican Church " and thus securing papal provisions for his protégés; but it is often forgotten that the Burgundians had practically abandoned the " Liberties " as soon as they seized the government in 1418. Much has also been said about the financial oppression practised by Bedford. It is true that he adopted the policy of making France support herself and pay for the operations against the Armagnacs. England had borne almost the whole expense of the war up to the death of Henry V, but she could not support the burden much longer, and, besides, Henry VI was ruling France, not as a conqueror but in accordance with a treaty made with the French Crown. There was nothing reprehensible in Bedford's frequent summons of provincial Estates, with the invariable sequel of a request for money. The request usually met with a generous response; but, except in Normandy, it was generally impossible to collect more than a very small proportion of the sum voted. Normandy, indeed, was heavily burdened; but it is questionable whether even there, all things considered, taxation was heavier than it had been in the dozen years before Henry V's invasion. The taxpayer might at least be assured that most of what he paid went into the public treasury; for there is no doubt that Bedford's financial administration was far more efficient and far less corrupt than Charles VI's. And Bedford certainly benefited his subjects by continuing the reform of the currency begun by Henry V.

Northern France was not indeed contented. At this time no part of France was likely to be contented for long. Each party vied with its rivals in promising great things. The evidence goes to show that the majority of Normans had been quite willing to settle down quietly under Henry V if he could give them better government than they had known under Charles VI. Subject to the same condition, most inhabitants of northern France were prepared to accept the Treaty of Troyes; some, in fact, such as the Parisians, welcomed it joyously. But when Bedford failed to bring peace, order, and prosperity, people began to hanker after a change. Things were very bad; perhaps the Dauphin might improve them. Such feelings, however, spread slowly. That the regions under Bedford's rule were seething with hatred of the English cannot be maintained when it is realized that since 1415 there had never been more than 12,000 English soldiers in France at one time; that during the years from 1422 to 1429 there were probably never more than 8,000, and rarely so many; and that the military help received by Bedford from the Duke of Burgundy was slight and rendered only at special crises. Eight thousand men cannot hold down a thoroughly disaffected population of some two millions.

Of the three divisions into which France at this time fell—the fiefs of the House of Burgundy, the "domain" of Henry VI, and the regions acknowledging Charles VII—the first probably enjoyed the most prosperity and order. Flanders and Artois, in particular, though subject to domestic disturbances, were not troubled by Armagnac raiders. As between the regions under Bedford and those under Charles, the advantage on the whole lay with the former. They at least had as their ruler an able, prudent, and public-spirited man; whereas the lands beyond the Loire were nominally under one of the most contemptible creatures that ever disgraced the title of king and actually under as sorry a set of knaves as ever abused the functions of government. Born in 1403, Charles VII was still quite a young man; but he looked, thought, moved, and lived like an old one. There was some doubt as to the identity of his father, and this may have had a paralysing effect on him. At all events, for the first years of his reign his main object was apparently to do nothing. He spent his time in various castles, mostly in or near the valley of the Loire, a prey to nervous terrors, and wholly under the influence of favourites whom he had not the energy to choose for himself, having them imposed on him by the fortune of court intrigue. At the beginning of his reign he was in the hands of a long-established gang, consisting of men deeply implicated in the murder at Montereau, headed by Jean Louvet and Tanguy du Chastel. Their sole object was to keep the king in his existing frame of mind and to batten on his resources.

*Charles VII*

*Factions at Charles VII's court*

Opposed to them was the King's mother-in-law, the Dowager Duchess of Anjou, who saw her son's fiefs in danger of being conquered by the English and was thus anxious that the war should be prosecuted with vigour. She allied herself with John V, Duke of Brittany, and his brother Arthur of Richemont, a brother-in-law of the Duke of Burgundy, and destined to be one of the heroes of the delivery of France from the English. Richemont was constantly advocating a reconciliation with Philip the Good. The court was the field of ceaseless intrigue and counter-intrigue, the upshot of which was the fall of Louvet, Tanguy, and their associates in 1425. Charles VII announced that he would henceforth govern with the counsel of the Duke of Brittany and his

*Arthur of Richemont*

brother. But, save for Richemont, the great nobles who now surrounded the king were as grasping and corrupt as the lesser men they had displaced. The King, furthermore, soon fell under the influence of Pierre de Giac, a member of the old gang, whom Richemont tolerated because he was supposed to have influence among the Burgundians which might promote an entente between the two parties. Before long, however, the two fell out. Giac was seized in the very residence of the King, carried off, subjected to a pretence of a trial, and drowned. Charles meekly accepted what had been done, and consoled himself with a new favourite, who a little later was murdered in his presence.

La Trémoille   The chief agent in these outrages was George, Lord of La Trémoille, a man in middle life, fat, greedy, lustful, with whom Richemont had foolishly allied himself. Richemont was a grim, active man, with a natural zeal for discipline and order, and he was continually trying to stir the King out of his inertia. Charles consequently hated him, and readily succumbed to the arts of La Trémoille, who approved the King's inaction, and by his embezzlement of public moneys rendered the government incapable of doing anything. La Trémoille indeed had the King deeply in his debt, having lent him money which ought really to have been in the royal treasury. Many of the court were in a similar plight.

Conditions in the regions recognizing Charles VII   Just as Richemont had quarrelled with Giac, so he soon quarrelled with La Trémoille. But the latter's influence prevailed with Charles, who in 1427 banished Richemont from court. There then began a private war between the rivals. When in the course of it La Trémoille was captured, his ransom was paid by Charles. Poitou was lamentably ravaged. The broil, which lasted intermittently for five years, caused no special scandal, for lesser men had long been behaving in the same way. The King might have his *Parlement* in Poitiers and his *Chambre des Comptes* in Bourges; his *Grand Conseil* might move from one to the other; hardly anyone heeded them. The nobles kidnapped and plundered their enemies with impunity; at least one actually employed English soldiers in his private quarrels. Mercenary captains, their pay and that of their men being always in arrear, ravaged indiscriminately. The very officers of the Crown, if less violent, were just as mischievous. Thus the Count of Foix, appointed lieutenant-general of the King in Languedoc, acted as if he were an independent sovereign, appropriated to his own uses a great part of the sums voted by the Estates to the King, oppressed his subjects in manifold ways, and ignored the King's command to render compensation. At the same time he failed to defend the frontier against the English in Guienne, and to protect the civil population against the armed bands that ranged Languedoc. Frenchmen under the sway of Bedford had little to hope from a transference of their allegiance to Charles VII.

There seemed, indeed, small prospect of any such change. For the "King of Bourges" had no money. While his favourites and nobles battened on him, he was sometimes reduced to dining off a plateful of mutton, putting new cuffs on his old tunics, and going with wet feet because he could not afford new boots: it is even said that the people of Tours once made the Queen a present of linen, because they had somehow heard that she needed new shifts. A king in such a plight could not hope to keep an army in the field for any length of time. He naturally relied on diplomacy rather than on arms. With Filippo Maria Visconti he entered in 1424 into an alliance which enabled him to reinforce the Milanese troops already serving on his side. In the same year a truce of four years was signed with Burgundy, and for some time there were good hopes of wholly detaching Duke Philip from his league with the English. But in 1428 the truce was not renewed.

*Helplessness of Charles VII*

The military achievements of the French had done nothing to restore their morale. Contemporary French chroniclers admit with no apparent shame that the French could not hope for success unless they were in greatly superior numbers. After the death of Henry V, it is true, the Dauphinists had for a while become bolder. In 1423, encouraged by their success at the fight of La Brossinière in Maine, they besieged Cravant, a town on the Yonne; but the Earl of Salisbury, at the head of a composite Anglo-Burgundian force, relieved the place and defeated them with great slaughter in battle. Next year, nevertheless, Charles's advisers attempted a big stroke. The feudal host was called up, and a large number of nobles obeyed the summons. Reinforcements had arrived from Scotland, and the Scottish contingent now numbered

*Military operations*

5,000 men. The army advanced towards Normandy, the first objective being Ivry, recently captured from the English, who were now trying to recover it. Bedford, warned of the danger, had put into the field every man he could muster, having even summoned the feudal host of Normandy. In all he may have had upwards of 9,000 fighting men. The armies met at Verneuil. Just before the battle a number of Normans deserted to the Dauphinists. The tactics of both sides were similar to those employed at Agincourt. The French made little use of their crossbowmen; their centre consisted of dismounted men-at-arms, while they had bodies of cavalry on the wings. The English, after their usual fashion, were all on foot, clumps of archers being interlaced with the men-at-arms. The battle began with a charge of the French horse against both wings of the English. The English right broke and was pursued a long way. Meanwhile a force of French got round the flank and plundered the English camp. Bedford's position became precarious, for when the two centres clashed neither could at first gain any marked advantage in the desperate hand-to-hand fighting that followed. But the English left, consisting mainly of archers, had broken and routed the French cavalry that charged them. At the critical moment they wheeled inward and took the French centre on the flank. What followed was a repetition of the closing stages of Agincourt. The English archers hacked and thrust and smote at the huddled mass. The Scottish force was nearly annihilated, and lost all its leaders. A great number of important men, French and Scots, were captured. Verneuil was to the military strength of France an even more deadly blow than Agincourt. Its importance has not been sufficiently recognized, probably was not fully understood at the time; for what specially pleased the English was the downfall " of these proude Scottes," seventeen thousand of whom, it was believed in London, " went to Dog-wash the same day." [1]

Had Bedford been able to follow up his victory, he might have broken French resistance, at any rate for a time. But he had very few men, and just at this moment he had to give his full attention to affairs in England and the territories of the Duke of Burgundy.

[1] *The Brut, or the Chronicles of England* (Ed. F. W. D. Brie), ii, 441.

Though Henry V had expressed the wish that Humphrey Duke of Gloucester should be protector of England, the English Parliament had insisted that this position should belong to Bedford. Gloucester, it is true, was to act as protector when his brother was out of the country, as of course he often would be; but his powers were narrowly restricted by the royal Council, and he was bitterly discontented. He attributed his disappointment to the machinations of his uncle Henry Beaufort, Bishop of Winchester, and the consequent rivalry of the two robbed the English government of much of its efficiency. *Dissension in England*

Gloucester's thwarted ambition sought a new field for its exercise. A few months after Henry V's death, he married Jacqueline of Hainault, whose husband, the Duke of Brabant, was still alive. He could have done nothing more annoying to the Duke of Burgundy or more embarrassing to the Duke of Bedford. *Humphrey of Gloucester and Jacqueline of Hainault*

Gloucester obtained from the anti-Pope Benedict XIII a pronouncement that Jacqueline's marriage to the Duke of Brabant was invalid, but this carried weight with only a handful of people. At the court of Rome, whither also the case was taken, it was not until 1428 that the cautious Martin V gave his decision against Gloucester. But Duke Humphrey cared little for ecclesiastical sanctions. In 1424 he led several thousand men, whom Bedford needed badly in France, to the conquest of Jacqueline's heritage of Hainault. The Anglo-Burgundian alliance almost snapped; the Duke of Burgundy sent a force of his subjects to resist Gloucester. The invasion was ill-conducted, and in 1425 Humphrey went home, leaving behind him Jacqueline, who was eventually taken prisoner. Bedford now stood a better chance of placating Philip the Good, but soon he had to go to England to restore harmony between Gloucester and Beaufort, whose rivalry had been on the point of blazing up into civil war. He did not return to France till 1427. *Gloucester's invasion of the Netherlands, 1424*

In the circumstances it is surprising that the English had been able to conquer Maine and extend their hold on the country south of Paris. But their grip on their new gains was insecure and their fortunes varied. Thus in 1427 Dunois Bastard of Orléans defeated the Earl of Warwick before *Warfare in France, 1424–8*

5

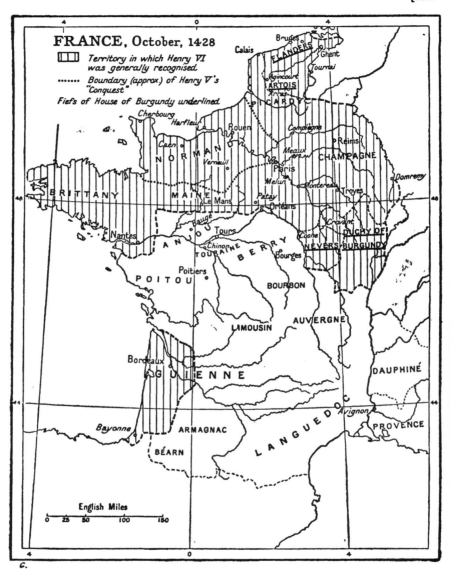

Montargis and relieved the town, while in the following year the French re-took Le Mans, though it was quickly recovered by Sir John Talbot, who was just becoming famous. The wise head of the Earl of Salisbury had already perceived that unless a decisive issue were forced England would fritter away her strength in petty operations. He won over the Council in Paris to consent to a big offensive, went to England in 1427 to raise reinforcements, and, returning in 1428 with about 2,700 fresh soldiers and a strong train of artillery, he led them, again with the countenance of the royal Council, towards Orléans, capturing numerous towns and castles on the way. Bedford did not approve of the undertaking; but his judgment was overborne. Salisbury might justly argue that the capture of Orléans would be a shattering blow to the cause of Charles VII. The siege began in October 1428; it ended in May 1429. In the meantime the fortune of the war had turned. Salisbury had been killed, and Joan of Arc had appeared.

*Orléans besieged, Oct. 1428*

Works on the subjects covered by chapters i and ii :—
i. Some original sources—
  *Ordonnances des Rois de France de la Troisième Race*, 22 vols., Paris, 1733, etc.
  *Les Grands Traités de la Guerre de Cent Ans*, ed. E. Cosneau, Paris, 1889.
  *Choix de Pièces Inédits relatives au règne de Charles VI*, ed. L. Douët d'Arcq, Société de l'Histoire de France, 2 vols., Paris, 1863–4.
  *Chronique du religieux de Saint-Denys*, ed. L. Bellaguet, Collection de documents inédits, 6 vols., Paris, 1839.
  Froissart, Jean : *Chroniques*, ed. Kervyn de Lettenhove, Brussels, 1867–77. There are many translations into English.
  *Henrici Quinti Angliae Regis Gesta*, ed. B. Williams, English Historical Society, London, 1850.
  Jean Jouvenel des Ursins : *Histoire de Charles VI*. In *Nouvelle Collection des Mémoires pour servir à l'histoire de France*, ed. J. F. Michaud and J. J. F. Poujoulat, vol. ii, Paris, 1836.
  *Journal de Clément de Fauquembergue, 1417–35*, ed. A. Tuetey and H. Lacaille, Soc. de l'Histoire de France, 3 vols., Paris, 1903–15.
  *Journal de Nicolas de Baye*, ed. A. Tuetey, Soc. de l'Hist. de France, 2 vols., Paris, 1885–8.
  *Journal d'un Bourgeois de Paris*, ed. A. Tuetey, Soc. de l'Hist. de Paris, Paris, 1881.
  Le Fèvre, Jean, seigneur de Saint-Remy : *Chronique*, ed. F. Morand, Soc. de l'Hist. de France, 2 vols., Paris, 1876–81.
  *Le livre des faicts du mareschal Boucicaut*. In *Nouvelle Collection des Mémoires*, ed. Michaud and Poujoulat, vol. ii, Paris, 1836.
  Monstrelet, Enguerrand de : *Chronique*, ed. L. Douët d'Arcq, Soc. de l'Hist. de France, 6 vols., Paris, 1857–62.

ii. Some modern works—
*Cambridge Medieval History*, vol. vii, ch. xiii, Cambridge, 1932.
*Histoire de France depuis les Origines jusqu'à la Révolution*, ed. E. Lavisse, vol. iv, pt. i (1328–1422), by A. Coville; pt. ii (1422–92), by Ch. Petit-Dutaillis, Paris, 1902.
*Histoire du Moyen Age*, ed. G. Glotz, vol. vii, by J. Calmette and E. Déprez, Paris, 1937.
Beaucourt, G. du Fresne de: *Histoire de Charles VII*, 6 vols., Paris, 1881–91. (The most thorough treatment of the subject.)
Bossuat, A.: *P. Gressart et F. de Surienne, agents d'Angleterre. Contribution à l'étude des relations de l'Angleterre et de la Bourgogne avec la France sous le règne de Charles VII*, Paris, 1936.
Colville, A.: *Jean Petit: La Question du tyrannicide au commencement du XV⁰ siècle*, Paris, 1932.
Jarry, E.: *La vie politique de Louis de France, duc d'Orléans*, Paris, 1889.
Luce, S.: *La France pendant la Guerre de Cent Ans*, 2 vols., Paris, 1890–3.
Petit, E.: *Ducs de Bourgogne de la maison de Valois*, Paris, 1909.
Thibault, M.: *Isabeau de Bavière, reine de France*, Paris, 1903.
Vallet de Viriville, A.: *Histoire de Charles VII*, 3 vols., Paris, 1862–5. (Less detailed than Beaucourt's work, but more stimulating.)
Wylie, J. H.: *History of England under Henry IV*, 4 vols., London, 1884–98. (Sheds valuable light on conditions in France.)
Wylie, J. H., and Waugh, W. T.: *The Reign of Henry V*, 3 vols., Cambridge, 1914–29. (Has as much to do with France as with England.)

## CHAPTER III

## FRANCE, 1429-1461

### EXPULSION OF THE ENGLISH, AND ESTABLISHMENT OF THE ROYAL AUTHORITY

GREAT as it was, the influence of Joan of Arc on the events of her own time has commonly been exaggerated. But her personality is so bewildering and her posthumous history so strange that she must be accorded more notice than her actual achievements merit. *Joan of Arc, 1412-31*

Her birthplace, at Domrémy on the Meuse, was on royal domain, but within a few yards of the duchy of Bar and within view of land which belonged to the duchy of Lorraine, and was thus subject to the Empire. It was not far from the frontiers of several other fiefs, and the neighbourhood was consequently the scene of much fighting. It saw little if anything of the English, though Domrémy, being on an important highway, must have heard a good deal about them. The village had a wide notoriety for its addiction to witchcraft. It had a tree and a fountain frequented by fairies, and near by there was a venerable wood—perhaps a remnant of the primeval forest—of which the villagers stood in superstitious awe. Joan was the daughter of a well-to-do farmer, and as a child she helped with the farm-work, tending the beasts in the fields. Nothing out of the ordinary seems to have happened to her till she was about thirteen, when she began to see visions and hear voices. These she identified, after some hesitation, as St. Michael, St. Catherine, and St. Margaret, and she thought, but was not sure, that the angel Gabriel was sometimes present too. She promised her visitants that she would keep her virginity as long as it should please God. For their part, they spoke of "the great pity that there was for the land of France," telling her that she must go thither but that her career thereafter would not be long. She concealed all these things from *Her childhood*

*Her "voices"*

everyone; but she became conspicuously quiet, thoughtful, and punctilious in religious devotion, and her neighbours began to ascribe to her the power of foretelling the future and curing disease; there were even rumours that she had been called to a military enterprise in "France." Her repute spread so far that shortly before she set out on her great mission, the Duke of Lorraine invited her to Nancy and consulted her about his health and fortune.

*Joan's convictions and mission*

Meanwhile Joan fell under the influence of two overmastering convictions—first, the English were the root of all the troubles afflicting France, and must be expelled; second, the "Dauphin" must have his legitimacy confirmed by coronation at Rheims. The latter conception is thoroughly medieval, but the former betrays a sentiment of nationality which in France was as yet extremely rare. The news of the siege of Orléans, it appears, caused a crisis in Joan. Her "voices" told her that she must go to the rescue of the city. After some hesitation and protest, she accepted the mission, and won the ear of Robert de Baudricourt, captain of Vaucouleurs, the principal officer of Charles VII in those parts. At first sceptical, if not derisive, Robert made inquiries into her antecedents and character, and also consulted the court; but in the end he sent her forth, with an escort of six men, on her journey of over 300 miles to Chinon. She arrived there on March 6, 1429.[1]

*Joan at Chinon and Poitiers, March–April 1429*

Charles and his advisers had stubborn doubts about Joan. Men and women claiming heavenly inspiration were common enough at that time. Many were palpable frauds; some were sorcerers or believed themselves such. Joan indeed seems to have made a good impression on the King at her first interview with him, perhaps because she claimed supernatural authority for the belief that he was the son of his reputed father. She had nevertheless to go to Poitiers and submit to an examination, lasting for about three weeks, by a commission of theologians. Their questions were very similar to those afterwards asked at her trial. She seems to have answered with the same boldness,

---

[1] This is the date commonly accepted by modern historians. M. P. Boissonade, however, has recently argued in favour of February 23 (*Une étape capitale de la Mission de Jeanne d'Arc*, in Revue des questions historiques, July, 1930).

not to say impudence, that she later showed at Rouen. For all that, the verdict was favourable. There was found in her " no evil, nothing but good, humility, virginity, devotion, honesty, and simplicity." Her interrogators, however, would not commit themselves to the opinion that she came from God. Nevertheless, Charles and his counsellors now granted her request that she might join the force that was mustering for the relief of Orléans.

That Orléans had not been relieved long before is enough proof of the demoralization of the French. The English operations were a travesty of a siege. The attack, it is true, had opened briskly, and on October 21, 1428, the English took the fort, known as the Tourelles, which stood close to the south end of the bridge from Orléans across the Loire. But an hour or two later the Earl of Salisbury was mortally wounded by a chance cannon-shot; active operations were suspended, and at the end of November the English, save for a few hundred men holding the Tourelles, went into winter quarters elsewhere. About the end of the year, indeed, the siege was resumed under the Earl of Suffolk, Lord Scales, and the celebrated but overrated warrior, Sir John Talbot. The English, however, could not even try to invest the town. They never had more than 5,000 fighting men before it, and they suffered continual loss by disease and desertion. They erected a number of small forts—" bastilles " or " boulevards "—and linked some of them by trenches; but there was always a great gap to the north-east of the town, and through this troops and provisions reached the defenders with little difficulty. Nevertheless, it seemed likely that the town would fall. Though the garrison equalled the besiegers in number and was commanded by the capable Dunois, it showed small resolution. When in February, aided by a force from Blois, it attempted to intercept a convoy of Lenten provisions which Sir John Fastolf was bringing to the English, the enterprise was grossly misconducted, and the small English escort beat off the attack brilliantly in the so-called Battle of the Herrings.

The relief expedition which Joan accompanied numbered about 10,000 men. No sooner did she join it than she tried to drive off the whores that always thronged French camps, to stop blasphemy, and to induce the soldiers to confess their sins and go to Mass; and, though these efforts fell short of their aim, the army seems to have felt that it had the aid of supernatural forces, an advantage which for long the French had attributed to their enemies. The English, weakened as they were by the recent withdrawal from the siege of the Burgundian contingent, several hundred strong, could not even try to prevent Joan's entry into Orléans.[1] She arrived on April 29, tumultuously welcomed by the citizens, who already knew all, and more than all, that was to be known about her.

*Joan's arrival at Orléans, April 29*

Joan had written to the English commanders, bidding them begone to their own country or abide her anger; but her message was unanswered. When she repeated it by word of mouth, she was received with jeers and insults. It is fair to remember that the names the English called her would have accurately described nine out of every ten women who accompanied the French army.

*Raising of the siege, May 4–8*

By noon on May 4 the whole of the relieving force had entered the town. Four days later the siege was over. First, on the afternoon of the 4th, the French made a demonstration against the English fort of St. Loup to the east of the city. Joan, arriving late, converted the operation into a serious assault. The work was stormed. It was no great exploit, for the garrison was small, but it had a profound moral effect on both sides. On May 6, a large part of the army, with many citizens of Orléans, crossed the river to attack the bridgehead, encouraged thereto by Joan against the will of the higher command. The attempt was fruitless till late in the afternoon, when an outwork was captured in a charge headed by Joan. Next day the French assailed a second fort covering the Tourelles. The garrison of 600 was outnumbered by ten to one, but resisted valiantly till evening, when a final desperate rush, again led by the Maid, carried the position. The defenders found no safety in the Tourelles, now attacked from two sides, and soon all had perished or fallen into the hands of the French. That night Joan, who had been wounded in the shoulder, entered Orléans by the bridge, as in the morning she had prophesied.

Next day the English offered battle in the fields west of

---

[1] Philip the Good was annoyed because Bedford would not allow him to take the town into his protection, as the citizens had asked him to do.

the town; but the French refused to fight, Joan declaring that it would be wrong to do so on Sunday. Then the besiegers evacuated their lines, and marched off unmolested.

The relief of Orléans, Joan's greatest exploit, was due in the main to the inspiration and enthusiasm which the French drew from her words, presence, and example. All attempts to prove that she was skilled in the art of war have broken down.[1] Her strategy and tactics might have been summed up in the familiar formula of a later age, "*l'audace, encore l'audace, et toujours l'audace.*" At Orléans it happened to be the right policy; and generally, in the circumstances of the time, bold tactics were likely to be the best for the French. But Joan never showed any capacity for discriminating between one situation and another; and her undiscerning aggressiveness was to lead to her undoing. *Joan's generalship*

When Orléans was relieved, Joan advised Charles VII to march forthwith to Rheims. But La Trémoille and the Archbishop of Rheims were much concerned at the prestige and popularity which Joan had gained. They did their best to belittle her share in the victory,[2] and to Charles they had much to say of the expense and risk of an expedition across Champagne. A precious month was wasted while the Duke of Bedford was concentrating his reserves and taking measures to raise fresh troops. When at length Joan was given more work to do, she was merely attached to a force of some 8,000 men which was to clear the line of the Loire. The enterprise, though uncongenial to Joan, was astonishingly successful. In the course of a week, Jargeau was stormed and Beaugency surrendered. An English army of relief, consisting of 5,000 men under Talbot and Fastolf, was approaching Beaugency when it heard of its fall. The English retreated, pursued by the French. On June 18, *Further victories: battle of Patay, June 18, 1429*

---

[1] Much has been made of the testimony of the Duke of Alençon as to her military skill, and in particular her able handling of artillery (*Procès de condamnation et de réhabilitation de Jeanne d'Arc*, ed. Quicherat, iii, 100); but the statement was made twenty-five years after her death, Alençon was a silly and stupid man, and the artillery of Joan's time was very easy to understand.

[2] This is well illustrated by a letter from the King to the people of Tournai, in which is described the relief of Orléans. At the end of the narrative comes the statement: "Et aus diz exploiz a toujours esté la Pucelle, laquelle est venue devers nous." There is no other allusion to Joan (Beaucourt, *Histoire de Charles VII*, iii, *Pièces Justificatives*, No. xxiii.).

by a stroke of luck, the French advance-guard surprised the English rear near Patay. Talbot was taken; Fastolf, with the main body, retreated precipitately. Panic set in; the English losses were very heavy, those of the French trivial. Joan was with the French rear, and had no influence on the course of the battle. But to the popular mind it was enough that she had been there, and her renown rose higher than ever.

*Charles VII crowned at Rheims, July 17, 1429* Charles now yielded to her pleadings: the march on Rheims was ordered, though many, with good show of reason, would have preferred to attack Paris or invade Normandy. No serious resistance was encountered as Charles, with the Maid and 12,000 fighting men, crossed Champagne. One or two places made a show of defending themselves, to insure against a possible change of fortune: but on July 16 Rheims admitted the King, and next day he was crowned in the cathedral. Joan was at his side throughout the ceremony, and when asked later why she had displayed her banner on so sacred an occasion, she replied, "It had done the work, and it was but just that it should have the honour."[1] She was at the peak of her fortune.

*Lost opportunities* For a moment it looked as though all northern France would fall into the hands of Charles. Almost the whole of the Île de France embraced his cause. Beauvais revolted against Henry VI; towns in Picardy sent messages offering allegiance if Charles would but come thither. Normandy was in a state of ferment. Even subjects of Philip the Good showed their readiness to accept Charles as king. Paris appeared to be wavering, and Joan wanted to go there at once. Charles and his intimates, however, wished to get back to their haunts on the Loire, urging with truth that they lacked money to pay their army. Their withdrawal was unexpectedly hindered by Bedford: he had diverted into English service 3,000 men raised by Cardinal Beaufort for a crusade against the Hussites, and with this reinforcement he manœuvred skilfully for some weeks in the region to the east of Paris. Neither side was disposed to run risks, and there was no great battle. Each was bargaining with Philip of Burgundy, who after some hesitation resolved to remain for the present on the side of the English and tricked Charles VII by signing a truce which checked the progress of

[1] *Procès de Condamnation de Jeanne d'Arc* (ed. Champion), i, 154.

his arms while giving the Burgundians a breathing-space. A French force, it is true, made a dash on Paris, occupied St. Denis, and on September 8 assaulted the city, trusting that Armagnac sympathizers within would open the gates. But the plot miscarried, and the ill-conceived and half-hearted attack was easily beaten off. Joan took it in deadly earnest, showed her customary reckless courage, and was wounded in the thigh. Though she had not planned the operation, she had made it her own; the failure dashed her spirits, tarnished her prestige, and, having occurred on a very holy day, gave her enemies a handle against her. *Failure of attack on Paris, Sept. 8, 1429*

After this Bedford let the French cross the Loire, and their army was disbanded. During the next few months their only notable undertaking was the siege of La Charité, which was well defended and feebly assailed. The collapse of this enterprise was a further blow to Joan. Though she knew it not, she had failed in her main purpose. The golden opportunity had been missed, and long years were to pass ere France saw the last of the English. *Joan further disappointed*

Though treated with honour, Joan found the winter's inactivity irksome, and in March 1430, acting on her own initiative, she led a small troop to the region eastward of Paris where desultory fighting had been going on ever since the previous autumn. Nothing of much note happened until, near the middle of May, the Duke of Burgundy laid siege to Compiègne. Joan made her way to the town, and on May 23 took part in a sortie against a village held by the besiegers. The operation was successful, but the troops lingered too long to plunder. Many were cut off from the town by English and Burgundian reinforcements: Joan herself was captured by an archer in the retinue of the Bastard of Wandomme, who handed her over to his commander, John of Luxemburg. *Joan captured, May 23, 1430*

This is not the place for an account of Joan's captivity, trial, and martyrdom, or for a discussion of the numerous controversies to which they have given birth. The hysterical patriotism of some writers, the unreflecting anti-clericalism of others, and the uncritical orthodoxy of yet more have produced bitter denunciation of her judges and the English. No one will deny that Joan's fate was a dreadful tragedy, but Mr. Bernard Shaw is justified in saying that there are no *Joan's captivity and trial* villains in the piece.[1] It is too often forgotten that Joan, besides being accused of sorcery and heresy, was a prisoner of war. Her purchase by the English from John of Luxemburg was a transaction of a very familiar kind. The determination of the English to retain her in their custody, even though she was acquitted by the ecclesiastical tribunal, was in no way reprehensible : why should she be released more quickly than other prisoners of war simply because she had been suspected of heresy ? It is now widely recognized—by Frenchmen, Catholics, and those who are neither—that her trial was regular, and no more " unfair " than any other fifteenth-century trial on similar charges. No doubt Joan's death was desired by both Burgundians and English; no doubt the latter in particular were eager to discredit Charles VII by securing her condemnation as a witch or a heretic. But Joan, in her innocence, ignorance, rashness, and self-confidence, saved them from the temptation to interfere with the course of law. Her evasive replies about her visions and " voices," and, above all, her claim to be directly inspired by God, with her consequent refusal to submit herself unreservedly to the judgment of the Church, were quite enough to ensure her condemnation. If there are any villains to be hissed, they are Charles VII and his favourites, who never lifted finger or voice to save her, but announced publicly that her capture was due to her self-will and that they had a successor—a shepherd lad from the Gévaudan—who was just as good.

*Joan at Rouen, Dec. 1430– May 1431*

It was not until November that Joan was handed over to the English. In the last days of the year she arrived in Rouen and was imprisoned in the castle. Already elaborate inquiries had been made concerning her, and much information collected. Formal proceedings against her opened on January 9, 1431; but it was not until February 21 that she was first interrogated. During the succeeding weeks she underwent numerous examinations, some public, some private. Her judges were Pierre Cauchon, Bishop of Beauvais, in whose diocese she had been captured, and the vicar of the Grand Inquisitor of France for the diocese of Rouen. According to custom they called to counsel them a number of assessors, more than a hundred figuring in the official

*Joan examined*

[1] *St. Joan*, Introduction, p. lv.

record.[1] Joan's ordeal was severe, and, all things considered, she came out amazingly well. Some of her answers to crucial questions could hardly have been bettered.[2] In April twelve articles, based on the process and other evidence, were drawn up. It was generally agreed by the assessors and other local clergy to whom they were submitted that they proved Joan to be guilty of sorcery[3] and heresy; but many wished them to be referred to the University of Paris. This was done, the report of the University being wholly unfavourable to Joan. After repeated admonitions, which apparently had no effect, she was taken on May 24 to the churchyard of the abbey of St. Ouen to receive sentence. Before the imminent threat of burning, Joan lost her confidence that she would somehow be rescued. She signed an abjuration, confessing that she had lied about her "voices," that she had practised sorcery, that she had sinned in claiming God's sanction for her irregular conduct. She submitted herself to the Church, promising to offend no more. She received her sentence of life imprisonment humbly, and donned women's clothes. But when she was back in prison her conscience smote her: convinced that she had betrayed her God, her "voices," and her king, she resumed men's dress, and, when questioned, defiantly reiterated her belief in her "voices." It was a clear case of relapse: she could look for no mercy, and on May 30 she heroically went to her doom in the market-place of Rouen. *Joan's abjuration, relapse, and death, May 30, 1431*

The death of Joan caused little outward concern at the court of Charles VII. The common people remembered her; and she had shown that the English hold on northern France was most insecure. But for some years after her death, there was small change in the military situation. It was not that the English performed any wonderful exploits. Their morale improved somewhat when Joan was gone; but the visit of Henry VI to France in 1430 and his coronation in Paris in December 1431, fell rather flat. With the Duke of Burgundy the relations of the English *No change on the English front*

---

[1] Of the six Englishmen among them, only one took a conspicuous part in the proceedings.

[2] For instance, in reply to the insidious question, "Are you in the grace of God?" she said, "If I am not, may God put me therein; if I am, God keep me there." (*Procès*, i, 48.)

[3] Little emphasis was laid on "witchcraft."

remained uneasy, and they received little military aid from him. Things were made worse by the death in 1432 of Bedford's wife, Philip's sister, and the widower's marriage to Jacquetta of Luxemburg, the sister of the Count of St. Pol, though expected to please Philip, was detrimental to some of his most cherished designs. Philip was known to be parleying with Charles VII; indeed, a six-years' truce between the two, signed in 1431, would probably have brought the Anglo-Burgundian alliance to a speedy end had not the proved complicity of La Trémoille in a plot against the Duke revived the latter's hatred of the French king. But English denunciations of Philip's treachery lose their impressiveness when it is remembered that in these years they themselves more than once entered into tentative negotiations for peace and were apparently quite ready to leave him in the lurch.[1]

*Continued confusion in Charles VII's territories*

In 1432 the English lost Chartres; Rouen castle was taken, though it was recovered after a few days; the French gained territory in Maine and Champagne. Normandy was terribly disturbed, and in 1434 Bedford authorized the peasants to arm themselves in order to put down brigandage. Exasperated by a demand for a heavy tax, they used their new weapons in a rebellion and actually besieged Caen. It was only after much slaughter that they were suppressed.

That the military situation changed little from 1431 to 1435 was due rather to Charles VII and his friends than to the English. When Joan of Arc was dead, they behaved just as they had done before her appearance. Nearly all the territory which acknowledged Charles was still racked by private war. La Trémoille went on fighting Arthur of Richemont, and in the prosecution of his private schemes and jealousies let loose on Auvergne and Anjou Rodrigo de Villandrando, one of the most notorious *Écorcheurs*, as the mercenaries of the time were called. Joan's friend, the Duke of Alençon, was at odds with Brittany. Another of her associates, Gilles de Rais, was plunging ever more deeply into the infamies that were to lead him to ruin. It was, however, to the good that in 1433 a plot in the interests of the house of Anjou brought about the fall of La Trémoille

[1] See *Letters and Papers illustrative of the Wars of the English in France* (ed. J. Stevenson), ii, 257 *seq.*

from power, and restored to influence Arthur of Richemont, who was friendly towards Burgundy.

It was perhaps because of this that in 1434 the negotiations with Duke Philip began to yield fruit. A truce was signed; and the effect on the Duke of the cry for peace, now to be heard everywhere, was increased by the conclusion of an alliance between Charles VII and the Emperor Sigismund which was notoriously intended to curb Burgundian ambitions. At a conference at Nevers, in January 1435, the representatives of the King and the Duke treated one another with great cordiality. The preliminaries of an agreement were settled, and Philip's abandonment of the English alliance was expressly treated as a contingency by no means remote. The English, for their part, declared that they wanted peace; the Pope and the Council of Basel used their good offices; and, after much preparatory negotiation, an imposing congress was held at Arras in August 1435. The papal legate and the cardinal of Cyprus acted as presidents and mediators. The French offered the English what they held in Guienne and the whole of Normandy in vassalage. The English, whose principal spokesman was Cardinal Beaufort, demanded all France north of the Loire in full sovereignty, but were willing to accept the territorial *status quo*, provided that Charles VII would hold his lands as vassal of Henry VI. The two sides were soon at a deadlock over the claim to the French crown, which neither would yield. Then the Duke of Burgundy let the English know that if they reached no agreement with Charles VII, he would make a separate peace. Neither prayers, persuasions, nor bribes availed to shake his resolution; and on September 6 the English envoys left the town in wrath. It was well for the Duke of Bedford that he died in Rouen nine days later, before the ruin of all his diplomacy became apparent. Once the English had gone, the two French factions soon came to terms; for it did not take long for the casuistries of the papal legate, supplemented by Richemont's bribes to Philip's counsellors, to remove the scruples felt by the Duke at breaking his oaths to revenge his father's murder and to uphold the Treaty of Troyes. Nevertheless, Philip drove a terrible bargain. Charles VII was made to denounce the murder of John the Fearless, to beg Philip's forgiveness on the ground of his youth, to promise to punish the perpetrators of the deed, and, besides other pious acts of expiation, to erect a cross on the bridge of Montereau. It was, to be sure, of more practical consequence that Charles yielded to the Duke the counties of Mâcon and Auxerre, the *prévôtés* of Péronne, Montdidier, and Roye, and " the towns of the Somme," a phrase that covered the county of Ponthieu and all the royal domain north of the river, save St. Amand and Tournai. Charles, it should be remembered, had the right to buy the " towns " back at a very high price; but on the other hand he gave up the claim to levy taxes in Artois and the lands now ceded. It was stipulated that the Duke of Burgundy should be exempt from all obligation of doing homage to the King of France, as long as either Charles or Philip should be alive. The Duke's vassals, it was further laid down, could not be called up for military service by the King; and Charles renounced his alliance with Sigismund against Philip and undertook to aid him if he were attacked by the English. The Treaty was signed on September 21. It dismayed and infuriated many of Charles VII's most faithful supporters. But the King ratified it.

*Tenacity of the English, 1435-53*

The English went on fighting. One may wish on every ground that they had concluded peace in 1435. But, considering their domestic dissensions and financial weakness, it was a marvellous military feat to prolong the struggle for eighteen years. It was accomplished by a mere handful of soldiers; in 1440, according to the statesman and historian Jean Jouvenel des Ursins, the fighting men upholding the English cause in France numbered in all four thousand.

One reason for the stubbornness of the English was their rage at Duke Philip's desertion of their cause. To take vengeance on " that foundour of new falsehede, distroubar of pees, capteine of cowardise," new taxes were voted by Parliament and desperate efforts made to raise recruits; and for a time, though not indeed for long, the strife of English factions ceased. But what nerved the English most was the evident reluctance of the French, despite the example of Joan of Arc, to meet them in pitched battle. It is true that after the Treaty of Arras the French seemed for a while to be carrying all before them. Early in 1436, they isolated Paris from her sources of supply. Many Parisians had long desired to submit to Charles VII; still more had always supported Philip the Good rather than Henry VI; nearly all were now sure that the English were going to lose. Faced with the threat of starvation, some of them conspired to admit the French. Arthur of Richemont, at the head of a body of troops, came to St. Denis; on April 13 a great part of the population of the city rose against the English garrison, and while bitter street-fighting went on, Richemont and his men entered by an open gate. The English took refuge in the Bastille, but soon surrendered and were allowed to withdraw to Normandy. Charles VII treated the Parisians leniently, and many of the officials who had served King Henry were retained in their posts. But Charles would never live in Paris, and did not even visit it until nineteen months after its capture. *Capture of Paris by Richemont, April 13, 1436*

Meanwhile the inhabitants of Caux in Normandy had risen, and within a short time almost the whole region, including Dieppe, Harfleur, and Fécamp, was lost to the English. Some of Charles VII's captains went to share in the plunder, but the soldiers maltreated the peasants, and the English took advantage of the consequent disunion to recover all that had been taken, except one or two towns. It was a very remarkable exploit, and the English were still more successful in dealing with another rising which a few months later broke out at the other end of the duchy, in the neighbourhood of Vire. Normandy, however, remained a prey to brigands and raiders: the English grew more ruthless in their efforts to crush rebellion and in their demands for money: the duchy was in a terrible state, for the English were not strong enough to govern it properly, nor the French to drive them out. *Norman risings suppressed, 1435-6*

For a year or two, indeed, the fortune of war turned in favour of the English. In 1437, under the vigorous leadership of Richard Duke of York, they re-captured Pontoise and several other places not far from Paris. Gloucester relieved Calais when it was besieged by the Burgundians, an achievement which caused immense exultation in England. In 1438 Warwick relieved Le Crotoy, and a French invasion of Gascony, after some initial success, broke down ignominiously. England, however, was increasingly war-weary; her leaders were again becoming more interested *English successes, 1437-8* in domestic intrigue than in foreign conflict; and there was growing up a generation which, having had little or no share in the triumphs of Henry V, could consider with coolness the abandonment of the fruits. Nevertheless, when a parley was attempted in 1439, the English still demanded vast tracts of French territory and flatly refused to give up the claim to the French crown.

Of course the main cause of the delay in the expulsion of the English was the inertia of Charles VII and the factious selfishness of the French nobles. The King did indeed wake up in 1437 and acquit himself valiantly at the capture of Montereau; but after that he almost vanished from view for some years. His inactivity, it must be admitted, is somewhat excused by the need of safeguarding himself against aristocratic machinations. The main centres of discontent were the Dukes of Bourbon and Alençon. Both were aggrieved by the King's growing reliance on low-born counsellors. An abortive plot in 1437 was followed three years later by a more formidable undertaking, commonly known as the *Praguerie*, a term coined to suggest a resemblance between the conspirators and the factious Hussites of Bohemia.

*The Praguerie, 1440*

Besides Bourbon and Alençon, the Duke of Brittany and La Trémoille were involved in the affair. Many mercenary captains, whose livelihood had been threatened by projected military reforms, were persuaded to take part; and it is probable, though not quite certain, that the plotters were in touch with the English. Their plan was to deprive Charles VII of power and to establish a regency under the Dauphin Louis, a disagreeable lad of sixteen, who lent himself readily to the design. But the King's councillors proved their mettle; the towns remained loyal; Arthur of Richemont hunted the rebels out of Poitou, the region where they were strongest; and though Alençon, Bourbon, and the Dauphin tried to prolong resistance in Auvergne, they soon had to yield. Nevertheless, the rebel leaders were treated with leniency, not to say favour, by Charles; while Louis was sent to govern Dauphiné.

Further plots

In 1441 there was more plotting. The Duke of Orléans, after twenty-five years as prisoner of war, had just been released by the English, who hoped that his return to France would intensify party strife there. He had been reconciled with the Duke of Burgundy, who had contributed largely to his ransom; and the two were soon parties to a new intrigue, in which Bourbon and Alençon again figured. But the King forestalled them by asking them to state their demands, promising remedies, and tampering with individual conspirators. For some years after this Charles had little trouble with his nobles. Orléans, old before his time, wanted a life of literary ease. Burgundy generally had plenty to do in his own lands. John V of Brittany died in 1442, and was succeeded by three short-lived dukes, all comparatively harmless. The Count of Armagnac, it is true, tried to assert his independence of the French Crown, but was overcome in 1444 by the Dauphin. It cost Charles VII a good deal in pensions and other favours to secure himself from further embarrassments of like nature, but the sequel showed that it was worth the expense.

For France as a whole the ten years after the re-capture of Paris were perhaps the worst of the Hundred Years War. Never had the *Écorcheurs* wrought so much harm. It must not be forgotten that, while some were foreigners (like the Castilian Rodrigo de Villandrando), most of them were French. Not a few were bastards of noble houses. Some of the most famous heroes of the struggle against the English, such as La Hire and Poton de Saintrailles, when not employed by the King, lived on plunder. As for the English themselves, they did their share of mischief, and as their hold on France weakened their commanders relaxed the discipline for which they had once been famous. But they were no more destructive than many of the French ravagers, and by this time their numbers were small and their range was limited. Altogether, the damage wrought was very great. Artois and Flanders escaped comparatively lightly, but no part of France went unscathed. In some districts rural life was utterly dislocated. Trade, internal and external, dwindled. But the speed of the subsequent recovery shows that the extent and completeness of the ruin have been exaggerated by modern patriots. It was seldom that land was deliberately and systematically laid waste. Villages would be sacked and burned, crops destroyed, beasts driven off; and for years in succession the peasants of certain regions might not think

*The Écorcheurs*

it worth while to till their fields. But things soon began to right themselves when the crisis was passed. The effects of the Hundred Years War on France were in no way as bad as those of the Thirty Years War on Germany.

*Revival of royal power*

Despite the gloom of the prospect, better times were approaching. The government was coming more and more into the hands of men of the middle-class, whose interests were bound up with the maintenance and increase of royal authority. And royal authority was growing, however slowly. One may indeed deplore some of the consequences. In the first years of the reign, the Estates-General of Languedoil met frequently, and no *taille* was collected without their sanction. After 1440, however, Charles never summoned them [1] : thenceforth the amount of the *taille* to be levied was decided, as occasion arose, by the royal Council. The Estates-General of Languedoc, it is true, remained more influential, and direct taxes were still voted by them. The Provincial Estates, too, had been summoned often and were still summoned sometimes : they occasionally secured a reduction of the share of taxation allotted to them ; they now and again authorized the levy of local taxes to serve local needs ; it was common for them to determine how financial burdens should be distributed within their respective spheres ; and at times they presented petitions or voiced complaints which the government could not ignore. But all these rights and powers were increasingly subject to challenge and encroachment by the King's officers. The financial position of the Crown had been enormously strengthened in 1436 by the restoration of the taxes on sales to which the term *aides* was especially applied. Charles had abandoned them in 1418 in a vain effort to win popularity. It must be recognized that public opinion in France approved of anything that would render more effective the authority of the central government, while the rights of the Estates, general or provincial, aroused little popular interest. The Pragmatic Sanction of Bourges, adopted in 1438, was another sign of the trend of French politics, for it was the Crown which stood to gain most advantage from it. Again,

*Decline of the Estates*

[1] In 1445 the towns north of the Seine and the Oise sent deputies to an assembly at Meaux, but this was not a true meeting of the Estates-General. There was also some kind of representative gathering at Tours in 1448, but its precise character is unknown.

the ordinance of 1439 for the enforcement of discipline on mercenary soldiers, though not effectual, was a notable step in a process that was to endow the Crown with an authority unequalled since the days of Philip the Fair.

The English military successes between 1437 and 1440 were not continued. In the latter year the French captured and held Évreux, thus gaining a new foothold in Normandy. Next year they besieged and took Pontoise, after it had been relieved several times by Talbot; and they never again lost their grip on the Île de France. In 1442 Charles VII once more invaded Guienne; and though bad weather, the heroic defence of the castle of La Réole, and the vigorous resistance of the civil population eventually forced the French to withdraw, their initial successes had been ominously widespread and easy. In 1443 a fresh English force, raised with great difficulty, was wasted through the incapacity of its commander, the Duke of Somerset. *French successes against the English*

Henry VI, now of age, was saintly and weak-minded, but favoured the faction headed by his kinsmen, the Beauforts, who with uncharacteristic wisdom wanted peace. Hence in 1444 a great effort was made to come to an understanding. Each side had received favourably the suggestion of the Duke of Orléans that a marriage might be arranged between Henry and Margaret, daughter of René, Duke of Anjou and Lorraine and titular King of Naples and Sicily. The English saw that they must give up the claim to the French crown, and merely demanded Normandy and Gascony in full sovereignty. But this concession the French refused to make, and the English representative, the Duke of Suffolk, could secure no more than a truce of twenty-two months and the betrothal of Margaret to Henry. Having reported to his King, Suffolk soon returned to escort Margaret to England. The French, however, affected a reluctance to entrust her to him, and the Duke, fearing lest he should have to go home without her, is said to have agreed in secret to the surrender of Maine, still largely in English hands, as the price of the completion of the agreement. Margaret brought Henry nothing, and the match was disliked in England even before Suffolk's concession was known. Nevertheless, the truce was prolonged more than once, and official hostilities between the two realms were suspended till 1449. *Marriage of Henry VI and Margaret of Anjou, 1445*

The French government used the interval to some purpose. If royal authority was to be effective anywhere in France, the " companies " must be suppressed. To achieve this—and also to expel the tenacious English—the King must have a strong permanent force of his own. In 1445, after prolonged discussion in the Council, drastic enactments were published.

*The compagnies d'ordonnance*

All captains, with their companies, were to appear before the Constable, who would retain such men as he chose. The rest would be escorted to their homes, or, if foreigners, to the frontier nearest to the place whence they came. From those kept in the royal service, new companies called *compagnies d'ordonnance* were to be formed. In theory each company consisted of 600 mounted men, of whom 100 were fully equipped men-at-arms and 200 archers, the rest being pages and men with inferior equipment, known as *coutillers* and *valets de guerre*. About twenty of these companies were maintained by Charles VII.

These troops were to dwell in billets in certain specified towns. They were to be paid adequately and regularly. Insubordination was to be punished very severely, great disciplinary power being vested in the captains.

The *compagnies d'ordonnance* consisted largely of men of noble or gentle blood. They contained the best soldiers in France, and willingly enforced the King's edicts against the rag, tag, and bobtail who had been discarded. Under Charles, being regularly paid, they remained loyal. They were expensive; and the *taille des gens de guerre*, the new tax which furnished their wages, was heavy and unpopular. But at once there was a great diminution of the disorder which had so afflicted France. Based in great measure on regulations of the fourteenth century, the reform is important, not because of its originality, but because it created a standing army which never afterwards ceased entirely to exist.

Twelve thousand men, though a formidable force, were not enough for the work to be done. When active warfare against the English was resumed, they had to be supplemented by *compagnies de petite ordonnance*, whose efficiency and pay were less. The King still called out the feudal host on occasion.

*The Free Archers*

It is amazing that no attempt was made to create a really formidable body of infantry. The civic militia which most

French towns maintained was seldom worth much, and the societies of bowmen which existed in some cities were often better at feasting than at fighting. It is true that Charles, again inspired by the example of former kings, instituted the famous " Free Archers." They came into being through two ordinances of 1448 and 1451: every fifty " hearths " belonging to *roturiers* must furnish an archer. The men were officially selected: they lived at home, had to possess a specified equipment, to practise on feast-days, and to serve when called upon. They were paid when on active service and were exempt from the *taille*. Under Charles VII there were 8,000 of them; they might have been very valuable but never were.

The neglect of infantry by the French was compensated by the attention which they gave to artillery. Henry V had made great use of siege engines, and some of his most notable exploits had been due largely to his guns. But in the later stages of the war, the English artillery was far surpassed by the French. Experts from all over Europe were attracted to France, but Charles owed most to the Bureau brothers, Gaspard and Jean, who were at once manufacturers, experts in ballistics, and gunners. Thanks to them, Charles VII became the possessor of field artillery capable of deciding battles, while his siege guns were the best hitherto known. His later military successes he owed to his artillery more than to any other single cause. French artillery

The effect of Charles's military reforms was sensationally apparent when fighting began again in 1449. Though Suffolk's promise was secretly confirmed by Henry VI, the King and his advisers, fearing with good reason the wrath of the English people, put off ordering the evacuation of Maine until the opportune death of Gloucester, the leader of the war party, in 1447. Even then the English on the spot demurred, and it was only in March 1448 that, menaced by a strong French army, the English garrison withdrew from Le Mans. In England Suffolk and his associates the Beauforts were generally execrated. Eager to rehabilitate himself, Suffolk lost his head, and early in 1449 instigated an unprovoked attack by English troops on the Breton town of Fougères, which was ruthlessly sacked. It was a flagrant breach of the truce, and the exultant French at once pounced upon Conquest of Normandy, 1449-50

Normandy. Assailed on every frontier, the English were overwhelmed. Town after town fell, the more obstinate being soon battered into surrender by the Bureau brothers. In October, aided by a popular rising within the walls, the French took Rouen: and at the end of the year scarce a dozen places in Normandy were in English hands. But the Duke of Somerset still clung to Caen, and a desperate effort was made to rescue him. Somehow a force of 2,500 men was raised in England and sent across the Channel under Sir Thomas Kyriel. On landing at Cherbourg it was joined by reinforcements scraped together from the remaining English garrisons in Normandy. Advancing through the Cotentin, the English made for Caen: but near Formigny they were intercepted by a French force of approximately equal size. The battle was very fiercely contested. The English adopted their time-honoured formation, in which they offered a splendid target for the few French cannon. An attempt to capture these brought about a savage hand-to-hand struggle, which was only decided by the arrival of about 1,800 fresh French troops. It was a terrible catastrophe for the English, five-sixths of them being killed or taken. In June 1450, Caen capitulated, and other towns soon did the like. At last, after a month's siege, Cherbourg was taken in August, and that was the end of English rule in Normandy.

**Conquest of Guienne, 1450-1**  Immediately afterwards the French once again attempted what seemed a much harder task—the expulsion of the English from Guienne, where their presence was not due to recent conquest and they were popular. For long, indeed, the English territory in Aquitaine had been greatly shrunken in comparison with its extent in Edward III's time; but the hold of the English on the Bordelais and the Landes was fairly complete. When, however, a French army invaded Guienne in the autumn of 1450, it was aided by many local lords and gained much success. Next year Dunois beset Bordeaux with a fleet and an army of 6,000 men; and, with no prospect of relief, the city surrendered towards autumn in the hope of saving the vintage. Very liberal terms were granted to the vanquished, and the conquest of the south-west was soon accomplished, Bayonne being captured on August 20, 1451.

But it was not long before Charles VII's officials—who in

the eyes of the Gascons were just as " foreign " as the English —brought home to the people that their new yoke was likely to be more oppressive than the old one. Learning that numerous nobles, burghers, and dispossessed functionaries of the region were corresponding with Henry VI, the French made their treason a pretext for withdrawing the privileges granted in the treaty of surrender. The consequence was a widespread conspiracy, whose leaders told Henry that if he would send an army, the whole countryside would rise for him. A force 8,000 strong was dispatched under the veteran Talbot, now Earl of Shrewsbury ; on its arrival the promised rebellion broke out, and in October 1452 Talbot entered Bordeaux. For several months the Bordelais was again English. But in the spring of 1458, three French armies invaded Guienne. One besieged Castillon, and Shrewsbury, wisely hoping to destroy his enemy in detail, led 8,000 men, mostly Gascons, against it. In face of the French superiority in artillery, he could devise no better tactics than a charge against the enemy's entrenchments. It was very gallantly made, but the dense ranks of his men-at-arms and archers were mown down by the French cannon. Shrewsbury himself was killed, his army nearly annihilated. Though attacked by a fourth French force, the Gascons continued to resist ; but the land was ravaged, and in October Bordeaux again surrendered.

Gascon rising : battle of Castillon, July 17, 1458

Hard measure was meted out to the rebels. Bordeaux was mulcted in a heavy indemnity. The administration of Guienne was assimilated to that of the royal domain. The prosperity of Bordeaux was gravely impaired by the measures which were taken to damage English trade. Many Gascons fled, not a few going to England. The French found it a hard task to hold the country, many plots being formed against them in the next few years, though all were put down.

The battle of Castillon and the final capture of Bordeaux are commonly treated by historians as marking the end of the Hundred Years War. But they were not followed by any formal treaty or by the abandonment of the English claims. The two countries were still officially at war ; there was much talk in England, and much apprehension in France, concerning an expedition that would recover everything. Nevertheless, the sequel showed that these events did mean that the

The Hundred Years War decided

attempt of the English to unite the two crowns had definitely failed, and that they were not even to have the consolation of annexing French territory. Though there was occasional fighting, as when in 1457 the English wasted the Île de Ré and the French sacked Sandwich, the Wars of the Roses soon deprived England of all capacity for foreign enterprises, and after a few years the House of Lancaster was actually seeking help from Charles VII.

*Charles VII's mistresses and counsellors*
The triumph over the English caused flatterers to call Charles *le victorieux*. It is true that for a while he had shown some energy; but the rapid rise in the fortunes of France was due to his counsellors far more than himself. In only one respect does he seem to have altered much. As a young man he had been singularly chaste, and unwavering in fidelity to his dull and ugly Queen. But after the death of his mother-in-law, Yolande of Anjou, in 1442, he became more and more addicted to women. Two years later he took as his acknowledged mistress the famous Agnes Sorel, who, on her death in 1450, was succeeded by her cousin Antoinette de Maignelais. The influence of Agnes on Charles seems in the main to have been good; it was certainly very great. After her death, however, he degenerated fast, became immoderately lascivious, and used to go about the country with a gorgeous harem. He was, personally, as contemptible at the end of his reign as at the beginning.

Even in his lifetime he was nicknamed Charles Le Bien Servy. Never was the Royal Council more assiduous than in the last twenty years of his rule. Agnes and Antoinette used their influence in favour of men very different from Charles's early advisers. The King relied much on Arthur of Richemont and Dunois, especially in military matters; but the first place in his confidence was held by Pierre de Brézé, a man of undistinguished though gentle birth, no genius or saint, but a great improvement on La Trémoille or Gilles de Rais. Most of the work on the Council, however, was done by men of quite humble origin, such as Jean Bureau, the artillery expert, who for some time was treasurer of France, and held several other posts in the royal service. Another councillor was the great financier Jacques Coeur, who, however, abused his position and was disgraced in 1451. Not a few of the most assiduous officials were lawyers by training, and these in particular held exalted theories of the royal prerogative. In this, and also in their lack of scruple, they recall the counsellors of Philip the Fair.

Charles made no material change in the organization of the central government. Henry V and Bedford had kept the old machinery substantially as they had found it; and all that Charles had to do after his victory was to adjust the relationship between the officials in Paris on the one hand, and those in Bourges or Poitiers on the other. Some attempt was made to accelerate and otherwise improve the procedure of the courts of justice, which nevertheless remained cumbrous and costly. The *Parlement* of Paris, recruited by co-optation, sometimes demurred at the registration of royal edicts, particularly those alienating royal domain; it could only delay, not frustrate, the execution of the King's will, but its criticism had a restraining effect on him and his Council.

*Central government*

Local administration was not much altered. The most remarkable innovation was the creation of provincial *parlements*, much to the chagrin of the *Parlement* of Paris. The first was the *Parlement* of Toulouse, established in 1420 and reconstituted in 1443 as a court of appeal for Languedoc and Guienne. A *Parlement* for Dauphiné, practically though not technically part of France, was set up by the Dauphin Louis and sanctioned by the King. Guienne was granted a special *Parlement* of its own in 1451, but forfeited it by rebelling in the following year. These precedents were fruitful, but they have been criticized on the ground that they perpetuated provincial diversity and hindered the unification of France.

*Local government*

These *Parlements* were of course primarily judicial bodies. For parliamentary institutions, in the English sense, the later years of Charles VII, as we have seen, were most unpropitious.

The strength of the Crown after the expulsion of the English was illustrated by its relations with the nobles. The humiliated Count of Armagnac died in 1450, and his son, Count John V, though permitted to hold his ancestral lands, claimed yet more, intrigued with the English, declared himself independent of the Crown, and alienated all decent people by living in incest with his sister. In 1455 royal troops occupied his lands, and he was subsequently sentenced to banishment and forfeiture.

*The nobility at the close of the reign*

More notorious, while really less formidable, was the treason of the Duke of Alençon. Restored to his duchy when Normandy was recovered, he was nevertheless soon intriguing with all Charles VII's enemies. In pursuit of his aims he collected artillery, practised magic, and formed conspiracies in Norman towns. In 1458 he was proved to have invited an English invasion. But, though condemned to death by the Court of Peers, he was reprieved and imprisoned at Loches, his duchy being confiscated.

The Dauphin Louis

Charles's chief source of anxiety in his last years was that objectionable but able young man, the Dauphin. After a brief spell of harmony with his father, Louis became jealous of the influence of Brézé and Agnes Sorel, and in 1446 plotted to set the King aside and make himself regent. His plan was detected, and he was again sent to Dauphiné. Though originally he was " banished " for only four months, he stayed in Dauphiné for nearly ten years, and he never saw his father again. In the administration of the province he showed the same characteristics and used the same methods as afterwards rendered memorable his rule of France. He raised the Dauphin's authority to an unprecedented height, and, though the country was heavily taxed, it enjoyed such peace and prosperity as it had not known for generations. Louis, however, found Dauphiné too small a sphere for the exercise of his ambitions. He was continually plotting in France, and he had his own foreign policy, which was often clean contrary to that of his father. It was, for example, in the teeth of Charles's prohibition that in 1451 he married Charlotte, daughter of the Duke of Savoy. He probably imagined that the King hated him as much as he hated the King, and when in 1455 Charles visited southern France with an army, he jumped to the conclusion that his misdeeds were the cause, and fled in ignominious panic to the Netherlands, where he threw himself upon the good-nature of the Duke of Burgundy. Philip harboured him hospitably for the rest of his father's life. The Duke doubtless thought he was making a friend of the future king and embarrassing the present one. This he was pleased to do, for Charles, it cannot be denied, had in many respects evaded the execution of the Treaty of Arras. The *Parlement* of Paris had entertained appeals from the Duke's subjects, and had even cited him before it. The Crown had

Grievances of Philip the Good against Charles VII

intervened between Philip and rebels against his authority; it had notoriously encouraged free-lance troops to raid his lands. Abroad, Charles was constantly thwarting Philip's most cherished schemes. On his side, Charles had grievances against the Duke. But neither wanted an open breach, and the trial of strength between France and Burgundy was deferred until both Charles and Philip were dead.

The relations of France at this time with other states of continental Europe do not require much comment. The old policy of interfering in the internal quarrels of Germany and nibbling at the German frontier was resumed. In 1444, when the government was eager to get the *Écorcheurs* out of France, the Dauphin led a force of them to aid the Emperor Frederick III against the Swiss. The immediate results of the expedition were disappointing to the French, but the prowess of the Swiss convinced Louis that he must always have them as friends, and the alliance which he speedily made with them was destined to have momentous consequences. Charles's foreign policy

About the same time Charles was conducting a campaign in Lorraine—a fief of the Empire—in support of Duke René, whose title was disputed by a rival and whose authority was defied by some of his subjects. The Duke's claims were vindicated. Épinal was constrained to swear fealty to Charles VII; Toul and Verdun had to recognize again that they were under the protection of the French King. These successes simply repeated what had been done long before in the days of Philip the Fair, and Charles VII, who seems to have set little store by them, probably regarded them as safeguards against the ambitions of Burgundy. It is certain that the intricate and unscrupulous intrigues which he later conducted in Germany had as their main object the thwarting of Duke Philip.

In Italy Charles had many interests but gained little success. The support which he lent to the Angevin claims to Naples yielded no fruit. French interference in the north on behalf of the Duke of Orléans was ineffective. In 1458, party strife in Genoa led to the city's being placed under the rule of Charles VII, but the French were soon driven out.

Despite minor setbacks, Charles VII, in his last years, was the most powerful sovereign in Europe. One very notable source of his strength was his influence on the Church. The Charles's ecclesiastical policy

Pragmatic Sanction of Bourges had raised this to a point at which it had not stood for centuries. Besides affirming the superiority of General Councils to the Pope in matters of faith and discipline and accepting various decrees of the Council of Basel concerning prevalent abuses, it declared invalid all papal provisions or reservations affecting France, forbade the exaction of annates there, and allowed appeals to the Papacy only when all lower courts had been tried. The blow to the authority of Eugenius IV was mitigated by practical concessions to him regarding taxation and the bestowal of benefices; but the Pragmatic Sanction did free the Church in France from much oppression. At the same time it increased the power of the French Crown and the French nobility, whose control over ecclesiastical appointments in the realm became much stronger.

At the beginning of the schism between the Papacy and the Council of Basel, Charles VII played a mediating part, and he contributed much towards the eventual restoration of unity. He refused, however, to withdraw the Pragmatic Sanction, notwithstanding the pleas and remonstrances of the Papacy. A great impression was made in 1450 by the production of the forgery called the Pragmatic Sanction of Saint Louis, which purported to be an ordinance of that king establishing the freedom of ecclesiastical elections and forbidding the levy of extraordinary taxation by the Papacy. When in 1460 Pius II declared that any prince appealing from the Pope to a General Council was liable to excommunication, the King's Procurator-General formally appealed to a General Council against this decree. The Papacy was much perturbed by the attitude of the French Crown, and its desire to conciliate French opinion is shown by the fact that in 1456 Calixtus III granted a demand, ostensibly from the family of

Rehabilitation of Joan of Arc, 1456

Joan of Arc, for a revision of the process against her. The commissioners appointed were all totally devoted to the King, and their object was to show that Joan was no sorceress or heretic but an ignorant and colourless country girl who owed all her ideas and force to divine inspiration. A great mass of evidence was collected, but its unconcealed bias robs it of much of the interest which it should have had. In general, people still alive were gently handled, and blame was concentrated on persons now dead, like Pierre Cauchon, or on the

English, whom it was both patriotic and safe to revile. The process of 1431 was ultimately declared to be irregular and Joan's condemnation to be unjustified.

The Crown of France had been freed from a stigma. But Charles continued to behave as though anxious to prove that his bygone association with a good woman had been a youthful indiscretion for which he wished to atone. He grew prematurely old, but, to the undissembled annoyance of his son, was an unconscionable time a-dying. At last, in July 1461, he had a stroke, and thereafter, it is said, refused food, asserting that the Dauphin was trying to poison him, a plausible but probably false accusation. His physician was imprisoned, but on July 22 he died. Seldom has so inglorious a king had so glorious a reign.

*Death of Charles VII, July 22, 1461*

Works on the subjects covered by chapter iii :—
i. Some original sources—
  Ordonnances des Rois (as for chaps. i and ii).
  Journal de Clément de Fauquembergue ; Journal d'un Bourgeois ; Le Fèvre, Chronique ; Monstrelet, Chronique (as for chaps. i and ii).
  Champion, Pierre : Procès de condamnation de Jeanne d'Arc, 2 vols., Paris, 1920.
  Letters and Papers illustrative of the Wars of the English in France during the reign of Henry VI, ed. J. Stevenson, Rolls Series, 3 vols., London, 1861–4.
  Quicherat, J. E. J. : Procès de condamnation et réhabilitation de Jeanne d'Arc, Société de l'Hist. de France, 5 vols., Paris, 1841–9. (This work must still be the basis of any serious investigation of the career of Joan of Arc.)
  Basin, T. : Histoire de Charles VII, ed. and trans. C. Samaran, Lat. and French, 2 vols., Paris, 1933. (Les Classiques de l'Histoire de France au Moyen Age, xv, xxi.)
  Bouvier, Gilles le, called the Herald Berry : Histoire Chronologique du Roy Charles VII, in D. Godefroy, Histoire de Charles VI et de VII, pp. 369–474, Paris, 1658–61.
  Cagny, Perceval de : Chroniques, ed. H. Moranvillé, Soc. de l'Hist. de France, Paris, 1902. (Very valuable for Joan of Arc.)
  Chartier, Jean : Chronique de Charles VII, ed. A. Vallet de Viriville, 3 vols., Paris, 1858.
  Cousinot, G. : Chronique de la Pucelle, ed. A. Vallet de Viriville, Paris, 1859.
  Escouchy, Matthieu d' : Chronique, ed. G. du Fresne de Beaucourt, Soc. de l'Hist. de France, 3 vols., Paris, 1863–4. (Continuation of Monstrelet.)
  Gruel, Guill. : Chronique d'Arthur de Richemont, ed. A. Le Vavasseur, Soc. de l'Hist. de France, Paris, 1890.
  Narratives of the expulsion of the English from Normandy, ed. J. Stevenson, Rolls Series, London, 1863.

ii. Some modern works—

The works of Petit-Dutaillis, Beaucourt, Vallet de Viriville, J. Calmette and E. Déprez, mentioned under chap. ii.

*Cambridge Medieval History*, vol. viii, ch. vii, Cambridge, 1936.

Ayroles, J. P. J.: *La vraie Jeanne d'Arc*, 5 vols., Paris, 1890–8. (Illustrates the extreme clerical and ultramontane attitude towards Joan.)

Cosneau, E.: *Le connétable de Richemont*, Paris, 1886.

France, Anatole: *Vie de Jeanne d'Arc*, 4 vols., Paris, 1910. (The revised edition of this famous work, first published in 1908, and written from an anti-clerical and sceptical standpoint. There is an English translation of the first edition.)

Jeanné, E.: *L'image de la Pucelle d'Orléans dans la littérature historique française depuis Voltaire*, Paris, 1935.

Lang, Andrew: *The Maid of France*, London, 1908. (Sentimental, but brings out some of the weaknesses of France's book.)

Lowell, F. C.: *Joan of Arc*, New York, 1896. (Though somewhat superseded by later research, this remains one of the most impartial, judicious, and accurate books on the subject.)

Luce, S.: *Jeanne d'Arc à Domrémy*, Paris, 1886.

Quicherat, J. E. J.: *Rodrigue de Villandrando*, Paris, 1879.

Shaw, George Bernard: *Saint Joan*, London, 1924. (Though many of its details have no historical foundation and there are anachronisms in the dialogue, Shaw's play probably gives a truer picture of Joan herself than any other modern work.)

Waldmann, M.: *Joan of Arc*, London, 1935.

## CHAPTER IV

## GERMANY, 1378–1410

### WENZEL AND RUPERT

FROM the old-fashioned political standpoint, it is natural *Character of* that modern writers should usually have spoken con- *German* temptuously of the history of Germany in the latter *history in the later* part of the Middle Ages. In the doings of the German em- *Middle Ages* perors, kings, and princes of the time there is little to arouse admiration or even interest; often they even lack important consequences. And depressing as the history of Germany becomes immediately after the fall of the Hohenstaufen, it grows yet more sordid in the hundred years that followed the death of the Emperor Charles IV. Of the men who wore the German crown in that time, only one—Sigismund—was fitted for his part, and so great were the weaknesses mingled with his virtues that what respect one may feel for him is very nearly counterbalanced by contempt. But no matter who was King of the Romans, his authority was so weak that the average German was little influenced by it. Far more effective was the power of the princes, and the history of Germany in the fourteenth and fifteenth centuries is really the history of a score of rival states, each for all practical purposes independent.

Nevertheless, Germany always had a king, called King of *The* the Romans and popularly termed Emperor, though properly *Monarchy* he had no right to assume the title until he had been crowned by the Pope. He was chosen by the seven Electors, whose rights, duties, and functions had been consolidated in the thirteenth century, and whose position had been authoritatively settled by Charles IV's Golden Bull. On election the fortunate candidate was as soon as possible crowned at Aachen, and thereafter he claimed the right to wield imperial power, not merely in Germany, but in all lands which fell within the sphere of the Holy Roman Empire; theoretically, indeed, he was lord of the whole world. But even regions which had for long recognized the Emperor had now ceased to do so. He was ignored in the kingdom of Burgundy or Arles, which was almost wholly under the rule of French potentates; while in Italy men only acknowledged his overlordship to serve their private ends, and the two visits of Charles IV had merely illustrated the fact that the Holy Roman Empire was still more of an anachronism there than in Germany. In one respect, on the other hand, the position of a King of the Romans was better in the fifteenth-century than it had been for many years previously. The Popes had long claimed that no King of the Romans possessed any lawful authority until his election had received papal confirmation. This doctrine had almost invariably been denied by the kings,[1] but since 1278 nearly all of them had found it advisable to seek papal approval, and the Holy See had used its opportunity to gain important concessions and to stir up trouble from time to time. Wenzel, Charles IV's successor, had been approved before the death of his father, and owing to a singular turn of events the Popes of the next hundred years were seldom able to press their old demands on the Empire, and king succeeded king with but small regard for their views.

In theory the King of the Romans was still very powerful in Germany. Subject to a few restrictions, he was entitled to legislate for all inhabitants of the kingdom. In practice, however, he was obliged to get the consent of the Electors and, as a rule, of the Diet, when he wished to make a new law; and in any event his legislation was likely to be ineffective, since he had no means of enforcing it. Financially he was in a sad plight. The lands attached to the Crown were small and scattered. The rule that the King might not alienate them without the consent of the Electors was often broken. The yield of the royal domain was consequently meagre, and other sources of revenue brought in little. The imperial cities owed regular contributions, but these were small and were paid reluctantly and irregularly. As for the exploitation of mines and the coining of money—for long supposed to be monopolies of the Crown—they had been surrendered to the Electors within the limits of their territories, and elsewhere did not yield much. The military obligations of the princes were no longer exacted. When a king wished to make war, he had to

[1] Albert I was the only one who expressly accepted it.

pay such of his vassals as condescended to serve under him, and as a rule he had no money for the purpose.

It followed from all this that the influence actually exercised by a king depended mainly on the extent and resources of his family possessions. He might indeed be a powerful man. But as the Crown was elective, the extra strength which he derived from his royal dignity was likely to be used to increase the territory of his house, not to consolidate the position of the monarchy. As a matter of fact, though the imperial crown remained in theory elective until the end of the Holy Roman Empire in 1806, it fell permanently into the hands of the Habsburgs during the period covered by this volume, while for nearly a hundred years before that happened it had been held by the House of Luxemburg. But no one at the time foresaw that in practice the German monarchy was to become hereditary, so that if princes of the fifteenth century coveted the crown, it was still merely because it might help them to get rich more quickly.

During the fourteenth century the power of the princes grew very great in relation to that of the King. But it must not be supposed that they were without troubles of their own. Their subjects often were as insubordinate towards them as they themselves were towards the Emperor. The actual authority of the princes in their respective territories varied greatly. A Count Palatine of the Rhine was in the fourteenth century a powerful monarch, whereas a Margrave of Brandenburg or a Count of Holland was frequently at his wits' end to maintain tolerable order in his lands. Like the King, the princes were often in great financial difficulties, which compelled them to ask their subjects for extraordinary subsidies, or *Notbeden*. It thus came about that in many principalities there were the rudiments of a real constitutional government ; for a prince's need of money compelled him to appeal to the three Estates of his territory, who took advantage of the situation to secure recognition of their right to consent to all extraordinary levies, and to gain a voice in legislation, the disposal of the prince's domain, and the succession to his title. By 1878 the *Landtage* of Germany were of more practical consequence to her people than the *Reichstag*. {The princes}

While at this time the princes of Germany could be numbered by the score, only a few were strong enough to have {The House of Luxemburg} much influence on the general fortunes of the country. In 1378 much the greatest family was the one that held the crown, the House of Luxemburg. Among its possessions, the county whence it took its name was now of but minor consequence. It is true that the strength which it derived from its vast domains had been impaired by the dispositions made by Charles IV; for Wenzel, the head of the house, ruled only Bohemia, Silesia, and part of Lusatia, while his brother Sigismund had Brandenburg, his brother John the duchy of Görlitz and the so-called Neumark, his uncle Wenzel Luxemburg, and his cousin Jost Moravia. It is also true that there was not much affection among these kinsmen. Nevertheless the House of Luxemburg remained the greatest political force in Germany.

The Electors  The influence of the Luxemburgs was based in no small measure on the fact that they held two of the seven electoral votes, those of Bohemia and Brandenburg. Of the other two lay Electors one, the Count Palatine of the Rhine, belonged to the House of Wittelsbach. His territorial resources made him formidable, for he was lord not only of his rich county in the Rhineland, but also of most of the Upper Palatinate, which adjoined Bavaria to the north. The Elector of Saxony carried less weight. He held the duchy of Saxe-Wittenberg, but the Ascanian family, to which he belonged, had for some time produced no men of much distinction, and its lands had been divided. There remained the three ecclesiastical Electors, the Archbishops of Mainz, Cologne, and Trier. Their very wealthy estates in western Germany placed them in the first class of the country's potentates. These prelates were usually just as worldly in their conduct and aims as the temporal princes. They could not indeed hand on their lands to their descendants, but they generally showed unbounded zeal for the territorial aggrandisement of their sees, while some of them contrived to do a great deal for the advancement of their kinsfolk.

The clergy  The part played by the clergy in political life was, it must be remembered, far more influential in Germany than in either England or France. In these countries bishops or abbots often held very rich temporalities; but they could not aspire to rule them regardless of the wishes of the King. In the Germany of late medieval times many bishops and some abbots were princes of the Empire ; they had usually been appointed, and generally exercised their authority, without any consideration for the interests of the Crown. A very large proportion of the soil of Germany belonged to the Church. Along the Main valley, ecclesiastical fiefs lay so thick that the region came to be known as the Priests' Lane. There was another nest of them in the north-west. No other ecclesiastical princes equalled the Rhenish archbishops in power, wealth, and splendour : but a Bishop of Strasbourg, of Speyer, of Würzburg, or an Archbishop of Magdeburg, did not come far behind. The abbots, though a few cut a great figure, were in general of much less consequence, and such moral authority as they had exerted was greatly reduced owing to the growing unpopularity of monasticism. Among the ecclesiastical principalities may be included the lands of the Teutonic Order of Knights in Prussia. Technically they lay outside the limits of Germany, but they constituted a most important outpost of German culture.

Of the dynasties which had not gained admission to the circle of the Electors, the most notable in 1378 was the House of Habsburg. It had passed through various vicissitudes since King Rudolf I had raised it to the front rank of German families, and it was now not quite so influential as it had been at the beginning of the century. But, with its original lands in Swabia, the vast possessions which Rudolf I had gained for it—Austria, Styria, and Carniola—and the more recently-acquired Carinthia and Tyrol, it was surpassed in resources by the Luxemburgs alone. Like many families the Habsburgs clung to the old German custom of dividing up a man's land among his sons. Thus in 1379, after a family dispute, the Habsburg possessions were shared between Albert III, who got Austria, and his younger and more vigorous brother Leopold, who took all the rest. The same practice had played havoc with the power of the Wittelsbachs, which the Emperor Lewis the Bavarian had raised to a high pitch, even after the separation of the Palatinate branch from the Bavarian branch of the house. In 1378 the Bavarian lands of the family were shared between three of the grandsons of Lewis, while the counties of Holland, Zeeland, and Hainault were ruled by his son Albert, who founded what was virtually a separate, though it proved a short-lived, dynasty. It was the lack of

*The Habsburgs and Wittelsbachs*

united devotion to the interests of the family which had cost it Brandenburg and Tyrol in the reign of Charles IV.

*Lesser dynasties*

Other princes that will demand our notice from time to time are the Counts of Würtemberg, the Welf Dukes of Brunswick, who also impaired their strength by the division of their lands, and members of the Wettin family, which dominated Thuringia, held the Mark of Meissen, and was destined to increase its power greatly during the fifteenth century. In the far north there were notable potentates, such as the Dukes of Mecklenburg and Pomerania; but they pursued their local ambitions with little regard for the Crown, which generally let them alone.

*The knights*

Besides the princes, there were countless nobles who acknowledged no overlord save the King. Their wealth, rights, and power varied greatly. The humblest grade was the class of knights, poor, proud, lawless, and turbulent. Their part in the social and economic life of Germany must be considered at some length elsewhere; but it should not be overlooked that in politics also they were an important element.

*The cities*

From the knights one passes to their bitter foes, the burghers. It was towards the end of the fourteenth century that the towns of Germany reached the climax of their political influence. From the standpoint of the statesman, they were on the whole a disintegrating force, notwithstanding their fondness for forming leagues. Very jealous of their privileges, which had generally been won with much effort and expense, they looked askance at any government, royal or princely, which promised to become truly effective. A distinction should be drawn between the imperial cities, which were, so to speak, corporate tenants-in-chief of the Crown, and the *Landstädte*, cities subject to the princes. In the political history of Germany during the fifteenth century, much more is heard of the imperial cities; but in number they were far inferior to the others, while for privileges, power, and riches many princely cities had little reason to envy them. There was no conscious rivalry between the two classes; members of each were to be found, for instance, in the Hanseatic League. It must not be supposed, however, that there was ever any attempt or even desire to form a national league of German cities. Each city thought of itself first, and if it joined others for common action, it was usually under the influence of a common fear, which rarely affected more than a limited area or preserved harmony for long.

All things considered, the prospects of King Wenzel, when he succeeded his father in 1378, were not very bright. It was indeed greatly to his advantage that the old Emperor's address and foresight had brought about the election of his heir before his death and secured papal approval of what had been done. Wenzel had therefore to cope with none of the troubles that usually beset an aspirant to the German throne. But it was certain that the Electors, who had voted for him reluctantly, would eye his doings critically, and that some of them would expect him to show his gratitude by lending his authority to their purposes. There was also a very general concern at the ascendancy which the cleverness of Charles IV had won for the House of Luxemburg, and many princes were awaiting the slightest opportunity of injuring the dangerous family. Furthermore, the Great Schism in the Roman Church had just begun, and it was already evident that it would greatly increase the difficulties which a German king inevitably had to face.

*Prospects of King Wenzel, 1378*

So far as could be judged, Wenzel's character and gifts warranted hopes of his success. He was indeed over young, scarcely eighteen. But he had been well educated; he knew Latin, French, German, and Czech, and took a genuine and active interest in art and learning. He was certainly no fool. There seemed no reason why he should fail to win popularity, for he was good-looking and naturally had pleasant manners. He soon let it be known that he wished to continue his father's policy—that is, to keep the peace in Germany by maintaining the *status quo* in co-operation with the Electors. Abroad, too, he was for cultivating friendship wherever he could. Like his father, he was on good terms with France, while in 1381 he consented to the marriage of his sister Anne and Richard II of England.

*His character*

*His policy*

It was not long, however, before Wenzel's conduct began to arouse discontent. He displayed a singular indolence, which grew worse as years went on. At first it probably seemed to the Germans greater than it really was, for Wenzel was not much interested in Germany or its crown, caring far more for Bohemia and the concerns of his family. In

Bohemia he spent nearly all his time, not crossing its western frontier for years together, and he gave his confidence almost exclusively to Czechs, some of whom, whether mentally or morally, were unworthy of it. Ere long, too, he began to drink so immoderately as to scandalize even medieval Germans.

<small>Hostility between princes and cities</small>

In the first years of Wenzel's reign the most troublesome problem for the German Crown arose from the relations between the cities and the princes of the south. There was in existence a league of the imperial cities of Swabia, formed towards the end of the reign of Charles IV. Its purpose was to defend the liberties of its members and in particular to preserve them from being given to princes by the Emperor as security for the fulfilment of imperial obligations or the payment of imperial debts—a common practice at the time and one which often had the effect of removing a city for ever from its direct relationship with the impotent crown and bringing it under the stricter rule of a local noble. The league had repelled an attempt of Charles IV to suppress it, and had fought successfully against the princes of south Germany. Shortly before the accession of Wenzel, peace had been patched up; but burghers and princes still glowered at one another suspiciously. Both parties were chagrined when Wenzel tried to maintain neutrality and showed little interest in the quarrel; and it was perhaps mainly because of their uncertainty as to his intentions that strife was averted for several years. When it finally did break out, it was occasioned by new factors in the situation. It happened that at this time the knights of southern Germany were more than usually conscious of their common grievances and thus more than usually disposed to unite for common action. Several new associations of knights were formed, the biggest being the Society of St. George, which originated in the Wetterau but spread along the Rhine and as far as Bavaria and Thuringia, being joined after a while by Count Ulrich of Würtemberg, numerous great lords of Swabia, two bishops, and even the city of Basel. In general, however, the south German cities considered the very existence of the society a threat to their interests. In 1381 several powerful cities on or near the Rhine—among them being Mainz, Frankfort, and Strasbourg—organized a new defensive league, which soon made an alliance with the Swabian league already mentioned. Almost immediately afterwards war broke out between the allied leagues and the knights. It was not a very serious struggle, and after a few months the mediation of Leopold of Habsburg led to peace. The knights were much discouraged; their princely allies had not helped them effectually, and the cities had revealed unexpected military strength and capacity. Of the new societies which the knights had formed, only that of St. George survived the war for long, and it never quite recovered its early strength. *War between cities and knights, 1381-2*

The two city leagues renewed their alliance and grew in power. The Swabian League came to an understanding with the Swiss Confederation, and both it and the Rhenish League were joined by many members of the nobility. Wenzel wavered. Immediately after the recent war, he inclined towards the princes, and after trying in vain to establish a *Landfriede* for the whole realm—an organization which would have rendered the city leagues unlawful—he promoted the formation of a league of princes. It was not long, however, before he began to show favour to the cities, and in 1384 he organized what was virtually a new *Landfriede*, to which the two city leagues and the princes of south Germany belonged. He declared that he would protect imperial cities against all who interfered with their rights, but negotiations for a closer agreement between them and the King led only to an organized robbery of the Jews in the cities of Swabia. Encouraged by Wenzel's friendliness, some cities would have resumed the war against the nobles; but there was a strong peace party among the burghers, especially in the Rhineland, and even when in 1386 there were hostilities between Leopold of Austria and the Swiss, the cities took no active part. The speedy overthrow of Leopold, however, increased their confidence, which rose yet higher when Wenzel repeated his promise to respect their privileges and announced that he would never dissolve their leagues. The crisis was precipitated in 1387, when Piligrim, Archbishop of Salzburg, a trusted counsellor of the King's and an ally of the Swabian League, was taken prisoner by his inveterate enemies the Bavarian Wittelsbachs. The undertakings which he gave to recover his freedom were repudiated by his cathedral chapter as soon as he was liberated. The Wittelsbachs again took up arms. The *Wenzel's vacillation*

*Renewed war in South Germany, 1388-9*

two city leagues supported the archbishop; the princes of Swabia and Franconia came to the rescue of the Wittelsbachs. In open fighting, the cities, which relied mainly on mercenaries, had the worse of it, and were badly beaten at the battle of Döffingen in Würtemberg. On the other hand, the princes were utterly unsuccessful in their siege operations. Each side consequently sought to injure the other by ravaging, and south Germany suffered enormous economic harm in a few months. It soon appeared that the nobles were holding together better than the cities; but the struggle might have continued for a long time had it not been for the intervention of King Wenzel. Though he had declared war on the Wittelsbachs, he had given no effective help to the cities but had stayed in Bohemia amusing himself. As the fighting went on and he saw that the cities were likely to lose, he began to lean towards the princes. In May 1389, he ordered both parties to make peace and unite in a *Landfriede*. As he pronounced the dissolution of the city leagues of central and southern Germany, and as the terms of the *Landfriede* were more favourable to nobles than to burghers, the princes were willing to comply. The cities, though aggrieved, feared lest resistance might lead to yet worse misfortune. Hostilities therefore ceased; the Swabian and Rhenish Leagues were disbanded; and never again did the cities of Germany form such formidable organizations for political objects. Though their end was somewhat ignominious, the two leagues might claim to have fulfilled their purpose, for the cities composing them had lost none of the privileges they had united to defend and they had obtained what they believed to be guarantees against being granted in pledge. But one may well understand that no one concerned was much pleased with Wenzel. Indeed, whatever popularity he had at first enjoyed in Germany had now vanished.

Unpopularity of Wenzel

Wenzel, in fact, had given his German subjects several grounds for annoyance. He had lent vigorous and decisive support, in both men and money, to his brother Sigismund's efforts to secure the Hungarian crown; but some German princes would have preferred another issue to that enterprise, and many were alarmed at the continued increase of Luxemburg power, while Wenzel's devotion to family interests had not only increased his indifference to Germany but had weakened his desire for the imperial crown, a decoration on which the Germans still set some store. The King's attitude towards the papal schism had also aroused adverse criticism. Nearly all Germany was in favour of the " Roman " Pope, Urban VI, and Wenzel remained outwardly loyal to him. But he was known to have given a friendly hearing to French representations in favour of Clement VII, the Pope at Avignon, and even to have had dealings with him. Furthermore, apart from the strife in the south, Germany was in a sadly disturbed state. In 1388 there was a serious war between the Welfs and the Elector of Saxony, and elsewhere there was an amount of petty disorder which had not been equalled since the Great Interregnum.

While Wenzel had thus furnished numerous pretexts for complaint, his real offences were that he had been over zealous for the aggrandizement of the House of Luxemburg and had shown no marked sympathy for the aims of any class in Germany. As early as 1384 there was talk among the Electors of appointing an imperial vicar to exercise his rights in the German kingdom. The idea won increasing favour, and in 1387 was perhaps formally suggested to Wenzel. The King, however, though too lazy to exert his royal authority, was determined not to surrender a particle of it, and as his critics could not agree on a candidate for the regency, the proposal hung fire for some years. But it was never out of sight. Doubtless the princes inimical to Wenzel were encouraged by contemporary events in France and England in each of which the central government, for different reasons, was for years under aristocratic control. So when they sought to shelve their king, they might plead that they were no worse than their neighbours.

In the last decade of the fourteenth century German politics were even more bewildering than usual. Wenzel's behaviour became increasingly contemptible, though now and then he had a spell of ferocious vigour. The French King was violent when mad, the German King when sober. Poor Wenzel, indeed, might have pointed to his kinsfolk as some excuse for his intemperance. Sigismund, so far from being grateful for all that his brother had done in his behalf, seized every chance of extorting concessions from him. Still more trouble was caused to Wenzel by his cousin Jost, Margrave of Moravia—a well-educated man and a sincere patron of learning, but a liar, traitor, and miser, who managed by intrigue and the judicious use of his wealth to gain great influence over both Wenzel and Sigismund. For some years both Luxemburg and Brandenburg were held by him in pledge, so that he was one of the most redoubtable potentates in Germany.

With the nobles and clergy of Bohemia Wenzel had many special difficulties, some of which will be noticed in another chapter. It must be borne in mind, however, that events in Germany and in Bohemia had a mutual influence on one another. Thus, when in 1394 Wenzel was imprisoned by Jost and a body of Bohemian nobles, much indignation was aroused among the Germans, who did not like to see their king maltreated by anybody but themselves; and the threats of the Elector Palatine, who was *ex officio* administrator of the Empire during the absence or incapacity of its lord, had much to do with Wenzel's speedy release.

All this while, nevertheless, the proposal to appoint a regent was under consideration, and not a few Germans were beginning to speak of downright deposition. It was partly with the object of anticipating his opponents that in 1396 Wenzel came to an understanding with Sigismund, recognizing him as the successor to the Empire and nominating him imperial vicar from that time on. In Germany, Sigismund's reputation was somewhat higher than facts warranted, and the arrangement might have placated many of Wenzel's critics. Unfortunately, the catastrophic battle of Nicopolis, which occurred a few weeks later, ruined Sigismund's prestige for a while, and, for this and other reasons, he was obliged to spend much time in Hungary during the next few years.

Wenzel and Gian Galeazzo of Milan

Not only did the agreement with Sigismund fail of its purpose, but Wenzel had lately given his enemies a new stick wherewith to beat him. He still had dreams of the imperial crown, and it was in part to facilitate its attainment that in 1395 he had recognized Gian Galeazzo Visconti as Duke of Milan. The Visconti had long been virtually absolute lords of Milan and its territory: but legally they were only vicars of the Emperor, and by making Gian Galeazzo a duke, Wenzel was technically creating a new fief out of imperial domain.

Such an act, according to the commonly accepted doctrine, required the consent of the Electors, and this had not been obtained.

What with annoyance at Wenzel's concession to Gian Galeazzo and his omission to take any action towards ending the Great Schism, the German princes were not disposed to handle him gently when in 1897 the Elector Palatine and the Archbishops of Cologne and Trier summoned to Frankfort a Diet which was asked to consider his case. It was an impressive gathering, the rival popes and several foreign rulers being represented by envoys. The German princes resolved that Wenzel should be asked to appoint a vicegerent, and drew up a list of their grievances against him. They also decided to advocate the resignation of both popes as the best means of ending the Schism.

Wenzel would not do as the Diet wished; but he visited Germany for the first time since 1387, and by proclaiming a new *Landfriede* and destroying some robber castles tried to convince his subjects that he was still fit for his job. He failed, however, to make much impression, and at a further assembly, in January 1898, the Electors presented him with additional complaints. These were largely concerned with French encroachments on imperial possessions in both Germany and Italy—the occupation of Genoa being especially denounced; and the grant of the ducal title to Gian Galeazzo was also criticized. But the evils which Wenzel was accused of countenancing were either trivial or beyond his power to remedy, and it is evident that the Electors were simply seeking pretexts for getting rid of him. He could do nothing right. When he proposed to discuss with Charles VI the method of ending the Schism which the Diet had commended to him, the Elector Palatine and the Archbishop of Mainz, who had changed their views, protested. *Wenzel's deposition considered*

Wenzel nevertheless attended the conference which Charles had planned at Rheims. Though drunk during a good part of the proceedings, he reached a close understanding with Louis of Orléans, and it was agreed that while both popes should be called upon to resign, neither France nor Germany should use force against them. Then Wenzel went back to Bohemia, where civil war was raging. He left things in Germany to take their course.

Very many Germans were now convinced that Wenzel must be deposed. The leading spirit in the events that followed was probably John of Nassau, Archbishop of Mainz, a man of much vigour, indifferent education, and no scruple. His chief supporter was the Elector Palatine, Rupert III. Early in 1899 the Archbishop of Cologne joined them in an alliance with the ostensible purpose of maintaining their rights and furthering the welfare of the Empire. At an assembly held at Forchheim in May they secured the concurrence of the Landgrave of Hesse, the Wettin family, one or two of the Wittelsbachs, and Frederick of Hohenzollern, Burgrave of Nürnberg. A little later the Archbishop of Trier and the Elector of Saxony came into line. In September the princes who had been at Forchheim issued a manifesto announcing their intention of deposing Wenzel. Further action, however, was delayed owing to differences of opinion as to who should be chosen in his stead: several princes held that Electors should be ineligible, and it was not until January 1400 that they agreed not to press their view. Wenzel made some advances to the princes, but in vain, and when he approached some of the cities it was hinted that help was not to be expected by those who would not help themselves. On the other hand, Wenzel's enemies failed to get the countenance of Pope Boniface IX, who when told of their intentions refused to commit himself.

In May 1400 there was another great gathering, this time at Frankfort. Many princes, lay and ecclesiastical, were present in person or by proxy. Numerous cities sent representatives. There also appeared embassies from France, Castile, and the University of Paris, who were there on business connected with the Schism, but were quite willing to remain even when they learned why the assembly had been summoned. Wenzel sent a message forbidding it to do anything in his absence which might affect the Church or the Empire and asking it to co-operate with him in arranging for a European Council to end the Schism. No effect was produced, but there was still some dispute as to the person of his supplanter. Many were in favour of the Elector Palatine, but Rudolf of Saxony and the Welf princes left Frankfort rather than consent to his nomination. On the way home their party was set upon by the Count of Waldeck,

Duke Frederick of Brunswick being murdered and the Elector of Saxony taken prisoner. The outrage was generally believed to have been instigated by the Archbishop of Mainz.

On June 4, the Rhenish Electors summoned Wenzel to appear before them and other princes at Oberlahnstein and there concert measures for the reform of the Empire, adding that if he declined, they would consider themselves absolved from their oath of allegiance. Wenzel refused to give way. He sought the assistance of Pope Boniface, of Charles VI, of his brother Sigismund. Boniface professed his devotion to the King, but did nothing; Charles was sympathetic and asked the Electors to defer action; Sigismund would only act at the price of concessions which Wenzel would not grant. In the end, Wenzel stayed in Bohemia. *Wenzel cited by Rhenish Electors, June 1400*

At Oberlahnstein there appeared in due course the Rhenish Electors, with Duke Stephen of Bavaria and Frederick of Hohenzollern. On August 20, 1400, the deposition of Wenzel was publicly pronounced by the Archbishop of Mainz, and it was proclaimed that all the King's subjects were freed from their allegiance. Next day, at Rense, the three archbishops elected as king of the Romans the Elector Palatine Rupert, whose consent was deemed to furnish the necessary majority. *Wenzel's deposition pronounced: election of Rupert, Aug. 1400*

There was no legal ground for the contention that the Electors had the right to depose their king. Under certain conditions, they might take judicial action against him, but they made no pretence of doing this. They drew up a statement of Wenzel's misdeeds and shortcomings. He had done nothing to restore peace to the Church. He had dismembered the Empire by creating the duchy of Milan: indeed many imperial lands and cities had been lost by his negligence. He had neglected to provide for the peace and order of Germany. Many of his subjects, both clergy and honourable laymen, had been barbarously put to death at his instance. Throughout the document there is reference to his sloth and untrustworthiness. The charges for the most part lack precision, in some there is manifest exaggeration, and altogether the case of the Electors is far from cogent. Nevertheless, what they had done was generally approved in Germany. While legally it was unwarrantable, morally there was much to be said for it. Had Wenzel been worth *Grounds of Wenzel's deposition* anything, his deposition, long discussed and accomplished openly and deliberately, would have aroused a little violent opposition. But we hear of no one who risked his neck in the King's behalf. When Wenzel himself learned what had happened, he blustered and vowed vengeance; but he still counted on Sigismund, and Sigismund still put his terms too high. So, after his wont, Wenzel did nothing.

<small>Rupert's defects and difficulties</small>

It was soon evident that Wenzel's substitute was no great improvement on Wenzel. He was indeed a man of reputable private life—upright and just, though inordinately pious. But he was rather stupid, his outlook and ideas were narrow, and he was ridiculously credulous and optimistic.

The weakness of his position soon became evident. The German princes were slow to accord him recognition, as they were not sure whether Wenzel might not after all reassert himself. The cities had similar misgivings, and naturally looked askance at a king who before his election had pledged himself not to increase their privileges. Frankfort, on the pretext of ancient custom, kept him waiting for forty-five days before it would admit him to undergo the traditional ceremony of being placed on the altar of St. Bartholomew's Church. Aachen, the proper place for the coronation, would have done the like, but Rupert would not wait and had himself crowned at Cologne. His attempts to obtain recognition abroad had varied results, but he managed to arrange a marriage between his son Lewis and Blanche, daughter of Henry IV of England, another king with a contested title, and he established friendly relations with the Burgundian party in France.

<small>Rupert's expedition to Italy, 1401-2</small>

Rupert owed his rise in part to Wenzel's policy towards Milan, and he was eager to fulfil the expectation that he would oust Gian Galeazzo from his duchy. He also hoped to receive the imperial crown. Though he would not accept the theory that the validity of his title to the throne depended on the confirmation of his election by the Pope, he nevertheless sought the approval of Boniface IX. While maintaining that only a pope might lawfully depose a king of the Romans, Boniface wished to avoid alienating Rupert and his supporters, and therefore postponed a pronouncement by asking for further information as to what had happened.

Despite the ambiguous conduct of the Pope, Rupert

pressed forward the preparations for his expedition to Italy. The main obstacle was his lack of money. It was believed that this was overcome when the republic of Florence, bitterly hostile to the Visconti, sent him an urgent invitation to visit Italy and backed it with pecuniary offers that seemed astonishingly liberal. Rupert's confidence had no bounds. But when he was at the point of departure, the sky clouded. A loan promised him by certain German merchants was not forthcoming, since the financiers on whom they were relying considered the risks too great. Florence, it transpired, did not want to hand over any money until Rupert and his men were in Italy. In the circumstances, it was sheer folly to start : but a large and fine army had assembled, and for very shame Rupert would not abandon his project. Nevertheless, though he scraped money together by every permissible device, he had perforce to dismiss about a third of his men.

In September 1401, Rupert set out, and reached Trent without mishap. There he wasted time awaiting money from Florence. When a small instalment arrived, it was instantly swallowed up. Meanwhile, Gian Galeazzo had collected strong forces which were guarding the exits from the mountains. The Germans, however, managed to reach Brescia late in October, and prepared to besiege it. Their operations were misconducted, but their prospects were not so gloomy as to excuse the despair which now seized a great part of the army. The Archbishop of Cologne and Leopold of Habsburg insisted on going home, and Rupert deemed it necessary to withdraw to Trent.

Most of the troops were now discharged, but Rupert, with a handful of men, managed to make his way to Padua. Though Florence was not disposed to supply him with further funds, Venice was friendly and he went thither in December. Having resumed negotiations with the Pope, he characteristically persuaded himself that Boniface was about to make a pronouncement in his favour. But sheer poverty, which the Venetians showed no inclination to remedy, forced him in January to leave for home. This move perturbed the Florentines, who sent after him and, having promised more money, induced him to go back to Venice. Rupert was now accompanied by no more than a modest suite, yet he fatuously expected that the Pope would shortly crown him Emperor.

Boniface of course perceived Rupert's helplessness, and raised his terms until they almost amounted to a downright refusal. At last, even Rupert saw that the game was up; but before he could go home he had to pawn all the valuables he had within reach, including his crown. In April 1402, he managed to recross the Alps, thus bringing to a tardy close one of the most ignominious expeditions to Italy ever made by a king of the Romans.

*Rupert "approved" by Boniface IX* — Rupert continued to negotiate with the Pope, and his position was somewhat improved by the death in September 1402 of his arch-enemy Gian Galeazzo. It happened also that Boniface's political embarrassments became very great, so that Rupert felt able to assume a stiffer attitude towards him. In October 1403 he at last received papal approbation. Boniface pretended that the Electors had deposed Wenzel relying on his subsequent confirmation of their action, which he now approved, together with their election of Rupert. This pronouncement, however, did Rupert little good in Germany.

*Sad plight of Germany* — In the years following Rupert's Italian expedition, Germany was in a deplorable state. Little respect was shown for either Rupert or Wenzel. The former remained pitifully hard up. He was driven to pledge much imperial property, and his frequent requests for money made him unpopular, especially in the cities. Many of these, having wasted money or men on the futile Italian enterprise, were not inclined to give anything more, though Rupert really did need large sums to pay legally contracted debts and to conduct the government of the country. Accustomed as they were to ineffectual government, the disorder prevailing at this time, and in particular the growing audacity of the knights, scandalized the majority of the German people.

Meanwhile, the affairs of the Luxemburg family were in utter confusion, or Wenzel would have stood a good chance of having his revenge on Rupert. Intrigue, reconciliation, and betrayal, with Wenzel, Sigismund, and Jost competing for the part of principal villain, followed in bewildering succession. It would be sheer waste of time to trace the ramifications of their domestic amenities. It is enough to mention that in 1402 Sigismund seized and imprisoned Wenzel, and, being in alliance with the Habsburgs, took him to Austria, where he was held in captivity. Sigismund, however, was as usual called away to Hungary, and Jost of Moravia, pretending to be on the side of Wenzel, was able for a time to act as leader of the House of Luxemburg in Germany and western Europe. He entered into relations with several German princes, and, since Rupert was friendly with the Burgundians in France, he came to an understanding with Louis of Orléans, who saw a chance of gaining some imperial territory. But in ordinary civil war Rupert knew how to take care of himself. He fell upon the Margrave of Baden, one of his principal enemies, and since Louis of Orléans was preoccupied with affairs in France, the German allies of Jost deemed it prudent to accept peace on the lenient terms which Rupert offered. Rupert, however, failed to make full use of his advantage or to turn to account the dissensions among the Luxemburgs. In 1403, the Habsburgs, playing Sigismund false, allowed Wenzel to escape. He returned to Bohemia, where he was generally welcomed as the least objectionable ruler available. There ensued further unedifying intrigue involving Wenzel, Sigismund, Jost, and the Habsburgs; but the upshot of all the confusion was that Wenzel was again in fairly secure possession of the Bohemian crown and thus capable of making himself very unpleasant to Rupert when opportunity served.

The sordidness, paltriness, and futility of German politics at this time are well illustrated by Rupert's relations with the Archbishop of Mainz. That prelate thought that his king should have given him effective help in a war which he was waging against Hesse and Brunswick. There were also several frontier disputes between the two men. Consequently in 1405 the Archbishop put himself at the head of what was called the League of Marbach, which included, among other malcontents, the Margrave of Baden, the Count of Würtemberg, and eighteen imperial cities. They pretended that they wished merely to form a *Landfriede* to uphold the welfare of the Empire and their own rights; but Rupert, after denouncing the organization as illegal, foolishly treated their complaints as a personal affront, met the leaders, and bandied arguments with them. Luckily the Archbishop of Cologne managed to mediate successfully, and the league became in reality the *Landfriede* it had professed to be. It

The League of Marbach

had perhaps served the turn of the Archbishop of Mainz, who had organized it to demonstrate his own importance, and it is true that thenceforward Rupert was less insistent in his demands for money and less free with the royal domain. But there had been much ado about very little.

For a while after this episode Rupert seemed more secure than he had ever been. There were even signs of an inclination to acknowledge him in regions where he had so far been ignored. But all his prospects were changed through the turn taken by the affairs of the Church.

*Rupert, Wenzel, and the Council of Pisa*

In 1408 the cardinals of the "Roman" Pope, Gregory XII, abandoned him, and pronounced themselves in favour of the summons of a General Council to end the Schism. When they communicated their views to Rupert, they received no reply. Wenzel, however, declared himself on their side. Rupert took expert advice, which was favourable to Gregory and thus agreeable to his own inclinations. Most Germans, on the other hand, approved of the cardinals, the Archbishops of Mainz and Cologne being especially vehement in their support. At a Diet held at Frankfort in January 1409 both Gregory and the cardinals were represented. There was much argument, but the assembly came to no clear decision. Rupert, however, consented to send envoys to a Council to see whether Gregory deserved to be repudiated. When the Diet was over, the envoy of the cardinals went on to Wenzel and promised that he would be recognized at the Council as true King of the Romans and that the future pope would oppose Rupert with all his power. Wenzel thereupon forbade his subjects to show obedience to Gregory.

Many Germans previously hostile to Wenzel were now disposed to reinstate him. Rupert mishandled the situation. He protested against the proceedings of the rebellious cardinals, and appealed in advance to a true Council and a true Pope. After visiting Gregory XII, his envoys appeared at the Council of Pisa, treated it disrespectfully, refused to submit their criticisms in writing, nailed a verbose protest to a church door, and left the city without saying farewell. The numerous Germans present were deeply chagrined.

*Death of Rupert, May 18, 1410*

In Germany itself Rupert's propaganda was wholly unsuccessful, and Wenzel's party was strong enough to threaten him with ruin. But in May 1410, before civil war actually began, Rupert died. He might be described, like the Emperor Galba and many other estimable men, as *omnium consensu capax imperii nisi imperasset.*

Some authorities for chapter iv :—

The original sources for the history of Germany in the later Middle Ages are much less attractive to the general reader than those for the history of France. Not only are the German chroniclers as a rule of inferior literary merit, but they concern themselves mainly with the affairs of comparatively small areas and treat national concerns incidentally. Research on German history in the period covered by this book consequently involves the investigation of a great many sources, most of which yield little of general interest. A great deal of the information about Germany in this book is based ultimately on the very valuable collection called *Die Chroniken der deutschen Städte von 14 bis ins 16 Jahrhundert* (35 vols., Leipzig, 1862, etc.). These shed a flood of light on the political, economic, and social condition of Germany during our period, but very few of them make pleasant reading like the works of Froissart, Commynes, and several other contemporary writers in France.

There are, however, a few German chronicles of the time which betray a keen interest in national or even European concerns. Such are the *Cosmidromius* of Gobelinus Persona (ed. M. Jansen, Münster, 1900), and the *Chronica novella* of Hermann Korner (ed. J. Schwalm, Göttingen, 1895); while the *Limburger Chronik* (ed. A. Wyss, Monumenta Germaniae historica, Chroniken, vol. iv, pt. 1, 1883) is particularly valuable for the student of social conditions.

Among the official records which have been printed, special mention must be made of the volumes of *Deutsche Reichstagsakten*—the proceedings of Imperial Diets (16 vols., ed. J. Weizsäcker and others, Munich, 1867, etc.).

Works by modern writers dealing with Germany as a whole during the reigns of Wenzel and Rupert are not numerous. Reference may be made to Th. Lindner's *Deutschland unter den Habsburgern und Luxemburgern* (in Bibliothek deutscher Geschichte, ed. H. von Zwiedineck-Südenhorst), 2 vols., Stuttgart, 1890–8 ; to the same writer's *Geschichte des deutschen Reiches unter König Wenzel,* 2 vols., Brunswick, 1875–80 ; to C. Hoefler's *Ruprecht von der Pfalz,* Freiburg, 1861 ; and to A. Hauck's *Kirchengeschichte Deutschlands,* vol. v, pt. 2, Leipzig, 1920.

## CHAPTER V

## THE GREAT SCHISM, 1378-1413

The condition of the Church

IN its earlier pages the previous volume of this series displays the medieval Church triumphant over its principal enemies, with the Papacy at the height of its power and repute, the Mendicant Orders at the peak of their zeal and influence, and the greatest of the schoolmen inspiring and directing the thought of Europe. Later, it has to trace a falling away: to show the Papacy, newly rid of an old foe, succumbing to the insolence of a new one, and going into captivity far away from the home to which, in the minds of nearly all Christians, it had been inseparably attached; to exhibit the religious orders, even the friars, yielding to sloth, luxury, and vice, and losing all hold on the regard of the devout; to describe the collapse of orthodox thought after Duns Scotus had discredited the alliance between faith and rationalism which had made the thirteenth century so prolific in intellectual achievement. The decline (which indeed was manifest throughout the Church) had gone far by the date at which this volume starts. Yet it will only be in the succeeding volume that the impending catastrophe will be described. If in the fifteenth century the Church grew no better, she did not grow much worse. It was not any new corruption or abuse that occasioned the revolt of the sixteenth century; it was a conviction that only by revolt could any improvement be effected. It took a long time for that belief to establish itself in the mind of Europe. For many years those most concerned about the abuses in the Church assumed that she could reform herself. It was this confidence that rendered possible the so-called Conciliar Movement.

Relations of Church and State

In surveying the history of the Church in the closing years of the Middle Ages, one must constantly bear in mind that the claim of the Papacy to dominate all things, temporal as well as ecclesiastical, had been defeated. True, the texts and pronouncements on which that claim was based remained part of the Canon Law. But in practice both ecclesiastical and secular authorities took it for granted that human affairs fell into two divisions, the spiritual and the temporal, the former being under the jurisdiction of the Church, the latter under that of the State. In normal circumstances each party refrained, often ostentatiously, from trespassing on the territory of the other. There was always, however, some dispute as to the whereabouts of the frontier between the two spheres. In most countries a working compromise was arranged on many of the points in dispute, but often there remained a debatable land which was the field of constant bickering. When it was strong enough the secular power would enforce its claims on the disputed territory, and enact legislation to deter and punish trespassers. But it must be clearly understood that in the period with which this volume is concerned no secular authority of catholic Christendom sought to interfere with things which were by general consent deemed spiritual. If kings and princes passed laws denying the claims or curtailing the privileges of the Pope or the clergy, it was on the ground that such claims or privileges encroached on the sphere of the State, which must repel the intruder and reassert its lawful authority. Thus we may find secular governments taking drastic measures in restraint of ecclesiastical pretensions and at the same time persecuting with savage zeal those who challenge the spiritual claims of pope or priest or who deviate by a hair's-breadth from the strait path of doctrinal orthodoxy. Similarly the public opinion of a country might be bitterly anti-clerical, while yet the preaching of heresy there excited violent resentment. In the latter part of the fourteenth century there were millions of people in Europe who told bawdy stories about their parish priest, denounced his rapacity, and would gladly have seen him deprived of his temporal property; but very few questioned his power "to make God's body," and the persecution of those who did roused no popular protest.

The encroachments resisted by secular governments were nearly all made by, or at the instance of, the Papacy. And in general it was the clergy who suffered most from them. The electoral rights of chapters, the claims of clerical patrons, were set aside more ruthlessly than those of laymen; and when kings forbade the dispatch of money to Rome or

*The Papacy and the clergy*

Avignon, it was mainly the possessions of the clergy that were affected. But though ecclesiastics were sometimes moved by anger to disobey a papal demand, it was seldom that any denied the Pope's authority to make it. Secretly they might rejoice when the secular power stepped in to restore their ancient prerogatives or preserve their property from taxation; but they very seldom ventured open assent to anti-papal measures, and frequently thought it discreet to make formal protest against them. Excommunication, and perhaps the stake, awaited those who advocated or countenanced disobedience to the Canon Law. Unless this is borne in mind, the significance of the Conciliar Movement cannot be fully grasped.

*Grounds of the demand for reform*

The ecclesiastical abuses of which earnest men were complaining in 1378 fall into two groups. There were some which were officially recognized as evils—clerical incontinence, the venality of ecclesiastical officials and courts, simony, non-residence, the holding of benefices in plurality, disregard of monastic rules, and numerous other irregularities about which one may read in the works of the satirists of those days. Against such there was already plenty of legislation, which as a rule would have been sufficient if it had been enforced. The difficulty was to find prelates who could or would enforce it. Men like Chaucer's Poor Priest were generally poor priests.

In the second place, however, there were evils which sprang from the dominant theory of papal authority. As the Papacy gradually lost the influence which in the days of Innocent III it had exercised over kings and emperors, it indemnified itself by increasing its control over the clergy. The Avignonese Popes made the government of the Church to all intents and purposes an absolute monarchy. According to them, all ecclesiastical authority was derived from the Pope; no member of the clergy had any rights as against him; he might give and take away at his will; he might legislate as and when it pleased him; if he sought the advice of his cardinals or of councils—general or local—it would be a gracious, nay perhaps a wise, act, but if he chose to dispense with all consultation of his inferiors, no one had any ground of complaint. No doubt such a theory was implicit in the utterances of Hildebrand, but it was not until the Babylonish

Captivity that it was thoroughly put into practice. And in applying it the Popes of Avignon were urged by the most practical motives. Short of money, they needed new financial resources. So they used to the full their control over all ecclesiastical appointments. The Pope might " provide " his nominee to any position in the Church, regardless of the rights of chapters or patrons; he might " reserve " for his nomination any office, dignity, or benefice whatsoever. It might be and was argued that the Pope was more likely to choose wisely than the persons whose rights he infringed. But in point of fact the Popes used their patronage in order to make money. If you wanted a provision or a reservation, you had to pay for it. And the obtaining of even a straightforward provision was no simple matter. Many formalities had to be fulfilled, and at every stage there was a fee to be paid. As for reservations of benefices not yet vacant, they were hardly less expensive and far more precarious. For after you had at great cost obtained your bull, someone else might offer a higher price and secure a reservation of the same benefice by a bull dated earlier than yours. Sometimes, in fact, the expectation of a benefice was thus sold five or six times over. And there was no redress, unless you were willing to invoke the secular authority, a course which was commonly regarded as treachery towards your own order.

Even if all went well and you entered into enjoyment of your hard-earned position, there were still dues to be rendered. Of these the most notable were the taxes known as first-fruits or annates. Everyone who received a benefice from the Pope must pay the equivalent of one year's revenue. The assessment of the amount was usually moderate, and it was payable in instalments; but it was a heavy burden. What made it the more galling was its novelty, for it had not been levied before the time of Clement V. The tax, however, had become one of the principal supports of the Papacy, and could not have been abandoned without a drastic modification of existing methods of Church government.

The Popes of course had other important sources of revenue. They made a great deal by dispensations to break the law. The most common were dispensations to marry within the prohibited degrees, to hold benefices in plurality, and to absent oneself from the benefice or benefices one held. The Papacy also had recourse to direct taxation of the clergy. Secular rulers in the Middle Ages usually obtained at least a show of consent from some body more or less representative of their subjects when they raised taxes; but in the fourteenth century the clergy were not consulted when the Pope wanted to collect a "tenth," and to make things more galling, the sum raised was often discreetly shared between the Pope and the temporal rulers of the districts where it was collected. The administration of justice was likewise very lucrative to the Papacy. Not only did the Popes encourage appeals from lower ecclesiastical courts, but they were willing to entertain suits on matters commonly deemed "temporal," and (what was still more important) the papal court might act as a court of first instance in any spiritual cause, and by the appointment of commissioners be brought, so to say, to one's doorstep. *Justitia magnum emolumentum:* so the Middle Ages believed it should be; and metropolitans, bishops, and archdeacons bewailed their lot as they saw fines and fees being diverted from themselves and their servants to the Pope and the staff of his *curia*.

The exactions of the Papacy caused widespread discontent. Those who had to pay naturally objected. Secular governments did not like to see the wealth of their subjects being sent to foreign parts, especially since the Papacy had come to be regarded as an institution rather French than catholic. And, apart from financial considerations, patrons did not wish to lose the influence which their rights had given them, nor were the ordinaries pleased to see their courts of justice set at naught. But, unless some temporal authority stepped in on the ground that the Papacy was encroaching on the temporal sphere, there seemed little chance of checking the usurpations of the Holy See, still less of undoing what it had done. The clergy could only restrain its power by adopting theories of Church government which for centuries had been advocated by none save heretics. Only a very desperate crisis could move any considerable number to go as far as that.

Such a crisis occurred at the very beginning of the period covered by this volume. It is commonly known as the Great Schism of the West.

In 1877 Pope Gregory XI went to Rome.  Early in 1378 he died.  There were in Rome sixteen cardinals, eleven of whom were French.  All the French probably wanted to go back to Avignon, and had they been united they would doubtless have chosen one of their fellow-countrymen, who would have gratified their wishes.  Their personal jealousies, however, made it impossible for them to agree upon a candidate.  The people of Rome were determined that the election should be made immediately and in the city; and the civic authorities took measures, ostensibly to protect the cardinals against lawless violence, which deprived them of all excuse for delay.  They accordingly entered the conclave on April 7, while a mob raged outside shouting, " A Roman, a Roman, we want a Roman, or at least an Italian."  Next morning the tumult increased, and eventually the mob invaded the rooms where the conclave was held.  Before this happened, however, the cardinals had deliberately rejected a proposal to choose a Roman cardinal and had elected Bartholomew Prignano, Archbishop of Bari, who took the name of Urban VI. *[margin: Election of Urban VI, April 8, 1378]*

The new Pope, though an Italian, had risen through French patronage.  He was expected to go back to Avignon.  At the same time, he was known to be on good terms with the civic authorities of Rome; and indeed, while the Romans were at first very angry at the choice that had been made, they soon reflected that they had been lucky to escape a Frenchman, and accepted Urban with a good grace.  The electors informed the cardinals still at Avignon of what had been done, stating quite superfluously that their votes had been given " freely and unanimously."

It was not long before Urban began to astonish and disgust them.  He showed no intention of returning to Avignon.  Instead of meekly deferring to the opinion of the Sacred College, as he had been expected to do, he displayed an independent and overbearing temper.  He treated the cardinals with contumely, reduced their revenues, and threatened to reform their luxurious mode of living.  At first they sought to placate him; but in the early summer the French cardinals, having (with the Pope's permission) gone to Anagni, declared that his election was invalid because they had been influenced by fear of the mob.  On August 9 they set forth *[margin: Rebellion among the cardinals, and election of Clement VII, Sept. 20, 1378]* this opinion in an encyclical, in which they called upon Urban to lay down his authority and all Christians to reject him. At Fondi, whither they soon moved, they were joined by their Italian colleagues, who wished to refer the whole problem to a General Council. But the plan did not commend itself to the majority, and on September 20 thirteen cardinals elected as Pope Robert of Geneva, who was himself a member of the Sacred College. The three Italian cardinals abstained from voting.

Thus began the Great Schism. The Church has never made a pronouncement as to the validity of either election, and historians still wrangle about them. It may be observed, however, that all the forms seem to have been correctly observed in the case of Urban, that he had been favourably considered by several cardinals before the conclave, that his election was at first believed by the cardinals to be extremely unpopular with the Roman people, that they went out of their way to declare that they had voted freely, that for several weeks they treated him with all outward respect and obsequiously sought favours from him, and that after leaving Rome the rebels hesitated for some time before denouncing his election. Urban was a foolish man, he made a bad pope, his behaviour towards the cardinals may well have been intolerable. But all that does not invalidate his election: and one may fairly wonder whether it would ever have been questioned had he acted as expected. On the other hand, it is unpleasant to think that a number of exalted ecclesiastics had so completely lost their self-respect as to accuse themselves falsely of cowardice.

Europe divided

Whichever side was right, the various countries of Europe made their choice on political rather than legal grounds. England, Germany (or nearly all of it), the northern countries generally, Bohemia, and Hungary, remained faithful to Urban. Italy was divided, Urban having at first a slight advantage. France, with the exception of Gascony and Flanders, eagerly embraced the cause of Clement VII, as Robert of Geneva called himself, and used all her influence to induce other states to do likewise. Scotland followed France and opposed England without misgiving. In the Iberian Peninsula there was more hesitation. Navarre, indeed, became Clementist almost at once. It was not, however, until 1381 that Castile officially ranged herself on the same side, while Aragon waited until 1387 before taking a decisive step. Portugal wavered to and fro for some years, according to the exigencies of her foreign policy; but after 1385, under the influence of England, she was definitely Urbanist.

The history of the first dozen years of the Schism is dull and unedifying. At first each side tried to win adherents by argument. It soon became evident, however, that the issue was not to be settled thus. For a year or two there was much talk of summoning a General Council, which should decide as between the rival Popes. Some of the cardinals, as we have seen, were in favour of this project. Charles V of France was said to have commended it on his deathbed. Distinguished publicists wrote treatises in support of it. In 1381 the University of Paris, which had committed itself to the Clementist cause with great reluctance, pronounced in favour of the plan, and Peter d'Ailly, one of its most famous doctors, tried to induce the French Government to reopen the question. But the Duke of Anjou, whose influence was then paramount, had strong personal reasons for desiring the complete victory of Clement; and the University was silenced. For several years little was heard of the scheme. *Futile advocacy of a General Council*

From the beginning each of the rivals and most of their supporters trusted mainly to force. Such spiritual weapons as excommunication and interdict, though freely employed, proved wholly ineffectual. For a time Clement hoped to capture Rome. But Urban hired the famous Italian mercenaries known as the Company of St. George, whose captain Alberigo da Barbiano gained military successes which constrained Clement to betake himself to Avignon in 1379. Thenceforward Urban, though often hard pressed, was never in serious danger of complete overthrow. As for Clement, he had little to fear from violence as long as France stood by him. *Clement VII at Avignon, 1379*

Clement hoped that the French would not only protect him but would oust his opponent from Italy. Louis of Anjou had shown particular enthusiasm for his cause, and in the hope of turning this to practical account Clement in 1379 bestowed on him, under the title of the Kingdom of *War in the Kingdom of Naples*

Adria, nearly all the Papal States, on condition that Louis should attempt to conquer his kingdom within two years. In 1380, thanks largely to Clement's mediation, Queen Joanna I of Naples adopted Louis as her heir, stipulating that he should defend her against Charles of Durazzo, the rival claimant to her throne, who was favoured by Pope Urban. Next year Charles invaded Naples, defeated and captured the Queen and her consort Otto of Brunswick and conquered the greater part of the kingdom. Urged to act by the French Council of Regency, Louis somewhat reluctantly invaded Italy in the summer of 1382. He met with no serious opposition until he reached Neapolitan territory. By then the Queen was dead, murdered, there is little doubt, at the instance of Charles; but many Neapolitan nobles joined Louis' army and acknowledged his claim to the crown. Charles of Durazzo, however, adopted Fabian tactics with success; disease and hunger played havoc with Louis' fine army; and though he won two or three small fights, marched far and wide through the country, and secured a firm hold on Apulia, he was unable in two years' campaigning to gain a decisive victory. He died in 1384; and notwithstanding the recognition of his son as king by many Neapolitans, his army dispersed, and for some years France had little influence on events in Naples. The Angevin cause, it is true, was kept alive by various leaders. But it was not until 1390 that Louis II of Anjou landed in the kingdom; by that time Urban had been succeeded by Boniface IX, and even if the Angevins had permanently conquered Naples, there is no reason to suppose that the cause of Boniface would have collapsed throughout Italy, still less in other countries. Louis II, indeed, was for a year or two remarkably successful, but as his strength spent itself, the tables were gradually turned by Ladislas, the young heir of Charles of Durazzo; and for many years the Angevin claim to Naples ceased to be of practical importance.

*Clement VII disappointed of French military aid* In his later years, indeed, Pope Clement trusted less in Louis of Anjou than in Louis Duke of Touraine, the French king's brother. Married in 1387 to Valentina Visconti, daughter of Gian Galeazzo, Lord of Milan, he had received the territory of Asti from Clement, and so had a double interest in northern Italy. The Pope sought to bring about his intervention against Urban by promising him a principality carved out of the States of the Church. Urged by both the Pope and his brother, Charles VI resolved to strike a decisive blow for the Clementist cause; but in 1391, as we saw above, his plans were completely frustrated. After Charles VI went mad, Clement tried to maintain the enthusiasm of Louis, who was now Duke of Orléans, by reviving in his favour the " kingdom of Adria," formerly used as a bait for Louis I of Anjou; but the terms on which this was offered were not acceptable to the Duke or the French Government. Before any agreement had been reached Clement died.

Urban VI had no compunction in using force against his rival, but he seems to have recognized from the outset that he had no chance of overthrowing him by purely military means. There was no reason why he should attempt to drive him out of Avignon, a place with no sanctity attaching to it; but it was vital that he himself should retain his hold on Rome. His diplomacy and warlike enterprises were thus mainly defensive in character. On the one hand, he strove to prevent the extension of his rival's influence in Italy, on the other to keep hostile states like France or Castile occupied in regions remote from Rome. Urban, however, was a most impolitic politician. The tactlessness and arrogance which had originally alienated the cardinals increased, and grew into insolence and brutality. So far from conciliating his foes, he wantonly alienated not a few of his friends.

*Policy of Urban VI*

The chief source of anxiety to Urban was Naples. Though it was at his instance that Charles of Durazzo attempted to make good his claim to the throne, he was made to pay heavily for the support of the Pope, who insisted that Charles should bestow rich territories on a disreputable nephew of his. When, after his initial successes, Charles delayed to fulfil this part of the bargain, Urban went to Naples in person with the intention of controlling his doings. Charles, resenting this, had the Pope put under arrest; and though an agreement was patched up, a secret enmity persisted between them. In 1384 Urban, with a large part of his court, fled from the capital and took refuge in Nocera. Thence he claimed the right, as Charles's overlord, to regulate the affairs of the Neapolitan kingdom, while Charles told the Pope to mind his own business. Some of Urban's cardinals,

*Urban VI and Charles of Durazzo*

disgusted with the position in which they found themselves, seem to have thought of subjecting the headstrong pope to the control of a council chosen by the Sacred College. Treachery revealed to Urban their inchoate plans; he had six cardinals arrested, imprisoned in a noisome dungeon, and tortured within his hearing. There was now open and ferocious war between Urban and Charles. For several months of 1385 Urban was besieged in the castle of Nocera. Neapolitan nobles hostile to Charles eventually rescued him; and after various vicissitudes he reached the Adriatic and was taken to Genoa by a squadron of galleys which had been sent to his aid. It was characteristic that he carried his captive cardinals with him.

*Urban's singular conduct*

Urban's violence, cruelty, and nepotism were in no wise diminished by the dangers and hardships into which they had already brought him. The rest of his life he devoted to schemes for increasing his temporal power in Italy. The maintenance or extension of his authority over the Church seems to have interested him but slightly. After over a year's sojourn in Genoa, he was politely asked to leave, the civic authorities finding his presence embarrassing. As it would have been troublesome to take with him the imprisoned cardinals, all of them save one—an Englishman for whom Richard II interceded—were killed before his departure. He spent nine months at Lucca, nearly a year at Perugia, plotting and intriguing all the time, and in the autumn of 1388 returned to Rome, his cause weaker and his reputation far lower than when he had left it five years before.

*Urban's crusades*

Charles of Durazzo's military operations against Louis of Anjou were not the only warlike enterprises declared by Urban to be a crusade. In 1382 he authorized Henry Despenser, Bishop of Norwich, to organize a crusade against the schismatics—in other words, the French. The fate of that grotesque undertaking has already been described. Strange to say, Urban's confidence in the English was not destroyed; for the expedition which John of Gaunt led to Castile in 1386 was also accounted a crusade. It was less scandalous than Bishop Despenser's, for its adversaries really were supporters of Clement VII, and its achievements were more creditable. But Gaunt soon recognized that he was not strong enough to expel John I of Castile from his throne.

He was bought off by a marriage alliance and an indemnity and withdrew to England in 1389. His expedition had confirmed Portugal in its adherence to Urban, but had not done any serious harm to the Clementist cause in Spain.

When Urban VI died, his cardinals chose as his successor Cardinal Piero Tomacelli, another Neapolitan, who took the title of Boniface IX. The new Pope owed his election to his reputation for amiability. He was no scholar, and had hitherto shown no interest in administration. To contemporaries his most astonishing characteristic was his chastity. He began his rule by trying to conciliate some of the supporters of the Roman Papacy whom Urban had treated as enemies. Thus he recognized the young Ladislas, son of Charles of Durazzo, as King of Naples, and sent help to the queen-mother in her resistance to the Angevin party. He reconciled Florence to the Holy See, gained some ground in the States of the Church, and by bestowing the title of Papal Vicar on usurpers of cities whom he could not oust, he at once won them to his side and affirmed his lordship over their stolen possessions. But Boniface was soon convinced of the need of increasing the papal revenues. Thanks to Urban's reckless policy, the Papacy had incurred unusually heavy expenses just when it was cut off from half its ordinary sources of revenue. Boniface was lucky in that Urban had proclaimed 1390 as a year of Jubilee, and the papal treasury rejoiced as the money of the pilgrims to Rome poured into it. So pleased was the Pope that he presently offered the Jubilee indulgence to those who, unable or unwilling to go to Rome, visited certain churches in Germany. It was the first sign of that unscrupulous and insatiable rapacity which characterized Boniface for the rest of his life.

Boniface IX, 1389-1404: his policy and ambitions

The success of the Jubilee seems to have made Boniface over-confident. He demanded from England the repeal of her anti-papal legislation and the abolition of certain legal processes which could be used to frustrate papal claims, and when dissatisfied with the response, he took coercive measures. The English parliament promptly told him that he was trespassing on the King's preserves; and the so-called Statute of Praemunire prescribed severe penalties for those who tried to give effect to the Pope's intentions. Simultaneously, the English Government was moving towards an *entente* with France. Boniface drew back, and thereafter used more discreet methods when dealing with his principal supporters. But English loyalty to him had been gravely impaired.

*Venality of the Roman curia*

Nevertheless, Boniface must have money, and the powers which in England he could only exercise with the connivance or licence of the King, he used without restraint elsewhere. Provisions and reservations, however, were a comparatively decent means of raising funds. The price charged for them had hitherto been collected under the guise of fees and taxes. But now there was an open market of benefices at the Roman court, and shameless use was made of the practice of selling the reservation of a benefice over and over again. Even more scandal was caused by the traffic in dispensations, which swelled far beyond its previous extent. There was scarcely a rule of Canon Law which might not be broken with impunity for a price. Boniface undoubtedly amassed vast sums; but he made the papal court stink in the nostrils of all good men and deeply injured the already falling prestige of the Papacy itself.

*Boniface IX and the city of Rome*

During the first years of his pontificate the chief source of anxiety for Boniface was not Pope Clement, the Angevins in Naples, or recalcitrant members of his own party, but the populace of the city of Rome. The republican party there was more powerful than usual, and twice in these years got the upper hand of Boniface. On the first occasion the Pope brought the Roman people to heel by residing for a year in Perugia. The absence of the Pope was ruinous to Rome, and the citizens eagerly welcomed him on his return in 1393, only to rise against him in the next year, when he was rescued by Ladislas of Naples. This insecurity of the Roman Pope in his own city had a strong influence on the course of the Schism. It was not long, however, before a still worse danger confronted Boniface. France fell out with his rival, and he paradoxically found himself in grave jeopardy.

*France concerned at the prolongation of the Schism*

Though France never showed any inclination to change sides, discontent with the extortionate policy of Clement spread widely among both clergy and laity. As years went on, too, the continuance of the Schism caused increasing concern. What if it should prove permanent, like the schism between the Latins and the Greeks?

This fear was particularly potent in the University of

Paris. After Charles VI had overset the rule of his uncles, it was not long before the University began to urge on him the necessity of taking action to end the Schism, even at the expense of his loyalty to Pope Clement. At first Charles merely ordered the University to keep silent: but many of its members refused to obey; both popes deemed it expedient to declare their zeal for the restoration of union; and at the beginning of 1894 the French Government announced that if the University could find any means of ending the Schism, it should be adopted. The problem was indeed difficult. According to the existing constitution of the Church, the Pope was an absolute monarch. It was asserted in the Canon Law and recognized by all save a few heretics that it was everyone's duty to obey him. That he could not err was not indeed an article of faith, but whoever denied it was likely to find himself in grave peril. Who then was to sit in judgment on a pope, and pronounce as to his right to the title?

The Church, however, was going to rack and ruin. Neither claimant to the Holy See had made any attempt to end the Schism save by the use of force, which had proved futile. Some peaceful means of restoring union must be sought, and at such a crisis, no matter what Canon Law might say, divine and natural law alike justified the coercion of a recalcitrant pope in the interests of the Church for whose good he was supposed to exist. The submission of the dispute to a General Council was again being advocated with much cogency. The most strenuous upholders of the *plenitudo potestatis* of the Pope admitted that if he were charged with heresy, it was for a General Council to make inquiry and pass judgment. Obstinate persistence in schism, it was now contended, amounted to heresy. Further, a Council dealing with schism must naturally take into account the causes which had produced it; hence a Council might introduce reforms affecting the Papacy with the object of preventing a recurrence of the calamity. Such views found favour with many who had no wish to restrict papal authority in normal circumstances and who held that ordinarily a pope was superior to a General Council. At the University of Paris the arguments outlined above were maintained by numerous doctors, among whom John Gerson, Peter d'Ailly, and John

Petit, destined to play important parts in the following years, were already renowned. It was manifest, however, that there were great obstacles to the assembling of a General Council. Properly, it should be summoned by a pope; but if either pope should refuse, what then? Some held that, failing the Pope, the cardinals might convoke a Council; but unless the cardinals of both popes agreed to co-operate, there was no chance of a general response. Others said that a Council might lawfully be summoned by an emperor: but would the supporters of Clement pay any attention to a summons from an emperor who recognized Boniface? It had been asserted by William of Ockham that if need arose a General Council might assemble without being summoned by anyone, but there was obviously little chance of such a thing happening. In face of these difficulties, other plans were sympathetically considered. What was called "the way of compromise" was supported by some. By "compromise" was meant what we should rather term "arbitration": each pope should appoint an equal number of representatives who should meet, argue, and come to an amicable agreement. Critics reasonably objected that it was highly improbable that such a procedure would lead to any agreement whatever. There was, thirdly, what was styled "the way of cession," or abdication. Each pope should graciously resign, and the two colleges of cardinals should unite and elect a pope whose legitimacy no one could challenge. Should either pope refuse to abdicate, the faithful might lawfully withdraw their obedience from him. This scheme found more and more adherents. At the beginning of 1894 the University of Paris officially approved the "via cessionis." The Duke of Burgundy supported the University —a fact of great moment; but the Pope's representative in Paris prevailed with the court; and the doctors were ordered to cease their agitation. The University declared a strike; but before anything more could be done on either side, Clement VII succumbed to a stroke of apoplexy.

Charles VI immediately wrote to the cardinals at Avignon calling on them to make no election until they had heard an embassy which he was about to send. But when the letter reached Avignon the cardinals were on the point of entering the conclave, and they discreetly decided not to read it until they had completed their business. Two days later, on September 28, 1894, they elected Peter de Luna, an Aragonese cardinal, who called himself Benedict XIII. Before voting eighteen of the twenty-one cardinals present had sworn, if elected pope, to resign on being required to do so by a majority of the Sacred College. Peter de Luna, it is said, declared that he would abdicate as easily as he would take off his hat. When he announced his election to Charles VI, he wrote that he had accepted the Papacy simply that he might use his position in order to end the Schism.

Benedict was a man of austere private life. He already had a reputation as a diplomatist; but his gifts for dissimulation and intrigue were soon proved to be even greater than men had supposed. For when in 1895 a most imposing embassy, containing three royal dukes, came to Avignon from Paris to urge him to abdicate, he soon showed that he had no intention of complying. His views, he said, were not quite what they had been when he was elected. Though nearly all his cardinals concurred with the French, he refused to give way, and the ambassadors had to go home baffled. They were angry, as well they might be. It must be recognized, however, that, while inviting Benedict to resign, they had offered no guarantee that Boniface would do so. {Benedict's refusal to abdicate}

In urging Benedict to abdicate the embassy had been giving effect to the recommendation of a council of the clergy of France which had solemnly approved the " way of cession." The Pope's attitude caused widespread disappointment and indignation. It was recognized, however, that before taking drastic action against Benedict, it would be well to secure the concurrence of other countries, including those of the Roman obedience. The government and the University of Paris both sent missions far and wide. In England and Germany little or no impression was made; Scotland showed no disposition to abandon Benedict, and in the Spanish kingdoms many felt that France was behaving with unwarrantable arrogance towards a Spanish pope. In France itself the propaganda of the University had more effect, and with its denunciations of Benedict it began to mingle demands for the reform of the Papacy. Meanwhile neither pope showed any intention of resigning. Both professed a desire to end the Schism, and ambassadors passed between them. But to each the end of {French propaganda for the " way of cession "} the Schism still meant the discomfiture of his rival, whether by argument or by force.

*Withdrawal of obedience to Benedict considered by France*

In the summer of 1396 there was held another council of the clergy of France. The immediate withdrawal of obedience from Benedict was powerfully advocated. But the assembly was under the control of the Duke of Orléans, who took care that the critics of the proposal had rather more than a fair chance in the discussions. It was decided to postpone action until Benedict had again been called upon to accept the " way of cession." There seemed some hope of shaking his obstinacy, for Castile had fallen into line with France, and Richard II of England promised to use his influence to secure the abdication of Boniface.

*Both popes obdurate*

Such optimism was vain. In 1397 a joint embassy from France, Castile, and England visited Benedict. They tried persuasion and threats, but all to no purpose. Benedict used every subterfuge in his repertory to gain time, and the ambassadors had to go away without a definite answer. They went on to Rome, but the English dealt very gently with Boniface IX, who was naturally not much moved by the pleas of the French and Castilians. Boniface's attitude was so much like Benedict's that the ambassadors had some ground for their suspicion that the two were in collusion.

*Ill-success of French diplomacy*

The French government, though indefatigable, had little to encourage it. It was believed that Scotland and Navarre had been won over to France's policy; but Aragon remained inflexible, and further efforts to secure the co-operation of Wenzel bore little fruit. Much was hoped from the interview between him and Charles VI which took place at Rheims early in 1398; but the effect of the conference on Wenzel's ecclesiastical policy was simply to make him more friendly towards the Clementists in imperial territory and to cause him to send to Avignon Peter d'Ailly, now Bishop of Cambrai, who respectfully suggested that in the interests of union Benedict might resign. On Boniface Wenzel apparently did not even attempt to make any impression. Simultaneously Richard II's zeal for union seems to have cooled. To estimate aright the step which France was about to take, it is essential to remember that she could expect little support elsewhere.

The French government had become more hostile to Benedict, who was increasingly provocative. So confident did he grow that in the spring of 1398 he refused to renew his permission of the levy of *aides* from the clergy by the French Crown, which had enjoyed this favour for some thirty years. In May a council of the Church in France met in Paris.

Rather more than two hundred ecclesiastics were present— archbishops, bishops, abbots, two representatives from each chapter and each university. The government kept a firm hold on the proceedings, and the clergy were plainly told that the King might have taken action without consulting them. No discussion of the " way of cession " was allowed ; the only question was whether the French should now withdraw their obedience from Benedict. There was no lack of keen debate. The opposition urged the practical inconveniences which would follow the adoption of the policy suggested, but insisted particularly on the fact that it would amount to rebellion against Christ's vicar. The other side asserted that it was the duty of Christians to renounce a pope who fell into heresy, fostered schism, or otherwise imperilled the Church. These conditions, they added, were fulfilled in the present case. It was objected that this could only be decided by a General Council, to which it was answered that the present council was virtually oecumenical in character and that in any event the King of France was competent to pronounce judgment on the matter. It is important to remember that the opponents of the official policy argued very powerfully, and that its defenders were driven into making some very dubious statements. At length the vote was taken. Each member of the council appeared alone before the royal dukes and one or two officials, stated his opinion, and recorded it—with a brief justification if he liked—on his voting paper. After an interval of several weeks, during which the Dukes of Berry and Burgundy wrangled with the Duke of Orléans, Charles VI, who had just emerged from a fit of lunacy, was told that the council had been decisively in favour of withdrawing obedience from Benedict, and immediately accepted what had been done. The result of the voting was then publicly announced. Two hundred and forty-seven votes, it was stated, had been cast in favour of immediate withdrawal of obedience, only fifty or thereabouts being adverse. This statement passed unchallenged for centuries ; but the voting papers are still

*Withdrawal of French obedience from Benedict XIII, July 27, 1398*

extant, and an examination of them towards the end of the nineteenth century showed that the figures had been drastically manipulated by the government. Only 123 members of the council had actually voted for immediate action. A large number of members of the University of Paris had been permitted to record votes, though each university was supposed to have only one; votes of the royal princes and of a few officials were also counted; and numerous members of the council who had given only a conditional assent to the proposed policy were reckoned as having expressed their unqualified approval. In reality, more than eighty were opposed to the immediate total withdrawal of obedience; and though this minority proposed various alternatives and was wholly lacking in unity, its existence helps to explain the events of the next few years. At the moment, however, it was ignored, and on July 27, 1898, a royal ordinance announced the withdrawal of the king, clergy, and people of France from Benedict's obedience. No one in France was to acknowledge his authority in any way, and measures were taken to prevent the life and administration of the Church in France from suffering through its sudden severance from its official head.

*Effects of France's action*

The revolt of France from the Papacy was an event of the highest moment. But its immediate consequences were disappointing to those who had advocated it. Nearly all Benedict's cardinals left him. The people of Avignon refused to defend him. When the Pope remained defiant, he was besieged in his palace by a French force under Geoffrey Boucicaut, brother of the famous Marshal of France. Castile, Provence, and several other imperial fiefs joined the rebellion. But Benedict held out in the strongly fortified palace at Avignon, and after two months a truce ended active hostilities. The King of Aragon intervened on behalf of Benedict, and the French government, whose complicity in the doings of Boucicaut is uncertain, discountenanced further violence. Negotiations were opened with Benedict, and early in 1399 he declared his approval of the "way of cession." But, besides deferring on countless pretexts the execution of an agreement which he had ostensibly accepted, he had recourse to a device which was very popular at the time, especially with the clergy: he drew up a formal but secret protestation that his consent to the agreement had been extorted by force and therefore was not binding, and even went so far as to invalidate in advance future concessions which he might be constrained to make. He actually protested that he would not consider himself bound by the precise terms of his protestations, so that not even the notary who drew them up or the witnesses who attested them knew exactly what he considered his obligations to be.

In view of Benedict's sense of honour, there is no need to pursue in detail the negotiations between him and the French in the following years. Benedict's object was to waste as much time as he could. The parties wrangled for long about the guardian who, according to his treaty with the French, was to watch over him. It was not until 1401 that Charles VI's brother, Louis of Orléans, was formally appointed, a choice suggested by the Pope himself.

All this while Benedict, while not subject to personal molestation, remained a virtual prisoner in the palace of Avignon. The majority of the cardinals and the population of the city were still hostile to him. The situation, however, was turning in his favour. The Duke of Orléans made no secret of his sympathy with Benedict. Voices in favour of returning to his obedience were heard in many quarters. The sudden removal of papal direction and control caused some confusion in the French Church, and the clergy occasionally found that freedom from the Pope meant increased subjection to the Crown or a great noble. Still, a very strong party, headed by the Duke of Burgundy, remained opposed to conciliation with Benedict. For a while there were hopes of uniting the nation in support of a proposal to hold a council representative of all the countries which had supported the Pope of Avignon; but this was wrecked on the obstinacy of Benedict, who evidently had no confidence in the judgment which such an assembly would pass upon him. Meanwhile the cause of the Pope of Rome prospered. In Italy his position grew stronger, he could count on the aid of Ladislas of Naples against the republicans in Rome, and he recovered some of the lost regions of the Papal States. Of the secular rulers who belonged to his party only Sigismund, King of Hungary, gave him serious apprehension. Sigismund had schemes in Italy which perturbed the Pope, who tried to keep him at home by supporting Ladislas in his claim to the kingdom of Hungary, and had only himself to thank when Sigismund forbade his subjects to pay any money to the papal treasury and stopped the introduction of papal bulls into the country. The House of Luxemburg, however, could not do the Pope much harm as long as Wenzel's title to the empire was disputed by Rupert of the Palatinate.

*Benedict's cause strongly maintained*

It became evident that the resignation of Benedict would only encourage Boniface. During 1402 the reaction in favour of the former progressed rapidly. The King of Castile was inclined towards reconciliation. The universities of Orléans, Toulouse, and Angers urged submission. The Duke of Orléans did all he could to commend their views to Charles VI. There were even doctors of Paris—Gerson among them— who took up their pens in behalf of Benedict, though it is true that there was still in the university a vast majority vehemently opposed to any change of front.

*Benedict's escape from Avignon, March 1403*

Benedict, who was of course fully alive to all this, resolved on a bold step. On March 11, 1403, he escaped in disguise from Avignon and made his way to Châteaurenard, only a few miles distant, but in the territory of Louis of Anjou. The Avignonese and Benedict's cardinals hastened to crave forgiveness, and were treated with unexpected forbearance. The citizens had to repair the damage done to the papal palace during the siege, but the Pope did not go back to live there, substituting for himself a strong garrison of Spanish soldiers.

*Restitution of French obedience to Benedict, May 28, 1403*

In April Castile resumed its allegiance to Benedict. In May, a council of French clergy, summoned by the government before Benedict's escape, met to consider the adoption of the same policy. It was clear at the outset that the issue would be fiercely contested. It happened that Charles VI was at the moment in exceptionally good health, and Louis of Orléans took advantage of the fact. He ordered the archbishops in the council to ascertain in private the views of the representatives of their respective provinces. Then he assembled a number of metropolitans, most of whom he knew to be on his side, and inquired the result of their investigations. It was as might have been predicted. The Duke forthwith had the King awakened from an afternoon nap, went to see him with an escort of the prelates whom he had just consulted, and showed him a list of clergy who desired the restitution of obedience to the Pope. Charles, evidently bewildered, answered that obedience must be restored, and swore it on the crucifix which his brother handed to him, while notaries made a record of the whole proceeding. When that evening the Dukes of Berry and Burgundy came to protest, the King read them a list of concessions which Benedict was said to have offered to the Duke of Orléans, including promises to abdicate in the event of the death, resignation, or overthrow of his rival, and to hold a council of the countries obedient to him. The two dukes were fain to acquiesce; the assembled clergy, whatever their sentiments, could hardly do otherwise; a royal ordinance immediately gave effect to the new policy, which was received in Paris with popular rejoicings. A day or two later Charles relapsed into lunacy.

It was not long before the French clergy began to realize how they had been tricked. Pressed to honour the promises which the Duke of Orléans had put into his mouth, Benedict would only undertake to resign when such a step would seem to promote union, and to summon a council at some time unspecified. He treated the French clergy as liable for arrears of taxes and dues which would normally have been paid during the past five years. As for the promotion of union, he now seemed to think that something might be achieved by bargaining with his rival, and envoys of his were actually in Rome when, on October 1, 1404, Boniface IX died. *Benedict's intransigence*

Rome was immediately in chaos. Papalists and republicans fought in the streets. Benedict's ambassadors were imprisoned for some days in the castle of St. Angelo by the captain, a kinsman of the dead Pope, and had to borrow from Florence in order to ransom themselves. On their release they begged for a postponement of the election of a successor to Boniface. But, having ascertained that it was useless to ask Benedict to resign at once, the Roman cardinals entered the conclave, each taking a similar oath to that sworn by the Avignonese cardinals before Benedict's election. After some days they chose Cosimo Migliorati, Cardinal of Bologna, the third Neapolitan in succession to occupy the Holy See. *Death of Boniface IX and election of Innocent VII, Oct. 1404*

The new Pope, who took the title of Innocent VII, was an old man, believed to be of a mild and kindly disposition. He proved to be much too weak to cope with the difficult situation in which he was placed. For the greater part of his short pontificate he was engaged in strife with the republicans of Rome. He did indeed get the better of them; but in November 1406, before he could turn his advantage to account, he died.

Innocent VII was never in a position to do much towards ending the Schism. For his evasive replies to Benedict's suggestions for a conference between the two, he can scarcely be blamed, seeing that his opponent was openly preparing a military expedition against him. It may readily be understood that Benedict's warlike preparations, though encouraged by the Duke of Orléans and Louis of Anjou, were generally viewed askance by the French. To pay for them he imposed on the French clergy a tenth, demanding payment from religious orders usually exempt and from members of universities. The new Duke of Burgundy, John the Fearless, soon proved himself quite as hostile to Benedict as his father had been. The University raised its voice again for a fresh repudiation of the Pope's authority. Benedict misjudged the situation, and in the spring of 1406 sent to Paris a cardinal who addressed the royal princes and principal ministers of State in a tone of arrogant remonstrance which caused intense irritation. The University of Paris found a pretext for raising before the *Parlement* the whole issue of Benedict's conduct, the liberties of the Gallican Church, and the best means of ending the Schism, and the judgment which the *Parlement* pronounced on the case ostensibly before it was really a condemnation of Benedict. The University sought to give practical effect to its victory by pleading that the withdrawal of obedience was still in force, since the restitution had been made irregularly and the Pope had not fulfilled its conditions. The *Parlement* declared illegal the collection of all sums due to the Papacy after the date of the decree of 1398 renouncing allegiance to Benedict. Public opinion turned against the Pope. In the autumn of 1406 a council of the French Church was again held in Paris, and listened to the now familiar arguments, John Petit being specially conspicuous for the violence of his language and also, it is fair to say, for the force of his reasoning. Much was heard of the liberties of the Gallican Church, which were of course represented as belonging to it of right, no matter what the state of the Church universal or the conduct of the ruling pope. The defenders of Benedict and the Papacy showed courage and ability, Peter d'Ailly being prominent on this side; but they were handicapped by the character and recent conduct of Benedict himself. Their best point was that the advocates of the withdrawal of obedience did not prove that it would promote the termination of the Schism. They so far prevailed that the council voted merely for what was called " partial withdrawal." In other words, the "liberties of the Gallican Church" were to be restored: the Pope was to make no ecclesiastical appointment in France, and to exact no taxes or dues from subjects of the French Crown.

Meanwhile, Innocent VII had died, and the Roman cardinals had tried to ensure that the promotion of union would not suffer through the appointment of a successor. During the conclave they took a solemn oath that whoever should be elected pope should resign when his rival did so, or died, and that, except in order to put the two Colleges on a numerical equality, he should create no new cardinals for fifteen months, and then only if the negotiations for union had broken down through the fault of the other side. As a further earnest of their sincerity, they elected the Cardinal of St. Mark, Angelo Correr, a Venetian, who was nearly eighty years old and renowned for his sincerity and uprightness. Within a week or two Gregory XII, as he called himself, wrote letters to the princes of Europe urging them to work for union, while he told Benedict that he was ready to arrange for a meeting of the two colleges of cardinals so that a successor to them both might be chosen after their resignation. In Paris the news of Gregory's zeal for union caused wild joy. Benedict's obstinacy seemed to stand in sharp contrast, and his opponents persuaded the government to embody the decision of the recent council in two ordinances dated February 18, 1407. The Duke of Orléans, however, succeeded in securing the postponement of their publication.

Meanwhile Benedict had replied to Gregory's overtures in a conciliatory, indeed cordial, tone. He was willing to meet Gregory and after the interview to resign, provided his rival

*Election of Gregory XII Nov. 30, 1406*

*Negotiations between Gregory and Benedict*

did so also. At Paris, however, some passages in this announcement were considered ambiguous, and a very imposing embassy, which was dispatched to both popes, was instructed to demand from Benedict a categorical written acceptance of the "way of cession," and in the event of his refusal to announce the withdrawal of French obedience. When the envoys reached Marseilles, where Benedict was residing, they found that a mission from Gregory had already concluded with Benedict an elaborate agreement whereby the two popes were shortly to meet at Savona. Consequently, despite Benedict's refusal to issue the bull demanded by the French ambassadors, they decided not to proceed to extremes, and held amicable discussions with him, unaware that he had drawn up a bull which inflicted excommunication and other penalties on all who renounced allegiance to him or appealed against his pronouncements. He held this in reserve, but its existence soon became known in Paris.

*Gregory XII's evasion*

Part of the French embassy appeared before Gregory in Rome. They soon found that the resolution of the old man had begun to waver. There was indeed some justification for his reluctance to ratify the treaty signed on his behalf. He was asked to concede far more than Benedict. Savona was in Benedict's obedience; it was in the territory of Genoa, the inveterate enemy of Venice, Gregory's native state; it was thus subject to the King of France. Ladislas of Naples was known to be hostile to any plan which might have the effect of establishing in the Holy See a pope friendly with the French, and Gregory had good reason to fear that as soon as he moved north Ladislas would attack the Papal States. Probably, too, the old pope's kinsfolk pressed him to abstain from any measure which might jeopardize his position and their prosperity.

Gregory still pretended to approve of Savona as a rendezvous, but alleged the existence of various difficulties which made it impossible for him to go there. The French ambassadors and envoys from Benedict offered the most generous concessions, guarantees, and safeguards; all met with objection. Numerous alternative schemes were advanced, only to be quickly abandoned. So unaccountable were some of Gregory's projects, so unreasonable some of his arguments, that the French ambassadors came to the conclusion that he was merely playing with them to gain time.

When Benedict heard of Gregory's tergiversations, his zeal for the interview was naturally redoubled. He refused Gregory's request for a modification of the treaty, and ostentatiously arrived at Savona five days before the appointed date. In France there was a revulsion of feeling in his favour. *Insincerity of both popes*

When Gregory should have been at Savona, he had got no farther than Siena. He offered Benedict fourteen new plans to choose from. According to the most promising, Benedict should go as far as Porto Venere, at the extreme limit of Genoese territory, while Gregory should advance to Pietrasanta, just within his own obedience; then, with only a few miles between them, they might conduct negotiations. This Benedict accepted, and, taking ship, he arrived at Porto Venere on January 3, 1408. But his rival then asserted that the Lord of Lucca, on whose territory Pietrasanta was situated, had refused to give sufficient guarantees of his safety, an excuse which did not prevent him from going to Lucca itself at the end of the month. Farther than that he would not stir. But while Gregory would not approach the coast, Benedict steadfastly refused to leave it. Contemporaries likened them to an elephant and a whale.

The behaviour of the popes caused general disgust. In France no one any longer believed in Benedict's sincerity. Strange stories circulated about secret and friendly dealings between the two popes, with a view to retaining their authority in their respective spheres. The murder of the Duke of Orléans removed from the royal Council the one influential man who could be trusted to offer a firm resistance to extreme measures.

The University increased its pressure on the government. In January 1408, an ordinance declared that if union was not restored to the Church by Ascension Day (May 24), Charles VI would adopt a policy of neutrality as between the two popes. This decision was not communicated to Benedict till April. At the moment the Pope had high hopes of winning Rome itself, for the Roman people, threatened by Ladislas of Naples, had appealed to him for help, and he was fitting out a naval and military expedition under Boucicaut. Possibly his optimism made him over-bold. At all events, with a letter of reproach which he addressed to Charles VI, he enclosed the *Neutrality of France declared, May 25, 1408* defiant bull, drawn up on May 19, 1407, but hitherto held in reserve. It was delivered to Charles on May 14. That very day the two ordinances, dated February 18, 1407, which restored the "liberties of the Church of France," were published. On May 21, before a great concourse of people, the King, the royal dukes, and a number of officials and prelates listened to a speech from Jean Courtecuisse, one of the most renowned and radical doctors of the University, who demonstrated the wickedness of Benedict and the uprightness of the government, declared that the author of the bull of excommunication and all concerned in its publication or distribution were guilty of *lèse-majesté*, and in the name of the University demanded that it should be destroyed, and that all who supported Benedict within the realm should be imprisoned. Courtecuisse's requests were straightway approved, and the bull was ceremoniously torn in pieces. Four days later the neutrality of Charles VI was proclaimed, all his subjects being forbidden to obey either pope.

**Rebellion among Gregory's cardinals**

Meanwhile Gregory XII had continued to evade acceptance of every proposal designed to promote union. Then there happened the catastrophe which Gregory had feared: Ladislas of Naples occupied Rome. This gave him a dominating position in Italian politics, and he announced that he meant to be present at any interview between the two popes, since he must safeguard his own interests and see to it that the negotiations did not lead to a new schism worse than the first. After this declaration the whole project of a double cession fell to the ground. Gregory abandoned all pretence of intending to abdicate. On May 9, 1408, he created four new cardinals. Two days afterwards, on the ground that he had thus broken the oath taken at his accession, eight cardinals left him and went to Pisa, whither they were soon followed by a ninth and by many officers of the *curia*. It was not long before they received from Charles VI a letter exhorting them to abandon Gregory and unite with the malcontents of the rival College.

At first Gregory's rebellious cardinals were disposed to treat with Benedict. Some of them met four of his cardinals at Leghorn. There the suggestion was thrown out that they should strive to assemble a General Council, regardless of Benedict's wishes. The Avignonese cardinals at first refused to consent to any scheme which might involve defying their Pope, and Benedict, believing in their loyalty, asserted his approval of the summons of a Council and encouraged them to continue their negotiations. But the news of what had happened in France had a powerful effect on their feelings; when Benedict ordered them to rejoin him, they refused. *[The rebels joined by Avignonese cardinals]*

Meanwhile Benedict, rightly expecting that the French would arrest him, was preparing to put himself out of their reach. On June 15, 1408, he set sail, and on the same day summoned a General Council to meet at Perpignan at All Saints'. A fortnight later he landed in Roussillon. *[General Council summoned to Perpignan by Benedict, June 15, 1408]*

The flight of Benedict was promptly followed by the formal union of the malcontents in both colleges of cardinals. On June 29, eight " Urbanist " and six " Clementist " cardinals issued a manifesto in which they declared themselves compelled to abandon their respective masters and announced their adhesion to the " Way of Cession and of General Council," meaning, it seems, that on the resignation of the popes the Council should decide what was to happen next, while, should either pope refuse to resign, the Council might depose him.

Gregory XII, recognizing that the rebels were in earnest, gave up hope of conciliating them, and moved to Siena, having himself, at the beginning of July, summoned a General Council to meet in north Italy. In anticipating the summons of a Council by the cardinals the two popes showed sound tactics. The delay of the rebels was due to the difficulty of inducing the Florentines to permit the Council to be held at Pisa, the place selected as most suitable. It was only on August 23 that their consent was obtained. The cardinals, indeed, pre-dated the letters convoking the assembly, but the device deceived nobody, and caused trouble to its authors later. *[General Council summoned by Gregory XII, July 1408]* *[General Council summoned to Pisa by cardinals, Aug. 1408]*

The great question now was, How would the different states of Europe respond to the threefold invitation? It soon became clear that there would be no unanimity. France, England, the greater part of Germany (headed by King Wenzel), and most of northern Italy supported the rebel cardinals. Castile, Aragon, and Scotland stood by Benedict. Gregory had the support of Naples, the greater part of the Papal States, the possessions of the Malatesta family, and *[European opinion divided]*

Venice; outside Italy, Sigismund of Hungary and Rupert of the Palatinate remained faithful to him, though the latter consented to send an embassy to the Council of Pisa. The cardinals had a stronger backing than either of the popes; but unless the Council summoned by them commanded the allegiance of an overwhelming majority of Catholic Christians, it would merely add to confusion. In any case, however, having committed themselves to rebellion, they could not draw back.

*Council of Perpignan, Nov. 1408–Feb. 1409*

The Council summoned by Benedict to Perpignan was formally opened by the Pope on November 16. Its numbers were not unimpressive, as it had about three hundred members. Nearly all, however, came from places in Spain. Even in these circumstances Benedict did not have his own way. The Council not only advised him to send an embassy to Pisa, but wanted him to give the envoys full powers to abdicate in his name. They also asked him to promise to resign if the Council of Pisa should depose Gregory. Benedict would only agree that his representatives might discuss a time and place where he might abdicate; and he refused to recognize Gregory's deposition unless it were made juridically and effectively. He showed his customary skill in wasting time; the members of the Council grew weary; they entrusted the negotiations with the Pope to a committee, which had dwindled to a very small body by the time that an agreement was reached. Benedict took care that the start of his envoys was delayed until after the Council of Pisa had begun. It is plain that he meant to concede nothing, and he continued to denounce all who should take any measures against him.

*French zeal for the Council of Pisa*

The attitude of the Council of Perpignan on the whole improved the outlook for the Council of Pisa. Meanwhile a council of the Church of France had approved the policy of neutrality and taken measures which, it was hoped, would obviate some of the disadvantages which had been felt when obedience to Benedict had been withdrawn ten years before. The assembly showed no lack of enthusiasm for the Council of Pisa, voting funds to cover the expenses of the French representatives. Delegates of the French Church were chosen, and instructed to concern themselves not merely with the healing of the Schism, but also with the re-establishment of the liberties of the Church and with the re-union of the Latins and the Greeks. While these things were being decided, partisans of Benedict were deprived of their benefices and, if they could be caught, imprisoned.

The prospects of the Council of Pisa were threatened more seriously by Gregory than by his rival. In November 1408, Gregory took refuge in Rimini, under the protection of the faithful Carlo Malatesta. But it was on Ladislas of Naples, formerly so much dreaded, the he relied to defeat the rebel cardinals. In March, with Gregory's countenance, Ladislas entered Rome, and a few weeks later set out northward with the object of scattering the Council then sitting at Pisa. The diplomatic skill of Cardinal Baldassare Cossa had formed a powerful league against him, with Florence at its head. Ladislas wasted his time in unprofitable sieges while at Pisa the Fathers went on with their business unperturbed. *Failure of Gregory XII's projects*

The Council of Pisa has been much derided. It was summoned irregularly. It acted precipitately. It not only failed of its purpose but left the Church in an even worse plight than before. Nevertheless, one cannot but admire the evident zeal and eagerness of the majority of its members. The fact that it opened on the appointed day (March 25)— a most unusual achievement for a medieval assembly—alone proves that its members were in earnest. Again, there was throughout its proceedings a singular concentration on great issues, a remarkable absence of petty bickerings, and a striking unanimity of opinion. In these respects it stands in favourable contrast with the Councils of Constance and Basel. *Opening of the Council of Pisa, March 25, 1409*

The Council was well attended. At its largest, about the beginning of June, it had some 500 members. Both obediences were well represented. The French were in great force and had a strong influence on the proceedings; it is not true, however, that they formed more than half the Council; indeed, they can rarely have numbered more than one-third of the total membership. Among the former supporters of Gregory Italians were the most numerous, and some of them were surprisingly strenuous in advocating the superiority of the Council to the Pope. While there were not many representatives from other countries, very few held aloof altogether. Embassies were sent by the King of the Romans, the Kings of France, England, Poland, Portugal, the Dukes of *Its composition and procedure*

Burgundy and Brabant, the Counts of Holland and Savoy, and many other potentates of consequence. Thirteen universities were represented, and the University of Bologna vied with that of Paris in upholding the doctrines whereby the existence of the Council was justified.

The presidency of the Council was at first entrusted to Guy de Malesset, the senior cardinal-bishop; later he was succeeded by Simon de Cramaud, Patriarch of Alexandria, who had played a prominent part in the ecclesiastical politics of France in recent years. The presidency, however, was not an arduous position, and neither occupant, so far as we can tell, was tempted to use it in the interests of his country.

To understand what happened at Pisa, and for that matter at Constance and Basel afterwards, it must be remembered that one of the worst vices of the clergy was a relentless verbosity. The speeches introducing business were long, ornate, and pompous. The great festivals of the Church and the arrival of embassies afforded pretexts for more set harangues and for innumerable sermons. It is true that the Council of Pisa lasted an astonishingly short time, considering the circumstances in which it met: but its work might have been done much more quickly had the Fathers been less fond of their own voices.

*Proceedings against the popes* At the first formal session, held in the cathedral on March 26, procurators and advocates were appointed to conduct the proceedings against the two popes, for it was taken for granted that both would have to be removed. It was formally ascertained that neither Peter de Luna nor Angelo Correr was present, and on March 30 they were declared contumacious.

Soon afterwards there arrived in Pisa a delegation from Rupert, King of the Romans. Their ill-mannered conduct has been noticed above. Both they and Carlo Malatesta, Pope Gregory's protector, who was in Pisa at the same time, proposed the removal of the Council to another place, where Gregory might be willing to appear. In the end, after long debate, the Council agreed to go to Pistoja, if Gregory undertook to attend there. Pistoja was on Florentine land, and Malatesta had little hope that Gregory would approve the choice, though he promised to recommend it. His misgivings were correct; Gregory jumped at the pretext for rejecting the whole project.

The Council of Pisa now devoted its attention to the process against the popes. There was read before it a long document describing how they had hindered union, and the Council nominated a commission to hear the evidence on which the charges were based. At least eighty-four witnesses were examined. Among them were many functionaries of the two papal courts, fourteen cardinals, and other ecclesiastical dignitaries secular and regular, most of whom were personally acquainted with one or other of the rivals. There was little difficulty in proving the truth of most of the facts alleged in the act of accusation; but did they warrant the deposition of a pope ? It was generally held that only heresy or its equivalent could do that. Some contended that obstinate persistence in schism amounted to heresy, but even among these there was a desire to put the issue beyond doubt, and the commission therefore sought to show that both popes had displayed culpable leniency towards heretics, Gregory, long before, having got into trouble with the Inquisition on this account, while Benedict had positively favoured people of shocking opinions. To make things worse, both popes were addicted to sorcery. There was, it is true, not much evidence about Gregory under this head; but numerous witnesses testified to Benedict's dealings with the devil. These charges seem to have been held in reserve and were not read in public; but doubtless many members of the Council had them in mind when they voted on the question of deposition.

The report of the commission was presented to the Council on May 22. The Archbishop of Pisa declared that all the charges had been proved. The several articles—except, it seems, those added during the inquiry—were read, and after each the number and rank (not the names) of the witnesses testifying upon it were stated. The report was referred to the committee of cardinals and others which the Council had appointed to prepare business.

Meanwhile there had been presented bulls from Benedict denouncing all who took measures against him. The bulls were treated with contempt, but were useful as proving that Benedict had received his summons to appear. The Council proceeded cautiously. New evidence was collected. Informal debates were organized to convince waverers and to throw light on the state of opinion. At last, however, on

**Deposition of both popes pronounced, June 5, 1409**

June 5, formal sentence of deposition was pronounced on the two popes as notorious and incorrigible schismatics, heretics, and perjurers. It was decreed that no member of the Council should go away without signing this sentence.

Just before preparations for electing a new pope were complete, some stir was created by the arrival of envoys from the King of Aragon and from Benedict XIII. The Aragonese embassy was heard by the Council, with civility on both sides; but its request that Benedict's representatives might also have a hearing was answered by the appointment of a small committee to find out what they had to say. The civic authorities and people of Pisa, however, were so threatening in their attitude towards them that their one meeting with the committee ended prematurely, and they left the city secretly next day. That afternoon the twenty-four cardinals present entered the conclave. Each had sworn that, if elected, he would continue the Council with a view to reforming the Church in head and members. On June 26, it was announced that they had unanimously elected Peter Philarghi, commonly called the Cardinal of Milan, a man of seventy, a good scholar, but reputed to be over-fond of the pleasures of the table. In the recent attempts of the cardinals to win the support of Europe, he had played a conspicuous part.

**Election of Alexander V, June 26, 1409**

**End of the Council of Pisa, Aug. 7, 1409**

The Council did not last long after the election of Alexander V, as the new Pope called himself. In a conciliar decree he declared his intention of proceeding to the reform of the Church, and called upon the members of the Council to submit proposals to him. But no one was really ready to set about so immense a task, and most members were fully satisfied by the decision to take up the matter seriously in a General Council which should open in April 1412. Before this date provincial councils should be held throughout the Church to consider what reforms were most needed. In any case, it was well to see the effect of the election of Alexander on those who had hitherto clung to Gregory or Benedict. Alexander did what he could to win popularity. He was very lavish with gifts of dignities, benefices, indulgences, dispensations; he pardoned all arrears due to the papal *camera* at the time of his election, and renounced some other payments which his predecessors had exacted; he even succeeded in persuading the cardinals to forgo part of their dues. He also granted a plenary indulgence to all who had taken part in the Council, including members' servants. He was doubtless generally liked when, on August 7, the Council was dissolved.

Notwithstanding the sincerity and zeal of the Fathers of Pisa, they had merely made confusion worse confounded. Benedict's supporters remained immovably loyal to him. Venice, it is true, recognized Alexander V, and thereby brought to an abrupt end the so-called General Council of Gregory's partisans. It had been opened in June at Cividale, but had never attracted more than a handful of clerics. Gregory used it as an occasion for announcing the preposterous terms on which he would resign. After the defection of Venice, he fled furtively to the protection of Ladislas, and fixed his abode at Gaeta. *Results of the Council*

The most notable success of Alexander V was gained by force, not by argument. Louis of Anjou had come to Pisa in the hope that the moment might prove propitious for the renewal of his designs on Naples. He was soon allied with the warlike Cardinal Cossa and the republics of Florence and Siena. Aided by treachery, their forces drove Ladislas out of almost all the papal territory which he had seized, and at the beginning of January took Rome in the name of Alexander V. The Pope, however, did not move thither; in January he went to Bologna, and it was there that on May 3, 1410, after a short illness, he died. Carlo Malatesta strove to induce the cardinals to defer choosing a successor until there had been time to discuss how the situation might be used to promote Church union, but Baldassare Cossa, whose influence was paramount in the Sacred College, met his pleas with plausible objections. On May 17 Cossa was himself elected, and took the name of John XXIII. *Death of Alexander V and election of John XXIII, May 1410*

It must remain uncertain how far Cossa had intrigued and bribed to bring about this result, but it is generally agreed that no more scandalous choice could have been made. John XXIII had first won renown as a pirate, in the early days of the conflict between Ladislas of Naples and the House of Anjou. Later he had studied at the University of Bologna, and though he was not distinguished as a scholar, he seems to have acquired a good working knowledge of Canon Law. But it was as an administrator and general that he had made himself famous. Raised to the cardinalate by Boniface IX, he *Personality of John XXIII* was sent as legate to Bologna, which he restored to the papal obedience and ruled for some years with a rod of iron. In capacity and morals he was not unlike many of the petty Italian tyrants of the age—on the whole, perhaps, more clever and wicked than most of them.

*His successes*

John thought of the Papacy in terms of political and military strength. For some time, doubtless, he considered that things were going very well. In Italy he organized a fresh offensive with Louis of Anjou, and in April 1411 he entered Rome, amid public rejoicing. Next month Louis won a crushing victory over Ladislas at Rocca Secca. The Duke, it is true, threw away the fruits by his lack of energy, and later in the year went back to Provence; but Ladislas had been much impressed by the resolution of Pope John, and peace was made between the two in 1412. John abandoned Louis of Anjou and recognized Ladislas as King of Naples and Sicily, while the King, after pretending to consult a small council of his clergy, accepted John as true pope. Gregory XII just managed to get to Rimini.

Meanwhile, events in Germany had apparently been no less propitious to John XXIII. Sigismund of Hungary had withheld recognition from the Council of Pisa, and maintained a neutral attitude for some time after; but in 1411 he formally recognized Pope John. It is true that the Elector Palatine, following his father's example, still upheld Gregory, but as he was not King of the Romans his influence was narrowly restricted.

Benedict's supporters, it must be recognized, were far more loyal than Gregory's. Still, in 1411, the palace of the popes at Avignon, which had been devotedly held by one of Benedict's nephews against a mixed force of French and papal troops and citizens of the town, was constrained by hunger to capitulate. John XXIII might boast that he was Pope of Avignon as well as Rome.

*Criticism of John XXIII*

In reality, nevertheless, the Pope's prospects were not bright. His very election had scandalized many. His manifest indifference to the cause of union caused wide concern. As for the modest reforms promised at the Council of Pisa, even Alexander V had disregarded some of them, and John ignored them all. The old abuses and exactions of the papal court continued. On every side complaints were heard.

The University of Paris again lifted up its voice for reform and the liberties of the Church. Far and wide there arose a cry for a new General Council which should deal impartially and fearlessly with the Church's desperate plight. Carlo Malatesta, who was constantly weaving new schemes to achieve union, urged Sigismund to intervene, and many voices echoed the plea. Sigismund listened readily enough. As Emperor-elect, was it not for him, like Constantine, to summon a Council when the Church was rent asunder? Might he not restore, nay surpass, the old-time glories of the Holy Roman Empire? The opportunity seemed the greater since France was torn by civil strife, and the Burgundian party in power showed itself strangely indifferent to the liberties and reform of the Church, and ready, at every juncture, to make a mutually remunerative compromise with Pope John.

John knew something of the state of public opinion, but miscalculated its intensity. Men wanted a General Council; so the Pope, faithful to the arrangement made at Pisa, summoned one to Rome for April 1, 1412. The opening had to be postponed more than once, and it was not until the beginning of 1413 that it took place. The Council was a fiasco. It is best remembered because of the story that at the opening session an owl came and perched over against the Pope. John XXIII and Ladislas were accused by contemporaries of purposely making the roads to Rome unsafe for travellers, and it is certain that the Council was poorly attended. Several countries had representatives, those of France being most numerous, but all seemed lacking in zeal and public spirit. The only notable decree of the Council condemned Wycliffe and his writings, which no one was to read or expound. In March 1413, John prorogued the Council till the following December, on the ground that the number of prelates attending did not warrant the discussion of the important questions with which the Council ought to deal. The place of reassembly was to be announced later. *Council of Rome, Feb. 10–March 3, 1413*

As soon as Ladislas heard that the Council might be recalled to a place removed from his influence, he broke his alliance with John, invaded the Papal States, and on June 8 took Rome by force. All the prospects of the Church were altered at a stroke. *Rome captured by Ladislas, June 8, 1413*

Some authorities for the Great Schism :—

i. Original sources—

See the authorities cited for chapters i, ii, and iv, many of which naturally throw much light on the history of the Schism. The following sources deal specifically with ecclesiastical affairs.

*Acta varia de schismate pontificum Avenionensium*, published by E. Martène and U. Durand in *Thesaurus novus anecdotorum*, ii, 1073 sqq. See also the same authors' *Veterum scriptorum et monumentorum . . . amplissima collectio*, vii, 416 sqq.

Baluze, E. : *Vitae paparum Avenionensium* (with a great collection of original documents), 2 vols., Paris, 1693.

Dietrich of Niem : *De schismate*, ed. G. Erler, Leipzig, 1890.

*Documents relatifs au Grand Schisme*, ed. L. Hanquet, U. Berlière and H. Nelis, (Analecta Vatico-Belgica, viii, xii, xiii), 1924, etc.

*Dokumente zur Geschichte des Grossen abendländischen Schismas*, 1385–95, ed. Steinherz, Prague, 1932.

Mansi, J. D. : *Sacrorum conciliorum nova et amplissima collectio*, vols. xxvi and xxvii, Venice, 1784.

Raynaldus, O. : *Annales ecclesiastici*, ed. D. G. and J. G. Mansi, vols. xxvi and xxvii, Lucca, 1752.

ii. Modern works—

Boüard, M. de : *Les origines des guerres d'Italie : La France et l'Italie au temps du Grand Schisme d'Occident*, Paris, 1936.

Creighton, M. : *History of the Papacy from the Great Schism to the Sack of Rome*, 3rd ed., vol. i, London, 1897.

Flick, A. C. : *The Decline of the Medieval Church*, vol. i, London, 1930. (Useful bibliographies.)

Haller, J. : *Papsttum und Kirchenreform*, Berlin, 1903.

Hauck, A. : *Kirchengeschichte Deutschlands*, vol. v, pt. 2, Leipzig, 1920.

Hefele, C. J. : *Histoire des Conciles*, trans. into French from the German and edited by H. Le Clercq, vols. vi, pt. 2, and vii, pt. 1, Paris, 1915.

Pastor, L. : *History of the Popes*, Engl. trans. ed. by F. I. Antrobus, vol. i, London, 1891.

Salembier, L. : *Le grand schisme d'Occident*, Paris, 1900.

Seppelt, F. X. : *Das Papsttum im Spätmittelalter und in der Zeit der Renaissance ; Geschichte der Päpste von Regierungantritt Bonifaz VIII bis zum Tode Klemens VII*, Leipzig, 1941.

Valois, N. : *La France et le grand schisme d'Occident*, 4 vols., Paris, 1896–1902.

## CHAPTER VI

## GERMANY, 1410–1437

### SIGISMUND

ON the death of King Rupert in 1410 the future of the German crown was uncertain. Wenzel, of course, still claimed to be King of the Romans. He had the support of the Elector of Saxony and of his cousin Jost, who was in possession of Brandenburg, though Sigismund contested his title to the electoral vote. The Rhenish Electors would not acknowledge Wenzel, but differences of opinion on the Schism prevented them from acting in concert. There was in any case small chance of anyone outside the Luxemburg family obtaining enough votes to give him a plausible claim to the throne.

The Elector Palatine and the Archbishop of Trier favoured Sigismund. He seems not to have been eager for the crown, though willing to accept it if offered. Frederick of Hohenzollern was sent to represent him at the election. To prevent his supporters from taking precipitate action, the Archbishop of Mainz laid Frankfort under an interdict. Nevertheless, on September 20, the Elector Palatine, the Archbishop of Trier, and Frederick met in the churchyard behind the choir of St. Bartholomew's and, as they alleged, elected Sigismund. Their proceedings were quite irregular and invalid.

*First Election of Sigismund, Sept. 20, 1410*

Meanwhile the Archbishops of Mainz and Cologne were working for Jost. Wenzel, strange to say, consented to cast the Bohemian vote for him, perhaps to spite Sigismund, and on October 1 another imperial election took place, this time in St. Bartholomew's church itself. The two archbishops in their own persons, with the representatives of Jost and Wenzel, elected Jost, the Elector of Saxony concurring later. Since Wenzel after all continued to act as King of the Romans, the Empire, like the Church, now had

*Election of Jost, Oct. 1, 1410*

157

three heads. But before much could be done to relieve it, Jost opportunely died.

There was now a very widespread feeling in favour of Sigismund. Wenzel suddenly became complaisant, and consented to vote for him on condition that he himself might retain the title of King of the Romans, with the exclusive claim to the imperial crown. To put Sigismund's rights beyond cavil, there was, on July 21, 1411, yet another election at Frankfort. Five Electors (including Wenzel for Bohemia and Sigismund for Brandenburg) cast their votes in person or by proxy. The Elector Palatine and the Archbishop of Trier absented themselves, not that they disapproved of Sigismund, but because they wished to cast no doubt upon the validity of his first election, from which, indeed, Sigismund always officially dated the beginning of his reign.

*Second Election of Sigismund, July 21, 1411*

Whatever Wenzel might call himself, Sigismund henceforth behaved and was regarded as sole king of the Romans. Few will deny that he was the most interesting of those who bore that title in the later Middle Ages, or that he was on the whole the best qualified for the position. For Sigismund was a man of parts. He looked a king from top to toe—tall and slender of stature, with fresh complexion, dancing eyes, and a long forked beard. Though no great general, he was a bonny fighter in both real and mimic warfare. He was, moreover, a keen sportsman, both by land and by water. But though very proud of his knightly accomplishments, he showed a genial bearing towards men of all ranks, and was usually much liked by burghers and peasants who had dealings with him. When he visited England in 1416, he was popularly regarded as a good fellow—a fit companion for King Henry, whose youthful indiscretions were still remembered by the public. He had, however, gifts that are less frequently found in kings. His mind was quick, alert, and receptive. He had been well educated. Like several others of the Luxemburg family, he was a first-rate linguist, speaking Czech, French, German, Polish, Hungarian, Italian, and Latin with fluency, though his Latin grammar was not above reproach. He patronized scholars, if not so generously as many contemporary princes; but he can hardly be called a scholar himself, notwithstanding his renown as an orator and the fact that he seems to

*Sigismund's character and attainments*

have composed his own speeches. While not really a religious man, and ever on his guard against encroachments of the Church on his lawful jurisdiction, he accepted fully the Church's authority in spiritual matters, was content to leave all theological questions to her judgment, and had a loathing of heresy. But, with the mind of a man of affairs, he saw that force was not always the best means of encountering heresy, and his willingness to try other methods exposed him to the unwarranted suspicion of being at heart inclined towards doubtful doctrine.

That Sigismund, notwithstanding his endowments, must be accounted a failure is due partly to circumstances for which he cannot be blamed, but no less to his many and great defects. His activity degenerated into restlessness: he was always doing something, but he seldom did the same thing for long. He was also the victim of an incorrigible optimism, something like that which afflicted Rupert. As a rule, he had far too many irons in the fire. He was constantly rushing headlong into the most ambitious projects, ignoring their difficulties and cost. There can have been few kings who failed in so many undertakings and learned so little from misfortune.

One characteristic of Sigismund's that especially aroused the contemptuous mirth of contemporaries was his constant impecuniosity. His financial incapacity was amazing. He would resort to the meanest and most undignified devices to raise money. When any was got, it would be instantly spent, for Sigismund was no miser like his kinsmen Wenzel and Jost. When on his travels he frequently had to stay in a place far longer than he intended because he could not pay his bills. On arriving in the Netherlands after his visit to England, he had to pawn part of the insignia of the Order of the Garter, just bestowed on him, in order to raise money for his journey back to Constance; and when he left that city at the close of the General Council, he gave the municipal authorities in pledge for the payment of his debts a quantity of linen which afterwards proved unsaleable because it was all stamped with the imperial arms. He and his court were often fain to wear shabby or tattered clothing, so that his poverty not only crippled his energy but also caused the men of his generation to despise him. What, however, caused still more astonishment was his licentiousness. Sigismund's devotion to women was even greater than Wenzel's to wine. His amours were indiscriminate and shameless; his behaviour, especially when he was imperfectly sober, was apt to become indecent. Much has been made of Sigismund's besetting weakness, and indeed it must have been sensational to shock that age. But his sexual irregularities do not seem to have impaired his health, still less to have damaged his political schemes. They are said by a biased authority to have contributed to the hostility which he aroused in Paris when he was there in 1416 trying to mediate between France and England: but it cannot be believed that the French court allowed such familiar phenomena to interfere with the course of political business. More serious for Europe at large were the treachery and promise-breaking of which Sigismund was often guilty. His behaviour towards Wenzel, to whom he owed much, had been abominable. In his latter days, indeed, he had his reward, for no one trusted him, and this was one of the main reasons why, the more power he seemed to acquire, the less successful he became.

*Sigismund's imperial policy*

Sigismund took his position as head of the Empire more seriously than anyone had done for a long time. He had ample possessions of his own, with the early prospect of more; and thus, especially since he had no son, he lacked any strong incentive to strive for the exaltation of his family. He really was interested in the authority of the German Crown. He wanted to enlarge and recover royal domain; he hoped to improve the Crown's financial position; the maintenance of public order, the abolition of private war, lay very near his heart; and for a time he seems actually to have hoped that the princes and the cities could be induced to aid him in the pursuit of such objects. Yet, when one tries to write of Sigismund's doings as German king, there is little to say. It is significant that, notwithstanding his concern for Germany, her interests were constantly being set aside in favour of something which seemed—and usually was—more urgent: the termination of the Schism, the reform of the Church, the defence of Hungary against the Turks, the suppression of the Hussites.

Sigismund's reign as King of the Romans may be divided into three parts. In the first, his main concern was the restoration of ecclesiastical unity. In the second, it was the overthrow of the Hussites. In the third, it was the Council of Basel. And all through there was Hungary in the background, continually demanding his attention, often determining his general policy, and sometimes compelling his presence. Still farther in the background was Germany. Sigismund's dealings with her may be treated summarily. They were rarely interesting in themselves, and they had few momentous consequences.

When Sigismund became King of the Romans, it was not necessary for him to trouble about securing recognition from any of the three rival popes: none could afford to offend him by denying the validity of his title. Nevertheless, his first important undertaking was an expedition to Italy. He hoped to receive the imperial crown; but the enterprise was really directed against Venice and was in the interests of Hungary rather than Germany, the Italian republic having lately bought Zara and Dalmatia from Sigismund's rival, Ladislas of Naples, a transaction which cut off Hungary from the Adriatic. In 1412 Sigismund crossed the Alps with an army and got as far as Udine; but, finding that victory, if attainable at all, would be slow and costly, he agreed to a truce. He also endeavoured to compel Filippo Maria Visconti of Milan to acknowledge his authority: but lack of money compelled him to desist from using force, and the ensuing negotiations led to nothing. Then came the opportunity of bringing about a General Council, and other interests fell into the background. Nevertheless, Sigismund did not wholly ignore his German kingdom: he visited Germany before the Council opened, and his arrival in Constance was delayed by his coronation at Aachen, which took place on November 8, 1414.

*Sigismund in Italy, 1412–14*

*Sigismund and the Council of Constance*

Sigismund's doings at the Council are described in another chapter. It should be remembered, however, that he announced his readiness to transact imperial business at Constance, and that the city became the temporary capital of Germany. It is well to bear in mind also that all the ecclesiastical business had its political aspect. The condemnation of John Hus meant not merely the destruction of a heretic; it was at the same time a victory of Germany over Bohemia. Similarly, the humiliation of Frederick of Habsburg, the protector of John XXIII, was more than a success for the theory of conciliar supremacy; it was also a notable triumph for the German crown. Sigismund's travels in western Europe in 1415 and 1416, though their original motive was the ending of the Schism and the promotion of international peace in the interests of harmony at Constance and the organization of a crusade, became a merely political enterprise, and the consequent alliance of Sigismund with England and Burgundy was undoubtedly one of the main causes of the Council's failure to achieve any adequate reform of the Church. Sigismund's policy, however, was generally approved in Germany, and all the Electors save his brother Wenzel confirmed the Treaty of Canterbury between him and Henry V. Of course that agreement never led to anything serious. Sigismund talked of the help he would give Henry, and countenanced the latter's effort to recruit soldiers in Germany. But the only German prince who really aided the English was Henry's brother-in-law, the Elector Palatine Lewis. He served at the head of a small contingent in 1420, and was very richly rewarded for his assistance.

When Pope Martin was elected in 1417, Sigismund paid him the traditional tokens of respect. He received the Pope's approval of his own election, and took the customary oath. Martin promised to bestow on him the imperial crown. Nothing was said of the Empire's feudal dependence on the Papacy, nor could Martin well suggest that Sigismund ought not to have acted as King of the Romans until his approval had been expressed. In relation to the Papacy, the position of the Empire was much more favourable than it had been a hundred years earlier.

In Germany, nevertheless, Sigismund was weaker at the end of the Council than he had been during its early months. While he was absent in France and England, Frederick of Habsburg had reasserted himself in Tyrol, and had incurred the Council's wrath for his attacks on the bishopric of Trent. Sigismund felt unable to suppress him, and in 1418 was reduced to the necessity of admitting him to pardon and restoring to him his forfeited lands, save a small piece kept by the Swiss Confederation. Sigismund's plans for reviving the power of the Empire had kindled the suspicion of both princes and cities. The Archbishop of Mainz and the Elector

Palatine were conspicuously unfriendly. South Germany was in confusion, principally owing to the intestine feuds of the Wittelsbach family, which even disturbed Constance during the Council. Sigismund's most trusted supporter was still Frederick of Hohenzollern, on whom in 1415 he bestowed the Mark of Brandenburg, an act which was to have far more momentous consequences than anyone suspected at the time. When in 1418 Sigismund was obliged to go to Hungary, he left Frederick as his lieutenant in Germany.

In 1419 the death of Wenzel forced Sigismund to give his attention to Bohemia. There followed the refusal of the Hussite party to accept his rule and the early victories of Zizka. In 1421, with many difficulties crowding upon him, he turned for help to the Electors. He could no longer count on the fidelity of Frederick of Hohenzollern, with whom he had fallen out owing to the margrave's policy of friendship with Sigismund's enemy Poland. It was a striking example of the incompatibility between the interests of the monarchy and those of the princes, and of the way in which regard for the welfare of a principality might impair even a loyal man's sense of duty to the crown. On the other hand, Sigismund's desire to suppress heresy appealed strongly to the four Rhenish Electors, who tried to form a league of all princes and cities for the prevention of the spread of Hussite doctrine into Germany, and, stimulated by a papal legate, authorized and encouraged the raising of a German army for a crusade. This was the first of the attempts of the Empire to uproot the Bohemian heresy. Its failure was complete, though not quite so ignominious as the fate of subsequent expeditions of a similar kind.

*The first German expedition against the Hussites, 1421*

The German princes were disposed to blame Sigismund for the disaster and there was talk of deposing him like his brother Wenzel. The discontent was manifest in 1422, when Sigismund met a German Diet. But an attack by the Poles on the Teutonic Knights convinced the princes that Sigismund's Polish policy was right and discredited Frederick of Hohenzollern, who had been stirring up opinion against his former patron. It was therefore decided by the Diet that all princes and cities should furnish troops for a Bohemian expedition according to their resources, and an attempt to make a complete and equitable assessment was initiated.

*German inefficiency*

It was discovered, however, that there was in existence no list of the tenants-in-chief or the imperial cities, and for this reason and others the assessment was imperfect. It was enacted, however, that those who had been overlooked must pay a property tax of one per cent.—the hundredth penny, as it was popularly called; indeed, anyone might commute his military obligations at that rate. But all these arrangements were to little purpose. On paper the army raised came to no more than 7,000 men, and far fewer actually assembled. A force destined to precede the main army promised to be larger. The commutation money was laboriously and inefficiently collected. It was in vain that Sigismund flattered the princes, curried favour with the knights, and cajoled the cities. Everyone was jealous and suspicious of everyone else, and nobody wished to sacrifice anything for the common cause. When Sigismund nominated the Archbishop of Mainz to act as vicegerent while he was out of Germany, the Elector Palatine refused to obey him, and on the advice of the other ecclesiastical Electors he resigned his position. In the end the whole expedition against the Hussites was abandoned.

Sigismund was away, disorder was increasing, the Hussites were becoming more dangerous. In 1424, therefore, the Electors met at Bingen to concert joint measures. They drew up an agreement which was in great part copied from a similar instrument drafted at a meeting of the Electors in 1399, when the deposition of Wenzel was in view. They promised to uphold one another in the enjoyment of their rights and to resist anything that made for the hurt of the Empire. The tone of the document is hostile to the King, but naturally a good deal of what is said is not very appropriate to the situation in 1424. The Electors did, however, add a section in which they deplored the triumph of the Bohemian heresy and asserted their intention of co-operating with the other princes for its extirpation. In all this there is nothing revolutionary, nor is there anything in the document to justify those historians who have supposed that the Electors were trying to constitute themselves a standing administrative Council of the Empire, with powers limiting the royal prerogative. Their complaint against Sigismund in fact was that he had failed to employ that prerogative

*Sigismund criticized adversely by the Electors, 1424*

effectively. As for his deposition, while it was doubtless considered, the evidence goes to show that the majority of the Electors were decidedly against it.

When the Electors communicated to him the result of their deliberations, Sigismund was angry. He maintained that he had done all he could, and that, if things had gone badly, the divisions among the princes were the main cause. For some time there seemed a likelihood of a complete breach between the King and the Electors. It was perhaps fortunate that efforts by Sigismund to win over the cities were wrecked by their suspicions and indifference to national interests. Gradually the situation improved. All parties could see the folly of quarrelling in face of the Hussites. Sigismund really wanted to do his royal duty. The Electors wished him no ill. Sigismund in fact had a new partisan among them in the Elector of Saxony, Frederick of Meissen, on whom the duchy of Saxe-Wittenberg had been bestowed in 1428, when its Ascanian line of rulers had died out.[1] Furthermore, Frederick of Brandenburg found that his hostility towards his old benefactor was losing him the sympathy of his fellow Electors and other princes, and the turn of politics in north Germany made him less anxious to maintain his friendship with Poland. So in 1426 Sigismund and Frederick were formally reconciled, and the King and the Electors renewed their efforts to remedy the ills of the Empire. A Diet at Nürnberg, however, failed to make adequate provision for the raising of a fresh army, mainly owing to the niggardliness of the cities. Soon afterwards came the great Hussite victory at Aussig. In 1427 the Electors therefore met by themselves at Frankfort. They declared that they had the same aims as in 1424, but this time there was no sign of animosity against Sigismund, and they took precautions for the maintenance of peace among themselves. They exhorted the princes and the cities to do all they could to swell the army which was about to invade Bohemia, and they drew up some admirable regulations for its conduct while on the march and in camp. The force that mustered was indeed of respectable size, but

*Sigismund and the Electors reconciled, 1426*

*A further disaster in Bohemia, 1427*

---

[1] Though other branches of the Ascanian family protested, the Wettins made good their hold on the Electorate, and held it until it was converted into the kingdom of Saxony, which in turn they ruled until 1918.

as soon as it got near the Hussites it ran away. This was the year in which the Hussites began to make systematic attacks on the parts of Germany adjacent to Bohemia.

At this crisis a vigorous lead was unexpectedly given by the papal legate in Germany, Cardinal Beaufort. It was at his instance that a Diet was summoned to Frankfort, and he even used the terrors of the Church to secure a good attendance. Beaufort, a notoriously shrewd business man, insisted that lack of money was the fundamental cause of the failure against the Hussites. In December 1427 the Diet was induced to vote the levy of a general tax. The feebleness of the central government may be gauged by the fact that this was thought a most drastic and daring expedient. Its purpose was said to be the provision of means for waging unremitting war against the heretics. To such a cause it was the manifest duty of every Christian to contribute according to his means.

*Diet of Frankfort; the "common penny," Dec. 1427*

The arrangements for raising the money were exceedingly complex, and based on several different principles. Ecclesiastics and religious foundations were to pay an income tax of five per cent. On the other hand, all lay people over fifteen, men and women, were at least to pay a poll-tax of a groschen; but those who possessed 200 gulden were to disburse half a gulden, while those who had 1,000 must pay one. Nobles were taxed at a flat rate according to their rank: a count, for instance, had to contribute twenty-five gulden. From every Jew one gulden was demanded. An elaborate scheme was devised for the collection of the cash, and ultimately all would be taken to Nürnberg, where it would be administered by the Electors with the aid of three representatives of the imperial cities.

Much careful thought had evidently been given to the tax, and it might have had momentous consequences, for it was a serious attempt to make everyone in Germany contribute towards a common purpose. But the scheme failed. This was due partly to its inherent defects: the scale of obligations was not equitably adjusted; nobles above the rank of count were exempted, the clergy were overburdened, the merchants (who could afford most) were let off lightly. But the main reason was that most people evaded payment if they could. The knights declared that they owed to the crown the service of their swords, but nothing else. The burghers showed their customary meanness when national concerns were in question. And, despite the exhortations which the parish clergy were instructed to deliver, ordinary people showed no great enthusiasm for the crusade. Heretics they were not, but they did not love the clergy, and a papal legate was an object of especial suspicion. Beaufort's threat of excommunication against those that would not pay caused such indignation that he had to withdraw it; and the machinery for collecting the money was not adequate for the coercion of the defaulters. In the end the yield of the " common penny " was grievously disappointing. The crusade which it was to have financed was perforce abandoned.

In the next years Sigismund was engaged mainly in fighting the Turks. He tacitly handed Germany over to the care of the Electors, who showed no fitness for the responsibility. There was much talk of political reform, but no concrete proposal stood any chance of being accepted. When at the end of 1429 Sigismund again came to Germany, no one had anything fresh to suggest. But the King had lately been in touch with the Hussite general Procop the Great, and a little later Frederick of Brandenburg actually made an agreement with a Hussite army. Such treatment of heretics roused much denunciation, but there was a spreading conviction that German soil must be saved from Hussite ravages, even at the cost of making terms with Antichrist. The situation was complicated by the approach of the date for the holding of a new General Council and the uncertainty as to the intentions of Martin V. That the Pope did eventually summon the Council was due in great measure to the general recognition in Germany that only through such an assembly could the Hussite problem be solved. Few people, however, really liked the idea of haggling with heretics, and before the Council met Sigismund persuaded a Diet to make one more attempt to settle the matter by the sword. *The Germans, the Hussites, and Martin V*

This time a very great effort was made. A quota of men-at-arms was demanded from each prince or city; and from the regions near Bohemia one man in twenty-five, from elsewhere one man in fifty, was to serve as a foot-soldier. *The Crusade of 1431*

The response—though far from complete, the cities being the worst defaulters—was sufficient to furnish a great and well-equipped army.

In the summer of 1431, under Frederick of Hohenzollern and the papal legate, Cesarini, it invaded Bohemia from the west. The disaster of Tauss speedily followed. After ten years of effort Germany gave up the attempt to suppress the Bohemian heresy. The question was left to the Council of Basel. Henceforth Germany as such had little to do with it.

<small>Sigismund again in Italy, 1431-8</small> As for Sigismund, he at first left the Council alone, having no wish to be embroiled in the ecclesiastical disputes which immediately began to afflict it. In the autumn of 1431 he carried out his long-cherished intention of going to Italy for the imperial crown, using the occasion to uphold or promote certain rights and interests of his own beyond the Alps. He remained in Italy until late in 1433, but there is no need to linger over his doings. He had with him few men and, as usual, little money. He was at war with Venice and Florence, and he soon fell out with Filippo Maria Visconti of Milan, on whose support he had mainly relied. He had a friendly reception in a few cities, notably Lucca and Siena, in each of which he made a long stay : but his position was for many months most embarrassing, not to say perilous. Pope Eugenius was openly hostile, and intrigued with his enemies both in Italy and beyond the Alps. Sigismund, however, benefited greatly through the quarrel between the Pope and the Council of Basel. He used the situation with great address, rendering himself indispensable to each side, striving to avert a complete breach between the Holy See and the Fathers, yet making it clear to Eugenius that he would lend himself to no schemes for the ruin of the Council. The Pope now mediated peace between the King and his foes, Venice and Florence, while Sigismund swore to defend the Church, to stand by Eugenius, and to maintain him in the enjoyment of all the territorial rights recog-
<small>Sigismund crowned Emperor, May 81, 1488</small> nized by previous kings of the Romans. After this Sigismund was permitted to enter Rome, and on Whitsun Day, 1433, he was crowned by the Pope at St. Peter's. It was the first imperial coronation in Rome since that of Frederick II, more than two hundred years before. Sigismund stayed

in Rome two months longer, but then news from Basel caused him to hasten thither in the hope of preventing the schism which now seemed imminent.

The Emperor's dealings with the Council are described in another chapter. During the few years that remained to him the ecclesiastical crisis and negotiations with the Bohemians occupied most of his attention. He did not, it is true, ignore the Empire. He summoned several Diets, at which plans for the cure of Germany's ills were discussed, and he was concerned to find means for checking the growth of Burgundian power at the Empire's expense. In 1434 Sigismund laid before the princes a comprehensive scheme of reform. He wished in particular to achieve his old desire of organizing a *Landfriede* which should embrace all Germany. His proposals were well received, but at the Diet which was to adopt them Sigismund did not appear, and the whole scheme fell to the ground. Further discussion in the following years was equally abortive. The truth was that while the princes were ready to talk about the reform of the Empire, they themselves were constantly doing the things that made reform necessary. Just as, at the Council of Basel, everyone was eager to reform his neighbour, but no one willing to sacrifice himself, so it was in the German Diet. *The Emperor's last years*

Sigismund was now an old man, sorely afflicted with gout. He remained wonderfully vigorous till he was on the verge of seventy. Then his magnificent constitution, which he had sorely tried, succumbed to the advance of his ailment. He had his wife imprisoned lest she should interfere with his plans for the succession, and then at Znaim, on December 9, 1437, he made an edifying end. *His death, Dec. 9, 1437*

He had not done much of lasting value for Germany, yet as lord of the Empire he had cut a great figure, and he had reminded not only foreigners but the Germans themselves that they were one people with a common sovereign. Though he had spent but little time in Germany—less than three years altogether after the Council of Constance—he left a kindly memory among the people. He lived long in German tradition as one of the great medieval Emperors.

Some authorities for chapter vi :—

In addition to the original sources mentioned under chapter iv, the following may be noticed :

*Die Urkunden Kaiser Sigmunds, 1410–37*, ed. W. Altmann, 2 vols., Innsbruck, 1896–1900.

*Andreas presbyter Ratisbonensis. Works*, ed. G. Leidinger, Munich, 1903 (*Quellen und Erörterungen zur Bayerischen und Deutschen Geschichte.* New Series, vol. i).

Windecke, Eberhard : *Denkwürdigkeiten zur Geschichte des Zeitalters Kaiser Sigmunds*, ed. W. Altmann, Berlin, 1893.

Besides the modern works named under chapter iv, see

J. Aschbach : *Geschichte Kaiser Sigmunds*, 4 vols., Hamburg, 1838–45.

See also the authorities for chapters vii and viii.

## CHAPTER VII
## THE COUNCIL OF CONSTANCE

LADISLAS King of Naples cared nothing for the unity of the Church, yet when he captured Rome in June 1413 he was doing more towards the termination of the Great Schism than anyone had so far accomplished. John XXIII and his *curia* had departed in confused flight. The Pope found a refuge in Florence and later in Bologna, but feeling still unsafe he turned for aid to the King of the Romans, at the moment in north Italy. Though Sigismund's support, as he knew, would have to be bought by the summons of a new General Council, to mention nothing else, he was confident that he could arrange for it to meet in a place where he could dominate its proceedings. But Sigismund swept his envoys off their feet; they agreed in the Pope's name that the Council should assemble at Constance on November 1, 1414; and before John knew of this arrangement, it had been published by Sigismund, who had invited to the Council John's two rivals and all Christian princes. The Pope dared not refuse compliance; and a few weeks later, on December 9, 1413, he issued bulls formally convoking the Council according to the terms of the agreement. He might not, indeed, have taken any further steps had not Ladislas, in the spring of 1414, again occupied Rome, and then advanced northward. On this John XXIII began to make active preparations for his journey to Germany, and urged the French and the English to participate in the Council. His mood changed once more on the death of Ladislas in August, and he would fain have gone back to Rome. But Europe was now thoroughly interested in the Council, and John's cardinals held him to his promise, rightly believing that to break it would mean ruin for him, if not for them. So, slowly and with many misgivings, he travelled to Constance, entering the city on October 28. On November 5 he solemnly opened the Council.

*Miscalculations of John XXIII*

*Opening of the Council, Nov. 5, 1414*

Alike in the numbers that attended it, in the length of time it sat, and in the importance of the business with which it dealt, the Council of Constance was one of the most notable assemblies in the history of the world. When at its largest it included three patriarchs, twenty-nine cardinals, thirty-three archbishops, one hundred and fifty bishops, more than a hundred abbots, and upwards of three hundred other ecclesiastics, nearly all of whom held a doctor's degree. Besides, the Council attracted to Constance a vast concourse of strangers who were not members, though some of them had much influence upon its proceedings. There were the suites of the great prelates and princes who were present; there were crowds of benefice-hunters and privilege-seekers; the business of the Empire, as well as that of the Church, was for many months officially transacted at Constance; and there were large profits to be made by pedlars, craftsmen, minstrels, harlots, and parasites of every kind. The most modest contemporary estimate of the numbers of this multitude gives 40,000, but one may prudently be sceptical as to this figure without denying that Constance successfully accommodated several times its normal population of some 6,000. Considering that the Council lasted for nearly three years and a half, that (while in such a mixed crowd a good deal of vice and crime was inevitable) there was very little open disorder, that the regulations laying down maximum prices for food and lodging were enforced and worked well, and that after the first winter there was no serious apprehension of a dearth of provisions, it cannot be denied that both among the Council's officials and among the municipal authorities there was very high organizing ability. Nor must the failure of the gathering to accomplish many of the things that it undertook lessen unduly our wonder that such an assembly could sit for so long, debate the most vital and controversial topics of that age, and, despite some narrow escapes of premature disintegration, separate peacefully, with much work achieved and its dignity and self-respect maintained. That the Council of Constance was possible is a measure of the zeal for the catholic Church which still animated Europe.

The Pope's punctuality was imitated by few, and up to the end of the year there was but a scant attendance. As for John's rivals, Gregory XII at first refused to countenance a schismatic gathering, but, under the urgings of his principal supporters, Carlo Malatesta and the Elector Palatine, he decided to send an embassy to meet the Council. Benedict XIII, despite pressure and persuasion, would do no more than promise to meet Sigismund in 1415 at Nice, where the question of union might be discussed. *Attitude of Gregory XII and Benedict XIII*

In the absence of Sigismund, who did not arrive until Christmas Eve, little formal business could be transacted. Some progress, however, was made with the case of John Hus, who had reached Constance as early as November 3. His trial and fate are described in another chapter, and call for attention here only in so far as they affected the general course of the Council. And on this their influence was much less than a modern student would naturally expect. The Bohemians of course were deeply interested, and so were many Germans. Subsequent events proved that nothing done by the Council was more momentous than its dealings with Hus. Protestant historians of the Council have justifiably treated the proceedings against him in great detail. But there was at Constance no desire to tamper with the Church's doctrine, and to the vast majority of those present Hus was merely a man suspected of heresy,[1] who, if found guilty, must of course undergo a heretic's punishment. To serious-minded persons, a criminal case like this, however sensational, was trivial compared with the hard problems raised by the Schism and the corruption of the Church. Even Sigismund, whose political prospects were involved, ranked the case of Hus among the "lesser matters" which must not be allowed to impede reform.[2] *Attitude of the Council towards Hus*

When the Council began, nearly all its members desired before everything the restoration of the Church's unity. Pope John was aware that his conduct had weakened the loyalty of many who had so far obeyed him, and that there was much support for the view that all three popes should be treated as on an equal footing. For a few weeks the Italians, *The Council and the three popes*

---
[1] Cf. the first reference to him in Cardinal Fillastre's journal (Finke: *Acta Concilii Constanciensis*, ii, 17): "Interim actum est contra quendam hereticum Boemum dictum Johannem Hus et de erroribus Johannis Wiclef Anglici." The journal of Cerretanus, an official of the *Curia*, does not mention Hus when it reaches the date of his death.

[2] Finke: *op. cit.*, ii, 208.

most of whom were disposed to stand by him, were in a majority, and some of them injudiciously proposed that if the Council confirmed the decrees of Pisa and arranged for the holding of further Councils every twenty-five years, it would have fulfilled its task and might be dissolved. This impudent suggestion brought into the open John's opponents, headed by two cardinals, D'Ailly and Fillastre, whom he had himself added to the Sacred College. They urged in both speech and writing that a General Council was superior to a pope, that the three rival popes should resign, and that, if John were obdurate, the Council might depose him. These views were approved by Sigismund, and were widely favoured by the members from northern and western Europe, who soon after the New Year began to appear in large numbers. Though Benedict XIII of course remained immovable, Gregory XII made a good impression by authorizing his envoys to say that he would resign if his rivals would.

*The four "nations"* John and his party struggled desperately. When, with the growth of the Council, definite rules of procedure had to be adopted, they proposed that at formal sessions individual votes should be counted and that only bishops and abbots might vote. Had this plan been accepted, the Italians would still have dominated the Council; but the Germans and English demanded that each " nation " should constitute a voting unit, after the fashion followed at many universities, and, with the agreement of the French, brought about the adoption of this arrangement. Four " nations " were recognized—the Italian, the French, the German (which included all from the north and east of continental Europe), and the English (under which head were counted all from the British Isles). Each " nation " seems to have decided who might share and vote in its deliberations, admitting, as a rule, all prelates, graduates in theology or law, and representatives of secular authorities, if in holy orders. When all four " nations " had made up their minds on an issue, it was laid before the whole Council, and the vote of each " nation " was recorded.

Defeated on the question of procedure, the Pope said that he would resign if, in the opinion of the Council, his doing so would give union to the Church, a condition which could hardly be fulfilled as long as Benedict XIII held out. Even in this mild concession he was probably insincere, since he was misled by disputes in the Council on other points into believing that a sudden shock would cause its disintegration. Rumours spread that he intended to run away, and on March 20 he assured Sigismund that he would rather die than flee. That night he left Constance disguised as a groom, and at Schaffhausen he was joined by Frederick of Habsburg, Count of Tyrol, whom the Pope had retained in his service before the opening of the Council in return for a promise of protection. *Flight of John XXIII, March 20, 1415*

John's stroke failed utterly. For a while the Council became almost unanimously hostile to him. The cardinals tried in vain to moderate its measures. A series of decrees on vitally important subjects was passed, culminating in those of the Fifth General Session, held on April 6, 1415. The Council, it was asserted, held its power immediately of God, and everyone must obey it in matters concerning the Faith, the extinction of Schism, and the reform of the Church in head and members. The Pope, it was enacted, must abdicate if and when the Council declared it to be in the interest of the Church that he should do so. Pope John was summoned to return, and threatened, in the event of refusal, with proceedings against him as a promoter of schism and heresy. *Council's superiority to Pope affirmed, April 6, 1415*

John's reply was to flee farther off and to make desperate efforts to reach territory belonging to the Duke of Burgundy, where—probably without much reason—he expected to find refuge. But Sigismund's military measures reduced Frederick of Habsburg to surrender ignominiously, and the Pope, who had begun to bargain about terms, found that he had exhausted the patience of the Council, which had decided to take judicial action against him for heresy, simony, moral turpitude, and waste of the Church's goods. *Proceedings against John XXIII*

On May 13 a commission of thirteen was appointed to examine witnesses on the charges brought against the Pope. Its initial inquiry was followed next day by his suspension from office. The detailed investigation ensued. There has recently been discovered a very full official report [1] of the depositions of the individual witnesses, so that the student of to-day can form a far better judgment on the process

---

[1] Printed by Finke: *Acta Concilii Constanciensis*, iv, 758 seqq.

against John XXIII than any historian was able to do for 500 years. Some seventy articles were laid to his charge. He had been an unruly and disobedient child. He owed his advancement to corruption. He was guilty of simony and fraud of all kinds both before and after he became pope. He had betrayed Rome to Ladislas. In his attempts to frustrate or break up the Council he had been actuated by a desire to prolong the Schism. He had practised several forms of sexual vice, had poisoned his predecessor Alexander V and that Pope's physician, and had denied the immortality of the soul. The principle that if you throw enough mud, some will stick, was thoroughly grasped in the Middle Ages, and a mere list of charges against a man never carries much weight. But we have a report of the evidence of thirty-nine witnesses, of whom six were cardinals and seven bishops—personages of weight and responsibility—while many were officials of the *curia*, for whom it would have been safer to keep silent. Only in the case of one or two witnesses is there any indication of personal animosity against the Pope. As a rule it is stated whether a witness is testifying from his personal knowledge or from hearsay. Though the procedure did not admit of the cross-examination of witnesses, the inquiry was careful and searching, and took altogether over eight days.

At the eleventh General Session of the Council, on May 25, the report of the commission was read, and fifty-four of the articles of accusation were declared to have been proved. John had already been arrested by order of the Council, and he declared that he submitted himself wholly to its judgment. On May 29, at its twelfth General Session, the Council formally stated that his flight from Constance had been detrimental to the Church, that he was a simoniac, that he had wasted the Church's goods, and that by his abominable life he had scandalized the Church of God and proved himself incorrigible. His deposition was solemnly pronounced, and was ratified by him two days later. He was kept in close confinement in various German castles until after the close of the Council.

*John's deposition pronounced, May 29*

The findings of the commission of inquiry were amply justified by the evidence which is now accessible to scholars. Whether they warranted the Council in deposing the Pope is a question of theology which may not be discussed here. But whatever may be thought of the action taken by the Council or the principles on which it was based, few will deny that its conduct at this crisis was marked by admirable dignity, firmness, and restraint.

A few days afterwards there arrived at Constance Carlo Malatesta, who was authorized to announce the resignation of Gregory XII. In the subsequent negotiations great care was taken to save the face of each side, but on July 4, Gregory's representatives and the Council were formally united, his abdication was proclaimed, and it was decreed that the election of a new pope should only be made as, when, and where the Council should deem good, and that Gregory and his cardinals should belong to the Sacred College. The Council named him legate of Ancona, and he lived in quiet dignity until his death in 1417. He had learned how to bow gracefully to the inevitable. *Abdication of Gregory XII, July 4, 1415*

Two days after Gregory's abdication John Hus was burned. The most pressing business was now the removal, by persuasion or force, of Benedict XIII. On July 18 Sigismund, with twelve delegates from the Council, left for Nice. *Sigismund's departure, July 18*

With Sigismund's departure the first phase of the Council's history ended. Its best days, in fact, were over. Hitherto, from its own standpoint, it had done well. It had made substantial progress towards the restoration of union. The execution of Hus was believed to be a deadly blow at heresy. It had achieved these results with remarkably little dissension, and it was full of confidence and zeal as it faced what remained for it to do.

Sigismund did not return until January 1417. He had asked that nothing of the first importance should be decided while he was away. Though this request could not be ignored, the effect of his prolonged absence has probably been exaggerated. No doubt it would have been better for the Council if he had returned to Constance as soon as he had completed his business with Pope Benedict and his supporters, instead of spending a year in fruitless mediation between France and England. But in any case the Council could not have done much towards union or decided anything respecting reform until it had been joined by representatives of the countries which had supported *Consequences of Sigismund's absence*

Benedict. And when Sigismund got back, the delegation of Castile, the most powerful of those countries, had not yet arrived.

*The first reform commission*

The Council, to do it justice, tried to press on with its proper tasks. The work of suppressing heresy was continued in the tortuous proceedings against Jerome of Prague, that clever, hot-headed, unstable, and eloquent admirer of Hus being put to death in May 1416. In the summer of 1415 the preparation of proposals for reform was entrusted to a commission of thirty-five—eight from each " nation," with three cardinals—which remained in being for two years. It worked hard, considered a vast number of suggestions, and while it seems never to have presented any formal report, it handed over a great deal of valuable material to its successor. But even if it had drawn up a cut-and-dried programme, it would have been idle for the Council to pronounce upon it until the summer of 1417.

*Sigismund and Benedict XIII*

The reason was the situation created by Sigismund's dealings with Benedict XIII. In the negotiations—conducted at Perpignan and not, after all, at Nice—the King of the Romans was conciliatory and tactful, though determined to bring about the Pope's unconditional surrender. But, while he won over most of Benedict's supporters who were present at the conference, including the King of Aragon, the old man remained obdurate, his head full of dreams, not only of regaining what he had lost, but of securing recognition from the whole of catholic Christendom. Eventually Sigismund broke off negotiations and withdrew to Narbonne. Benedict retired to the impregnable castle of Peñiscola, near Valencia.

*The Capitulation of Narbonne, Dec. 1415*

The Pope had presumed too far. The envoys of several states in his obedience continued discussions with Sigismund, and on December 13 the Capitulation of Narbonne was accepted by the delegates of Castile, Aragon, Navarre, and Foix, on the one hand, and on the other by Sigismund, the Council's delegation, and a representative of the King of France. The Council sitting at Constance and the followers of Benedict were to unite and seek means of ending the Schism. No new pope should be chosen until the Council had been formally joined by Benedict's supporters and he had been formally deposed, as he might lawfully be if he still refused to abdicate.

The Council promptly accepted the agreement and ratified it. But owing to opposition from some of the Aragonese clergy and delays caused by the death of the King, it was not until September 1416 that the representatives of Aragon reached Constance. In December embassies from the Count of Foix and the King of Navarre joined the Council; but strong opposition to the Capitulation among the clergy of Castile prevented the arrival of envoys from that country until March 1417, and even then it was some time before they would allow themselves to be incorporated in the Council. As for the Regent of Scotland and the Count of Armagnac, they refused to recognize the Capitulation at all.

*Benedict's supporters at Constance*

It is thus in a sense true that for nearly two years the Council had too little to do. But it may also be said that it was doing a great deal too much. For this it cannot be altogether blamed. The Papacy was in abeyance, but the administration of the Church must be carried on. The cardinals might have performed many of the Pope's functions, but, though some of them had taken the lead in the proceedings against John XXIII and had expressed themselves strongly in favour of conciliar supremacy, the majority were regarded by the Council as reactionary and for some time were thrust into the background. It was the Council itself which tried to take the Pope's place. A great deliberative assembly, however judiciously it might delegate its powers, was not fitted for such a task. The burden soon became too heavy, and the minds of many of the Fathers were preoccupied with petty details. What was still more serious, the Council was thus involved in controversies that were political rather than religious. For instance, shortly before the Council opened, the Duke of Burgundy had appealed to the Pope against the sentence of an ecclesiastical assembly at Paris which had condemned John Petit's "Justification" of the Duke for the murder of Louis of Orléans. The Armagnacs, headed on this issue by Gerson, pressed violently for a denunciation of Petit by the Council, which did not feel strong enough to ignore the matter altogether. It wisely evaded an official pronouncement on Petit, limiting itself to a condemnation of tyrannicide in general terms, but the question troubled the Council at intervals until its end, wasting time, straining tempers, and reviving political

*Injudicious policy of the Council*

animosities which at first the Fathers seemed disposed to lay aside. Similar effects were produced by the similar case of John of Falkenberg, who in vindicating the Teutonic Order against the Poles had asserted the murder of princes to be justified in certain contingencies. In other cases the Council lost much prestige by failing to enforce its decisions. It was in fact defied with impunity by the civic authorities of Strasbourg, whose differences with their bishop had been laid before it, and even by John XXIII's old protector, Frederick of Habsburg, who had been encroaching on the rights of the Bishop of Trent.

That the Council should have meddled with these and like matters was the more regrettable since it became more and more desirable that it should hold itself aloof from political controversy. Every political aspiration had its spokesman at Constance, and every occurrence of political moment had its repercussion there. The renewal of active hostilities between England and France in the summer of 1415 naturally put a severe strain on the harmony of the Council. That strain became still more serious when Sigismund's attempt to mediate broke down, and he became the open ally of the King of England and, it was justly suspected, the secret supporter of the Duke of Burgundy. Opinion at Constance grouped itself increasingly along national lines. After the signing of the Treaty of Canterbury in August 1416 the Germans and the English were under instructions from their respective sovereigns to co-operate as far as possible. The French—or such of the French " nation " as obeyed Charles VI [1]—seem about the same time to have lost much of their interest in the real work of the Council and to have thought mainly of scoring political points off the English. They were greatly aided by Cardinals d'Ailly and Fillastre, whom Charles VI had appointed as his proctors at the Council. These two, particularly d'Ailly, had lost the zeal for the Council which they had once shown, offended by the discourtesy and suspicion, not to say contempt, with which the Sacred College was treated by the conciliar party after the deposition of John XXIII. The objects of the two men seem now to have been the election of a pope as soon as might be, the rehabilitation of the Sacred College, and the

*Political dissensions at Constance*

[1] Many of the French " nation " were subjects of the Empire.

humiliation, by whatever means, of the Germans and English. Before long there grew up a firmly-grounded *entente* between the College of Cardinals and the French.

D'Ailly's policy was much assisted by the arrival, in September 1416, of the envoys from Aragon, who in the following month, in association with the Portuguese, were formed into a "Spanish nation." It should be understood that none of the former supporters of Pope Benedict viewed the Capitulation of Narbonne with enthusiasm; they never cared anything about the authority of the Council of Constance or, to judge by their conduct, about the reform of the Church: they would make some sacrifices in the interests of union, but they were very jealous of the dignity of their respective countries and very eager to harvest whatever political advantages were to be reaped in the field of ecclesiastical controversy. The great majority of the members of the Council dreaded above everything the prolongation of the Schism, so that a body of men who cared little whether the Schism went on or not was in a very strong position. Thus the Aragonese, and later the Castilians, were able to exert an influence quite out of proportion to their numbers and ability, or the size, power, and prestige of the states they represented.

As soon as the Aragonese reached Constance, they began to raise questions of precedence, especially as between them and the English, of whom they were specially jealous. It happened that d'Ailly had lately been criticizing the procedure of the Council and investigating the right of the English, who certainly were very few in number, to form a separate "nation." Encouraged by the attitude of the Aragonese, he became so vehemently hostile towards the English that even the French tried to restrain him. Feelings rose to a high pitch, causing disorder in the Council's sessions and threatening armed conflict in the streets. Unfortunately this was not a dispute which the return of Sigismund, on January 27, 1417, was likely to compose. To the French he was an enemy, and indeed he was almost ostentatious in his friendliness towards the English. He still, it is true, wished to further the successful accomplishment of the Council's task, but his efforts to this end were regarded in many quarters as moves in a political game.

Henceforth, it must be recognized, d'Ailly, many of the other cardinals, and not a few of the French, particularly the envoys of the King, wanted to wreck the Council. The attack on the English continued. It led to no change in the Council's organization, for the English defended themselves stoutly, and were backed by Sigismund, the Germans, and the representatives of Burgundian territories. But it kept political passions alight, and increased the nervous strain which was beginning to tell on many of the members. There was abroad a feeling of weariness and disillusionment. Nothing much could be done until the Castilians came, and the proceedings of the commission on reform had aroused much doubt whether it could ever frame an adequate report which the Council would accept. There had been and still was an immense output of treatises and sermons advocating reform, but while few denied its necessity, nearly everyone fixed his attention on the shortcomings of all classes save his own. The most difficult problems were those raised by the Papacy's pecuniary demands and its encroachments on the patronage rights of corporations or individuals. The Italians were opposed to any drastic regulations on such matters. The English, who were all delegates of the Crown and took their orders from Henry V, were comparatively indifferent on the question of papal authority, knowing that the King of England had ample powers for checking papal encroachments in his territories. The German "nation" was perhaps more thoroughly in favour of drastic remedies than any other. Among the French zealous reformers abounded, but on the question of papal rights there was wide difference of opinion, the universities, headed by Paris, being generally hostile towards restriction of papal control over patronage. To complicate the work of reform, the autumn of 1416 saw a revival of the dispute as to the authority of a General Council in relation to the Papacy.

*Obstacles to reform*

The prospects of the Council were thus not very bright when on March 30, 1417, the envoys of Castile at last made their appearance. They said that they could not join the Council until they had received answers to certain questions, the most important being, how would the election of the new pope be conducted? There had lately been some debate as to when a new pope should be elected. The reform party held strongly that the election should be deferred until the Council had finished its work, but the old papal party, supported by the cardinals and many of the French, contended that it should take place as soon as possible. The inquiry of the Castilians brought the whole issue into the forefront, and emboldened the papalists to press their opinions. The reformers, on the other hand, declared that all talk about the election was premature. In this view they had the support of Sigismund.

*Dispute concerning the election of a new pope*

There followed a period of much confused and obscure intrigue. The Castilians stood firm, and evidently did not care if they broke the Council. Near the end of May, d'Ailly, in the treatise *Ad laudem*, suggested that the new pope should be chosen by the cardinals and an equal number of other members of the Council. The Castilians approved of the principle. So did the majority of the Italians and the French, while the Aragonese promised to accept it if the Castilians would unite with the Council. This they did on June 18.

Proceedings against Benedict XIII had been formally initiated at Constance in the previous autumn, and it was now possible to complete them. On July 26, he was deposed as a heretic and an incorrigible promoter of schism.

*Deposition of Benedict XIII, July 26, 1417*

Meanwhile, however, the Council had fallen into two fairly well-defined parties, whose relations tended to grow worse. On the one side were the cardinals and the majority of the three Latin "nations," on the other Sigismund, with the Germans and the English, supported by the Burgundians and other minorities. More than once during the summer the Council seemed on the point of breaking up, but Sigismund's genuine zeal for its success and the general desire to restore unity to the Church averted an irremediable catastrophe. In July the cardinals allayed passions by declaring that they were willing to reform the Papacy and the *curia* before making arrangements for a papal election. A new reform commission, to which each "nation" contributed five representatives, took up the work and perplexities of the one which had been sitting for the past two years.

*Increasing dissension in the Council*

**Change in the policy of the English**

It was not long, however, before the papal party, regardless of the recent undertaking of the cardinals, renewed its agitation for a speedy election. In September the English lost their influential, skilful, and widely respected leader Robert Hallam, Bishop of Salisbury, and almost simultaneously received new instructions from Henry V. Just what these were is not known, but the English suddenly consented to accept representation on a committee to consider arrangements for a papal election. Though this was a notable success for the papalists, a long and bitter struggle was still in prospect when about the beginning of October there arrived in Constance Henry Beaufort, Bishop of Winchester, Henry V's uncle, who was ostensibly breaking his journey as a pilgrim to Jerusalem. He had evidently been enjoined to influence Sigismund in favour of an early papal election on the ground that he was then in a specially good position to secure the choice of someone acceptable to himself and Henry. Beaufort's mediation was astonishingly effective, for in a few days it was arranged that the election should be held as soon as possible, that such reforms as the Council was willing to adopt should at once be enacted, and that the new pope, aided by the Council or a special commission, should reform the Papacy and the *curia*.

**The decree *Frequens*, Oct. 9, 1417**

Accordingly, a number of decrees received formal approval on October 9, at the Council's 39th General Session. In the most important, the decree *Frequens*, it was laid down that General Councils were to be held periodically, the first five years after the termination of the Council of Constance, the second seven years after the first, and the third and following at intervals of ten years. Another decree sought to provide for the automatic assembly of a General Council in the event of a new schism. Every new pope, it was enacted, should make a profession of his faith, and there were restrictions on the pope's power to translate bishops and on one or two of his financial claims. Though not to be despised, these decrees were not an impressive yield considering that the reform of the Church was one of the Council's main duties and that it had been sitting nearly three years.

A committee was chosen to settle the precise mode in which the pope should be elected, and its recommendations

were approved by the Council on October 30. All the
cardinals were to take part in the voting, and also six representatives of each "nation." To be elected a candidate must have two-thirds of the cardinals' votes and, besides, four from each of the national delegations. It was further decreed that, before the dissolution of the Council, the new pope should introduce reforms on eighteen specified points, the most notable being the number and character of the cardinals, papal taxation, annates, the collation of benefices, appeals to the *curia*, and the punishment of bad popes.

The conclave began on November 8, and three days later Cardinal Otto Colonna obtained the necessary majorities, the French delegation being the last to adhere to him. He had been known as a moderate supporter of the conciliar party, but at Constance had successfully run with the hare and hunted with the hounds. Men thought him amiable, but he was in no sense a popular or commanding figure. His election, nevertheless, caused enthusiastic rejoicing. Many members of the Council felt that their work was done.

Pope Martin V, as he called himself, lost no time in giving effect to his views on the powers of the Holy See. On the day after his election he laid down for the conduct of the papal chancery rules which gave him greater control over ecclesiastical appointments than that claimed by John XXIII. These regulations, however, were not published for three months, and at first it was generally believed that Martin was a friend of the moderate reformers. A new Reform Commission, consisting of six from each "nation" and six cardinals, was chosen to confer with the Pope concerning the eighteen points enumerated in the decree of October 30. But it was again impossible to obtain agreement on anything that really mattered; before Christmas the Commission suspended its proceedings for a month; and, with the object of discovering the highest common factor of the various views on reform, each "nation" was invited by the Pope to draw up a memorandum of suggestions respecting the eighteen points. In January Martin submitted to the Council a number of projected decrees. On few of these, however, was there any approach to agreement; and though Martin, whether sincerely or not, pressed for unanimous decisions, his exhortations had little effect.

He had good ground for entering into negotiations with the several nations for the arrangement of concordats.

Almost all the members of the Council now wanted above everything to go home. A deputation from the Eastern Church, which alleged its desire to restore the unity of all Christendom, was heard and answered with bare politeness. The Pope, with general approval, evaded a renewed demand for a definite pronouncement on the cases of Petit and Falkenberg. At the 43rd General Session, held on March 21, 1417, the fruit of the Pope's reforming activities was approved by the Council. Seven decrees were passed: they concerned the union and incorporation of churches, the revenues of vacant benefices, simony, dispensations, papal taxes, and the life and honour of the clergy. Though the Pope renounced one or two financial claims, his power was scarcely affected, and he had already declared that the memoranda of the nations revealed no desire for legislation as to the punishment or deposition of an unworthy pontiff. Most of the new decrees, indeed, did little but enjoin obedience to the existing law. Nevertheless, the Council acquiesced in Martin's pronouncement that the purpose of the decree of October 30, 1417, had now been fulfilled.

These measures were supplemented by three concordats, one for the Latin "nations," one for the Germans, one for the English. None was of any practical consequence. The first two bear a close resemblance to each other. They purport to restrict the number of cardinals, to limit the papal control over appointments to benefices, and to lighten the burden of annates. Each, however, had a time limit of five years, and neither was anywhere effectually applied. The English concordat was to endure for ever, as well it might, considering the triviality of its contents. It was soon forgotten.

Having announced that the next General Council would be held at Pavia after five years, Martin dissolved the Council of Constance. At the final session, on April 22, 1418, the Poles, dissatisfied with the Pope's attitude towards the Falkenberg case, appealed from him "to a future Council." It was an unpleasant but wholesome reminder that since Martin V's election the relation between himself and a General Council had never been explicitly defined.

Some authorities for chapter vii :—

i. Original sources—
  Mansi : *Sacrorum conciliorum collectio*, vols. xxvii and xxviii ; Raynaldus, *Annales*, vol. xxvii : see under chap. v.
  Arendt, P. : *Die Predigten des Konstanzer Konzils*, Freiburg, 1933.
  Dietrich von Niem : *De modis uniendi et reformandi ecclesiam in concilio universali*, ed. H. Heimpel (*Quellen zur Geistesgeschichte des Mittelalters und der Renaissance*, ed. W. Goetz, Bd. iii), Leipzig, 1933.
  Finke, H. : *Acta Concilii Constanciensis*, 4 vols., Munster, 1896–1928. (A most valuable collection of material.)
  Hardt, H. von der : *Magnum Oecumenicum Constantiense Concilium*, 7 vols., Helmstädt, 1697–1740. (Another invaluable collection. With this and Finke's alone an excellent history of the Council might be written.)
  Richental, U. von : *Chronik des Constanzer Concils*, ed. M. R. Buck, Tübingen, 1882.
  Windecke, E. : see under chap. vi.

ii. Works by modern writers—
  See the works of Creighton (vol. ii), Flick (vol. ii), Hauck, Hefele (vol. vii, pt. 1), Pastor, and Valois, under chap. v.
  Heimpel, H. : *Dietrich von Niem*, Münster, 1932.
  Huebler, B. : *Die Constanzer Reformation und die Concordate von 1418*, Leipzig, 1867.
  Jacob, E. F. : *Essays in the Conciliar Epoch*, Manchester, 1943.
  Kitts, E. J. : *In the Days of the Councils*, London, 1908 ; *Pope John XXIII and Master John Hus of Bohemia*, London, 1910.
  Wylie, J. H. : *The Council of Constance to the Death of John Hus*, London, 1900.

CHAPTER VIII

## THE COUNCILS OF SIENA AND BASEL

THE reform party had not shown to advantage in the closing stages of the Council of Constance. But it was far from being destroyed. If for a while many would-be reformers seemed to have lost some of their zeal, it was largely because the intentions of Pope Martin were still misunderstood. After all, it could be plausibly argued that the failure of the Council to accomplish an effective reform had been due almost wholly to its own dissensions, which the Pope had vainly striven to compose. Might not Martin, then, administer the medicine which the Council had withheld?

*Aims and policy of Martin V*

The real intentions of Martin were very simple. He wanted to recover for the Papacy all the temporal and spiritual power which had been so gravely impaired by the Babylonish captivity and the Schism. His achievements in the Papal States belong to the political history of Italy and are best considered elsewhere. But it must constantly be remembered that in secular politics Martin was extraordinarily successful. It was not until more than two years after the end of the Council of Constance that he was able to enter the dilapidated city of Rome, but in the next decade, with remarkably little strain upon his own resources, he reasserted papal authority over the States of the Church and gave them better government than they had enjoyed for generations.

Unfortunately this able Italian prince made but an indifferent head of the Christian Church. In that capacity Martin contented himself with a stubborn and unprincipled conservatism. The need for reform was acknowledged by all thoughtful men. And Martin was in a most favourable position to inaugurate a thorough cleansing. He had little to fear from rivals. The previous supporters of Gregory XII and John XXIII had submitted, and the latter, ransomed from prison by Martin himself, had accepted him as pope and died a short time afterwards. Benedict XIII remained obdurate till his belated death in 1422 or 1423, and he had a successor called Clement VIII, but though they had the nominal support of the King of Aragon and the Count of Armagnac, neither was ever really dangerous to Martin. Indeed, had he needed to kindle devotion to himself as against an opponent, he could have done nothing better than head an attack on abuses.

Nevertheless Martin set his face against any measures that would have materially changed existing conditions. Attempts to palliate his conduct only reveal the more clearly that both at Constance and afterwards he consented only to such reforms as were futile or unavoidable. From his own standpoint such conduct was foolish, for it imperilled the very office whose interests he imagined himself to be upholding. What seems to have led Martin astray was a confusion in his mind between a desire for reform and a belief in the superiority of General Councils to popes. Whether Martin was justified in his resistance to the doctrine of conciliar supremacy turns on points of theology which do not concern us here. There has been much dispute as to whether, before the end of the Council of Constance, Martin did formally accept that doctrine. The truth probably is that he never did so expressly, but that he deliberately tried to give the impression that he approved of it. At all events Martin, as Pope, hated Councils ; and as many who were eager for reform were also advocates of conciliar supremacy, he concluded, quite erroneously, that the two parties were identical. If, during his pontificate, they tended to become so, it was largely due to his own attitude. The doctrine of the superiority of a General Council to the pope appealed in itself to none but a few ecclesiastical politicians and a few students of political philosophy. Most of those who accepted it were led to do so by the suspicion, amply justified by Martin, that it was only through a General Council and in the teeth of the Papacy that any real reform would be achieved. But it was merely reform that they wanted ; they cared little whence it came ; and if Martin had headed them in an attack on abuses, the chances are that they would soon have forgotten their constitutional theories.

To such considerations Martin shut his eyes. He knew,

nevertheless. that he must walk warily. It was a General Council that had put him where he was, and he had the fate of John XXIII to remind him of what a General Council might do with him thereafter. Before he actually left Constance, in fact, he received a sharp warning. Alarmed by the appeal of the Poles to a future Council, he caused to be read in consistory, on May 10, 1418, a bull which declared it unlawful to appeal from judgments or pronouncements of the pope on any subject. The outcry was prompt and startling. There was talk of heresy; and the great Gerson wrote a treatise in which he argued that if Martin's declaration was accepted, the Councils of Pisa and Constance were void, and either Benedict XIII or John XXIII was the true pope. Nothing more was heard of the bull, and Martin never again raised the issue in plain terms. Naturally, therefore, he did not dare to defy the decree *Frequens* or to disregard his announcement that the next General Council would be held at Pavia in 1423. The choice of Pavia, however, he regretted because of the enmity that subsisted between him and the Duke of Milan, and though the Council was opened there by papal legates on April 23, reasons were soon found for transferring it to Siena, where it would be more amenable to papal influence. At the moment, indeed, it could not cause much concern to anyone. It contained only four members of the German " nation " and only six of the French, and while the English were rather more numerous, the only Italians present apart from local ecclesiastics were the papal legates, and there were no Spaniards at all.

Even had Martin been friendly to the Council, it could hardly have been successful. The keenest reformers had not recovered their vigour after the wearisome strain of the Council of Constance. There was no fresh schism to heal, no new heresy to condemn. The most powerful states of Europe had political preoccupations of unusual urgency. Nevertheless, but for the Pope's machinations, the Council might have done much better.

Though the first formal session was held at Siena in July 1423, the second did not take place till November. There was difficulty in arranging satisfactory safe-conducts for the timid and suspicious " fathers," and the Pope, probably on purpose, caused delay by promising to attend in person and then failing to do so. At the second session, attended by two cardinals and twenty-five mitred prelates, heresy was denounced, the decrees of Constance against Wycliffe and Hus were confirmed, and Benedict and his followers were once more condemned. Union with the Greeks (one of the official tasks of the Council) was asserted to be impracticable at the moment, and the Council therefore turned to the work of reform.

Very soon the old differences of opinion made themselves felt. After some wrangling, it was resolved that each nation should draw up its own programme of reform, so that the Council might know for certain how much agreement there was. The French were ready first. They demanded the "liberties" of the French Church and proposed that the Pope should levy no taxes whatever save on the laity of the Papal States; but for the most part their suggestions were no more drastic than those made by advanced reformers at Constance. The legates, however, were much perturbed, and soon after the beginning of 1424 it became known that they would seize the first opportunity to dissolve the Council.

The reform party made but a poor defence. The unity of the French nation was impaired, partly by intrigue, partly by the addition to it of a number of French officials from the *curia*, partly by the singular conduct of the Archbishop of Rouen, who arrived as an envoy from the Duke of Bedford, and, after being welcomed and made president of the French "nation" as an enthusiastic reformer, lent himself to the schemes of the Pope. The other "nations" seemed to despair; members of the Council began to go away; and those that remained designated Basel as the seat of the next Council. A handful of die-hards, mostly French, tried to carry on business, but on March 7 the papal legates fled and proclaimed the dissolution of the Council. A few protests were raised, but nearly all the remaining members acquiesced. *The Council defeated by the Pope: its end, March 7, 1424*

Martin had attained his end. Only by a detailed examination of the original sources relating to the Council can one form a just impression of his influence on its fortune. Henceforth, at all events, the reform party had no illusions about him; he was an enemy. It was idle for him to appoint a committee of cardinals to inquire into and amend abuses in the *curia* and the Church, and to base on their report a long constitution which, even if put into effect, would have been ludicrously inadequate. The reformers fixed their hopes on the next Council, which, according to the decree *Frequens*, must be held in 1431. If Martin had hoped that he might evade it, he was grievously disappointed. Apart from would-be reformers, everyone who wished for his own purposes to put pressure on the Pope urged the early summons of the dreaded assembly—Sigismund in 1424, the Duke of Bedford in 1425, perhaps Charles VII in the following year. The sensational victories of the Hussites, too, added to the demand for the Council. The secular arm served well enough against a solitary Hus or Jerome, but Zizka and Procop brought home to many its defects as a theological argument. Still, the Pope's intentions remained obscure until the last moment, despite the pleas and exhortations and protests that poured in upon him during 1430. One of these, an anonymous manifesto backed by two princes and placarded in several places in Rome, threatened plainly that if Martin did not promote the success of the Council by every means in his power, he would suffer the lot of John XXIII. The princes were almost certainly important German potentates; the document dismayed the papalist party, heartened their opponents, and caused the Sacred College to press Martin urgently to fulfil his duty. Accordingly, albeit with a heavy heart, Martin, on February 1, 1431, named as president of the Council Julian Cesarini, who as papal legate was about to head a new crusade against the Hussites. Cesarini was a cardinal of noble birth, only thirty-two years old, a fine scholar, a tactful diplomatist, and specially renowned for his continence, which seemed to contemporaries singular in a member of the Sacred College. Before Cesarini heard of his new appointment Martin V, on February 20, died of apoplexy.

On March 3 the cardinals elected Cardinal Gabriel Condolmaro, a Venetian of forty-seven, nephew of Gregory XII. He was of no distinction as a scholar; but he had proved himself a competent administrator, his private life was respectable, he was thought to be in favour of reform, and he had advocated the summons of the Council of Basel. He was bound by an agreement into which all the cardinals had entered before the conclave—namely, that the new pope should reform the Holy See and the *curia* with the advice of the Sacred College, and that the reforms undertaken by the Council should concern only the rest of the clergy and the laity.

The General Council should have been sitting through March, but at the end of the following month only a mere handful of strangers had appeared at Basel. On May 30, however, the new Pope, who called himself Eugenius IV, authorized Cesarini to preside if a sufficient number of prelates attended. At last, on July 23, 1431, the Council was officially opened by two deputy-presidents. But the attendance was still miserably thin, and the Council's life would doubtless have been short had not the Pope been preoccupied by civil strife in and around Rome. Before he was able to seize the opportunity of infanticide, the Hussites had been heard approaching by the crusaders near Tauss, and a few weeks later Cesarini appeared at Basel convinced that a General Council was the one means of dealing with the Bohemian heresy. At his instance the Pope was begged to come in person. The clergy of the whole Church were exhorted to assemble in haste. And on October 15 the Council wrote to the Hussite leaders inviting them to send to Basel a delegation which should discuss with the assembled Fathers, freely and on an equal footing, the restoration of unity.

*The Council of Basel opened, July 28, 1431*

*The Hussites invited to Basel, October 1431*

At Basel enthusiasm was running high, and a spirit of optimism was abroad. At the Council's first formal session, held on December 14, 1431, the decree *Frequens* was renewed, and the objects of the Council were declared to be the extirpation of heresy, the re-establishment of peace in Europe, and the reform of the Church. One may imagine therefore the dismayed chagrin with which the members learned that an emissary from the Pope had brought a bull dissolving the Council. It happened that just at this juncture communication between Rome and Basel was inexplicably slow ; each side in the ensuing dispute had misleading notions about the mood and intentions of the other ; and the consequence was that rash things were said and done which would have been avoided had the Pope and the Council been in

*Dissolution of the Council announced by Eugenius IV*

closer touch. The events of this winter are bewildering. But it slowly became clear that the Pope had issued two bulls, the purport of which was that the Council was dissolved, that all prelates were to assemble at Bologna in 1433 to hold an extra Council, that the third Council under the decree *Frequens* should meet at Avignon in ten years' time, and that the war against the Czechs should continue. Eugenius was determined to get the Council on to papal territory, and he shrank with horror from the idea of bargaining with excommunicated heretics. He had, however, wholly misapprehended the situation. The Council refused to dissolve. It vindicated its disobedience by appealing to the decrees of Constance, and passed new ones denying anyone's right to dissolve or transfer it.

*Eugenius defied by the Council*

The subsequent history of the Council of Basel falls into three main divisions. Throughout 1432 and 1433 it was engaged in a bitter conflict with Eugenius, which ended early in 1434 with the Council's victory. From 1434 to 1436 the Council was at the height of its power and reputation, and its relations with the Pope were outwardly amicable. During 1436, however, they again became bad, and by the end of the year the two were in undissembled enmity. The Pope soon began to get the upper hand, but the Council—or part of it—struggled tenaciously though vainly for many years and did not finally capitulate until 1449. But for long its fortunes had depended on people whose pleasure it had to await and whom it scarcely influenced.

In the first phase of the conflict with the Pope, the honours unquestionably lay with the Council. Not only did it win, but it acted with a firmness and dignity which stand in admirable contrast with the duplicity and vacillation of Eugenius. At Basel the ruling motive was a desire for reform. The chief enemy of reform, it was believed, was the Papacy. So conciliar supremacy must be maintained, in order that Eugenius might be lawfully overridden. At the outset the Council was not revolutionary in temper, but the maladroit obstinacy of the Pope stirred up strong passions, and some very radical opinions were expressed. But while there was for a time an almost unanimous denial of the absolute claims put forward by the Pope, there was never any agreement

*Conflict of Pope and Council, 1432–4*

concerning the position which was rightly his. All the principal views propounded during the Schism were represented at Basel. This diversity of opinion on constructive policy was naturally a grave handicap to the Council in the long run, but at first, when it was fighting for its existence, negative convictions sufficed to hold it together.

On the Pope the Council steadily and relentlessly increased its pressure. In April 1432 it renewed the decrees of the fifth session of the Council of Constance, and cited the Pope to appear at Basel. It denied his right to create cardinals as long as he stayed away, and summoned the existing cardinals to attend. The Pope, impressed at last, sought to conciliate the Council by some practical concessions, but was answered by a stern reassertion of the principle of conciliar sovereignty. Most of the cardinals made their peace with the Council, and in September 1432 Cesarini, who had remained in Basel after obeying the Pope's command to resign the presidency in the previous winter, accepted the Council's invitation to resume that position. In the following December the Council passed a decree in which it demanded the withdrawal of the bull of dissolution and the adherence of the Pope to the Council within sixty days. In case of non-compliance it would act as the Holy Ghost should inspire. This threat unnerved the members of the *curia*, and, backed as it was by urgent representations from the German Electors, it forced Eugenius to admit defeat. On February 14, 1433, he issued a bull authorizing the holding of a General Council at Basel, alleging that many of his previous objections to the place had been modified by the course of events.

To the astonishment of Eugenius the Council was unmoved. The Pope had said nothing of what the Council had already done. Before it would accept the presidents whom he had nominated, he must acknowledge that it had been a true Council ever since its beginning and must revoke his bulls of dissolution. It voted that if he failed to attend or to send representatives empowered to act for him, he would be liable to suspension or even deposition. In the summer of 1433 the Council, by 363 votes to 23, decided in favour of prompt action against him.

That it still delayed was due to the restraining influence

of Sigismund, who had been crowned Emperor by the Pope in May, and of the other temporal rulers represented at Basel. On the whole they were on the side of the Council, but they dreaded a new schism and were opposed to all precipitate action. The Council deferred to them impatiently, but it was mainly the folly of the Pope that caused the abandonment of their efforts to save him from humiliation. Believing that he had won Sigismund over to his cause, Eugenius resolved on a counter-attack, and in the summer of 1433 issued a series of bulls which showed clearly the true value of the concessions of the preceding winter. He forbade the Council to attempt anything apart from its three tasks of suppressing heresy, restoring European peace, and reforming the Church. A little later he annulled everything it had done outside its proper field, including in this category all its acts against himself, the Holy See, and the *curia*. Provided that it should recognize such acts as null and void and accept the presidents named by him,[1] he would graciously deem the Council to have been valid from the first and would withdraw the bull of dissolution. A few days afterwards, on the receipt of disagreeable news from Basel, he sent to the temporal authorities of Europe a circular letter in which he denounced the Council's conduct, and he annulled a number of decrees in which the Council had lately confirmed the principles laid down at Constance about papal authority. If the so-called bull *Deus novit*, dated September 13, is genuine [2]—and the evidence is on the whole in its favour—he proceeded to declare that the conduct of the Council approximated to heresy, to deny that it had had a continuous existence since its opening, to assert the authority of the Pope over all Councils, to denounce as heretical any doctrine to the contrary, and to hint that Christian princes ought to use the secular arm against the " Fathers."

**Victory of the Council, April 1434**  Again Eugenius had miscalculated. The kings and princes of Europe were unfavourably impressed, and from quarters which he had believed friendly came advice to sur-

---

[1] There was a version of the bull (*Dudum sacrum*), shown to Sigismund, from which the provisoes were omitted.

[2] The Pope afterwards denied it, but his bare word unfortunately goes for little. The document was widely published and discussed.

render. In Italy, the condottieri Sforza and Fortebraccio, probably at the instance of the Duke of Milan, occupied part of the Papal States. The Pope decided to forestall further measures by the Council, and in December 1433, by the second bull *Dudum sacrum*, he recognized that the Council had been canonical throughout, that his dissolution of it was invalid, and that it ought to continue in order to deal with its three tasks; he declared, further, that he would loyally promote the success of the Council and revoked everything he had done to its detriment. On February 5, 1434, the Council declared that Eugenius had given full satisfaction. In April, after a little dispute respecting the oath to be taken by them, the presidents named by the Pope were admitted. Peace was officially established.

This striking victory of the Council could not have been gained but that public opinion in Europe was generally on its side. During 1432 the number of those attending became respectable. The secular potentates of western and central Europe one by one acknowledged it and sent embassies to represent them. As we have seen, they more than once brought political pressure to bear on Eugenius, though on the other hand there was a risk that the Council would fall overmuch under their influence.

At the same time European opinion never became deeply concerned over the relations between the Council and the Papacy. It was affected far more by the Council's handling of the Hussite problem. What impressed Europe most was the Convention of Eger, of May 1432, whereby the terrible Hussites agreed to send representatives to discuss with the Council the possibility of reconciliation, and the actual appearance at Basel, in January 1433, of fifteen Bohemian delegates, including the great Procop himself. It was not merely that the "Fathers" of Basel deigned to debate with condemned heretics, but in deference to Hussite prejudice harlots were kept off the Basel streets and members of the Council were instructed to avoid drunkenness, dancing, and gambling. The heretics were allowed to state their views fully, and treated as a rule with a politeness which approached cordiality. But, convinced after some weeks that their hopes of converting the Council were vain, they declared that they had not been authorized to make any concessions,

*The Hussites at Basel, Jan.-April 1433*

and that, if the negotiations were to go further, the Council must send a mission to Bohemia to confer with the Diet.

*Strife in Bohemia: battle of Lipan, May 30, 1434*

The Hussites left Basel in April 1433. Between then and the end of the year, two embassies of the Council visited Bohemia, where they cleverly fomented the quarrels among the Hussites. The number of Bohemians who favoured conciliation grew rapidly. Civil war broke out between them and the more advanced reformers, and on May 30, 1434, the latter were overwhelmed at the battle of Lipan. Everyone outside Bohemia rightly judged that the aggressive force of the Hussite cause was gone. And in the opinion of Europe it was the Council that was chiefly to be thanked for this happy result.

*Strength and organization of the Council*

Triumphant and respected, the Council had a chance of making reforms of real and lasting value. It now had about five hundred members. There were many French and Germans, Italians were less numerous, Spaniards and English relatively rare. Such comparisons, however, were of less interest than they had been at Constance, for at Basel the division into "nations" was not officially adopted. It is true that national animosities often ran high, and that the members tended to form themselves into national groups, which sometimes had much influence on the Council's actions. But for the formal transaction of business the Council was divided into four committees or "deputations," which dealt respectively with the suppression of heresy, the pacification of Europe, the reform of the Church, and matters of organization, personnel, and sudden emergency. The representatives of each nation were distributed equally among the committees. Of course every proposal had to be submitted to the whole Council before it could be promulgated as a decree. In the Deputations ample opportunity for discussion seems to have been given, and very humble members might turn the course of a debate. There were never more than 105 mitred prelates at Basel, and they were far outnumbered by a very miscellaneous crowd of other clergy. Rules concerning admission had been made, but the imposing committee charged with their application seems to have paid little heed to them, and though the cooks and grooms mentioned by Aeneas Sylvius among the

"Fathers" may have been merely rhetorical figures, we know that the Council included many who were clergy only in name, and some who were not even that.

In the day of its prosperity this mixed assemblage flung away many of its claims to respect. Some of its members were moved by personal hatred of Eugenius; others liked to feel that they were lording it over the Church; and the Pope himself was continually giving ground for the suspicion that his surrender was not sincere. At all events, the Council acted as though the Papacy had been suspended, entertaining judicial causes, receiving money from papal collectors, demanding taxes from the clergy, and meddling in all sorts of matters for which machinery was already provided or which did not concern it at all. Such behaviour wasted time, alienated public opinion, and convinced Eugenius that conciliation only encouraged radicalism. *Unwise behaviour of the Council*

It has often been said that the Council's folly was due to its democratic organization. It is an attractive and plausible theory, but there is little concrete evidence in favour of it. The most extravagant views found spokesmen at Basel in bishops and even cardinals. The truth rather is that the councillors of Basel, with a few striking exceptions, were not men of high moral or intellectual calibre. They could endure adversity but not success, and their fine principles seldom resisted for long the allurements of practical expediency.

Nevertheless, from 1434 to 1436 things seemed to be going well with the Council. Though the negotiations with the Hussites were unexpectedly prolonged, Bohemia was officially reconciled with the Church at Iglau in July 1436. The accomplishment of this hollow formality was due to Sigismund rather than the Council, but the Council's envoys had been conspicuous throughout the negotiations and were widely supposed to have played a decisive part.

The Council also addressed itself, somewhat tardily, to the work of reform. On this there was less dissension than there had been at Constance, most conservatives having shunned the Council; but it was temptingly easy to reform the absent and those who were weakly represented. Thus, in November 1433, there had been passed a decree prescribing the regular holding of provincial and diocesan synods which should control metropolitans and bishops just as General *The Council's reforming decrees of June 1435*

Councils were to control the pope. For the next eighteen months, however, no reforms of any consequence were announced, and the Council incurred much criticism for its apparent inactivity. But in June 1435 the Council, along with ten decrees of small moment, issued one which threatened to turn the existing order upside down. No payment was to be demanded at any stage of an appointment to an ecclesiastical benefice, or for the sealing of bulls, or under the name of annates or any similar title. If the Pope resisted this decree, the Council would take appropriate measures.

Had the decree been executed, the Papacy, in the sense attached to the name since the days of Hildebrand, would have ceased to exist. It is true that the Council declared its readiness to compensate the Pope and the cardinals for what they were losing; but when asked what it proposed to do, it refused to give an immediate answer, insisting that Eugenius must confirm the decree irrespective of the Council's further intentions. This the Pope would not do, but for a while he assumed a non-committal attitude, taking the blow much more coolly than had been expected. Really he was feeling much more confident than he had been for some time. Driven from Rome in the spring of 1434, he had been in Florence ever since, but of late the political situation in Italy had turned in his favour. He was informed, too, that many members of the Council thought that the majority was going too far. And he was particularly encouraged by his relations with the Greeks.

The Council, the Pope, and the Eastern Church

It was in fact Eugenius himself who had brought to the fore the question of union with the Eastern Church. The Byzantine Emperor and his leading prelates welcomed his overtures in the hope that the subsequent negotiations might enable them to get substantial aid from the west against the Turk. The Council of Basel dared not allow the Pope a free hand in the matter. For some three years, in fact, the Council and the Pope had each been trying to convince the Greeks that no good could come out of dealings with the other. After much tortuous bargaining, it was agreed between the Council and the Greeks, in the autumn of 1435, that the conference to discuss union should be held in a town on the coast, as the Greeks steadfastly refused to go to Basel itself, that the Council should pay the expenses of the Greek delegation, and that the Pope should be present in person. The Council, in fact, was being driven to accept conditions very agreeable to Eugenius.

The Council became the more eager to show the Greeks that the Pope was really of but small account. The more hotheaded of its members began a new offensive against him. It was not hard to show that he had ignored some of the Council's reforming measures and had countenanced vexatious and frivolous proceedings in the *curia* against some of its members. In January 1436 he was called upon to withdraw everything he had done against the Council and to confirm all its decrees. He was subjected to obloquy in a circular addressed to all Christian princes. New reforming decrees, enacted in March, laid down rules about the conduct, personal and official, of pope and cardinals, and imposed on the pope a novel form of oath. In April, notwithstanding bitter opposition from both papalists and reformers, the Council voted a plenary indulgence to all who should contribute towards the expenses of the projected Council of Union with the Greeks. To the Pope's overtures on annates and the Greek question, uncompromising and aggressive answers were returned. *Renewed quarrel between Council and Pope, 1436*

Eugenius for some time continued to treat the Council politely. But in the summer of 1436 he took up its challenge. In a letter to the princes of Europe he accused the Council of interfering in matters beyond its competence, of sterility even within its usurped sphere, and of a desire to destroy the authority of the Pope and make the government of the Church a democracy.

As if it were not enough to break with the Pope, the Council proceeded to exasperate the Greeks. With incomprehensible folly it tried to go back on the agreement of the previous year, and to insist that the conference should be held, if not at Basel, then at Avignon, regardless of a Greek envoy who asserted plainly that the treaty must be observed. Through the winter of 1436–7 there was fierce strife over this at Basel. Cesarini and a large following urged that an Italian city should be chosen; but the majority, under the leadership of Louis d'Aleman, Cardinal of Arles, refused to change its mind. So high did feeling run in the spring of 1437 that at the twenty-fifth session, held on May 7, each party tried to *Dissension in the Council* seize the high altar of Basel cathedral and the president's chair, swords were drawn, and blows struck. Eventually two bishops started simultaneously to read rival decrees. The minority, whose decree was the shorter, sang *Te Deum* as soon as its recital was ended, but the majority were in time to start the hymn before their opponents had finished. The majority decree stated that the Council of Union was to be at Basel, or, if the Greeks were obdurately opposed to that, at Avignon or somewhere in Savoy. The minority resolved that it should be at a town named in earlier negotiations and agreeable to the Pope and the Greeks.

After this session, the Council would have done well to dissolve itself. It was irremediably split, and both parties had lost their self-respect and sense of proportion. Nevertheless they acted together for a little longer, and one of them still had years of undistinguished life before it. Over the sequel there is fortunately no need to linger.

Surrender or attack were the only alternatives before the Council. On July 31, 1437, though Cesarini refused to preside, Eugenius was cited to answer charges of having refused to introduce reform, raised new scandals in the Church, and caused schism by disregarding the decrees of the Council. As the Pope made no response, he was, on October 1, pronounced guilty of contumacy.

Meanwhile the Pope had issued the bull *Doctoris gentium* of September 18, 1437. If the Council persisted in its action against the Pope it was to be transferred to Ferrara after thirty days, and in any event it must move thither as soon as the Greeks reached Italy. The Council defiantly answered the bull point by point, announcing that unless Eugenius gave way, he would be suspended at the end of four months after the issue of his last bull and deposed at the end of six.

*The Pope's success with the Greeks*

At such threats, however, the Pope could laugh, for he had decisively worsted the Council in the competition for the confidence of the Greeks. A deputation, chosen partly by Eugenius and partly by the minority at Basel, had reached Constantinople early in the autumn of 1437, bringing troops for the defence of the city and ships for the transport of the Greek representatives to the Council of Union. Envoys and ships sent soon afterwards by the Basel majority made no impression on the Greeks, whose envoys embarked in

November on the vessels belonging to the other party. When this was known at Basel, Cesarini made a last effort to induce the Council to meet the Greeks at Ferrara, and on his failure left the city with numerous supporters, to be warmly welcomed in Italy.

For the next eighteen months the discussions with the Greeks at Ferrara and Florence interested Europe more than what went on at Basel, but the truth is that both councils were futile. The chief motive of nearly all the Greeks was political, while the Pope was thinking mainly of exalting the prestige of the Holy See, especially at the expense of the Fathers at Basel. *The Greeks at Ferrara and Florence, March 1438–July 1439*

The Eastern Emperor, the Patriarch of Constantinople, and twenty-two Orthodox bishops, with a train of priests, officials, and others, numbering in all seven hundred persons, reached Ferrara in the spring of 1438. The Greeks deliberately wasted time, for their Emperor hoped to secure military aid from western Europe without risking a defeat of his Church in theological controversy, and it was not until the autumn that, perceiving the futility of this policy, he allowed his clergy to deal seriously with the crucial difficulty—the doctrine of the procession of the Holy Ghost. Was it ever lawful for a section of the Church to make an addition to the Creed, as the Latins had done ? And if it were, was it true that the Holy Ghost proceeded from the Son as well as from the Father ? The debate continued at great length, both sides showing much theological learning and dialectical acumen, together with a dignity and good temper abnormal in religious controversy. In the winter the Pope persuaded the Council to move to Florence, where it was undoubtedly in greater security and comfort; but the removal suspended proceedings for nearly two months. There was as yet no agreement about the Holy Ghost, but some of the Greeks, fearing to go home without achieving anything, became more compliant, and in June 1439 a majority accepted a formula stating that the disputed addition to the Creed was warranted by the Fathers and that the Holy Ghost proceeded from the Father and the Son as from one origin and cause. At the last moment, however, when several minor questions had been easily settled, there was nearly a complete breach over papal supremacy. All the Greeks wished their Church to retain a considerable measure of autonomy, while Eugenius for some time insisted that the Papacy must wield as much authority in the East as in the West. In the end, however, the adoption of an inconclusive and indeed meaningless formula enabled 115 Catholic prelates and all the Greek prelates in Florence save one to sign the decree of Union on July 5, 1439. Though Eugenius wanted the Greeks to discuss other matters, they promptly went home.

*The Union rejected in the East*

When the terms of the Union became known, they provoked an outburst of furious anger in what was left of the Eastern Empire. The Emperor, while never repudiating the agreement, did not venture to promulgate it officially. Isidore, Archbishop of Kieff, and Bessarion, Archbishop of Nicaea, identified themselves with the western Church and received cardinals' hats. A few Russian dioceses accepted the Union, but otherwise the Orthodox Church scarcely noticed what had been done at Ferrara and Florence.

*Continuance of the Council of Florence*

The Council of Florence did not end when the Greeks left it. On September 4, 1439, in the important decree *Moyses*, it denied the assertions, lately reiterated at Basel, that a General Council was superior to a pope, and that a pope might not dissolve, adjourn, or transfer a General Council. It was kept officially alive for six more years, perhaps longer, though after 1443 it was formally transferred to Rome. Its sole function was to pass decrees of union with eastern sects, but Eugenius liked to be able to say that he was in consultation with a General Council. How and when it ended is not known.

*Eugenius IV suspended by the Council of Basel, Jan. 24, 1438*

Meanwhile the depleted Council of Basel kept up its fight with more success than might have been anticipated. On January 24, 1438, it declared Eugenius suspended from the exercise of his papal functions, but under political pressure it deferred further measures against him for more than a year. In the summer of this year the French promulgated the Pragmatic Sanction of Bourges, which accepted for the French Church the most notable of the reforming decrees passed at Basel and, while refraining from any repudiation of Eugenius, favoured the Council's views on ecclesiastical authority. The German Electors had already declared their neutrality as between Eugenius and the Council, but early in 1439, at a Diet at Mainz, they announced that they accepted the Basel decrees about the supremacy of General Councils, papal provisions and reservations, the freedom of ecclesiastical elections, annates, and other matters.

The Council of Basel was emboldened to resume proceedings against Eugenius. In May 1439, the theory of conciliar sovereignty was solemnly proclaimed a dogma of the Church. The strong party which advocated further delay was outwitted by Louis d'Aleman, commonly called the Cardinal of Arles, and outvoted by the lesser clergy who supported him. On June 23, 1439, Eugenius was formally declared a heretic for denying the doctrine that a General Council had authority over all Christians. Two days later, in the presence of thirty-nine prelates and about 200 of the lower clergy, he was solemnly deposed. *His deposition announced, June 25, 1439*

The election of a new pope was deferred until November, when an electoral commission, specially appointed by the Council, chose Amadeus, Duke of Savoy, who took the name of Felix V. Amadeus had ruled Savoy successfully for forty years, but since 1431 he had secluded himself with seven companions at Ripaille, where he led an existence which, however devout, was certainly not austere. He had shown a special interest in the Council, and his election was not unexpected. But the sequel was disappointing to both parties. Felix was not content with the power and dignity which the radicals at the Council were willing to accord him. He insisted in particular that a proper revenue should be allotted to him and his court, and the Council, which had hoped that Felix would support the Papacy out of his private fortune, was forced to transgress some of its own decrees to raise the money. Nevertheless, Felix continued to complain of niggardly treatment, while the Council criticized him for lack of vigour and his officers for rapacity. The election of an antipope, in fact, was a failure. Felix was recognized by a number of universities, by a few German princes, and by Elizabeth of Hungary, widow of Albert King of the Romans. Aragon and Milan deliberately wavered in their attitude. But France, Castile, England, and most of Italy continued to acknowledge Eugenius as true pope, even though they might not always be willing to support him as against the Council of Basel. The ambiguous policy of Germany kept the Council in existence and Felix on his throne, but near the *Election of Felix V, Nov. 5, 1439* end of 1442, tired of the petty bickerings at Basel, the Pope went to live at Lausanne.

**The last years of the Council**

On May 16, 1443, the Council at Basel, at its 45th General Session, decreed that in three years a new General Council should meet at Lyons, until when it should itself continue to sit at Basel. But this proved to be the last General Session held there. Henceforth, with dwindling numbers, the Council busied itself with little save petty litigation. Its zeal for reform had virtually vanished some years earlier.

As few people showed any interest in the projected Council at Lyons, the Council of Basel still clung to life after 1446. What brought it to an end was the reconciliation of Germany with the Papacy in 1447, which is described below. In the negotiations which led to it, the Council had from time to time sought to make itself felt, but never with any effect. No sooner had Germany restored its obedience to Rome than Frederick III ordered the civic authorities of Basel to expel the remnant of the Council; but it was not until June 1448, when Frederick's command had been repeated, with a threat of the ban of the Empire, that the Fathers were asked to depart.

**The Council transferred to Lausanne, July 1448**

On July 7, 1448, they were escorted to Lausanne, whither they declared the Council to have been transferred. They soon held a formal session, in which they proclaimed themselves ready to do all they could to restore peace and unity to the Church. Just as things were becoming comic, however, the mediation of the Kings of France and England brought them to a seemly end. Eugenius IV had died the year before, and the new pope, Nicolas V, was disposed to be gracious, while Felix was willing to abdicate. After friendly bargaining, Felix, on April 7, 1449, in the Second General Session of the Council of Lausanne, solemnly announced his resignation. On April 19 the Council elected as pope Thomas of Sarzana (called in his obedience Nicolas V), having been assured of his belief that a General Council holds its authority immediately of Christ and that all Christians must obey it in things which concern the Faith, the extirpation of schism, and the reform of the Church in head and members.

**The Council dissolved, April 25, 1449**

Six days later the Council voted its own dissolution. It made a timely and gallant ending, and had it always faced facts and consulted its own dignity as it did in its last days, it would have accomplished more and left a better name behind it.

Its end marked the failure of a great movement and rendered inevitable one even more momentous.

Some authorities for chapter viii:—
i. Original sources—
   Bartôs, E. M. : *Orationes quibus Nicolaus de Pelhrimov, Taboritarum Episcopus, et Ulricus de Zuginio, Orphanorum Sacerdos, articulos de peccatis publicis puniendis et libertate verbi Dei in Concilio Basiliensi anno 1433 in eunte defenderunt*, Tabor, 1935.
   Mansi : *Sacrorum conciliorum collectio*, vols. xxviii-xxxii ; Raynaldus, *Annales*, vols. xxvii-xxix : see under chap. v.
   Aeneas Sylvius Piccolomini : De rebus Basileae gestis Commentarius, ed. C. Fea, Rome, 1823.
   Concilium Basiliense : *Studien und Quellen zur Geschichte des Konzils von Basel*, ed. J. Haller and others, 8 vols., Basel, 1896–1936. (A most important collection, which has never been thoroughly explored.)
   *Monumenta conciliorum generalium seculi decimi quinti*, 3 vols., Vienna, 1857–96. (These volumes contain the histories of the Council by John of Ragusa and John of Segovia.)
   Traversari, Ambrogio : *Latinae epistolae*, ed. L. Méhus, 1759.
ii. Modern works—
   See the works of Creighton (vols. ii, iii, iv), Hauck, Hefele (vol. vii, pts. 1 and 2), and Pastor, under chap. v ; and add
   N. Valois : *Le Pape et le Concile*, 2 vols., Paris, 1909. (A work of considerable value, especially for its account of the Council of Siena, but not so successful as the author's earlier work on the Great Schism.)

[1378–

## CHAPTER IX

## JOHN HUS AND HIS FOLLOWERS

Political status of Bohemia

DURING the Council of Constance, the affairs of the kingdom of Bohemia forced themselves on the attention of all Europe. Bohemia, with its dependency the margraviate of Moravia, held an anomalous position. Though a kingdom, it was ruled by a vassal of the King of the Germans. The King of Bohemia was one of the seven Electors, yet he had for long enjoyed a measure of independence which no other German prince possessed. While the Bohemian throne was elective, the family of the Přemyslids had held it until its extinction in 1305, and thereafter it had descended from father to son in the House of Luxemburg. At the same time, owing to the growth—albeit tardy—of feudalism, the actual authority of the Bohemian king was greatly restricted.

Its population

The population of the country was mainly Czech and therefore Slavonic in blood, and though its neighbours on three sides were German-speaking, it had felt the pressure of the German advance eastward less than any of the other Slavonic territories bordering on Germany. Still, there was a German element in its population. German princesses, married to Bohemian dukes or kings, had brought with them German noblemen and officials who had settled in the country. In the twelfth and thirteenth centuries German colonists had established themselves, mainly near the frontiers, but also occasionally in small pockets in the heart of the kingdom. They had tenaciously maintained their customs and language, as they do to this day. German merchants had arrived also, and the urban population was predominantly German. Bohemia being a comparatively backward country, the influence of German culture on its people was considerable. Just as the nobles of western Germany imitated the French, so did the nobles of Bohemia imitate the Germans. Some of them had actually Germanized their names.

Until the middle of the fourteenth century Bohemia formed part of the ecclesiastical province of Mainz; there were numerous Germans among the Bohemian clergy, and German influence on the Church in Bohemia had long been great. Nevertheless, it had for a great part of the Middle Ages possessed a marked individuality, and even in the fourteenth century displayed some peculiarities of its own. Christianity had first been firmly implanted among the Czechs by Cyril and Methodius, two missionaries of the Eastern Church. Rome had soon asserted its authority over the country; the connexion with Constantinople had been severed; and the conversion of Bohemia had been completed by German clergy. Attempts to prove that throughout the Middle Ages there was a party in Bohemia which kept in touch with the Eastern Church and followed its teaching have not been convincing. But it is possible that certain characteristics of the Church in Bohemia may be ultimately traced to Eastern influence. For long the dukes and the kings retained a control over the clergy which was flatly contrary to the Canon Law and paralleled in no other Catholic country. For long, too, the clergy resisted the centralizing policy of the Papacy, and in the fourteenth century the provision and reservation of benefices by the Pope seems to have aroused more resentment in Bohemia than elsewhere. The efforts of the reforming popes of the eleventh century to enforce the rule of the celibacy of the clergy created special indignation there; it was not until the thirteenth century that the principle was consistently upheld by the ecclesiastical authorities of the country; and thereafter, it appears, a very large number of priests lived with women who legally might be merely concubines but whom public opinion regarded as wives, a state of affairs which was usual in all other lands of central and western Europe, though probably less so than in Bohemia. A notable peculiarity was that the laity of Bohemia were in the habit of taking the Communion oftener than was usual elsewhere or was countenanced by Catholic teaching. There was, furthermore, a certain amount of real heresy in the country, the Waldenses being probably more influential there than anywhere else outside their Alpine homes.

*The Church in Bohemia*

**Bohemian nationalism**

Thus papal authority was not so well established in Bohemia as in most other countries of Europe, and in religious matters the Bohemian people displayed an independent temper which might readily lead to a serious conflict with Rome. The likelihood of this was much increased by the rise of a sentiment of nationality among the Czechs. It has become customary to speak of the national principle as a modern discovery. In point of fact, national feeling is one of many motives which have influenced mankind for centuries. It may be strong in one country and absent in the next. It may determine the conduct of a people at one time and then be superseded by another force. In the Middle Ages, it was seldom very powerful, but it is a mistake to suppose that it was wholly absent. It is doubtless true that it often grew out of unworthy passions, if indeed it is not an unworthy passion itself. At all events, the first manifestations of a national consciousness in Bohemia seem to have been due to the jealousy felt by the nobles, who were mainly Czech, towards the burghers in the towns, who were mainly German. Ill-considered interference by German kings and princes towards the end of the thirteenth century helped to intensify and spread the sentiment. As yet men felt hatred of the German rather than pride in being Czech. It is paradoxical that it was not until the native dynasty of Přemysl had died out and been replaced by the alien House of Luxemburg that a positive sense of nationality arose among the Czech people. It was the Emperor

**Influence of the Emperor Charles IV**

Charles IV who, more than any other man, was the cause of this. For the Holy Roman Empire he cared little; his interest centred in his kingdom of Bohemia. By his vigorous and well-organized administration, he gave her unprecedented order and quiet. His legislation fostered her trade and industry. He persuaded the Papacy to elevate the see of Prague to the rank of an archbishopric, so that in ecclesiastical affairs Bohemia was independent of all external authority save Rome itself. He founded a university at Prague, the first in central Europe, and it was soon thronged by students from all neighbouring countries. The town itself was enlarged and beautified by his munificence. Charles, moreover, showed a high regard for the Czech people. He flattered them, spoke their tongue, surrounded himself with Czech officials and counsellors. He was himself far more French than German in upbringing and tastes; and he made no secret of the fact that he valued Bohemia more than all his other dominions. It is worth noting that he founded in Prague a monastery for Slavonic monks, where worship was conducted according to the Slavonic liturgy, which had been introduced into Bohemia by Cyril and Methodius but long since banned by Rome. It must not be imagined that the devout Charles had any notion of revolting from the Papacy and leading his subjects into the fold of the Orthodox Church; but his new foundation must have put new ideas into critical heads. The effect of his reign was that the Czechs began to hold their heads high. Previously they had acknowledged the superiority of German culture; now, with an Emperor who was more Czech than German, they felt that their country possessed political hegemony in central Europe, and, with their new university, that they had turned the tables on the Germans.

It was mere coincidence that the rise of national enthusiasm in the reign of Charles IV was accompanied by a growing concern about the condition of the Church. Similar alarm was voiced in all countries, and everywhere there were some who vehemently denounced abuses and demanded reform. Historians of the Hussite movement, while quite properly pointing out that Hus had his forerunners, have often written as though such men were to be found only in Bohemia at that time. In themselves they were not particularly remarkable. What gave the Hussite movement a unique position among all the attempts to reform the Church was the personality of Hus himself, together with the circumstances of his fate and the mingling of religious and patriotic aims among the Czechs. *Advocates of religious reform*

Among those who, in the latter half of the fourteenth century, raised their voices for the reform of the Church in Bohemia, four men stand out. These were Conrad of Waldhausen, Milic of Kremsier, Thomas of Stitny, and Matthias of Janow. Conrad, an Austin canon, German in race and speech, won great renown by his sermons de-

*Conrad of Waldhausen*

nouncing the luxury and immorality of the clergy; he was specially severe on simony, which, he said, tainted the whole life of the Church. Though he incurred the bitter hostility of the mendicant friars, he retained the favour of Charles IV, who made him rector of the Tyn Church, one of the most important in Prague, and upheld him there until his death in 1369. He was succeeded by Milic, a

*Milic of Kremsier*

Czech, who was already famous for his diatribes against vice, whether in laity or clergy, for his personal asceticism, and for his conviction that the end of the world was at hand, his researches into prophecy having once led him to call Charles IV Antichrist to his face. The most stormy period of his career was, indeed, over; for in 1367 he had gone to Rome to tell the Pope about Antichrist, had been imprisoned by the Inquisition, and, having been released at the instance of the Cardinal of Albano, had been treated very honourably by that prudent dignitary, an experience which greatly modified some of his more violent opinions. Milic, however, retained his puritan fervour and his zeal for good works. There was nothing heretical about his teaching, and the only charge against him which had any serious foundation was that he encouraged the over-frequent reception of the Eucharist. He died at Avignon in 1374, having gone thither to rebut accusations brought against him by some of the parish clergy and friars of Bohemia, a task in which he had been brilliantly successful. He was tri-lingual, but spoke and wrote by preference in Czech, and his influence over his fellow-countrymen was thus greater than that of Conrad.

*Thomas of Stitny*

Thomas of Stitny, who lived from 1331 to 1401, was a man of a very different type. Though he had been a successful student of Prague University, he never took holy orders, but being a member of the lesser nobility, dwelt on his estates, where he lived a retired life. His literary works were numerous. He wrote entirely in Czech, being the first author to use that tongue for the scientific discussion of theological and philosophical problems. He is very bitter about the state of the Church, praises Conrad and Milic in enthusiastic terms, advocates the frequent reception of the Communion by the laity, and lays great emphasis on the authority of the Bible. He had no intention of rebelling against the Church, nor does he seem ever to have held heretical views unwittingly. His historical importance is due to the influence which his writings had on men of his own class.

Matthias of Janow was of noble birth, like Thomas, whom he rivalled in zeal for religious reform. Matthias, it should be noted, studied arts and theology at Paris. He seems never to have been so closely in touch with his fellow-countrymen as the reformers just mentioned, and it was to scholars that he mainly appealed, both in speech and in writing. While he condemns in bitter language the abuses prevailing in the Church and predicts the early advent of Antichrist, he is particularly notable for his reasoned defence of frequent, even daily, Communion, his denunciation of the use of images and pictures in worship, his appeal to Scripture in preference to ecclesiastical tradition, and his advocacy of the doctrine of justification by faith. In some ways he was more radical than Hus himself. But it took some time for the views of Matthias to produce much effect. His writings are prolix and not always consistent with one another, and Matthias, who seems to have been a man of querulous temper, discredited himself by twice retracting his opinions when accused of heresy before the Archbishop of Prague. But he deserves to be remembered as perhaps the most original thinker produced by the reform movement in Bohemia.  *Matthias of Janow*

Writers and preachers like those mentioned—and there were many of less note—had stirred up in Bohemia a good deal of religious excitement, and had accustomed men to denunciations of the clergy. Thus, it was possible for John Hus to go far without causing special alarm. Hus was probably born in 1369: he was therefore only about forty-six at his death. His parents were peasants of Husinec, a village near the Bavarian frontier, in a region where the Czech and German languages contended for mastery. Very little is known of Hus's early life. While still a boy, he resolved to become a priest, and so entered Prague University. He became a Bachelor of Arts in 1393 and a Bachelor of Divinity in the following year. In 1396 he took the degree of Master of Arts. He never attained the doctorate of Divinity, and there is no reason to suppose that he was a particularly  *Early life of John Hus (1369–1415)* distinguished student. That his record was creditable and that he was personally popular may however be inferred from his selection in 1402 as rector of the University.

**Hus at the Bethlehem Chapel in Prague**

By this time Hus was a priest and had made some reputation as a preacher. He was also known as an advocate of the principle, Bohemia for the Bohemians. Both his eloquence and his patriotism probably had something to do with his appointment in 1402 as incumbent of the Bethlehem Chapel in Prague, founded eleven years before for the preaching of sermons in Czech. It was already famous, but the renown of Hus soon eclipsed that of his predecessors, and the chapel was crowded to overflowing with admiring listeners of every class, the Queen often attending. Hus had already begun to range himself with the reform party in Bohemia. He shared the puritanical outlook of such men as Conrad of Waldhausen and Milic of Kremsier; like them and the other leaders mentioned above, he laid on the authority of the Bible an emphasis unusual for a medieval theologian; and he was unsparing in his rebukes of the shortcomings of the clergy. Up to this time, however, he had neither done nor said anything that could bring him under a serious accusation of heresy.

**Influence of Wycliffe on Hus**

In 1403 there occurred an incident which foreshadowed the course of Hus's later life. The marriage of Anne of Bohemia, sister of the reigning King Wenzel, to Richard II of England had stimulated intercourse between the two countries. There was also an endowment for poor Bohemian scholars studying at Oxford. There the reputation of John Wycliffe stood high, notwithstanding the condemnation of his doctrines by the ecclesiastical authorities of England; and many Bohemians seem to have been strangely attracted by his writings. His philosophical works were probably known to Hus before he took his degree, and some of Wycliffe's theological writings were apparently brought to Prague in the first years of the fifteenth century. At all events, in 1403 a number of articles extracted from Wycliffe's works, some of them having been officially condemned in England, were laid by the chapter of Prague Cathedral before the university, which was asked to pronounce an opinion upon them. The views of the masters differed widely. Broadly, it may be said that the Germans were for condemnation, the Czechs against. Several of the Czechs, among them Hus, asserted that the assertions attributed to Wycliffe had been garbled; some, however, seem to have been ready to defend them all as they stood. It was resolved, nevertheless, that no one should teach or affirm the controverted articles. This decision was apparently ineffectual, and in any case the Bohemian "nation" at the University voted some years later, at the instance of Hus, that no member of that "nation" should defend the articles in a "false, erroneous, or heretical sense" —a formula which obviously had no practical value whatever.

The incident raises the question of the relation of Hus to Wycliffe. About this there has been savage controversy, in which a regard for truth has been less prominent than religious and political fanaticism. But a survey of the course of the conflict and the temper of the combatants seems to warrant one in concluding that Hus was not a man of profound or original thought, that he owed a very great deal to Wycliffe, that some of his works—notably the very important *De Ecclesia*—are in great part transcribed from works of Wycliffe, that he nevertheless was no blind follower of the Englishman, that on several questions of the first importance (notably transubstantiation) he differed from him altogether, and that the fiery, enthusiastic, emotional, indiscreet Czech could not possibly have been the blind votary of the cool, dry, logical, academic Englishman. It should be pointed out that Hus's plagiarism from Wycliffe must not be judged according to modern ideas. Medieval scholars (Wycliffe among them) habitually quoted at great length from other writers without making any acknowledgment. Again, the scholastic method of argument reduced philosophical or theological discussion to little more than the dexterous handling of fixed formulæ. Two scholars, without having read a line of each other, might yet treat a problem in almost identical terms, just as two mathematicians will employ identical words and symbols to explain a rule of algebra. But while Hus used his own judgment on all questions and produced numerous works in which there is little or no trace of Wycliffe's influence, it was probably the teaching and example of the

Englishman that impelled him so far in advance of his Bohemian predecessors that he suffered a fate which they had escaped.

Hus's attitude in the controversy of 1403 did not get him into any trouble. Others had gone further in their acceptance of Wycliffe's doctrines, even to the denial of transubstantiation. Hus indeed was still regarded favourably by such authorities as had power to injure him. The Archbishop of Prague, Zbynek of Hasenburg—a nobleman who knew more about war than theology but was honest and well-intentioned—regarded him with approval, invited him to report irregularities that came under his notice, appointed him preacher to the synod of Prague, and commissioned him with others to investigate an alleged miracle which was recurring in a town of Brandenburg. Hus was also made a chaplain to the court and became confessor to the Queen. He continued to denounce the clergy and to support the Wycliffite party in the university, until in 1408 the opposition which he thus excited brought to an end his days of ease and prosperity.

*Growing influence of Hus*

The Archbishop, who was determined to uphold orthodoxy even though he did not understand it, had been ordered by Pope Innocent VII to check the spread of Wycliffe's doctrines in Bohemia. He had tried to stop the growing practice of frequently receiving the Communion, but otherwise had not been able to do much, and in the matter of teaching Wycliffe's opinions the Bohemian " nation " of the University had politely defied him. Thus when in 1408 a number of Prague clergy formally accused Hus of falsely and maliciously bringing them and their fellows throughout the country into contempt by his denunciations, the Archbishop listened. Hus replied vigorously, and beyond depriving him of the position of synodal preacher, the Archbishop took no action against him ; but the old friendliness between them was never renewed. Just at this time Bohemia was called upon to decide its policy towards the rebellion of the cardinals against Gregory XII and Benedict XIII. King Wenzel was for the cardinals and the General Council which they summoned. The Archbishop stood by Gregory. At the University the Bohemians were for the cardinals, the Germans generally for the Pope. Now when

*Beginning of his troubles, 1408*

deciding questions of common policy, the University masters voted by "nations," of which there were four—Bohemian, Bavarian, Saxon, and Polish, the last consisting in fact mainly of Germans. Thus the Germans had three votes, the Czechs only one. This state of affairs, which had not been designed when the university constitution was made, had long been bitterly resented by the Czech masters. What now happened is not quite clear; but Wenzel, annoyed at the attitude of the Germans, was prevailed upon to sign a decree which conferred upon the Czech nation three votes, leaving only one to be exercised jointly by the three Teutonic "nations." After futile protests, nearly all the German masters left Prague and founded at Leipzig a university which continues to this day. Though Hus seems to have had no direct influence on the course of events, he rejoiced at what had happened. But, whether it was just or not, Wenzel's policy led to the impoverishment of the university and exacerbated the hatred between Germans and Czechs.

*Secession of the Germans from Prague University, 1409*

Hus was now at the height of his influence and popularity. After some months, however, the Archbishop wearied of playing Becket, recognized Alexander V as Pope, and made his peace with the King. He then, encouraged and supported by Alexander, resumed his attack on Hus. New accusations were brought against him, and there is no doubt that views which he never held were now attributed to him in reports to the Pope. In 1410, acting under orders from Alexander which embodied suggestions of his own, the Archbishop forbade preaching anywhere but in cathedral, collegiate, monastic, and parish churches, ordered that all copies of Wycliffe's books should be surrendered, and had two hundred publicly burned; further, since Hus defiantly continued to preach in the Bethlehem Chapel, he excommunicated him. Prague was in a state of ferment, and both sides used violence. But the King was still disposed to favour Hus; he resented the imputation of heresy made against his subjects; and both he and the Queen wrote to John XXIII asking for the annulment of the recent proceedings. Some of Hus's influential friends among the nobility also addressed the Pope on his behalf. The situation in both Church and Empire was precarious, and John XXIII had to walk circumspectly, but in the end

*Hus excommunicated, 1410*

Hus's enemies prevailed, he was summoned to the papal court, and when, though sending proctors, he failed to appear, he was in 1411 excommunicated again. But this made his position no worse than before.

*Attempted reconciliation*

Soon afterwards there was a serious attempt to make peace in Bohemia. The Pope dared not offend the King, who seemed at the moment more than ever disposed to support Hus; and it was arranged that Wenzel should arbitrate between Hus and the Archbishop. Wenzel behaved very well, maintained a judicial temper, took the best counsel available, and induced the parties to accept an agreement. The Archbishop was to declare that there were no heresies in Bohemia, to withdraw sentences of excommunication which he had pronounced against Hus and his followers and an interdict which he had (somewhat ineffectually) laid on the city of Prague, and to ask the Pope, for his part, to absolve Hus and other excommunicated Bohemians. Every one was to have restored to him any property, rights, or privileges which had been lost or impaired during the recent controversies. The King, with the advice of his spiritual and temporal councillors, was to inquire into the shortcomings of the clergy in faith and morals and to take appropriate action. These arrangements were manifestly more favourable to Hus than to the Archbishop, who soon began to raise difficulties about their execution. But before further trouble arose, he died.

*Dispute over indulgences*

His successor, an easygoing man, might have had a soothing effect on the controversy. But in 1412 there appeared in Prague vendors of the plenary indulgence which John XXIII had just offered in order to raise funds for his so-called crusade against Ladislas of Naples. Such traffic was unfamiliar to the Bohemians, and it was conducted with cynical unscrupulousness. Hus and his friends raised vehement protests, and argued against the whole theory of indulgences in disputations at the University. That radical aristocrat, Jerome of Prague, threw all the weight of his learning and all the force of his invective into inflammatory speeches which incited a crowd of students to burn a papal bull in public. The city of Prague was in a turmoil, and Wenzel's efforts to maintain order resulted in the execution of three young men who had interrupted sermons in which the salesmen were recommending their wares. When the doings in Prague came to the ears of the Pope, he issued bulls laying Hus under the greater excommunication, ordering his arrest, condemnation, and execution, and enjoining the demolition of the Bethlehem Chapel. Prague was also subjected to an interdict, which this time was fairly effectual. Hus appealed from the Pope to Christ, and continued to preach; his partisans were ready to uphold him by force; but in the autumn of 1412, at the request of the King, he withdrew from the city. For the next two years, though he remained in Bohemia, his visits to Prague were rare and private; he spent most of the time at castles belonging to sympathizers among the nobility, and busied himself with literary work, in both German and Czech; it was now that he wrote his *De Ecclesia*, his most famous work, though it is little more than a transcription of passages from writings of Wycliffe. Meanwhile, attempts to reconcile the rival parties came to nothing. The situation changed little until, in the autumn of 1414, Hus accepted Sigismund's suggestion that he should appear before the Council of Constance. Sigismund gave him a safe-conduct which covered his journey to Constance, his stay there, and his return to Bohemia. *Hus in retirement, 1412–14*

When Hus and his small band of companions, Czech nobles and clergy, reached Constance on November 3, Sigismund was not there. For three weeks Hus lived a secluded life in a private lodging. During this time his Bohemian enemies incessantly calumniated him to the Pope and the cardinals. Their accusations took effect, and on November 28, at the instance of the cardinals, he was arrested, notwithstanding the vigorous protests of his friends. He was taken to the Dominican friary, situated on an island in the lake, where for a time he was lodged in a damp and gloomy dungeon close to the mouth of a sewer. A commission was appointed to investigate and report upon his case; it examined witnesses, interrogated Hus in his prison (although he had fallen sick), and drew up a schedule of charges against him. The Council, it should be remarked, in its dealings with Hus, followed scrupulously the rules observed by the Inquisition. His treatment was neither better nor worse than that accorded to victims of that tribunal. *Arrival of Hus at Constance, Nov. 3, 1414* *His arrest, Nov. 28*

*Sigismund and Hus*

When Sigismund arrived at Christmas, he professed great indignation at what had befallen Hus, and requested the Pope to release him. John XXIII represented, truly enough, that the cardinals and the Council would not allow him to do so. There was mutual remonstrance and argument. It was urged against Sigismund that no bargain with a heretic was binding; it was hinted that his pleas for Hus exposed his own orthodoxy to suspicion; he feared, not without reason, that if he insisted on the release of the prisoner the Council might dissolve. Gradually he yielded and acquiesced in what had been done. It must be remembered that to the vast majority of men in that age, a heretic was a public enemy of the worst kind. To most members of the Council the case of Hus was a simple matter. They would certainly not release a heretic at the behest of a temporal monarch; but they had far more important topics to consider. Sigismund himself thought them more important, and was not willing to wreck the Council, which owed its existence mainly to him, for a point of honour. So when, on the flight of John XXIII, everything was in confusion, and he might have released Hus without attracting notice, he not only failed to do so, but helped to arrange for his transference to the castle of Gottlieben, which belonged to the Bishop of Constance. For some time previously Hus had been in fairly sanitary quarters at the Dominican friary, and his new cell was healthy enough. But he was chained to a post day and night, he was insufficiently fed, and his guards, Germans, treated him with contempt if not brutality.

When it had recovered from the shock caused by the flight of John XXIII, the Council, eager to prove its orthodoxy, resumed its proceedings against heresy and appointed a new commission to deal with Hus. Early in May it passed a decree condemning 251 articles said to have been taken from the writings of Wycliffe, whose works were all to be burned and whose bones were to be dug up and scattered on unconsecrated ground. Meanwhile, the friends of Hus continued to protest vehemently against his

*Hus granted a public audience, June 1415*

treatment and to demand that he should be permitted to state his case before the whole Council. Eventually a public audience was conceded; it occupied three days in the early part of June. It was inevitably futile. Hus thought that he would be allowed to state and argue his views; the Council intended to limit him to a repudiation of the heretical and erroneous opinions ascribed to him. Hus and his accusers were soon at cross purposes. For he declared that many of the views attributed to him were not his, and when asked to renounce them, refused on the ground that to do so would be equivalent to an admission that he had held them. Throughout Hus hotly repudiated the charge of heresy, and, for that matter, Gerson, one of his chief adversaries, said later that if he had had an advocate he would never have been condemned. It is certain that some of the doctrines ascribed to Hus were not held by him. On the theory of transubstantiation he was quite orthodox: indeed, he succeeded in convincing the Council that this was so. Nor had he ever taught that sacraments administered by a sinful priest are invalid. The recklessness of some of his opponents—especially his fellow-countrymen— is shown by the charge, brought on the day of his final condemnation, that he had declared himself to be the Fourth Person of the Godhead. But his views concerning the nature of the Church, though he apparently would not have applied them in practice, struck at the foundations of the existing ecclesiastical order, and led logically to an ecclesiastical democracy such as was afterwards striven for by the most extreme Protestant sects. In the case of Hus, however, as in the case of Joan of Arc and nearly all those accused of heresy in this and the following age, the crucial question was, would he submit himself unreservedly to the judgment of the Church, accepting the assumption that the Church was speaking through his judges. Despite his asseverations of devotion to the Church's teaching, Hus refused to comply. In short, he asserted the right of private judgment.

There is no need to linger on the wretched business. At the public audience the Council treated Hus with that bullying discourtesy which ecclesiastical assemblies so often display towards those who differ from them. Hus, for his part, was provocative; perhaps he was bewildered, as well he might have been, but much of what he said sounded disingenuous and evasive. The result of the three days' wrangling was to confirm the Council in its hostility towards him. Four weeks passed in attempts to induce him to

*Hus condemned and burned, July 6, 1415*

yield. They made no impression: indeed, from the tone of his answers and his letters at this time one may suspect that he desired martyrdom. On July 6 he attained it. Before the whole Council, assembled in the cathedral, he was formally condemned for heresy, solemnly divested of his clerical status, and handed over to the secular arm, everything being done with that ceremonious elaboration of symbolism which the Roman Church can use with such tremendous appropriateness. He was straightway taken outside the city and burned, meeting his fate with dignified fortitude.

*Effects of Hus's death in Bohemia*

The trouble which Hus caused the Church during his life was small compared with the trouble he caused her when dead. Numerous protests against its treatment of Hus had reached the Council from Bohemia, and when it was known that he had been burned, the fury of the Czechs was terrible. Many denounced the Council for its disregard of Hus's safe-conduct. It must be remembered, however, that the safe-conduct had not been granted by the Council but by Sigismund. It is true that all the Fathers had come to Constance trusting to his protection and that Hus would never have appeared but for his confidence in it; but if it is consequently argued that honour commanded the Council to respect the safe-conduct, one may well ask what is honour in comparison with the Faith. In any case, it is Sigismund who has incurred most obloquy. It was his promise that had been violated. Perhaps he could not have prevented the condemnation of Hus without using unwarrantable violence against the Council: but he might have insisted that he should be handed over to the temporal authorities of Bohemia. Not only did he acquiesce in the Council's proceedings against Hus, but friends of the reformer had overheard him urging prominent men of the Council to resort to the sternest measures. It has been well said that these unguarded words cost Sigismund the Bohemian crown and indeed ruined all his ambitions.

In September 1415 a number of Bohemian and Moravian nobles met in Prague, and drew up a letter to the Council in which they asserted their belief in Hus's goodness and freedom from heresy and denounced as traitors all who should allege that heresy existed in Bohemia or Moravia.

Before being despatched the letter was signed by 450 nobles and knights. A number of them entered into a solemn covenant, pledging themselves to uphold freedom of preaching, to defend priests who were unjustly excommunicated, and to resist any attack that might be made on the country because of its support of their views. There was, indeed, a party which fully accepted the authority of the Council, and its leading men formed an opposition league. But though it included some of the greatest Bohemian nobles, it was far weaker than the league of the Hussites.

*The Council defied by the Hussites*

For two or three years the prospects of Bohemia were quite uncertain. Wenzel nominally adhered to the conservative or Catholic party; but his queen was known to have strong Hussite leanings, he himself regarded the proceedings against Hus at Constance as a slight on his own authority, and he was jealous of Sigismund. So at first the Hussites had nothing to fear from him.

Meanwhile the Council, by burning Jerome of Prague, by ordering the execution of its decrees against the Wycliffite and Hussite heresies, and by hinting at the organization of a crusade against Bohemia, had sought to cow the rebels into submission. Martin V continued its policy. The Hussites were quite unperturbed. Already, however, there had begun to appear among them those divisions which were to cripple their strength. There was indeed not much to hold them together. Their strongest bond was that of nationality: they were almost all Czechs. Hus's affection for the Czech people, his love of the Czech language, the efforts he made, by example and precept, to purify it from foreign intrusions and to raise its value as a medium of expression, seem out of place in the fifteenth century; but Hus the nationalist has influenced modern Bohemia more than Hus the reformer. Apart from nationalist fervour—which often, it is true, amounted to little more than dislike of Germans—the only link uniting all Hussites was the demand that the laity, as well as the clergy, should be permitted to partake of the wine in the Eucharist, a practice that had been continued in Bohemia until the fourteenth century. Its revival had of late been strongly urged by several Czech scholars, conspicuous among them being Jakobek of Mies, a supporter of Hus. The question

*Divisions among the Hussites*

seemed to Hus himself of no great consequence, but he had written from Constance approving of the practice, and his words carried far more weight in Bohemia than the Council's decree forbidding it. The Bohemians came to attach extraordinary importance to the principle, the chalice becoming the emblem of the entire Hussite party. There was a general demand among the Hussites for a reform of clerical morals and a reduction of ecclesiastical wealth; but on these matters many orthodox Catholics agreed with them. On questions of doctrine and organization factions began to form immediately after Hus's death. What may be termed the right wing of the party, soon to be known as the Utraquists or Calixtines, insisted on the necessity of receiving the Communion under both kinds, but otherwise were Catholic in belief, and had no wish to separate from the Church, though they mostly hoped to secure a great measure of ecclesiastical autonomy for Bohemia and Moravia. At the other extreme were reformers who held views much like those of the later Calvinists, rejecting the doctrine of the Real Presence, belief in purgatory, indulgences, the veneration of the Virgin or the saints, and the use of images in worship, condemning the whole Catholic system of government, insisting on the true priesthood of all believers, and barely tolerating, for convenience' sake, a regular ministry. Those with advanced opinions came to be styled Taborites. They were sternly puritanical in their moral teaching, and many of them held communistic opinions in politics. In Bohemia, as in all European countries, there had always been a certain amount of wild heresy, and some of the extravagant sects already in existence have often been treated as Hussites by writers hostile to the party. Such, for instance, were the Adamites, who claimed to be in a state of innocency, went about naked, and disregarded conventional morality; their worst enemies, in actual fact, were the Taborites, who virtually exterminated them. It must be understood that there was never any hard and fast division between the various sections of the Hussites: between the most cautious Utraquist and the most radical Taborite could be found infinite gradations of belief and disbelief. The term Taborite in particular was used to cover people of a wide variety of views. While, then, their differences made it difficult for the Hussites to pursue a common policy, the absence of sharply defined distinctions among them rendered possible their co-operation when threatened by a common danger.

In 1419 the ferment in Bohemia reached a crisis. Wenzel, after long hesitation, took vigorous action on the Catholic side. He ordered Hussite priests to leave Prague, and would permit the administration of the Sacrament under both kinds in only three churches. The Hussites took to holding meetings in the fields, some of them being attended by many thousands of people. Encouraged by this, the Hussites of Prague, after hearing an inflammatory sermon from a priest of Taborite leanings, demonstrated in procession through the city streets, and demanded of the magistrates of the New Town the release of certain Hussites who had been arrested. The city councillors foolishly treated the request with contempt and someone, hurling a stone, knocked out of the hand of a Hussite priest the chalice which he was symbolically holding aloft. The furious crowd stormed the City Hall; the councillors were thrown out of the window, and those that survived the fall were lynched. The news so shocked Wenzel that he soon afterwards had two apoplectic strokes, and on August 16 died " with a roar as of a lion." *Breach between Wenzel and the Hussites, 1419* *Wenzel's death, Aug. 16, 1419*

His heir was the hated Sigismund. The Bohemians pointed out that the crown was elective, and began to bargain with him. They demanded permission for the Eucharist to be everywhere celebrated according to their views, and requested that only Czechs should be admitted to public office in the kingdom. Sigismund evasively replied that he would govern like his father, Charles IV. Being detained in Hungary, he agreed that the popular Queen Sophia, Wenzel's widow, should act as regent. *Negotiations of the Bohemians with Sigismund*

In the next months the Taborites, who expected nothing of Sigismund, organized resistance. Their leaders were Nicolas of Husinec and John Zizka of Trocnov, both of noble birth, who had gained political experience in the service of Wenzel. Nicolas is best remembered as an organizer and diplomatist; but there is reason to believe that his military abilities were considerable. Zizka, of course, has the name of one of the greatest generals in history. *Nicolas of Husinec and John Zizka*

At this juncture, however, he overestimated his strength, and an attempt to occupy Prague by force failed owing to lack of sympathy on the part of the citizens.

Gradually the temper of the capital changed. For some months Sigismund temporized, but in the end he showed his hand prematurely. It became known that he was promoting a crusade which the Pope had proclaimed against the Hussites. At the same time, while at Breslau in Silesia he dealt very harshly with Hussites there. On this there was a general rising of the Hussites in Bohemia. But the Taborite section began destroying churches and monasteries, to the disgust of the Utraquists, many of whom reconciled themselves to Sigismund. When therefore he entered Bohemia, he felt strong enough to call upon the citizens of Prague to surrender to him unconditionally.

*Hussite rising, Spring, 1420*

Meanwhile Zizka had been operating in south-western Bohemia, where he had gained some striking local successes against adherents of Sigismund. The extreme party among the Hussites had chosen as a place of refuge a high and precipitous peninsula, protected on three sides by a lake and a stream. This, with their fondness for Scriptural names, they called Mount Tabor, and thence the advanced Hussites derived their popular designation. Zizka, invited thither, had begun to fortify the place scientifically, and a town, afterwards of considerable size, was beginning to rise within the walls. When Sigismund and the crusaders, a large and motley host, entered Bohemia, Zizka's fame consequently stood high, and in their straits the citizens of Prague appealed to him for help. Towards the end of May 1420 he entered the city with 9,000 of his own troops.

*Tabor fortified by Zizka, 1420*

At the beginning of July the siege of Prague began in earnest. Two weeks later the attackers tried to take the Witkow Hill, a position of much strategic value to the north-east of the city, held and fortified by the Hussites. After a sharp fight, they were repulsed with much loss. The crusading host, which had no natural cohesion, resounded with recriminations; it had lost confidence in Sigismund, and showed signs of breaking up. The University of Prague seized the moment to attempt a reconciliation. With some difficulty all sections of the Hussites were induced to adopt what became famous as the Four Articles of Prague.

*Prague besieged by Sigismund, July–Nov. 1420*

These demanded freedom of preaching by Christian priests throughout the kingdom, the administration of the Sacrament in both kinds, the confiscation of the property of the clergy until they were in a state of "apostolic poverty," and the punishment of mortal sin, especially if committed publicly, by the appropriate authority. Except for the second, on the Eucharist, the articles were open to various interpretations; and from the standpoint of the Taborites they were far too mild. Sigismund might have accepted them, but the papal representatives with the army refused even to discuss them. *The Four Articles of Prague*

Sigismund tried to strengthen his moral authority by having himself crowned King of Bohemia; but no one seemed impressed. Then the Hussites laid siege to the Wyssehrad, a height surmounted by a castle, on the outskirts of Prague. The place being on the point of surrender, Sigismund tried to relieve it by force. On November 1, however, his men-at-arms were beaten back by the Hussite peasants and suffered very heavy losses in the ensuing flight. The Wyssehrad having fallen, Sigismund withdrew from the neighbourhood of the capital. Zizka had not been present at the fight of November 1, having returned to southern Bohemia, where before the end of the year he gained further local victories.

It was now evident that the Hussite revolt was a very serious matter, not only for Sigismund but also for the Church. It is true that there had as yet been no big battles; but the operations of 1420 had bestowed on the Hussites that moral ascendancy which was a leading cause of their sensational victories. Undoubtedly they owed much to Zizka. It has been argued, on the basis of recent research, that Zizka's abilities were not really remarkable, and that his part in the Hussite movement was comparatively insignificant. It is of course certain that many of the tales told about him, even by contemporaries, are false, and that Catholic propaganda afterwards made of him a legendary bogy. But enough trustworthy testimony remains to warrant our regarding him as a commander of astonishing talent. Wherein that talent consisted is not so easy to discover. Zizka's fame has chiefly rested on his supposed invention of a new system of tactics, in which the main *Strategy and tactics of Zizka* factor was the transport wagon. That the Hussite armies when camping in the field or when threatened with attack disposed their baggage train as a fortification there can be no doubt; but the device, though they perhaps used it more scientifically than anyone before them, was not original, being in fact familiar in the warfare of eastern Europe. Few reasonable people now believe the story that Zizka employed wagons for offensive purposes, like warchariots. Zizka was one of the first soldiers to attach much value to small fire-arms, and his rampart of wagons was always manned with soldiers trained in the use of hand-guns. Within the square formed by the wagons there was artillery, more extensively used for field operations by Zizka than by any previous general. Thus prepared the Hussites awaited attack, and there is no record of one of their laagers having been carried by assault. As soon as the attackers showed signs of confusion, there issued from sally-ports swarms of infantry armed with spears, clubs, and war-flails, the latter (a Bohemian speciality) being particularly dreaded. Falling on the already shaken enemy, they usually encountered small resistance and inflicted frightful casualties. Thus were the Hussite victories won, according to the military historians. But if we examine their several triumphs, it appears that in many—including some of the most famous—the *wagenburg* did not figure at all, while often it was the Hussites who first took the offensive. And though good tactics had much to do with the Hussite success, their main cause was unquestionably the enthusiastic devotion of the rank-and-file of their armies. They were mostly peasants, untrained when the Hussites first took the field, and throughout, save for the hand-gun men, equipped with weapons which were technically inferior to the long-bows of the English or the pikes and halberds of the Swiss. They owed a great deal to the half-heartedness and incapacity usually shown by their opponents, and after their early successes they expected victory and their enemies defeat. They believed that God, their enemies that the devil, was fighting for them. The terror caused by the atrocities they frequently committed—usually under instructions from the Higher Command—also facilitated their operations. But when all is said, these Hussite warriors, who held half Europe

*The Hussite warriors*

at bay for fourteen years and forced the Church to bargain with them, deserve enduring renown for an astounding feat of arms.

During the winter of 1420-21, the Hussites continued their victorious operations, until they controlled nearly the whole land. In April Sigismund went to Hungary to collect new forces. Soon afterwards no less a personage than the Archbishop of Prague accepted the Four Articles, and the Utraquists, to their joy, found themselves enabled to establish an independent Bohemian Church without breaking the apostolic succession. In the summer a largely-attended Diet met at Caslav. It declared Sigismund unfit to be king, and set up a provisional government, in which there were men of every substantial party in Bohemia. Shortly afterwards, the Grand Duke Witold of Lithuania, with whom the moderate Hussites had already been negotiating, was proclaimed king. *Sigismund rejected by the Bohemians, June 1421*

In the autumn the military peril again became serious. A great army raised by the German princes entered Bohemia from the west, while Sigismund returned from the east. The Germans laid siege to the town of Zatec, or Saaz. The place held out valiantly, and Zizka led the main Hussite army to the rescue. The Germans would not abide its coming; such (said a contemporary) was their horror of heretics that they would not look one in the face. Then Zizka turned to deal with Sigismund. He was now totally blind. For long he had had but one eye, and he had lost that in the fighting of the previous summer. His military insight, however, seemed to be no whit impaired. To those who have their sight, there is often something uncanny about the activities of a blind man, and Zizka's blindness probably increased the terror which he created among his enemies. At all events, his next exploit was probably his most brilliant. He threw himself into Kuttenberg, which was attacked by Sigismund. On December 21, 1421, he left the town, formed his wagons into a square, and challenged attack. Sigismund's troops were repulsed, but managed to cut off Zizka from the town, into which they were admitted by the Catholic faction of the inhabitants. The Hussites were in a perilous situation; but Zizka, who displayed tactical versatility that bewildered his enemies, *Hussite victory at Saaz, Oct. 1421* cut his way through, and brought his army to Kolin. There he rested his men and collected recruits. In the first week of January, bitter though the weather was, he returned towards Kuttenberg. On his approach Sigismund's troops, with many civilians, left the town in a panic. The Hussites pursued for three days; Sigismund's officers repeatedly tried to fight a rearguard action, but their men would never stand. Sigismund and a part of his army finally got away, but many of his troops were overtaken at Deutschbrod, which was stormed by the Hussites, who perpetrated a terrible massacre. Between Kuttenberg and the Moravian frontier, Sigismund lost 12,000 men.

*Zizka's triumph over Sigismund at Kuttenberg, Jan. 1422*

Though Martin V, Sigismund, and the German princes were always planning further operations against the Hussites, it was not until 1426 that Bohemia was again seriously troubled by invasion from abroad. In the meantime, however, the internal dissensions of the Hussites had become more bitter, causing ferocious civil war. The party strife of these years is extremely complicated, but luckily it is not necessary to follow it closely. In 1422 the chief centre of interest was Prince Korybut, nephew of both Ladislas King of Poland and Witold Grand Duke of Lithuania. Witold had accepted the offer of the Bohemian crown and sent Korybut to uphold his interests. It is possible that Witold and some of the Hussite nobles had dreams of a united Slavonic State embracing the lands of the Bohemian Crown, Poland, and Lithuania, a state which would finally check the German advance eastward and might even recover some of the lands once held by Slavs and now lost. Such ideas, however were not sufficiently widespread to have much influence on the course of events. Korybut, who accepted the Four Articles of Prague, was welcomed by the Utraquist party. Zizka, too, after some hesitation, recognized his authority; but the bulk of the Taborites viewed him askance. They suspected him—rightly—of a readiness to compromise with the Catholics, and the ill-success of such military operations as he undertook confirmed them in their mistrust. Meanwhile, the Pope had been urging on Korybut's two uncles the dangers, spiritual and temporal, of trafficking with heretics. Towards the end of the year, therefore, Witold, alleging that he had accepted

*Civil war in Bohemia*

the Bohemian crown in the belief that most of the Hussites had returned or were about to return to the true faith, abandoned his Bohemian schemes and ordered Korybut to leave the country.

Dismayed by the loss of their leader, the moderate Hussites entered into closer relations with the Catholics and began to negotiate with Sigismund. This was too much for Zizka, who could not abide the King of the Romans. He took the field at the head of a Taborite army. For the first time Hussite fought Hussite. Zizka and his men showed all their former skill, courage, and ruthlessness, and after one or two heavy defeats the Utraquists abandoned the Catholics and succeeded in making an accommodation with the victors. It was decided, among other things, that Zizka should lead a Hussite army into Moravia, where Catholicism was still relatively strong. Moravia offered no serious resistance, and Zizka was encouraged to invade Hungary. Little is known of what followed. The Hussites apparently reached the Danube in the neighbourhood of Gran, but being then assailed by vast numbers of Hungarian horsemen, were forced to withdraw. The retreat was accomplished with such amazing skill that the campaign on the whole enhanced Zizka's reputation. *Zizka's invasion of Hungary, 1423*

In Zizka's absence some of the Utraquist nobles had resumed their dealings with the Catholics and Sigismund. The general was furious, and 1424 was long remembered in Bohemia as the bloody year of Zizka. After a series of victories, mostly gained against heavy odds, he encamped with his army before Prague, which had recently received Prince Korybut, who had returned to Bohemia, ostensibly on his own initiative. But before the Taborites assaulted the city, Zizka was persuaded to accept a provisional agreement and to accompany a united Hussite army to Moravia, where the Archduke Albert of Austria had been gaining ground for the Catholics. When near the Moravian frontier, Zizka stopped to besiege the castle of Pribyslav. There he was attacked by the plague, and on October 11 he died. The campaign was continued, and the Hussites gained possession of nearly all Moravia. But Zizka's loss was a terrible one—not only because of his military skill, but also because of the moderation of his religious and political views, *Zizka's bloody year, 1424*

*His death, Oct. 11*

which enabled him to co-operate with Utraquists, even though his sympathies were in the main with the Taborites. It is significant that after his death the divisions among the Hussites became more sharply defined. The Taborite party definitely split into two, the more moderate section calling themselves Orphans, in allusion to their dead leader.

The year 1425 saw unsuccessful negotiations between the various Hussite factions, and between the Utraquists, headed by Korybut, and the Catholics. There was not much fighting. As a military enterprise seemed the only way of obtaining harmony among the Hussites, another expedition to Moravia was organized in the autumn. It was so successful that the army pressed forward into Austria and took the town of Retz. It was, however, impossible for the victors to hold the occupied country.

*Procop the Great*

The commander of the Taborites had been killed in the campaign, and they now chose as their leader Procop, commonly called "the Great" to distinguish him from another Hussite general of the same name. Procop, the son of a Prague merchant, was of gentle blood on his mother's side. He was well educated, had travelled much, and was in priest's orders. As a clergyman, he would not carry weapons or take actual part in fighting. Historians have usually disparaged him in relation to Zizka—it is hard to see why, for Procop's victories were as remarkable as Zizka's and his strategy seems to have been more far-sighted. In his religious and political views Procop belonged rather to the Orphans than to the radicals, whose confidence, nevertheless, he usually commanded.

Procop wanted peace for Bohemia. He knew that the Hussites would again be attacked from abroad. They must therefore maintain the offensive, and so terrorize their enemies that all—Germans, Sigismund, nay the very Catholic Church—would be willing to come to terms. It must be recognized that Procop's policy was completely successful for a while, and might have been permanently successful but for the disunion of the Bohemians.

*Hussite victory at Aussig, June 1426*

Now began the most terrible phase of the Hussite wars. In 1426 the Hussites besieged the Bohemian town of Aussig, on the Elbe, which was held by the Elector of Saxony, to whom Sigismund had granted it in pawn. An army of

Germans entered Bohemia to relieve the town. The Hussites sank their differences and powerful reinforcements got to Aussig before the invaders. Korybut was present; but Procop was put in command, and, adopting Zizka's famous wagon formation, gained a resounding victory over a vastly more numerous enemy. The Germans lost terribly, especially in their flight; for, having announced that they would give no quarter, they got none. Next year, urged by Cardinal Beaufort, the German Diet organized a new crusade. A large army invaded Bohemia; but it lacked nerve and zeal, and was badly led. It laid siege to Mies, but ran away without a blow when the main Hussite army approached. The Cardinal, accustomed to be on the winning side, strove hard to rally the crusaders at Tachau, but again they fled, though this time not fast enough to escape very severe loss at the hands of their remorseless pursuers. *A crusade routed, 1427*

Before these things happened, the internal situation of Bohemia had been unexpectedly changed. Prince Korybut, though (so far as we can judge) loyal to the Hussite cause, was anxious to effect a reconciliation with the Papacy. He opened negotiations with Martin V, who, as usual, would offer no concessions. The Utraquist nobles were willing to go to great lengths in order to secure peace; but the citizens of Prague, though mostly very moderate in their views, were determined not to bate a jot of the Four Articles. Convinced by John Rokycana, the most eloquent preacher of the Utraquists, that Korybut was about to betray their cause, they suddenly rose in rebellion, seized Korybut, and kept him in prison. There he remained from April 1427 until September, when some of his supporters made a feeble attempt to restore his authority. Thereupon his captors had him escorted across the frontier. Owing to Korybut's fall and to his own brilliant successes, Procop was for a time the most influential man in the country. He used to the full the opportunity of carrying out his military policy. *Overthrow of peace party in Bohemia*

In the last year or two raiding parties of Hussites had caused alarm in the lands bordering on Bohemia. But in 1428 Procop himself, at the head of the main Hussite army, led two expeditions abroad, the first into Hungary, the second into Silesia. Both penetrated far into the invaded land, spreading terror and destruction, though, in accordance *Procop takes the offensive, 1428* with Procop's plan, the Hussites did not try to occupy territory or even to capture fortified towns. Simultaneously Hussite detachments continued to raid in other directions. The effect appeared when in April 1429 a conference was held at Pressburg between Sigismund and representatives of all the parties in Bohemia, and it was suggested to the Hussites that all religious differences might be submitted to a General Council. They accepted the proposal in principle, but added stipulations which neither Sigismund nor the ecclesiastical authorities could concede. The negotiations broke down, but they had encouraged Procop to give another turn to the screw.

**Great invasion of Germany, 1429-30**

In 1429 a new crusade was abandoned because the English troops raised for it by Cardinal Beaufort were sent to fight Joan of Arc. In the autumn Procop prepared a great offensive, and in December the finest army ever put into the field by the Hussites crossed the frontier into the lands of the Elector of Saxony. None dared meet them in the field. Procop sent out bands which ravaged far and wide in north Germany. With the main force he marched through Thuringia and into Franconia. There Frederick of Hohenzollern, Elector of Brandenburg, entered into negotiations: Procop consented to go back to Bohemia for a heavy indemnity, and Frederick undertook to promote discussions between the Hussites and the Church on the basis of the Articles of Prague. The Hussite army returned to the Bohemian capital in February 1430. It had convinced a majority of Germans that peace must be attained by negotiation. Much farther afield, too, a great impression had been made, and the necessity of a General Council to deal with the Hussite peril was widely recognized.

**Abortive negotiations, 1430**

There is no need to recount the raiding operations of the Hussites during the remainder of 1430. They had more result than the negotiations that went on between the Hussites and Sigismund, the Hussites and Poland, and among the Hussites themselves. The Pope did not want to discuss anything with heretics; Sigismund would not agree to the terms on which alone they would consent to attend a Council. Martin V was organizing another crusade, and Sigismund and the German princes agreed to await its issue.

The crusade was led by Cardinal Cesarini, who had been appointed President of the Council of Basel. Its military commander was Frederick of Hohenzollern. In numbers it was imposing. In August 1431 it entered Bohemia from the west. Procop advanced against it with an army inferior but yet large in numbers, the Taborites being most strongly represented in its ranks. On August 14, near Tauss, at the sound of the Hussite battle-hymn "All ye warriors of God," the warriors of the Church bolted without shot or stroke. Again the carnage during the flight was appalling. *(Fate of the Crusade of 1431)*

Thus ended the war of the Hussites against foreign enemies. Soon afterwards came an invitation from the Council to send representatives to Basel with the object of reaching some agreement. There was a preliminary conference at Eger, at which envoys of both sides discussed the conditions on which the debates at Basel were to be conducted. It was agreed that the basis of negotiation should be the Four Articles of Prague. The Bohemians were given ample guarantees of their personal security, and they were to be permitted to state and argue their views freely. In the summer of 1432 the leaders of the principal sections of the Hussites accepted the terms. There was undeniably a general desire for peace in Bohemia. Every effort was made to minimize the differences between the various factions. Although victorious, the Hussites had suffered heavy losses. Bohemia had been grievously ravaged, mainly in the civil strife. Further, the quality of the Hussite armies had deteriorated. The recent plundering raids had demoralized many of the warriors of God; and numerous mercenaries had been attracted to the Hussite banner from all parts of Europe. Procop could not trust his men as once he had done. Even the more extreme enthusiasts were consequently in a conciliatory mood, and the delegation sent to Basel, consisting of seven nobles and eight priests, included men of all shades of Hussite opinion. The most notable men among them were the orator John Rokycana, Procop himself, and the English Lollard Peter Payne. *(The Convention of Eger, May 1432)*

The Hussite mission reached Basel on January 4, 1433. Its members were on the whole fairly and courteously treated. In the next three months they were given ample opportunity to propound and vindicate their views on the *(The Hussite embassy at the Council of Basel, Jan.–April 1433)*

Articles of Prague, and it was acknowledged on all sides that they had acquitted themselves well. But it soon became evident that no agreement could be reached then and there. The Council naturally detected signs of the differences among the envoys, and sought to amplify them by raising questions which were not covered by the Articles of Prague. The Bohemians were wary, declaring that they were not authorized to discuss anything else. In April, therefore, they went home, accompanied by a commission appointed by the Council, nominally to confer with the Bohemian Diet, really to spy out the land and see how cheaply the submission of the Bohemians might be purchased. Nothing definite resulted from the ensuing negotiations. The Diet held together astonishingly well in face of the attempts of the Council's envoys to multiply its divisions. The Utraquist nobles, however, were much attracted by the unofficial suggestion that the Council would concede the cup to the Bohemian laity if the Hussites would incorporate themselves with the Council before discussing other matters. Eventually, envoys of the Diet went back to Basel with the envoys of the Council. The Bohemians were not allowed to do much beyond submitting an explanation of what the Bohemian Diet understood the Articles of Prague to mean. It was at this stage that the Council resolved to grant Communion under both kinds to the Bohemians, but the decision was kept secret for the time.

*Intrigues of the Council's envoys*

Meanwhile the Council's plans were being furthered by events in Bohemia. All the Hussites wished to make the reception of Communion under both kinds obligatory throughout the kingdom. It was therefore very desirable that any places which still upheld Catholicism should be conquered. The town of Pilsen, though more than once attacked, had never abandoned the Catholic cause or its allegiance to Sigismund; so in the summer of 1433 a Hussite army under Procop laid siege to it. The operations did not prosper. The town was too strong to storm, and was not completely invested. Soon the besiegers were more in need of food than the besieged. The Hussite soldiery—many of whom were now foreigners—plundered the countryside and infuriated the peasantry. A raiding party of some 2,000 men, sent into Bavaria, was cut off and almost

*Pilsen unsuccessfully besieged by the Hussites, 1433*

wiped out. This disaster caused a mutiny in the Hussite camp. Procop was wounded in the head by a stool which was hurled at him; he was put under arrest, and declared to have forfeited his command. Though very soon released, he would not resume leadership of the army for some months.

In the autumn of this eventful year a deputation from Basel was again conferring with the Bohemian Diet. The Council, it was now stated, would permit the administration of Communion under both kinds to those who desired it. On the other points in the Articles of Prague, ambiguous undertakings were given. Though it was not found possible to reach formal agreement, it was manifest that a very large and growing party would make peace on the terms suggested. Still, there followed a good deal of wrangling between the Council and the ambassador sent to Basel by the Bohemian Diet to discuss outstanding questions. *Growth of Bohemian peace party*

But now the Hussites destroyed their own cause. The Utraquist nobles and the men of Prague desired peace more and more. The soldiers who called themselves Orphans or Taborites became increasingly mutinous and destructive. Moderate opinion inclined towards reconciliation with Sigismund, who might restore some measure of order. In April 1434, a league was formed for the restoration and maintenance of peace; it was joined by nearly all the nobles of Bohemia and Moravia, whether Catholic or Utraquist, and by the burghers of the Old Town of Prague. The provisional government ordered all armed forces to disband; but Procop placed himself at the head of the troops of the more advanced factions. The line of division between the two sides was not merely religious. The League was conservative in temper, in favour of the old political arrangements and the maintenance of the privileges of the nobles and cities, whereas among Procop's followers democratic and even communistic notions had much influence. The campaign was short. On May 30 the two armies met near Lipan. Procop's army, which was outnumbered in the proportion of two to three, used the wagon fortress in the classic manner, and flung back the first attack of the enemy. But the League general was an old officer of Zizka's, and Procop's troops were not the equal of those who had victoriously defied Catholic Europe. A feigned flight *War between Utraquists and Taborites* *Battle of Lipan, May 30, 1434* enticed the defenders prematurely from the shelter of the wagons; simultaneously the fortress was pierced from the flanks. Procop and the greater part of his men were cut off. They fought for a day and a night, and nearly all perished. Bohemian historians have proudly reflected that only Czechs could beat Czechs: but Procop was dead and so were the men from whom the crusaders had run away. The Hussite cause had lost its pith and marrow.

During the next two years there were several wordy and acrimonious conferences in which the spokesmen of the Utraquists chaffered with envoys from the Council and with the Emperor Sigismund; but though they often threatened to break off the negotiations, they never did. The chief difficulties arose from the demand that the administration of Communion in both kinds should be obligatory in Bohemia and Moravia, and from the desire to secure for the Bohemians a considerable measure of ecclesiastical autonomy, in particular the right to elect their own bishops. On both these subjects the Council was obdurate. In regard to the first, it won. The treaty of peace between the Hussites and the Council embodied what are known as the Compacts of Prague, which had been under consideration since 1433. The Bohemians and Moravians were to make peace with all men, and on submission would be restored to the unity of the Church. It was conceded by the Church that the Sacrament was to be given in both kinds to all in Bohemia and Moravia who desired it. Mortal sins were to be punished by those authorized to do so. The word of God was to be freely preached by those duly appointed for that purpose. As regards ecclesiastical property—the fourth point in the Articles of Prague—it was asserted that it ought to be administered according to the teachings of the Fathers; but its lawfulness was expressly admitted. From the Church, in short, the Hussites got nothing but permission to receive the Communion under both kinds. It was, as we have seen, a matter about which Hus himself had cared little. Whether it was worth all the blood that had been shed because of it we are fortunately not called upon to judge.

The Utraquists seemed to have done better in their dealings with Sigismund, who was desperately anxious to secure recognition as King of Bohemia. The Emperor agreed that no foreigner should grant benefices in Bohemia

*The Compacts of Prague signed at Iglau, July 1436*

or Moravia, that no inhabitant of those lands should be cited before a foreign tribunal, and that the archbishops and bishops of the Bohemian Church should be elected by the Bohemian clergy and people. He also promised to be guided in the government of the land by Bohemian councillors, to admit only Bohemians to public office, and to grant an amnesty for all that had happened since the death of Wenzel. In August 1436 the nobles swore fealty to him, and he entered Prague in state. We know that he did not intend to observe the concessions which he had made, but he did not live long enough for his perfidy to be fully revealed to his subjects. It at once became evident, however, that the Council would stand on the bare letter of the Compacts, and would not advance an iota beyond them. As for an autonomous Bohemian Church, it would consider no such thing, and its legates immediately began to enforce the observance of Catholic ritual and practice, save in regard to the administration of the Sacrament. But the progress of the dispute was checked by the death of Sigismund and the renewed breach between the Council and the Pope.

*The Utraquists reconciled with Sigismund, July 1436*

Some authorities for chapter ix :—
*Cambridge Medieval History*, vol. viii, chaps. ii, iii, Cambridge, 1936.
Bachmann, A. : *Geschichte Böhmens*, vols. i and ii, Gotha, 1899–1905.
Betts, R. R. : *English and Czech influences in the Hussite Movement* (TRHS 4th Series, vol. 21), 1939.
Bezold, F. von : *König Sigmund und die Reichskriege gegen die Hussiten*, 3 vols., Munich, 1872–7.
Creighton, M. : *History of the Papacy*, vols. ii and iii. See under chap. v.
Denis, E. : *Hus et la guerre des Hussites*, Paris, 1930.
Hefele, C. J. : *Histoire des Conciles*, vol. vii, pts. 1 and 2. See under chap. v.
Kitts, E. J. : *Pope John XXIII and Master John Hus of Bohemia*, London, 1910.
Loserth, J. : *Huss und Wiclif*, 2nd ed., Munich and Berlin, 1925.
Lützow, Count F. : *The Life and Times of Master John Hus*, London, 1909, new ed., 1921 ; *The Hussite Wars*, London, 1914.
*Magister Joannis Hus opera omnia*, ed. W. Flajshans, Prague, 1904, etc.
Palacky, F. : *Documenta magistri Joannis Hus vitam, doctrinam, causam in Constantiensi concilio actam et controversias de religione in Bohemia . . . illustrantia*, Prague, 1869 ; *Geschichte von Böhmen*, 5 vols., Prague, 1836–67.
Schaff, D. S. : *John Huss : his life, teachings, and death*, New York, 1915.
Seton-Watson, R. W. : *A History of the Czechs and Slovaks*, London, 1943.
Vischer, M. : *Jan Hus, sin Leben und seine Zeit*, Frankfurt-am-Main, 1940.
Workman, H. B. : *The Letters of John Hus*, London, 1904.
The original authorities mentioned under chaps. vii and viii contain much information about Hus and the Hussites. There are, of course, many important works on the subject, both medieval and modern, written in Czech.

## CHAPTER X

## FRANCE, 1461–1494

**Louis XI, 1461-83**

AS soon as Charles VII was dead, Louis XI entered France, encountering a general eagerness to welcome or conciliate him. The army with which the Duke of Burgundy had followed him was not needed. Louis soon began to act with little regard for his recent host, and the Duke, after an ostentatious display of his magnificence and wealth at Rheims and Paris, found that his most dignified course was to go home.

**His tastes and character**

The new King was a singularly unpleasant person. In appearance he was as unprepossessing as his father. His sharp-featured face was robbed of all chance of pleasing by a long, ill-formed nose. He had lanky legs, and his gait was ungainly. His personal disadvantages were emphasized by the habitual shabbiness of his clothes. He had a natural aversion from pomp and formality, though as he grew older his indifference to dress and dislike of ceremony became less marked. Paris he avoided, and like his father lived by preference in Touraine, especially at his new château of Plessis-les-Tours. But he seldom remained long in any place, for he was an indefatigable traveller, wandering restlessly about his realm with a small train and lodging in houses of burghers in the towns through which he passed. Official receptions he abhorred, and sometimes rebuffed with brutal rudeness the loyal efforts of his subjects to welcome him. But in bourgeois circles he made himself at home and was popular, notwithstanding the habitual freedom and frequent grossness of his conversation with their women-folk.

Louis had been an undutiful son : he was a bad husband : he was solicitous for his children only because they served political ends. He had many mistresses and bastards, and apparently no affection for any of them. Sincerity, loyalty, trustworthiness he despised ; self-interest, in the crudest sense, was the only motive he understood. What he sought above all was power. Though he prized money and spent little on what most men regard as pleasures, he was no miser but would spend lavishly in order to gain some political end. In his pursuit of power he would use every resource—violence, bribery, treachery, cajolery, bluster. Zealous service he always rewarded well. When he liked he could be most winning in manner, and his apparent ingenuousness got him out of many a tight corner. He was most happy when conducting some complicated intrigue: contemporaries called him "the universal spider," but the webs which he wove were stronger and more intricate than the metaphor suggests.

In this repulsive character there were strange anomalies. This lover of dark and crooked ways, of subtle plots, of tergiversation and make-believe, was a chattering bore; ambassadors sometimes had to listen to him for two hours before they could get in a word. Again, this daring schemer was a bundle of nerves, liable to sudden fits of panic. Perverted though many of his tastes might be, his favourite recreation was a healthy and honest one—hunting; and he was genuinely fond of his hounds and hawks. He knew no pity, yet he was assiduously religious—a prodigal benefactor of churches and shrines, a hardened pilgrim, and a steady purchaser of masses. His piety was actuated by exactly the same motives and directed towards exactly the same ends as his secular doings. He must have Heaven and its hosts on his side, and when they served him well it was prudent to reward them. He was expert in corrupting the saints of his enemies, whom he sometimes induced to be neutral or even to transfer their patronage.[1]

Chauvinist writers have palliated Louis' defects because he added territory to France, strengthened her central government, and combated disruptive elements among her people. Others will be more likely to deplore the outrage to decent human feeling which is caused by the spectacle of such a man's success.

The reign of Louis XI falls into four main divisions. Up to 1465 he was showing his subjects what he was like and what he meant to do. Thence until 1472 he was faced by a

---

[1] Contemporary estimates of Louis naturally varied; but the most famous and favourable—that of Commynes (*Mémoires* [ed. Calmette], i, 67 *seqq.)*—leaves on the whole a disagreeable impression.

series of hostile coalitions of the nobility. From 1472 to 1477 came his final conflict with the House of Burgundy. After that Louis was mainly occupied in attempts to exploit his triumph.

Among Louis' passions was an inordinate love of revenge. This got the better of him at his accession. He had hated his father, and he therefore hated his father's servants. A great many of Charles VII's wisest counsellors were summarily dismissed, some, such as Pierre de Brézé, being imprisoned. It was indeed natural that Louis should try to make room for friends of his exile whom he wished to reward, but he went so far that he endangered the continuity of administrative tradition. He did not, however, lose all power of discrimination. The famous Tristan Lermite, who had served Charles VII as provost marshal, was continued in office. And it was not long before Louis' brain cooled: most of the prisoners were soon released, and a few, conspicuous among them being the Count of Dammartin, were raised to posts of honour. As a rule Louis used anyone who seemed disposed to serve him well. He had in his employ a number of foreigners, and he often attracted into his service men who had been in the confidence of his enemies, like Philippe de Commynes, for years a chamberlain to Charles the Bold. If only a servant showed zeal for the interests of the crown, Louis cared little about the rest of his doings. Hence he frequently bestowed high positions on disreputable persons, who abused their authority and oppressed those under them. It has been pleaded that he was ignorant of most of the maladministration and corruption that disgraced the public services during his reign; but there is no doubt that he winked at a great deal, and he was notoriously clever at finding out what he wanted to know.

When he became king, Louis was popular with the humbler classes, who as usual supposed that a new king meant lighter taxes. But instead of abolishing the *taille* and the *gabelle*, as rumour said he intended to do, he approved the execution of inhabitants of Angers and Rheims who had resisted his tax-collectors, and limited his reforms to some futile and short-lived changes in the methods of raising revenue. Among the richer bourgeoisie he gained and kept much favour by restoring, confirming, or enlarging the privileges of numerous towns. But this was the only class that at first he tried to please, and within two or three years he had kindled bitter anger among the most influential sections of his subjects. The clergy were annoyed when in November 1461 he withdrew the Pragmatic Sanction, partly because it was a measure of his father's, partly because he hoped to get something from the Pope in return. But though he acknowledged the *plenitudo potestatis* of the Papacy in terms which seemed to leave no place for the liberties of the Gallican Church, he soon showed that he did not intend his action to impair the power of the French crown. When in 1464 he realized that the Papacy was not going to offer what he considered to be adequate recompense, he prohibited the despatch of money from France to the *curia*, forbade the reservation of French benefices by the Pope, and revived the Pragmatic Sanction in Dauphiné. At the same time his hand bore heavily upon the clergy, who saw some of their privileges ignored and others threatened. The University of Paris he treated with contemptuous insolence, and though its learning, public spirit, and renown had declined, it was still a dangerous force to antagonize.

Yet more overbearing was the King's behaviour towards the French nobles. With scarcely an exception, it is true, they were selfish, factious, and stupid. But they were powerful, and it behoved a king to meddle warily with their ambitions and rights. In the early years of his reign, Louis showed no concern for either. In his passion for sport, he issued a monstrous decree forbidding anyone to hunt save with royal licence; and a gentleman of Normandy had an ear cut off for killing a hare on his own land. Louis' unconcealed preference for humble society, the dullness of his court, his indifference to chivalrous exercises and pageantry, also alienated the nobles. But it was perhaps the King's capricious conduct towards individuals that aroused most annoyance. Men lost their offices or pensions simply because they had been faithful to the King's father. Some were soon restored to favour, but some were not; and it was hard to see how Louis drew his distinctions. What exposed Louis to the greatest risk, however, was his policy in relation to his two greatest subjects—the dukes of Brittany and Burgundy.

*Louis and the French nobility*

The days were long past when Brittany had preserved its prosperity by acting as a neutral in the Hundred Years War. Duke Francis II, who had succeeded his uncle the famous Arthur of Richemont in 1458, had been on good terms with Charles VII, and had no inclination to depart from loyalty to the French crown. But, though an easy-going and pleasure-loving man, he was not willing to bate any of the claims of his predecessors, under whom Brittany had been linked to France by nothing but the bond of homage. This virtual independence of the duchy Louis was bent on destroying, a desire intensified by his strong personal dislike of Francis. The Duke soon grasped that the King was trying to provoke a quarrel. Louis was now supporting the unlucky Lancastrian party in England; the sympathies of Francis were on the same side, but the commercial interests of Brittany forbade him to wage formal war on any *de facto* government of England. After angering the Duke by claiming regalian rights over Breton bishoprics and abbeys, the King in 1463 signed a year's truce with Edward IV, and asserted that Francis II, as a French subject, was included in it, though not expressly mentioned. This view the Duke denied, but as he could not afford to quarrel with Edward, he felt himself obliged to negotiate a separate truce between England and Brittany, thus adding force to the charges of treason which the King was already voicing against him.

Mutual recriminations followed. Francis appealed for help to his fellow-nobles. Louis, having assembled them at Tours, flattered and cajoled them into a promise of loyal service and an assertion that the Duke's accusations against the King were false. A few days later some of these same men entered into a league against Louis and invited the Duke of Brittany to join. He was already in alliance with Burgundy, and gladly fell in with the plans of the conspirators.

The hostility of Burgundy was even more serious to Louis than that of Brittany. It must be recognized that he had himself done much to provoke it. The ingratitude which he showed towards Philip the Good, however, does not seem to have had much effect on the course of events, for after 1462 the Duke was a broken man, and with his heir Charles the Bold, Count of Charolais, Louis had never been on really friendly terms. The purchase of the Somme towns by Louis in

1463, according to the terms of the Treaty of Arras, infuriated Charles, who was not yet quite powerful enough to prevent it. The interference of Louis in the affairs of Liége poured oil on the fire of Charles's wrath. As after 1464 Burgundian policy was virtually under Charles's direction, he thus became the leading spirit in the rebellion of 1465, commonly called the War of the Public Weal, to which the insurgents were constantly protesting their devotion.

The conflict was precipitated by the flight from Louis' court of his young brother Charles, Duke of Berry, who sought refuge with the Duke of Brittany. This was in March 1465, and in the same month the Duke of Bourbon took the field. Henceforth pretence was cast off on both sides.

In their manifestoes the rebel lords had much to say of the King's misgovernment and the intolerable burden of taxation. What they meant to do if victorious is obscure, but it seems that most of them aimed at making the King a puppet, while State finance, the army, and appointments to public office should be in the hands of a council of nobles, and the Estates-General should be allowed to make suggestions for the reform of abuses. The official leader of the revolt was Charles of Berry, whom some wished to make regent; but this youth of eighteen, feeble in mind and body, was quite overshadowed by the great Count of Charolais. The Duke of Brittany, when it came to the point, did little, risking few men and not much money. The League, however, had some notable adherents—the Duke of Bourbon, John Duke of Lorraine and Calabria (the son of old King René, who sat on the fence), that inveterate plotter the Duke of Alençon, the veteran warrior Dunois, the disreputable Count of Armagnac, besides many other lords whose rights —real or fancied—had been injured by Louis. Some who had stood by him when he was Dauphin, such as Jacques d'Armagnac, now Duke of Nemours, turned against him. Indeed, of the great nobles only Gaston of Foix really backed the King, though some waited to see which way the cat would jump. The lesser nobles, when they dared, stayed at home. The clergy were divided, and mostly kept aloof. The towns generally remained quiet; but both rich and poor townsfolk inclined towards the King. The rebels were said by contemporaries to have 50,000 men in the field, and though this is doubtless an exaggeration, their forces probably outnumbered the King's. But he had the standing army, which remained almost wholly loyal, and he was aided by his ally the Duke of Milan with several thousand men.

On Louis' side were unity and brains. The initial move of the Duke of Bourbon was premature, and Louis, striking at him instantly, occupied Berry and the Bourbonnais with little trouble. Meanwhile, the army of Charles of Burgundy had marched on Paris, but the city, contrary to his expectations, showed a stout front, and he impatiently advanced to meet Louis, who was hastening back from the south. The armies collided near Montlhéry on July 15, and a confusing series of petty fights followed. There was not much generalship on either side, but Louis fought bravely and rallied a part of his army when it was on the brink of panic. On each side a number of men ran away, and both the King and Charles—who was wounded—claimed the victory. The Burgundians could boast [1] that they held the field, but it was an empty triumph, for, with characteristic indifference to conventional ideas of honour, the King slipped away by night, and marched by a circuitous route to Paris. A few days too late Charles was strongly reinforced by the King's brother, the Dukes of Brittany and Lorraine, and numerous other lords. But their united forces, though formidable, could do no more than beset the capital on the east.

There ensued many weeks of deadlock. Some prominent Parisians plotted to admit the rebels, but their plan was frustrated: the insurgent nobles dared not risk an assault, the King would not fight a battle. But though the army of the League became straitened for victuals and money, several waverers among the nobility now joined it, and a great part of Normandy declared itself against the King. Louis therefore opened negotiations which led to the treaties of Conflans and St. Maur-les-Fossés, signed in October 1465.

The King's brother exchanged Berry for Normandy, and the whole of the north coast of France was now in the hands of Louis' foes. For Charles the Bold recovered the

---

[1] Commynes, who was present, has a most vivid and amusing account of the battle as seen by him (*Mémoires*, i, 19 *seqq.*). He speaks at length of Charles's childish pride in his " victory " and of the inflated self-confidence which it engendered in him.

Somme towns; only after his death might they be re-purchased for 200,000 crowns. He received other lands in the same quarter, and Louis agreed that he might deal as he liked with Liége. The Duke of Brittany's claims over the Church were conceded, and he was to be allowed to coin gold money. Bourbon was made lieutenant-general of a vast area in central France. Other lords were placated by gifts, promises of favour, or the restoration of forfeited possessions; but one or two, notably the Count of Armagnac and the Duke of Nemours, got nothing.

The treaties multiplied grounds for mutual jealousies among the lords of the Public Weal. Their ostensible aims were almost wholly ignored. Louis had indeed to promise to reform the government with the aid of a committee, but he never summoned it to do its work. The authority of the crown was left virtually intact. Louis still had his army. And, as soon as the rebels separated, he began to undo the treaties. His brother Charles having fallen out with the Duke of Brittany, Louis, on the pretext of aiding him, entered Normandy with an army and soon was in occupation of almost the whole duchy. Heavy punishments were inflicted on Normans who had served or supported Charles. It was in vain that the young man reconciled himself with Duke Francis; the King held Normandy fast and turned a deaf ear to all his complaints. Soon, moreover, Louis took his revenge on one or two prominent men whose treachery towards him had been particularly flagrant; while he employed every conceivable excuse and subterfuge to prevent Charles the Bold from profiting by the concessions made to him. It was not long before Charles was boiling with anger. In 1467 he inherited all his father's possessions, and, rendered thus more formidable than ever, he formed a fresh league against the King with the disappointed Prince Charles, and the Dukes of Brittany and Alençon. Louis characteristically gained a breathing-space by offering a truce, which his principal adversaries foolishly accepted. He lured the silly Alençon out of the confederacy. Then he secured from the Estates-General, assembled at Tours in April 1468, a declaration that his brother's demands were excessive, and that it was not within the authority of the crown to alienate Normandy from the royal domain. He further appealed

*Royal reprisals*

*Renewed breach with Burgundy*

to popular sympathy by an ordinance amending the organization and discipline of the army.

*Interview between Louis XI and Charles the Bold at Péronne, Oct. 1468*

Louis' position, nevertheless, was precarious. In this year, 1468, Charles the Bold married Margaret of York, sister of Edward IV of England, who was openly planning an invasion of France. But the Duke fatuously agreed to a prolongation of the truce without consulting his Breton ally, so that Louis was free to invade Brittany and constrain Duke Francis to sign the Treaty of Ancenis, whereby he abandoned his alliances with Burgundy and England, promising loyalty to the King. The treaty was made in September 1468; the truce with Burgundy had just expired, and Charles, at the head of an army, was about to march on Paris. Louis tried in vain to buy him off, and then, to the general amazement, begged a safe-conduct for a personal interview. The Duke condescendingly agreed, and on October 9, Louis, with an escort of about a hundred men, entered Péronne, Charles's headquarters. Thus began one of the most dramatic episodes in the history of Europe. Louis soon grew uneasy, for there were in the town many Burgundians with personal grievances against him; and it was at his own request that his lodgings were transferred from a private house to the castle. Conversations between him and Charles were in progress, when news came that the people of Liége, instigated by agents of Louis, had revolted and killed their bishop.[1] Louis, it seems, was so accustomed to having secret emissaries at Liége that he had overlooked the advisability of keeping them quiet while he was at the mercy of Charles.

The Duke's rage was terrible. For two days and three nights the fate of the frightened king hung in the balance. Some of Charles's counsellors urged him to hold Louis a prisoner; but others, not uninfluenced perhaps by the lavish bribes which the King caused to be judiciously distributed, spoke of the sanctity of safe-conducts and argued that if Louis would accept the Duke's terms, he should be allowed to go. On the third day, Charles, after a sleepless night, with limbs scarcely under control, his voice trembling, his face grim and hard, went to see the King. Louis' one concern was to

---

[1] The bishop had not really been killed. Everyone interested in Louis XI and Charles the Bold should read Commynes' incomparable account of the Péronne meeting (*Mémoires*, i, 125 *seqq.*).

escape from the trap, at whatever cost to his honour and dignity. He agreed to everything. He would accompany Charles on a punitive expedition against Liége. He would restore any lands of Charles or his allies which his officers had seized. New territory south of the Somme should be ceded to Charles. All the Duke's subjects should be exempt from military service to the crown. For eight years Flanders should be free from the jurisdiction of the *Parlement* of Paris. And there were other conditions of less note.

Next day Louis, with his Scottish guard and a few other men, set out with Charles and his army for Liége. Until the city was taken, he made himself most agreeable to the Duke, so that when immediately after the Burgundian triumph Louis suggested that he might now go home, Charles could think of no valid objection. Louis had his treaty with Charles formally registered by the *Parlement*. He put a good face on his humiliation, but he was not the man to forgive it. *Louis XI with the Burgundian army at Liége*

Louis had promised Charles to bestow Champagne on his brother in compensation for the loss of Normandy. The Duke would thus have friendly territory between Picardy and Burgundy. The King persuaded the Duke of Brittany to consent to another arrangement. Then he imprisoned two of his principal councillors, Cardinal Balue and Guillaume de Harancourt, Bishop of Verdun, on charges of having conspired against him with both Charles of France and Charles of Burgundy. He next suggested to his brother that he should accept Guienne instead of Champagne, a proposal supplemented by other attractive offers of land in south-west France, a long way from Burgundy. The weak young man agreed, and swore a deadly oath that he would never plot against Louis again or marry the Duke of Burgundy's daughter. An interview between the two brothers is said to have been most affecting. *Louis and his brother reconciled*

Louis had now realized that he could achieve nothing until he had broken the power of Burgundy. Hitherto, for all his subtlety, he had been rash. But his humiliations had taught him a lesson, and henceforth he played his game with great caution and increasing skill.

In the next years both Louis and Charles the Bold gave

much attention to affairs in England. It delighted Louis when in 1469 Edward IV fell into the hands of his old friend the great Earl of Warwick. Next year the tables were turned, and Warwick, with his ally the Duke of Clarence, brother of the English King, fled to France : but Louis skilfully turned the situation to his own advantage by bringing about an alliance between the Earl and Queen Margaret, long a refugee in France ; and it was with the aid of French money and French ships that in the autumn of 1470 Warwick was able to return to England, drive out Edward IV, and restore Henry VI to his throne.

*Louis XI allied with the Earl of Warwick*

No sooner was Warwick's victory known than Louis struck at Burgundy. He had been preparing the ground by intrigues with the Duke's subjects, and now he assembled at Tours a carefully picked gathering of magnates and officials, who, having listened to a recital of the misdoings of Charles the Bold, declared that the King was not bound by treaties made with such a traitor and informed the Duke of Brittany that he ought to avoid such associates, advice which kept him quiet for a time. Immediately afterwards Louis took the field. Charles was not ready, many of the towns of Picardy were disloyal to him, and in a few weeks St. Quentin, Amiens, Montdidier, and other important places were in the King's possession. The duchy of Burgundy was likewise invaded with success. When the Duke came to the defence of his precious Picard frontier, Louis refused battle, and Charles failed to recover Amiens after a siege of six weeks. Discouraged, he proposed a truce, which in April 1471 was signed for a year, the King retaining St. Quentin and Amiens.

*Charles the Bold attacked by Louis, 1471*

Why Charles was so pusillanimous it is hard to fathom ; for Edward IV had gone back to England, and soon he had overthrown Warwick at Barnet and Margaret at Tewkesbury and was again firmly seated on the throne. For Louis the prospect seemed darker than ever. His brother Charles was petitioning the Pope to release him from his oath not to marry Mary of Burgundy. The Count of Armagnac and other malcontents were in arms in the south. Francis II of Brittany was making great military preparations. Charles the Bold was reorganizing his army. The confederates had powerful allies abroad. Edward IV was to invade France and to be rewarded with the lands that had once

*New confederacy against the King*

belonged to Henry II. John II of Aragon promised aid; so did Yolande, Duchess of Savoy, though Louis was her brother. The King, said the plotters, would have "so many greyhounds at his tail that he would not know where to run."

But there was no mutual confidence among the allies, nor had they any concerted plan of action. Besides, Louis' luck was in, for in May 1472 his brother died, probably from natural causes, though many men thought otherwise. Louis instantly occupied Guienne, scattered privileges among the towns, and placated Bordeaux by restoring its *Parlement*. *Death of the King's brother, May 1472*

Charles the Bold was already on the move, but Louis coolly turned on Brittany. Several places fell before his arms, but the King showed his customary reluctance to risk a pitched battle. Once more he negotiated a truce, which successive prolongations were to extend to 1475.

Meanwhile Charles the Bold, with an army which excited the special admiration of military experts, had invaded the royal domain and had begun, contrary to his previous custom, to lay it waste. Early in June he took Nesle-en-Vermandois to the accompaniment of much frightfulness. He was held up, however, by the heroic defence of Beauvais, where the weakness of the garrison was compensated by the valour of the townsfolk, men and women alike. Charles showed his usual incompetence in siege warfare, even allowing reinforcements to enter the town. After about a month he acknowledged his failure, betook himself to Upper Normandy, and mercilessly ravaged the region of Caux. But the King would not face him in the open, and in the autumn, his army being weary, disheartened, and short of food, he signed a five months' truce and withdrew to his own lands. *Abortive campaign of Charles the Bold, 1472*

The other enemies of Louis in France had fared even worse. The Duke of Alençon had been seized and sentenced to death by the *Parlement* of Paris. For a second time he was reprieved, and three years later he was actually set free. But in 1476 he ended his foolish life. More tragic was the fate of the Count of Armagnac, who in 1473 was slain in his town of Lectoure, which had just been taken by the King's troops. His heritage was divided among a score of Louis' supporters. *Defeat of other rebels*

The truth was, though naturally none realized it at the

moment, that the crisis of Louis' fortunes was past. It is true that he had mere truces with his worst enemies, and that Burgundy, Brittany, and England were still in league against him. But Charles the Bold, his most dangerous foe, gave most of his attention henceforth to his ambitions in the Empire. He consequently consented to repeated prolongations of his truce with Louis, and it was not until 1475 that the King had again to undertake military operations.

He used the interval effectively, winning the good graces of his fickle capital, fortifying towns near the frontiers, putting subtle obstacles in the way of Charles the Bold's schemes. As ever, he wished to avoid fighting. But in 1474 Edward IV undertook to invade France with 10,000 men in the next year. Charles the Bold and Francis of Brittany were to aid him with powerful forces. When all was over, Edward would be king of France, but would bestow on Charles all Picardy and Champagne in full sovereignty. Edward and Charles meant business; but their plans were known all over Europe, so that in the spring of 1475 Louis was able to take the initiative. He laid waste Picardy, dismantling a number of towns which he captured. His forces also wrought much havoc in the duchy and county of Burgundy.

*English invasion of France, 1475*

Early in the summer 13,000 men—a very great force for England to send overseas—landed at Calais. In July, the Burgundian contingent having joined them, King Edward and the Duke led the army to the Somme. Then disenchantment came upon the English. The force brought by Charles the Bold was smaller than they had expected. The Duke of Brittany sat still. The victualling of the army began to present great difficulty. Soon, to Edward's chagrin, Charles went off to his army in Lorraine. Louis seized the opportunity to suggest an accommodation. It at once became evident that the English might be bought off. The English soldiers were admitted to Amiens, and lavishly entertained with food and drink for some days at the expense of Louis. The Duke had got wind of what was happening and rushed back to stop it; but his prayers and bluster alike left Edward unmoved. Finally, on August 29, the two kings reached a definitive settlement in an interview on a bridge at Picquigny, where they conversed through a stout wooden trellis. The two realms were to be at peace with each other for seven

*The Treaty of Picquigny, August 1475*

years. Edward should receive an immediate indemnity of 75,000 crowns and a yearly pension of 50,000. Neither king would aid rebel subjects of the other. The Dauphin should marry Edward's daughter Elizabeth.

The English went home as soon as they could. The Duke of Burgundy, troubles thickening around him, was fain to agree to a nine years' truce. Louis' promise that he would not aid the Lorrainers or the Swiss against him was of course not meant to be kept. Though Francis of Brittany had utterly failed his allies, Edward saved him from severe punishment. Louis let him off with the Treaty of Senlis, whereby he made perpetual peace with the King of France and renounced all alliances that he had hitherto entered.

Louis' dangers were ended. Charles the Bold went to conquer Lorraine, and then on his fatal enterprise against the Swiss. Though Louis kept an army on the eastern frontier and watched events closely, he refrained from military interference in these affairs; but the money which he freely spent was no small factor among the causes of the Duke's discomfiture. Meanwhile, his hand fell heavily on some who had betrayed or failed him. The Count of St. Pol, who had played false with both sides, was handed over by Charles, condemned by the *Parlement* of Paris, and beheaded. Jacques d'Armagnac, Duke of Nemours, was constrained to surrender, shut up in a cage in the Bastille, and executed in 1477. The Duke of Bourbon, who had merely temporized in 1475, had to cede Beaujolais and thus give the king command of his communications with Burgundy. But though it pleased him to punish men like these, Louis probably never felt such joy as when he heard "the good and agreeable news" of Charles the Bold's death at Nancy on January 5, 1477. *Louis triumphant*

Louis was a bully. Though not a physical coward, he naturally cringed to the strong and trampled on the weak. Strange to say, his surrenders, cunningly timed and conditioned, usually turned to his advantage in the end, whereas his violence, dictated by passion, frequently defeated its own purposes. So it was at this juncture. Faced by two women, Mary, the dead duke's daughter, and her stepmother Margaret of York, Louis threw restraint to the winds. A *Louis and the Burgundian succession, 1477* pathetic letter appealing to his generosity was not even answered. Philippe de Commynes, who counselled moderation, was dismissed from court.

Though Mary had been betrothed to Maximilian of Austria and the Dauphin to Elizabeth of England, Louis was resolved that his son should marry Charles's daughter. Charles's French fiefs, he said, had been forfeited by his treason. Besides, he alleged quite falsely, none of the Duke's possessions was heritable by a woman. He proposed to annex to his domain, not only all Charles's lands in France, but also Hainault and Franche-Comté, which, he asserted, were incorrectly regarded as fiefs of the Empire. The rest of Charles's territories might serve to attach to Louis' cause some of the princes of Germany, and even the English might be allowed a little. René of Lorraine, Sigismund of Habsburg, and the Swiss, who had shown an unwelcome interest in the future of the two Burgundies, were warned or bought off. The price of the Swiss, as usual, was high; and as Louis was not a little afraid of them, they did very well out of him for the rest of his reign.

*The duchy and county of Burgundy seized*

Louis' prospects seemed good, for Charles had not been popular with his subjects, and Mary was faced with much disaffection. The two Burgundies, in particular, had resented the indifference which both Philip and Charles had shown towards them, except when they wanted money. Within a few days of the Duke's death, the King's emissaries were cajoling the people of Dijon and distributing favours among the nobles and towns of the duchy. Thus, at the end of January 1477 a thinly attended meeting of the Estates of the duchy agreed that until Mary's marriage Louis should conduct the government. The county was less amenable, but there too the Estates soon assented to Louis' claims. When, however, the protests of Mary became generally known and the troops introduced by Louis' officials began to behave as though in a conquered land, the county rose in general insurrection, and parts of the duchy followed its lead. In the duchy the rising was soon quelled, and Louis conciliated its people by confirming privileges, enacting measures to promote economic prosperity, and exempting them from the jurisdiction of the *Parlement* of Paris. But in the county Louis' troops suffered more than one sharp reverse, and resistance was only broken after four years' hard and destructive conflict.

Farther north Louis had acted with even more brutal precipitancy. Picardy, never very firmly attached to Burgundy, was occupied with little trouble. But in Artois several places made a stout defence. Among them was Arras, which was to be a victim of the futile ruthlessness which often marked the King's conduct. When the town surrendered, it was condemned to pay a large indemnity and its walls were destroyed. The officers set over the place were tyrannical, the population remained restive, and Louis, to his annoyance, had to keep a big garrison there. In 1479 he therefore exiled all the inhabitants. The place was to be repopulated by compulsory emigration from other parts of France, and to be known thenceforward as "Franchise," in allusion to the wide commercial privileges which it was to enjoy. But many of the newcomers were ne'er-do-wells, few liked their new home, few showed any zeal for work, and the place did not flourish. Towards the end of 1482 the old inhabitants were allowed to return. But Arras never recovered its former prosperity. *Harsh treatment of Arras*

Notwithstanding inevitable difficulties and his own folly, Louis got a fairly secure hold on Artois. In Flanders, however, he overreached himself. The shrewd Flemings saw through an attempt of his to convince them that Mary was hostile to their liberties. They firmly rejected the Dauphin as her future husband, and in August 1477 she was married to Maximilian. This was a blow to Louis, though he little thought how seriously it would affect his successors  Meanwhile, he had invaded Hainault—a fief of the Empire—where the harvest had been systematically ravaged, while Avesnes had been taken and its population massacred. The Hainaulters were the more determined not to pass under the rule of France, and their resistance, together with Mary's marriage, constrained Louis to sign a truce. *Failure of Louis in Flanders* *Marriage of Mary of Burgundy and Maximilian of Habsburg, Aug. 1477*

In 1478 and 1479 there was further fighting near the north-eastern frontier of France, but Louis gained little by it. Maximilian, though no genius, was soon recognized by Louis as a more formidable foe than Charles the Bold. In August 1479 a battle was fought at Guinegate, near St. Omer, in which Maximilian's infantry flung off the attacks of the French, and remained in possession of the field. Louis took the reverse very seriously. He reorganized the army, abolishing the Free Archers, who had become proverbial for insubordination and licence; but it was significant that henceforth the proportion of foot-soldiers to horsemen was to be greatly increased. Nevertheless, Louis was more reluctant than ever to put his fate to the touch of battle. The next year or two were full of negotiations with Maximilian, Edward IV, and the Duke of Brittany. Louis was often hard pressed, and in 1481 an alliance between his three chief enemies might have ruined him but for the characteristic slackness of the King of England. Louis' health was failing, and his foes were waiting for his end, when their expectations were confounded by the death, in March 1482, of Mary of Burgundy, at the age of twenty-five. The Flemings made it clear that they would tolerate Maximilian only as guardian of his little son Philip, and showed a desire for peace, which Louis shared. The result was a treaty signed at Arras in the December of the same year. The Dauphin Charles was to marry Maximilian's daughter Margaret, whose dowry would be Franche-Comté and Artois. The duchy of Burgundy and Picardy were tacitly left to Louis. Enraged at the repudiation of the Treaty of Picquigny, Edward IV prepared for war; but in the following April he too died.

Louis might boast that he had freed the French crown from the incubus of Burgundy. But his gains fell short of his ambitions, and through his folly the House of Habsburg was established on the confines of France, nay, within her borders.

It was to Burgundy and Brittany that Louis devoted most of his diplomatic skill and warlike activity. Among foreign powers the one he feared most was England. But he had dealings with many others. His relations with Germany were in the main subsidiary to his policy towards Burgundy. His intrigues in Savoy continued plans which he had initiated when dauphin; they brought him no substantial advantage, and drove his very sister Yolande, wife of Duke Amadeus IX, to ally herself for years with Charles the Bold. Louis was constantly interfering in Italian affairs; but though he influenced them more than any other foreign ruler, he achieved nothing of material benefit to himself or France. He was usually on friendly terms with the Sforza and Medici families, and showed small practical concern for the Italian ambitions of his kinsmen, the Dukes of Orléans and Anjou.

Much more noteworthy were the dealings of Louis with Spain. Here again his diplomacy was unscrupulous and his conduct imprudently violent. When he became king, Catalonia was in fierce revolt against John II of Aragon. Louis' offer to help the rebels was refused, and he then made a secret treaty with John, promising some modest military aid in consideration of 200,000 gold crowns, for the payment of which John mortgaged the counties of Roussillon and Cerdagne. The Catalans, with the aid of Castile, put up a desperate defence, and in the end frustrated the efforts of the French to conquer them. Louis tried in vain to cajole them into accepting him as their lord, and later he hoped to get control over them through René of Anjou, whom they asked to become their ruler. But after the death in 1470 of René's vigorous son, John of Calabria, Louis, beset with domestic trouble, gave up his Catalonian ambitions. *His relations with the Spanish kingdoms*

In Roussillon and Cerdagne Louis was more successful. In 1463 the French seized them, Louis justifying his action, not by his treaty with John of Aragon, but by the right of conquest. He was so foolish as to govern the two counties harshly, ignoring their long-established liberties. In 1472 they rebelled, and it took the French three years to restore their rule. After that Louis acted with more moderation, and succeeded in holding his acquisitions until his death. *His acquisition of Roussillon and Cerdagne*

Louis for some time had a wild hope of uniting France and Castile through a marriage alliance. But his intricate intrigues towards that end bore no fruit. He failed to prevent the marriage of Ferdinand of Aragon and Isabella of Castile and to make a match between their daughter and the Dauphin. In Navarre, though a sister of his for some time exercised the regency for her infant son, Louis' persistent interference gained him no substantial advantages. A general survey of his dealings with foreign countries makes one question whether his contemporaries did not overrate his diplomatic skill.

Besides Burgundy there was a noble house of France which counted among its possessions lands which lay outside the realm. René of Anjou was lord not only of Anjou but *Louis and René of Anjou* also of Bar, both French and Imperial, of Lorraine, and of Provence, while his title of king came from his claim to the throne of Naples. He was a poet, a patron of letters, and an ornament of chivalry; but in politics he was timid, and in his latter years he dwelt in Provence, his main concern being to avoid trouble. Nevertheless, he had his full share of misfortune, for his promising son, John of Calabria, died in 1470, and John's son Nicolas in 1473. René proposed to divide his possessions between his nephew, Charles Count of Maine, and a grandson, also called René, son of his daughter Yolande. King Louis disapproved of the suggested arrangement, declaring it illegal in so far as it concerned French fiefs: he seized René's French lands and terrified the old man by accusing him of intrigues with Charles the Bold. A reconciliation followed, and René got back his confiscated territories, but it is probable that he promised to bequeath Anjou and Bar to the King. At all events, when in 1480 René died, Louis at once annexed them. Provence had been left to Charles of Maine, who had promised to devise it to Louis. Charles died next year, and the crown got both Maine and Provence, most welcome additions to its domain.

*Provence annexed, 1481*

Within the royal domain—and in his last years little of France lay outside it—Louis' rule was as despotic as it could well be. He had no great minister, nor any adviser whose influence was deep or lasting. He probably trusted Commynes as much as anybody, but Commynes was disgraced as soon as he gave unpalatable advice on important matters. The Count of Dammartin—the bourgeois expert in finance, Pierre Doriole, for many years chancellor—indeed almost all his confidants, were discarded sooner or later. Towards the end of the reign the Lord of Beaujeu, his son-in-law, was accorded an unusual measure of trust. But throughout his life Louis' schemes and intrigues were the fruit of his own mind.

*Character of Louis' government*

Notwithstanding the independence of his judgment, Louis liked to take counsel with others. But he favoured unconventional methods of doing so. The meeting of the Estates-General at Tours in 1468 was the only one during his reign. Some of the deputies of the sixty-four towns represented ventured to hint at the existence of grievances, but they

*Louis and the Estates*

were bluntly told that they had been summoned to pronounce against the alienation of Normandy. This, as we have seen, the Estates obsequiously did, adding that if Louis were attacked by any enemy, he might raise such men and money as he deemed necessary without consulting anyone. As for the Provincial Estates, Louis assembled them but rarely, and when they did meet they seldom showed any spirit. But while exhibiting characteristic suspicion of established institutions which might restrict his powers, the King often convoked *gens entendus et expers* to advise him on specific problems. Thus he summoned to Tours in 1470 a few great nobles and prelates and a number of councillors and officials, sixty persons in all, and secured from them an assertion that he might justly disregard the treaties of Conflans and Péronne. Of more real service were such gatherings as that of 1479, at which each of the " good towns " was represented by two burghers specially qualified to advise the government as to the best means of maintaining a sound currency.

Under Louis the royal Council was concerned mainly with administrative routine. But it had to go on working regularly; its composition remained much as it was under Charles VII; and its judicial activity actually increased. The King was still of course the fount of justice, and therefore any case might be removed from one of the regular courts and committed to the royal Council. In its judicial capacity this institution was coming to be called the " Grand Conseil." The personnel of the " Grand Conseil " was now, at least in part, differentiated from that of the administrative section of the Council, often called the *Conseil étroit* or *Conseil ordinaire*.[1] The Grand Conseil decided disputes between the ordinary law-courts; it served as a court of appeal; but much of its work came from cases evoked by the King from other tribunals or entrusted to it from the first. Louis often used it to circumvent the *Parlement*, which could not always be trusted to give the judgments he desired. Its activity aroused some resentment, and the Estates-General

The Royal Council

[1] It was also sometimes called the " Grand Conseil." The terminology employed by contemporaries when speaking of the Council is characteristically medieval in its illogicality and inconsistency. On the whole question, see Viollet: *Histoire des Institutions politiques et administratives de la France*, iii, 893 *seqq.*

of 1484 demanded its suppression. But it continued to function with scarcely reduced vigour, and in 1497 it was officially constituted a distinct court of justice.

Louis sometimes appointed special commissions to deal with cases in which he was specially interested. It was, however, difficult to man these except from the ranks of the *Parlement*, and they did not always do what he wanted. At times he dealt drastically with the recalcitrant, as when he dismissed from their offices three members of the *Parlement* who refused to consent to the execution of the Duke of Nemours.

*Heavy taxation*

A general review of Louis' administration reveals little ground for the customary praise of him as a benefactor to the country. Local government was oppressive and corrupt, and the King did not care so long as the officials served his interests. Owing to the civil strife that began in 1465, the disorder quelled by Charles VII was to a great extent renewed. It was hard to put down, even after Louis had overcome his enemies, for heavy taxation and extortionate officials drove many people into crime. The regular army, though its pay fell into arrears, became bigger than ever, notwithstanding the abolition of the Free Archers, and, in addition, Louis had in his service some thousands of Swiss mercenaries. The amount of the *taille*, which the King levied at will, rose from 1,200,000 livres in 1462 to 4,600,000 in 1481. And Louis also raised cash by forced loans, the abuse of feudal rights, and the sale of privileges and concessions. Despite his personal frugality, his court had always been expensive, and when in his later years he became more inclined to pomp and ostentation, its cost naturally increased.

*Louis' last days*

Louis' death was in keeping with his life. He came of a poor stock and aged early. He had always been something of an hypochondriac, and was continually consulting physicians, though for the cure of his ailments he trusted to miracle rather than medicine. After one or two minor strokes, he had a bad seizure in 1481, losing speech and memory for several days, and though he rallied he was thereafter a broken man. But he still travelled about, he retained an active interest in every aspect of government, and he was as keen on hunting as ever. His infirmities nevertheless grew upon him; and after the autumn of 1482 he had to live in strict seclusion. His retreat was at Plessis-les-Tours, in the château which, built by himself, had long been his favourite residence. The house itself was comfortable, and even luxurious, with spacious and well-lighted rooms—nothing like the grim fortalice of legend—but its outer defences were strong and in the King's last days it was guarded by forty crossbowmen. There Louis awaited his end, wearing gorgeous apparel, but attended by only a few servitors and afflicted with an unsightly skin disease. He tried to convince the nation that he was still fit to rule: he punished incompetent ministers and officials, sent diplomatic missions to and fro, purchased horses, hounds, and deer. But he knew that his case was serious. He tried to placate the heavenly powers; he had already released Cardinal Balue, and he forgave others of his enemies. His benefactions were as liberal as ever. For some time he had been on friendly terms with Pope Sixtus IV, who now showed his good-will by sending him Moses' rod, allowing him to borrow from Rheims the ampulla containing the sacred oil used at the coronation of French kings, and inducing the holy Francis de Paul to visit him. But the most desperate remedies failed of their purpose: even the blood of Cape Verde tortoises was of no avail. At last Louis surrendered. He summoned his son-in-law, entrusted to him and his wife the regency, and urged him to keep France at peace until the Dauphin came of age. When he felt the end approaching he declared that he would sing the mercy of the Lord for ever. He died chattering on August 30, 1483. *His death, Aug. 30, 1483*

The new king Charles, a delicate boy of thirteen, had been brought up in careful seclusion at Amboise. His father had taken care that he should have a good education; was he not heir apparent? But the two had rarely met, and to Louis he was apparently a political institution rather than a son. *Charles VIII, 1483-98*

It was disputed whether a French king came of age on his fourteenth birthday or when he entered his fourteenth year. If Charles was still a minor, there must be a regent, and according to precedent the position should belong to the first prince of the Blood, in this case Louis Duke of Orléans. But if Charles was already of age, only a guardian of the Royal Person need be appointed. The King's sister

Anne seemed to have the best claim to act in this capacity, especially as Louis had entrusted Charles to the care of her husband. At all events, the two forthwith took charge of the King, and for about seven years they virtually held the regency.

**Anne and Peter of Beaujeu**

There has been some controversy as to the relative influence of Anne and Peter of Beaujeu during this time. Anne was only twenty-two when her father died. Peter, who was a brother of the Duke of Bourbon and heir-presumptive to the duchy, was an experienced man of forty-three and had of late been as deep as anyone in the confidence of Louis. Contemporaries and the men of the next generation seem nevertheless to have believed almost unanimously that the leading spirit was Anne; and their opinion cannot be rejected. Peter, a loyal, upright and intelligent administrator, was yet lacking in subtlety and force. Anne, on the other hand, had much of her father's patience, adroitness, and his insight into character and motive, with not a little of his cynicism. In some ways she was his superior. She was not so liable to be carried away by passion or panic. In appearance she was handsome and dignified. Her chief vice was said to be avarice; and she was plausibly accused of having used her position to feather her own nest. Her brother the King went in terror of her. She was indeed a very formidable young woman.

**Policy of the Beaujeus**

Anne and Peter, having the support of most of the late King's servants, kept the majority of them in office. Some of the most unpopular, however, they thought it discreet to degrade, and the *Parlement* of Paris, which Louis had treated slightingly, was given the opportunity of sentencing one or two of them to death and forfeiture. No doubt such men as the disreputable upstart Jean de Doyat and Olivier le Daim, ex-barber and Count of Meulan, deserved drastic punishment; but it was regrettable that the former should have happened to be a personal enemy of the Duke of Bourbon, and that the proceedings against the latter should have taken an irregular course at the instance of the Duke of Orléans, who subsequently got much of the victim's property. The ruin of these men pleased the people, who also rejoiced when the army was cut down, the Swiss troops were dismissed, and the *taille* was consequently reduced. Alienations of royal domain made by Louis were all revoked, a measure which was not thoroughly carried out but must still have caused much unmerited hardship. Many towns, on the other hand, had their privileges confirmed. The Beaujeus, however, had not much to fear from the middle and lower classes. It was the nobles who threatened danger.

Towards the nobility Anne and Peter were at first conciliatory. Some of Louis' political prisoners were set free; others of his victims recovered their forfeited property or were recalled from banishment. Certain nobles from whom trouble was specially to be apprehended were lavishly bribed to be good. The Duke of Orléans, for instance, received the governorship of Paris, Île-de-France, Champagne, and Brie, together with vast financial privileges and grants in cash.

The most vital question for the Beaujeus was the composition of the Council. They had at first accepted a Council consisting almost entirely of magnates, the majority of whom were unfriendly. But these noblemen were seldom willing to give regular attention to administrative work; and the Beaujeus gradually and cleverly added to them a number of men trained under Louis XI in law, administration, and finance. The nobles soon perceived that power was slipping out of their hands. They could not beat the professionals at their own game; they were not yet prepared to use force; so they had recourse to the Estates-General, which was convoked at their request.

The Estates-General of 1484 proved one of the most notable on record. It was a large assembly, 284 members being present. Apparently with the object of diminishing the influence of the discontented nobility, the government had ordered that in each *bailliage* or *sénéchaussée* the three Estates should meet and jointly elect representatives of each. This arrangement was adopted in many parts; but some provinces, especially those newly annexed to the royal domain, rejected it as derogatory to their liberties, and in certain other regions the clergy and the nobles insisted on choosing their own representatives. The bishops, moreover, asserted their right to attend, alleging with truth that hitherto they had always been summoned individually to meetings of the Estates-General, and some of them were actually present though not elected. It would have been well for France if

*The Estates-General of 1484*

the proposed method of election had been generally and permanently adopted.

In the chancellor's opening speech, on January 15, the misdeeds of Louis XI were deplored, and the Estates were invited to co-operate in the work of reform already begun by the government. The deputies, who had brought numerous petitions with them, divided themselves into ten committees, and strove to draw up a common set of demands. When, however, they were asked to nominate the royal Council, some were for avoiding the responsibility, saying that the princes of the blood should have the tutelage of the young king and select his councillors. This view was denounced by Philippe Pot, Lord of La Roche-Nolay and Seneschal of Burgundy, in a speech which was to become famous. The crown, he said, was an office, created originally by the people to serve their own interests. When the King is incapable of governing, power reverts to the people—that is, all the King's subjects, noble or common—who for the time have the right of administering the realm through their nominees. These assertions, startling though they may sound to those unfamiliar with the Middle Ages, have been aptly described as "commonplaces of the schools," and indeed there is little doubt that Pot was a partisan of the Beaujeus and speaking in their interests. In the end, the Estates merely asked the King to add to his Council twelve of themselves. The question of the guardianship of Charles was left open.

Towards the middle of February the "cahiers" of the Estates were presented. Their proposals were grouped under six heads. Under the first, abuses in the Church were detailed—papal exactions, provisions and reservations, simony, and pluralities receiving special mention; the remedy prescribed was the enforcement of the Pragmatic Sanction. The second chapter—on the Nobility—asked for due recognition of its privileges : the nobles also wanted pay for military service and the revision of contracts into which they had entered for the conditional sale of land ; in nothing did they betray any public spirit or political capacity. With respect to taxation, the Estates denounced the extravagance of the government, the increase of its demands, the unfair distribution of the burden of taxation among the provinces, and the arbitrariness of the collectors. Much was said about the venality and pluralism which stained the administration of justice. Judicial officers should be chosen by their prospective colleagues, should receive adequate salaries, and should be irremovable. Interference with the ordinary courts of law should cease. The codification of customary law— long advocated and officially though abortively initiated thirty years before—was also urged. Regarding trade, the Estates proposed the abolition of tolls and duties within the kingdom, an evil which had much increased under Louis XI. The views of the Estates on the Council have been indicated above.

The Beaujeus proposed to examine the complaints and requests in the "cahiers" with the aid of a committee nominated by the Council; this body, when chosen, was found to consist entirely of men who would acquiesce in whatever the government wanted. This discovery, together with the unconcealed intention of the Beaujeus to dissolve the assembly forthwith, caused such indignation that the Beaujeus had to make a show of deference. The deputies were asked for advice on national defence. To their denunciation of mercenaries and request for the reduction of the standing army to its strength under Charles VII, the government replied that it must have at least 12,500 horse and 6,000 foot. The Estates then stated that before deciding whether such a force could be supported, they must be told the entire estimated expenditure for the ensuing year. When in response a Budget was presented, Jean Masselin, president of the Norman deputies, denounced it as over-estimating the needs of the government and under-estimating the ordinary revenue. The Estates voted a grant of 1,200,000 livres for each of the next two years, after which, it was stipulated, they were to consider afresh the necessities of the State. The government received the offer ungraciously, but managed by discreet pressure on individuals and provincial groups to secure 300,000 livres in addition. Vigorous protests against the proposed allotment of the tax among the provinces cancelled one another, and caused so much bad blood between the deputies that the government deemed it safe to order a dissolution. So on March 12 the members were told that their wages would cease after the morrow.

Thus ended an assembly which for vigour, outspokenness, and courage was to have no parallel in France until 1789. Yet it had shown small political capacity. The three Estates were jealous of one another. "Treat these rogues to anything but heavy taxes," said a lord, speaking of the *tiers état*, "and they grow arrogant. . . . They are unfit for freedom, and you must hold them down." Within each Estate, too, there was no unity. Local rivalries weighed more than national interest. Many deputies were timeservers and grafters, and on such the machinations of the government naturally had great effect. The practical results of the assembly were of little moment. The Beaujeus thought it well to conciliate certain nobles and towns by restoring lands or confirming privileges. There were some minor, and largely ineffectual reforms of judicial abuses. But the *taille* was continued and increased, and the consultation of provincial Estates about it was only a pretence. The new members admitted to the Council were all men who had served Louis XI, and the Beaujeus held power more firmly than ever. This may well have been for the good of France: at all events, the people at large showed no concern over what had happened.

*Hostility of the nobles to the Beaujeus*

During the next few years the attention of the Beaujeus was devoted mainly to the discomfiture of hostile nobles and the maintenance of the interests of the crown in Brittany. There is no need to dwell upon the intricate and generally barren intrigues into which both they and their enemies plunged.

*The Duke of Orléans and Brittany*

The head of the aristocratic opposition was the dissipated and unstable Duke of Orléans, heir-presumptive to the throne. While he was not above intriguing with Maximilian, it was on the Duke of Brittany that he chiefly relied for support. Though barely fifty, Duke Francis was physically and mentally decrepit. He was wholly under the dominance of his treasurer, Pierre Landais, the son of a tailor, a strong upholder of Breton autonomy and therefore of alliance with England. His arrogance, harshness, and avarice gained him many enemies among the Breton nobles. In 1484 he managed to drive his principal foes into exile: he then arranged a marriage between Louis of Orléans and the Duke's elder daughter Anne, and formed an alliance with Maximilian and

Richard III of England, the object being, in effect, the partition of France.

The danger to the Beaujeus was not really very great. There was no bond of unity among their enemies. By cajoling here, bribing there, and terrifying in some quarters, they diminished the danger from domestic disloyalty. The discontented nobles had little popular sympathy. Consequently the so-called "Silly War" (*la Guerre Folle*), which occurred early in 1485, consisted of a few fruitless military demonstrations, which collapsed when Anne of Beaujeu took the field in person at the head of a royal army. In Brittany Landais was unexpectedly overthrown by a conspiracy between the exiles and nobles whom he had imagined to be friendly to him, and was hanged out of hand without the Duke's knowledge. A little later Richard III was killed at Bosworth. Shortly after this Louis of Orléans submitted—for the second time in this rising—and the whole movement broke down. *La Guerre Folle*, 1485

It was not long before it was repeated. There was another league of French nobles, Louis of Orléans being of course its head. The leading nobles of Brittany, much more united among themselves now that Landais was dead, belonged to it. Maximilian was once more concerned; so, this time, were the King of Navarre and the Duke of Lorraine. The Beaujeus were equal to the occasion. Royal troops occupied the disaffected parts of Guienne and Picardy, where the confederates were particularly strong, and the government fomented a formidable and temporarily successful rising against Maximilian in Flanders. Brittany, it is true, required more force than usual. Early in 1487 the Duke of Orléans and other notable rebels fled thither and were welcomed by the Duke. But the Marshal Rieux and his faction, the former enemies of Landais, were jealous of the intruders and agreed to co-operate with a French force against them. In the ensuing campaign, the French overran a great part of eastern Brittany and took Vannes. But their Breton allies declared that in various ways they had broken the treaty, Breton patriotism was stirred by the invasion, and during the winter almost the whole duchy rallied to the cause of the Duke. In the spring of 1488 Louis de la Trémoille, a general of much ability, led into Brittany Further disturbances

Brittany invaded by a royal army, 1487

an army of 15,000 men, including 7,000 Swiss mercenaries. Near St. Aubin-du-Cormier he came face to face with the Duke's force, some 13,000 in number, of whom 8,000 were Bretons, the remainder being Gascons, Spaniards, Germans, or English. Lord Scales was the commander of the English, who were there in defiance of the orders of King Henry VII; there were only 500 of them, but they were valued very highly by the Bretons. The French, of course, had the advantage in organization, training, and discipline, and the issue was quickly decided in their favour. The Duke of Orléans was captured and consigned to prison. St. Malo having been taken soon afterwards, Duke Francis sued for mercy. Anne of Beaujeu would have dealt hardly with Brittany, but Charles VIII, who was just beginning to assert himself, listened to counsels of leniency. By the Treaty of Sablé, Francis promised that he would arrange no marriage for either of his daughters without the consent of the King, and the French, while holding some towns as security, withdrew from the rest of the duchy. But in September the Duke's death plunged the whole Breton question into fresh uncertainty.

For some time there was great diplomatic activity and much blustering talk by foreign governments. In 1489, Spain, England, and the Empire formed an alliance to protect the young Duchess Anne from French aggression. The duchy, meanwhile, was rent by faction, fomented by the French. Spanish, German, and English troops landed in Brittany, and there was indecisive fighting between them and the forces of Charles VIII. The duchy suffered much, and the patriotic party among the Bretons came to the conclusion that the best way to secure peace was for the Duchess to marry Maximilian. After some intricate negotiation, the two were espoused by proxy in December 1490.

The French government now cast off all show of forbearance. Negotiations having broken down, a very large army entered the duchy. The situation of the Bretons, for whom Maximilian did nothing of any value, soon became desperate. At last, yielding to the solicitations of her advisers, the Duchess Anne agreed to exchange Maximilian for Charles. She married him in December 1491. The King made some concessions to Breton self-esteem; but in effect this was the end of Brittany as an autonomous fief. The situation was well accepted by the Bretons; in 1492 there was a rising by nobles who had favoured the French and thought their rewards insufficient, but it was soon suppressed.

It remained for Charles to avert the vengeance of the powers who had miscalled themselves protectors of Brittany. He wished to give his whole mind to the invasion of Italy which he had begun to plan. The influence of the Beaujeus had been waning since 1488, and after 1491, when Charles released Louis of Orléans, it was almost negligible. Anne would never have agreed to the concessions whereby Charles disarmed his enemies. By the Peace of Étaples (November 3, 1492), he got rid of a great army which Henry VII had landed in France. Each king undertook not to aid the other's enemies. Charles promised to pay the debt which his queen had incurred for help given her by England when she was Duchess of Brittany, and to pay 125,000 crowns as arrears of the pension which Louis XI, in like circumstances, had pledged himself to pay to Edward IV. On January 6, 1493, the Treaty of Barcelona, besides stipulating for mutual aid and succour, ceded to Spain Roussillon and Cerdagne. Yet more of Louis XI's work was undone by the Treaty of Senlis, signed on May 23 following. Maximilian's daughter Margaret, the discarded bride of Charles VIII, was to be honourably restored to her father, and so were Franche-Comté, Artois, Charolais, and other districts received as her dowry. The arrangement may have been just, but it was not for that reason that Charles accepted it.

*Preparations for an expedition to Italy*

*Treaty of Étaples, Nov. 1492*

*Treaty of Barcelona, Jan. 1493*

*Treaty of Senlis, May 1493*

Notwithstanding these strange treaties, France was at the moment the strongest and most-feared state in Europe. The power of the crown was probably higher than it had ever been. But Charles and his successors were about to squander these advantages in hare-brained adventure. For the French nation the sixteenth century was to be largely wasted.

Works on the subjects covered by chapter x :—
i. Some original sources—
    Basin, T. : *De rebus gestis Caroli VII et Ludovici XI Historiarum libri xii*, ed. J. Quicherat, Soc. de l'Hist. de France, 4 vols., Paris, 1855–9.
    Commynes, Philippe de : *Mémoires*. (There are many editions, in both French and English, of this deservedly renowned work. The references in the footnotes are to that of J. Calmette, 4 vols., Paris, 1924–6.)

Gaguin, Robert : *Compendium de origine et gestis Francorum*, written between 1483 and 1495 ; often published.

La Marche, Olivier de : *Mémoires*, ed. H. Beaune and J. d'Arbaumont, Soc. de l'Hist. de France, 4 vols., Paris, 1883–8.

*Journal de Jean de Roye*, commonly known as the *Chronique scandaleuse*, Soc. de l'Hist. de France, ed. B. de Mandrot, 2 vols., Paris, 1894.

*Lettres de Louis XI, roi de France*, ed. J. Vaesen and E. Charavay, Soc. de l'Hist. de France, 11 vols., Paris, 1883–1909.

See also the list of works for chapter xi.

ii. Some modern works—

Ch. Petit-Dutaillis' volume in Lavisse's *Histoire de France*, and pt. ii of vol. of J. Calmette and E. Déprez : Glotz' *Histoire du Moyen Age* (see under chap. ii).

*Cambridge Medieval History*, vol. viii, chap. viii, Cambridge, 1936.

Bailly, A. : *Louis XI*, Paris, 1936.

Bridge, J. S. C. : *A History of France from the death of Louis XI*, 4 vols., Oxford, 1921, etc.

Calmette, J. : *Le grand règne de Louis XI*, Paris, 1938.

Calmette, J., and Périnelle, G. : *Louis XI et Angleterre (1461–83)* ; *Mémoires et documents publiés par la Société de l'Ecole de Chartres, xi*, Paris, 1930.

Champion, P. : *Le roi Louis XI*, Paris, 1936. (A more concise work than his *Louis XI* [Paris, 1927] which was translated into English in 1929.)

Haut-Jussé, B. A. Pocqué du : *Deux féodaux, Bourgogne et Bretagne (1363–1491)*, Paris, 1935.

Stein, H. : *Charles de France, frère de Louis XI*, Paris, 1919.

CHAPTER XI

## THE GREATNESS AND DOWNFALL OF BURGUNDY

WE have already had frequent occasion to refer to the part played by the Dukes of Burgundy in the history of fifteenth-century Europe. For about three-quarters of that century, in fact, they ranked with the greatest potentates of the world. Historians have had much to say about the anomaly of their position, pointing out that, for all their power, they were vassals of the Emperor or the King of France for every inch of territory they held. But as long as feudal theories survived, it was always possible to find rulers of the first importance who nowhere enjoyed sovereign authority. What distinguished fifteenth-century Burgundy were the number and variety of the elements of which its strength was composed and the resources in men and riches which they placed at the disposal of the Dukes, who were thereby enabled to indulge the most extravagant ambitions and come very near attaining them. {Bases of Burgundian power}

The diplomatic history of the later Middle Ages consists largely of negotiations for marriages. These negotiations usually failed : when they succeeded, the marriage rarely brought the expected advantage to either party. But the persistence with which the rulers of that time sought after matrimonial alliances is explained by the fact that one or two states drew great prizes in the lottery. The matrimonial good-fortune of Austria was for long proverbial ; but it is often forgotten that Austria became a really great power by stepping into the shoes of the even luckier Burgundy.

The first of the Valois Dukes of Burgundy was Philip the Bold, on whom his father King John of France bestowed the duchy in 1363, claiming to be its heir. John would have done better to retain it for the Crown ; but the grant in itself did not raise Philip to dangerous power, and Charles V kept him in his place without much difficulty. With the accession of {Philip the Bold, 1363–1404} the young Charles VI his influence naturally increased; but it was not until 1384 that he became one of the leading potentates of Europe through the death of Louis de Maele, Count of Flanders, Artois, Nevers, Rethel, and Burgundy, whose only child, Margaret, was Philip's wife. The Burgundian power was still substantially French, the Free County of Burgundy (Franche-Comté) being Philip's only important possession in the Empire; but in 1385 the foundation was laid for momentous future development. William of Ostrevant, son of Albert of Wittelsbach, Count of Holland, Zeeland, and Hainault, married Philip's daughter Margaret, while the Duke's son John married a daughter of Albert.

*John the Fearless, 1404–19*

Enough has been said elsewhere concerning the character and policy of Philip the Bold. John the Fearless, too, and the mischief he wrought in France, have already been sufficiently discussed. It should merely be mentioned that in 1406, the duchy of Brabant was bequeathed by an aunt of his mother to his younger brother Antony. On Antony's death at Agincourt in 1415, Brabant was inherited by his son John, a feeble youth. Next year died William Count of Holland, the Duke of Burgundy's brother-in-law. In 1418 John the Fearless brought about a marriage between William's daughter and heiress, Jacqueline, and the impotent young Duke of Brabant. He thus strengthened the likelihood that not only Brabant, but also Holland, Hainault, and Zeeland would fall into his clutches.

*Philip the Good, 1419–67*

*Philip's early acquisitions*

Next year John was murdered at Montereau, and soon afterwards Jacqueline, a lively and resolute young woman, ran away to England, where she was harboured by Henry V. Henry's brother Humphrey, Duke of Gloucester, as we saw above, took up her cause,[1] married her, and in 1424 invaded Hainault. But Duke Philip the Good easily repulsed him, and he soon returned ignominiously to England, leaving Jacqueline to struggle alone. In 1427 John of Brabant died, to be followed three years later by his only brother. Philip the Good, declaring himself sole heir (regardless of the claims of another branch of the family), possessed himself of Brabant and Limburg. Meanwhile Pope Martin V had pronounced against the validity of the marriage of Jacqueline and Gloucester. Despairing of securing aid from anyone, she

[1] See Chapter II.

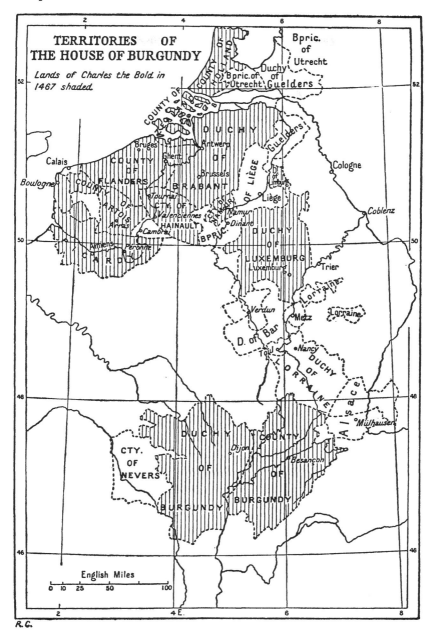

recognized Philip as her heir, and granted him the administration of her lands. In 1433, to save the life of her fourth husband, she abdicated, and, except for the Emperor's negligible claims to overlordship, Philip came into full ownership of Holland, Zeeland, and Hainault. Having in 1421 purchased the county of Namur, he was now lord of nearly all the Netherlands.

*Philip's position after the Treaty of Arras, 1435*

In 1435 Philip signed the Treaty of Arras, and we have seen what enormous concessions he thereby extracted from the King of France. In the next years he was easily the richest of European rulers. Probably, too, his possessions were on the whole better governed than any other part of Europe; it is at least certain that Flanders and Artois were the most orderly and prosperous regions of France. Nevertheless, as Philip knew, there were grave weaknesses in his situation. His territory was a bundle of heterogeneous provinces, each with its own traditions, customs, laws, and organs of government. They had no common political institutions; Philip himself was the only force that held them together. Again, they did not even form a solid block of land; there was a wide gap between Philip's Netherlands possessions and the duchy and county of Burgundy.

It was unwise of Philip to sign the Treaty of Arras. He has of course been much praised for patriotically withdrawing from his alliance with his country's enemies; but there was not much patriotism apparent in the hard bargain which he drove with Charles VII, and he took little part in the subsequent fighting against the English, with whom indeed he made a truce as early as 1439. In his own interests—and he had nothing else in view—he should never have given Charles the opportunity to restore the power of the French Crown. His main reason for concluding the Treaty was probably a desire for freedom to pursue his schemes in the Empire. Philip was always a Frenchman, but thenceforward his attention was turned mainly towards Germany.

*Character and abilities of Philip the Good*

It will have been gathered that Philip the Good's goodness was purely conventional. In the later Middle Ages the epithet was earned by a pleasant manner, a love of ostentation, and an addiction to the carnal vices. For the welfare of his subjects, save in so far as it promoted his own, Philip cared nothing; he was in fact a hard and exacting ruler. In his political dealings he was merciless, faithless, and insatiable. In private life the variety of his inclinations, in Gibbon's phrase, was attested by the finest library in northern Europe and twenty-four acknowledged mistresses, whose offspring played a conspicuous part in the social and chivalrous life of the times. His abilities were no greater than his virtue. He was neither industrious nor clever. What success he gained was due partly to the skill and devotion of his servants, and partly to an ambitious pertinacity which often carried him to his goal if the opposition were irresolute or unintelligent. It pleased him to receive the homage of artists and men of letters —he could turn a verse himself—and his patronage of the writers of his time has been rewarded by the fame which Chastellain, Wavrin, La Marche and others have bestowed on him. In wider circles his renown was based largely on the magnificence and pomp with which his resources enabled him to surround himself. It was not merely that in its furniture and appointments the Burgundian court was the most splendid in Europe, that its feasts and pageants were the most extravagant, that for long it was regarded as the very focus of chivalry. All its activities were regulated by a ceremonious etiquette, the like of which had never been seen before in western Europe. It set the pattern of behaviour for the courts of emperors and kings. Its influence was not unlike that of Versailles in the seventeenth century: indeed many of the rules of conduct enforced at Versailles originated in the palaces of Philip the Good. *[Splendour of the Burgundian court]*

Philip was no great organizer. He strove, it is true, to introduce a measure of unity into the administration of his lands. For financial purposes they were divided into four parts and placed under the direction of four *chambres des comptes*, situated respectively at Dijon, Lille, Brussels and the Hague. Over all there was a *Grand Conseil*, which, besides supervising everything, tried to make itself a supreme court of appeal, analogous to the *Parlement* of Paris. But all these bodies, manned though they were by legists steeped in the absolutist principles of Roman Law, were hampered at every turn by the customs and privileges of the provinces and municipalities. Philip had no respect for such things; when he dared, they were declared invalid or simply ignored; but it behoved him to be careful. It is true that, owing largely to *[Government of Philip's lands]* the class and party dissensions that everywhere existed, no rebellion against him succeeded. But one or two gave him much trouble, diverted his energies from schemes for enlarging his power, and, what was worse, afforded an opening for the machinations of the French. There were disturbances in 1436 at Bruges, where quiet was not fully restored until 1440. Ghent, as always, was restless and quick to resent encroachments on its rights, real or imaginary. A demand for a new salt-tax in 1447 was met with a downright refusal. Philip resorted to indirect methods of getting his way, and began to tamper with the civic elections in order to secure amenable magistrates. The annoyance thus generated burst into revolution in 1452, when the insurgents set up a democratic government and openly defied the Duke. When, after some difficulty, Philip approached the city with a force collected from all parts of his dominions, the men of Ghent, who were aided by many of the peasants of the vicinity, showed a bold and aggressive spirit. In the fighting that followed, Cornelius, the most influential of the Duke's bastards, and Jacques de Lalaing, who had a European reputation as the mirror of knighthood, were killed. For a while the rebels gave as much as they got; but in 1453 they made an ill-considered attack on Philip's army at Gaveren, and were cut to pieces. They had to yield and accept the Duke's terms; the city's autonomy was curtailed, and the burghers had to pay an indemnity and undergo various humiliations. But it is significant that the salt-tax was not imposed, and that soon afterwards Philip bestowed certain favours on the city. He had in fact been seriously alarmed, especially by the appeal which Ghent had made to Charles VII as its sovereign lord.

Such episodes were particularly irritating to Philip since he needed all his time, energy, and resources for the pursuit of his main ambitions. He naturally wanted to round off his territories in the Netherlands. In 1455, despite the opposition of the clergy and people concerned, he prevailed on the Pope to provide his bastard son David, Bishop of Thérouanne, to the bishopric of Utrecht, the temporalities of which amounted to a good-sized principality. Next year he managed to secure the election of his nephew, Louis of Bourbon, a dissolute and ignorant youth of eighteen, as bishop of the still richer see of Liége. It was not easy, however, for

Philip to impose his will on the city of Liége, a populous and flourishing place, with a great measure of self-government. Infuriated by the misrule and vices of their new bishop, the Liégeois entered into relations with Louis XI, and in 1465 there began a rebellion which was to have momentous consequences.

What Philip above all desired was to link his Netherlands fiefs with Burgundy itself. He took a step towards his goal when he bought the duchy of Luxemburg from his aunt Elizabeth of Görlitz, niece of the Emperor Sigismund. William of Saxony disputed her right to the duchy, but in 1443 Burgundian forces occupied the country with little difficulty, and Philip held it for the rest of his life, notwithstanding intrigues by Charles VII and the claims of various members of the Luxemburg family. The inhabitants of the duchy, it is fair to say, seem to have been tolerably content with their new ruler. Philip also had designs on the duchy of Lorraine, on the adjacent bishoprics, and on parts of Alsace. In 1431 he warred against René of Anjou in support of the Count of Vaudemont's claims to Lorraine; but having taken René prisoner, he let him go some years later without having turned his opportunity to much account. In 1444 Charles VII established René's authority in the teeth of the recalcitrant Lorrainers, while the doings of the Dauphin Louis in Alsace were detrimental to Burgundian influence there. It was in fact Charles VII who hindered Philip's designs in Germany rather than the Emperor. But, though Frederick III, resenting the French King's interference, became more favourably disposed towards Philip than he otherwise might have been, he would not go so far as to comply with the Duke's request that the old realm of Lothair, as created by the Treaty of Verdun in 843, should be revived for him. On the other hand, the Emperor's offer of the title of King of Brabant was not good enough for Philip.

*Luxemburg occupied, 1443*

*Philip's designs on Lorraine*

*His desire for a royal title*

Notwithstanding his disappointments, Philip had some ground for self-complacency. His epitaph is one of the most boastful ever written, but it is in the main true. It was a magnificent heritage that he bequeathed to his son. Though Philip did not die until 1467, his bodily infirmities had compelled him for some years to leave the conduct of Burgundian policy to Charles, who thus took the lead against Louis XI in the War of the Public Weal and conducted the operations against Liége and its associates in 1465 and 1466.

*Characteristics of Charles the Bold*

Charles was very different from his father, to whom his character owed less than to his Portuguese mother. He was a sturdy and somewhat thickset man, rather under medium height. He stooped slightly and his walk was a little awkward. He had an eager open face, with flashing black eyes; but when he was annoyed or worried, his features assumed a sulky cast which was unpleasant without being impressive. His good qualities were many. He was a man of his word, temperate in food and drink, and his strict continence excited the amazement of all and the derision of many. On the other hand, he was hard, arrogant, and resentful. His wrath was quickly kindled, and he was often carried away by it—a weakness which grew upon him. Yet, despite his impulsive nature, he was accused of avarice and was certainly far less open-handed than his father. In manner he was stiff and formal, and he attached enormous importance to ceremony and etiquette, on which he was an expert. He had an exalted opinion of his own consequence, took advice reluctantly, and was so conscious of his good intentions that opposition filled him with indignant perplexity. It will readily be understood that though in many ways he was a much better man than his father, he was not half so popular. What made his defects disastrous was his stupidity. In the famous phrase of Commynes, "il n'avait pas assez de sens ni de malice pour conduire ses entreprises." He was a wretched diplomatist. Though he was personally a good fighting man, his generalship was contemptible. Needless to say, he had no idea of this, and it must be admitted that most of his contemporaries thought him an able commander. Unfortunately for Charles, Louis XI was one of those who judged him aright.

*His aims in the Empire*

We have already traced Charles's relations with Louis. The struggle between the two is very famous, and Louis is remembered as Charles's arch-enemy and the chief agent of his downfall. But the projects—inherited from Philip—which Charles had most at heart concerned the Empire rather than France; and his policy towards Louis was defensive in purpose. If there had been on the French throne a king who could be trusted not to meddle with him, Charles for his part would probably have left France alone and given his exclusive attention to his schemes in the kingdom of Germany. It is these that must now be considered.

When the rebellion of Liége against its bishop broke out in 1465, the War of the Public Weal was in progress. The insurgents had relied much on promises from Louis XI, but in the Treaty of Conflans he mentioned them only to apologize for having had any dealings with them. Charles the Bold promptly led his army against the city, which despaired of resistance and accepted humiliating terms. The bishop's authority was restored, and the Dukes of Burgundy were recognized as hereditary " protectors " of Liége, a euphemism which misled nobody. Dinant, which was in the bishopric, was not included in the peace, for it had not only rebelled but had burnt Charles in effigy and hinted that he had been begotten in adultery. So in the summer of 1466 Charles took his father to witness its punishment. It was bombarded into surrender, and then subjected to an organized programme of frightfulness, for Charles was a just man and a disciplinarian, and abhorred haphazard rape and pillage. Unfortunately an unauthorized fire presently broke out and destroyed the greater part of the place. It was disappointing that, notwithstanding Charles's triumphs, a number of irreconcilables kept up an irregular warfare in the less accessible parts of the bishopric. *Suppression of Liége and Dinant, 1466*

Still more ominous were the risings which occurred in several towns of the Netherlands when in 1467 Charles formally succeeded his father. The most formidable was at Ghent, where the Duke was in peril of his life. The cause of these movements was a general discontent, aroused mainly by heavy taxation; but that they occurred at this moment indicated an apprehension that things would be worse under Charles than they had been under Philip. About the same time there was renewed trouble at Liége, which was punished by the dismantling of its fortifications. But even when defenceless the city was not cowed, and next year, owing to Louis XI's renewed promises and the belief that he was going to make war on Burgundy, there occurred the capture of the bishop which so infuriated Charles when, grossly exaggerated, it was reported to him during his meeting with Louis at Péronne. Then followed the joint-expedition of the King and the Duke against the city, which was soon taken by *Risings at Ghent and elsewhere, 1467* *Further rising and chastisement of Liége, 1468* assault. On this occasion Charles let his troops do much as they liked, and deliberately had the place burned, sparing only churches and other ecclesiastical establishments. The miserable inhabitants who clung pathetically to their ruined dwellings were a little later ordered by him to pay their taxes to the bishop as usual. Soon afterwards came the formal reconciliation of the Duke with Ghent. "The Grand Privilege," Ghent's most cherished charter, was publicly cut in pieces, and various penalties were imposed; but what strikes one most is the determination of Charles to subject the city's authorities and representatives to the greatest possible amount of public humiliation. It is well to note these early doings of the Duke against his subjects and neighbours. They stirred up widespread feeling against him. Henceforth the burgher class, especially in Germany, feared and hated him. The events just described undoubtedly had much to do with the unexpected obstinacy of the resistance which often confronted him later on.

*Unpopularity of Charles the Bold*

It is true that in the next years Charles tried to ingratiate himself with his subjects, especially the middle and poorer classes, by personally dispensing justice to them and allowing easy access to his presence. But he had no popular gifts or graces, and his justice was too just for the public taste. And any favourable impression that may here and there have been made was quite obliterated by his demands for money. Resistance and remonstrance he met with passionate, scornful speech. Thus, when in 1469 he was trying to establish a small standing army, he asked for a large aid from each of his Netherlands provinces. The Estates of Flanders demurred, and politely suggested that the duchy and county of Burgundy should pay their share. Charles replied personally to the deputation in a vehement and brusque speech, denouncing the meanness of the Flemings and the thickness of their skulls. He probably thought that he had done wisely, for he got his money; but he gave lasting offence. His unpopularity was increased by measures which he took towards completing that centralization of government which his father had begun.

At the same time Charles was not liked by his nobles, officials, and courtiers. They thought him unduly affable with low people. They despised him for his indifference to women. They wearied, very reasonably, of the ceremonies and formalities which he imposed on the court, where the etiquette had been strict enough in the days of Philip the Good. With ample justification they yawned under the long sententious speeches which he loved to make in council and on all public occasions. Many missed grievously the extravagant liberality of Duke Philip. And even the aged and prudent Chastellain, who defends Charles's alleged parsimony, joined in the widespread condemnation of his devotion to public business and the cares of State. " His taste for hard work," he wrote, " is excessive, but in other respects his good sense has ruled him, at least up to the present. It is to be hoped that as his reign proceeds he will restrain his overzealous industry." One cannot but feel sorry for Charles when his very virtues are cast in his teeth ; but that his good qualities won him so little affection shows how singularly unattractive his personality must somehow have been.

In the first years of his rule Charles's foreign policy was concerned principally with France. His animosity against that country was very bitter. He was wont to declare that he was no Frenchman and to boast of his Portuguese ancestry and the English strain in his blood. He advertised his hatred of France in 1468 by marrying Margaret of York, sister of the English King Edward IV, notwithstanding the fact that ties of kinship attached him to the dispossessed House of Lancaster. We have already seen his lack of success in his subsequent dealings with the French King. To contemporaries, however, his failure was scarcely apparent. After all, he suffered no loss of territory, nor was his influence appreciably less. The civil strife in England from 1469 to 1471 was throughout profoundly influenced by the aid which the factions respectively received from Louis and Charles ; and the issue was not only a victory of York over Lancaster, but also of Burgundy over France. Meanwhile Charles was acquiring new lands in Germany. *Charles's hatred of France*

It was in 1469 that Charles's evil genius tempted him to listen to overtures from Sigismund, lord of the Habsburg lands in Tyrol, Swabia, and Alsace. Over his nominal domains in the two last regions his control was very slight. His vassals did what they liked. Some of the towns enjoyed extensive privileges, which enabled them to ignore Sigismund, but did *Charles and Sigismund of Habsburg* not save them from the depredations of the nobility. Their insecurity led certain of them to ally themselves with the Swiss Confederation. But it was an imperial city, Mülhausen, which in 1466 invoked the aid of Berne, thus giving the latter, confident of the backing of its fellow-members of the Confederation, a pretext for seizing the city of Waldshut, on the Rhine. The Bernese offered to restore Waldshut to Sigismund for a ransom of 10,000 florins, a sum which he could not raise. He sought the aid of Louis XI, but Louis had been bitten by the Swiss once and was always shy of meddling with their concerns. So Sigismund visited Charles in Flanders. There the scope of his suggestions broadened. He spoke of a marriage between the Duke's daughter Mary and the Emperor's son Maximilian, and hinted that the election of Charles as King of the Romans might be arranged. He likewise offered, for an advance of 50,000 florins, to bestow on the Duke in pledge all his rights in Alsace, the county of Ferrette, and certain other areas on or beyond the Rhine. Charles consented. The loan, it was stipulated, should be discharged in a lump sum, to which must be added the expenses incurred in the administration of the mortgaged property. It seemed most unlikely that these stipulations would ever be fulfilled. A treaty embodying the bargain was signed at St. Omer, and Charles at once began to act as though the territories and rights concerned were his in full lordship.

*Treaty of St. Omer, May 1469*

*Difficulties of Charles in his new territories*

Charles soon encountered bewildering complications. The Habsburg lands in south-west Germany did not form a solid block, but were cut up by other seignories. The rights of the Habsburgs over them had originated at various times and in various ways, and were of varying character. Many of them had been pawned, some for generations. And it was a long time since any part of these Habsburg territories had been under efficient administration.

Instead of deriving from his new acquisition the profits which he expected, Charles speedily found that it was costing him a large amount of money. He resolved, nevertheless, to make it pay for itself. The Treaty of St. Omer empowered him to redeem all mortgages on Habsburg property in the ceded areas. Charles wished to do this, and should have done so immediately, but he hoped to pay for the transaction out of the revenues of the unpledged parts of his new possessions.

It was, however, hard to ascertain precisely what his rights were, for the Habsburg lands were not like those inherited by Charles, where everything was organized and registered. It was consequently necessary for him to appoint successive commissions of inquiry, whose investigations caused much uneasiness. A tried official, Peter of Hagenbach, was made lieutenant-governor, with instructions to get as much as possible out of Charles's new property. He was a licentious and otherwise unpleasant man, but he deserves a measure of pity, for he had to choose between Charles's wrath and popular odium. For some years, however, his subjects remained quiet; they had not loved the Habsburgs, and hoped that, despite an unpromising start, their new masters would please them better.

In 1473 Charles was able to make an addition to the northern block of his territories. Ten years before the Duke of Guelders, Arnold, had been seized and imprisoned by his son Adolf. The old man was harshly treated; great scandal was caused; and Charles, having summoned both father and son to his court, proposed an accommodation, which Adolf would not accept. Charles took the two with him to France in 1472, but Adolf escaped. When he was soon afterwards recaptured, his case was submitted to the Order of the Golden Fleece, of which he was a member. Meanwhile, Arnold had been prevailed upon to make over to Charles all his administrative rights in the duchy of Guelders in return for a cash payment and a life interest in half its revenues. Three months later (March 1473) he died. The Order of the Golden Fleece declared that the agreement entitled Charles to enter forthwith into possession of Guelders, and sentenced Adolf to imprisonment for life. Some of the people of Guelders upheld the rights of Adolf's little son Charles; but a great Burgundian army encountered no serious resistance save at Nimwegen, which put up a stout though vain defence. On its surrender it was subjected to the usual humiliations, and the leaders of the opposition to Charles the Bold were executed. The annexation of the duchy was formally approved by the Emperor. *Annexation of Guelders, 1473*

Between Frederick III and Charles there had been intermittent negotiations since 1469. The Emperor was attracted by the proposal of a marriage between his son Maximilian and

**Meeting of Charles the Bold and the Emperor Frederick III at Trier, Sept.–Nov. 1473**

Mary of Burgundy. The Duke, having no lack of suitors for his daughter's hand, stipulated that the price of Mary was his election as King of the Romans, and he even suggested that Frederick might vacate the imperial throne to make room for him. Frederick, who had not the least intention of abdicating and knew that in any case he had little influence over the Electors, answered evasively, but offered to make the Burgundian possessions into a kingdom. At the time this was not enough for Charles, and for a while the negotiations hung fire. But they were renewed about the time when Guelders was seized, and a meeting between Frederick and Charles was arranged. This took place at Trier in the autumn of 1473. Charles went thither with an army, and throughout encompassed himself with a magnificence such as western Europe had not seen for a thousand years. He entered the city clad from head to foot in gleaming armour, his mantle ablaze with diamonds and other jewels. Frederick, contrary to his custom and inclination, did what he could to make a brave show, but was utterly eclipsed by Charles. There was not much cordiality between the Germans and the Burgundians. The Germans thought the Burgundians offensively ostentatious, the Burgundians thought the Germans repulsively barbarous. Yet at first business seemed to be going well, though it is likely that the Emperor was at his favourite game of playing for time. It was agreed that the projected marriage should take place, that Charles should participate in a Crusade, and that in his favour the Emperor would create a kingdom, which, besides his existing dominions, should include the bishoprics of Utrecht, Liége, Toul, and Verdun, and the duchies of Cleves, Lorraine, and Savoy. These were all imperial fiefs; the new realm indeed would be held of the Empire; and it was a question whether the scheme could legally be carried out without the consent of the Electors. Charles, in any case, wanted to get it, though he knew that he might fail. But as the Electors present at Trier declared that it was not for them to discuss the limits of the Emperor's authority, it was generally taken for granted that the business was settled. An elaborate account of Charles's coronation was actually circulated in parts of Germany and Italy.

At the last moment something went wrong—what, will

probably never be known. According to some, the difficulties had all been smoothed over, and Charles was to be crowned on November 25; according to others, the creation of the new kingdom was after all to await electoral approval and there was simply to be a farewell ceremony. What is certain is that early in the morning of the 25th, it was discovered that the Emperor had left Trier and was miles down the Moselle in a boat. Charles sent after him, but Frederick would not return. Nothing whatever had been formally settled. For some time, it seems likely, Frederick had resolved to reject Charles's demands. Emissaries from Louis XI are known to have been in the city, and he may have been influenced by them. At all events, he had tricked Charles as effectually, if not perhaps as artistically, as Louis could have done.

The rest of Charles's history is little but folly and misfortune. Troubles crowded upon him thick and fast. While at Trier, his restless ambition had exposed him to fresh strokes of fate. Nicolas, Duke of Lorraine, had lately died. He was succeeded by his aunt Yolande, daughter of René of Anjou, who forthwith abdicated in favour of her son, also called René. There was in Lorraine a party friendly to Burgundy, and, under its influence, the young Duke, in October 1473, signed a treaty in which he recognized Charles the Bold as his protector, gave permission for Burgundian troops to traverse Lorraine, and promised that in places on the route between the two blocks of Charles's territories he would appoint officials sworn to be faithful to the Duke of Burgundy. This treaty was approved by a large number of Lorraine nobles; but when soon afterwards Charles visited the duchy, he began to interpret it in a way which they had never expected, putting Burgundian garrisons in many towns, to the great annoyance of the populace and the neighbouring peasantry. Popular feeling turned strongly against Burgundy. *Multiplying troubles of Charles*

At the same time Charles's fortunes in Alsace were not prospering. Charles's officials, to do them justice, had brought to the Habsburg lands unprecedented peace and order; but their demands were heavy, and Burgundian rule was disliked, especially in the towns. The Swiss were apprehensive and unfriendly, while the Burgundian officials were openly hostile and contemptuous towards them. Early in *Disaffection in Alsace*

1473, Charles's wish to redeem the mortgages which he had taken over from the Habsburgs led Hagenbach to impose a new tax on wine, commonly called the Bad Penny. It was illegal, for it was levied without the consent of the local Estates, whose rights had been expressly protected by the Treaty of St. Omer. Resistance was offered in certain towns, and Hagenbach had to besiege Thann, which was very savagely punished when captured. Just when feelings were thus inflamed, the imperial city of Mülhausen, threatened by Hagenbach with forcible subjection to Burgundian authority, appealed for help to the Swiss and to other towns which had reason to fear a like fate. The Swiss, while friendly, were reluctant to act at the moment; but the appeal of Mülhausen led to the formation of a league, for the defence of common interests, between several towns, bishoprics, and seignories of south-west Germany. It was known as the Lower Union and played an influential part in the events of the ensuing years.

*Formation of the Lower Union, 1473*

Before anything startling occurred as a result of the new situation, Charles visited Alsace in the winter of 1473-4. On the one hand, he tried to overawe the malcontents by a display of might and magnificence; on the other, he tried to placate the people in general by a show of affability. He made small impression, for popular suspicions of his intentions were kept alive by two abortive attempts to get possession of Basel by treachery, and though Charles was ready to listen to complaints, it soon became clear that he did not intend to provide remedies. When he was gone, Hagenbach continued to levy the Bad Penny, coercing defaulters more sternly than ever, and at the same time his own proclivities increased his unpopularity. The Lower Union was bargaining with the Swiss; agents of Louis XI were here and there; and men were beginning to talk of the restoration of Sigismund.

*The Swiss, the Lower Union and Sigismund allied against Charles, March–April 1474*

The outcome of some obscure negotiations was that in the spring of 1474 it was agreed at Constance between the Lower Union, the Swiss, and Sigismund that the Habsburg lands should be redeemed from Charles, a defensive alliance between the parties being likewise signed. The money was somehow raised, and put at Sigismund's disposal. The arrangements for its payment, when communicated to Charles, proved to be slightly at variance with the stipulations of the Treaty of St.

Omer. He pointed this out, and said that the whole question must be investigated.

At Easter, however, before anything further was done, Hagenbach's exactions provoked a violent outbreak at Breisach, where he was seized. At first the townsfolk protested their loyalty to Charles, but they refused to deliver Hagenbach to him, and shortly afterwards received Sigismund as their lord. Hagenbach, tried by a court containing representatives of the members of the Lower Union, was condemned and beheaded. His brother Stephen was sent with troops to take vengeance, and did so ferociously; but the effect was to strengthen and extend the revolt. *Peter of Hagenbach killed*

Charles, let it be remembered, had continually to keep an eye on Louis XI, and at this very time he was planning a great invasion of France with Edward IV. But, as if he had not enough irons in the fire, he must needs involve himself in the disturbed affairs of the archbishopric of Cologne. On this important electorate the Dukes of Burgundy had long cast longing eyes, and Philip the Good had tried to secure control over it by the same means that he had used at Utrecht and Liége. He had, however, failed; and when Charles the Bold became duke, the Archbishop was a brother of the Elector Palatine. He was on bad terms with his chapter, and in 1467 asked for Charles's aid. The Duke was busy elsewhere, and merely told the chapter to behave itself. The quarrel dragged on, and the city of Cologne took the side of the chapter. Charles's rebukes to the Archbishop's enemies were disregarded, and presently almost the whole of the electorate was in revolt against him. The mediation of the Emperor was expected; but Frederick, as usual, was reluctant to commit himself, and at the end of 1473 Charles, anxious after the Trier fiasco to prove himself a better man than the Emperor, announced that the Archbishop was in the right and that he, Charles, would defend him. Next summer he invaded the electorate, and in July laid siege to the small town of Neuss. His expectation that it would fall in three days was characteristic, but his subsequent dispositions were much admired by military experts. He had a marvellous camp, larger and more comfortable than many a German town. The discipline of his troops was good; they were well cared for; losses through disease were astonishingly few. Nothing was lacking *Charles and the archbishopric of Cologne*

*Siege of Neuss, July 1474– June 1475*

but success. After some time an imperial army came to the relief of the town. But it did little, and the only operation which at all resembled a battle had no decisive result. There was general amazement that Charles should continue to waste his time on an operation which would not gain him much even if successful; but it was not until June 1475 that a truce was signed between Charles and the Emperor, and the siege was raised.

During the siege troubles had poured upon the Duke. The agents and gold of Louis XI were at work in every quarter that threatened danger to Charles. It was mainly owing to them that in October 1474 the Swiss openly declared war and invaded Alsace, defeating a strong force of Charles's mercenaries and forcing Stephen Hagenbach to surrender at Héricourt. Sigismund was now generally accepted as lord in his old territories. In the following April, René of Lorraine joined the hostile alliance.

*The Swiss declare war on Charles, Oct. 1474*

*Conquest of Lorraine by Charles, 1475*

Charles was not dismayed, for the great English expedition was at last on foot, and he counted on gains in France which would more than compensate for his misfortunes elsewhere. The futile termination of the enterprise, as he betrayed in public, was a bitter blow to him, but it was due in great measure to his own fault. However, in the treaty which Louis now signed with him, the French King threw over his ally the Duke of Lorraine. Charles at once fell upon René, and after a few weeks captured Nancy—a surprising issue to a siege conducted by him. He behaved as though Lorraine were his by conquest, but he treated his new subjects well and was generally accepted with little apparent reluctance.

*Charles attacks the Swiss*

Meanwhile the Swiss were ravaging in the county of Burgundy and in the lands of Yolande Duchess of Savoy, who was at enmity with her brother Louis XI. There were half-hearted negotiations for peace; but Charles wanted revenge, and Louis' money kept the Swiss up to scratch. The headstrong Duke entered on a winter campaign against them. He crossed the Jura without mishap, and then, instead of making straight for Berne, one of his most dangerous enemies, he laid siege to Granson on Lake Neuchâtel. After ten days of brave resistance the little garrison surrendered unconditionally, and Charles hanged them all—an act which was intended to terrify his enemies and merely infuriated them. On March 2,

1476, he was attacked on the spot by the Swiss army. To Charles's force half the countries of Europe had contributed some of the troops for which they were most renowned; but, like many a cricket or football team of "stars," the army lacked cohesion and mutual confidence. The Swiss came on with their usual reckless fury. Charles foolishly tried to check their leading column by cavalry charges, and when these were shattered on the pikes, he attempted to lure the attackers into a trap by withdrawing his centre while making a converging movement with his wings. It is a manœuvre which can only succeed with highly-disciplined troops possessing absolute confidence in their leaders. At Granson, the wings thought that the centre was broken, and their precipitate flight soon involved the whole army. There was not much real fighting; the Burgundians had few casualties; but Charles lost his excellent artillery, his baggage, and a large amount of treasure. It was a heavy blow; though Charles was justified in belittling the significance of the actual engagement, and as yet had no grounds for despair. *Battle of Granson, Mar. 2, 1476*

In June the Duke again advanced towards Berne. His army numbered some 20,000 men, rather more than had fled at Granson. It was better organized and drilled. Unfortunately he again forfeited the initiative through his foolish propensity for conducting unnecessary sieges. He beleaguered the small town of Morat, on the lake of that name, and there on June 22 he was attacked by a relieving force which was somewhat larger than his own army and included cavalry from south Germany and Lorraine as well as the Swiss pikemen and halberdiers. The Duke's dispositions were such as an experienced but stupid soldier might be expected to make. His main position was strong in itself and was stockaded and entrenched; but it had the lake behind and a dense wood in front. Owing to the proximity of the wood, Charles's right—the more important wing—was surprised; the key position of his lines was rushed with little loss; his centre was isolated and cut to bits; only his left got away, and that with great difficulty. The Swiss, as usual, gave no quarter, and the slaughter among the Burgundians was appalling. *Battle of Morat, June 22, 1476*

Charles put a bold face on the catastrophe. But he had been ill after Granson, and now he became odd in manner and took to drinking more than he could carry. His judgment, *Charles's restlessness and difficulties* never very sound, broke down pitiably. He should have left the Swiss alone for a time and recruited his strength. But he could not rest until he had taken vengeance, for which he immediately began to prepare. His prospects were most gloomy, for there was no enthusiasm for his cause among his subjects. After the siege of Neuss, the Estates of Flanders had refused to furnish any more men or money for offensive operations. He now wished to recruit new mercenaries, to summon the feudal host, and to call up for military service such able-bodied men as he required. But an assembly representing all his Netherlands territories refused to sanction or finance any such measures, pointing out that in 1473, when he had been granted 500,000 crowns annually for six years, he had promised to ask for no more until the end of that term. Long negotiations failed to move the deputies to make any but the most trivial offers. The Estates of the two Burgundies, though addressed by Charles himself in a most eloquent and learned speech which did great credit to its unknown author, would do no more than take certain defensive measures. It was ominous, too, that his few allies were leaving him. The Duke of Milan was inclining towards Louis XI. Yolande of Savoy fled to her brother's court and was reconciled to him. There was a general feeling that Charles's star was setting, and it was not merely because of his lack of funds that he found it hard to raise an adequate army.

**Lorraine lost, Oct. 1476**

Charles's projected attack on the Swiss never took place. For René of Lorraine, aided by the Lower Union and encouraged by Louis XI, invaded his lost duchy, and in October, assisted probably by treachery, recaptured Nancy. Simultaneously, thanks to French gold, a new and close alliance was concluded between him and the Swiss. With all his efforts Charles could not raise much more than 10,000 men to cope with the crisis. Nevertheless, he pushed René back, and by the end of October was before Nancy. He laid siege to the town, a hazardous undertaking, for winter was setting in, his communications were insecure, and the fidelity of some of his most prized mercenaries had been undermined by Louis XI. Charles no doubt hoped to storm Nancy quickly, but several assaults were repelled. Meanwhile René was enlisting volunteers among the Swiss, and in December they entered Lorraine,

# THE FINAL STROKE

where they were joined by a contingent of Alsatians and 4,000 of René's own subjects. The united forces were far superior in numbers to Charles's army, and they advanced confidently to the rescue of Nancy.

*Quem Deus vult perdere prius dementat:* the tag was often on men's lips in Charles's last years, and now indeed he seemed to have lost his remaining wits. Rejecting the advice to raise the siege, avoid battle, and return after the inevitable dispersion of René's ill-compacted army, Charles went to meet the enemy. He neglected to reconnoitre, and chose a position which had all the defects of the one he had held at Morat, with several others. On January 5, 1477, he was outmanœuvred and surprised. About half his army betrayed him, the rest was overwhelmed. The slaughter was frightful, but occurred mostly during the flight. Charles himself did not flee. Two days later his naked body was found, encompassed by the corpses of famous Burgundian nobles, embedded in frozen mud, the head cleft from brow to chin by a halberd, the face gnawed by wolves and unrecognizable. For long there was doubt in many quarters as to the identity of these pitiful remains, and many believed that the great Duke was still alive and would return to his dominions. *Battle of Nancy, Jan. 5, 1477*

What followed in Charles's lands has been described elsewhere. With his death the might of Burgundy as a separate power came to an end. Never again—even in the time of Napoleon—were all the territories over which he ruled united under one hand. Yet the strength of Burgundy, though concealed among the far-flung resources of Holy Roman Emperors and Kings of Spain, affected the course of European history in the sixteenth century no less than in the fifteenth. It is indeed unwise to assume, as so many historians have done, that Charles the Bold was attempting the impossible. His calamities were due in the main to his own folly. Had he not involved himself in the tangle of Habsburg affairs in south-west Germany, he might never have incurred the enmity of the Swiss, and though he was no general, he was not likely to suffer decisive military defeat at the hands of anyone else. He was of course unlucky in having to match himself in the diplomatic field with such an adversary as Louis XI, and, even without the Swiss, Louis might have ruined him. But Louis was the older man; Charles at his death was only forty- *The fate of Burgundy* four; in less than seven years he would have been rid of his arch-enemy; and can we say that he might not then have realized his dream of reviving the old Middle Kingdom ? A ramshackle state it would have been, no doubt, viewed in the light of our nationalist assumptions. But at the same time the Habsburgs were building up a ramshackle state which lasted four hundred years.

Works on the subjects covered by chapter xi :—
See also the lists for chaps. i, ii, iii, and x. The works of Monstrelet, Le Fèvre, La Marche, and Commynes are particularly important for Burgundian history. The following original sources are also conspicuously valuable :

Gachard, L. P. (ed.), *Analectes belgiques*, vol. i, Brussels, 1830 ; *Documents inédits concernant l'histoire de la Belgique*, 3 vols., Brussels, 1833.

Chastellain, Georges : *Œuvres*, ed. Kervyn de Lettenhove, 8 vols., Brussels, 1863–6.

*Chronique de Jean Molinet*, ed. G. Doutrepont and O. Jodogne, Brussels, 1935–7.

Duclercq, Jacques : *Mémoires*, ed. Baron de Reiffenberg, 4 vols., Brussels, 1823. Also in Michaud and Poujoulat, *Mémoires*, vol. iii.

*Le livre des trahisons de France*, ed. Kervyn de Lettenhove, in *Chroniques relatives à l'Histoire de Belgique sous la domination des ducs de Bourgogne*, vol. ii, Brussels, 1873.

Among the works of modern writers the following may be noted :

*Cambridge Medieval History*, vol. viii, chap. ix, Cambridge, 1936.

Barante, M. de : *Histoire des ducs de Bourgogne de la maison de Valois*, 10 vols., Brussels, 1835. (A very important work in its time, and still not without value.)

Cartellieri, O. : *Geschichte der Herzöge von Burgund*, vol. i, Philipp der Kühne, Leipzig, 1910 ; *The Court of Burgundy. Studies in the history of civilization.* Trans. by M. Letts, London, 1929.

Huizinga, J. : *The Waning of the Middle Ages*. Trans. from the Dutch by F. Hopman, London, 1924. (This book purports to deal with medieval civilization in general, but is particularly full and interesting on conditions in the Burgundian territories.)

Huizinga, J. : *L'Etat bourguignon, ses rapports avec la France et les origines d'une nationalité néerlandaise* (Le Moyen Age, 1930).

Kirk, J. F. : *History of Charles the Bold*, 3 vols., Philadelphia, 1864–8. (The most thorough life of Charles in English.)

Laurent, H., and Quicke, F. : *Les origines de l'état bourguignon. L'accession de la maison de Bourgogne aux duchés de Brabant et de Limburg (1383–1407)*, Brussels, 1939.

Pirenne, H. : *Histoire de Belgique*, vols. i and ii, Brussels, 1903.

Putnam, Ruth : *A Mediaeval Princess*, New York, 1904 (Jacqueline of Hainault) ; *Charles the Bold* (Heroes of the Nations), New York, 1908.

## CHAPTER XII

## FRANCE

### ECONOMIC AND SOCIAL CONDITIONS

AT the beginning of the fourteenth century France had been the best governed, the most prosperous, the most feared, and the most admired country in Europe. It did not take long for the war with England to deprive her of this enviable position, and the recovery brought about by Charles V did not wholly restore her fortunes. And, as we have seen, with the accession of Charles VI she entered a time of great confusion and distress, when it was hard to say whether domestic strife or foreign invasion did the more harm. We have already examined the efforts of Charles VII and Louis XI to re-establish sound administration and the authority of the Crown; it remains to see how the economic and social life of France fared during the period surveyed.

Naturally the return of prosperity lagged behind the restoration of order, and at the end of the fifteenth century the economic convalescence of France was not yet complete. Paradoxically, the very efficiency of French government at the beginning of the Hundred Years War had served to intensify the sufferings of her people. In the first half of the fourteenth century, a very great part of France was included in the royal domain, and the King exercised real authority over nearly all the French nobility. Thus, when the King of England declared war on him, almost the whole land was exposed to the English attack, which proved to be far more formidable and destructive than anyone had anticipated. It was only in regions which preserved a considerable measure of feudal independence that the population avoided the worst consequences of the war. Such were Flanders, and, in the second part of the struggle, Brittany. The trade of these with England was vital to their existence; considering the length of the war, it underwent astonishingly little inter-*Economic effects of the Hundred Years War* ruption; and they emerged from the conflict with their commerce and industries unimpaired. But the inhabitants of such favoured areas numbered but a small fraction of the total population of France. Had it been Germany which Edward III and Henry V attacked, some powerful feudatories would have sided with them and many would have remained neutral, and the principalities of all these would have been immune from English raids. How Germany would have expelled the English is another question.

*Rural life*

Something has already been said of the ill that befell nearly every province of France in the reign of Charles VI and the earlier years of Charles VII. Over wide areas rural life was utterly dislocated. Many villages were altogether destroyed, large districts were left untilled, and even where agriculture was continued, the peasants often cultivated no more than sufficed for their own bare needs, knowing well that everything sown might be destroyed before it was reaped. Even in parts which escaped lightly, the absence of the *seigneur* at the wars might throw all into confusion, and of course many peasants were tempted to turn soldier or brigand in the hope of making a quick fortune. Making full allowance for the exaggeration into which contemporary French writers naturally fell, and remembering that during the whole of this time ten million people contrived to live somehow in France, one cannot doubt that at the middle of the fifteenth century French agriculture was in a grievous plight. The increase in the number and boldness of wolves, which was remarked almost everywhere, is in itself striking evidence of the decrease in the number and vigour of the peasants.

*The peasants*

For many generations before the Hundred Years War, the lot of the peasants in most parts of France had steadily improved. Serfs there still were; but many peasants whose ancestors had been serfs in the twelfth century were now free from the most irksome and degrading incidents of serfdom, and, though attached to the soil, paid a fixed rent in money or kind for their holdings, from which they could be evicted only by process at law. Numerous lords, moreover, had been constrained by financial difficulties to sell their rights over their tenants, and thus there had grown up a class of small freeholders. Tenant farmers also existed, less secure in the enjoyment of their possessions, as their leases were seldom long. And there had also appeared a class of agricultural labourers, with little or no land which they possessed themselves, who hired their services to *seigneurs* or big farmers.

During the wars peasants of every sort suffered, but there was no formal change in the relations between them and their lords. When comparative peace returned, however, conditions again favoured an amelioration of the peasants' lot. Much land had gone to waste, and must be cleared, and for that—and indeed ordinary agricultural work—there was a shortage of labour. The old tenants were able to insist on a revision of their obligations; farmers were not to be found at the old rents; labourers got higher wages than ever before. Those who undertook to clear land often extorted such advantageous terms that to all intents and purposes they became independent proprietors. As for real serfs, still to be found in Champagne, Burgundy, Berry, and a few other regions, they too turned the situation to their profit, and thousands were enfranchised in the years following the expulsion of the English. The central government did little towards the restoration of agriculture, and when it interfered generally aimed at restoring pre-war conditions. But it could not stem the prevailing tendency.

The status of the rural population was raised more rapidly than its standard of living. Enfranchisement was no safeguard against famine. It is often assumed that after 1453 prosperity migrated to France from England, distracted by the Wars of the Roses. But the Wars of the Roses, judged by French standards, were no more than a series of brawls between two factions of nobles and their retainers; they made little difference to the life of the English cultivator. And the injuries wrought in France since the middle of the previous century were too deep to be cured quickly. One of the shrewdest Englishmen of the time, a man who knew France well, writing about the middle of the reign of Louis XI, speaks of the French people thus: *An English view of the French peasant*

"The commons there ... be so impoverished and destroyed that they may unneth [scarcely] live. They drink water, they eat apples, with bread right brown made of rye; they eat no flesh but if it be right seldom a little lard, or of the entrails and heads of beasts slain for the nobles and merchants of the land. They wear no woollen, but if it be a poor coat under their uttermost garment, made of great canvas, and called a frock. Their hose be of like canvas and pass not their knee, wherefore they be gartered and their thighs bare. Their wives and children go barefoot; they may in no other wise live. For some of them that were wont to pay to his lord for his tenement, which he hireth by the year, a scute [crown], payeth now to the king over that scute v. scutes. Wherethrough they be arted [forced] by necessity so to watch, labour, and grub in the ground for their sustenance, that their nature is wasted. . . . They go crooked, and be feeble, not able to fight, nor to defend the realm; nor they have weapon, nor money to buy them weapon withal. But verily they live in the most extreme poverty and misery, and yet dwell they in one the most fertile realm of the world." [1]

We may believe in the accuracy of Fortescue's observation, even though we cannot agree when he ascribes all the wretchedness of the French to the heavy and arbitrary taxation imposed on them by the Crown.

The towns
The towns of France suffered less than the open country during the Hundred Years War, but of course they were hard hit. Few, however, underwent serious material damage, even when besieged or sacked. Their inhabitants might undergo great privations, lose many of their goods, even be raped or massacred; but the artillery of the time, though rapidly improving, was not capable of doing widespread harm, and it was rare for the victorious commander of a besieging force to authorize deliberate destruction. Thus, when peace returned, the towns were still there, and the restoration of normal life was more rapid in them than in rural districts.

In France, towns were not so important a factor as they were in Italy or Germany. They were numerous, they had prospered, many of them possessed extensive franchises. Politically, however, their status was much below that of the Italian and German towns. Only in Flanders did any medieval French town seem likely to become an autonomous city state. Towns in the royal domain, protected and favoured though they might be, had their government regulated by the Crown and were subject, in greater or lesser degree, to royal officials. Those in the fiefs of great nobles were likewise as a rule kept well in hand. Even Ghent and Bruges, for all their truculence and turbulence, seemed downtrodden communities to many a German city which legally was subject to a prince of very small account. The burgher class was humbler and less confident in France than in Germany; it could not go about its business regardless of the

[1] Sir John Fortescue: *The Governance of England* (ed. Plummer), 114 *seqq*. The spelling has been modernized.

quarrels of other classes, nor could it by itself ensure the progress of French culture.

The end of our period therefore saw the towns of France very much where they were at its beginning. In most of them [1] industry was still controlled by the local craft gilds. Where these had perished or languished during the troubles, they were usually revived; indeed many new ones were created in the latter half of the fifteenth century. If there was any change in their character, it was for the worse. Their regulations became more rigid and left less room for healthy competition. Their government tended increasingly towards oligarchy. The mastership became harder than ever to attain; in many gilds it was virtually hereditary. The rules about apprenticeship were still enforced, but unless he was the son of a master, the apprentice at the end of his term had little to anticipate but the life of a journeyman for the remainder of his days. A journeyman's membership of his craft gild was now of small use to him; for he had no control over its policy, which was under the direction of men whom he was wont to consider his worst enemies. This cleavage between capital and labour was not a new phenomenon in medieval industry; it had appeared long before the Hundred Years War. But the bitterness was now deeper on both sides. The central government, if it interfered at all by legislation, did so in the interest of the consumer or the employer. When the journeymen formed their own associations, the masters strained every nerve to put them down, and often, with the aid of municipal or royal authorities, succeeded. The struggle had some interesting consequences. It became much more common than previously for a man to leave the town where he had been trained and seek work elsewhere. Many journeymen acquired the nomadic habit, and rarely stayed long at a job. For the protection of their interests they needed something more than local associations. There thus came into existence unions of workers which, though confined to a single industry, had members all over the country. They were of course frowned upon by officials and employers, and their existence had to be kept half secret. They were consequently not able to do much bargaining for

[1] In certain large towns, such as Lyons and Bordeaux, the craft gilds were few and unimportant. They were weak also in central France and Brittany.

improvement of wages and conditions; but they acted as friendly societies and helped their members to find work. Such unions were to become more important later on, and some of them, such as that of the Freemasons, were completely to change their character; but there is no warrant for regarding them as the ancestors of the trade unions of to-day, which are of quite different and much later origin. It was the wandering journeymen who originated the so-called *Tour de France*, which in course of time became obligatory on the young artisan.

Rise of capitalism

The conditions of the period were not favourable to the accumulation of wealth, and the capitalization of industry progressed more slowly than in Italy or Germany. The cloth industry of Flanders, however, was largely under the control of rich merchants, who bought the wool, distributed it to the workers—spinners, weavers, fullers, carders—and then sold the finished product. The famous Jacques Coeur ran various industrial enterprises, such as a dyeworks and a paper factory. He also owned mines; indeed, the mining industry, in France as elsewhere, was more under the direction of big capital than any other. There was a great and growing demand for all kinds of metals, and the poorest deposits were lucrative to work. Over most of France mining could only be carried on with royal licence and on condition that one-tenth of the output went to the Crown, and in one or two great fiefs where it was controlled by the duke or count, it was commonly conducted on similar terms. The immediate lord of the land where the mine lay naturally received something too. Some mining concessions were very extensive and valuable. There were coal mines in Languedoc which had been exploited by a company in the thirteenth century and were still flourishing at the end of the fifteenth. Jacques Coeur was granted the right of working all mines of silver, copper, and lead in the Lyonnais and Beaujolais. He had an army of officials and workers, many of them brought from abroad, particularly from Germany, which was reputed to have the most skilful miners. His employees were elaborately organized; they were well paid, fed, housed, and clothed; they had free medical attendance when sick, chapels were built for them, and they were provided with small holdings of land to cultivate. They were at the same time subjected to a regimen which, if paternal, was austere. Reading the regulations one is often reminded of the discipline imposed on the Hanse merchants in their foreign factories. It must not be supposed that many mineowners were able or wishful to imitate the arrangements of Jacques Coeur. In France, moreover, the mining industry was eclipsed in importance by many others in which the big capitalist had little or no place.

The troubles of the times perhaps injured commerce more than industry. One may not indeed separate the two completely, for under the gild system the master-craftsman usually sold his products to the consumer. Thus most commerce, like most manufacture, was localized. The fortunes of the two rose and fell in close agreement, and national calamities affected neither as much as might have been thought. Still, France had imported and exported certain commodities, and there had been a good deal of trade between widely separated French provinces. Naturally all commerce which necessitated the transportation of goods between distant points was very nearly ruined, things going from bad to worse when the Treaty of Troyes virtually divided France into two hostile states. And when disorder was checked, there were many obstacles to the recovery of trade. The roads had fallen into disrepair, bridges had been broken down, the channels of rivers had become choked, harbours had silted up. The great fairs—especially those of Champagne and Lyons—had been suspended, and foreign merchants who had once frequented them had become accustomed to go elsewhere. Other foreigners had dropped their dealings with France: the Hanse merchants, for example, no longer visited La Rochelle, which had formerly had a large trade with them. It happened, too, that about the middle of the fifteenth century piracy was very rife in the North Sea, the English Channel, and the Mediterranean. It is not astonishing that the revival of French commerce was slow. The royal government did its best, showing far more interest in trade than in agriculture or manufacture. It repaired roads, dredged rivers, abolished tolls, tried by legislation to draw traffic to decaying ports. Both Charles VII and Louis XI signed commercial treaties with most of the states of Europe and attempted by diplomacy to promote trade with the East. Numerous new fairs and markets were created; and though new methods of business

*Decline of French trade*

were robbing fairs of their former international importance, so that it was not possible to resuscitate the celebrated fairs of Champagne, Louis had the satisfaction of ruining the Duke of Savoy's fair at Geneva to the profit of his own at Lyons. Ships were fitted out to destroy pirates and make reprisals on the vessels of other countries whose subjects had injured French merchants and sailors. The coinage was improved, and, in accordance with the economic doctrines of the time, efforts were made to prevent the exportation of precious metals. Such measures were not fruitless, but they could not obviate the effects of the long dislocation which French trade had undergone. To the end of the century, France, as a commercial country, could not vie with Italy, Germany or even Aragon.

*Jacques Coeur*

One is liable to get an exaggerated notion of the vigour and remunerativeness of French commerce from the doings of that most remarkable man Jacques Coeur, especially as his successes were all achieved before the end of the Hundred Years War. The son of a furrier of Bourges, Jacques inherited little from his father. His first attempt to attain wealth was in every way unhappy, for he associated himself with the master of the Bourges mint in a scheme for the unauthorized debasement of the coinage, was detected, and put on his trial.[1] It may be suspected, however, that he had already made something out of his misdoing, for he and his accomplices procured their pardon, which, at a time when La Trémoille was in power, was certainly not to be had cheaply. His next venture, though more respectable, was yet more unfortunate. He went to the Levant, intending to buy spices, always in great demand in the Middle Ages, but of late scarce and dear in France. On the way back he was shipwrecked, and lost everything. But the voyage had taught him much about Mediterranean trade, and he later turned his knowledge to good account.

Somehow he made his way into the good graces of Charles VII. In 1438 he was appointed treasurer of the royal household, an office which gave him ample opportunity of feathering his own nest. He used his gains to embark on new commercial enterprises, in which through his persuasion many

[1] This happened in 1429, but attempts to prove that the offence had been committed in order to provide funds for the enterprises of Joan of Arc are based on mere prejudice and imagination.

great men, nay the King himself, became financially interested. Jacques Coeur became a member of the royal Council and was granted various influential posts in Languedoc. He was undoubtedly a man with a natural turn for big business, exceptional organizing ability, and a commanding personality, and, being totally devoid of scruple, he acquired an enormous influence throughout southern France. The main source of his huge fortune was his trade with the East, which he conducted with his own ships, first from Montpellier, later from Marseilles. He also ran passenger services, and trafficked in slaves. He was even charged (on weak evidence, it is true) with having shipped arms to the Moslems, against whom western Europe was continually planning crusades. So far as possible he dispensed with middlemen, buying his goods direct from the producers. His industrial undertakings, which were not confined to France, would alone have brought him a fortune; mention has already been made of some of them, notably his mines. While his success was no doubt due in the main to his initiative and shrewdness, it must be confessed that his methods did not become more honest as he grew older. He was the master of every kind of graft, and more than once he paid foreign creditors with large amounts of debased silver, with which he had tampered himself. For the conduct of his extensive operations, he of course required an enormous staff of assistants and agents; he trained them most efficiently and they usually served him with loyalty and skill; but the means whereby he attached them to his interests will not always bear examination. He exploited his offices to the full: important towns paid heavily for his favour, and the Estates of Languedoc were at his beck and call, granting him privileges, modifying taxation to serve his purposes, and even voting him sums of money.

Jacques became extremely famous, and it wanted but little to establish his fame as a popular hero like Dick Whittington. His operations in the Levant were the beginning of an active commercial intercourse between that region and France, whose prestige in the East, after an interval of eclipse, was now revived. His services to his country were really great. He helped materially in the reorganization of French finances, and but for his money the reconquest of Normandy would have taken much longer. The peak of his fortunes was reached when, on the capture of Rouen, he, Dunois, and Brézé rode into the city side by side.

Despite the precautions he had taken, Jacques Coeur's position was not as secure as it looked. Men like him inevitably make countless enemies. The French nobles hated him as an upstart. Good men, like Charles VII's faithful minister, Jean Jouvenel des Ursins, thought him no better than a brigand. Those whom he had pushed aside or trampled down in his upward progress longed for revenge. He had lent money right and left among the needy nobility; even the Queen was believed to be in his debt. Thus no doubt his power was for a while increased, but so was the number of those who desired his overthrow. In 1451 all this hostility broke upon him. The King's trust in him having been shaken by a report that he was intriguing with the Dauphin, he was arrested on the charge of having poisoned Agnes Sorel, who had died the year before. The commission which tried him dismissed this charge, but for having supplied arms to enemies of the Faith, for having exported French coin, and for having embezzled public funds, he was sentenced to banishment for life, to forfeiture of his goods and a fine of 400,000 crowns, and to imprisonment until it was paid. Jacques Coeur, however, escaped to Italy after a series of melodramatic adventures, and was in the service of the Pope when in 1456 he died in the Ægean island of Chios. Little of his immense fortune went to the victims of his unscrupulous transactions, and not much to the State. It was the courtiers who benefited by his fall.

It is unlikely that there was in France another man who could have achieved such success as Jacques Coeur. And those who might have tried to imitate him were naturally dismayed by his fall. Thus, though conditions soon became more favourable to trade than they had been during his career, French commerce did not expand with the rapidity which one might have expected. It is true, however, that the memory of his exploits, exaggerated as they inevitably were, was to prove a powerful stimulus to French maritime and commercial enterprise at a later time.

The downfall of Jacques Coeur was the work of a singularly worthless nobility, conscious that its influence was precarious and thus disposed to repel ruthlessly any low-born intruder on what it deemed to be its exclusive preserves. We have seen enough of the doings of the nobles in the fifteenth century to realize how little gratitude France owed them. Taken as a class they were factious, greedy, dissolute, treacherous, and incompetent. Even those who distinguished themselves in the expulsion of the English were for the most part stupid blackguards. It is easy indeed to be misled by the talk about chivalry in the works of military or courtly writers such as Froissart, Monstrelet, Le Fèvre de St. Remy, Chastellain, the Herald Berry, or Olivier de la Marche. Though these men declare their intention of writing of chivalrous exploits, and constantly describe the characters in their pages as models of knighthood, the deeds they narrate are commonly quite unaffected by the rules of chivalry. Chivalry in reality had long ceased to be of any practical consequence. It might occasionally cause sentimental young men to do fantastic things; it might sometimes lead a man to keep a promise, even to his own hurt; and at times it restrained a warrior from slaying a fallen or fleeing enemy. But the very age which saw the foundation of the most celebrated Orders of knighthood, the age in which the tournament and the joust reached the height of their popularity and magnificence, the age in which more was written in praise of chivalry than ever before or since, was also an age notable for the ruthlessness of its warfare, the butchery of prisoners, the breaking of promises, for conspiracy, assassination, treachery, torture, and general licence. It has been suggested that men, bent on selfish enjoyment and yet still professing the belief that the world was evil and its pleasures a snare, sought to soothe their consciences by rendering lip-service to an unattainable ideal and by pretending to imitate the life of a bygone heroic age, of Arthur and his knights or Charlemagne and his paladins. Perhaps, indeed, they often beguiled themselves into believing that they were noble in conduct as in title. At all events, the conviction that a man of noble blood possessed an innate virtue which raised him above the merchant and the peasant remained powerful, even in quarters where one would have looked for scepticism. When Henry V was Regent of France, he hanged an incredibly ferocious ruffian known as the Bastard of Vaurus, who came into his hands at the fall of Meaux. Jean Jouvenel des Ursins, a man of middle-class extraction, who often shows concern for the interests of the poor, says that while some thought the Bastard's fate divine retribution for his cruelty, others blamed Henry for treating a gentleman as he did. To Jean Jouvenel the latter view was evidently quite reasonable. The Burgundian Georges Chastellain, too, born in Flanders and serving a master whose power was principally based on manufacture and commerce, speaks of the nobles as the only members of society capable of upholding order and virtue, of defending religion, and of conducting beneficent government.

*Mirrors of chivalry*

*The Marshal Boucicaut*

*Jacques de Lalaing*

The few French noblemen of this period who merit admiration fall into two main groups. There were in the first place the warriors who sincerely strove to live up to the chivalric ideal. One of the most famous of these was Jean le Maingre, called Boucicaut. He was temperate in food and drink, almost ridiculously courteous to women, and morbidly punctilious in the performance of what he considered his religious duties. He fought the Turk, and was present at the catastrophe of Nicopolis. At the same time he was a practical man of affairs, and served his king for years as governor of Genoa. His active career ended at Agincourt, where he was captured, to die six years later a prisoner in England. A generation afterward Jacques de Lalaing excited equal admiration. A Hainaulter by birth, he was not a subject of the King of France, but in speech, training, habits, and ideas he was essentially a Frenchman. It is to be noticed, however, that while Boucicaut's strivings after chivalrous perfection took him to Nicopolis, Genoa, and Agincourt, where serious business was afoot, Jacques de Lalaing's exploits were almost all performed in the lists. It is no doubt true that he visited every country of western Europe in search of knightly adventure and the most doughty adversaries, and his reputation as a warrior was not lightly earned; but there was something self-conscious and artificial in his doings. It cannot be good for a man to be continually fighting for ladies he does not admire and against enemies he does not hate. A recent writer has called him " an antique curiosity," and the phrase may be defended. But it must not be inferred that contemporaries thought him quaint or eccentric: they regarded him as something to be imitated, though with little chance of success. There was a grim irony in the fate which befell this paladin at the age of thirty-two, for his head was smashed in by a bourgeois cannon-ball while he was fighting for his duke against the Ghent rebels in 1453.

The second type of noble worthy of praise is exemplified by Charles of Orléans and René of Anjou.[1] The nobleman with literary or artistic ability, even with literary or artistic judgment, was rare in fifteenth-century France. For a while, thanks largely to the example of Philip the Good, it was fashionable to patronize writers and painters, and even to write verses oneself. But it was seldom that real merit was encouraged and still more seldom that real poetry was produced. Charles of Orléans, however, deserves honourable mention, for he could sing easily, pleasantly, and aptly on themes of everlasting interest—youth, love, and old age; and the tragedy of his life—his youth shadowed by the murder of his father, his manhood wasted in English prisons, his later years passed on his half-ruined estates and among people who had almost forgotten him or been born during his captivity—informed his reflections with a certain gentle melancholy which gives them no small charm. But it must be confessed that he had little power or imagination and no originality, and he was a singularly bad judge of the work of others. As a patron, indeed, René of Anjou had a much more discriminating taste, and he was much the more versatile man. He wrote respectably in prose as well as in verse; and among his works were a treatise on tournaments, an allegory, *Coeur d'amour épris*, and a manual of Christian morals, part prose, part verse, called the *Mortifiement de vaine plaisance*, besides a vast number of short poems on very various subjects. Perhaps the most charming of his verses are those which describe, with evident affection, ordinary rural scenes and occurrences, subjects which rarely attracted medieval man. But René, though often pleasing and usually interesting for his technical dexterity, had hardly more creative power than Charles of Orléans. His pictures—for he could paint as well as write—seem to have been numerous, but it is improbable that any of them has survived. There is no reason to suppose that they possessed much merit. René neverthe-

---

[1] Despite René's claims to royal titles and his possession of lands outside France, he owed whatever authority and importance he enjoyed to the fact that he belonged to a noble French family.

less was an enlightened patron of good artists, and employed a number to decorate his palaces and châteaux. He was interested in the Italian work of his time, though, rightly or wrongly, he preferred and encouraged painters of the Flemish school. René had an active and inquiring mind. He loved good craftsmanship in any calling, and delighted in curiosities, alive or other, from foreign lands. The same trait appears in several prominent men of our period. The Duke of Berry, Charles VI's uncle, was an indefatigable collector of books, jewels, metal-work, furniture, birds, and plants—anything in fact that sprang from cunning workmanship or was unfamiliar in France. Even Louis XI had a touch of the same passion, though his taste ran rather to wild beasts and sacred relics. René, perhaps because he was never very rich, showed better discrimination than other collectors of his day.

*Social importance of the bourgeoisie*

When everything in their favour has been weighed, it nevertheless remains clear that the nobility were decadent and that their contribution to French life in the fifteenth century was worth little. As in nearly all the lands of central and western Europe, it was the middle class that showed most vitality. The rise in the status and influence of the *bourgeoisie* was striking. It was due in great measure to the misfortunes of the nobility. The wealth of the aristocracy lay mainly in their landed estates and most of these had been terribly ravaged. Again, a great many French nobles were taken prisoners by the English, and to secure their liberty paid enormous ransoms, which sometimes permanently impoverished their families. The Duke of Orléans, as we have seen, was a prisoner for twenty-five years, and though the Crown helped to find his ransom, was a poor man for the rest of his days. It may readily be understood that lesser men were often driven to sell or mortgage part of their lands, usually to the advantage of members of the *bourgeoisie*. Among the more prosperous of the middle classes, once the Hundred Years War was over, there was a general eagerness to acquire land, partly because under existing conditions it seemed a good investment and partly because of the social distinction conferred by the possession of landed estates. Thus it came about that in many parts the principal landowners were not of noble or even gentle blood; and though a few of the greater nobility might turn their backs upon the intruders, it would not be long before intermarriage between the two classes began. In short, the line between the lesser nobility and the upper middle class was becoming blurred.

A further reason for this was that many nobles were entering the learned professions, particularly law, and even engaging in trade. Some crafts, such as iron-founding and glass-making, might be practised by a noble without loss of caste ; but many cared nothing for such considerations and sought a living where it could be had.

But what specially benefited the middle classes was the favour shown them by the Crown. Without that, their position would have improved but little. In his later years, as we have seen, Charles VII relied largely on men of middle-class origin, and they were the only section of French society that Louis XI really liked and trusted. When a bourgeois rose to great influence, it was always due to royal or princely patronage. The first step was to get office. It was in the royal service that the family of Jouvenel des Ursins rose to the top of the tree. Jacques Coeur's prosperity was based on royal favour and collapsed as soon as it was withdrawn. The Bureau brothers owed their fortunes to the fact that they were indispensable to Charles VII. Nicolas Rolin, one of the most famous climbers of the time, was an undistinguished lawyer who rose in state service—in his case Burgundian—until he became Chancellor to Philip the Good. Such examples stimulated immensely the ambition, enterprise, and industry of the French *bourgeoisie*. The eagerness for public office, however humble, became almost comical, and gave rise to much corruption. There were, indeed, plenty of openings for the middle class from the Peace of Arras to the end of the reign of Louis XI. And many a bourgeois official was rewarded for his good work by being ennobled. In this way, again, the dividing line between the old classes was being obliterated.

Great bourgeois officials lived in the same style as nobles with resounding titles. In the rural districts, bourgeois landowners were likely to be housed more comfortably and to fare more sumptuously than their aristocratic neighbours. And the rich merchants of the towns had a standard of living quite as high as that of the average noble. One must, indeed, be on one's guard against the tendency to draw a sharp contrast between the factious, profligate, and lazy noble, and the law-abiding, thrifty, industrious bourgeois. The middle class included all sorts of men. The famous handbook of domestic science known as the *Menagier de Paris* reveals the comfortable, orderly, and dull household which was the ideal of the upright, pious, kindly old bore who wrote it. But some of the stories that he tells, besides plenty of other evidence, show that many of the *bourgeoisie*, when they waxed fat, kicked. The middle classes were as much given to the lusts of the flesh as the nobility, and among them there was no veneer of chivalry to rob vice of its grossness. Overmuch has been made of the pious expressions and dispositions which appear in middle-class wills at this time; a careful examination of these documents reveals that a great deal of the edifying sentiment is mere common form and that many of the religious or charitable bequests are meant to atone for sad irregularities of life. The Middle Ages abounded with paradoxes; but it is startling to read of hospitals in the south of France harbouring the bastard children of slave-girls, Moslem or Christian, and their bourgeois masters, and to learn that there was a revival of slavery in the commercial towns of southern France during late medieval times.

All things considered, the middle classes affected the intellectual life of France less than might have been expected. They betrayed no particular interest in art, literature, or education; and humanism in France owed little to their patronage. In the towns mystery and miracle plays were popular, and in many places there were formed clubs or societies—called in the north *Chambres de Rhétorique*—whose members read their verses to one another and helped to produce plays and pageants written by themselves. But these bodies were as a rule more convivial than intellectual.

**Prevalence of crime**  As for the poorer classes, the economic state of the peasants and the journeymen and labourers in the towns has already been discussed. There was no nett improvement in their standards of living during the period under review, though they rose in its latter half after a time of depression. Despite their sufferings, the only notable peasants' rising was one which occurred in 1431 in Forez and Velay. There, stirred up by preachers of a crude communism, they asserted that all men, being descended from Adam, should work, and that all superfluous clergy should be abolished, leaving one priest for each parish. They maltreated ecclesiastics and besieged a number of castles ; but the nobles of the vicinity, aided by mercenary troops, put them down with little trouble. The evils of the time, however, drove many peasants to crime. They took to the woods and became brigands, or to the roads and became beggars, or to the towns and became thieves, the three callings being hardly distinguishable. In the latter years of the Hundred Years War there was an alarming increase in the numbers of the criminal class. What made the situation particularly disquieting was the existence of elaborate organizations of law-breakers. In 1455 the authorities arrested at Dijon numerous members of a society called the "Coquillarts," or Pilgrims. It had several hundred members, and its activities extended over a very wide area. It was organized somewhat like a craft-gild, had a hierarchy of officials and a grade of apprentices, and the "masters" were divided into several groups, according to the type of crimes in which they respectively specialized. The beggars, too, had a huge union, which they called their kingdom, with a king at its head, officers analogous to the *baillis* in each province, and even deliberative assemblies. A vivid picture of the life of the French underworld at this time may be derived from the poems of that disreputable vagabond, drunkard, thief, and murderer, François Villon, the greatest French poet of the fifteenth century. It was not merely among the professional criminals that violence and disorder were to be found. They were far more prevalent than before among people who were ordinarily law-abiding. That, of course, was to be expected after a long war. Towards the end of the century the amount of crime became less, and France was probably as orderly as any of its neighbours.

*Societies of law-breakers and beggars*

Nothing has yet been said about one of the Three Estates— the clergy. The truth is that, so far from stemming the evils that prevailed, they were carried away by them. In the wars ecclesiastical property was ravaged, churches and monasteries were ruined, tithes often ceased to be paid. Many of the clergy became destitute vagabonds, living on their wits. The more fortunate sought by accumulating benefices in their hands to make up for the general fall in values. Every abuse that had been denounced before the war remained and became worse. The Great Schism of course intensified the

*The clergy*

confusion, and when it was over there came the conflict between the Papacy and the Council of Basel, and its offshoot, the dispute between the Papal and Gallican parties in France. Under the conditions, it is not astonishing that the morale and discipline of the French Church became contemptible. Respect for the clergy, great and small, sank lower than ever.

When the country became comparatively peaceful again the condition of the Church did not improve much. As agriculture slowly recovered, she regained, it is true, some of her material prosperity. But there was no revival of spiritual zeal. The upholders of Gallican liberties had expressed great enthusiasm for reform; but they showed little eagerness to proceed from words to deeds, though they might plead in excuse that the Pragmatic Sanction of Bourges was imperfectly and spasmodically applied. In any case, the example of the Popes of the latter half of the fifteenth century was not likely to foster moral and spiritual fervour among the clergy. It was indeed a long time since bishops, archdeacons, cathedral chapters, and parish priests had commanded general respect by their walk and conversation. But what was considered the highest ideal of the Christian life had been upheld by the Orders of monks and friars to which successive movements for reform had given rise. The return of peace, however, brought no revival of monastic enthusiasm. Numerous religious houses remained in ruins, others were almost empty, most of the rest were in great financial embarrassment, very many were guilty of habitual disregard of the most vital precepts of their rules. No new Order of any consequence was founded as a rallying-point for the few who were resolved to lead a life of abnegation or devotion. Very rarely was a new foundation added to any of the old Orders. The monastic ideal, in short, had ceased to make any widespread appeal. The rich layman, full of zealous piety or remorseful generosity, no longer put his money into monks or friars: he might invest it in a hospital or a chantry, but was more likely to spend it on pilgrimages or relics. It goes without saying that monasteries had long since ceased to play a leading part in the intellectual life of the country. Such monastic schools as had survived until the fourteenth century were mostly abandoned during the Hundred Years War, and few were subsequently revived. The secular clergy, too, were losing their ascendancy in learning. Of the famous chroniclers and poets of the time the majority were laymen. This is not to say that the intellectual life of France was declining. Several new universities were founded in France during the fifteenth century, two of them— Caen and Bordeaux—in regions which at the time were held by the English. Patriotic French historians, eager to make the most of the harm wrought by the English invasion and to belittle the importance of an institution which helped to condemn Joan of Arc, have said far too much about the decay of the University of Paris. In the first two decades of the century its influence on Europe at large was probably greater than ever before, and under Charles VII and even Louis XI its prestige stood very high and the number of its members remained very great. During the years when Paris was in English hands the University still took the lead in the Conciliar movement, and its opinion on theological questions continued to be regarded as authoritative far beyond the borders of France. If its numbers fell, it must be remembered that a great part of France was under a government which, not being recognized at Paris, naturally did not desire its subjects to pursue learning there. Unable to prove any serious diminution in the University's renown or efficiency, some writers have urged that its obstinate adherence to the established curriculum and to established methods of teaching and learning was a sign of decadence. If, they say, the University noticed the rising tide of Humanism, it was to try to stem it. The charge, true or not, would lie against almost every university in Europe north of the Alps. The tide of Humanism, furthermore, was a feeble trickle in France until quite late in the century. Perhaps the University should have tried to remove obstacles to its flow. But the value of Humanism in comparison with the old studies is not so obvious now that we can blame the scholars of that time for failing to acknowledge its superiority. At all events, it shows a complete misapprehension of medieval culture to assume that the conservatism which Paris shared with other universities proves it to have been on the decline, and it is certain that its academic policy had little effect on its general repute. Any fall in its prestige is amply explained by the growing disregard for clerical authority.

For this indifference to the claims of the clergy was wide-

*Anti-clericalism and witchcraft*

spread and deep. The nature of the prevalent anti-clericalism must not indeed be misunderstood. There was still very little disposition to question accepted doctrine. The parishioners of a greedy and dissolute priest might hate him, but they fully believed that he was able to perform a stupendous miracle. And they deemed it their duty to go and see him do it, though they might behave most irreverently during the greater part of the ceremony. Nor must one attach undue significance to the growth of witchcraft and sorcery. There were undoubtedly a good many people in France—mostly women—who belonged to societies or covins which met at regular intervals for the rites and orgies called the Witch's Sabbath and believed themselves endowed, through the might of the Devil, with supernatural powers. Their beliefs and observances may really have been survivals of a very primitive religion, but they had usually taken the form of a travesty of Christian doctrine and worship. What is most remarkable, however, is that many of those who believed themselves to be wizards or witches, owing their powers to Satan, still professed and called themselves Christians, and that in complete sincerity. The illicit cult supplemented, it did not replace, the lawful cult. This paradox is strikingly exemplified in Gilles de Rais, the great Breton noble, who fought valiantly against the English when the fortunes of Charles VII were at their lowest ebb, was one of the warmest supporters of Joan of Arc, and was made Marshal of France at Charles's coronation. What befell him then, no one can tell; but he took to drink, astrology, alchemy, magic, unnatural vice, sadism, and murder. This is no place to describe or discuss his doings. It is enough to say that in the space of a few years, he did to death, wantonly and often with horrible refinements of cruelty, scores and probably hundreds of children whom he and his agents had kidnapped or enticed into his clutches. In 1440, at the instance of the Bishop of Nantes, he was brought to trial before both the secular and the ecclesiastical tribunals, and after the most sensational revelations, convicted of both murder and sorcery. He was executed, and his last words expressed the hope that he and one of his accomplices would meet in Heaven. For he had always been, in his own estimation, a good Christian. He communicated devoutly at Easter, endowed masses in honour

*Gilles de Rais*

of the Holy Innocents, and planned a pilgrimage to Jerusalem, though he never accomplished it. He was much astonished when told that by practising sorcery he had technically been guilty of heresy. Doubtless he was mad; but so, in that case, were scores of less famous wretches who shared his delusions without imitating his crimes.

There were of course many people of genuine piety who defied the Devil instead of trying to make terms with him. Some of these contented themselves with the ordinary means of grace, others fell under the influence of mystics like the Brethren of the Common Life. And even the indifferent multitude could be stirred to religious fervour by an emotional preacher like the Spanish Saint Vincent Ferrer, the Carmelite Thomas Couette, or the Franciscan Friar Richard, who was at the height of his fame during the career of Joan of Arc, and, after some hesitation, approved her mission. But the effect produced by itinerant evangelists was seldom lasting, and it did but little to counteract the growing hostility towards the clergy. *Popular piety*

At the end of the fifteenth century the temper of the French people was on the whole rather pessimistic. They were restless and uneasy. The state of the country was improving, albeit slowly, but they did not understand that. They were inclined to look with regret to a remote past rather than with hope to the future. They still, in fact, had the medieval outlook on human affairs.

Authorities for chapter xii :—
    See the works mentioned under chaps. i, ii, iii, x, xi. Reference may also be made to the following :
Bloch, M. : *Les caractères originaux de l'histoire rurale française* (Instituttet for Sammenlignende Kulturforskning, série B, Skrifter xix), Oslo, 1931.
Champion, Pierre : *Vie de Charles d'Orléans*, Paris, 1911.
*La Chronique de Philippe de Vigneulles*, ed. C. Bruneau, Metz, 1929–32.
Clément, P. : *Jacques Cœur et Charles VII*, Paris, 1873.
Gandilhon, R. : *Politique économique de Louis XI*, Paris, 1941.
Guiraud, L. : *Recherches et conclusions nouvelles sur le prétendu rôle de Jacques Cœur*, Paris, 1900.
Lecoy de la Marche : *Le roi Réné*, 2 vols., Paris, 1875.
Lizernand, G. : *Le régime rural de l'ancienne France*, Paris, 1942.
Paris, G. : *Villon*, Paris, 1901.
Prutz, H. : *Jacques Cœur von Bourges*, Berlin, 1911.
Seé, Henri : *Histoire économique de la France*, I. Le Moyen Age et l'Ancien Régime, Paris, 1939.
Viollet, P. : *Histoire des Institutions politiques et administratives de la France*, 3 vols., Paris, 1890–1903.

## CHAPTER XIII

## GERMANY, 1437–1493

### KINGS AND PRINCES

Election of Albert II, Mar. 1438

SIGISMUND left no male heir. But he had let it be known that he hoped to be succeeded in all his titles and possessions by Albert of Austria, the husband of his only daughter Elizabeth. Albert was soon accepted in Hungary, and the Catholic party in Bohemia was ready to support his election as king of that country. Like the Electors, he wished to remain neutral in the dispute between the Pope and General Council. He was a very powerful man, whose support was worth having. At the same time, his strength, like Sigismund's, lay for the most part outside Germany. Thus he pleased the Electors better than Frederick of Brandenburg, who was favoured by many German adherents of the Conciliar party. Accordingly, in March 1438, Albert was elected.

Albert proved to be the first of a line of Habsburg Emperors which continued unbroken, save for an interval of three years, until the Holy Roman Empire came to an end. In 1438, of course, no one supposed that anything specially notable was being done. It looked as if the conditions of Sigismund's time would be prolonged. Albert, indeed, was a capable, upright and vigorous man, who might, if given the opportunity, have raised the status of the German Crown.

His death, Oct. 1439

But whatever the expectations of the Electors, they were unfulfilled; for Albert was called away to fight the Turks in Hungary, fell sick during the campaign, and died on October 27, 1439, before he could reach home.

Declaration of Diet of Mainz on Church Reform, Mar. 26, 1439

Meanwhile, although the Electors had renewed their profession of neutrality as between the warring parties in the Church, they and the other princes had accepted the reforming decrees of the Council of Basel in a declaration very similar to the Pragmatic Sanction adopted by the French in the previous year. If they were in earnest, their action meant that they would carry out a reform of the German Church, even in the teeth of the Pope.

On the death of Albert, the Electors turned to the new head of the Habsburg family, and without much delay chose as King Frederick, Duke of Styria, Carinthia, and Carniola, which he ruled jointly but unharmoniously with his brother Albert. Frederick was guardian of Sigismund, the young son of Frederick the Penniless, who had given so much trouble at the Council of Constance, and he thus directed the administration of Tyrol and the old Habsburg lands in Swabia. He was about twenty-four years old, good-looking, and apparently vigorous. He owed his election in great measure to the support of his brother-in-law, the Elector of Saxony, who was desperately afraid lest a Hohenzollern should be chosen. *Election of Frederick III, Feb. 1, 1440*

Three weeks after Frederick's election there occurred an event which gravely affected the prospects of all central Europe. The widow of Albert II gave birth to a son, commonly known as Ladislas Postumus. Though heir to Austria and Hungary, it was only in the former that he was at first accepted. He was, however, soon elected King by the Bohemians. Frederick acted as guardian of Ladislas in Austria, but he was not suffered to exercise any authority in Bohemia, which made its own arrangements for a regency. *Birth of Ladislas Postumus*

Frederick's relations with Ladislas and the territories under the boy's nominal rule soon became extremely complicated. More will be said about them in another chapter. His dealings with Germany, on the other hand, require little explanation. For Frederick is remembered as perhaps the most contemptible creature that ever pretended to govern the Holy Roman Empire. He had but one principle of conduct—to do nothing. In the affairs of his German kingdom he did not seem to be even interested. For years at a stretch he never left Habsburg territory. Till late in his reign he never attended a German Diet. He was no warrior —indeed, he was widely accused of physical cowardice, a charge probably false, for though he did once or twice run away from a difficult situation, it was rather moral than physical fear that impelled him. He was most happy when secluded in one of his castles pursuing his favourite studies *Character and aims of Frederick* of alchemy and astrology, or gloating over his collections of precious stones and rare plants. He is often compared to Wenzel, and the two resembled each other in their inertia. But Wenzel had his outbursts of ferocious energy, and he drank heroically; Frederick was never energetic or heroic.

Frederick might be a *roi fainéant*, and he might care nothing about the welfare of Germany or the Empire. But he was deeply concerned about the welfare of the House of Habsburg. His schemes were all woven, his sins of commission and omission all perpetrated, in the interests of his family. In the destiny of his House the stars taught him to believe without misgiving. Towards the end of his life he was wont to adorn his dwellings, his furniture, and his books with the anagram, AEIOU—*Alles Erdreich ist Österreich unterthan*, or, in Latin, *Austria est imperare orbi universo*. And, by a singular turn of fortune, he saw his House become one of the Great Powers of Europe, with the prospect of rising to yet loftier heights. Historians have marvelled over this, and have argued therefrom that Frederick cannot have been such a fool as he seemed. It is true that the power of his family at his death was mainly based on the marriage which he had arranged between his son Maximilian and the heiress of Burgundy, but that this alliance had yielded any practical advantage was entirely due to the energy of Maximilian. Had its political results depended on Frederick himself, the match would not have brought the Habsburgs a pennyworth of profit. Frederick, it is true, was not without guile, but it was luck rather than cunning that enabled him to do so much for the exaltation of his family.

It was not long after his accession that Frederick's attitude towards Germany became manifest. For some years the burning question in the country was the reform of the Church. While still reluctant to take sides in the new Schism, the Electors indicated that they would acknowledge no pope who was unwilling to introduce drastic reforms. Frederick, however, did nothing to put pressure on Eugenius IV. The Schism continued, to the great concern of all serious Germans, and in 1444, at a Diet at Nürnberg, it was announced that, while the princes would remain neutral for the present, unity must be restored to the Church within a year, failing which a Council should meet in Frederick's

*Frederick and Eugenius IV*

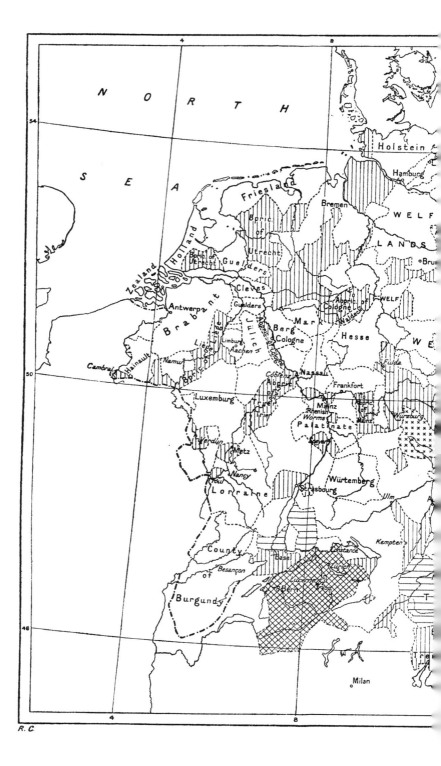

presence somewhere in Germany and settle the whole matter. At the Diet Frederick was criticized for his apparent indifference to the question, and at the same time his reputation was under a cloud owing to the depredations of the so-called Armagnacs—the French mercenaries whom the Dauphin Louis had led to Frederick's assistance in a war against the Swiss. It has been supposed that he was so deeply wounded by the reproaches flung at him on this occasion that he resolved to trouble himself no more about the Empire and think only of his own family. Though this view is not wholly accurate, it is clear that he now set himself to turn the situation to his personal advantage, his plan being to strike a bargain with Eugenius behind the backs of the Electors. His agent was Aeneas Sylvius, who had lately deserted the Council and entered his service. Sent to Rome to report the resolutions of the Nürnberg Diet, Aeneas seized the opportunity to ingratiate himself with Eugenius and disclose Frederick's real intentions. After secret negotiations in Vienna during 1445, Frederick agreed to recognize Eugenius in return for the promise of the imperial crown, a tenth of the revenue of all German benefices to pay the expense of his journey to Italy, 220,000 ducats in cash, and the right of nominating to a vast number of sees and benefices in the Habsburg lands, besides other valuable concessions.

Now that Eugenius could count on Frederick, he became bolder in his behaviour towards the Electors, excommunicating the Archbishops of Cologne and Trier, who supported Felix V. The other Electors were enraged, and after deliberations in March 1446, sent to Eugenius an ultimatum calling upon him to recognize the supremacy of General Councils, accept the Basel reforms, and summon a fresh Council within a year. If he complied, they would return to his obedience: otherwise, they would adhere to the Council of Basel, subject to certain conditions which the members of that assembly were only too eager to satisfy.

*The Electors outmanœuvred by the Pope*

In the following September the Pope's reply was reported at a Diet. It was decidedly unfavourable. But Frederick was now openly on the side of Eugenius, the papal agents were busy with secret intrigues, the Archbishop of Cologne was corruptly won over, and the plausible tongue of Aeneas Sylvius persuaded the princes that the Pope's answer offered a basis for a reasonable and honourable compromise. In the end a deputation was sent to Rome to complete an understanding. When this was drawn up, in February 1447, it barely touched upon reform, for the accomplishment of which a legate was to visit Germany; and the Pope's most important concessions were so worded that they practically amounted to nothing, were announced in such a way that his successor would not be bound by them, and were further emasculated by his formal and secret protestation that they were perhaps unwarrantable and were not to stand if contrary to the teaching of the Fathers and the rights of the Apostolic See. Immediately afterwards Eugenius died; and at Aschaffenburg, in the following July, Nicolas V was accepted by nearly all the German princes without demur. The recalcitrants were soon cajoled or bought, though it must be admitted that some princes charged a high price.

The Concordat of Vienna, 1448

There soon began the negotiations between a papal legate and Frederick which in February 1448 produced the Concordat of Vienna. It represented a complete victory of the *curia* over the reform party. It was concerned solely with papal provisions and reservations, and it was on the whole more favourable to the Papacy than the similar Concordat of 1418. In short, it gave the Pope more control over the Church in Germany than in any other country. Nevertheless, modern historians have often exaggerated the extent of the papal triumph. It was at the cost of many sacrifices to the secular power that the Holy See had re-established its authority over the restive German clergy. It is significant that whereas the Concordat of 1418 had been made with the German Church, the Concordat of 1448 was made with the German State. As we have seen, Frederick's compliance had been dearly purchased, and henceforth the control of the Habsburgs over the Church within their lands was such as would have horrified a Gregory VII or an Innocent III. And other German princes, while they did not get so much, now enjoyed privileges which seriously impaired the authority exercised by the Papacy in their territories. The Conciliar Movement, it is true, was scotched. The reform party in Germany was defeated and demoralized. But it was not destroyed, and its aims had not been forgotten. Henceforth, however, it was recognized that no serious reform could be expected from the Papacy, and that the clergy in general were neither earnest nor strong enough to effect one. It was to the Emperor, or rather to the princes, that men began to look. As the Church would not reform, she must be reformed.

In the forty years following Frederick's surrender to the Papacy, Germany's plight was as bad as it ever had been since the tenth century. Her sovereign almost ignored her. It is true that in 1452 he took the trouble to receive the imperial crown, and thereby gained the distinction of being the last Emperor to be crowned at Rome. But Frederick's expedition, though it achieved its main purpose, did his reputation no good. He left Austria in rebellion; people said that he was running away. When in Italy, he was manifestly and comically anxious to avoid meddling with anything that might kindle strife. He aroused contempt by his characteristic meanness. It must be admitted that, thanks to the hospitality and presents that he received, he did fairly well out of his excursion; but success of that kind further debased his reputation. His so-called pilgrimage to Rome in 1468 was of small political moment, though the insults which he meekly accepted from the Pope might have served as trouble-making precedents had this not been the last visit of a Holy Roman Emperor to his nominal capital. *Frederick crowned Emperor, 1452*

The year after Frederick's coronation the Turks took Constantinople: it is one of the ironies of History that Frederick III was the first lord of the Holy Roman Empire to hold his title without a rival. But it soon looked as if the Empire of the West would succumb to the same fate as the Empire of the East. Turkish pressure on Hungary increased, and before long Carinthia, Styria, and even Austria proper were afflicted by Turkish raids. In the west Burgundy had been absorbing province after province, and though her acquisitions might technically remain imperial fiefs, in fact they were lost to the Empire, as everybody knew. Nevertheless, it was from her own sons that Germany suffered most. Never had there been a worse time for internal strife. Some of the feuds became long and widespread wars. While prince often fought prince, this was a period of specially bitter hostility between princes and cities. Particularly notable was a war between Albert Achilles, third son of *Deplorable plight of Germany*

Frederick I of Brandenburg, and the cities of Franconia, headed by Nürnberg: it began in 1449, and spread over a great part of south Germany. Albert Achilles and his noble supporters had the better of it in the open, though they failed in their sieges. In 1450, however, they lost a pitched battle near Pillenreuth, and soon afterwards deemed it well to make peace on the basis of the *status quo ante*. The conflict had been waged with exceptional ferocity, and large parts of central and south Germany had suffered grievous damage.

At the same time there was in progress a struggle which became famous in German song and story as the *Soester Fehde*. On the one side was the city of Soest, whose liberties were threatened by the Archbishop of Cologne, together with most of the towns of Westphalia and Duke Adolf of Cleves; on the other, the Archbishop-Elector, a number of neighbouring princes and bishops, and a few cities, tempted by local ambitions and jealousies to be false to their order. The Emperor actually intervened so far as to put Soest under the imperial ban, a totally ineffective measure. The war, which was savagely conducted, lasted for five years. The Archbishop caused some scandal by hiring Bohemian mercenaries, remnants of the Hussite armies of twenty years before. Nevertheless, the heroic defence of Soest forced him to give up his claims.

Similar conflicts, though usually on a smaller scale, were to be witnessed in all parts of Germany. There were some conspicuously fierce and destructive feuds between rival members of the same family. The Wittelsbachs became notorious for the frequency and bitterness of their domestic broils; and the House of Wettin suffered great hurt in a family war which lasted from 1446 to 1451.

People had long ceased to think of the German monarchy as a force capable of preventing or punishing such occurrences. Yet the uselessness of the Crown was obscured by talk about the reform of the Empire. Much was said on this theme,

*Abortive discussion of reform in Church and State*

for instance, at two Diets held in 1454, when the final downfall of the Eastern Empire had drawn special attention to the perils of the Western. The remedy of abuses in the Church and the organization of a Crusade were also debated. But the Emperor, as usual, was absent, and nothing was done. Next year it looked as if the Electors really meant business, for in the name of all (save the Elector of Saxony) the Archbishop of Trier laid before Frederick at Wiener Neustadt a programme of reform. It was proposed to set up an imperial court of justice, the judgments of which should be enforced by the princes whose territories they concerned. Closer relations between the Emperor and the Electors were to be maintained. The cost of the projected changes was to be covered by a general tax, though no measures for raising it were suggested. The summons of a General Council was also declared to be desirable. Frederick protested against the inroads on his authority which the Electors were contemplating, and opposed to their demands an obdurate passivity which finally baffled them. A further storm, accompanied by threats of deposition, broke out on the death of Pope Nicolas V in 1455, owing to the Emperor's failure to use the occasion to the advantage of the German Church. But Frederick now had the support of the Electors of Saxony and Brandenburg, there was no likelihood that his opponents would agree on a substitute for him, and in the next few years the party friendly to him tended to grow. Zeal for reform was for a while diverted towards the Church. But any real amendment, whether of Church or Empire, was impossible in face of the prevailing lack of personal integrity. The need of reform in the Empire made a good pretext for pressing private interests at the expense of Frederick, and the crying abuses in the Church gave the unscrupulous welcome opportunity for succumbing to papal corruption.

At the beginning of the seventh decade of the century, it looked indeed as though both Emperor and Pope would be hard put to it to avoid disaster. In 1460 a war between the Hohenzollerns and the Wittelsbachs ended in a severe defeat for the former. The Hohenzollerns were friendly towards Frederick, the Wittelsbachs hostile, and the victors seized their moment of triumph to suggest the replacement of the Emperor by George of Podiebrad, the King of Bohemia. The Wettins as well as the Hohenzollerns would not have brooked the rule of Podiebrad, and there was never any serious likelihood of his success; but he was a very able man, and his unscrupulous diplomacy kept the plan alive for some years. The scheme against the Emperor was closely linked with a renewal of animosity against the Pope, occasioned in the first place by the pecuniary demands of Pius II and stimulated by his deposition of Diether, Archbishop of Mainz, a talkative "reformer." The deposed prelate was upheld by the Elector Palatine and other leaders of the Wittelsbach family, and the cause of his supplanter, nominated of course by Pius, was consequently taken up by the Hohenzollerns and their party. Hence there arose yet another civil war in south Germany. Frederick III roused himself sufficiently to pronounce against the Wittelsbachs, but this did not save Albert Achilles of Hohenzollern from a severe reverse at Giengen in 1462, a disaster which constrained him to submit to the so-called arbitration of George of Podiebrad, an ally of his Wittelsbach enemies. Meanwhile, however, Adolf of Nassau, the Pope's nominee, got possession of Mainz, and maintained himself there. In the end, therefore, notwithstanding his military successes, the Elector Palatine was forced to recognize Adolf, and the war, having caused immense mischief in south Germany and the Rhineland, ended in 1463 with the discomfiture of the Wittelsbach faction. In the following years George of Podiebrad's energy was fully absorbed by civil strife in Bohemia, where, at the instigation of the Papacy, the Catholic party was trying to overthrow him. The schemes of the reformers, secular or religious, were temporarily ruined, and for many years Frederick had no trouble from the princes of Germany.

Frederick's new troubles

Nevertheless his repute fell lower than ever. Neither Bohemia nor Hungary had wanted him as king on the death of his young cousin Ladislas Postumus in 1457, and his participation in the attempt to oust George of Podiebrad from the Bohemian throne was quite ineffectual. After the death of George in 1471, Bohemia was disputed between Matthias Corvinus of Hungary and Ladislas of Poland; but Frederick's intervention on the side of Ladislas was brief and disastrous, and he was ignored when in 1478 the disputed territories were partitioned between the protagonists. To all intents and purposes, Bohemia had been severed from the Empire.

Frederick's reputation was yet further impaired by his dealings with Charles the Bold, which are described elsewhere. In the end, they did the Empire no harm, but for that no credit is due to Frederick, whose conduct in his relations with Burgundy had been a singular mixture of cunning, cowardice, meanness, greed, and shamelessness. Even in his own lands, though he really prized them, he failed to cope with the troubles that beset him. In 1468 the death of his brother Albert left him undisputed lord of Austria and the Habsburg lands to the south. There was, however, much disaffection among the nobility of these regions, many of them allying with George of Podiebrad. What was worse, the Habsburg lands were now exposed to Turkish raids, and neither Frederick nor the nobles seemed able to stir themselves to any effective resistance. Frederick's crowning misfortune, however, was deferred until 1485, when Matthias Corvinus, who had resumed the war against the Emperor some years before, captured Vienna. Frederick, whose noble vassals had betrayed him, wandered pitifully through Germany begging help from the princes. Even in his extremity he refused to surrender a foot of Habsburg land, but he received so little aid that he was fain to consent to the occupation of the eastern half of Austria by Matthias pending the payment of a heavy indemnity. *The Emperor driven from Austria, 1485*

Though the princes had failed the Emperor, his plight caused them some concern. The demand for reform was again heard. It was recognized that nothing would ever be done by Frederick, and, headed by Berthold of Henneberg, Archbishop of Mainz, the Electors proposed to supplant the old Emperor by his son Maximilian. Frederick at first resisted the suggestion. But seeing at length that the Electors really meant business, he reluctantly complied, having received an assurance that while Maximilian should bear the title of King of the Romans, his own authority should be unimpaired. The election took place in 1486. Save for the Bohemian vote, which was not cast, it was unanimous. *Election of Maximilian, Feb. 16, 1486*

Notwithstanding the assurances of the Electors, Frederick was thenceforth shelved, and Maximilian acted as if he were sole monarch. He was a very different man from his father —lively, active and warlike. It is true that he was unstable and flighty, and that his intellectual powers were but moderate. Still, he was a great improvement on Frederick.

Maximilian was destined to leave a deep mark on Germany, but most of his doings belong to a time with which this volume is not concerned. Though he was eager to reform the government of the Empire, his views on the subject were not in agreement with those of the Electors. Thus no material changes could be made during the first few years of his rule. The achievement that made most stir in Germany was the formation in 1488 of a new Swabian League. It included twenty-two cities, a number of knights and prelates, and two great princes—Sigismund of Habsburg and Eberhard of Würtemberg. It had a federal council of two chambers, each elected annually, the first containing nine representatives of the clergy and the knights, the second nine representatives of the cities. When the Council ordered, each of the three groups in the League—princes, prelates and knights, and cities—had to furnish 3,000 foot and 300 horse, and in case of need there was to be a levy *en masse*. There was a federal treasury, to which each member had to contribute. The League, it is evident, was more than a *Landfriede* of the familiar type; it was the beginning of a real federation. It was originally established for eight years, but that term was prolonged, and the organization soon began to extend itself beyond the limits of Swabia. Its founders hoped that it would be imitated in many parts of Germany. Its later fortunes may not be described here, though it may be said that in the end its results were disappointing. Nevertheless for some years it was the most promising political experiment that Germany had seen for a long time.

Meanwhile, Maximilian was winning notable successes as head of the House of Habsburg. Against France, as we have seen, he vindicated the claims of his young son Philip to the greater part of the Burgundian inheritance. In 1490 his kinsman Sigismund handed over Tyrol and his lands in Swabia and Alsace; so that all the possessions of the House were now in Maximilian's hand. What was yet more important, Maximilian freed the Habsburg lands from the Hungarians and the Turks, and in 1491 forced Ladislas of Bohemia and Hungary to sign a treaty which eventually brought those realms under Habsburg rule. All this while Frederick III remained in obscurity, pursuing his hobbies and observing with pleasure though not surprise the rising fortunes of his House. His death on August 19, 1493, while it made little stir, was important in that it left

Maximilian free to press forward with his efforts, already begun, for the strengthening of the administration in the Habsburg territories.

The attention given by Maximilian to the government of his own property illustrates a tendency which was widespread in Germany towards the close of the period with which we are dealing. It has been mentioned already that the difficulties of the Emperor in relation to the princes were in great measure experienced by the princes in relation to their own subjects. In one or two respects indeed the power of the princes was somewhat reduced during the fifteenth century. In several principalities, for instance, the control of the Estates over the central government became greater: this was so in the Habsburg lands, in Brandenburg, in the Welf lands, in Hesse, in Pomerania, to name no others; in Bavaria the Estates maintained their influence, already considerable at the beginning of the century; in the Wettin lands it was in its latter half that they first began to meet. In some ecclesiastical principalities, too, the power of the *Landtag* was very great. Though many a prince found the interference of the Estates irksome and strove to avert or frustrate it, most *Landtage* exerted a wholesome influence on the territory where they operated. A *Landtag* was as a rule a unifying, not a disintegrating, force; it was after all an organ of the central government. In general, the Estates of fifteenth-century Germany were opposed to the partition of principalities; they were eager for peace, internal and external; and they encouraged sound administration and the employment of capable officials. Thus, while apparently placing limitations on a prince's authority, they were often really helping to increase it. It is well for Englishmen, who are inclined to regard their Parliament as a unique phenomenon, to remember the existence of these numerous and vigorous assemblies in Germany during the confused fifteenth century. The worst criticism that can be levelled against them is that they showed complete indifference, not to say hostility, towards the claims of the Emperor and the interests of Germany as a whole.

It has been necessary to dwell upon the position of the *Landtage* in order to explain how the fifteenth century witnessed the imposition of a check upon the

**Disintegration of principalities checked**

disintegration which had been proceeding in the several principalities. In all parts of Germany a great many of the functions of government had fallen, legally or not, into the hands of the *Grundherren*—lords of manors they would have been called in England—or of the cities. The extent of this decentralization varied from state to state; it was on the whole worse in the east than in the west. In addition, many principalities fell into a condition of chronic disorder; at the beginning of the century, for example, Brandenburg was terrorized by robber barons. By the year 1500, however, several states had experienced a change for the better. Nowhere, it is true, had the reaction gone far; but whereas in the thirteenth and fourteenth centuries the tendency had almost everywhere been centrifugal, it was now in the opposite direction.

Many of Germany's troubles had been caused by the time-honoured custom of dividing a prince's lands among his sons. In the fifteenth century there were signs that the practice was at last losing favour, and that men were beginning to draw a distinction between a principality and a private estate. It has generally been assumed that this change was rendered inevitable by Charles IV's Golden Bull, which laid down that the rule of primogeniture should apply in the territories to which the electoral right was attached. But if the Golden Bull stimulated the rulers of other principalities to alter their policy, the effect appeared very slowly. Thus, it was not until 1473 that the Elector Albert Achilles made his famous pronouncement—known as the *Dispositio Achillea*—that the Hohenzollern possessions in Brandenburg and the adjacent Marks, with all subsequent additions to them, should be for ever inseparable and should be inherited according to the rule of primogeniture; while the family's Franconian lands were to go to younger sons, provided that they should never be divided into more than two parts, Ansbach and Bayreuth. Though this arrangement was not rigidly observed thereafter, its influence on later German history has been enormous. About the same time, by a series of family agreements, the county of Würtemberg recovered its unity; and a few years after, as we have seen, all the Habsburg possessions came under one hand. The Wittelsbachs, who had suffered much through the repeated division of their territories, at last became convinced of its folly, though their change of view did not produce important results until the following century. Some families, indeed, held to the old ways: in 1486 the Wettin family split into the Albertine and Ernestine lines; its lands were divided and were never reunited. Still, the new policy was approved by most German princes and was soon to have momentous results.

Up to the beginning of the fifteenth century the continual struggle for power between the princes and noble subjects had on the whole gone in favour of the latter. Now the progress of the nobility was in many regions checked, and here and there they lost ground. The strife was particularly intense in Brandenburg and Bavaria. The first Hohenzollern rulers of the Mark found the nobles in a most unruly condition. They deemed it well to go to work circumspectly. They tried to ingratiate themselves and to dazzle the rough northern barons with displays of the splendour and culture of Franconia. At the same time they scrupulously enforced their legal rights, intervened in disputes between nobles and their tenants, and confiscated lands when it seemed safe and advantageous, occasionally, though seldom, using naked force. In the latter part of the century, however, circumstances prevented the Electors from giving adequate attention to the curbing of their over-mighty subjects; and it has to be recognized that during the years with which this volume is concerned, the power of the Brandenburg aristocracy was little impaired. In Bavaria, too, the resistance of the dukes to the nobles, though determined, had few positive results; while in the Habsburg lands the nobility held its ground well until the time of Maximilian. Nevertheless, the stand made by the families mentioned and by others proved to be the prelude to striking victories of princes over nobles in the early part of the sixteenth century.

Strong as it was, the hostility between the princes and their noble vassals was not so great as that between the princes and the cities. The imperial cities of course feared and hated the great princes, whom they justly suspected of a wish to annex them. But it was the cities legally subject to some prince which were the most bitter. Their relations to their overlords varied much. Some *Landstädte* were virtually independent, whereas in certain states—Saxony and Bavaria, for example—the central authority kept a firm control over the cities. In any case they were fiercely jealous of their privileges, and they usually put their own local interests before any others. Their narrowness of outlook was in some measure excusable, since culture, comfort, and quiet were hardly to be found outside the towns in fifteenth-century Germany. It was commonly the object of a prince to destroy civic privileges in his territories. Sometimes he claimed that they existed merely at his good pleasure. Often he strove to secure financial control over his cities, or he might aim at obtaining a dominating influence on elections to city councils. Frequently he tried to prevent them from forming leagues with one another or with cities belonging to other princes. The enmity of the princes was specially conspicuous in the north, where the Hohenzollerns were the leading foes of municipal privilege. They and their neighbours, in fact, sometimes met to concert a common policy against the cities of their lands. The *esprit de corps* of the princes, it must be admitted, was greater than that of the burgher class. They could count, too, in this instance on the sympathy and often the support of the lesser nobility. Seven thousand men of gentle blood are said to have helped Albert Achilles of Hohenzollern in his war against Nürnberg in 1449.

On the whole the cities put up a stout resistance to the attacks on their liberties. Some of their confederacies long remained powerful. In the fifth decade there was a great league of south German cities, which took part in the war between Nürnberg and Albert Achilles. In the north there was of course the Hansa, and throughout the century there was generally a league of " Saxon " cities under the lead of Brunswick and Magdeburg. There were two main periods of conflict, the fifth decade and the years from 1470 to 1490. In the first the initiative on the princely side was taken by the Hohenzollerns, who in 1442 worsted a league of Brandenburg cities and deprived Berlin and Köln of most of their franchises. Their success caused several neighbouring princes to attempt to imitate them, with results on the whole unsatisfactory to the cities. A revolt by Berlin in 1448 was put down; but the ill-fortune of Albert Achilles in his war with Nürnberg cooled the confidence of the princes, who in the next twenty years were less aggressive. Then, however, a series of conflicts began, ending as a rule in the discomfiture of some city. Thus the Wettin family reduced the almost independent Halle to the obedience of its feudal lord the Archbishop of Magdeburg, who at the time was a Wettin himself. The same archbishop greatly diminished the autonomy of his own cathedral city. John Cicero, Elector of Brandenburg, defeated the towns of the Altmark when they rebelled against an excise on beer voted by the Estates, and many of them were constrained to accept changes in their constitutions. From 1487 to 1491 the wealthy city of Rostock waged a stubborn and complicated fight with the Dukes of Mecklenburg, only in the end to suffer defeat and humiliation. On the other hand, Hildesheim successfully withstood its bishop when he sought to impose a new beer-tax, and with the aid of several cities of Brunswick and a few princes of western Germany survived two sieges by the bishop and the Duke of Brunswick, emerging victoriously from the war in 1486. A few years later the city of Brunswick defeated an attempt of its duke to deprive it of its most precious liberties. By this time, nevertheless, there were signs of a decline in the morale of the burgher class. The cities became increasingly reluctant to co-operate. Even the Hansa could hardly be moved to do anything, and more than once denied help to members of the league who were in conflict with princes. It was a time, too, when party strife in the towns was very virulent, and to gain an advantage a faction would sometimes betray the interests of the community. Towards the end of the century there was a growing tendency to bargain with dangerous princes instead of defying them after the old fashion. At the end of our period, in fact, Germany was about to witness a sudden and marked decline in the political importance of her cities. The more intelligent and public-spirited of the burghers understood what was coming to pass and bewailed it bitterly. Often, it must be recognized, they exaggerated the catastrophe. Even when most completely defeated, the cities usually kept many advantages. The object of the prince was to subordinate them to himself. If he felt sure that he could make his will prevail, he was glad to save himself trouble and money by allowing them to manage their local affairs.

And it is to be remembered that most of these places were, according to our standards, mere villages, and that not a few were quite unfitted for autonomy. A city would often be better governed by its overlord than by its inhabitants. The wiser princes naturally did what they could to promote the prosperity of their cities, which sometimes flourished more after being subjected than they had done before. It was observed, on the other hand, that the burghers of such places often lost their enterprise and tended to rely overmuch on the prince's government. And, all things considered, it is fair to say that in the long run the loss of the political privileges of the cities was detrimental to their economic welfare.

The princes and the Church

The most serious restrictions on a prince's authority were imposed by the Church. The Church in Germany was enormously wealthy, and its political influence much greater than in either France or England. As against the temporal power, imperial or princely, it had been singularly successful in making good its claims. In no other country was the scope of ecclesiastical jurisdiction so wide. "Benefit of clergy" was no doubt a scandal in England during the later Middle Ages, but it meant far less than in Germany, where none of the clergy might be haled before a lay court for any cause. Furthermore, the Church courts in Germany had trespassed on ground which even the Canon Law did not claim for them. It must be acknowledged that laymen sometimes preferred to bring purely secular matters before them, finding them quicker, cheaper, and less corrupt than the secular tribunals. Nevertheless, there was plenty of complaint against the church's dignitaries and officers. Besides the usual charges of immorality, dishonesty, and neglect of duty, it was alleged that they used spiritual weapons —excommunication and interdict—for the furtherance of political and other temporal objects. Criticism of this kind began quite early in the Middle Ages, but for long public opinion had generally approved of the Church's claims and even of her usurpations; and the extension of her power continued. In the fourteenth century, however, owing to the Babylonish Captivity, growing corruption, and other causes, the popularity of the Church declined rapidly, and the German princes were able to make a stand against ecclesiastical encroachments. The Schism and the Conciliar

Movement gave them further opportunity, and the fifteenth century consequently witnessed a great increase in the influence of the temporal authorities on ecclesiastical affairs. Not only did the princes succeed better than heretofore in vindicating their authority in temporal things, but some of them ventured to trespass on ground which had commonly been deemed spiritual. This change of fortune was due in great measure to the weakness of the Papacy. The Holy See had indeed emerged from the crisis of the Conciliar Movement with its authority over the clergy virtually unimpaired. But it paid for its victory by great concessions to the secular power in many parts of Europe, and it had been so badly shaken that for the rest of the century it rarely ventured to oppose or denounce a temporal ruler for high-handed conduct towards the Church. And it soon became evident that, without the backing of the Papacy, the clergy had no chance against kings and princes.

One of the main objects of a German prince was to secure his territory from any interference from outside. It often happened that a principality was subject in ecclesiastical matters to a bishop whose see was beyond its limits. In that case it was natural that the prince should do his utmost to secure control over appointments to that see. Some of the princes were very successful in such efforts. The Elector Palatine, for instance, seldom had any trouble with the Bishops of Worms and Speyer, who shared episcopal jurisdiction over his territories; the Wettins, too, generally had a trustworthy man in the archbishopric of Magdeburg, while the Habsburgs kept a tight hold on Salzburg and Passau. Over ecclesiastical appointments within their own borders the princes found it yet easier to get control. Sometimes indeed the Papacy lent itself to their purposes. Thus at one time or another the Emperor Frederick III received from the Papacy the right to nominate to nine bishoprics; in the case of eight the right was to pass to his heirs. He was granted similar authority in respect of numerous lesser dignities or benefices: thus in 1474 and 1475 Sixtus IV bestowed on him the presentation to 300 benefices in the Empire. Lesser princes, such as the Electors of Brandenburg and Saxony, were granted like favours on a smaller scale. But there were many other ways of securing control over ecclesiastical elections, collations, and presentations; and so it often happened that the clergy of a principality, great and small, were mostly men who owed their positions to the secular authority. The Papacy looked the other way and cared not if Hildebrand turned in his grave.

In regard to the Church courts the princes were less successful. On this ground the local authorities of the Church were more concerned to make a stand; *Justitia est enim magnum emolumentum*. In many states, however, the Church courts were expelled from the ground which they had filched from the temporal sphere; and in some regions the clergy were made amenable to the secular tribunals in civil causes concerning secular matters. In certain principalities the Church lost part of its jurisdiction over matrimonial and testamentary suits. Numerous princes protected their subjects against the misuse of the Church's penal weapons, and regulated the right of appeal to the court of Rome. The Habsburgs, who even in the fourteenth century had exercised a very firm control over the Church in their lands, continued to make successful inroads on ecclesiastical jurisdiction. Under Frederick III, weak as he was, the secular courts of his lands secured jurisdiction in causes concerning tithes; and the Archbishop of Salzburg and his suffragans were actually made subject to them in secular causes. The Elector Palatine pursued a similar policy with great, and the Elector of Brandenburg with moderate, success. One must be on one's guard against exaggerating the effect of what was achieved. The Church courts remained very powerful, with a very wide jurisdiction, and in some principalities their losses had been trivial. Still, they were on the whole distinctly less strong at the end of the century than they had been at the beginning; men were accustomed to seeing their claims successfully defied; and the policy of the princes towards them was generally approved by lay opinion.

According to Canon Law, no temporal authority might tax the clergy without their consent. This principle was not infringed in fifteenth-century Germany; but in many principalities, notably in the Habsburg lands, so many extraordinary taxes were demanded and conceded—often under great pressure—that the exemption was of small practical importance. It was vain for the clergy to look to the Pope for aid. He taxed them too, and without the compliance of the temporal power (which sometimes got a share) could not hope to collect his money. Thus the wealth of the German Church, though still perhaps increasing, was somewhat precarious.

In the religious activity of the Church many princes took a keen and active interest. We hear of them encouraging local attempts at reform, exhorting parish priests to do their duty, coercing them when delinquent. They frequently appointed administrators of monasteries which had fallen into financial difficulties, a fate which many of them suffered, in Germany as elsewhere, in the fifteenth century. Now and again princes possibly meddled in matters that were properly spiritual, in the sense then generally accepted, but such actions as those just mentioned belonged to their bounden duty, and the better sort of clergy encouraged them. It is nevertheless true that the secular princes were now far more influential in the religious life of Germany than they had ever been. To many of the clergy they mattered more than the Pope. The German Church, it is true, was still an integral part of the Church Catholic; no principality had a *Landeskirche*, nor, so far as we know, did any prince think of creating one. But the way was being prepared for the changes which the Reformation was to cause in the relations between Church and State—changes which in practice were far less revolutionary than has commonly been supposed.

Most German princes at the close of the Middle Ages were not content to break down the privileges of classes or institutions which hampered their authority. They wisely sought to promote the public welfare by legislation, usually with the consent of their *Landtage*, on economic and social matters, and if many of their laws were foolishly restrictive of individual enterprise and liberty, they were in that respect following the most approved medieval models. Some princes tried to improve their courts of justice, an essential step if the judicial power of the Church and the local nobility was to be broken. In most principalities, too, the administrative activity of the central government was increased. Nevertheless, the results of these efforts were disappointing. The truth was that no great improvement in government could

*Political reforms attempted*

be accomplished until new machinery was created. In the typical principality some of the local officials were hereditary; very many farmed their posts; rarely were any of them subject to efficient supervision. At the centre the prince's private and public capacities were seldom differentiated; the judiciary and the executive were not distinguished; the administration was directed by the chief household officers or their deputies and by the prince's Council, which remained as it had been since the beginning of the fourteenth century—a body of sworn and paid advisers, some of them officers of the court, some local functionaries, some ecclesiastics, some noblemen with no office, and some laymen of the burgher class, generally trained lawyers. Only a few of these would be with the prince at any given moment; some members did not attend unless individually summoned; and in certain principalities there were what were called *Landräte*, councillors who were expected to appear only when the prince visited the region where they dwelt. No part of the Council met regularly as a matter of course. There was no division of labour among the counsellors, who were all general practitioners. Such an institution was manifestly unfitted to shoulder the increasing burden of government; but down to the end of the fifteenth century attempts to adapt it to changing conditions seldom met with much success. Sometimes the Estates took the initiative: thus in Cleves they imposed on the Duke a permanent Council, and it was at the instance of the *Landtag* that in 1466 a similar body was appointed in Lower Bavaria. But counsellors forced on a prince were not likely to wield much influence when the crisis which caused their appointment had passed away. Probably the most valuable reforms in administration were those achieved by the Hohenzollerns in Brandenburg. They characteristically devoted special attention to finance, adapting to the Mark methods which they had already used in Franconia. They separated the public finances from their domestic income and expenditure; they had a budget carefully drawn up every year, and compelled all officials who handled money to render systematic accounts —a precaution rarely employed in medieval Germany. At the very end of our period, Maximilian had just inaugurated changes which were to transform the administration of the

Habsburg lands; but the accomplishment of his plans lies beyond the limits of our survey. It happened, indeed, that drastic and momentous reforms were carried out in several states during the twenty-five years following the death of Frederick III.

The alleviation of Germany's political ills was in the end to come through the development of the authority of the princes. For many generations before the year 1400 the political decomposition of Germany had been going on with little intermission. It was in the fifteenth century that the process was checked. For long the turn of the tide was scarcely perceptible. When Frederick III died the princes were very far from being absolute in their respective territories. But in all parts of Germany they had begun to recover and consolidate their rights, and most of them had realized the necessity of creating new organs of government for the maintenance and increase of their authority. It was not long before the Reformation gave them opportunities of which they had scarcely dreamed; but the Reformation only accelerated a process which had begun years before. The princes of fifteenth-century Germany were for the most part neither clever nor good; few were actuated by anything but a narrow selfishness; but in striving to increase their power, they were, all things considered, working for the advantage of Germany. *Importance of the fifteenth century in Germany's political history*

It is hard to make generalizations about fifteenth-century Germany, and those that at first seem plausible are almost sure to be invalidated by the Swiss Confederation. Its fortunes must be treated as part of the History of Germany, for in 1378 its members were wholly German, and though during the following century it began to extend its control over French and Italian areas, it remained predominantly German in character. The Confederation offers an example, unique in that age, of the extension of German rule over alien regions; among all the leagues and associations of fifteenth-century Germany it was the only one that attained a lasting political eminence; and not only did it afford an instance of successful republicanism in a country and at a time when, as we have seen, monarchical power was generally increasing, but, within its own ranks, a struggle between democratic and oligarchic elements confirmed the ascendancy of the former. *The Swiss Confederation*

The years with which we are concerned wrought many and great changes in the position of the Swiss. At the end, as at the beginning of the period, their great enemy was the House of Habsburg. But the relations of the two parties had been reversed: instead of the Swiss living in terror of the Habsburgs, it was the Habsburgs who went in fear of the Swiss. Before 1378 the Confederation had of course gained several resounding victories, but it was not until shortly afterwards that it wrested the initiative from its traditional foe. The occasion was the attempt of Leopold of Habsburg, ruler of all his family's lands save Austria, to chastise the insolent peasants and burghers for alleged infringements of the peace which was supposed to exist between him and them. In 1386 Leopold was utterly overthrown by the men of Lucerne and the three Forest Cantons at Sempach, the battle, it is to be feared, being best remembered for the legendary heroism of Arnold Winkelried, though really memorable as an astonishing triumph of lightly equipped peasants over panoplied knights and men-at-arms. In 1388 an army seeking revenge was defeated at Näfels by the men of Glarus and Schweiz, the consequence being that in 1389 the Habsburgs accepted a treaty which practically marked the abandonment of their claims to lordship over any of the existing members of the Confederation. There were to be several wars between the two in the following century, but, whatever their occasion, the fundamental cause of them all was Swiss aggression.

*The battle of Sempach, 1386*

In the hundred years after the battle of Sempach, the Swiss Confederation, from being a petty league of merely local importance, rose to be a great force in international politics. There were no additions to its eight members until 1481, when Freiburg and Solothurn were admitted. But it had long since begun to attract allies and associates, and also to seize territory by force. Its main objects were to acquire the comparatively level lands lying northward towards the Rhine, and to secure control of the passes over the High Alps. By the end of the period under review, the Confederation had two kinds of dependencies. There were "associates," *socii*, such as the abbey of St. Gall, the canton of Appenzell, the region of Valais—the first French-speaking area to become Swiss—the town of Schaffhausen

*The Confederation's allies and dependencies*

and its territory, and the town of Mülhausen in Alsace, whose relations with the Swiss were the source of the trouble between them and Charles the Bold. There were also the subject lands, some under the rule of individual cantons, others—the " common bailiwicks "—administered jointly by the Federal Diet. Of these the most notable were the Aargau, acquired during the Council of Constance at the expense of Frederick of Habsburg, the friend of Pope John XXIII, and the Thurgau, unscrupulously conquered from Frederick's son Sigismund, in a war which lasted from 1458 to 1461. Among the conquered lands may be mentioned the Val Leventina, attached to the canton of Uri since 1440.

Throughout the period which concerns us, the Confederation remained a loose one. In the Diet, its members had two votes apiece; *socii* had one; subject lands were not represented at all. Except on questions affecting the common bailiwicks, the minority was not bound by the decision of the majority. In any case few matters came within the competence of the Diet. The Compact of Stans, accepted in 1481, increased and tightened the bonds uniting the members and probably averted a conflict between the burghers and the peasants of the Confederation; but it was concerned with little save methods of determining foreign policy and the conditions under which mutual military assistance was to be rendered. Each member or associate of the Confederation was free to determine its own constitution and make what arrangements it liked for carrying out its obligations to the rest. {Constitution of the Confederation}

The Confederation had but a short career as a Great Power. Its renown and influence were based entirely on its military exploits. Its early victories, though very remarkable, had attracted little notice outside southern Germany. The battle of Sempach made a wider stir; but it had been fought in a quarrel that interested only a narrow circle. In the first decade of the fifteenth century, however, the Swiss began to encroach on the southern slopes of the Bernese Oberland, and thus provoked the anger of Milan. The war which followed was for the Swiss the least successful of the century; in 1422 they were defeated by the great *condottiere* captain Carmagnola at the battle of Arbedo; and when peace {Growth of the military reputation of the Swiss} was made in 1426, they had to disgorge the Italian territory they had previously seized. They profited by their reverses, as they proved in the so-called War of the Toggenburg Succession, waged from 1436 to 1440 between Zürich and several other members of the League; but this was primarily a civil conflict, and added little to their prestige. A year or two later, Zürich, the defeated party, renewed the strife in alliance with the Habsburgs and many Swabian nobles, who enlisted in their cause a great host of *Écorcheurs* from France under the Dauphin Louis. At the battle of St. Jakob, near Basel, in 1444, some 1,300 Swiss attacked a force of " Armagnacs " at least ten times as numerous, and when brought to a stand defended themselves for hours against a series of furious charges supported by a hail of missiles. The little troop was almost annihilated, but only after inflicting on the mercenaries losses much greater than its own numbers. Louis was deeply impressed, and took care thereafter to avoid hostilities with the Swiss, the first treaty between the Confederation and France being signed in 1452. But what made the Swiss universally famous was of course their astounding series of victories over Charles the Bold. For many years afterwards they were believed and believed themselves to be invincible, and it was hard to get troops to face them. Thousands of them were hired by Louis XI in the closing years of his reign, and within a short time the greatest kings and princes of Europe were competing for their assistance.

**Swiss tactics**

The Swiss fought almost without exception on foot, in deep columns, usually three in number, which entered battle in *échelon*. They attacked whenever they could. The rank and file wore little or no body armour, so that a Swiss army was astonishingly mobile. The arms on which they relied in their greatest days were the long pike, measuring eighteen feet from butt to point, and the halberd, once their main weapon, but in the second half of the fifteenth century carried only by the banner-guard in the midst of each column. Before the front rank of a Swiss column there projected four rows of pike-heads, a steel thicket impenetrable by cavalry. If the front ranks became closely engaged, the banner-guard issued from the flanks of the column and fell upon the enemy with their terrible halberds, which could crash through the best plate-armour. The Swiss had a well-earned reputation as very savage fighters, and prided themselves on giving no quarter.

The Swiss have never been surpassed for headlong courage, and they were undeniably most formidable warriors. But their military fame was somewhat cheaply earned. The operations of a Swiss army were directed by a Council of War consisting of the captains of the cantonal contingents, who, when a battle was imminent, appointed a commander-in-chief to conduct it. Swiss strategy was consequently crude and Swiss tactics, though very effective under favourable conditions, lacked flexibility and had certain defects which should have been obvious to enemy commanders. For years, however, the Swiss were opposed by contemptible generalship. Charles the Bold, in particular, played straight into their hands. Their enemies usually relied on primitive shock tactics, instead of putting their trust in missile weapons, though a Swiss column was the sort of target that an English longbowman saw only in his most roseate dreams. Once the Swiss were confronted by generals with brains in command of troops of good morale, their day was over; and this fate was to befall them early in the sixteenth century. They justly retained their name as stout soldiers, but their military hegemony was never regained. Yet in the days of their highest renown, as the following volume will narrate, the Confederation had made itself a virtually independent State, and thus, German though most of its members were, had dealt a fresh blow to the political integrity of Germany.

*Weaknesses of the Swiss*

Authorities for chapter xiii:—
Interest in national concerns fell even lower under Frederick III than in the previous reigns. The city chronicles, though mainly occupied with local affairs, shed occasional light on the state and fortunes of the country at large (see under chap. iv: *Chroniken der deutschen Städte*). The following contemporary authorities may likewise be mentioned:

Aeneas Sylvius Piccolomini: *De rebus et gestis Friderici III*, ed. A. F. Kollar, in *Analecta monumentorum omnis aevi Vindobonensia*, vol. ii, Vienna, 1762.

Nauclerus, J.: *Memorabilium omnis aetatis . . . chronici commentarii*, Tübingen, 1516. Frequently printed.

Rolewinck, Werner: *Fasciculus temporum*; often printed.

Modern works—
Bachmann, A.: *Deutsche Reichsgeschichte im Zeitalter Friedrichs III und Maximilians I*, 2 vols., Leipzig, 1884–94.

Bemmann, R.: *Zur Geschichte des Reichstages im 15 Jahrhundert*, Leipzig, 1907.

Chmel, J. : *Geschichte Kaiser Friedrichs IV (sc. III) und seines Sohnes Maximilian I*, 2 vols., Hamburg, 1840–2.

Haller, J. : *Epochs of German History*, London, 1930.

Kallen, G. : *Aeneas Silvicus Piccolomini als Publizist in der Epistola de Ortu et Auctoritate Imperii Romani*, Köln, 1939.

Kraus, V. von, and Kaser, K. : *Deutsche Geschichte im Ausgange des Mittelalters (1438–1519)*, in *Bibliothek deutscher Geschichte*, ed. H. von Zwiedineck-Südenhorst, 2 vols., Stuttgart, 1888–1912.

Ulmann, H. : *Kaiser Maximilian I*, 2 vols., Stuttgart, 1884–91.

Wostry, W. : *König Albrecht II*, 2 vols., Prague, 1906–7.

Works on the history of Switzerland—

Partly because the field was narrowly circumscribed, partly because the achievements of the Swiss aroused much interest and enthusiasm, there are several chronicles of note relating to the Swiss Confederation in the fifteenth century. It was at this time that many of the most famous Swiss legends took shape.

The following contemporary sources are noteworthy :

*Chronik des Weissen Buches*, ed. F. Vetter, Zürich, 1891.

Etterlin, Petermann : *Kronika von der loblichen Eidgenotschaft*, ed. J. J. Spreng, Basel, 1752–64.

Justinger, K. : *Berner Chronik*, ed. G. Studer, Bern, 1871.

Knebel, Johannes : *Diarium (1473–9)*, ed. W. Vischer and H. Boos in *Basler Chroniken*, vols. i and ii, Basel, 1880 and 1887.

Russ, Melchior : *Luzerner Chronik*, ed. J. Schneller, Bern, 1834.

Schilling, D., senior : *Berner Chronik, 1468–84*, ed. G. Tobler, 2 vols., Bern, 1897–1901.

Schilling, D., junior : *Luzerner Chronik*, Lucerne, 1862.

*Tschachtlans Chronik*, ed. G. Studer, in *Quellen zur Schweizerischen Geschichte*, vol. i, Basel, 1877.

Among modern works may be mentioned :

*Cambridge Medieval History*, vol. vii, chap. vii, Cambridge, 1932.

Dändliker, K. : *Geschichte der Schweiz*, 3 vols., Zürich, 1884–1903.

Dierauer, J. : *Geschichte der Schweizerischen Eidgenossenschaft*, 5 vols., Gotha, 1887, etc.

Dürr, E. : *La politique des Confédérés au XIV et au XV siècle*, Berne, 1935.

Gagliardi, E. : *Geschichte der Schweiz*, 3 vols., Zürich, 1920–7.

Van Muyden, B. : *Histoire de la nation Suisse*, 3 vols., Lausanne and Paris, 1899–1901.

Nabholz, H., Muratt, L. von, Feller, R., Dürr, E. : *Geschichte der Schweiz*, vol. i, Zürich, 1932.

There is a singular lack of good English books on the period of Swiss history with which we are concerned.

## CHAPTER XIV

# GERMANY

### SOCIAL AND ECONOMIC CONDITIONS

NO one is now content to define History as "past politics," and it is astonishing that so ignoble an estimate of Clio could have been countenanced by anyone acquainted, however slightly, with the past of Germany. For to confine one's attention to her political vicissitudes is to get a totally false impression of the experiences and achievements of the German people. English or French students of history are particularly prone to draw false inferences from political conditions when dealing with Germany. In their countries a period of weak or corrupt government has usually been marked by general slackness or decadence. In Germany the people have repeatedly shown astonishing vigour, enterprise, and creative power just when her political ills seemed desperate.

It must be confessed that a fifteenth-century German had many grounds for pessimism. The Emperor did little or nothing for him. The princes filled the land with strife; their efforts to establish order in their own territories had not yet gone far, and, for that matter, alarmed some of the best elements in German society. During the greater part of the century the House of Burgundy was extending its power in the west; its culture and outlook were essentially French; and nearly all its gains were made at the expense of Germany. In the south the Swiss Confederation, no longer wholly German in membership, became to all intents and purposes an independent power. To the east, Bohemia, legally an electoral state of the German kingdom, became for a time the scourge of Germany, and thereafter went about its own affairs with but little regard for what was happening further west. Poland rose to a position of unprecedented might, not only bringing the *Drang nach Osten* to a

*Germany's troubles and losses*

stand, but defeating the Teutonic Order and eventually depriving it of West Prussia. In the north Slesvig and Holstein became attached to the Danish Crown. On all hands, the area where German culture might freely develop had been cut short.

*Influence of the princes*

It has to be recognized, too, that little was done for the benefit of the country by the so-called upper classes. The political activities of the princes we have already considered. Not a few of them tried to improve the economic state of their lands; but their measures were as a rule so rigidly protectionist and restrictive that they did more harm than good. The mining industry perhaps profited most from their efforts. Their attempts at social reform generally took the shape of sumptuary laws or regulations for the betterment of the private morals of their subjects, some of the latter measures anticipating the most impudent enactments of modern America and producing even less effect. As patrons of art and learning a few princes gained a reputation; but the majority cared little for such things, and if it had awaited princely encouragement the Italian Renaissance would have affected Germany more tardily than it did.

*The knights*

The nobles below princely rank were of widely varying status and influence. Among them the class of knights—both tenants-in-chief of the Emperor and others—was extremely numerous and constituted a highly perplexing problem. At one time the knights had been the leaders of German culture, while their military prowess had been the admiration of Europe. They still pretended to uphold their traditions, but for the most part were quite unfitted to do so. Most of them were poor; few of them possessed any culture or indeed education, many affecting to despise all refinement of mind or manners; and owing to changes in the art of war their military value had greatly declined. But they were still very proud; the most poverty-stricken knight was of noble blood, and so were all his sons; as a boy he had undergone the most brutal discipline, but when a man he must, so far as possible, avoid obedience to any authority; and he must of course maintain himself by his sword and the revenues of his lands, participating if he liked in the more dignified forms of agricultural labour but on no account demeaning himself by engaging in trade. With such views and aims, the knights were commonly on bad terms with the princes and sometimes at open strife with them. Their bitterest hatred, however, was reserved for the towns. They owed it to their class to despise the burghers for their vulgar blood. At the same time they were jealous of the wealth which these louts had amassed and of the peace and comfort which were to be found only in the cities. Some of them were resentfully conscious that when art and literature fled from the knight's castle they had taken refuge behind city walls. In any case, the riches of burghers were fair game for the decayed gentleman, and some cities were in a state of chronic feud with the knights of the surrounding country. For the truth is that many of these gentry were no better than highwaymen. It was not uncommon for a well-to-do merchant, travelling on his lawful occasions, to be waylaid, carried off to his captor's castle, thrust into a dungeon, and, under the threat of torture, compelled to write to his friends begging them to raise his ransom. The affair was frequently so managed that when the victim was set free, he did not know where he had been or who had seized him. It must not be supposed that the dens of these brigands were magnificent or formidable strongholds. Ulrich von Hutten has left a vivid picture of the conditions under which a typical German knight lived, and what he says will apply in all essentials to the century before he wrote. The knight's castle was usually a dilapidated structure, barely defensible against a modest force. Within, it was wholly devoid of comfort. The lord and his family dwelt in two or three bare rooms, their ears assailed by the noise, their noses by the smell, of the live stock that occupied the adjacent stables and fouled the yard under the windows. There was a constant going and coming of retainers and farm-hands. In summer wagons rumbled to and fro between the castle court and the fields outside; in winter wolves howled in the woods around. Malefactors in such reduced circumstances could not have escaped punishment for long, had it not been for the remarkable *esprit de corps* which the knights habitually showed. Something has already been said of the big societies which they from time to time formed. These of course were generally designed to secure their ends by force; but it is just to remember that some of them existed to protect the interests of the class at law, and that at the end of the century there was a party among the knights which repudiated " direct action " and limited itself to legal measures. Such moderation was not popular among the knights in general; indeed, it was difficult to hold even the militant associations together for long, many of their members finding the regulations irksome. Nevertheless, the knights of a particular locality were generally ready to co-operate with one another when occasion arose; had it been otherwise, the secrecy which was so essential to the success of many of their crimes could not have been maintained. But while this class loyalty partly accounts for the failure of the princes to bring the knights to heel, it is also true that few of them could altogether dispense with knightly support; the knights were still useful for military purposes, and their aid was worth having when a prince was at odds with his towns. So their poverty, their desperation, and their insolence continued to increase. It reached unprecedented heights in the early years of the sixteenth century and boiled over into the Knights' War of 1523.

The clergy  If the claim of the nobles to be the leaders of the German people in temporal matters was but little justified by their deeds, still less did the walk and conversation of the clergy warrant their pretensions in the religious sphere. Their discipline and morals do not seem to have deteriorated much in the fifteenth century, and there was plenty of genuine devotion and piety to be found, especially among the laity. But the old abuses continued: the clergy as a class remained worldly, avaricious, corrupt, lazy, and licentious. Anticlericalism, which had long been prevalent, increased; and the feeling had in it a revolutionary ingredient which had hitherto been rare. It was intensified by the fact that, as in other countries, the religious ideals which had appealed to earlier generations were ceasing to satisfy. Very few monasteries were founded in Germany in the century preceding the Reformation, and attempts to reform those that existed seldom came to anything. Bishops and abbots, furthermore, were accused of being the most oppressive landlords. Nine Germans out of ten still professed to be orthodox Catholics in belief. But the political and social doctrines of the more extreme Hussites had spread far and wide in Germany, and those who favoured them had often been infected by the religious heresy out of which they had sprung in Bohemia. Towards the end of the century, moreover, one or two fanatical outbursts showed that criticism of the behaviour of the clergy easily passed into criticism of their teaching. Unless the German Church could produce some great leader of conservative views, the ascendancy of the clergy, such as it was, could hardly be maintained much longer.

It was in the burgher class that most of the vitality of the race was concentrated. So much has been written in praise of the German towns of the later Middle Ages that there is some danger lest their merits should be over-estimated. It should be remembered, in the first place, that by modern standards they were all quite small. It is unlikely that the population of any was over 40,000 : Nürnberg, one of the biggest and most renowned, had 20,000 inhabitants about 1450. The streets of even prosperous towns were narrow and foul. Most of the houses were made of lath and plaster on a timber framework ; they were small, with narrow gabled fronts and usually with thatched roofs. It should be noted that most of the German towns which are to-day shown to tourists as " medieval " owe their picturesque appearance to the sixteenth and seventeenth centuries; it is only in two or three, such as Hildesheim and Rotenburg, that fifteenth-century buildings are preserved in any number. The outlook of the burghers was commonly just as narrow and selfish as that of the nobles or the clergy—perhaps as a rule more so, for they frequently thought only of the immediate advantage of their own city and were with difficulty persuaded to co-operate with the inhabitants of others. In many a town, too, the spirit of faction ran high ; and municipal politicians of medieval Germany knew all the less creditable tricks of their trade. Yet the fact remains that it was only in the towns that reasoned and orderly government was to be found ; it was there alone that peace and comfort were attainable. The houses of the burghers were in general far superior to the cottages of the peasants and the cheerless lairs of the knights ; those of the wealthiest merchants excelled the palaces of princes in luxury and magnificence. The average level of education was much

*The burghers*

higher in the towns; some civic authorities maintained schools for the children of citizens; in other places private endowment often placed at least an elementary education within reach of those who wanted it. The art of writing was not a rare accomplishment, as it was elsewhere. Consequently a city's by-laws were commonly written down, and records of official proceedings were kept, one result being the establishment of civic archives, some of which have survived for the enlightenment of the modern historian. The administration of the public finances was much more scientific in the towns than elsewhere. In the fifteenth century civic finance was usually on a money basis, and in some places the officials had the handling of large sums. Medieval government was normally a hand-to-mouth business, and the municipal officials of Germany were for the most part men of their age; but they did sometimes try to carry out a reasoned, systematic, and continuous policy, such as could seldom be traced outside the cities.

Party strife in the towns, though there was plenty in the fifteenth century, was perhaps not so frequent and fierce as it had been in the previous period. In many places the constitutional struggle between the merchant aristocracy and the craft-gilds had been settled. Sometimes the merchants vindicated their exclusive control over the Council, sometimes they were fain to share power with the artisans, sometimes the government of the town had fallen entirely into the hands of the gilds. As a rule the aristocracies had held their ground better in the north than in the south. In very few places, however, could the government be called democratic; for the craft-gilds were an ever-narrowing oligarchy, just as jealous of their privileges as the merchants had been. In the fifteenth century, indeed, the journeymen and other elements of the unenfranchised populace frequently conducted against them an agitation of exactly the same character as they themselves had formerly directed against the merchants. The attitude of a city towards the outside world seems to have been little affected by the nature of its constitution; merchants and craftsmen were equally zealous in maintaining its rights, though the former were perhaps the more willing to enter into leagues with other places.

Every town that desired to maintain its autonomy had

to give much attention to military defence. The kernel of a town's fighting force consisted of the craftsmen of the gilds, who had to join in repelling attack and to take part in expeditions which did not occasion more than a day's march from home. For more extensive operations mercenaries were employed by the richer cities in the fifteenth century. In field warfare, as might have been expected, the towns seldom did well, but they stood sieges admirably and were rarely taken. And towards the end of the century their wealth enabled them to purchase fire-arms, with which they could batter down the strongholds of the lesser nobility. The development of artillery, on the other hand, placed them at a disadvantage in relation to the greater princes.

A flourishing German town of the later Middle Ages, with its sound and steady government, its fortifications, its stately churches, its charitable foundations, its public baths, its municipal brothel, its frequent festivals, its gorgeous pageantry, its lively and intemperate social life, had an immense attraction for many sorts of men outside. To the serf it must have seemed Paradise, for whosoever had eaten his bread unmolested for a year and a day in a town was free. The towns had to restrict immigration, and there are not a few places in Germany which had more inhabitants in the fifteenth century than they have now.

All this prosperity and magnificence depended of course upon trade and industry. The channels of German trade remained much as they had been since the thirteenth century. The south German towns retained their specially close connexion with Venice. Even when German kings were officially at war with the Italian republic, this traffic was little affected. The goods brought into Germany across the Alps were much the same as they had been earlier in the Middle Ages, and the victories of the Turks, though they disturbed intercourse with the East, did not stop it. The geographical discoveries of the fifteenth century made small difference to German commerce until after the end of the period with which we are concerned.

While it is true that Germany exported and imported the same commodities as before and bought and sold in most of the old markets, the century witnessed vital changes in the organization of her economic life. There was a great develop-

Rise of capitalism
ment of capitalism. This was less evident in industry than in commerce; for the craft-gilds remained powerful, and in many towns the master-craftsmen were able to hold their own against big capitalist undertakings. In mining, however, capitalism made much headway. There were great mining companies whose operations extended far afield, sometimes beyond the bounds of Germany. Again, new industries, such as paper-making and printing, were as a rule organized on a capitalistic basis. But it would be misleading to speak of trade and industry as though they were conducted by quite different people. The German business man of the later Middle Ages was a versatile fellow. The goods sold by the merchant were often of his own manufacture, and his profits were not seldom invested in land. Some merchants practised money-lending or banking. As for the companies which began to abound in Germany at this time, many of them were family concerns, but some were of much wider scope, with members belonging to various cities or principalities, and the joint-stock company was also known. Great capitalistic organizations, whether in the hands of an individual or of a number of shareholders, were generally unpopular—eyed with jealousy by the princes, with covetousness by the knights, with reprobation by the clergy, with fear by the craftsmen and peasants. But there was no stopping their advance, and at the end of the fifteenth century many of them were enjoying great, and on the threshold of much greater prosperity. Such, in particular, was the position of what is perhaps the most renowned family in the whole of Germany's economic history. The Fuggers had already been established in Augsburg for more than a hundred years. At first weavers in a humble way, they had become wool-merchants by the end of the fourteenth century, and thenceforward they steadily amassed profits, much of which they invested in houses and land. In the middle of the fifteenth century, they split into two branches, one of which came to grief in 1494. But the other, now headed by the famous Jacob Fugger, was just entering upon the period of its greatest power, having laid the foundation of its later political influence by loans to Sigismund of Tyrol.

It is not, however, of Augsburg or Nürnberg, of south or central Germany, that the modern German especially thinks when reminded of the commercial achievements of his countrymen during the Middle Ages. It is the Hanseatic League that has quickened the enthusiasm and confidence of such German business men as have looked for encouragement to the past. The origin and rise of the Hansa are treated in another volume of this series. At the beginning of the period to which we are here limited, the League had just reached the summit of its strength; for it had lately emerged from a war in which, after various turns of fortune, it had worsted and bent to its will the kingdom of Denmark.

*The Hanseatic League*

Throughout the ensuing century the League remained very prosperous and powerful. From the standpoint of the governments of northern and western Europe, it was a rival state which had to be treated with great respect. Yet the fifteenth century saw a marked decline in the League's strength and fortunes. The victory over Denmark may easily give an exaggerated impression of its power. The League was never a real federation; it was only an unusually extensive and lasting alliance. The bond between its members was loose. The towns belonging to it lay scattered over a vast area, and varied immensely in size, institutions, prosperity, and history. The purpose of the League was purely commercial—to maintain the privileges of the merchants of the cities which composed it; and it was seldom that so many privileges were simultaneously in jeopardy that more than a few Hanse towns felt themselves urgently concerned. Thus the Hansa was quite different from such a body as the Swabian League which gave so much trouble to King Wenzel: it did not exist for the maintenance of civic rights as such, whether against the Emperor or the princes or the knights. The Hansa, indeed, hardly noticed the Emperor's existence; it was no part of its policy to incite members to resist their princely overlords; and in north Germany the class of knights was of relatively small account.

There were, indeed, those who wanted to give the League a more closely knit organization and to use its strength for the promotion of their political ends. Many of the Hanseatic towns were rent by domestic strife. In the most influential the aristocratic party usually had the upper hand, and an attempt was made to use the League for the frustration of revolutionary ambitions. Thus in 1418 it was enacted by the common assembly of the League that any member whose governing Council was deprived, wholly or partially, of its authority should be " put outside the Hansa." From time to time, generally at the instance of Lübeck, cities of democratic leanings suffered economic excommunication in accordance with this policy, though it could not be applied consistently. It was of course a two-edged weapon. Though originally forged for the chastisement of democrats, it might equally well be used for the frustration of princes. The Hanse towns looked askance at rebellion and were always reluctant to interfere between a fellow-member and its lord; but few would have disputed that the League ought to stand by a member threatened with the loss of its autonomy, and in 1430 the League assembly resolved that if a member were unjustly attacked, it should be aided with both men and money, each Hanseatic town contributing according to its means and its distance from the seat of conflict. This pronouncement, however, had little practical consequence, and the princes of north Germany were not much hampered by the Hansa in their efforts to assert authority over unruly cities. Thus the subjection into which the towns of Brandenburg were reduced by the Hohenzollerns was such that at the end of the fifteenth century only two, Stendal and Salzwedel, were still members of the League. The wars waged by allied Hanseatic towns against princes were nearly always conducted by small groups, which would very likely have formed themselves even if the Hansa had never existed.

Schemes to turn the League's strength to political purposes might fail, and yet the members might have been willing to create new machinery for the readier attainment of their commercial ends. In fact, however, they were strangely reluctant to do so. During our period general assemblies were from time to time held, and these, as we have seen, might enact ordinances or pass resolutions which were supposed to bind all members. The first great general ordinance, which dealt with a number of heterogeneous topics of vital moment to the League, was enacted in 1418, and was several times re-issued, amended, and enlarged. But as legislation had to be carried unanimously, it was rare, and contentious matters were likely to be shelved. Further, though every city summoned to a general assembly was legally required to send representatives or undergo punishment, it was hard to secure a good attendance. In 1430 it was ordained that such an assembly should be held every three years. Immediately afterwards, however, it was conceded to the Prussian and Lithuanian groups of cities that they might discharge their obligations by sending two delegates each. Moreover, among the towns in general two classes quickly formed themselves and soon received tacit recognition, one consisting of cities which appointed representatives to general assemblies, the other of lesser places which were content to entrust their interests to one of their neighbours. At the biggest assembly on record (that of 1447), thirty-eight towns were represented. How many figured in the second class it is impossible to say, as no complete list of Hanse towns has survived; but as long as the League remained prosperous, the second class was probably about as large as the first.[1] It is likely that during the fifteenth century the membership of the Hansa declined somewhat in numbers, for some towns ceased to belong to it, while it became harder to secure admission, since all applications had to be accepted by a general assembly and the existing members were increasingly reluctant to share their advantages with new-comers. It was perhaps natural in the circumstances that the rule about the frequency of general assemblies should fall into disregard. Between 1440 and 1480 only seven were held.

The attempt to unite the members of the League more closely had thus failed. The Hansa had no officials, no treasury, no armed forces. It actually lacked a common flag and a common seal. Its members might form alliances with princes or with cities outside the League if the terms were not detrimental to the Hansa. In such conditions the League could hardly be expected to have a consistent or even a common policy towards the states with which its commercial activities brought it into contact. It would probably have flown asunder but for the influence of the so-called Wendish cities and, in particular, of Lübeck. It was at Lübeck that the general assembly met; it was Lübeck which summoned it, carried on indispensable correspondence with

[1] We know of 164 towns which at one time or another belonged to the League, but it is unlikely that there were ever more than half so many members simultaneously.

its fellow-members, and, with their consent, took action in emergencies.

Even in the great war against Denmark, numerous Hanseatic cities had done nothing. And the difficulty of stimulating even a few into joint action was strikingly shown over and over again in the following century. This reluctance to co-operate was the more regrettable since the international politics of northern Europe soon took a turn which involved the League in grave difficulty. The success of Olaf of Norway and his mother Margaret in making good their claims to the Danish and Norwegian thrones was favourably regarded by most members of the League ; [1] but when in 1389 Albert of Sweden was dethroned and replaced by Margaret of Denmark and Norway, the sympathies of the Hansa were divided, and it could not intervene effectively in the ensuing war. Nevertheless, it could not remain indifferent, for Mecklenburg, to whose ducal family the deposed King of Sweden belonged, threw open its harbours to all who would fight against Margaret. This resulted in the activities of the Victualling Brothers, so-called because at first their main purpose was to convey provisions into Stockholm, which Margaret's partisans were besieging. They quickly degenerated into mere pirates, and the trade of the Baltic suffered grievously at their hands. Here, one might have supposed, was a situation in which the interests of all the Hanseatic cities were identical. But the League altogether failed to restore the security of its trading routes. For some years the freebooters had things their own way, actually capturing Bornholm and Gothland. When the Union of Kalmar brought no cessation of their activities, it was not the Hansa but the Teutonic Order which in 1398 sent a great expedition to Wisby and took it by storm, so shaking the confidence of the rovers that for the most part they soon betook themselves to the North Sea. The knights held Gothland for seven years and then gave it back to Denmark.

The presence of pirates in the North Sea, where the Frisian coast was their headquarters, prevented a complete recovery of the Hansa's trade. Some of the towns fitted out special ships to deal with them, but when, in the second

*The Victualling Brothers*

[1] See below, Chapter XV.

decade of the fifteenth century, war broke out between Denmark and Holstein, each side was glad to enlist these lawless resolutes in its service, and for some years they did as much mischief as ever. Again the sympathies of the Hanseatic cities towards the combatants were divided, and when the imposition of a new toll in the Sound by King Eric of Denmark caused six of the greatest to make war on him, they did not scruple to use the freebooters themselves. It is true that when, towards the end of the war, the pirates again withdrew to the North Sea, Hamburg seized and fortified their principal base, Emden, a blow from which they never wholly recovered; but the harm already done to Hanseatic trade could not be fully repaired. The war of the six cities against Denmark, furthermore, had not gone well. Apart from Hamburg, only Wendish cities had taken active part in it; most of the rest had shown no interest in the struggle; some had continued to trade with Denmark. The fighting had opened badly for the Hanse towns with a severe naval defeat off Copenhagen, and though subsequently they did better, they failed to win any decisive success. Two of them, Stralsund and Rostock, were constrained by domestic discord to make a separate peace, and the other four were lucky to secure the confirmation of their existing privileges when the war was formally ended in 1435 by the Peace of Wordingborg. The conflict had injured the prestige of the Hansa and impaired the confidence of its members. What was worse from its point of view was the loss of that virtual monopoly of Baltic trade which it had for many years enjoyed. Taking advantage of the preoccupation of the most formidable champions of the Hansa, English and Dutch traders had crept in, and though as yet their operations were comparatively small, they were never to be ousted.

*War of the Hansa with Denmark, 1426-35*

The prosperity of the Hansa came to depend increasingly on the Wendish group of cities. Those farther east mostly fell on evil days in the fifteenth century. The Livonian members suffered from the disturbed condition of their country. After the defeat of the Teutonic Order by Poland, Königsberg was the only Hanseatic town under the rule of the knights. The other Hanseatic towns of Prussia remained in the League, but Danzig, recognized as a free city by Poland, was the only Hanse town east of the Oder which showed any vitality.

Piracy in the North Sea and the disturbed state of the Lower Rhineland and the Netherlands greatly reduced the Baltic trade of the Rhenish and Westphalian cities, whose connexion with the Wendish group became looser and looser. Of still more serious moment was the decline of some of those foreign settlements or factories which had played so important a part in bringing about the formation of the League. One of the earliest and greatest of these, Novgorod, suffered throughout the century from the growing competition of Russian traders. It nevertheless maintained its autonomy, remaining a little German sanctuary in the heart of Russia, and it continued to be fairly prosperous, until Ivan III of Muscovy took action against it, forced it to surrender unconditionally, and cancelled its liberties. The German merchants, indeed, were allowed to remain if they wished; but under Swedish persuasion, and in revenge for alleged offences by other Germans, Ivan again attacked the settlement in 1494, imprisoned the merchants found there, and carried off their treasure and stock to Moscow. Maximilian secured the release of the captives, and in 1514 Ivan's son, Wassili IV, permitted the settlement to be revived; but the place never approached its former importance.

*The foreign factories of the Hansa*

*Novgorod*

Very different from the Petershof at Novgorod, but hardly less valuable to the Hansa, were the seasonal settlements of the members of the League on the coast of Scania. Enormous shoals of herrings frequented this part of the Baltic Sea in the Middle Ages, and the business of catching and preserving the fish attracted thither a vast concourse of people towards the end of every summer. The little towns of Skanör and Falsterbo were the centres of activity. Tradition, diplomacy, and private bargaining had brought it about that each Hanse town had a little strip of land for its merchants, the Baltic towns clustering near Falsterbo, the North Sea towns near Skanör. The visitors were of course not exclusively concerned in the fish trade; the region in fact became a great market or fair, in which all kinds of traffic were carried on. In 1463 it was estimated that 20,000 strangers were present. They were not all Germans, and the settlements were all under the jurisdiction of the Danish Crown; but the Hanseatic merchants were extremely numerous and possessed privileges of special value. Towards the close

*Scania*

of the century, however, their numbers fell. About the year 1425 the herrings had begun to leave the coast of Scania and to betake themselves for spawning to the North Sea. Navigation, moreover, was becoming more adventurous, and many traders shipped their goods direct to their final destination, instead of meeting their customers at some common trading-ground. And, as we have seen, the Hanse towns of north-western Germany were ceasing to be interested in the Baltic.

During the fourteenth century one of the chief sources of the prosperity and prestige of the Hansa was its factory at Bruges. Here the German merchants did not live apart in a settlement of their own; but they enjoyed very extensive liberties and formed a society with a common business centre, a common treasury, and elaborate regulations. To Bruges came traders from all parts of Europe, but for long the Hansa held its ground well against every kind of competition. In the fifteenth century, however, a certain falling away became manifest. The Dukes of Burgundy were not always friendly, and more than once the German merchants left Bruges and settled in other Netherlands cities. They always returned, and at the end of the century they still possessed their old rights; but the community had suffered much damage through the frequent wars which affected Flanders, the rivalry of Antwerp, and competition by the English. The old *esprit de corps*, moreover, had weakened, and many merchants from Hanse towns forfeited the privileges to which they might have been entitled rather than conform to the League's regulations which were the condition of their enjoyment. *Bruges*

In London, the Hanseatic settlement—the famous Steelyard—likewise had its troubles, though it maintained its position with a considerable measure of success. Like the Petershof at Novgorod, it was an enclave wherein dwelt the German merchants and their assistants, ruled by their own officers and subject to a strict, nay austere, discipline. When the Steelyard was founded, the Hanse merchants had been welcome in England; but now their privileges, which gave them the advantage, not only over other foreigners but in many respects over English traders, excited bitter jealousy. Their hospitality and munificence usually kept them in the *The London Steelyard* good graces of the influential classes: but by the populace they were hated. It was this growing animosity, as much as alleged offences against English ships by members of the League, that led the English Government in 1447 to withdraw the privileges of the Hansards throughout the country. There followed an irregular war between the English and some of the Hanse cities, notably Lübeck. This was still proceeding when Edward IV came to the throne. The new King was much concerned to promote English commerce, and viewed the League with dislike. He did indeed confirm its privileges, but only after much delay and for a brief term, which was reluctantly extended from time to time while efforts were made to reach a definitive accord, each party having grievances against the other and the English demanding concessions commensurate with the franchises enjoyed by the Hansa. For years the negotiations bore no fruit, and in 1468 Edward, asserting that the Hansa had broken a truce, arrested a number of German merchants, sequestrated their goods, and closed the London Steelyard. The city of Cologne, which had refrained from hostilities, convinced Edward of its innocence, and was put into exclusive possession of the Steelyard as a reward. Denounced as a traitor, it was expelled from the League, and the Wendish towns fought England with increased vigour. The strife which afflicted England in 1470 and 1471 was naturally favourable to the League; indeed Edward IV was glad of its help when he was driven from England by the Earl of Warwick, and the ships which escorted him when he returned had mostly been hired from Hanse towns. The war, it is true, continued after he had recovered his throne. But Edward came to the conclusion that the English stood to lose more than they would gain by the continuance of hostilities; negotiations were resumed; and though the English envoys bluffed and blustered heroically, the treaty which in the end they signed was altogether favourable to the League, which was restored to the enjoyment of its old privileges in England, and received an indemnity for some of the damage it had sustained. The men of Cologne had to surrender the Steelyard, though they were soon afterwards restored to membership of the League. It was a notable victory for the Hansa, which upheld its position in England during what was left of the rule of the House of York. But its unpopularity was unabated, and after the accession of the House of Tudor fresh blows assailed it. These, however, may not be described here.

The success of the Hanseatic League in its conflict with England is a warning against exaggerating its weaknesses. Here and there, indeed, it gained. Thus it was in the fifteenth century that the great Hanse settlement on the shores of Bergen harbour reached the height of its prosperity. Here, as in Novgorod, the Germans were pioneers of culture amid a ruder people. Their thirty houses, each of three stories and including offices, store-rooms, and cramped accommodation for a hundred men and boys, constituted what passed in medieval Norway for a good-sized town. The Hansards of Bergen lived a rough celibate life; new-comers underwent an initiation of ingenious brutality; the only authorized recreation seems to have been drinking. But their *esprit de corps* was high, and they maintained themselves well, both in speech and in deed, against their Norwegian neighbours, who, to tell the truth, could not do without them. The settlement was still flourishing at the end of the century. {.sidenote: Bergen}

The rise of the Hansa to the peak of its fortunes had been due to the lack of rivals rather than its own strength. When competition grew, as it did in various quarters during the fifteenth century, the ascendancy of the League was quickly impaired. But it remained a mighty force to the end of the Middle Ages and beyond; and the decline which the modern historian can discern was hardly perceptible to contemporaries. It was of the arrogance and aggressiveness of the Hansards that Englishmen complained at the end of our period.

The commodities in which the Hanse towns trafficked were remarkably heterogeneous; but what particularly distinguished their trade from that of south Germany was the position occupied in it by raw materials and foodstuffs. It was not, in the main, a carrying trade. Very often the goods in a Hanseatic ship had been bought and would be sold by the owner of the vessel; the rest would mostly be consigned to or by Hanseatic merchants. Of the exports from the Baltic lands, furs held the first place in value. Hides and leather were also sent westward in great quantities. {.sidenote: Character of Hanseatic trade}

There was a good market for the timber which Sweden and Russia could supply without limit; and it is a little surprising to find that the longbows wherewith the English archers won their victories were made of yew which was largely imported in Hanseatic bottoms and came from the Carpathians. Ores—especially Swedish iron—were a source of profit to many Hanse merchants. There was some trade in live stock. Numerous horses went to England from Prussia and Sweden, and the Baltic countries were an important source of the sporting hawks which were in demand all over Europe. The Hansa did a tremendous trade in wax, mainly from Russia. Grain—principally oats and wheat—was exported in great quantities from north Germany, and several Hanse towns made much profit from their beer. In bulk the import trade of the Hanseatic towns was far less. It consisted of manufactured goods of all kinds, wines, the highly prized spices of southern Europe and the East, sugar, southern fruits, and other luxuries.

The towns of the Hansa of course had a certain amount of overland trade. But the main purpose of the League was to uphold the privileges and interests of its members in lands which they could reach most readily by sea; its leading cities were seaports and even its inland members faced, as it were, seaward. The Hansa had astonishingly little direct intercourse with the cities of south Germany. Its policy was actuated by no sentiment of nationality. If a citizen of Nürnberg or Augsburg tried to avail himself of the privileges accorded to the Hansa in Flanders or England, he was regarded as an interloper and sometimes subjected to violence. The history of the League has been much used by modern propagandists to stimulate German enthusiasm for commercial enterprise and naval expansion, yet it was one of the many disintegrating forces that were destroying Germany's political unity in the later Middle Ages. Nevertheless, it rendered great services to Germany. It brought economic prosperity to thousands of her people, and, what was still more important, helped to maintain their morale and self-respect. As long as the Hansa flourished, the north German could hold his head high in any company. The noble town-halls, the spacious churches, the stately dwellings which arose in its cities and survive in no small number to this day testify eloquently to the munificence, public spirit, and sturdy ambition of the merchants whose welfare it fostered.

It is tempting to linger over the German cities of the later Middle Ages, for few phases of European life at that time are so attractive. But it remains true that only a small proportion of the German people lived in cities; the vast majority were peasants. There has been much controversy as to the position of the German peasant in the later Middle Ages, one school representing him as enjoying a prosperity which was destroyed by the changes wrought at the time of the Reformation, the other dwelling upon his wrongs and sufferings, many of which are alleged to have been due, directly or indirectly, to the Church. The truth is that one ought not to generalize at all about the state of the German peasant in the fifteenth century. The peasant class fell into numerous subdivisions. Its lot varied from one part of Germany to another. War and pestilence were frequent, and a region flourishing in one decade might be poverty-stricken in the next. In south and central Germany and over a good part of the west, the peasants, on an average, were not badly off. There actually remained a number of free peasants, who had no feudal lord. And though the great majority were imperfectly free, to describe them indiscriminately as serfs would be to give a misleading idea of their status. The tendency for some time before the beginning of the century had been to assimilate the different grades of serfdom, the result being that the average status of the peasant was raised. He might now as a rule leave his lord's estate if he liked. His possession of his holding was secured by custom, if not by law; custom or law likewise fixed the amount of his rent and dues, which remained stationary while the prices of land and produce were rising. Many peasants had thus been able to raise themselves to a position of great comfort. But in some parts there was a different tale to tell. In the extreme south-west, for instance, there was some congestion of population, and here many peasants fell back into the bondage from which their ancestors had escaped. Towards the east, too, where big estates were numerous, the peasant's freedom remained much restricted. But he was rarely in abject misery. Most peasants had

*The German peasants*

enough to be ambitious for more. There is a consensus of testimony that those who became well-off were ostentatious, arrogant, and quarrelsome. They were in a mood to smell a grievance in everything and to see in the operation of economic laws evidence of deliberate plots against their welfare.

And it is probable that, taken all round, the lot of the German peasant became a little worse during the fifteenth century. He suffered much through the Hussite and Turkish invasions. The so-called private wars of this century, too, were not only very numerous but inflicted immense harm on non-combatants. For that matter, as he rose from serfdom the peasant became liable for military service, and as the victories of the Hussites and the Swiss gradually convinced the German nobles that foot-soldiers were not useless, his skin as well as his goods was often endangered if his prince was at odds with a neighbour. There is no doubt that many lords sought to remedy their financial troubles at the expense of their peasants. Traditional rights grounded in custom, such as those which gave the peasant access to commons, woods, or streams, would be gradually withdrawn. A voluntary payment or service would be treated as compulsory, a temporary one as permanent. Obsolete demands would be revived. Here a little and there a little would be added to the peasant's obligations. The peasant might grumble, protest, appeal to tradition, demand written authority; but if he went to law, he was probably judged by his lord. This same lord, moreover, might be his most formidable competitor when he tried to sell his surplus produce; for at this time it was more common than previously for a lord to exploit his domain with a view to pecuniary profit. The right of hunting, too, now became restricted to the nobility; the peasant thus lost a source of food and, what was more serious, a means of amusement. But what remedy had he short of force? He could look for no sympathy from other classes. The clergy were exacting in their demands and neglectful of their duties, and, despite fervent denials, the evidence leaves no doubt that ecclesiastical landlords were conspicuously harsh and grasping. The burghers, who tried to destroy village industries and would scarce allow him to sell agricultural produce in their towns, the peasant viewed with hatred. He loathed the new class of capitalists, he was jealous of the miners whom they pampered, he feared his prince, who was always laying taxes upon him. He often had a vague notion that the Emperor would render him justice if he but knew the facts. That, however, was small consolation, and, on the whole, he drew more encouragement from the exploits of the peasants of Switzerland and Bohemia.

The great explosion of discontent did not come until 1525. But in the latter half of the fifteenth century numerous minor outbreaks gave warning of what was to follow. It was in the south that most of the disturbances occurred. Thus in 1458 there was a rising against the Archbishop of Salzburg, who had demanded a tax on cattle and debased the coinage; the rebels got most of their demands. Four years later there was renewed trouble in the same area; the dispute was submitted to Duke Lewis of Bavaria, whose decision was in the main favourable to the peasants. The Habsburg lands were the field of much discontent. Some of them were afflicted by the Turks, with whom the nobles were accused of being in league. In 1478 there was a formidable outbreak of the peasants of Carinthia. They protested against the debasement of the coinage by Frederick III, and, if their enemies are to be believed, displayed a violent anti-clericalism and advocated social and economic revolution. They were well organized; but they rashly attempted to repel a Turkish invasion and were annihilated. In the neighbouring Styria there was also much unrest, though it produced no big movement until 1515. Many contemporaries ascribed Hussite opinions to anyone who rebelled against constituted authority, and there is little doubt that the political and social teachings of the more extreme Hussites made a strong appeal in various parts of Germany. But in every medieval country there was always a certain amount of heresy and fanaticism, and one need not attribute to Hussite influence the vagaries of Hans Böhm, a young shepherd who claimed to have had a special revelation from the Virgin and in 1476 attracted enormous multitudes to Niklashausen in Franconia, where he proclaimed the approach of better times, advocated a communistic reorganization of society, criticized emperors, popes, and princes, and denounced the clergy. With the central doctrines of the Church he apparently had no quarrel, though some of his teaching was logically incon-

*Peasants' risings*

sistent with one or two of them. There is little doubt that he was a foolish and stupid young man, who was exploited by cleverer people in the background. After a short run of immense popularity, he was arrested by the Bishop of Würzburg and burned at the stake. His admirers showed no desire to share his lot, but hostility to the clergy soon reappeared in movements that had more resolution behind them. In 1491, for instance, there was a rising against the great abbey of Kempten, which for years had been notorious for its unscrupulous severity towards its tenants. The insurgents stood on their rights, and appealed for help to the Swabian League; but though the city of Kempten aided them, they were put down. About the same time there was much unrest in Alsace, where the peasants first used as their badge the "Bundschuh," the rough brogue bound with thongs which was the usual footwear of the rural labourer. In 1493 there was a rising under this badge headed by a certain Hans Ulman. There was a burgher element in the movement, but most of those concerned were peasants. The Jews were to be exiled; the local courts of justice, spiritual and temporal, were to be suppressed; no one in future should pay more than four Pfennig a year in dues and taxes; no priest should have more than one benefice, and the confessional should be abolished. Ulman's plans were discovered before they were ripe, and the insurrection collapsed. But it was soon to be followed by others in the same region, and its abortive programme gives one a good notion of the bewildered discontent which actuated thousands of German peasants at this time.

No review of the condition of Germany in the later Middle Ages would be complete without some reference to the courts of the Vehme. The *Vehmgericht* has been surrounded with an atmosphere of romance by writers who should have known better, until in popular belief it has become one of the most mysterious, efficient, and ruthless of all secret societies, more terrible than the Camorra, the Mafia, or the original Ku Klux Klan, and yet an instrument of rough justice in a country and at a time when justice of any sort was rare. But though the origin of the Vehmic courts is still disputed, there was little mystery about their doings in the fourteenth and fifteenth centuries. They were always held by day in

The *Vehmgericht*

the open air; to most of their proceedings the public were admitted; their judges and other officers were never disguised. *Veme*—the correct form of the word—simply means "society" or "association." The Vehmic tribunals were descended from the old communal courts of Westphalia. These had long fallen into private hands. This, of course, had happened to the administration of local justice almost everywhere in Germany; but Westphalia was peculiar in that the Emperors had expressly bestowed judicial authority on the officials—called *Freigrafen*—appointed by the feudal lords to exercise their jurisdiction. On this imperial grant the Westphalian courts seem to have based their claim to sit in judgment on all the Emperor's subjects. They retained many traces of their antiquity. They met at traditional places of assembly—on a highway, on a bridge, in the courtyard of a castle, in the market-place of a town, beside a church, under a tree. Much primitive procedure was retained. The *Freigraf* presided; but he must be aided by at least seven "free judges"—*Freischöffen*—who determined the sentence, a relic of the times when the "suitors" of a court—those with the right or duty of attendance—were the judges. There were a great many of these *Freischöffen*, any free man being eligible for the position. The actual conduct of a case was very ceremonious, almost liturgical in fact, great importance being attached to the recitation of the correct formulæ by everyone concerned. The issue was normally decided by swearing. An accused man had to produce "oath-helpers" who would testify that he was swearing the truth. Here appeared one of the great advantages of belonging to the Vehme as one of its "free judges," for a *Freischöffe* under accusation could clear himself by his unaided oath, and, whichever side he was on, his oath counted for far more than that of an outsider. Nevertheless, the power of the Vehmic courts was subject to very restrictive conditions. They might act only when the ordinary tribunals could not provide a remedy or had failed to do so, and if a man summoned before them appeared and offered to go before the regular courts, they were legally obliged to let him. For long they dealt only with cases of theft, perjury, and murder, though later, by various devices and fictions, almost everything was brought within their scope. Heresy, however, they left alone. They never tried clergy, and they ignored Jews as unworthy of appearing before such honourable tribunals.

Anyone accused before a Vehmic court was summoned in writing, and as it was often difficult or dangerous to serve the document on the defendant in person, it sufficed to affix or leave it where he would be likely to see it or hear of it. Often the name of the accuser was not mentioned, nor was the nature of the charge indicated. Should the accused appear, the proceeding would usually be solemn but straightforward, as we have said ; if found guilty, he would probably be hanged forthwith. But the odds were heavy against the defendant in a Vehmic court, unless he belonged to the society himself, and most of those summoned preferred to keep out of the way. Proceedings against absentees were always held in secret, that is to say, only *Freischöffen* might be present. The case was solemnly considered, and the accused might be sentenced to death. Hanging was the authorized mode of execution, and it was the duty of every "free judge" to carry out the sentence if he had an opportunity of doing so, though it was laid down that at least three *Freischöffen* must be present when the offender underwent his fate. Thus it sometimes happened that a man's neighbours would find his body hanging from a tree, with near at hand a token that this was the handiwork of the Vehme, and no one would know when or why his fate had befallen him. It took few cases of this kind to instil into the credulous peasants a shuddering dread of the Vehme and an exaggerated notion of its power and effectiveness. In point of fact, most of the Vehmic sentences on absentees were not carried out at all.

It was in the reign of the Emperor Charles IV that these Westphalian courts first became of more than local importance. Their ambitions were much stimulated when in 1372 Charles made them in part responsible for the maintenance of a *Landfriede* which had been established in north-west Germany. Their functions as upholders of the public peace were renewed by Wenzel, who extended them over a large area of the north and centre. The Vehmic courts abused their powers and their doings excited violent protests, so that in 1387 Wenzel dissolved the *Landfriede* in question,

Meanwhile, however, the Vehme had made itself felt over a great part of Germany; it now tried to apply its claim to jurisdiction over all subjects of the Emperor; and its influence continued to grow. King Rupert gave it semi-official recognition; but its golden age was the reign of Sigismund. The Emperor himself was admitted as a *Freischöffe*, and encouraged other princes to follow his example. The Archbishop of Cologne was the official head of the organization. It became fashionable to belong to the Vehme, even though one had to journey to Westphalia to be initiated. Its citations went all over the country and were addressed to great princes; it actually passed sentence of death on two Dukes of Bavaria, though in each case without effect. An attempt was made at the instance of Sigismund to give the Vehme a constitution and to subject all its tribunals to general rules. The Archbishop of Cologne was supposed to hold an annual meeting of all the *Freigrafen*, and at one of these, in 1430, a set of general regulations was drawn up. Some years later these were amended, supplemented, and ratified by the Emperor Frederick III.

In the days of Sigismund the Vehme was both feared and respected. But thereafter its prestige rapidly declined. It administered no body of scientific law, and its proceedings were based partly upon laws designed for a long-vanished social order, partly upon custom and tradition, partly upon rule of thumb. Attempts to frame new laws to meet new conditions had little success, and the judgments of the *Freigrafen* and *Freischöffen*, who were seldom educated men, became more and more arbitrary and capricious. What made this the more serious was that in theory all Vehmic courts were of equal authority, so that it sometimes happened that a man defeated in one would take his case successfully to another. The different tribunals, indeed, began to compete with one another. Whereas at first a Vehmic court had usually been upright, corruption now became rife. The lords, to whom the courts legally belonged, were generally poor, and could not resist the temptation of using this unexpected opportunity of making profits. The *Freigrafen* took their share of the gains. There came indeed to be a number of unattached *Freigrafen*, who would hold a court as and when hired to do so. When *Freischöffen* were to be found in all parts of Germany, it became advisable to have some means of identifying them, and this led to the adoption of secret passwords and signs. They evidently liked the atmosphere of mystery with which they thus surrounded themselves, and began to behave as if they were merely a secret society, admitting new members reluctantly and only after an elaborate initiation, and putting the interests of their organization above the claims of justice. By the second half of the fifteenth century, corruption had gone to such lengths that some princes and cities retained Vehmic courts in their service. Others more wisely got charters of exemption from its jurisdiction, which could be obtained from either the Emperor or the Pope. As its real influence declined, the claims of the Vehme became more fantastic; one tribunal actually summoned the Emperor Frederick before it. Such doings only hastened the decline of its reputation. When its courts became conspicuously expensive and unjust, no one had any reason for resorting to them, and their growing unpopularity rendered it unsafe for members of the Vehme to execute the sentences passed against those who disobeyed their summons. The relapse of the Vehmic courts into insignificance was not to be regretted. In their best days they may now and then have brought to justice a malefactor who would otherwise have escaped retribution; but the disorder and lawlessness prevalent in Germany were not to be alleviated, still less cured, by an institution whose authority was either obsolete or usurped.

*Intellectual and artistic activity*

The doings of the Vehme draw one's attention to the darkest side of German life in the fifteenth century. Its brightest side comes to the front when we consider the artistic and intellectual activity of the time. It was naturally in the cities that this was most evident. Several princes established universities during our period; some founded valuable libraries; a few patronized scholars who were trying to spread the Humanism of Italy. But throughout the century art and learning owed far more to burghers than to nobles or clergy. The finest architecture of fifteenth-century Germany is not to be seen in cathedrals or monasteries, but in town churches built by craft-gilds, religious fraternities of laymen, or the merchant princes of the Hansa, and in the town-halls which many municipal authorities were rich and public-spirited enough to erect. Another art that flourished notably in the towns was music, where such societies as the Mastersingers of Nürnberg were full of enthusiasm and highly esteemed. It was in the towns that the New Learning from Italy was most liberally patronized and that the art of printing won its first triumphs. But of such things more must be said in another place.

Authorities for chapter xiv :—
Most of the works mentioned under the other chapters on Germany throw light on social and economic matters. To them may be added the following :
Andreas, W. : *Deutschland vor der Reformation*, Stuttgart and Berlin, 1932.
Hegel, K. : *Städte und Gilden der Germanischen Völker im Mittelalter*, 2 vols., Leipzig, 1891.
Lamprecht, K. : *Deutsches Wirtschaftsleben im Mittelalter*, 4 vols., Leipzig, 1885–6.
Lindner, Th. : *Die Feme*, Münster and Paderborn, 1888.
Schultz, A. : *Deutsches Leben im 14 und 15 Jahrhundert*, Leipzig, 1892.
Weider, M. : *Das Recht der deutschen Kaufmannsgilden im Mittelalter*, Breslau, 1931.
There are, of course, in addition, a vast number of works dealing with the economic and social life of individual towns.
Authorities on the Hansa are numerous. Among original sources the following are specially notable :
*Die Recesse und andere Akten der Hansetage von 1256–1430*, ed. K. Koppmann, 8 vols., Leipzig, 1870–97.
*Hanseakten aus England, 1275–1412*, ed. K. Kuntze, Halle, 1891.
*Hanserecesse*, ed. G. von der Ropp and D. Schäfer, 16 vols., Leipzig, 1876, etc.
*Hansisches Urkundenbuch*, ed. K. Höhlbaum and others, 11 vols., Halle, 1876, etc.
Modern works on the Hansa include the following :
*Cambridge Medieval History*, vol. vii, ch. viii, Cambridge, 1932.
Daenell, E. : *Die Blütezeit der deutschen Hanse*, 2 vols., Berlin, 1905–6.
Lindner, Th. : *Die deutsche Hanse*, 2nd ed., Leipzig, 1911.
Nash, E. G. : *The Hansa : its history and romance*, London, 1929.
Rörig, F. : *Les raisons intellectuelles d'une supériorité commerciale : la Hanse*. (Annales d'histoire économique et sociale, t. ii, 1930.)
Schäfer, D. : *Die deutsche Hanse*, Leipzig, 1925.
Schulz, F. : *Die Hanse und England*, Berlin, 1911.
Zimmern, H. : *The Hansa Towns* (Story of the Nations), London, 1889.

CHAPTER XV

# THE SCANDINAVIAN COUNTRIES

**Comparative insignificance of the Scandinavian countries in the later Middle Ages**

FROM time to time the Scandinavian peoples have been a great force in the affairs of Europe. Everyone knows of their achievements in the Viking Age. They left their stamp upon all the British Isles, upon France, Italy, and Russia, and indeed affected to some extent the fortunes of every country in Europe and some in Asia, to say nothing of America. Again, in the seventeenth century they played no small part in international affairs; indeed, for a time Sweden ranked as a Great Power. But between these two periods of prominence, they passed through a phase of comparative obscurity and insignificance, and during the centuries when medieval culture reached its climax, they lagged behind the countries which they had once scourged and exerted but little influence upon them. After all, they dwelt in lands which were not for the most part fertile, and as late as the beginning of the fifteenth century they numbered altogether only about one and a half millions. Of these probably half belonged to Denmark, which then included three provinces of what is now Sweden. None of the Scandinavian peoples could be expected to have very widespread foreign interests. Norway, the least important of the three countries, maintained fairly close relations with Scotland; but the external interests of Denmark and Sweden had become increasingly confined to the Baltic. Their foreign policies were thus principally concerned with one another, with the principalities of northern Germany, and, above all, with the Hanseatic League.

**Their government and social conditions**

In Denmark, the national assembly possessed extensive powers by charter, but had been practically superseded by the *Rigsraad*, a council of prelates and nobles selected by the king. Sweden had a Council of State and a Diet, the nobles having a preponderating influence in both. But the real limitations on royal authority in all the kingdoms were feudal rather than constitutional. In Norway, where feudalism had developed later than in Denmark or Sweden, the nobility were less influential, but still a formidable hindrance to the effective assertion of royal power. In the other two countries, they were not only able to flout the central authority, but had the right of electing the king. In the fourteenth century, while the Scandinavian peasants were mostly subject to lords and suffered under many irksome disabilities, serfdom hardly existed in any of the kingdoms; in 1335, indeed, it was formally abolished in Sweden; but during our period the lot of the Danish peasants became much worse, and at the end of the fifteenth century many of them might correctly have been termed serfs. Towns were few and small, and the burgher class, though represented in the Swedish Diet, carried little weight. Trade was mainly in the hands of Germans from the Hanse towns.

In 1375 occurred the death of Waldemar III of Denmark, who, after reviving the decayed power of his realm, had been badly worsted in his famous war with the Hansa. In the Treaty of Stralsund, which ended that conflict, it had been laid down that no one should succeed to the Danish throne without the consent of the League. Waldemar left no sons, but he had two grandsons, one, Albert, the son of his elder daughter Ingeborg and Henry of Mecklenburg, the other, Olaf, the son of a younger daughter Margaret and King Hakon VI of Norway. The Danes, fearing the intrusion of German influence, chose Olaf, though he was only five years old. The Hanseatic League, which had no love for the Dukes of Mecklenburg, approved. *Situation in 1375*

Olaf's mother Margaret was accepted as regent, and when in 1380 his father died, she acted in that capacity in Norway also. She acquitted herself so well that when in 1387 King Olaf died she was invited by both kingdoms to continue in the exercise of royal authority. Shortly before, a formidable rebellion had broken out in Sweden, where the King, Albert of Mecklenburg, had angered the powerful nobility by the favours which he lavished on his German friends. Olaf's death having frustrated the rebels' intention of making him their king, they offered the regency of Sweden to Margaret, who accepted it. Despite his trusted German mercenaries, King Albert was soon defeated and taken prisoner, remaining *The Regent Margaret* in captivity until in 1396 he paid a ransom and abdicated. Stockholm, however, offered a prolonged resistance, and was aided by Mecklenburg and the freebooters who, as we saw, caused so much concern to the Hanse merchants at this time. Nevertheless, in 1395 Stockholm was handed over to the Hansa, in pledge for Albert's ransom, which the League had advanced. Three years later, it was surrendered to Margaret.

The woman who thus became ruler of all three countries is one of the greatest figures in Scandinavian history. Her ability was well matched by her energy. It was her statesmanlike ambition to render permanent the political union of the three realms. Such a policy was far more practicable then than it would be to-day. The languages spoken in the three countries differed from one another much less than they do now. There were no vital differences between their customs, institutions, and interests. One must not deny the existence of a sense of nationality in each, but it was not a strong motive force, and it might easily be extinguished by other considerations. That it must nevertheless be handled carefully was shown in 1397, when Margaret assembled at Kalmar representatives of the three kingdoms. Her adopted heir, Eric of Pomerania, grandson of her sister Ingeborg, was crowned king, and a document was drawn up embodying the terms of a permanent union of his realms. Though it has figured conspicuously in the writings of later historians, this was no more than a draft. A certain mystery attaches to its fate, for while it certainly never acquired legal force, the reasons for its rejection are obscure. Probably the limits it imposed on the authority of the Crown and the provision it made for safeguarding the separate identity of each of the three kingdoms, were unpleasing to Margaret, while some at least of the delegates—especially, it seems, the Norwegians—thought that, notwithstanding the precautions which it enshrined, it went too far in the direction of union. Nevertheless, since Eric was the crowned king of the three countries, and in that capacity used a single seal, Margaret had some ground for hoping that she had laid the foundation of a lasting Scandinavian Empire.

*The so-called " Union " of Kalmar, 1397*

It was at the same time true that only very wise and wary administration could accomplish the achievement of Margaret's aim. If the three peoples concerned felt no animosity against one another, neither did they love one another very much. The event showed, it is true, that Denmark and Norway might live in peace under the same rule; but there was much mutual suspicion between Denmark and Sweden. Even the statesmanlike Margaret impaired the prospects of the Union by treating Sweden and Norway as though they were subject to Denmark; in those countries offices and lands were lavishly bestowed on Danes, but in Denmark there were no such things for Swedes or Norwegians. Margaret, furthermore, gravely impaired Eric's prospects by bequeathing to him a wholly unnecessary war. In 1386, she had bought off the hostility of the Count of Holstein—a prince nearly as powerful as a Danish king—by granting him the region of Slesvig, to be held, it is true, as a fief of Denmark. She thus wove the first strands of one of the most complicated webs that ever entangled European diplomatists. But the Slesvig-Holstein complication might never have arisen had not Margaret, on the Count's death in 1404, tried to recover the fief for the Danish Crown, at the expense of his young sons. The result was war between Holstein and Denmark. The conflict lasted altogether for thirty years. In 1412 Queen Margaret died; Eric of Pomerania became king in fact as well as name, and continued the struggle with great tenacity. Piracy and privateering once again became rife in the Baltic and the North Sea, and eventually, as we have seen, some of the Hanse towns took up arms against Denmark. Neither side did anything to boast of; but the war probably harmed Denmark more than her adversaries. Her resources were not equal to maintaining so prolonged a contest. Taxation was heavy, the coinage was debased, the support of the nobles had to be purchased by extravagant gifts and concessions. Sweden and Norway resented requests for money to pay for something in which they felt no interest. All three kingdoms were offended by the evident partiality shown by Eric for his Pomeranian kinsfolk; the Swedes and Norwegians had in addition to endure much misgovernment at the hands of Danish officials. Finally, a rising in Sweden impelled the King to procure peace in 1435 by recognizing Adolf Count of Holstein as Duke of Slesvig.

*War of Denmark and Holstein*

**Rising in Sweden: Engelbrekt Engelbrektsson**

The rebellion in Sweden was notable by reason of the prominent part taken in it by the peasants. They were led by Engelbrekt Engelbrektsson, a man of gentle birth, who belonged to a family engaged in the privileged mining industry. The Swedish Council of State was constrained to declare King Eric deposed; and in 1435 Engelbrekt summoned a Diet in which the peasantry had special representatives—a precedent frequently followed thereafter, the Swedish Diet being in fact the only assembly of the kind in which the peasants appeared as a distinct Estate. Engelbrekt, however, was not so strong as he seemed, for even among the rebels there was great difference of opinion as to what ought to be done next. Many of the nobility disapproved of the rising, and the revolt of the peasants had been limited to a comparatively small region. King Eric therefore had a promising field for intrigue, and he exploited it to the full. It was a triumph for him when he won over Karl Knutsson, the most influential of the Swedish nobles, the result being that the Council of State, going back on its former decision, confirmed the union of the three realms. Engelbrekt was by this time odious to the majority of the jealous nobles, and it was at the instance of one of them that this very remarkable man, a national hero to the modern Swedes, was murdered in 1436. Meanwhile, some of the Norwegians had begun a rising which, while forcing Eric to make concessions, had no lasting effects. The discontent of Denmark, however, though less well-founded, proved more stubborn, and Eric did little to allay it by his conduct after the end of the war with Holstein. In 1439 the Danish *Rigsraad* pronounced his deposition. No one in any of his three kingdoms seemed willing to risk anything in his behalf, and, after trying to support himself by piracy in the Baltic, he withdrew to Pomerania, where he ended his days long afterwards.

The Danes now chose as their king Christopher of Wittelsbach, Eric's sister's son. The Swedish Diet was corrupted into compliance, though the Swedish nobility exacted a heavy price. For some time the Norwegians were disposed to remain loyal to Eric, but they acknowledged Christopher in 1442. Under Christopher's rule the bond between the three realms was very loose; the authority of the Crown, moreover, was everywhere much impaired, especially in

Sweden, where the nobles were even more unruly than before. And even the nominal unity of Scandinavia was not preserved for long; since, when Christopher died in 1448, the anti-Danish party in Sweden, backed by the populace of Stockholm, got the upper hand, and elected as king Karl Knutsson, the old rival of Engelbrekt and for many years the most powerful man in the country. The Danes, for their part, offered the crown to Christian of Oldenburg, who was descended in the female line from Eric Glipping, a Danish king of the thirteenth century. He had to pay for his election by concessions which greatly increased the powers of the *Rigsraad*, and his uncle, the Count of Holstein, who had recommended him to the Danish nobles, compelled him to grant a charter which declared that the duchy of Slesvig should never be united to the kingdom of Denmark so as to become an integral part of the kingdom. The question now was whether Norway would follow Denmark or Sweden or assert her independence. There was little likelihood of her taking the last course, and it soon became clear that the issue would be settled by the result of a conflict between a pro-Danish and a pro-Swedish party. The cause of Karl Knutsson prospered for a time, and he was crowned in Trondhjem Cathedral; but in the end, thanks in great measure to Karl's opponents among the Swedish nobility, his enemies got the upper hand, and the Norwegian assembly ordained that Denmark and Norway should be perpetually united. Strange to say, the union lasted until 1814. Its effects are far from having been obliterated.

King Christian was an ambitious man, but not a very wise one. The restless nobles and clergy of Sweden soon wearied of the rule of Karl Knutsson, and a malcontent party offered the crown to the King of Denmark. He would have been well advised to decline; but he accepted, Karl was driven out, and in 1458, at the cost of extravagant concessions to the nobles, Christian was crowned and secured recognition of his son as heir to the Swedish throne. Then in 1459 Adolf of Holstein died, leaving no male issue. Christian claimed both Holstein and Slesvig as lawful heir, and it was further contended that Slesvig, a Danish fief, had escheated to the Danish Crown. The claim was disputed by other kinsmen of the dead duke, and the Estates of the two fiefs settled the question. In 1460 they accepted Christian, who had, however, to buy off the claims of his rivals—the Danes being taxed for the purpose—and, moreover, agreed to the stipulations of the Estates that Holstein and Slesvig should for ever be united and that thereafter they might elect as their ruler any member of the royal family and not necessarily the King of Denmark. Thus was yet further perplexity laid up for the men of the nineteenth century.

To outward seeming, Christian was now an extremely powerful sovereign. But he owed all his titles to elections for which he had been obliged to pay heavily. Apart from this, he was an improvident and extravagant man; he was usually hard up, and his efforts to raise money were often undignified and unscrupulous. In each of his kingdoms, royal authority had been gravely damaged and was on the decline. And in Sweden even the concessions which he had made could not secure for him the loyalty of his subjects. There was always a party hostile to the Danish connexion, and Christian's own supporters constantly made him feel that he owed his crown to them, and that his retention of it depended on their good pleasure. It is not surprising that after a few years he fell out with John Oxenstierna, Archbishop of Upsala, who had headed the rising against Karl Knutsson and carried more weight in Sweden than the King himself. At the same time popular discontent was aroused by the taxation which Christian imposed for objects in which the Swedes had no interest. In 1464 the King, trying to suppress a rising, was defeated by the peasants of Dalecarlia. Nevertheless, Karl Knutsson, who seized the opportunity to return from his exile in Danzig, met with so little success that he had again to leave the country. But in 1467, after much confusion and bewildering intrigue, the anti-Danish party secured a commanding ascendancy; Knut was invited by the *Riksdag* to try his fortune again, and this time he re-established himself on the throne with little difficulty, maintaining himself there until his death three years later. Karl was not a great man, and his aims seldom transcended the interests of his class; but he deserves to be remembered as the exponent of a national sentiment which, if not very potent, was sufficiently sincere to affect seriously the course of Scandinavian affairs.

On Knutsson's death, the Swedes chose as their ruler his nephew Sten Sture, though they gave him only the title of regent. Christian tried to reassert his rights over Sweden by force, but was disastrously defeated at the battle of Brunkebjerg. This event convinced many of the "unionist" nobles of Sweden that their cause was hopeless. Sten Sture's power rested mainly on the support of the common people, and he made much use of Diets in which burghers and peasants were represented. For some years patriotic feeling ran high for those days, its most notable outcome being the foundation of the University of Upsala in 1477. As for Christian, the Swedes had little to fear from him, seeing that it was all he could do to keep his hold on Denmark and Norway. But it was not long before faction again began to determine the conduct of the Swedish nobility, and Christian's son John, who succeeded to the Danish throne in 1481, managed with their aid to restore the union in 1497. He was, however, ousted by Sten Sture in 1501. With that event, save for a brief and violent interlude, ended the union of Sweden and Denmark. King John, in fact, was an unlucky ruler. He had much trouble from his ambitious younger brother Frederick, the favourite of the queen-mother, and his attempt to reduce to obedience the unruly peasants of the Ditmarsh region was an ignominious failure.

*Sten Sture, regent of Sweden, 1470*

*John, King of Denmark and Norway, 1481–1513, and of Sweden, 1497–1501*

The so-called Union of Kalmar was really the beginning of a protracted attempt to impose Danish rule on the other Scandinavian peoples. The resentment aroused among the Swedes caused the political history of Sweden in the fifteenth century to be more eventful than that of her neighbours. Though there was much factious narrow-mindedness among her people, Sweden may look back on the century with more satisfaction than either Norway or Denmark. For Norway the period was one of decadence. She was treated more and more as a mere dependency of Denmark, a fate in which she acquiesced with little protest. The most pleasing feature of Norwegian society was the continued prominence of the yeomanry and free peasantry; but her history affords additional proof of the inertness and helplessness of those classes in the Middle Ages unless they had aristocratic leadership. And in Norway the nobility was weak and growing weaker. Conditions favoured the establishment of a strong monarchical

*Fifteenth-century Norway*

rule; but the kings were interested mainly in the affairs of more prosperous and civilized Denmark or in their efforts to uphold their authority over Sweden. They thus neglected the interests of Norway, giving a very free hand to the Danish officials, not always competent or upright, whom they sent to administer the country. Meanwhile Norwegian trade had become almost monopolized by the Germans, the great Hanse settlement at Bergen reaching the height of its prosperity towards the end of the century. At the same time Norway's connexion with her overseas settlements became very slight, and, as regards some of them, ceased altogether. From 1410 to the end of the century no ship is recorded to have made the voyage from Norway to Greenland, and one of the few remaining relics of the Viking conquests was lost when in 1469 the Orkney and Shetland Islands were handed over to James III of Scotland as security for the dowry of his bride, Christian I's daughter Margaret—a pledge which was never to be redeemed.

**Condition of Denmark at end of fifteenth century**

Denmark itself, though the predominant partner in the Scandinavian union, was on the whole in a less healthy state at the end of the century than at its beginning. Owing partly to the nationality of her kings, partly to the intimate connexion with Holstein, partly to the influence of the Hansa in her economic life, the Germanization of Denmark proceeded rapidly. The energies of her kings were wasted on efforts to maintain the political union of Scandinavia and on the Slesvig-Holstein entanglement. In the course of the century the Crown grew weaker, the nobles stronger, and in 1481, owing to concessions by King John, the *Rigsraad* became the controlling force in the government. It was largely owing to the increased power of the nobility that the lot of the Danish peasantry changed so much for the worse. Yet among the Danes, as among the other Scandinavian peoples, there remained plenty of ability and vigour, as succeeding centuries were amply to demonstrate.

Some works on the history of Scandinavia :—
    Apart from works written in the Scandinavian languages, which there seems little point in mentioning, there are few histories which shed any adequate light on the later medieval period. The sole recent monograph appears to be: Nordmann, V. A.: *Albrecht, Herzog von Mecklenburg, König von Schweden* (Annales Academiae scientarum Fennicae, vol. xii, i), Helsinki, 1938.

There is also, in the *Cambridge Medieval History*, vol. viii, chap. xvii, a useful chapter on Scandinavian history of the fourteenth and fifteenth centuries. Otherwise, reliance must be placed on works dealing with the entire history of the different Scandinavian countries, none of which deals in any exhaustive way with their history in the later Middle Ages. Reference may be made to the following:

Allen, C. G.: *Histoire de Danemark*. Translated into French from the seventh edition of the Danish by E. Beauvois, vol. i, Copenhagen, 1878.

Dahlmann, F. C.: *Geschichte von Dännemark*, vols. ii and iii, Hamburg, 1841–3.

(Both these works, though in some measure superseded by later research, were of very high merit when first published, and they remain useful.)

Gjerset, K.: *History of the Norwegian people*, 2 vols., New York, 1915.

Hallendorff, C., and Schück, A.: *History of Sweden*. Trans. from the Swedish, London, 1929.

Svanström, S., and Palmstierna, C. F.: *Short History of Sweden*, trans. Joan Bulmer, Oxford, 1934.

## CHAPTER XVI

## SPAIN

THE political status of no European country changed during our period so much as that of Spain. In 1878, apart from the little Pyrenean kingdom of Navarre, the Iberian peninsula was divided between the Christian states of Castile, Aragon, and Portugal, and the Moorish kingdom of Granada, just as it had been since the middle of the thirteenth century. And well-nigh another hundred years elapsed before there was any modification of that arrangement. Meanwhile, the four kingdoms had exerted even less influence on Europe at large than they had usually done in earlier medieval times. Castile had been generally sunk in disorder, Portugal had turned her mind to maritime exploration, and Aragon, though her doings abroad were destined to have momentous consequences, had hardly increased her international prestige or her intrinsic strength. As for Granada, it was still there, a little smaller, but only very little. And then, in the space of a few years, all was altered. Instead of four kingdoms there were now two, both Christian, and one of them a great European power. Each of them, furthermore, had an overseas Empire, not wholly new, but with prospects that had just become dazzling in their magnificence. The sordid history of the century which preceded the great change may not be ignored, but little profit is to be gained by lingering over it.

*Provincialism in medieval Spain*

On a small-scale map the Iberian peninsula looks very compact, but actually its geographical configuration favours the growth and persistence of local diversity. And the country's experiences had reinforced this tendency. The first rally of Christian Spain against triumphant Islam had been due very largely to private and local enterprise, and in the process there had arisen a provincial patriotism, and a corresponding variety of traditions, customs, institutions, and laws, which profoundly affected the character and fortunes of the Christian kingdoms of the later Middle Ages. In none of these Christian states was there a strong central government; in all, the subjects of the Crown possessed an influence on the conduct of public affairs which was surpassed nowhere else in Europe.

By far the biggest of the Christian kingdoms was Castile, which was very often spoken of simply as "Spain." Castile had taken the leading part in the wars against Islam, and in the later Middle Ages she alone bordered on Moslem territory. On the whole, too, she had been most in touch with other European countries. In 1379, when King John I succeeded his father, Henry of Trastamara, her future seemed promising. She had just emerged from a time of civil war, in which Henry, albeit of illegitimate birth, had worsted his half-brother, Peter the Cruel, and other rivals. Castile was in alliance with France, and had caused a stir by her naval successes against England. In the next years things went fairly well. An attempted conquest of Portugal, it is true, was foiled in 1385 at the battle of Aljubarotta; but two years later the so-called crusade of John of Gaunt, uncle of the King of England, and son-in-law of Peter the Cruel, was easily repelled. Fortune seemed to have turned against Castile when in 1390 John I was killed through a fall from his horse; but the boy who succeeded him grew up to be an extremely able and vigorous ruler, reducing the nobles to an exceptional state of subordination. He had, too, wider interests than Castilian kings usually possessed. It was in his reign that Castile acquired the lordship of the Canary Islands, and he entered into friendly diplomatic relations with Tamerlane, whose court at Samarcand was visited by a Castilian embassy in the last months of the great conqueror's life. But Henry III died in 1406 at the age of twenty-seven. The next seventy years were among the most gloomy in the whole history of Castile.

*Castile*

*John I, 1379-90*

*Henry III, 1390-1406*

The government of Castile was legally a limited monarchy. The Cortes was an institution of great age and much power, which was probably at the height of its influence about the beginning of our period. It consisted of three Estates, nobles, clergy, and towns. It had come into being to promote the government of the realm by the King, and though in course of time it had won an authority of its

*Government of Castile*

*The Cortes* own, it never lost its character of a royal council. It could meet only when summoned by the King, who was not bound to summon it at all. All nobles, however humble, were liable to be summoned to the Cortes; but which were called to any particular meeting depended entirely on the King's choice. Nor had any of the clergy a legal claim to a summons; the King invited whom he chose from among the archbishops, bishops, and heads of the great Military Orders. Similarly, it rested with the King whether a given town should be asked to send representatives. Forty-nine towns had proctors at the Cortes of 1391, but during the following century the number tended to fall. The members of the Third Estate were mere delegates obliged to act strictly in accordance with the instructions which they brought with them. There was no general rule as to the method whereby they were chosen, the procedure varying much from place to place.

Members of the Cortes enjoyed freedom from arrest and freedom of speech. No extraordinary direct taxation might be levied without its consent. In the latter part of the fourteenth century it sometimes successfully demanded an audit of the royal accounts. More than once, too, it enforced a claim to appropriate to particular purposes the sums it had voted. Over legislation its control was comparatively weak. The King remained the law-maker, alike in theory and practice. No law, however, might be repealed without the approval of the Cortes; and many new laws were based on petitions of one or other of the Estates. The Cortes unfortunately did not insist that the King should reply to petitions before it voted supply: indeed, the presentation of petitions was commonly the last act of a session. The right of petition thus had far less value than in the English Parliament. In theory the King was under the obligation of consulting the Cortes on all matters concerning the general welfare of the realm; but this duty was interpreted somewhat laxly, though at times the Estates were even asked for their opinion on questions of foreign policy. At the end of the fourteenth century the powers of the Castilian Cortes were much like those of the contemporary English Parliament. At the opening of a session the Cortes, like Parliament, appeared as one body before the King; thereafter the

Estates debated separately, and, it seems, no further joint-sittings were held. It is clear, at all events, that the gulf between the Third Estate and the others was much deeper than that between the Commons and the Lords in England. This was partly due to the fact that the Third Estate consisted entirely of burghers; the lesser nobility sat with their mightier fellows.

Notwithstanding the rights and claims of the Cortes, the Castilian Crown was in theory very powerful. In practice, however, during the greater part of the period with which we are concerned, it was usually very weak. At every turn its authority was restricted by the privileges and exemptions enjoyed by the nobles, the clergy, and the cities. The nobility were exempt from nearly every form of direct taxation. They might not be imprisoned, nor might their property be confiscated, for debt. Nobles of the highest grade, the so-called *ricos hombres*, might renounce their allegiance to the King at any moment. But it was not these common privileges which rendered the nobles so hard to control; the relation of each to the Crown was determined by a bargain struck by him or an ancestor. In the days when the recovery of Spain for Christendom had depended on the zeal and initiative of the individual noble, kings had been lavish in granting lands, jurisdiction, and immunities; and their successors were now bearing the cost. It must not be inferred that Castile had been thoroughly feudalized. Indeed, systematized feudal law, such as for long prevailed in many parts of France, had never been introduced into Spain. The fact that a man held land from another did not involve the two in the mutual obligations characteristic of medieval feudalism; and there was in Spain no such feudal hierarchy, with its well-marked grades between king and serf, as might be seen in France, England, or Germany.

As for the clergy, they were in a singularly happy position. Their services in promoting the holy war against Islam had been amply rewarded. Their freedom from taxation extended even farther than that of the nobles. They possessed lands of vast extent and great wealth; the higher clergy enjoyed wide jurisdiction within their estates, and even possessed, subject to certain conditions, the right of waging private war in their defence. The clergy in general profited, too, by almost all the claims made by the Canon Law for their advantage. Their numbers were consequently very great, for countless people rushed into Minor Orders in order to secure the immunities which these conferred. Special notice should be taken of the great Military Orders of Calatrava, Santiago, and Alcantara. Their members claimed the privileges of both the nobility and the clergy, and their Grand Masters were the most powerful subjects of the King. Taken all round, the Castilian clergy, in the latter part of the Middle Ages, were worldly, corrupt, licentious, and ill-reputed.

**The Castilian towns**

The towns of Castile constituted another serious check upon the King. As each strip of territory had been won back for Christendom, it had been necessary to secure it against Moslem counter-attack by the erection of cities with special attractions for settlers. The rights, powers, and constitutions of the cities varied according to the terms of their respective charters; but many of them were almost independent republics, and in most there was a strong democratic element in the system of government. They claimed and had often exercised the right of forming *hermandades*—brotherhoods or leagues—for the maintenance of their interests or the preservation of the public peace. There are many analogies between the Castilian cities and those of Germany; but the former lacked the economic importance of the German towns. By the end of the fourteenth century, furthermore, they had passed their best days. The Crown was beginning to encroach upon their liberties. The usual device was to appoint a *corregidor*, an agent of the King whose duty it was to aid the officials of a town which had got into difficulties. He usually became a permanent factor in the city government and eventually pushed the other magistrates into the background. There were other methods of encroaching on municipal autonomy; but the towns, though they often protested, were seldom in a position to resist effectively, for they were exposed to the jealousy and covetousness of nobles whose control would be worse than the King's. Besides towns directly subject to the Crown, there were others on the domains of the nobility or clergy: on the whole, these were of minor importance, and the liberties they enjoyed were of only indirect concern to the central government.

With its powers trammelled in the ways described, the

Crown would have needed great resources to be able to surmount its difficulties. And it lacked both the machinery and the resources for enforcing its will. The royal council, hitherto a body whose composition changed at the King's caprice, was organized by John I, who defined its duties and decreed that it should contain four representatives from each of the Three Estates; but the arrangement was not carried out, and such councillors as were appointed lacked the traditions and experience which are essential to administrative efficiency. The revenues of the Crown, impressive on paper, fell far short of their nominal amount. It was not easy to increase them; for new direct taxes must be voted by the Cortes, and customs duties, tolls, the sales tax —all of which, with other indirect imposts, figured among the Crown's resources—were not very fruitful in a country where trade and industry never flourished greatly. The army consisted of the nobles and their retinues, the contingents due from the estates of the clergy, and the levies of the towns; it could not be turned against its leaders, and the kings were too poor to hire an adequate force of mercenaries. Nor was it possible for the Crown to rely on the non-privileged classes. In the first place, the rural population was small in proportion to the size of the country; for the soil was generally poor, and stock-raising, which requires comparatively little labour, was far more remunerative than agriculture. Again, rural society in Castile was a bewildering medley. Every type of economic and social status was to be found, from the independence of a *behetria,* a group which claimed the right of changing its lord at will, down through all the grades of serfdom, to sheer slavery at the base. With local diversity added to economic heterogeneity, there were no common interests to which the kings could appeal. Strange to say, it was on the non-Christian elements of the population that the Crown might most reasonably have relied. For the greater part of the Middle Ages the Moors and the Jews, who remained in great numbers in the territory recovered from Islam, were well treated by the Castilians. They were, it is true, segregated in special quarters of the towns, forbidden to have any social relations with Christians, and subjected to extra taxation: but the Moors were given some measure of autonomy and permitted to regulate their own affairs by their own law, both they and the Jews were allowed complete freedom of worship, and members of both races were sometimes given public office, the Jews in particular being employed as tax-collectors. The position of the Moors, though a few new restrictions were imposed on them, did not change much until the last quarter of the fifteenth century. The Church, however, had long been growing more insistently intolerant, and from the reign of John I onward massacres of the Jews occurred from time to time. They were not authorized by the State, but were due to popular hatred, fanned by the zeal of the clergy for the Faith. Thousands of Jews accepted Christianity as the one means of escape; but they soon found that it was their wealth rather than their unbelief that had really given offence, and as time went on the religious pretext tended to disappear and racial hatred appeared unashamed. Many thousands of Jews, " converted " and others, left the country. But they had been very numerous in Castile, and there were estimated to be 12,000 Jewish families on which Ferdinand and Isabella were able to exhibit their Christian zeal.

The Castilian kings were as weak in relation to their subjects as any contemporary sovereigns save the Holy Roman Emperor. Under a capable man like John I or Henry III the Castilians might retain some respect for the royal dignity, and the forces making for disorder were restrained. But in the reigns of the next two kings, John II and Henry IV, Castile fell into a worse plight than ever before. From 1406 to 1412, it is true, the realm was well governed by the little king's uncle Ferdinand. But in 1412 he became King of Aragon, and though John II's mother tried to continue his policy and methods, it was not long before things began to go wrong. What caused calamity, however, was the character of John, who proved both lazy, feeble, and incompetent. When he grew up, he speedily fell utterly under the sway of his favourite Alvaro de Luna, Grand Master of the Order of Santiago. For a generation Alvaro was the real King of Castile. He was a man of parts— a pattern of chivalry (or so reputed), a respectable general, a subtle intriguer, a most ostentatious, extravagant, unscrupulous, and charming man. In his own interests he tried to increase the effective power of the Crown; but having no concern for what would happen after his time, he trampled right and left on the rights and pretensions of the privileged classes. He thus excited against himself a resentment over and above the jealousy which is always felt towards a king's favourite, and the time of his ascendancy was filled with plots against him which sometimes led to civil war. Alvaro, however, was strong and capable enough to baffle or overthrow all his enemies, until he believed himself beyond the reach of misfortune. Meanwhile, the public administration, where it worked at all, was rife with corruption, and Castile's status as a European power fell into the depths. Finally, Alvaro overreached himself. In 1445 John II was left a widower by the death of Queen Maria, daughter of his uncle Ferdinand of Aragon, and two years later, at Alvaro's bidding, he married Isabella, a cousin of the King of Portugal. Alvaro, having made the match, apparently thought it within his province to control the most intimate relations of the wedded pair. His arrogance, at all events, soon became intolerable to the high-spirited Queen, and as even the King began to think it irksome, she managed to excite him to revolt. In 1453 Alvaro was arrested by royal order and executed after a pretence of a trial. John II himself died in the next year.

The new king, Henry IV, born in 1425, was the offspring of John's first marriage. Isabella of Portugal had borne two children—a girl, also called Isabella, born in 1451, and a boy, Alfonso, only eight months old at the death of his father. Henry, feeble in both body and mind, was surnamed "the Impotent" by his subjects, and proved to be as bad a king as Castile ever had. Like his father, he fell completely under the influence of a favourite, Beltran de la Cueva; but Henry's evil genius, while not lacking in dash and brilliance, possessed few of the solid qualities which had enabled Alvaro to hold his place for so long. It was not long before his friendship with the Queen, Joanna of Portugal, caused tongues to wag, and when in 1462, seven years after her marriage to Henry, she gave birth to a daughter, her first-born child, it was generally believed that Beltran was the father, the poor infant, though christened Joanna, being commonly known as *La Beltraneja*. Henry, however, acknowledged her as his daughter and heiress, and the Cortes took an oath of allegiance to her as prospective ruler of Castile. The doubts as to her

Henry IV, "the Impotent," 1454–74

paternity offered a pretext to malcontents among the nobility who resented the ascendancy of Beltran. Supported by the King of Aragon, who had designs of his own concerning the succession to the Castilian throne, they raised a rebellion in 1464, declared Henry deposed for his manifold crimes, and proclaimed his half-brother Alfonso as king. Civil war began; but negotiations between the two parties delayed serious fighting until 1467, when the rebels, though defeated at the battle of Olmedo, took Segovia and got possession of the Princess Isabella. Among them there were now many who saw with alarm that Alfonso was likely to grow up into an able and energetic ruler; but it was maladroit of them to announce his death three days before he succumbed to the plague. Isabella was now put forward as heiress of her brother's rights. She at once showed that she had a will of her own by lending her support to the faction among her followers who favoured an accommodation with the King. By the Treaty of Toros de Guisando of September 1468 it was agreed that Henry should retain the crown during his life, but that he should be succeeded by Isabella. To understand the sequel, one must turn to the history of Aragon.

*Rebellion in Castile, 1464*

*The Princess Isabella and the Treaty of Toros de Guisando, 1468*

*The kingdom of Aragon*

That kingdom, though much smaller than Castile, was even less united. It was composed of three provinces—once entirely separate from one another—Aragon, Catalonia, and Valencia, each retaining its own institutions, laws, and administration. In each division the inhabitants enjoyed a large measure of political liberty. The constitution of Aragon, in particular, placed the strictest limitations on the power of the King. The Cortes presented the peculiarity of being divided into four " arms " or Estates—the greater nobles, the lesser nobles, the clergy, and the towns, an arrangement which added much to the influence of the aristocracy, already great through their very extensive privileges. The clergy, on the other hand, were not so powerful as in Castile, and the relative importance of the towns was much less. But the Cortes, taken as a whole, was a formidable body. Every nobleman had the right to attend; the representation of the clergy was fixed by law; any town once called upon to send representatives had the right to do so thereafter. Thus the King had far less control over the composition of the assembly than he had in Castile. The Cortes must give its consent before

*The Cortes of Aragon*

any extraordinary direct taxation might be levied, nor could any new impost whatsoever be exacted without its approval. All new legislation required its sanction. The *Diputacion del Reyno*, a committee of two representatives of each Estate, watched over the execution of the laws and informed the Cortes of any neglect. Usually declarations of war and treaties of peace were submitted to the Cortes. It had frequently exercised much influence on the appointment of ministers of the Crown, and it had asserted its right to investigate injustice and abuses in the government of the country. This brings us to a very remarkable personage—the *Justicia*. After much dispute the right of appointing this dignitary remained with the King, but he was obliged to select a member of the lesser nobility. He was at the head of the judicial system and alone might judge public officials. His main function, however, was to supervise the execution of the laws and to preserve everyone in the enjoyment of his rights. At the appeal of anyone who had reason to fear that justice was being denied him or that he was threatened with wrong, the *Justicia* would intervene and see to it that the law was obeyed. It was also his duty to prevent arbitrary taxation. In the discharge of his duties, the *Justicia* had sometimes to act as arbitrator between the King and the nobles—a function which, though really incidental, has attracted particular attention. The powers of the *Justicia*, when all summed up, were indeed most impressive. At the end of the fourteenth century a holder of the position said that it was "the greatest lay office that existed anywhere in the world."

The social organization of Aragon did not differ greatly from that of Castile. The rural population was on the whole in worse case, serfdom of a somewhat extreme type being prevalent. On the other hand, the Jews were rather better treated, and there was less racial prejudice against them, those who had been converted sometimes attaining high public office.

Though the kingdom took its name from Aragon, it owed its energy and influence mainly to Catalonia. That region has always had a marked individuality. It had for long been attached to the Frankish Empire; there was much French blood among its nobility; and it had been more thoroughly feudalized than any other part of Spain. By the second half of the fourteenth century the power of the nobles had been considerably reduced; but it still remained great, and in proportion to the area of the royal domain in Catalonia the lands of the nobles were very extensive. The lot of the Catalonian serfs had been conspicuously miserable, but was being rapidly ameliorated in the fourteenth and fifteenth centuries. The Cortes of Catalonia consisted of the usual Three Estates. Only about a dozen towns sent representatives, but their influence was powerful. The consent of the Cortes was necessary for the levy of extraordinary direct taxation and the enactment of new laws, and it is probable that its effective power was greater than that of the Cortes in Castile and Aragon, for one of the most notable institutions of the province was the *Diputacion General de Cataluña*, a standing committee on which each Estate of the Cortes was represented; this body collected and administered a great part of the public revenue, supervised the execution of the laws, judged disputes between private individuals and officials, and furnished arms to the military forces of the country and naval defence for its coasts and shipping. The Catalonian navy had for long been one of the most formidable in Europe.

*The Cortes of Catalonia*

*Barcelona*

If it was Catalonia which enabled the kings of Aragon to cut a figure in Europe, it was the city of Barcelona which was the heart and soul of Catalonia. Barcelona enjoyed such extensive rights of self-government as to be virtually a city-republic, and its boundaries stretched far beyond its walls. Its constitution, while giving all classes a voice in the government, cunningly avoided the evils of democracy. The members of the executive council, one of whom was a working man, enjoyed privileges which placed them on the same footing as the greatest nobles of the province; and, apart from its officers, the city had a recognized nobility of its own, which was socially and politically equal to the lesser nobles of feudal society. The wealth of Barcelona was fabulous. Her merchants dealt with every part of the Mediterranean world, penetrated far into the Orient, and trafficked briskly with northern countries, having a "factory" at Bruges. The most notable exports of Barcelona were raw wool and cloth, the latter mainly from her own looms. The industry, commerce, and shipping of Barcelona were carefully protected by tariffs and navigation laws. Her shipyards were the finest in the Mediterranean, her shipwrights equalled only by those of Venice. Barcelona, from the thirteenth century, had maintained consuls in the lands with which her merchants had dealings, and the Crown used them as its representatives. What gave her still wider renown was the code of maritime and commercial law drawn up by Catalonian seamen and merchants in the thirteenth century. It was adopted all over the Mediterranean, and had very great influence in every part of Europe.

Thanks to the pre-eminence of Barcelona in its life, Catalonia was active, enterprising, and progressive, utterly different in spirit from Aragon, which conceived of liberty as exemption from duties and obligations rather than a condition precedent to great achievements. But the two together made a very strong and formidable combination.

Of the old kingdom of Valencia there is less to be said. Valencia It had not been completely reconquered for Christendom until the thirteenth century, and there had followed a struggle between the Aragonese nobles and the Catalonian burghers for ascendancy within its borders. Thanks largely to the support of the Crown, the Catalans had gained the upper hand by the end of the fourteenth century. The Cortes was very similar to that of Catalonia; but the Third Estate was dominated by the city of Valencia. Each Estate, by a peculiar custom, had the right of meeting separately without being summoned by the Crown, though on such occasions the Third Estate consisted exclusively of representatives of the city of Valencia. At these assemblies each Estate might discuss its common concerns and present the Crown with petitions concerning them. In one respect Valencia resembled Castile more than the other parts of the realm of Aragon; it had a large population of Moors and Jews, and while the Moors, who were mostly agriculturists, were treated fairly well, the Jews, who dwelt in the towns, were subjected, from the latter part of the fourteenth century onward, to frequent and brutal persecution.

Occasionally, though not often, the Cortes of the three component parts of the Aragonese realm held a joint session, along with representatives of the Balearic Islands, to deal with matters of common concern. To allay local jealousy, it was decided in 1383 that the King's speech opening the proceedings should always be in Catalan, and that the heir to the throne should reply, on behalf of the assembly, in Aragonese. The arrangement is a reminder of the need for constant wariness on the part of the Crown lest provincial self-esteem should be offended.

*Aragon's overseas Empire*

Besides the Balearic Islands, the Crown of Aragon ruled Sardinia, where at the beginning of our period its authority was still fiercely contested by the natives. It also claimed Corsica, though down to the end of the fourteenth century nothing had been done to enforce its title, which rested on a grant of Pope Boniface VIII. The island of Sicily had been ruled since 1302 by a junior branch of the Aragonese royal house. For the maintenance of these overseas interests, the kings of Aragon relied mainly on Catalonia and, in a lesser degree, on Valencia. The inhabitants of Aragon proper took little interest in foreign affairs, and resented requests for money to promote the foreign ambitions of their kings.

*Peter IV of Aragon, 1336–87*

In 1378 the long and stormy reign of Peter IV, called the Ceremonious, was nearing its end. It was he who had annexed the Balearic Islands to the Aragonese Crown and worsted the Genoese in a long conflict for the possession of Sardinia. He had likewise defeated the nobles of his Spanish realm in a civil war, and had fought successfully against Peter the Cruel of Castile. In 1377, the male line of the Sicilian branch of his family having come to an end, he laid claim to the Sicilian throne, though he took no steps to force himself on the recalcitrant Sicilians and indeed in 1380 transferred his rights to his son Martin. He died in 1387, leaving a reputation for vigour, guile, and unscrupulousness which has led many historians to compare him to Louis XI of France.

The next king, Peter's son John, was a patron of music and a keen sportsman; but when he died in 1395 he had made little mark on the country. Meanwhile, however, his nephew Martin had married Maria, heiress to Sicily, who had been captured and held in captivity by Peter IV; and the bridegroom, with his father (also called Martin), had gone to Sicily to enforce their rights to the throne. Owing to stubborn resistance by the Sicilians, they had made little headway.

*Martin I of Aragon, 1395–1410*

But when in 1395 the elder Martin succeeded his brother John on the Aragonese throne, he was able to support his son so effectively that by the end of 1397 the island was reduced to obedience. The younger Martin was an able and attractive man, who soon made himself popular with the Sicilians; but in 1409 he died, leaving no issue. His heir was his father, in whose hand all the possessions of the royal house of Aragon were now united. But Martin I himself died in 1410, and as he had no direct heirs, Aragon was exposed for two years to the troubles which usually attend a disputed succession. A committee composed of three representatives of each of the three Cortes of the realm weighed the rights of the three claimants. It was a complicated case, and its details need not concern us. In 1412 the choice of the committee fell upon Ferdinand of Antequera, son of John I of Castile and Eleanor, Martin of Aragon's sister. He was nearer in descent to King Martin than either of his two rivals; otherwise both had a better hereditary claim. One reason for the choice was the success of Ferdinand's rule as regent for his nephew, the young John II of Castile. The House of Trastamara now held the sovereignty of both Castile and Aragon. The union of the two was well within the sphere of practical politics, and plans for bringing it about had much influence on the course of events in Spain from that time onward.

*Aragon and Sicily united, 1409*

*Ferdinand I of Aragon, 1412–16*

The reign of Ferdinand I lasted only four years. He is best remembered for the part he played in terminating the Great Schism by withdrawing his obedience from Pope Benedict XIII. He also put down a revolt in Sicily, and arranged a match between his second son John and Joanna, Queen of Naples, though Joanna broke her word and married the Count de la Marche. These doings, however, determined the policy of Ferdinand's son Alfonso, who succeeded to all his father's dominions and claims. He was a very brilliant and ambitious man—a capable soldier, a clever diplomatist, and a keen and discriminating patron of the art and learning of the Italian Renaissance. Though an attempt of his to make good the Aragonese claim to Corsica was defeated by the Genoese, he succeeded in consolidating his authority in Sardinia. His great achievement, however, was the conquest of Naples—a task which took twenty-two years and exposed him to many caprices of fortune. The doings of Alfonso concern Italy rather than Spain. In his realm of Aragon he spent little time, and after his hold on Naples was

*Alfonso V, King of Aragon, 1416–58, King of Naples after 1435*

secure it became his regular place of residence. His Aragonese subjects viewed his doings with disapproval, for he showed that he preferred Italy to Spain, he had demanded their services and money in the prosecution of his foreign projects, and he had tampered with their constitutional liberties. The character and behaviour of his brother John, who acted as regent for Alfonso, did not tend to soothe their tempers. The Catalans, in particular, were ready for mischief when, on Alfonso's death in 1458, John became king of all his dominions save Naples, which Alfonso had bequeathed to his bastard son Ferrante.

*John II, King of Aragon, 1458-79*

John II of Aragon had abilities hardly inferior to those of his brother, and if he lacked his brother's popular gifts, he also lacked his few scruples. Long before he succeeded to the throne of Aragon, he had become involved in a conflict with his son, Charles of Viana, for the crown of the kingdom of Navarre, which Charles inherited from his mother. There would be little purpose in tracing the wars and intrigues which the question engendered between 1441, when Blanche of Navarre died, and 1458; it is enough to say that when John became King of Aragon, he was in actual possession of Navarre, while Charles, an amiable but rather feeble man,

*John II and Charles of Viana*

had withdrawn to Sicily. The situation was complicated by the existence of Ferdinand, King John's son by his second wife, Joanna Enriquez, daughter of a Castilian grandee. Queen Joanna, a masterful woman, hoped to secure the whole Aragonese Empire for her son, and John II, who hated Charles of Viana, was fully in sympathy with her ambition. In 1460 Charles, who had returned to Spain, was induced to sign a treaty in which he by implication resigned his rights as heir to the throne. But his cause was vigorously taken up by the Catalonians, who thought that there had been too much disregard of law, tradition, and treaties on the part of the King. When John had the prince arrested they rose in open rebellion and compelled his release; the King was actually constrained to make him Governor of Catalonia. But in 1461 he died, whether by poison or not is uncertain. The Catalans had no doubts, however; they renewed their revolt, besieged the Queen and her son Ferdinand in Gerona, and reduced King John to accept the aid of Louis XI of France, who drove a bargain which, as we have seen, promised

*Rebellion of Catalonia, 1461-72*

to secure France in permanent possession of Roussillon and Cerdagne. Louis also approved an arrangement which John had made with his younger daughter Eleanor, whereby he was to hold Navarre during his lifetime, after which it was to pass to Eleanor and her husband, Gaston de Foix. John's elder daughter Blanche was placed in Eleanor's custody and soon, like so many prominent Spaniards about this time, died very opportunely.

The Catalans resisted Louis stubbornly. They offered the throne to Henry IV of Castile, who sent a military force to their aid. Louis XI insinuated himself as arbitrator between the two Spanish kings, and his award offended both. The Castilians indeed withdrew from Catalonia, but in his irritation Henry IV ended the long-established alliance between Castile and France, and in 1467 signed a treaty with Edward IV of England. It was a change of front destined to have far-reaching consequences. All this, nevertheless, had little effect on the relations between the Catalans and their king. The rebels offered the crown to a Portuguese prince, who proved to be feeble and foolish; they then transferred their allegiance to René of Anjou, who thus added Catalonia to the list of the dominions which he did not possess. René sent his dashing and capable son, John of Calabria, whose forces occupied a good part of Catalonia. The fortunes of John of Aragon sank low: his queen died in 1468, and he himself was nearly blind. But he refused to bate a jot of his claims, and presently his luck turned. In 1470 death removed John of Calabria; and in 1472 the resistance of the Catalans was worn down and Barcelona fell. With singular forbearance, the King confirmed the province and the city in the enjoyment of its liberties.

Meanwhile, John II had won a still greater triumph in his dealings with Castile. It had long been his hope to unite the two realms through a marriage between his son Ferdinand and Isabella, the half-sister of the Castilian king, Henry the Impotent. On the death of Isabella's brother Alfonso, John at once made a formal proposal of the alliance. Isabella showed herself favourable, and in January 1469 a marriage agreement was signed. Louis XI tried desperately to destroy the treaty, but paid the penalty for his headstrong policy towards Spain a few years before. On the other hand, *Marriage of Ferdinand of Aragon and Isabella of Castile, Oct. 19, 1469* the arrangement was nearly wrecked by the Castilian nobles, most of whom foresaw that the union of the two kingdoms would enormously strengthen the Crown. A large number of them repudiated the recent Treaty of Toros de Guisando, declared themselves supporters of *La Beltraneja*, and won over the King to their side. Isabella, it is true, had enough support to save her from instant ruin. But for several months she was in a parlous plight. Her friends recognized that the marriage should take place as quickly as might be. Ferdinand was summoned; but his father's resources were wholly involved in the war with the Catalans, and the prince had to enter Castile with but a few companions, all disguised as merchants. He made his way to Valladolid, where Isabella had taken refuge; and there in October 1469, in a private house, with no pomp or ceremony, the modest expenses being paid with borrowed money, the most momentous royal marriage of the century was solemnized.

In his rage Henry the Impotent forgot his grievances against France, and accepted the project of a marriage between *La Beltraneja* and Louis XI's brother Charles of Guienne. But the plan speedily broke down, and all notion of reviving it was perforce ended on Charles's death in 1472. Meanwhile, the alliance with Louis had alienated many Castilians, who feared France more than Aragon. Thus Isabella and Ferdinand were just able to hold their own. But Castile, as may be imagined, fell into unexampled anarchy. When King Henry died, at the end of 1474, the situation seemed no whit improved; for he had to the end upheld the claims of his daughter, and her party was still in the ascendant. It is true that some of Isabella's former opponents—among them the reputed father of her rival— now went over to her side, believing that she was going to win; but what she thus gained was counterbalanced by the hostility of the King of Portugal, Affonso the African, who made an alliance with Louis XI, invaded Castile, and was betrothed to *La Beltraneja*. The ensuing conflict was more critical for Spain, and indeed Europe, than any of the combatants suspected. Victory for Affonso would have united Castile with Portugal; the two realms would have shared the results of the great discoveries and conquests that were occurring and about to occur in Africa, Asia, and America, and Castile would probably have avoided entanglement in the feuds of Italy. But, owing mainly to his own incompetence, Affonso failed; in 1479 he signed treaties in which he left Castile to Isabella. *La Beltraneja* was offered the choice of marrying a son of her supplanter or becoming a nun. She took the veil. *Defeat of Affonso of Portugal, 1479*

The same year saw the death of John II of Aragon, after his long and chequered career. He was succeeded in all his dominions save Navarre by Ferdinand. Aragon and Castile were at last under a common rule. *Ferdinand, King of Aragon, 1479*

With the achievement of the union of the two realms, the history of medieval Spain comes to an end. Between 1479 and 1494 Ferdinand and Isabella did many important things, but as the latter date marks no change in their policy, it seems advisable to devote only a few words to these years, which are best treated in close relation to the sixteenth century. The conquest of Granada, however, demands more than a bare mention, for it was the completion of a characteristically medieval undertaking.

For over two centuries Granada had been tributary to Castile. Its boundaries had changed little for a long time, the most recent Christian success being the capture of Gibraltar in 1462. It is doubtful whether Ferdinand and Isabella would have troubled about Granada, had not its king, believing Castile to be crippled, refused his tribute in 1476, and in 1481 captured a Castilian frontier fortress. In 1482 Ferdinand and Isabella began the systematic reduction of the country, realizing, of course, that a common victory over the traditional enemy would promote good feeling between their two realms. The odds were overwhelmingly in favour of the Spaniards, even had the Moors not been crippled throughout by their domestic dissensions. Nevertheless, the operations were conducted with great deliberation and with a regard for military science hitherto rare in Spanish warfare. The decisive event of the invasion was the capture of Malaga after a long siege in 1487, nearly all the inhabitants being enslaved, though some were afterwards exchanged for Christian prisoners in Africa. Then the Spaniards, full of confidence and piety, steadily closed in on Granada, the Moors here and there resisting valiantly but to little purpose. The city of Granada was beleaguered for about eighteen *The Conquest of Granada* months, until in the autumn of 1491 the defenders lost heart and entered into negotiations which led to the surrender of the place on January 2, 1492. The terms were very liberal, leaving the Moors in the enjoyment of their religion, laws, and customs; but it was not long before the temper of the victors changed, and with it the lot of the vanquished, a tragedy which fortunately lies beyond our view.

Thus ended a notable chapter in the history of Europe. A new one was about to open, for on October 12, 1492, Columbus landed in the Bahamas. Next year Alexander VI's famous bull *Inter caetera* bestowed on Spain all lands beyond a line drawn from north to south a hundred leagues west of the Azores, a grant modified in 1494 by the Treaty of Tordesillas between Spain and Portugal whereby the line was moved some 270 leagues farther west. The skin having thus been divided, it remained for Spain to go after the bear.

**Domestic policy of Ferdinand and Isabella**  Meanwhile, Ferdinand and Isabella had been conquering the Canary Islands [1] and busying themselves with the domestic concerns of their hereditary lands. The union of the two kingdoms was merely a personal one. Their customs and institutions were legally unaffected; their administration remained separate. The marriage treaty had imposed severe restrictions on Ferdinand's rights in Castile; in Aragon, Isabella was simply Queen-consort, with no greater prerogatives than her predecessors in that position. In actual fact, however, Castile soon became the predominant partner, and from the first the two sovereigns gave it the greater share of their attention. This was partly because the Crown had become weaker there than in Aragon, and the forces of disorder stronger. No sooner had Isabella succeeded Henry the Impotent than she and Ferdinand began an attempt to establish an absolute monarchy. By cleverly playing off the towns against the nobility, they brought the latter to heel, while by judicious cajolery and flattery and by maintaining privileges which, however injurious to society, were not directly dangerous to the Crown, they on the whole kept them in a loyal frame of mind and averted any lasting resentment.

Ferdinand and Isabella are remembered as devout and indeed fanatical Catholics. But they were not willing to

[1] See below, p. 507 *seq.*

brook any insubordination on the part of the clergy or to tolerate interference by the Pope in the affairs of their realms. They managed, partly through an understanding with the Holy See, partly through indirect means, to secure almost full control over ecclesiastical appointments within their dominions. The grand-masterships of the three great Military Orders were bestowed (under pressure) on Ferdinand. The clergy in general were subjected to a measure of royal control quite without precedent in Spain; and it cannot be denied that the effect on their walk and conversation was most beneficial. But nothing so affected the life of Spain at this time as the establishment of the terrible Spanish Inquisition, sanctioned by a papal bull in 1478. Even the comparatively ineffective papal Inquisition had never been admitted to Castile, and while it had for a time functioned in Aragon, it had for long been in virtual abeyance there. It may then be imagined what impression was made by the new organization, an instrument which served the interests of the Crown no less than those of the Church, for the Crown controlled the appointment of all its officials and was the force behind all its activity. At first its energies were largely devoted to recently converted Jews, many of whom were suspected of secret adherence to their old beliefs. The effect of its vigour was that conversions from Judaism to Christianity ceased; indeed, some of the converts returned to the faith of their fathers. It became clear to Ferdinand and Isabella that, if Spain was to be purged of their detestable belief, they must be expelled. Zealous propaganda prepared the mind of the nation for this step, so contrary to the country's tradition; and as a thank-offering to God for the capture of Granada, the decree of expulsion was promulgated. About 200,000 Jews had to go into exile, and since no time was given them to settle their affairs, most of them lost nearly all their property. The economic injury inflicted on Spain was immense.

*The Spanish Inquisition established, 1478*

*Expulsion of the Jews*

The harm wrought by the bigotry of the two sovereigns was not evident for some time. For they reformed the financial administration of Castile, relieved the conditions of the serfs in both their realms, and by various measures promoted industry and commerce, so that the economic state of Castile seemed better than it had ever been. At their

*Beneficial reforms*

instance the codification of the law of Castile was taken in hand; they reorganized the administration of justice in the kingdom; and by remodelling the Royal Council and ignoring the Castilian Cortes as much as they dared, they strove to ensure that the Crown would always have counsel and assistance at hand without exposing itself to criticism and hindrance. Their work was scarcely half complete by 1494; but already they had fundamentally altered the condition and prospects of their dominions and had started Spain well on the way to her brief hegemony of Europe.

*Portugal*

We saw that for some years it was touch and go whether Castile would be united to Aragon or to Portugal. The issue was decided by the fortune of war and politics. The other solution would have been just as reasonable and natural; for in origin, history, and traditions Castile resembled Portugal as much as Aragon.

*The Portuguese Crown*

In Portugal, as in Castile, the power of the Crown was theoretically great. The Cortes, indeed, hampered it somewhat, the Three Estates having much the same powers as they enjoyed in Castile. But what most restricted its authority in practice were the extensive privileges of the nobles and the franchises of the towns. Portugal, for that matter, was more thoroughly feudalized than her neighbour.

*Ferdinand the Handsome, 1367–83*

At the beginning of the period with which this book is concerned, Portugal was in turmoil through the misdeeds of Ferdinand the Handsome's unscrupulous queen, Leonor Telles de Menezes. Before long the situation became worse, for Ferdinand had a claim to the crown of Castile and, attempting to make this good with the support of an English army under Edward Duke of York, he exposed his country to invasion by the Castilian King John. Ferdinand saved himself by signing a treaty whereby his daughter was to marry the King of Castile, and Queen Leonor was to be regent after his own death. He died a few months later, in October 1383; but when the Queen assumed the regency, there was a formidable rebellion, headed by John the Bastard, Ferdinand's half-brother. Portugal was invaded by the King of Castile, but he besieged Lisbon in vain and lost a battle in 1384. Early next year the Cortes declared the Portuguese throne to be elective, and chose John the Bastard as king.

*John I, 1385–1433*

He signalized his accession by a brilliant victory over the Castilians at Aljubarotta, a battle won by a contingent of English archers, but notable also as the first occasion when firearms were used in the Iberian peninsula. Next year yet another John, the English Duke of Lancaster, appeared on the scene, and though his " crusade " was unsuccessful, he was able to negotiate a long truce, destined to become a formal peace, between Castile and his Portuguese ally.

John I of Portugal, often called "the Great," remained on the throne until 1433. The main principles of his policy were to maintain his alliance with England and to avoid involving himself in the affairs of his neighbours. Thanks to his firm and sensible administration, Portugal became extremely prosperous, her trade growing rapidly; so that the King's rash liberality towards his nobles seemed to be harmless. He was a patron of learning, and his introduction of the Portuguese language into the law-courts encouraged the growth of a national literature which was one of the most striking features of the time. What, however, won him most renown in the eyes of Europe was the capture in 1415 of the Moorish stronghold of Ceuta, a notorious nest of pirates, a feat accomplished by an expedition in which men of many nations took part, though its personnel was mainly Portuguese and it was led by King John's sons.

It was shortly after this that John's third son began to take that fruitful interest in exploration which has caused him to be remembered as Prince Henry the Navigator. The consequent achievements of the Portuguese sailors are best treated in a general survey of the maritime enterprise of the period. They of course added more lustre to the name of Portugal than anything else that the country ever accomplished. The opinions and projects of Prince Henry were encouraged by his father and by his brother Edward, the next king. Unfortunately it seemed to many Portuguese that military conquest was more glorious and profitable than exploration, and even Edward, who in the main was a prudent ruler, was persuaded to lead an expedition against Tangier. The Portuguese army was cut off from its ships, and it was only when Prince Ferdinand, the King's youngest brother and Master of the Military Order of Aviz, offered himself as a hostage that the Moors agreed to let Edward and his troops

*Prince Henry the Navigator*

*King Edward, 1433-8*

go home. In 1438 the broken-spirited king died; five years later, Ferdinand, still in captivity, followed him.

*Affonso V, 1438-81*

Edward's heir, Affonso V, ascended the throne at the age of six. A dispute over the regency led to a series of destructive civil wars which undid much of the good wrought by the administration of the two previous kings. When he grew up Affonso proved to be vain, credulous, and extravagant, albeit a dashing warrior. He is known as Affonso "the African," a title gained through his three expeditions to that continent. The third of these captured Tangier and other places; but the total result of these ambitious undertakings was miserably small in proportion to their cost in men and money. Affonso also hoped to secure the Crown of Castile: his rather ignominious efforts towards that end have already been noticed. Though the work of exploration went on, his reign was on the whole mischievous; he lavished gifts and favours on the nobles, who got out of hand, so that his son, John II, was faced on his accession with domestic problems very like those that confronted Ferdinand and Isabella in Castile.

*John II, 1481-95*

In his foreign relations John II imitated his great-grandfather John I. He maintained the *entente* with England, despite a change of dynasty there, and he carefully kept the peace with his Spanish neighbours. At home, however, he was much affected by the example of Louis XI. He broke the power of the Portuguese nobility by the most drastic and ruthless methods; it is estimated that eighty of them were executed in the first six years of his reign. His success was rendered possible by the support of the Third Estate in the Cortes; but as soon as he felt secure, he ignored that body and ruled despotically. Yet he ruled so well that he remained generally popular and left behind him the reputation of a "perfect king." He had all Prince Henry's zeal for navigation, and his reign witnessed some of the most noteworthy exploits of Portuguese explorers. He did, it is true, miss a great opportunity when he refused his patronage to Christopher Columbus; but his decision was reasonable though mistaken. When he died, Portugal was rich and happy. No country in Europe seemed to have brighter prospects. The kings of the House of Aviz had all been enlightened patrons of art and learning, with the result that the intellectual life of Portugal was vigorous and that the Italian Renaissance had probably exercised more influence there than anywhere else outside its native land. How and why Portugal failed to respond to the beckonings of fortune must be told in another volume.

Some works on Spain and Portugal :—
> *Cambridge Medieval History*, vol. vii, chap. xx, vol. viii, chaps. xv, xvi, Cambridge, 1932 and 1936.
> *Histoire du Moyen Age*, ed. G. Glotz, vol. vii, pt. ii, by J. Calmette and E. Déprez, Paris, 1939.
> Mariana, Juan de : *Historia de Rebus Hispaniae*. English translation by John Stevens, London, 1699. (This work is a classic, and the translation, from the literary point of view, no less attractive than the original.)
> Zurita, Jeronimo : *Anales de la Corona de Aragon*, 6 vols., Saragossa, 1610.
> Altamira, R. : *Historia de España y de la Civilizacion Española*, 4 vols., 1913–4.
> Chaytor, H. J. : *A History of Aragon and Catalonia*, London, 1933.
> Diercks, G. : *Geschichte Spaniens*, 2 vols., Berlin, 1895–6.
> Irving, Washington : *Chronicle of the Conquest of Granada*. First published in 1829. Often reprinted. (Now of literary rather than historical value.)
> Merriman, R. B. : *The Rise of the Spanish Empire*, vols. i and ii, New York, 1918. (The best book on the subject in English.)
> Plunket, I. L. : *Isabel of Castile* (Heroes of the Nations), New York, 1915.
> Prescott, W. H. : *History of the Reign of Ferdinand and Isabella*, 4th ed., 3 vols., London, 1846. (A classic, which still possesses much historical value.)
> Vincke, J. : *Staat und Kirche in Katalonien und Aragon während des Mittelalters*, Pt. I, Münster, 1931.

## CHAPTER XVII

## EASTERN EUROPE

<small>Racial and religious confusion in Eastern Europe</small>

EASTWARD of Germany there lay in the later Middle Ages a number of states which the English student of history is apt to ignore. Nevertheless, they were very active and restless, and for some of them the period which we are surveying was particularly momentous, giving birth to events which profoundly affect Europe to-day. Most of the countries in question were inhabited by peoples of Slavonic stock, the chief exceptions being East Prussia, which was mainly German, Hungary, which was mostly Magyar, and South Russia, where Tatars or kindred peoples predominated. But in every state more than one nationality was represented, and the mixture of races had gone much further in these regions than in western Europe. Another source of confusion was diversity of religion. Whereas in western Europe, save for a few Jews, a handful of Moslems in one small area, and a certain number of scattered heretics, all were Catholics, in the east there were, besides, very many Orthodox Christians and no small number of downright pagans. The main reason for this singular mixture of races and beliefs was that eastern Europe had been exposed to barbarian invasion far longer than the west. Since the beginning of the Christian era, it had been traversed by successive waves of Teutons, then by still more numerous waves of Slavs, and at intervals by various kinds of Mongols, from the Huns to the Tatars. Such civilization as these various invaders had acquired was derived largely from Constantinople, whose proximity accounts also for the influence of Orthodox Christianity among those who had abandoned paganism. But eastern Europe had also experienced penetration, both forcible and peaceful, from the west. This was due mainly to the German *Drang nach Osten* from the tenth century onward. Many regions once peopled by Slavs were now occupied and governed by Germans. And German settlers had pushed far beyond the limits which the German kingdom had attained in the fourteenth century, and had established themselves in parts which remained predominantly Slavonic or Magyar in population. There were many Germans in the lands bordering on the Baltic as far north as the Gulf of Riga; they were numerous in Poland and in Hungary, where there were flourishing German colonies as far east as Transylvania. In the Middle Ages the Cross was always closely associated with the sword and the plough, and one phase of the western counter-attack on the east was the conversion of certain eastern peoples to Catholicism. Thus Poland and Hungary were both Catholic, and their proximity to regions where schism and paganism flourished made them conspicuously enthusiastic upholders of their faith.

Everything conspired to keep eastern Europe in a condition of turmoil, to hinder the creation of strong and stable states, and to retard the advance of its backward culture. Thus the Teutonic Knights in Prussia and the Poles were good Catholics who had a common foe in the pagan Lithuanians; but the knights were Germans and the Poles Slavs, and the two hated each other accordingly. Likewise the Poles and the Hungarians were allied in religion and hostile through race. In blood the Poles were closely akin to the inhabitants of central, western, and northern Russia; but these were schismatics, adhering to the Greek Church, and to be abhorred by Catholics. It might have been thought that a permanent union, or at least a permanent entente, might have been formed between Poland and Bohemia, which in race, language, and religion were closely akin. But Bohemia was attached—loosely, it is true—to the German kingdom and the Holy Roman Empire; and up to 1378 the foreign policy of her Luxemburg kings had been far more concerned with the west than with the east. It is not surprising, therefore, to find that the relations between the states of eastern Europe in the fourteenth and fifteenth centuries are extremely bewildering, and that the internal history of each is as a rule dull and unedifying. Nevertheless, it was in the fifteenth century that the *Drang nach Osten* was halted, and that the Slavs attempted, not without success, to recover some of the ground that they had lost. We have already seen something of this Slavonic reaction, for the Hussite movement was in great measure nationalism nationalist in temper. Despite the religious dissensions among them, the vast majority of the Bohemian people would always unite to resist a foreign invasion, and that the Hussite leaders regarded the wars which they waged as to some extent a phase of the age-long rivalry of Teuton and Slav is shown by their persistent efforts to ally themselves with Poland, though that country never betrayed any leanings towards Hussite views on religion. The victories of Zizka and Procop were by far the most spectacular triumphs ever gained by Slavs against Teutons; but to understand the impression they made in Germany and the confidence with which the Czechs engaged their enemies, it is necessary to consider the turn recently taken in the dispute between the Poles and the Teutonic Knights.

*Poland in the fourteenth century*

At the beginning of the fourteenth century Poland had been in danger of losing her political identity, but from this fate she was saved by two vigorous kings, Ladislas I and Casimir III, not unjustly called "the Great." Though Casimir had enlarged Poland's territories, it is as a statesman rather than a warrior that he is famous. He reorganized—or, rather, re-created—the administration, he reduced the power of the nobility, favoured the peasants, encouraged the building of towns, fostered trade and industry, founded a university at Cracow, and established in Poland such peace and order as had never been known before. For the first time the monarchs of western Europe had to deal with a King of Poland as with an equal. Casimir died in 1370. With dubious wisdom he had chosen as his heir his nephew Lewis II,

*Lewis of Hungary, King of Poland, 1370–82*

King of Hungary—an arrangement to which the Polish nobles had only given their consent after extorting from Lewis promises very damaging to his royal authority. Lewis had too many irons in the fire to be able to give much time to Poland. He entrusted the government of the country to his mother, Elizabeth, Casimir III's sister, and when her rule provoked opposition he tried to allay it by yet more concessions, the most notable being the Pact of Koszyce of 1374, whereby the whole body of Polish nobles, great and small—numbering many thousands—were exempted from almost every duty or obligation to the State. Notwithstanding his weakness, his rule gave offence to the nobles of the province of Great Poland, and they rose in rebellion. In 1382, while the

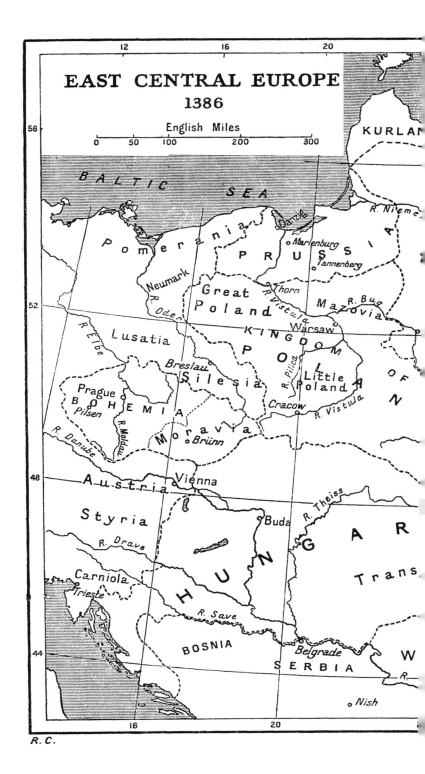

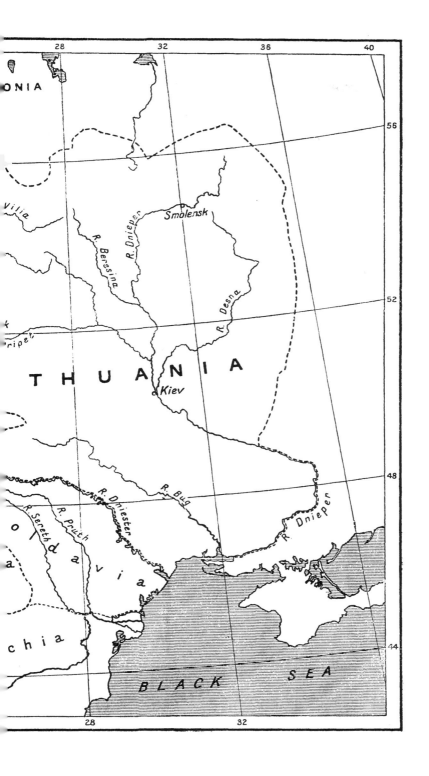

revolt was in progress, Lewis died. Confusion was worse confounded, and many of the benefits derived from the sound rule of Casimir were swept away.

King Lewis left two daughters, the elder, Mary, betrothed to Sigismund, brother of Wenzel, King of the Romans, the younger, Jadwiga, betrothed to William of Habsburg, son of Leopold, Duke of Styria. Sigismund had hopes of securing both the crowns of his father-in-law; but the Poles were opposed to union with Hungary, and feared, moreover, that Sigismund, with the power of the House of Luxemburg behind him, would prove an unpleasantly efficient king. In 1384, therefore, a majority of the Polish nobles accepted Jadwiga as Queen. They did not, however, want a Habsburg as her consort, and favoured the suit of Jagello, Grand-duke of Lithuania, especially as he promised to renounce his paganism in order to win the princess. The unfortunate girl, terrified at the prospect of wedding a heathen savage, begged William to come to her rescue. He went to Poland, and his marriage with Jadwiga was consummated without being solemnized. According to the letter of Canon Law this rendered invalid the marriage of Jadwiga to anyone else as long as William was alive; but the Poles drove him out of the country and subjected Jadwiga to such unchivalrous pressure that in 1386 she yielded. Jagello, true to his word, embraced Christianity as well. The tragedy of Jadwiga and William still furnishes a theme for poets, and the union of Poland and Lithuania a problem for diplomatists. *Union of Poland and Lithuania, 1386*

The origin of the Lithuanians no one knows for certain. Dwelling among the forests and marshes around the upper reaches of the Niemen river, they had long defied invasion, and had preserved their primitive savagery more completely than any other European people except perhaps the Lapps. Their country was the last extensive stronghold of heathenism in Europe, a distinction which it had enjoyed for a long time. The Lithuanians were much feared by all neighbouring peoples. In the century and a half before the union with Poland, they had made many conquests, and had become rulers of a vast empire, which just touched the Baltic near Memel and stretched southwards to the Black Sea, including its coasts from the Dniester to the Bug, while it reached eastward from Brest Litovsk to a somewhat indeterminate line *The Lithuanians* in the heart of modern Russia, well beyond the river Desna. Most of the expansion of Lithuania had been at the expense of Russia, and the majority of her new subjects were Christians of the Orthodox Church. Of late years the Lithuanian rulers had been a sore trouble to the Dukes of Muscovy, and more than once had besieged Moscow, though without success. The principal motive of Jagello in seeking marriage with Jadwiga had been to prevent the acquisition of Poland by a German prince who might ally her forces with those of the Teutonic Order. The union of the two states was merely personal, and many of the Lithuanians disliked it. But the great majority of them obeyed their sovereign and believed the Catholic faith.

Ladislas II (Jagello), King of Poland, 1386–1434

Jagello, or Ladislas, as he called himself after his conversion, was almost as conciliatory towards the Polish nobility as his predecessor had been, and the Polish Crown consequently suffered further damage. Nevertheless, Ladislas managed to raise the prestige of Poland to unprecedented heights in the course of his long reign. His most notable successes were gained in Prussia at the expense of the Teutonic Knights.

The Teutonic Order in Prussia

For that Military Order the union of Poland and Lithuania was a grave matter. It was not merely that two enemies, hitherto mutually hostile, had now joined forces. But the purpose of the Order was to fight the infidel; it was to do so that it had originally come to the coasts of the Baltic. And now there were no more infidels for it to fight. Of course for a long time the Order had been sovereign of large and settled territories in Prussia, Livonia, Esthonia, and Kurland; in that capacity it had waged wars against Christian princes; it might remain as one of the Great Powers of eastern Europe, even though it no longer fulfilled the aims of its founders. All the same, however great its preoccupation with purely political matters, it had always kept up the crusade against heathendom with decent energy. It had thus attracted into its armies, whether as full members of the Order or as temporary auxiliaries, many of the warriors of western Europe who wished to acquire merit by striking a blow for Christianity. Chaucer evidently felt it incumbent upon him to make service in Prussia and Lithuania a part of the career of his " very perfect, gentle knight." But when the

Teutonic Order had no more pagans to fight, it naturally got no more recruits of this sort. It was simply a corporate prince, and its position was more precarious than that of most German princes. For one thing, it is hard for a corporation to command the loyalty and devotion that may attach themselves to a personal sovereign : respect it may indeed evoke ; but when it ceases to fulfil the function for which it was created, respect is almost certain to disappear. There is no doubt, too, that the Knights had become corrupt and profligate. Still, these weaknesses might have been counteracted if they and their subjects had been held together by common interests. The conquered Slavonic population of Prussia could hardly be expected to feel much affection for their masters, but those masters never tried to create a feeling that, after all, they were probably better than any that were likely to replace them. Besides Slavs, there were of course in Prussia many Germans, descendants of colonists who had been encouraged to immigrate when the land was conquered. They belonged to every social class. But none had any share in the government of the regions subject to the Knights, the latest recruit to the Order having more control over its affairs than the greatest of the resident nobles. In these circumstances, it is not astonishing that the inhabitants of Prussia, in their common dislike of their rulers, tended to draw together regardless of their racial diversity. This process went on most quickly in the rural districts. In the towns the population was mainly German ; but all the greater towns, except Memel, belonged to the Hanseatic League, and where the interests of the League conflicted with those of the Knights they would be likely to support the former. Furthermore, it was not merely that the Order was an autocrat ; its members were regarded as foreigners. Not only were they of course vowed to celibacy, but it was a rule that no one born in Prussia was accepted as a recruit. Most of the Knights came from central and south Germany ; most of the German settlers had come from the north : and the two classes could hardly understand one another's speech. Thus even the German inhabitants had little reason to support the Knights in a war with Poland.

To make its prospects worse, the Order displayed the characteristic defects of an oligarchy. Its members were despotic collectively; individually, all—even the Grand Master—were let and hindered at every turn. The government was not even well centralized, for the Provincial Masters had a great deal of authority. Thus, all things considered, the Order was ill-prepared to face a serious crisis. Its strength lay in its wealth and, above all, in its military prowess, still very great.

From the moment when the Teutonic Knights revealed their ambition of establishing themselves as rulers of Prussia, the Poles had resented their presence in the country. That feeling grew into bitter hatred when at the beginning of the fourteenth century, the Order, which had hitherto operated east of the Vistula, secured the province of Pomerellia, including the town of Danzig, by some sharp practice at the expense of Poland. In the wars that followed, however, the Knights had held their ground, though with growing difficulty. It was only to be expected, therefore, that Ladislas II would renew the conflict as soon as possible. But when hostilities began in 1391, the successes of the Poles fell far short of their expectations. This was due partly to the valour of the Knights, but still more to their diplomacy, for they fomented a rebellion in Lithuania under the leadership of Ladislas' cousin Witold, a very able and totally unscrupulous man. In 1401 Ladislas was fain to recognize Witold as Grand-duke of Lithuania, the two agreeing to pursue a common policy, while it was stipulated that on Witold's death Lithuania should revert to Ladislas or his heirs and that thereafter both states should concur in the choice of a common ruler. After this the Teutonic Order soon found it advisable to make peace. But though it sold the region of Dobrzyn to Poland, it kept Samogitia, which Witold's rising had enabled it to seize from Lithuania. In 1409, however, Ladislas and Witold jointly renewed the conflict. Next year a great battle was fought near Tannenberg, a place destined to have its fame revived a little more than five centuries later by another battle between Teuton and Slav in which the issue was very different. For in the medieval battle of Tannenberg, the Slavs gained an overwhelming victory, the Grand Master of the Order and great numbers of his Knights being slain. The victors seemed to have Prussia at their mercy. But Witold and his Lithuanians went away to cope with a threatened Tatar attack on their country; the great fortress of Marienburg held out heroically; Sigismund, who had just been elected King of the Romans, entered Poland in the south; and in 1411 Ladislas deemed it wise to sign the Peace of Thorn. The Knights escaped with the surrender of Samogitia and the payment of an indemnity. It was a disappointment to Poland. But both sides have rightly regarded Tannenberg as a turning-point in their relations. Henceforth, in their wars with the Order, the Poles had the moral ascendancy, and the Knights felt in their hearts that theirs was a losing cause.

*Peace of Thorn, 1411*

Ladislas II was a man of parts and, elderly as he already was, had many years of life before him. But though he increased the prestige of Poland, and wielded a great influence in the affairs of eastern and central Europe, his achievements were hardly commensurate with his activity. Lithuania continued to be a source of trouble. In 1413 the Union of Horodlo defined more precisely the relations between her and Poland. The Grand-duke of Lithuania was declared to be the equal of the King of Poland; both potentates were to be chosen by the joint Diets of both states. The administration of Lithuania was to be precisely assimilated to that of Poland, and the newly-created Lithuanian nobles, provided that they were Catholic Christians, were to enjoy all the privileges of the Polish nobles. But this measure naturally offended the considerable Ruthenian population in the domains of Witold, seeing that they belonged to the Eastern Church, and the Teutonic Knights, with the connivance and occasional support of Sigismund of Hungary, succeeded in keeping alive the separatist party in the country and even in winning over Witold to their schemes. They seemed to be at the point of success when Witold died in 1430. His successor, Swidrigiello, though a brother of King Ladislas, tried to continue his policy, but his abilities were poor, and the Poles drove him out and replaced him by Sigismund Korybut, nephew of both Witold and Ladislas II, a prince who had already figured prominently in the controversies of Bohemia. Korybut adopted a policy of conciliation towards his own subjects, adherents of the Orthodox Church being placed on the same footing as Catholics. He likewise agreed that the Grand-dukes of Lithuania were removable at the will of the Kings of Poland. When the Teutonic Knights went to war to

*Uneasy relations between Poland and Lithuania*

defeat this treaty, they were worsted and in 1435 promised to refrain from interference between Poland and Lithuania.

*Effect of Ladislas II's policy on Poland*

Ladislas II lived just long enough to conclude his treaty with Korybut, and he might congratulate himself warmly on having, after so many vicissitudes, preserved the connexion between Lithuania and Poland. He had, however, missed a great opportunity when he refused the offer of the Bohemian Crown which the Hussites made on their rebellion against Sigismund. Ladislas had been actuated by religious motives, which had afterwards led him to urge the recall of Korybut from Bohemia, to withhold all support from the Hussite cause, and to take measures for the suppression of such Poles as accepted Hussite teachings. For good or evil, his policy decided that Poland should remain an eastern state; it also, as the event proved, prepared the way for another eastward surge of German power. And in his own kingdom, his actions furthered that decline of the central authority which was to be Poland's undoing. He lavished favours on the clergy with more than a convert's ingenuousness. The lay nobles, in their jealousy, took steps of their own to counterbalance the advantages gained by the Church. The King's frequent need of money for his wars was exploited by the nobility to the full. It was at this time that provincial Diets came into existence and began to claim the right of being consulted on all matters which affected their respective spheres. The result was that the central Diet, no very effective body at best, was seriously crippled, and the lesser nobility, with their narrow local interests, grew stronger in relation to the greater lords, who were more likely to look at things from a national standpoint. It was from Ladislas that the Polish nobility gained their much-prized privilege of freedom from arrest except after judicial process, an immunity which defeated any attempt by the Crown to govern effectually.

*Ladislas III of Poland, 1434-44*

Ladislas II was succeeded by his son of the same name, a boy of nine, who had been born when his father was seventy-four. The regency was nominally in the hands of the Queen-mother and a council of nobles, but real power belonged to Zbigniev, Bishop of Cracow, a restless, capable, and unscrupulous man, whose influence had been paramount during the last years of the old king. Naturally the power of the

Crown tended to fall, and when Ladislas III grew up he did nothing to improve its prospects, for by a singular turn of events he was elected King of Hungary, to which he devoted nearly all his attention for the rest of his short life. To understand what happened it is necessary to glance at the fortunes of Hungary during the previous half-century.

We have seen that, at the beginning of the period with which this volume has to do, Poland and Hungary were ruled by the same king. When he died in 1382 his elder daughter, Mary, betrothed to Sigismund of Luxemburg, was crowned Queen of Hungary. But Sigismund's expectations were nearly frustrated by the Queen-mother, Elizabeth, who had no wish to see herself pushed aside by an energetic and ambitious son-in-law, and was furthermore opposed to an extension of German influence. The position in Hungary was more complicated than in Poland, because Mary's claim was disputed by Charles of Durazzo, who, as we saw above, had a claim (also disputed) to the kingdom of Naples. Thus the question of the Hungarian succession was involved with the intricate politics of Italy and, to confound confusion, with the manœuvres of the rival Popes of the Great Schism. *Dispute concerning the succession to Hungary, 1382–7*

Luckily there is no need to pursue the details of the strife in Hungary. Sigismund, suspecting that the Queen-mother aimed at putting off his marriage for ever, strove to enlist the great resources of the Luxemburg family in his support. Elizabeth, recognizing that Mary must have some husband to protect her, entered into negotiations with France, and arranged a marriage between the heiress and Louis, brother of Charles VI. Some Hungarians were for Sigismund, some for Louis, some for Charles of Durazzo. Sigismund was the quickest. Entering Hungary with an army, he found that Elizabeth was frightened by the landing of Charles in Dalmatia and willing to acquiesce in his marriage, which he had otherwise resolved to accomplish by force. In October 1385 the ceremony was performed, but Sigismund immediately left the country to raise more troops for the war with Charles of Durazzo. That prince succeeded in having himself crowned, but was soon afterwards trapped and murdered by the amiable Elizabeth. She now plotted to dispense with Sigismund, but King Wenzel, with unwonted resolution, brought him back to Hungary with an army, and constrained Elizabeth and Mary to sign a treaty satisfactory to him. The two brothers, however, at once went away on other urgent business, and thereupon some of the Croatian supporters of Charles's heir Ladislas kidnapped the two Queens and imprisoned them in a castle on the Croatian coast. There was now great confusion throughout Hungary; the Turks were very menacing to the south; so that most of the population were willing to accept Sigismund when in 1387, having again returned with an army, he was crowned. As for the two Queens, Elizabeth was murdered by her captors, but Mary was rescued by the Venetians, who had taken up Sigismund's cause for fear of a union between Hungary and Naples.

*Sigismund of Luxemburg crowned King of Hungary, 1387*

Sigismund was King of Hungary for the next fifty years. If it is true that he failed to do himself credit in that capacity, it must be admitted that his task was no easy one. For many years he had in Ladislas of Naples a threatening rival. And even had his title to the throne been undisputed, he would have found it hard to assert his authority over the Hungarian nobility—numerous, powerful, and insubordinate. Yet it was difficult to work with them, for they were split into mutually hostile factions; the gentry were jealous of the great magnates; and the Diet was an unwieldy and tumultuous assembly, since every noble was entitled to attend, and very large numbers sometimes did. If Hungary had been feudalized, the position of the Crown would have been better, for under feudalism a man's relations to his fellows are regulated by well-known rules or at any rate carefully defined: but the power of the Hungarian nobles was based on privileges extorted from the Crown, and their duties were meagre in comparison with their rights. Apart from difficulties within the realm, Sigismund had to cope with the Turkish menace, which was enough in itself to exhaust the energies of any man. Still, it cannot be denied that Sigismund was partly to blame for his ill-success. His characteristic fault of busying himself with too many projects at once was one of the main reasons why his government of Hungary must be included in the list of the numerous things which he did badly.

*Policy and difficulties of Sigismund*

After his coronation and the recovery of his Queen, Sigismund put down the rebels of Croatia and Bosnia, taking a bloody and treacherous revenge on the murderers of his mother-in-law. He had then to give his mind to the Turks.

Sigismund's contests with them, usually unsuccessful, are noticed below, as they cannot be followed without constant reference to the affairs of the Balkan Peninsula. It should be noted, however, that the reckless campaign which led to the disaster of Nicopolis was due partly to Sigismund's desire to impress his critical subjects. Its effect was naturally the reverse of what had been hoped; when he returned to his kingdom, the southern part was in rebellion; many had believed him dead, and there was talk of electing a successor. Sigismund's measures in face of the widespread disaffection were unwise. He tried to win supporters by extravagant grants of the royal domain, and at the same time, in the hope of guarding himself against treachery, he surrounded himself with foreigners and appointed them to high offices. The consequence was that in 1401 he was seized at Buda by a number of malcontent nobles. The plotters, however, could not agree as to a substitute, and Sigismund, having been liberated by loyalists, managed after a short civil war to recover his former authority. He treated his defeated enemies with prudent leniency, and thenceforth avoided the worst of the mistakes that had caused the revolt.

Sigismund's position in Hungary was nevertheless always somewhat precarious, for his wife had died in 1395, and some of those who had acknowledged her right to be queen would not recognize that her widower had any lawful authority in the kingdom. After some years a rebellion was raised by the partisans of Ladislas of Naples, who invaded the country in 1402, received the crown from the Archbishop of Gran, and met with no small measure of support from the people. Sigismund, however, was strong enough to defeat the movement, and Ladislas went back to Italy and thereafter confined himself to the affairs of that country. In 1408 Sigismund married Barbara of Cilly, daughter of the Count Palatine of Hungary, the most powerful noble of the kingdom. She was deemed extraordinarily beautiful, but, owing to her fondness for both amorous and political intrigue, the marriage did not realize Sigismund's expectations.

Up to 1410, despite occasional intervention in the affairs of Bohemia, Hungary was Sigismund's main concern; but after his election as King of the Romans, the country only saw him at intervals. He appeared when disaffection ran high or when the Turks were unusually threatening; but, just as the Germans blamed him for devoting too much time to Hungary, so did the Hungarians denounce him for devoting too much to Germany. On the whole, the Germans had more ground for complaint. It was as King of Hungary that Sigismund waged against Venice a war that lasted altogether from 1409 to 1421. Ladislas of Naples had sold to the republic the rights which, as King of Hungary, he possessed in Dalmatia, and Sigismund strove to prevent the bargain from taking effect. At first he was victorious; but his attention was distracted from the conflict, first by the Council of Constance and then by the Hussite revolt in Bohemia, so that in the end Venice got possession of almost the whole coast-line of Dalmatia. Later, his struggles against the Turks undoubtedly hindered his operations against the Hussites.

*Albert of Austria, King of Hungary, 1437–9*

By Barbara of Cilly, Sigismund had one daughter, Elizabeth, who was married to Albert, Duke of Austria. Many of the Hungarian nobility had been persuaded to recognize Albert as heir to the throne, and when in 1437 the Emperor died, he was generally accepted as king. Albert was already well known in Hungary as a resolute foe of the Turks, and a great part of his short reign was spent in fighting them. On his premature death in 1439 the succession to the throne was quite uncertain. Albert left two daughters, but no one seemed to take their claims seriously. Some were in favour of awaiting the birth of his unborn child. But the majority, having no love for the connexion with Austria, chose the young King of Poland, Ladislas III.

*Ladislas of Poland and Ladislas Postumus*

When, early in 1440, Albert's widow, Elizabeth, gave birth to a son—christened Ladislas with callous indifference to the sorrows of future students of history—she withdrew the consent which she had given to the Polish King's accession and upheld the claims of her baby. The Polish Ladislas, however, had the upper hand, and after Elizabeth's death in 1442 his position looked secure, and there seemed a possibility of a permanent union between Hungary and Poland. As yet, indeed, the two peoples did not love each other: the Poles resented their King's devotion to Hungarian concerns, and in 1444, so widespread was the feeling against the projected invasion of the Ottoman dominions that very few Poles took part in the expedition that culminated in the catastrophe of Varna, where the King perished. In the circumstances, it is not surprising that the Hungarians ignored the intentions of the Poles, and now recognized the title of the little Ladislas of Austria, commonly called Ladislas Postumus. There were many, however, who would have preferred the great soldier, John Hunyadi, already a national hero through his exploits against the Turks and in no wise discredited by the disaster of Varna, which he had nearly averted. But Hunyadi, a man of gentle but not distinguished birth, could not have commanded the allegiance of the great magnates; and the Hungarians took the wise course when they merely made him regent for the boy-king. Thus Hungary, severed from Poland, was linked to Austria and Bohemia. But the union was nominally no more than a personal one, and in reality hardly that. In Hungary there was a national hero as regent : in Austria, a German, Frederick, King of the Romans : in Bohemia there was for some years civil war between factions aspiring to control the government, but in the end victory fell to the Czech noble, George of Podiebrad. For many years Hungary, Bohemia, and Poland followed their own concerns without paying much regard to one another.

On the death of Ladislas III the Polish nobles could not agree upon a successor, and the land fell into a condition of anarchy which many of them doubtless found congenial. It was, however, prolonged beyond the wishes of the majority, for the late King's brother, Casimir, Grand-duke of Lithuania, at first refused the crown when it was offered to him, and only accepted it after extorting the cession of Volhynia and Podolia from Poland to Lithuania. Even after his coronation at Cracow in 1447, he dwelt mainly in Lithuania for several years. The Poles were incensed, and the all-important nobility were disquieted by Casimir's delay in confirming their privileges and by the somewhat ambiguous language in which he finally acceded to their wishes. They were soon to make him pay for his independent behaviour. Casimir's conduct, however, was based upon sound motives. It was obviously desirable, whether feasible or not, to recover some of the power which the Crown of Poland had lost to the nobles. His attitude towards Lithuania was dictated by his resolve to maintain the union between the two countries. There was much more feeling against it in Lithuania than in Poland;

further, Lithuania was a harder country to hold together, since there was always some danger lest the Orthodox Ruthenians and Russians, who formed so large a part of the population, would break away and attach themselves to one of the Orthodox principalities farther east. It was therefore advisable to humour the Lithuanians and to keep in close touch with them. It is to Casimir's credit that he preserved the union, though he did not fully convince the Lithuanians that it was desirable.

Casimir was a sober and level-headed man, not naturally fond of fighting. For many years he resisted the temptation of trying to fish in the disturbed waters of Bohemia or Hungary. He proved himself able to defend his territories by repelling and punishing an attack on Lithuania by the Grand-duke of Muscovy, and he reasserted an old Polish claim to suzerainty over Moldavia. But he will always be best remembered for his war against the Teutonic Order.

Position of the Teutonic Order

Since their defeat by Ladislas II the troubles of the Knights had increased apace. In the hope of recovering their ascendancy they had waged against Poland several indecisive wars which had seriously strained their resources. It was becoming harder to find recruits, and they were driven to employ mercenaries, who were of course costly and untrustworthy. With their subjects their relations had grown worse. Even before the end of the fourteenth century some of the nobles and towns of Prussia had formed a society called the League of the Lizard, which had behaved treacherously at the battle of Tannenberg. When peace was made, the Grand Master had established a *Landtag*, through which the Estates might influence the conduct of the government. But he had acted without the concurrence of his chapter; it was not hard to show that the *Landtag* was irregular in origin, if not indeed contrary to Canon Law, which forbade the giving of counsel to priests by laymen. The new institution consequently languished, while the grievances of the population increased. To pay for their wars the Knights levied an export duty at the seaports. The Order had for long traded on its own behalf, especially in amber, of which it had a monopoly within its territories; but now, pressed for money, it became less scrupulous in its methods, and thus added to the jealousy with which it was regarded by the merchants of the Prussian towns. It seems, too, that the morals of the Knights declined with their power. They were no longer of any value as protectors of the subject population, for since the conversion of Lithuania there were no foreigners to be particularly dreaded; indeed, many came to think that Polish or Lithuanian conquest of Prussia would make a pleasant change. In 1440, the growing exasperation led a number of nobles and about a score of towns to form the so-called Prussian League, an organization which soon became more formidable than the previous League of the Lizard. At the instance of the Grand Master, the Pope threatened its members with excommunication unless they dissolved it. The League then turned to the Emperor, Frederick III, but he, too, declared it unlawful. Faced with forcible suppression the League appealed for help to Casimir of Poland, offering to recognize his suzerainty over Prussia. Without awaiting his formal reply—though no doubt it knew what to expect—the League renounced allegiance to the Teutonic Order, and took possession of more than fifty Prussian towns. A month later, in March 1454, Casimir declared Prussia annexed to Poland, confirming the rights of the Prussian *Landtag* and promising, besides, to grant to the inhabitants of the country a wide measure of autonomy. But when Casimir prepared to back the rebels by force, he found that disloyalty was not limited to Prussia. For military purposes, Poland was practically a federal state, and before he could raise money and men he had to apply to six provincial Diets, all dominated by the lesser nobles whom he had annoyed. At first only the nobles of the province bordering on Prussia—the so-called Great Poland—would take the field, and even they would not move until Casimir had confirmed and enlarged their privileges. Further disillusionment was in store for the King, for they were promptly and ignominiously routed by the Knights. Early in the next year, the nobles of Little Poland, after likewise driving a hard bargain with the King, met with a similar fate. Casimir thenceforth relied mainly on Czech mercenaries, but as the nobles would only vote him inadequate supplies, he had to resort to desperate shifts in order to pay the troops he hired. For a time the operations were indecisive. In 1457 treachery admitted the Poles to the great fortress of Marienburg, the headquarters of the Order, but after a few weeks the towns-

*War between Casimir IV and the Knights, 1454-66*

folk readmitted the Knights, and the place thereafter held out for three years. But for the support he received from the Prussian League, Casimir would certainly have been defeated. At last, the Czechs inflicted on the Knights, at the battle of Puck in 1462, a blow from which they never recovered. In 1466 the Order was constrained to agree to the second Peace of Thorn. The Knights surrendered West Prussia, and the districts of Kulm, Marienburg, and Ermeland; but they were allowed to retain the greater part of East Prussia as a vassal-state of Poland. The terms were more generous than Casimir would have granted but for his domestic difficulties, which rendered him glad to get out of the war. But the lands of the Order were now severed from Germany, both juridically and physically, while the Poles had gained an outlet to the sea, obtained control of the river Vistula, and secured one of the greatest Baltic ports, Danzig, which they allowed to govern itself as a free city. The military honours of the war lay mainly with the Teutonic Order, but the result was one of the worst blows that Germany has ever received in her conflict with the Slavonic countries. It has not yet ceased to affect the fortunes of central Europe.

*Casimir IV intervenes in Bohemia*

Casimir's experiences in the war against the Teutonic Order should have disposed him to avoid disputes with his neighbours, and it is true that he kept the peace with the Grand-duchy of Muscovy and refused the Pope's invitation to accept the Bohemian crown in place of the heretical George of Podiebrad. In Poland he bestowed favours on the cities in the hope of creating a counterpoise to the nobles. In Lithuania he sought to remove a cause of disunion by promoting the spread of Catholicism, a policy which had less effect than he had hoped. But he flung away the fruits of his restraint and discretion when in 1469 he countenanced the acceptance of the succession to the Bohemian throne by his son Ladislas. He thus incurred the enmity of Matthias Corvinus, King of Hungary, and involved himself in strife which lasted the rest of his life.

*Ladislas Postumus, King of Bohemia, 1440–57*

In 1438, after the death of the Emperor Sigismund, there had been a short civil war in Bohemia between Albert of Austria and a party which preferred Casimir of Poland, then a boy. Albert's victory was soon followed by his death, and the Bohemians accepted Ladislas Postumus as their king.

Over the regency a conflict arose. The Bohemians had discovered that the Papacy was disinclined to give effect to the Compacts which they believed it to have accepted and that it would not confirm the election of John Rokycana to the archbishopric of Prague. The Utraquist and nationalist party therefore closed its ranks and resolved to get control of the government. Opposed to it was a party of Catholics, consisting largely of Germans and generally favourable to the maintenance and spread of German influence in the country. Owing to the rivalry of the two, no regency could be set up and great confusion afflicted the whole land. Eventually avowed war broke out between the Utraquists and the Catholics, the former being led by the Czech noble, George of Podiebrad, the latter by Ulrich of Rosenberg. After about three years, the national cause won, and in 1451 the Diet (in which during the recent troubles the cities had secured representation) recognized George as regent. He proved a very able ruler and gave the land such peace as it had not enjoyed for many a long day. The Utraquists were now beginning to realize that their so-called reconciliation with the Church had been a snare—a conviction which caused a revival of more advanced views in the country, these years witnessing the foundation of the Unity of the Brethren, a body known to-day in Britain and America as the Moravian Church and destined in the sixteenth and seventeenth centuries to attain to great influence in the land of its birth. Though the young King swore before his coronation in 1453 to uphold the Compacts, he soon showed his dislike of them, especially when he returned to Bohemia after his campaign with John Hunyadi against the Turks in 1456. But in the next year he died of the plague.

*Success of the Utraquists: George of Podiebrad regent, 1451*

By hereditary right the Emperor Frederick was heir to the Bohemian throne. He had several rivals who claimed it on other grounds. The Bohemian Estates rejected them all and chose George of Podiebrad. John Rokycana, whose influence at the time was very great, declared publicly that he would rather have seen Bohemia a republic than subjected, even by her own choice, to a foreigner. The nationalist fervour of the Czechs of the fifteenth century was equal to that of their descendants in the twentieth.

*George of Podiebrad chosen King, 1458*

George of Podiebrad is one of the heroes of the Czech people and on the whole he deserves the honour in which they hold him. The first years of his reign were happy and prosperous. He maintained a close friendship with Matthias Corvinus, King of Hungary, through whose good offices he was crowned by a Catholic bishop. His head was perhaps a little turned by his success, for, as we saw above, he allowed himself to be lured into a scheme for making him King of the Romans in place of Frederick III. In pursuance of this plan, he tried to gain the favour of the Papacy by persecuting the Unity of the Brethren and other advanced Hussites. But it was in vain. Pope Pius II, who knew Bohemia well, denounced the Compacts and called upon the Bohemians to conform in all respects to the doctrine and practice of the Catholic Church. George perceived that his hold over the Czechs had been somewhat shaken by his conciliatory attitude towards the Pope and his efforts to win a German crown. Faced with the intransigence of the Holy See, he dropped his German projects, and declared that he was ready to die in defence of Utraquist principles. Thus the pretence of reconciliation was abandoned, and the Bohemians had to face a repetition of the Hussite wars. George vainly tried to make his peace with Rome by offering almost every conceivable concession short of abandoning the demand for Communion in both kinds. A number of Bohemian nobles, Catholics and others, renounced allegiance to him, charging him with illegal and oppressive acts, though everyone knew that personal jealousy and religious or racial animosity were the real motives of their conduct. Thus civil war had begun even before Pope Paul II in 1466 announced the King's excommunication. George's prospects seemed desperate. Besides the rebels in Bohemia and Moravia, most of the inhabitants of Silesia and Lusatia were against him, and the ranks of his enemies were augmented by the Emperor and Matthias Corvinus, King of Hungary, who was both orthodox and ambitious. But King George, in hard fighting during 1467, defeated his domestic foes, and turned the tables on Frederick III by invading Austria. Next year, however, Matthias conquered the greater part of Moravia, and in 1469 was proclaimed King of Bohemia by the Bohemian faction hostile to George of Podiebrad. It was now that the latter, abandoning his hopes of founding a dynasty, recognized Ladislas of Poland as his successor. The choice was

largely determined by racial considerations, for Ladislas was
quite as good a Catholic as Matthias. The war now took a *Ladislas of*
turn more favourable to George, who in 1470 recovered nearly *Poland*
all Moravia. But in 1471 he died, and the Bohemian Estates, *recognized as King of*
after some hesitation, confirmed their recognition of Ladislas as *Bohemia,*
his heir, though Matthias and his party continued the struggle. *1471*

It now becomes necessary to consider what had been
happening in Hungary since the recognition of Ladislas
Postumus as king in 1445. Until 1453 John Hunyadi was *John*
officially regent of the country, and thereafter, as commander *Hunyadi*
of the Hungarian armies, he was virtually ruler until his death. *regent of Hungary,*
Hunyadi is probably to most Hungarians their greatest *1445-53*
national hero; and it is therefore difficult to discern the real
man through the mist of tradition, legend, and even superstition that has enshrouded him. His exploits against the
Turks belong to another chapter, and there is thus little to be
said about him here, for the man was before anything a
soldier, a very fine soldier and a capable general, but not, so
far as we can tell, at all remarkable as an administrator. It
would indeed have been hard for him to suppress aristocratic
insubordination, for he was of Wallachian origin and obscure
family. He must have had a commanding and attractive
personality, and his military gifts rendered him almost indispensable to Hungary; but for all that there was a strong party
of great nobles hostile to him, and one of them, the Count of
Cilly, gained the ear of the young king. Had Hunyadi failed
to relieve Belgrade in 1456, his enemies would probably have
struck him down; as it was, his death immediately afterwards relieved them of any embarrassment caused by his
great triumph. But somehow Hunyadi's sons had got wind *Death of*
of their enemies' plot. They secured the persons of the King *John Hunyadi,*
and the Count of Cilly, who was promptly executed. The King *1456, and*
affected indifference, but took the first opportunity of seizing *of Ladislas*
the brothers, the elder of whom (called Ladislas) was tried and *Postumus,*
put to death for Cilly's murder. The younger, Matthias, was *1457*
kept in custody until King Ladislas died a few months later.
He was then, owing to the influence of the lesser nobles,
chosen as king by the Hungarian Diet. *Matthias*

Matthias, called Corvinus, ruled Hungary from 1458 to *Corvinus*
1490. In the popular tradition of the Hungarian people, he *King of Hungary,*
is the greatest king they ever had. As a national hero he *1458-90*

stands hardly second to John Hunyadi. And Matthias, though not so brilliant a leader as his father, was unquestionably a good soldier, besides being a skilful diplomatist, a keen administrator, an intelligent legislator, and a discriminating patron of art and letters. He left a high reputation for justice, gained probably through his accessibility to the humble and his fondness for rough and ready interference with the course of law. He was, in fact, a would-be despot, of the type so common in the fifteenth century. His diplomatic methods remind one of Louis XI. He kept (illegally, it seems) a small standing army, and in general showed small concern for the rights of his neighbours or his more dangerous subjects. What perhaps impressed contemporaries most was his extravagant ostentation: his court exceeded in splendour anything seen in Hungary before. It may be doubted whether on the whole his reign was beneficial to the country. He angered the nobles without really reducing their power. Against the Turks he fought successfully, conquering the northern part of Bosnia and repelling their raids into Hungary; but if he had put all his strength into an offensive when the feeble Bajazet II became Sultan, he might have saved his country from the disasters of the following century. His failure to seize his chance was due in the main to his preoccupation with the affairs of Bohemia, which he had much better have left alone.

War between Matthias and Ladislas of Poland, 1471-8

From 1471 to the end of our period the fortunes of Poland, Bohemia, and Hungary are inextricably intertwined. For seven years Matthias and Ladislas of Poland contended for the Bohemian crown. The Emperor took the side of Ladislas, and Matthias had trouble with malcontents at home; but he stirred up the Teutonic Knights against the Poles, and acquitted himself so well in the rather petty warfare that ensued that in 1478, by the Treaty of Olmütz, while acknowledging Ladislas as King of Bohemia, he received for himself Moravia, Silesia, and Lusatia.

Poland, Bohemia, and Hungary under different kings, 1478-90

In the next decade each kingdom had its own king, though the bond between Bohemia and Poland was naturally close. Matthias was much concerned at the intervention of Casimir IV in Moldavia, even though it was directed against the Turks, and the invasion of Lithuanian territory in 1487 and 1490 by bands of Tatars and other peoples was probably due to the machinations of the King of Hungary. Casimir, however, outlived him, and died in 1492, leaving a name as one of the greatest of all Polish kings. His policy, which was pacific and cautious, was however much wiser than his deeds, which were often grasping and ill-considered. On his death the Lithuanians, regardless of the Union of Horodlo, chose as their Grand-duke, Alexander, Casimir's fourth son, while the Poles elected his third son, John Albert. The eldest son, Ladislas, King of Bohemia, was passed over because as ruler of both kingdoms he would have been too powerful for the taste of the Polish nobles.

*Union of Poland and Lithuania broken, 1492*

Ladislas continued to rule Bohemia until 1516. In the part of his reign which concerns us, the religious differences of the country again caused trouble. Ladislas openly favoured the Catholic party and seemed inclined to encourage the persecution of Utraquists. His conduct caused the formation of a league among the Utraquist nobility, followed by a popular rising in Prague, in which several magistrates and numerous Germans and Jews were massacred. On this, the two parties came to an understanding, the Catholics consenting to the application of the famous Compacts. The Utraquists desired reconciliation with Rome, and an attempt to bring it about was made in 1493. But that ornament of the Faith, Pope Alexander VI, insisted on the renunciation of the Compacts, a demand flatly rejected by the Bohemian Diet.

*Ladislas II of Bohemia and the Utraquists*

Thus, at the end of our period, the greater part of the Bohemian people were still defying Rome. Their views were very moderate, and to the later Protestants they seemed to be straining at gnats and swallowing camels. But the significance of their obstinacy must not be overlooked. At the same time, as it happened, they were reducing their capacity for resistance. The victories of Zizka and Procop had been won by armies consisting mainly of free peasants; but during the century the great nobles had gained more and more influence upon the government, and a series of measures reduced the status of both the free and the half-free cultivators until in 1487 the Diet passed an enactment which virtually bound the peasant to the soil. Simultaneously, an attempt was made to curtail the privileges and influence of the towns. The evil effect of the selfish policy of the nobility was not fully evident for a long time, but it appeared very plainly at the beginning of the Thirty Years War, when the national party had to rely mainly on foreign mercenaries.

In the first years of the reign of Ladislas, it looked as if the bond between Bohemia and the Holy Roman Empire was about to snap. The Emperor Frederick, who at the best of times could not command the respect of the Bohemian people, was not consulted when the Peace of Olmütz was made. Matthias Corvinus later made vigorous war upon him, and in 1485, as we have seen, took Vienna, occupied Lower Austria, and forced the Emperor to beg for help round Germany. Thus when Matthias died in 1490, he left far-spreading dominions to his successor. But he had no legitimate son, and the bastard John Corvinus, though supported by some, could not command a majority in the assembly of nobles that met to choose a king. The Emperor's son, Maximilian, commended himself to many, but in the end an invitation went to Ladislas of Bohemia, who accepted it. The House of Jagellon had indeed risen high. Casimir of Poland and his son together ruled an immense Empire, which included some of the most warlike peoples and some of the best agricultural land in Europe.

*Victories of Matthias Corvinus over the Emperor Frederick III*

*Ladislas II of Bohemia elected King of Hungary, 1490*

But Maximilian had already recovered Lower Austria for his father, and in 1491, beset by many difficulties incidental to his succession to the Hungarian throne, Ladislas agreed to the Treaty of Pressburg, whereby he restored to the Habsburgs all that Matthias had taken from them and agreed that if there should be a failure of male heirs among his own descendants, all his territories should pass to the Habsburg family. This was one of the most fateful agreements we have had to record; not only did it take effect, and that unexpectedly soon, but its consequences were ruinous to the Slavonic peoples and it was the true foundation of the Austro-Hungarian Empire.

*The Treaty of Pressburg, 1491*

Ladislas may perhaps be fairly blamed for signing the Treaty of Pressburg, but it seems unjust to condemn his father, Casimir of Poland, for failing to foresee in the Grand-duchy of Muscovy the embryo of a power which, albeit Slav, was to prove the chief oppressor of his people. At the middle of the fifteenth century south Russia was still in the hands of the Tatars, and Muscovy was only one of several small states which owed them tribute. It was, however, under Ivan III,

*The Grand-duchy of Muscovy*

her Grand-duke from 1462 till 1505, that her rise really began. Ivan, a crookback of sinister appearance, reduced and annexed the Republic of Novgorod, once the most powerful state in Russia, after a prolonged struggle; he also seized the principality of Tver, and constrained Lithuania to cede a small piece of territory. Eastward he extended his influence to the Urals, and it was in his time that changes of fortune in the south freed Muscovy from dependence on the Tatars. He assumed the title of Gospodar—or sovereign— of all Russia, and having in 1472 married as his second wife a niece of the last Byzantine Emperor, he deemed himself the inheritor of the traditions and prerogatives of Constantinople, and assumed a dignity and state in dealing with his subjects such as Russia had never seen. How little all these doings and aspirations meant to western Europe may be judged from the fact that a German traveller astonished Vienna by announcing that northern Russia was not just a remote part of Poland but under the rule of a formidable and independent potentate.

## KINGS OF POLAND, BOHEMIA, AND HUNGARY
### POLAND
Lewis (also King of Hungary), 1370–82.
Ladislas II (Jagello), 1386–1434.
Ladislas III (also King of Hungary), 1434–44.
Casimir IV, 1447–92.
John Albert, 1492–1501.

### BOHEMIA
Wenzel, King of the Romans, 1378–1419.
Sigismund, Emperor (also King of Hungary), 1420–37.
Albert, King of the Romans (also King of Hungary), 1438–9.
Ladislas Postumus (also King of Hungary), 1440–57.
George of Podiebrad, 1458–71.
Ladislas II (son of Casimir IV of Poland), 1471–1516.

### HUNGARY
Lewis II (also King of Poland), 1342–82.
Sigismund, Emperor (also King of Bohemia), 1387–1437.
Albert, King of the Romans (also King of Bohemia), 1437–9.
Ladislas V (also King of Poland), 1440–4.

Ladislas VI, Postumus (also King of Bohemia), 1445–57.
Matthias Corvinus, 1458–90.
Ladislas VII (also King of Bohemia), 1490–1516.

Some authorities for the subjects covered in chapter xvii :—
There is a lamentable dearth of writings in English on the history of East Central Europe, and it seemed to me useless to name books written in Czech, Polish, or Hungarian.

### BOHEMIA

See the histories of Bachmann, Palacky and Seton-Watson, noted under chapter ix, and also :
> *Cambridge Medieval History*, vol. vii, chap. vi, vol. viii, chap. iii, Cambridge, 1932 and 1936.
> Denis, E. : *Fin de l'indépendence bohême*, vol. i, new edition, Paris, 1930.
> Thomson, S. Harrison : *Czechoslovakia in European History*, London, 1943.

### POLAND

*Cambridge Medieval History*, vol. viii, chap. xviii, Cambridge, 1936.
Dyboski, R. : *Outlines of Polish History*, 2nd ed., 1931.
Gardner, M. M. : Queen Jadwiga of Poland, Ouseley, 1934.
Grappin, H. : *Histoire de la Pologne*, Paris, 1923.
Halecki, O. : *The History of Poland*, trans. M. M. Gardner and M. Corbridge-Patkaniowska, London, 1942.
Roepell, R., Caro, J., Zivier, E. : *Geschichte Polens*, 5 vols., 1840–1915.
Slocombe, G. E. : *Poland* (The Nations' Histories), London, 1916.
Whitton, F. E. : *A History of Poland*, London, 1917.

### HUNGARY

*Cambridge Medieval History*, vol. viii, chap. xix, Cambridge, 1936.
Domanovsky, A. : *Die Geschichte Ungarns*, Munich, 1923.
Fraknoi, W. : *Mathias Corvinus*, Freiburg i. B., 1891.
Yolland, A. B. : *Hungary* (The Nations' Histories), London, 1917.

### TEUTONIC ORDER

See the works on the general history of Germany, noted under chapters iv, vi, and xiii, and also :
> *Cambridge Medieval History*, vol. vii, chap. ix, Cambridge, 1932.
> Greiser, R. : *Hans von Baysen : Ein Staatsman aus der Zeit des Niedergangs der Ordenherrschaft in Preussen*, Leipzig, 1936.
> Mortensen, H., and Mortensen, G. : *Die Besiedlung des nordöstlichen Ostpreussens bis zum Beginn des 17 Jahrhunderts*, Pt. I, (Deutschland und der Osten, vol. vii), Leipzig, 1937.

CHAPTER XVIII

## THE FALL OF THE BYZANTINE EMPIRE AND THE TURKISH CONQUEST OF THE BALKAN PENINSULA

THE capture of Constantinople by the Turks is one of the most famous catastrophes in history. And it is probable that more important consequences have been erroneously ascribed to it than to any other historical event. It is true that it caused a great shock to the whole of Christendom; but it made very little difference to the relations or prospects of the states of Europe. And though the circumstances attending the fall of the great city lent the catastrophe a certain tragic dignity, the events which led up to it arouse little admiration for any of those concerned. The history of the Balkan Peninsula during the last century of the Middle Ages can scarcely be matched for folly, treachery and cruelty. There was, as we have seen, no lack of brutality and rapine in western and central Europe in those days; but the wars of France or Germany seem chivalrous and humane when compared with the contemporary conflicts of southeastern Europe. Here and there gleams of heroism relieve the gloom; but too often one finds that the hero is no more than a brave blackguard. Why any of the peoples involved care to dwell on their doings in this period is incomprehensible.

The Byzantine Empire had been a magnificent state, and had rendered eminent services to the cause of European civilization, both by the example of its own life and also by its resistance—for long successful—to barbarian or Moslem invaders. But it had been well for its renown if it had never revived after its overthrow by the Fourth Crusade in 1204. For it was never again anything but a quaking ruin, dependent for its continuance more upon the weakness or dissension of its foes than upon its own courage or merits. In the first part of the fourteenth *The Byzantine Empire in the first part of the fourteenth century*

century it held little more on the European mainland than the province of Rumelia—or eastern Thrace—the peninsula of Chalcidice, the city of Salonica, and a small part of the Morea, while in Asia it possessed but a few square miles of land on the shores of the Bosphorus and the Sea of Marmora, together with one or two cities. Its European territories were constantly threatened and often cut short by the Bulgarians and the Serbians, who successively established powerful empires. Central and southern Greece were for the most part under rulers of western origin, Catholic in religion. The republic of Venice had occupied various points on the coast, and many of the Ionian and Ægean islands were held by her or Genoa. And in Asia Minor the Empire was confronted with the rapidly growing power of the Ottoman Turks, who had possessed the ascendancy over their rivals, Christian or Moslem, since the closing years of the previous century. Europeans frequently think of these Turks as though they were ill-disciplined barbarians, formidable through their numbers and ferocity. In reality, the Turkish army had no superior in training, organization, and equipment, and Turkish generalship was quite as good as any with which it was likely to be called upon to cope.

In face of its numerous enemies, the Byzantine Empire cut a wretched figure. Its subjects were more interested in amusements and in silly theological bickerings than in the defence of its territories. The Emperors were without exception poor creatures, and the members of the royal family were so stupid, selfish, and treacherous that they dissipated what little strength the Empire retained in strife which sometimes amounted to civil war. So insensate were their mutual hatreds that rival leaders sometimes allied themselves with Turks and invited Turkish troops to Europe. It is small wonder that Moslem raids into Europe became common. They were successful and destructive, but up to 1350 they had not led to any Turkish settlement on European soil.

*First Ottoman successes in Europe*

Soon after the middle of the century momentous changes occurred. In 1353 a force of Turks crossed the Dardanelles, and in the following year established themselves in Gallipoli. It was the beginning of their permanent settlement in Europe.

## WEAKNESS OF THE EASTERN EMPIRE

In 1357 the Turks took Adrianople, which was the capital of their European territories from 1365 to 1453. In the next years vast numbers of them entered Europe and pressed far to the north and west. The Byzantine Empire scarcely resisted. Amadeus VI, Count of Savoy, at the head of a force of crusaders, recaptured Gallipoli; but the Emperor gave it back to the Turks. Adrianople, recovered for a while by bargaining, was soon reoccupied by the Sultan Murad I, who succeeded his father Orkhan in 1359. In 1369 the Emperor John V went to Italy and France to seek help. He professed himself a Catholic, and was allowed to recruit troops; but his mission was a failure, and in 1373 he recognized Murad as his suzerain and promised him military service. Immediately afterwards he accompanied the Sultan on a campaign in Asia Minor. A little later there was the extraordinary spectacle of an Emperor and a Sultan fighting together against a rebellion headed by a son of each. When John V was restored to Constantinople, which the rebels had for some time held, the Sultan put on the screw. John had to undertake to pay an annual tribute of 30,000 gold bezants, to furnish 12,000 fighting men, and to surrender the Asiatic city of Philadelphia, hitherto faithful to the Empire, a stipulation which could only be carried out after Byzantine troops had coerced the wretched inhabitants of the place into compliance. In the next years the Turks extended their grasp on Greece and the Ægean islands. They took Salonica in 1387.

The Empire being in such a plight, it may well be asked why it was not until 1453 that it was finally overthrown. The reason is that it was the least formidable of the many foes with whom the Turks had to contend. Their invasion of Europe had soon brought them into conflict with the Serbians and the Bulgars, who were much more to be dreaded than the Greeks. Had the great Serbian Emperor, Stephen Dushan, not died in 1356, the Turks might indeed have long been held in check. But Stephen's Empire, which stretched from the Danube to Thermopylæ and from the Adriatic Sea to the river Struma, broke up quickly after his death. The Balkan Peninsula was filled with strife, and the Turks were thus easily victorious in their first encounters with both Serbs and Bulgars. In 1371

*Wars of the Turks with Serbs and Bulgars*

the King of Southern Serbia essayed a counter-attack on the Turks, but his army was cut to bits on the Maritza river. Macedonia now became tributary to Murad, and the Tsar of Bulgaria, in his helplessness, promised military support to the Turks and contributed a sister of his to Murad's harem. There followed further inroads on both Bulgarian and Serbian territory. But a great league against the Turks was formed, headed by the King of Bosnia, Tvrtko, who had raised his state to the hegemony of the Balkans, and the Moslems were heavily defeated at a battle on the river Toplica in 1387. The Bulgarians and Wallachians now joined the alliance, and its army received reinforcements from many other peoples. Murad soon struck back. He first overcame the Bulgarians. Then he advanced against the Bosnians and Serbs, whom he met at Kossovo on June 15, 1389. The battle that followed ended in overwhelming victory for the Turks. Just before the fight, a Serbian noble who pretended to have deserted his fellow-countrymen, stabbed and fatally wounded the Sultan, and when Lazar, the Serbian Prince, was taken prisoner, he was killed in revenge. The disaster is still mourned by the Serbs and Montenegrins, and plays a great part in their folk-lore and ballads. The son of Lazar was allowed to occupy his father's throne on condition of rendering tribute and military service; other princes ruling over Serbs received similar terms. Bosnia was left alone for the moment, and seemed to have profited by the downfall of Serbia; but in 1391 King Tvrtko died, and his ill-compacted realm at once began to break up.

Murad's successor was his son Bajazet, commonly called the Thunderbolt, from the rapidity of his movements in war. He conquered Wallachia, and made it tributary to himself. In 1393 he fell upon Bulgaria, suppressed its autonomy, and annexed it to his Empire. He extended the grip of the Turks in Asia Minor. He mercilessly bullied the Byzantine Emperor, who at his behest demolished new fortifications which he had erected at Constantinople. Bajazet is known to have intended the capture of the great city, and would doubtless have achieved it but for two perils which he was called upon to face.

The progress of the Turks had at last seriously alarmed

western Europe. Sigismund, King of Hungary, gained some successes over them, and succeeded in restoring the Prince of Wallachia to his country. In response to his appeal and the urgings of the Church, a force of knights and men-at-arms from Italy, Germany, England, and France—principally the last—came to aid him in driving the Turk from Europe. After some minor successes the Christian allies laid siege to Nicopolis on the Danube. Bajazet led his army to relieve the town, and the Christians left their lines and took the offensive. The battle was fiercely contested, and it is hard to make out exactly what happened. The mail-clad horsemen from the west, led by John of Burgundy, son of Duke Philip the Bold, broke through their enemies, but, after their fashion, pursued too fast and too far, and were taken at a disadvantage by the Turkish cavalry reserves. Sigismund and the Hungarians advanced in the hope of restoring the fortunes of the day, but after bitter fighting they were put to flight by a charge of the Serbian horse under the Serbian despot, Stephen Lazarevic. Sigismund just managed to escape in a boat down the Danube, and eventually reached Constantinople; but John of Burgundy and many other notable men were captured and held to ransom.

*Battle of Nicopolis, Sept. 25, 1396*

The battle of Nicopolis caused dismay in western Europe, which for the first time grasped that the Ottoman Turks owed their success to their own merits as much as to the defects of their adversaries. The battle, indeed, illustrates several of the causes of the amazing series of Turkish triumphs which marked the latter half of the fourteenth century. The strategy and the tactics of Bajazet were both superior to those of the crusaders. His army was a co-ordinated machine, under a single effective command. He had in the Janissaries troops which had no superiors and hardly any equals at the time. On the other hand, the Christians lacked discipline. The headlong charge of the French was made in defiance of the wishes of Sigismund. The Christian force came into action piecemeal, and its tactics were throughout wretched. The issue, further, was manifestly not a straight one between Cross and Crescent. There were numerous Christians in Bajazet's ranks, and though they were serving under a treaty imposed on them by force, the Serbs fought with the utmost vigour and devotion. The Janissaries themselves were not Turks, but sons of Christian subjects of the Sultan, levied as tribute when children. The Prince of Wallachia was fighting on Sigismund's side at Nicopolis, but otherwise the crusaders seem to have received no help worthy of notice from any of the Balkan peoples. The Byzantine Emperor never lifted a finger to aid his would-be rescuers.

The pusillanimity of the Emperor Manuel availed him nothing, for Bajazet immediately began to prepare for the capture of Constantinople. The arrival of the great Boucicaut from France gave him pause, for he feared that it might presage a new Crusade. The Emperor used the respite by going to western Europe on a begging tour, accompanied by Boucicaut. Manuel offered to become the vassal of the King of France, a proposal which was assuredly the *reductio ad absurdum* of the Byzantine Empire. He was well received in both France and England, but got little save fair words. Charles VI, however, did supply 1,200 men-at-arms for a year, and with these Boucicaut went back to Constantinople in 1399. On his way, in conjunction with Genoese and Venetian squadrons, he gained a notable naval victory near Gallipoli; he then relieved Galata in the nick of time; and in the next year the French fought brilliantly against the Turks on Asiatic soil. But they were too few to gain any decisive success; nearly all went home when their year's service was over; and Boucicaut departed also in order to raise reinforcements, leaving behind at Constantinople a small French garrison. The Turks had meanwhile pursued their conquests, having in 1398 defeated the Bosnians, and now they began to close in on the city. At the beginning of 1402 the Emperor held hardly anything beyond its walls; but when Bajazet summoned the place to surrender, threatening in the event of resistance to massacre the entire population, he received a humble but explicit refusal.

There seemed but one possible issue. The stoat might seize the rabbit when he liked. And then Bajazet was called upon to defend himself against a far more formidable foe than any he had yet encountered. The terrible Timur, or Tamerlane—the conqueror of India, Persia,

Syria, and Armenia—commanded him to restore to the Greeks all that he had taken from them. Bajazet sent an insulting answer, and hurried eastward to meet Timur's advance. The two armies clashed near Angora on July 28, 1402. Bajazet committed many of the mistakes which had ruined the crusaders at Nicopolis, and suffered a similar catastrophe. The Serbian contingent in his army acquitted itself best, cut its way out of the battle, and saved the Sultan's eldest son, Suleiman. Bajazet himself was taken prisoner; his life was spared and he was not harshly treated, but he was closely confined and carried about in the train of his conqueror until his death early in 1403. The Byzantine Emperor hastened to offer tribute to Timur, and the Tatar host never tried to invade Europe. But it overran all Asia Minor, perpetrating atrocities from which even the Turks would have shrunk, and it captured Smyrna, which had been held for many years by the Knights of St. John. Before long, however, Timur led his hordes eastward, with the intention, it is said, of subduing China. But he was now over seventy, and in 1405 he died.

*Bajazet and Timur: battle of Angora, July 28, 1402*

The departure of Timur was followed by a series of civil wars between Bajazet's sons. The Christian peoples of the Balkan Peninsula had an excellent opportunity of throwing off the Turkish yoke. But instead of uniting in a common effort, they preferred to seek advantages by intrigue, bargaining, and the changing of sides. Unfortunately their leaders, though quite unscrupulous, were not very adept at the game; and it was largely owing to support received from the Byzantines and Serbians that in 1413 the most able of Bajazet's sons, Mohammed, found himself victorious. He restored some territory to both the Empire and Serbia in return for their aid, and during his reign neither was attacked. Mohammed indeed was an organizer rather than a conqueror. He forced Wallachia, which had fought against him, to return to its tributary status; it was in his reign that the Turks secured a footing in Bosnia; and he led one or two raids into Hungary. But in a naval war with Venice the Turks were worsted, and in 1419 King Sigismund invaded Serbia and gained a notable victory at Nish. Nevertheless, Mohammed I, whom the Turks called "the Gentleman," holds a very

*Turkish power restored by Mohammed I, 1413–21*

high place in the traditions of his people—and rightly so, for his judicious rule made the Ottoman state a great power again, and prepared the way for the exploits of the next two Sultans.

*Murad II, 1421-51*

Murad II, who was Sultan from 1421 to 1451, was a vigorous and warlike ruler. It was highly characteristic that he fell out almost at once with the Byzantine Emperor, and in 1422 besieged Constantinople, which was saved by the outbreak in Asia of a formidable rebellion against the Sultan. The Turks extended their hold over southern Greece, and in 1430 Salonica, which since the beginning of the century had changed hands in a most bewildering way, was taken from the Venetians, to be held by Turks until the twentieth century. As regards Serbia, Murad respected the treaty made by his predecessor with Stephen Lazarevic, but when in 1427 that astute time-server died and was succeeded by his nephew, George Brankovic, the Sultan declared himself to be the lawful heir to the country. George tried to satisfy him by promising tribute, troops, land, and his daughter; but owing to some delay in the execution of the terms, the Sultan invaded the country, and George only saved himself by agreeing to surrender a great part of it. He received permission, however, to build a new fortress at Semendria on the Danube. Then he offered to exchange Belgrade for certain lands in Hungary. It was an astute move, for in the event of a new Turkish attack on Serbia, he would have a place of refuge, while Hungary would probably be drawn into the conflict. Events fell out much as he expected. Not long afterwards Murad, having been persuaded that he had let the unbeliever off too lightly, demanded the cession of Semendria, and while George was trying to secure Hungarian help, besieged and took it. After a few more operations, Serbia was declared to be a province of the Turkish Empire, and in 1440 Murad laid siege to Belgrade. But the city was well fortified and well equipped with artillery, and after six months the Turkish army was fain to withdraw.

*His acquisitions*

*Unsuccessful siege of Belgrade, 1440*

Hitherto the struggle between Christian and Moslem on European soil had been singularly devoid of heroic figures. But now, in the space of a few years, there arose two of the most famous fighting-men in the age-long warfare between East and West. In 1441 John Hunyadi, a Wallachian noble in the service of Hungary, was appointed *voivode* or governor of Transylvania. On the frontiers of that region there was constant fighting, and in this Hunyadi soon gained striking successes. His renown rose so quickly that in 1443 he was appointed the virtual commander-in-chief of a great expedition which was being organized, under papal patronage, for the expulsion of the Turk from Europe. Ladislas V of Hungary took part, so did the exiled George of Serbia, and the Prince of Wallachia contributed a contingent. The army passed through Serbia and penetrated far into Bulgaria. Murad, however, blocked the way with a force which Hunyadi felt incapable of dislodging, and he had to retreat. A Turkish attack on his rearguard at Kunovica near Nish developed into a battle in which the Christians were brilliantly victorious. Bad news from Asia increased the chagrin of Murad, who in July 1444 consented to a treaty whereby George of Serbia got back his territory—only, it is true, in consideration of a crushing tribute, while both the King of Hungary and the Sultan promised not to cross the Danube for warlike purposes. The expedition, though it had not accomplished all it desired, had been on the whole successful. But the papal legate, the celebrated Cardinal Cesarini, was not satisfied: Murad was in Asia, and it seemed to him that now was the time to finish with the Turk for ever. George of Serbia protested against the foolish treachery. Hunyadi, who (according to contemporary apologists) had not sworn to the treaty, was eager to strike again; and the scruples of Ladislas were overborne by the Cardinal, whose learning and sanctity gave irresistible force to his argument that it was no sin to break treaties with unbelievers. Part of the army had disbanded; George of Serbia not only refused to follow but prevented the great Scanderbeg of Albania from joining Hunyadi; and it was really an inadequate force which marched unopposed to Varna on the Black Sea. There, to the general astonishment, they were confronted by Murad, who had returned in haste from Asia at the head of a superior army. The prowess of Hunyadi nearly snatched a victory; but in the end the Christians met with the overthrow that they deserved, the King of Hungary and the mischievous Cardinal being slain.

In 1448 the indefatigable Hunyadi again attacked the Turks. Again George of Serbia refused to help, and sent a warning to Murad. The Hungarians invaded Serbia and met the Turkish army on the already historic field of Kossovo. The battle lasted for three days, but on the third Hunyadi's Wallachian allies deserted him, and the Hungarians, who had been fighting against odds even before, gave way. In the flight Hunyadi fell into the hands of George of Serbia, who had held aloof until he saw which way the cat would jump. Hunyadi gained his freedom by promising a ransom and pledging himself never to cross Serbia again with an army—both undertakings being disregarded.

Meanwhile, the Byzantine Emperor, John VIII, had been trying to secure protection from the west by uniting the Orthodox and Catholic Churches. The negotiations at Ferrara and Florence have been described elsewhere. The aid subsequently sent by the Papacy was insufficient to make any material difference to the prospects of the Empire, and owing to the disaffection caused in Constantinople by attempts to carry out the decree of union, the episode on the whole did the Empire more harm than good. Murad left Constantinople alone; but his armies laid waste central and southern Greece, and he exacted tribute from the Morea. The only shadow on the splendour of his last years came from Albania, where Scanderbeg repulsed one Turkish army after another.

When Murad died in 1451, he was succeeded by his son, Mohammed II. The new Sultan was an even more able man than his predecessor, a shrewd statesman, a careful administrator, a sound general, and (what is exceptional among Turkish Sultans) a patron of learning and art and a respectable scholar. He was, too, a man of austere life, but, like most Sultans, he was utterly merciless and wantonly cruel. It was his aim to consolidate the Empire which he inherited and then to extend it as far as he could. The first step must be the capture of Constantinople.

There is something sinister in the way in which Mohammed prepared for his great undertaking. He made no secret of his intentions. With Hungary, Bosnia, and Venice he made agreements which secured him from their intervention. He slowly but ostentatiously amassed munitions, and had a monster bombard—the " Big Bertha " of its day— constructed at Adrianople. He built a great fortress on the European shore of the Bosphorus, to render secure his control over the strait. He systematically gathered the harvest of the country round Constantinople, and then laid it waste. The Byzantines looked on helpless. The protests of the Emperor, Constantine XI, were ignored; his efforts to placate the conqueror had no effect. In the early autumn of 1452, war was declared, and all seemed ready; but Mohammed still had some finishing touches to put to his preparations, and he contemptuously allowed the city to live through the winter.

*Mohammed's preparations against Constantinople*

Within the city the psychological effect of Mohammed's conduct was just what he desired. The inhabitants, despairing of themselves, relied on the miraculous intervention of the Virgin Mary. In their own rulers and leaders they had no confidence, especially after December 12, when at the instance of the Pope, the union of the Eastern and Western Churches was inaugurated by a solemn service at St. Sophia. Riots broke out in the city, and the great church was deserted until the very end of the siege. While it cannot be shown that treachery had anything to do with the final catastrophe, there is no doubt that disapproval of the Emperor's religious policy weakened the resistance which was offered. A great Byzantine noble was heard to say that he would rather see a Turkish turban in Constantinople than a cardinal's hat; and many of the Greek clergy, aware that their fellows in the lands conquered by the Turks had been well treated and indeed regarded as magistrates of their flocks, viewed with equanimity the threatened change of ruler. Indeed, what vigour the defence showed—and it was great—came from certain foreigners— two hundred soldiers sent by the Pope, the contingents of six Venetian vessels whose commander had consented to serve the Emperor, and (most important of all) seven hundred first-rate troops under the Genoese captain, John

*Disaffection in Constantinople*

Giustiniani, who was made the Emperor's chief of staff. All told, these foreigners were not numerous. With the native troops, the garrison amounted to some 8,000 men. The Turkish army numbered scores of thousands.

*Opening of the siege, April, 1453*

The siege began early in April 1453. The Turks directed their main attack on the western defences, which consisted of the great triple wall running from the Golden Horn to the Sea of Marmora; it was over a thousand years old, a masterpiece of military engineering, and had never yet been pierced. Against it Mohammed brought the most formidable body of fire-arms that had yet been seen in action. There were fourteen four-gun batteries. Some of the guns were too small to have much effect on the fortifications, and the biggest gun, which threw a shot weighing 1,200 pounds, soon got out of order; but there were weapons of lesser calibre, though still very large according to contemporary standards, which wrought terrible havoc. There is general agreement among contemporaries that it was the Turkish artillery that decided the issue. There was some naval fighting: the Turks failed to break the boom which blocked the entrance to the Golden Horn, and were defeated in a great fight when they tried to intercept three Genoese ships bringing munitions to the defenders. A very wonderful engineering feat, on the other hand, was accomplished by the Turks when they conveyed seventy ships over a specially constructed tramway from the Bosphorus to the west end of the Golden Horn, thus depriving the defenders of their command of the harbour. But none of these operations was decisive; the fate of the city turned on the result of the attack on the western wall. A great bombardment was concentrated against its weakest point, about a mile from its northern end. The guns did such harm that as early as April 18, the Turks tried, though in vain, to carry the defences by storm. Soon afterwards a breach some 300 yards wide was made in both the outer and middle walls. But the Genoese constructed a strong barricade to fill the gap, and on May 7 a second general assault was beaten back. Further attacks, on a smaller scale, were defeated; attempts to mine the walls were foiled; the Turks could not drive the Christians from the Golden

*The Turkish artillery*

*Assaults repulsed*

Horn. Mohammed and some of his advisers became apprehensive. At a Council of War held on May 27, alarmist reports of the approach of relieving forces and the meagreness of the results hitherto achieved caused some important voices to advocate the abandonment of the siege. In the end, however, it was resolved to try a final grand assault two days later. Preparations for this supreme effort were made openly. In face of the peril, dissension within the city was stilled, and on the evening of May 28 a solemn service, in which both Orthodox and Catholic joined, was celebrated in St. Sophia—the last time it was to be used as a Christian church. Soon after midnight the Turks began the attack. The defence was magnificent, and two separate waves of assailants were flung back from the great barricade. A third charge, preceded by a terrific bombardment with all sorts of missiles, and headed by the famous Janissaries, was at first held in check. But Giustiniani was wounded and had to withdraw, and very shortly afterwards the Turks succeeded in gaining a footing within the defences, and in entering the city through a gate in the third wall. In face of their overwhelming numbers, the resistance of the Christians collapsed. The Emperor Constantine perished heroically in the final onset, as became the last sovereign of a State which, whatever its faults, was the inheritor of the glory of Greece and grandeur of Rome, had breasted the barbarian torrent when it threatened to submerge all Europe, and for centuries had held back the ambitious East and been the safeguard of the West. Towards noon of May 29, Mohammed made a ceremonious entry into the New Rome: and then the humbled city was delivered to the infidel soldiery for a three days' sack.

*Final attack, May 29, 1453*

While it is doubtless true that Constantinople might have been saved but for the mutual jealousies of the Christian Powers, it ill befits any moderns to throw stones, seeing that in our own day similar jealousies have secured the Turk, even when defeated and helpless, in the continued enjoyment of his prey. The catastrophe caused dismay throughout Europe, and crusading fervour became more loquacious than it had been for a long time. In a year or two, however, Christian princes were thinking more of holding back the further advance of the Turks than of taking their conquests from them. Mohammed II believed in annexing conquered regions. In the year after the capture of Constantinople he sent to George of Serbia an ultimatum which plainly betrayed his intention of seizing the country.

*Mohammed's aggressive policy*

To the man who had captured Constantinople nothing seemed impossible. But though Mohammed has left a great name as a conqueror, and though under him the terror of Turkish arms became more intense than before, his gains must have seemed to him disappointing. He met with stubborn resistance from three sources. In the first place there were the Hungarians; secondly, the Albanians under Scanderbeg; thirdly, the Venetians. Mohammed proved the mettle of the Hungarians as soon as he essayed the conquest of Serbia. Even before he could reach the frontier, John Hunyadi had raided Bulgaria and retired safely with much booty. Mohammed showed the same cool deliberation that he had displayed before and during the siege of Constantinople. He met with one or two reverses, but by the summer of 1456 all Serbia was his, and he was before Belgrade with a powerful train of artillery. Hunyadi, however, came with a great relieving force, consisting largely of Hungarian peasants who had been filled with crusading zeal by the preaching of Capistrano, a Franciscan friar. Hunyadi overcame the Turkish fleet which was blockading Belgrade on the river-front, and flung his army into the city. The Sultan then tried to take the place by storm, and was within an ace of success when a headlong sortie, led by Hunyadi and Capistrano themselves, flung the Turks back, rushed their camp, and drove them off in a flight that was stayed only at Sofia. The Turkish losses in men and material were enormous, and the victory saved the line of the Danube for over half a century. But Hunyadi and Capistrano both died a few weeks later: the Serbs and the Hungarians quarrelled; before the end of the year George of Serbia was dead; before the end of the next, Ladislas of Hungary; and in both countries there was doubt and dispute as to the succession to the throne. So, aided by treachery, Mohammed soon recovered Serbia, which in 1459 became a Turkish province. Four

*The Turks stoutly resisted*

*Relief of Belgrade by John Hunyadi, 1456*

years later he conquered Bosnia. That country had been much afflicted by political and religious broils, and the district thereafter known as the Herzegovina had secured its independence. The task of the Turks was therefore far easier than the geographical features of the land might lead one to suppose. The circumstances of the conquest led to one singular result. The majority of the Bosnians had for centuries adhered to the Bogomile heresy. Their last three kings, however, had embraced Catholicism and had persecuted those of their subjects who had not followed their example. Most of the nobles had remained Bogomiles, nevertheless, and after the Turkish conquest many of them, together with thousands of humbler folk, turned Moslem. It thus came about that in Bosnia there was an aristocracy, Slav in blood but Mohammedan in faith, to which the Sultans allowed great authority. Its members became very loyal to their rulers and very enthusiastic Moslems. *[margin: Serbia recovered, and Bosnia conquered by the Turks]*

The Turkish advance northward from Bosnia was checked by Hungary. Hunyadi's son, Matthias Corvinus —who was dreaded by the Turks nearly as much as his father—led a counter-attack, and succeeded in occupying and holding two *banats* of lower Bosnia, which Hungary retained for some sixty years. This, however, did not prevent the Turks from raiding far afield, and it was now that they began to afflict the lands of the Habsburgs. *[margin: Resistance of Matthias Corvinus]*

To the south of Bosnia, Mohammed met with no less stubborn resistance. Notwithstanding repeated efforts, he failed to conquer the Herzegovina, a feat which was only achieved in 1483 by his successor, Bajazet II. The region called Montenegro remained unsubdued until the very end of the century. It was, however, the resistance of Albania that caused most concern and loss to the Sultan and excited most admiration and enthusiasm among the Christians of the time. *[margin: Defence of the Herzegovina and Montenegro]*

George Castriota, the hero of the Albanian struggle against the Turks, was of Serbian origin on his father's side, though born in Albania. When he was a boy, Albania was invaded and conquered by the Turks, and he was sent as a hostage to Adrianople, where he was educated as a Moslem and trained as a soldier. He was called Iskander *[margin: Scanderbeg]*

—the Turkish corruption of Alexander—and later received the title of *Beg*; hence the name Scanderbeg, which was applied to him afterwards by his fellow-countrymen. In 1443, contrary to the rule that children of Christians brought up in the Turkish service were conspicuous for their devotion to Islam and the Sultan, he deserted from the Ottoman army, made his way to Albania, then in revolt, renounced Mohammedanism, and soon gained widespread recognition as leader of the national resistance to the oppressor. He received help from Venice, Naples, and the Papacy; but his successes were due mainly to his marvellous skill in guerrilla warfare and to the strength of his rock-fortress of Kroja, often besieged by the Turks, but never taken as long as Scanderbeg was alive. Murad II could make nothing of him. In 1449, he made a supreme effort to quell him; but Scanderbeg beat back four Turkish armies, and successfully endured a siege at Kroja. Mohammed II, it is true, was a more formidable adversary, for he combined guile with force, tampered successfully with some of the Albanian chiefs whose jealousy Scanderbeg had aroused, and gained a victory which seemed to have ruined Albanian liberty. But Scanderbeg escaped, reappeared after a while, easily excited a new rising, and inflicted such blows on the Turks that in 1461 he actually constrained Mohammed to conclude a ten years' truce. Unfortunately for his fame and his cause, Scanderbeg (like Ladislas of Hungary in 1444) was willing to defer to the Church on a question of honour. Pius II assured him that he might break his promises to Mohammed without sin; and in 1463, trusting in the aid which the projected crusade would afford him, he recommenced warfare. The death of the Pope and the abandonment of the crusade forced him to face retribution unsupported. Nevertheless, he remained unconquered, withstanding two further sieges at Kroja before his death in 1468. His genius is best illustrated by the sequel: for the Turks speedily overran all Albania, except Scutari and Kroja, which the Venetians had occupied, and the towns which they had long held on the coast. All these places, save Durazzo, were yielded ten years later.

The mention of the Venetians is a reminder that the great Adriatic republic was tardily taking a leading part in the defence of the West. Up to the fall of Constantinople, the share of Venice in the conflict between Christendom and Islam had been anything but heroic. She had exploited the weakness of the Byzantine Empire without mercy. Against the Turks she had done little. She had warred against them successfully in the time of Mohammed I; she had given aid, mainly financial, to Scanderbeg; and some of her subjects, as we have seen, took part in the final defence of Constantinople. But when the Turks were victorious, she hastened to strike a bargain with them, remaining in occupation of her possessions in Greece and the Ægean islands, and receiving valuable trading privileges. It suited Mohammed's convenience to keep Venice quiet for a while: what pleased Venetians most was that they had scored a point over the Genoese, who had hitherto enjoyed more favour from the Turks and had anticipated increased advantages after the fall of Constantinople. At this time Venice held or controlled all the eastern shores of the Adriatic and the island of Corfu: on the mainland she had Lepanto and several towns on the coast of the Morea; while in the Ægean and its approaches she ruled the islands of Cerigo, Crete, Ægina, Negropont, and others of lesser importance. But her satisfaction with the situation was short-lived. Save for her possessions, the Morea was at the moment held by two Greek "despots," brothers of the dead Emperor Constantine XI. They were tributary to the Sultan; but with inexplicable folly they failed to pay their dues. Mohammed II consequently invaded the Morea in 1458, and annexed about a third of it. Even now the Greek rulers, whom Mohammed had treated with singular forbearance, would not perform their obligations; so in 1460 the peninsula was again entered by a Turkish army, and this time was definitively annexed. The Venetian colonies were spared; indeed, the republic seemed to have profited, for the inhabitants of the impregnable fortress of Monemvasia transferred themselves to her allegiance. But she now realized that Mohammed's desire for conquest had no limit: indeed, he put to death the Florentine Duke of Athens, and ended the last shreds of autonomy retained by that principality, which thus closed a chequered existence of two centuries and a half. Still more disquieting perhaps was the capture of the island of Lesbos from the Genoese family which had ruled it for generations. Thus it came about that in 1462 Venice broke with the Sultan and entered upon a war which lasted for seventeen years. Like Scanderbeg about the same time, she was much influenced by the plans of Pope Pius II for a great crusade; and when they fell through she found herself fighting against odds which she would probably never have deliberately challenged. For all that, she acquitted herself valiantly: indeed, for some years she had the better of the struggle, and actually conquered Lesbos, with neighbouring islands, Athens, and a great part of the Morea. But the tide turned: her ally Scanderbeg was dead; the slackness of one of her admirals lost her the island of Negropont; the Morea was recovered by the enemy; and in 1479 exhaustion compelled her to make peace. She had to surrender her gains and to cede Negropont, Argos, Pteleon, and her possessions in Albania, except Durazzo. But she kept her trading rights in the Levant and her special quarter in Constantinople for an annual tribute. She remained in fact very powerful and, as later events were to show, a serious obstacle to Turkish advance. In 1489, moreover, she received compensation for her recent losses in the acquisition of Cyprus, handed over by its Venetian queen.

In 1480 Mohammed II filled western Europe with consternation by despatching across the mouth of the Adriatic a force which seized and held Otranto. It was believed to be the advance-guard of a mighty Turkish host; but the apprehensions of the Papacy were relieved when in the following year the Sultan died, and the invaders were recalled. The next Sultan, Bajazet II, was the least able and active that had ruled the Turks for a long time. Under him, as we have seen, the resistance of the Herzegovina was broken down, but otherwise the Turkish dominions received no notable accession until the end of the period with which we are concerned. The Turkish Empire in Europe then covered practically the whole of the Balkan Peninsula south of the Save and the Lower Danube, while it exacted tribute from Wallachia, beyond the latter river. As yet, however, its command of the waters of the eastern Mediterranean was successfully disputed; and it shared possession of the islands with the Knights of St. John, who held Rhodes, with Genoa, which held in particular Chios and Naxos, and above all with Venice. But it was exceedingly great and strong, and there seemed no power, Christian or Moslem, capable of stemming its advance when it should again have a Sultan like Murad II or Mohammed II. No one at the time could have guessed that the despised Emperor of the West was laying the foundations of the power which, two hundred years later, was to hurl back the descendants of the terrible Sultan who had overthrown the Emperor of the East.

Some authorities for chapter xviii :—
*Cambridge Medieval History*, vol. iv, chaps. xvii, xviii, xxi, xxiv. Revised edition. Cambridge, 1927, (Extremely valuable : supersedes anything previously written in English on the subjects treated. Contains very full bibliographies.)
*Histoire du Moyen Age*, ed. G. Glotz, vol. ix, pt. i, by C. Diehl, L. Oeconomos, R. Guilland, R. Grousset, Paris, 1945.
Atiyah, A. S. : *The Crusades in the Later Middle Ages*, London, 1938.
Diehl, C. : *Byzance : grandeur et decadence*, Paris, 1919 ; *Histoire de l'empire byzantin*, Paris, 1919.
Jirecek, C. J. : *Geschichte der Bulgaren*, Prague, 1876.
Jorga, N. : *Geschichte des osmanischen Reiches*, 5 vols., Gotha, 1908–13.
Lane-Poole, S. : *Turkey* (Story of the Nations), London, 1903.
Miller, W. : *The Latins in the Levant*, London, 1908.
Ostrogorsky, G. : *Geschichte des Byzantinischen Staates*, Munich, 1940.
Pears, E. : *The destruction of the Greek Empire*, London, 1903.
Runciman, S. : *Byzantine Civilisation*, London, 1938.
Temperley, H. W. V. : *History of Serbia*, London, 1917.

## CHAPTER XIX

## ITALIAN POLITICS

IT has been customary for writers on the last centuries of the Middle Ages to devote a very large share of their space to the political history of Italy. As long as it was still believed by scholars that the Middle Ages were a howling wilderness of brutality, lust, and superstition, and that manners, virtue, and learning were restored by the Humanists of the fifteenth century, it was natural that historians should be strongly attracted towards all that was then happening in Italy, especially as information about it was abundant, accessible, and written in Ciceronian, not " monkish " Latin. But now that our knowledge of European history is better adjusted, there seems little reason for lingering over the abortive squabbles and intrigues with which the political history of fifteenth-century Italy abounds. It is well to see something of the background to the intellectual and artistic activity of the country, and to know something of the conditions under which Italy became the battlefield of foreign powers. But in themselves the bickerings between, say, Florence and Milan are no more important than those between Saxe-Wittenberg and Saxe-Lauenburg.

The "Great Powers" of Italy

The political history of Italy in the thirteenth and fourteenth centuries is comparatively interesting because of the vigorous life of the cities. Their rejection of aristocratic control, their defiance of imperial authority, their experiments in constitution-making, their ferocious party struggles (ridiculous as they often were), their progress in commerce and industry—in fact, every manifestation of their restless throbbing energy—cannot but appeal strongly to all with a sympathetic feeling for the strivings of medieval man to better his environment. But by the beginning of the period which concerns us the Italian cities had passed their best days. Nearly all of them had succumbed to the usurpations of tyrants, or dictators. Nor could many of these tyrants maintain their independence for long. Already most of them could only survive by playing off one of the greater states against another. In 1378 the "Great Powers" of Italy numbered four—the republics of Venice and Florence, Milan —nominally ruled by an imperial vicar, actually under the despotism of the Visconti—and the kingdom of Naples. They were to be joined by the Papal States before long, but at the time the future of the Papacy was dark and uncertain, and its temporal authority at a very low ebb. The political history of Italy in the ensuing century consists in the attempts of these Powers to get the better of one another and to gobble up such of their weaker neighbours as had hitherto escaped. In this struggle for aggrandisement, no great principle was even advanced as a pretext. The very names of Guelph and Ghibelline, which had at least a venerable etymology, were scarcely used as labels any more. In fifteenth-century Italy it was every state for itself, and devil take the honest or weak. The strife was carried on mainly by Italians and interested few outside Italy. Not for many generations had Italy been so free from foreign interference, and until the nineteenth century she was never to be so free again. No Emperor ever seriously threatened to lay his yoke upon her. Rupert's invasion was ignominiously fruitless; Sigismund's war with Venice concerned the possession of Dalmatia, not any part of Italy. During their visits to Italy to receive the imperial crown both Sigismund and Frederick III refrained as far as possible from doing anything that might offend anyone. It is true that from time to time Angevin or Aragonese princes sought by armed force to give effect to their claims to Naples; but Naples had been contested by foreigners since the time of the Hohenstaufen. Further, whereas in the fourteenth century the wars of Italy had been conducted mainly by foreign mercenaries, towards its close these began to be replaced by native *condottieri*, and after John Hawkwood's death in 1394 all the great mercenary captains were Italians. And the people of Italy themselves were seldom much concerned about anything that went on outside their own country.

*Isolation of Italy*

Nothing illustrates better the isolation of Italy from the rest of Europe than the wars which were waged among her numerous states. They were frequent, and some of them lasted many years. Yet one justifiably thinks of the fifteenth

*Italian warfare in the fifteenth century*

century as one of the most splendid periods in the history of Italy, and that because of her material prosperity as well as her intellectual and artistic achievements. The solution of the paradox is that the fighting was nearly all done by mercenary armies, which, though composed mainly of Italians, seldom felt any personal ardour for their cause. The professional captains who led them were sometimes good strategists, and generally skilled tacticians. They would try to win, because defeat would lower their market value, but they did not want to beat the enemy too much. He was in the same trade, and cut-throat competition was bad for every one in the long run. Besides, a war soon ended might mean unemployment for a long spell; it was far better to make it last, giving your employers just enough success to make them expect decisive victory in the near future. It was naturally more profitable to capture your enemies than to kill them; but best of all was victory without any fighting whatever, for in that case you kept your men—your stock-in-trade—intact. So, if in smaller numbers, you clung to impregnable positions; if you were in superior force, you manœuvred the foe out of the territory you wished to occupy. A victorious campaign of that sort was far more becoming than one of those bloody brawls which were called battles beyond the Alps. And at every turn, of course, you did the minimum for your pay. The mercenary captains, wrote Machiavelli in a famous passage,

"used every art to lessen fatigue and danger to themselves and their soldiers, not killing in the fray, but taking prisoners without exchange of blows. They did not attack towns at night, nor did the garrisons of the towns attack encampments at night; they did not stockade or entrench a camp, nor did they conduct campaigns in winter. All these things were sanctioned by their rules of war, and devised by them, as I have said, to avoid fatigue and peril; and thereby they have brought Italy to slavery and shame."

Elsewhere he tells of a great battle in which three men lost their lives by being suffocated in a muddy ditch; and another author says that at the battle of Molinella in 1467 armies numbering in all some 20,000 combatants fought for several hours with a total of three hundred casualties. Furthermore, there was little plunder and ravaging; a captain who allowed it would soon be " resting "; besides, it was obvious folly to kill the geese that laid the golden eggs. So, while Milan,

Florence, or Venice waged war year after year, the citizens of those states carried on business as usual.

It was not merely that the wars were conducted according to a code peculiar to the professionals concerned in them; when fighting did take place, the combatants followed oldfashioned tactics. The armies consisted almost wholly of cavalry. Time was when the civic militia of Italian cities, fighting on foot, had acquitted themselves well against the Hohenstaufen emperors; but as wars became longer and more frequent, and as wealth increased, the burghers very reasonably evaded military service whenever they could. When the city fell under the rule of a despot, he naturally approved of this aversion from martial activity. It thus came about that by the beginning of the fifteenth century, the employment of the civic militia was almost obsolete, and when it was revived the result was commonly disastrous. As long as foreign mercenaries were used, the tactics in vogue beyond the Alps affected warfare in Italy. The famous English captain, John Hawkwood, had a force of archers who fought on foot, and both he and the French commanders, who were numerous in fourteenth-century Italy, often dismounted their men-at-arms in battle. But when Italians took up the military trade, they ignored infantry altogether. For one thing, it is necessary to have large numbers of footsoldiers if they are to be of much use. They have to be very carefully and effectively trained if they are to withstand cavalry charges. Further, you can make a brave show with comparatively few mounted men, and obviously it is more comfortable to go campaigning on horseback, besides being much safer in days when a man-at-arms in full armour was nearly invulnerable. So there was a tacit understanding among the Italian captains that, whatever rumours might reach them of the doings of Englishmen, Swiss, Czechs, or Turks, they would uphold the dignity of a chivalrous profession.

Machiavelli and other Italians of a later time, echoed by most modern historians, have treated the wars of fifteenthcentury Italy with great ridicule. Yet there is much to be said in their favour. Such warfare was not a bad method of settling disputes between states. In modern war, it has been urged, no one can win; in Italian war of the later Middle

Ages, it was seldom that anyone lost. A defeated cause would almost certainly be protected from ruin by its conquerors. Yet the vanquished, mourning the vain expenditure of some thousands of ducats and (it might be) the surrender of a few square miles of territory, could soothe their pride with the reflection that it was the fortune of war and that honour at any rate had been saved. So far as can be judged, if the people of Italy had all been subject to conscription and if (like the trans-Alpine barbarians) they had fought to kill, the relative positions of the different states at the end of the fifteenth century would have been very much as they actually were. But, absolutely, the lot of Italy would have been piteous.

*Weakness of Italy in relation to other countries*

That the professional soldiers brought Italy, as Machiavelli alleged, to " slavery and shame " was due to the fact that she was not inaccessible. Like a debased coinage or an inflated paper currency, a military system based on conventions will lead to disaster as soon as those who have adopted it have dealings with foreigners. The Italians might despise the other peoples of Europe as barbarous; but their military science availed them nothing against warriors who charged home with lance and pike, and would even kill a fleeing foe. Even their over-estimated diplomacy was of little service when everyone was aware that there was no force at its back. And, for that matter, there was not much to choose between Italian diplomacy and any other in point of skill. What distinguished the politicians of Italy was rather an utter lack of scruple such as rarely appeared among other peoples. The rules of chivalry were much in men's mouths in northern Europe, and though it is true that, the more they were talked of, the less they were followed, there were still some things from which most statesmen north of the Alps would shrink. But it would be hard to find any prominent politician in Italy during the fifteenth century who ever allowed considerations of morality or honour to influence his conduct of public affairs. The reputation which the Italians gained for remorseless duplicity explains in great measure the dislike and contempt which were shown towards them by the peoples who invaded their country.

To understand the history of Italy in the century after 1378, it must be grasped that the Middle Ages ended there much earlier than elsewhere in Europe. Italy, indeed, had never been so thoroughly medievalized as France, Germany or Spain. She had never accepted the ideals of the Holy Roman Empire with any enthusiasm, and had been the first land to rebel openly against them. Feudalism had never flourished in Italy, Naples being the only state where it really took root, and there it was always an exotic growth with peculiar features derived from the soil and climate to which it had been transplanted. The characteristic learning of the Middle Ages, Scholasticism, was a product of France rather than of Italy, and if the greatest schoolman of them all, Thomas Aquinas, was an Italian, it was at Paris that he acquired his knowledge and made his name. Similarly, Gothic architecture, the greatest artistic achievement of medieval times, was French in origin, and though it spread to Italy, the Italians never took to it kindly. Even the Roman Church, as a religious institution, lost its hold on Italy sooner than elsewhere. By the end of the fourteenth century the Pope's spiritual authority counted for nothing in Italian politics. The influence of the Ancient World had always been more vital in Italy than anywhere else except the Byzantine Empire; in the fourteenth and fifteenth centuries it was increased through the Humanists. Classical ideas and standards partly replaced the feeble precepts and principles of medieval religion and culture, but many Italians plunged forward without any guide, classical or medieval, save their own tastes and passions. Historians point out with superfluous iteration that there are no sharp dividing lines between one period and another, but they are prone to forget that different countries do not advance abreast, that one may have emerged from the Middle Ages while another is still marching through and a third has scarcely entered them.

It luckily happens that the year 1878 was a really important one for Italy. It presented the Italians with several weighty questions, the answers to which were quite uncertain. In the first place, would the Papacy remain in Rome? The answer, as we have seen above, was unexpected. Italy was again to be the seat of the Papacy, but it was many years before the Popes could resume their place in the front rank of Italian temporal potentates.

Secondly, what would be the outcome of the war between

**The war of Venice and Genoa**

Venice and Genoa which was just beginning? The repeated conflicts between these inveterate rivals had hitherto been indecisive, the balance of advantage inclining slightly towards Genoa. In the new struggle, Venice was nearly captured, but the besieging force was itself besieged in Chioggia, and in 1381 the war ended with the complete defeat of the Genoese. Genoa ceased to belong to the first class of Italian powers; a few years later she was fain to sacrifice her independence. But Venice, too, suffered through the war. She lost her possessions on the Italian mainland; in her attempts, perfectly reasonable, to get them back, she succumbed to the lure of territorial expansion, with consequences most fateful to all Italy. Further, having now the whip hand of the Genoese at sea and in the Levant, she was perhaps disposed to relax her energy and alertness in those spheres, as though her interests would now take care of themselves.

**Milan**

Another problem of great interest was furnished by the death in 1378 of Galeazzo Visconti, who had shared the rule of Milan with his brother, Bernabo. Would the family split into two lines? If so, there would be an end of Milan as a first-rate force in Italian affairs. The problem was solved in 1385 by Galeazzo's son, Gian Galeazzo, who had been quietly ruling his share of Milanese territory from its centre at Pavia. Gian Galeazzo trapped his uncle, murdered him, and assumed the rule of the whole duchy.

**Florence**

Further, would the long dominant oligarchy continue to direct the fortunes of Florence? That republic had an extraordinarily complicated constitution, which placed all power in the hands of the *popolo grasso*, the members of the seven greater gilds—the cloth-merchants, weavers, bankers, silk-manufacturers, physicians, furriers, and lawyers. The government, in short, was a plutocracy. To make matters worse, it had become a monopoly not merely of the rich, but of a faction of the rich, known as the Albizzi, from the name of the family which dominated it. In 1378 an attempt to change the constitution, headed by Salvestro de' Medici, who belonged to the rival faction of the Ricci, was met with a resistance which provoked a rising of the Florentine mob. The government was reorganized on a much more democratic basis. The Medici family soon withdrew from active politics, perhaps alarmed at the upheaval Salvestro had occasioned; but to the popular mind of Florence they were henceforth the natural leaders of the poor and unprivileged. Their withdrawal at this juncture was well timed, for it was not long before the misgovernment of the new administrators provoked a reaction. In 1382 the old oligarchy was restored; at first it was a little wider than it had been before the crisis, but within a few years a series of constitutional changes made it narrower than ever.

From his *coup d'état* in 1385 to the end of the century the dominating figure in Italian politics was Gian Galeazzo of Milan. His object was to make a kingdom for himself in north Italy. It is noteworthy that the unification of the whole country was apparently beyond the wildest dreams of any Italian of these times. But Gian Galeazzo came within measurable distance of his limited objective. Circumstances were favourable. Naples was distracted by the feuds of the rival branches of the House of Anjou.[1] The Roman Pope's attention was largely claimed by the Schism, and, especially after the marriage of Gian Galeazzo's daughter Valentina to Louis of Touraine in 1387, he was terrified lest Milan should go over to the side of Avignon. Wenzel, the Emperor-elect, was for various reasons disposed to be friendly; indeed, in 1395 he bestowed on Gian Galeazzo the title of Duke of Milan, therefore giving the Visconti a legal right to the position they had held for generations.

Gian Galeazzo allied with Francesco Carrara, lord of Padua, to overthrow Antonio della Scala, head of the famous family which had long ruled Verona and Vicenza. Then he made war on Carrara in alliance with Venice, which thus got back Treviso and the approaches to the Alpine passes whereby its precious trade with Germany was conducted. Gian Galeazzo had contrived by various means to terrorize, disarm, or conciliate all other states in northern Italy. Next he turned against Florence, with which he was at war from 1390 to 1392. It is notable that he relied mainly on Italian generals and troops, whom the Florentines confronted with the Count of Armagnac, in command of a French force, and the great John Hawkwood, renowned not merely for his military skill but even more for his fidelity to his employers. Before the military operations had produced decisive results a revolution

[1] On the course and results of these, see Chapter V above.

in Padua upset Gian Galeazzo's schemes, and he agreed to a treaty wherein each party promised not to interfere in the other's sphere of influence. But in the next few years, by means of diplomacy and intrigue, he strove to isolate and encircle Florence. He got possession of Pisa, Perugia, Siena, and other places, while Genoa only escaped by putting herself under the protection of Charles VI of France. The Florentines hoped for much from the expedition of Rupert, King of the Romans; but when in 1401 Gian Galeazzo defeated him and followed up this success by capturing their ally Bologna, they fell into despair. Then came the unexpected news of Gian Galeazzo's death, which happened in September 1402. The Visconti family underwent an eclipse, and never afterwards attained the heights to which Gian Galeazzo had raised it.

*Decline of Milan after Gian Galeazzo's death, 1402*

The death of the great Duke of Milan was followed by some twenty years in which Florence and Venice took advantage of the disintegration of the territories of Milan. By allying with Gian Galeazzo's widow, who had been named by him as regent but was beset by enemies domestic and foreign, Venice got possession of north-east Italy as far as the river Adige. Next she was involved in a long war with Sigismund, King of the Romans, whereby she gained Friuli and nearly the whole of the coast of Dalmatia. Meanwhile, in 1406, Florence had conquered Pisa, her ancient enemy. She had been at war with Ladislas of Naples[1]—a conflict closely connected with the papal Schism—and had got Cortona out of it. In 1421 she bought Leghorn from the decadent Genoa.

While these things were happening, one of Gian Galeazzo's sons, the cowardly and crafty Filippo Maria, had contrived, by treachery, diplomacy, or force, to reunite under his rule all his father's lands from Piedmont to the Adige. Presently he turned against Florence, which was soon hard pressed and begged aid from Venice. Now it was obvious that Filippo Maria, if victorious over Florence, would next try to recover what had been seized from his father's territories by Venice. On the other hand, if Venice was to dispute the leadership of northern Italy with Milan, she could hardly hope to maintain her commercial ascendancy in the eastern Mediterranean, still

*Triumph of militarist party in Venice, 1425*

---

[1] Ladislas, like Gian Galeazzo, had tried to conquer central Italy. For his doings and ambitions, see Chapters V and XVII above.

less to hold her overseas possessions against the Turks. At the moment, Venice stood at a crisis of her fortunes. She was rich, powerful, and respected. Her far-spread trade was flourishing, her splendidly organized industries were still progressing. Her oligarchic institutions were well adapted to a persistent, shrewd, safe policy. They ensured for her a sound steady government, and her long immunity from violent revolution filled the rest of Italy with admiration. If, however, she embraced a policy of aggrandisement at the expense of her Italian neighbours, flattering envy would be turned into a jealous malice such as no other state provoked. The question split Venice into two parties. One was for continental aggression, urging that the present frontier was useless, and that unless Venice pressed forward she would lose all her possessions on the mainland. That, indeed, was a contingency which the other side would not countenance, but it contended that it was possible for Venice to retain what land she needed to protect her Alpine communications and no more, and that she should devote her main strength to upholding her maritime and commercial interests. But the militarists, headed by the Doge Francesco Foscari, had their way; in 1425 Venice joined Florence against Filippo Maria Visconti. At first the war went very well for her; but after a brief interval of peace fortune changed, and the renewed conflict dragged on for year after year without any decisive events. The truth was that neither party could trust its *condottieri* generals. Venice, whose wars had mostly been fought at sea by her citizens, was less accustomed to the little ways of the *condottieri* and less disposed to tolerate them. In 1432 her authorities caused a tremendous sensation by executing Carmagnola, the most famous captain of his time, for treachery. But the Venetians were ready to profit by the treachery of others, and it was the betrayal of his Milanese employer's interests in 1441 by Francesco Sforza that enabled Venice to emerge from the war with the river Adda as her western frontier. But as she had not gained a foot of land since 1428, she had little cause for satisfaction, and, for that matter, it was not long before hostilities again broke out. The ensuing events are very hard to understand, and luckily there is little need to dwell upon them. Milan, Venice, Florence, and the Papacy, besides some minor

Tortuous policy of Francesco Sforza

powers, were involved in the war, which became extremely confused through the tergiversations of Sforza, who, though the son-in-law of Filippo Maria Visconti, was seldom on good terms with him and was working to secure the succession to Milan, if not to supplant the Duke in his lifetime. When, in 1447, Filippo Maria opportunely died, Sforza happened to be well situated for achieving his ambition.

<small>The Papacy and the States of the Church</small>

Meanwhile, the conditions under which Italian diplomatists had to work had been greatly altered through occurrences farther south. Martin V had restored papal authority in the States of the Church, giving them such law and order as had not been known there for generations and beginning the establishment of a centralized administration. It is true that the folly and misfortunes of Eugenius IV undid much of what Martin had accomplished. Venice laid hands on Ravenna; Milan encroached on the Romagna; Eugenius was forced to flee from Rome itself. The city was soon recovered for the Pope, but when peace was signed between Eugenius and his enemies in 1441, the Romagna was in revolt against him, and the march of Ancona was held by Sforza. However, Eugenius, having now got the better of the Council of Basel, was very formidable when soon afterwards he resumed his efforts to recover all his lost territories. There is no need to trace his political fortunes in the next years. It is enough to note that by 1447 the Papacy had got back Ancona. It was henceforth one of the great Powers of Italy.

In Naples there had likewise been momentous changes. King Ladislas, the arch-enemy of John XXIII, had left no legitimate issue. He was succeeded by his sister, Joanna II, a woman of exceptionally unbridled lasciviousness. She was childless, and there were numerous candidates for recognition as her heir. For many years much additional confusion was caused in the kingdom by the rivalries of the *condottieri* Braccio da Montone and Attendolo Sforza. The latter, with the encouragement of Pope Martin V, declared himself an advocate of the claims of Louis III of Anjou; but the Queen adopted as her son Alfonso, King of Aragon and Sicily. Alfonso's military operations, however, were not very successful, and he fell out with his adoptive mother, who consequently bestowed her favour on Louis of Anjou. When he died in 1434, she transferred his rights to his more famous

<small>Naples conquered by Alfonso V of Aragon</small>

brother René. Joanna herself died in 1435, and Alfonso of Aragon now reasserted the ancient claim of his House with much vigour. At first fortune was unfriendly to him; he was severely defeated in a naval action and taken prisoner by the Genoese allies of his rival. But he came into the hands of Filippo Maria Visconti, suzerain of Genoa, and won him over to the view that it would be advantageous for Milan to have the Aragonese in Naples rather than the French. After his release, the cause of Alfonso prospered, and in 1442 he entered the city of Naples and was recognized as king, thus restoring the unity of the old kingdom of the Normans and the Hohenstaufen after it had been split into two for 160 years. Alfonso, a great lover of pomp and splendour, an enthusiastic and discriminating patron of art and letters, and withal a highly capable and unscrupulous politician, identified himself entirely with his new kingdom, where he spent nearly all his time until his death in 1458. The House of Anjou gave him no more serious trouble, but it must not be supposed that it had abandoned its claims.

During the second quarter of the fifteenth century there had also been notable changes at Florence, though outwardly her position had altered little since the beginning of her wars with Filippo Maria. The very narrow oligarchy that ruled the city at the opening of the century, though selfish and corrupt, provided tolerable government, and, as we have seen, made additions to Florentine territory. As long as it was successful, its continuance was assured. But though there was little political agitation in Florence, the populace still thought of the Medici family as their leaders. From about 1410 onwards a certain Giovanni de' Medici was reputed to be at the head of the opposition to the Albizzi. He was a banker and very rich. It seems certain that, using his wealth adroitly, he became what might be called a political "boss," but he was very cautious and had done nothing overtly against the existing order when he died in 1429.

By this time the Albizzi were much discredited owing to their ill-success in a costly war. To recover their prestige they organized an unwarranted attack on the coveted city of Lucca; and on its failure, the military plight of Florence became worse than ever. A son of Giovanni de' Medici, Cosimo, now openly appeared as an opponent of the Albizzi.

*Florence: rise of the Medici family*

But their hold on the political machine was still strong, and they were able to bring about the exile of Cosimo and his brother Lorenzo. Unfortunately for the Albizzi, further military misfortunes befell Florence. In 1434 they were overthrown by a rising of the exasperated populace; Cosimo returned, and seized the opportunity to get a grasp of the government which he never relaxed.

*Florence controlled by Cosimo de' Medici, 1434-64* The government of Florence by the Medici is one of the most memorable examples of political make-believe. It was founded on "graft," graft so extensive and so efficient as to become respectable. The comical constitution of Florence continued to function. Cosimo, it is true, made great use of certain devices which had been designed for special emergencies; but he was not breaking the law in so doing. Never was a dictatorship so carefully veiled. Cosimo did not hold any permanent magistracy, like the early Roman Emperors; nor did he, like Pericles, secure election year after year to some dominant public office. He lived and behaved like a private citizen, avoiding not merely all pomp but also any ostentatious display of his wealth. But that wealth he used with great judgment. He surrounded himself with a large body of adherents, taking care to choose them from every class of society, so that the government of the city appeared more democratic than it had been. The elections of State officials were of course carefully manipulated by Cosimo, though as a rule the dirty work was actually done by others. Cosimo cultivated a reputation for mildness, but in reality he was very severe towards his opponents. They were mercilessly taxed; many were banished, and were not free from persecution even in exile, for Cosimo's money gave him great influence throughout Italy and in some states outside. As a banker, Cosimo naturally disliked disorder and war, and the Medici were generally a pacific influence in Italian affairs.

*The succession to Milan, 1447* On the death of Filippo Maria Visconti in 1447, the future of Milan aroused much concern throughout Italy. There were three claimants to the succession. In the first place there was Sforza, the husband of Filippo Maria's daughter Bianca. Other considerations apart, there was the obvious objection that she was illegitimate. Charles, Duke of Orléans, claimed through his mother Valentina, Filippo Maria's sister. A third candidate was Frederick, King of the Romans, whose claim was derived from his grandmother Virida, daughter of Bernabo Visconti, whom Gian Galeazzo had removed in 1385. But as Wenzel, when creating the duchy, had limited it to heirs in the male line, none of these claims was worth much. Frederick III, indeed, asserted that he was entitled to dispose of Milan as an escheated imperial fief—a contention probably sound in law though unenforceable in practice. The people of Milan, who also argued that the ducal authority had lapsed, proclaimed a republic. Though Sforza was on the spot, his plans might have been frustrated but for the folly of Venice. There the party in favour of territorial expansion had lately been under a cloud; they were eager to retrieve their reputation, and the young Milanese republic seemed fair game. But when they attacked it, the Milanese were driven to seek the aid of Sforza, who repelled the Venetians without much difficulty. The Venetian authorities then offered to leave him a free hand in return for the cession of some Milanese territory. Sforza next turned against the republic of Milan, and in 1450 the helpless citizens were fain to accept him as duke. This result the Venetians, strange to say, had not anticipated; they saw that as Duke of Milan Sforza would be a more formidable obstacle to their ambitions than even the Visconti had been, and, regardless of their recent bargain, they attacked him. Again they were defeated, and the news of the capture of Constantinople increased their eagerness to get out of the entanglement. They were lucky, when peace was signed at Lodi in 1454, to be allowed to retain what they had held at the death of Filippo Maria. The failure of Venice in her dealings with Sforza led to the enforced abdication of the old doge Foscari, who for thirty years had been the leading exponent of that policy of territorial aggrandizement which had won her so little and caused her to neglect her threatened interests in the East. These almost monopolized her attention during the twenty-five years that followed the Peace of Lodi. From 1462 to 1479 she was engaged in the first of her great wars against the Turks, from which she emerged, not without honour, but sorely injured.

Francesco Sforza forbore to take advantage of the preoccupations of Venice. Once he was duke, in fact, it became his object to maintain peace. He had long been on good terms with Cosimo de' Medici. With Alfonso of Naples he

*Francesco Sforza established as Duke of Milan, 1450*

*Venice at war with the Turks, 1462-79*

*Policy of Francesco Sforza*

made an alliance, cemented by a marriage between his daughter and Alfonso's grandson. Sforza had formerly been a supporter of the Angevin party in Naples, but the claim of the Duke of Orléans to Milan made him anxious to keep the French altogether out of Italy. This he had of course to do without exasperating them. He was thus in a difficult position when in 1460 Naples was invaded by John of Calabria, son of René of Anjou. But Louis XI, who became King of France next year, was himself opposed to the aggrandizement of the Angevins; and relations between him and Sforza, which had long been friendly, were for some time very close. Louis indeed surrendered to Sforza the French claims to Genoa, which had been tossed about between France and Milan for three-quarters of a century.

For many years Italian inter-state politics turned on the maintenance of the triple alliance between Milan, Florence, and Naples. On the death of King Alfonso in 1458, Naples passed under his will to his bastard son Ferrante; having acquired the kingdom himself, he claimed the right to dispose of it as he wished; but Aragon and Sicily, which he had inherited, went according to law to his brother John. Ferrante's accession was soon followed by the expedition of John of Calabria, mentioned above. The Angevins received a good deal of support in the invaded kingdom, but Ferrante gradually got the upper hand, and in 1464 John went home. Ferrante enjoyed a period of security, during which he ruled with the cruel unscrupulousness that he had shown before John's attack. He did nothing, however, to imperil the alliance with Florence and Milan.

<small>Angevin invasion of Naples, 1460–4</small>

Cosimo de' Medici, the most influential wire-puller in Italian politics, died in 1464. Six years previously his hold on Florence had been strengthened by a stroke of sharp practice which historians have sometimes unwarrantably called a revolution. He had characteristically kept out of sight, and it is possible that this shrinking from publicity led some of his more conspicuous subordinates into the belief that they might supplant him. There was certainly in his later years some disaffection smouldering among his followers. Cosimo, who doubtless was aware of their feelings, could afford to ignore them. But when his son Piero tried to step into his shoes, the malcontents deemed themselves strong enough to move. At first they sought to set Piero aside by constitutional means, but being at variance among themselves as to their ultimate aims, they made small progress. They therefore turned to Venice, which was much embarrassed by the triple alliance and welcomed a chance of rupturing it. A plot was formed for the removal of Piero, which was to be followed by the military intervention of Venice in behalf of the conspirators. But Piero had enough hold on the populace of Florence to foil the plotters by means which kept on the windy side of the law, and most of the ringleaders were exiled. In the next year they tried to return with the aid of *condottieri* paid by Venice and one or two petty princes, but were worsted by the forces of Florence and her allies in a campaign which was a classic example of the artificiality of Italian warfare. The Medici were firmly seated in power again, and when in 1469 Piero died, his son Lorenzo was invited by the leading citizens of Florence to succeed him. *(Unsuccessful plot against the Medici, 1466)*

Lorenzo, as his familiar title "the Magnificent" implies, threw off much of the pretence that had been maintained by Cosimo and Piero. He had a cultivated and luxurious court. He excelled his predecessors and all contemporary potentates as a patron of art and letters. Changes in form and practice were accompanied by changes in law which for ten years deprived the people of control over legislation and narrowed the circle associated with the Medici family in working the government. With few exceptions the people of Florence seemed content. *(Lorenzo the Magnificent in power at Florence, 1469-92)*

After a short spell of power, Lorenzo became over-confident, and tried experiments in foreign policy. He sought to establish friendly relations with Venice and the Papacy, believing that if they were favourable to the Medici, he might make himself the arbiter of Italy. He managed for a while to win the good graces of Pope Sixtus IV, and in 1474 he arranged with Venice an alliance in which Milan also participated. This alarmed Ferrante of Naples, who greatly feared Venice as a rival to himself in the Adriatic. He had for some time been on good terms with the Pope, and he soon turned Sixtus against Lorenzo, the more readily since the Medici had shown some concern at certain schemes of the Pope's for the aggrandizement of his family in central Italy. *(Indiscreet policy of Lorenzo)*

At this juncture the enemies of the Medici were encouraged

by conditions in Milan. Francesco Sforza died in 1466, and was succeeded by his son Galeazzo Maria. Except that he allied himself for some years with Charles the Bold of Burgundy, Galeazzo Maria followed the main lines of his father's policy. Nevertheless, he was far more unpopular than Francesco, for like so many of his ancestors of the Visconti family, he was extremely licentious and cruel. These characteristics led to his murder in 1476, and though, after some confusion, the succession was secured for his son Gian Galeazzo, a boy of eight for whom his mother acted as regent, the new government was not very stable. It could not be expected to do much for the allies of Milan.

The Florentine malcontents, headed by the Pazzi family, and the kinsmen of Sixtus IV resolved to seize the opportunity. Both the Pope and the King of Naples connived at their doings. They were to begin by the murder of Lorenzo de' Medici and his brother Giuliano. The two were set upon one Sunday in Florence Cathedral by hired assassins and some of the conspirators. Giuliano was killed, but Lorenzo, though wounded, just managed to escape. An attempt to seize the civic magistrates was foiled, and the populace rose against the plotters, several of whom were lynched. In Florence itself Lorenzo was now more secure than ever. But he was attacked openly by the Pope and the King of Naples, angry at having failed and been found out. He received aid from Milan and Venice, but the territory of Florence was invaded, Ferrante stirred up a revolution in Milan, Venice just then suffered serious reverses in her war with the Turks. The city of Florence seemed likely to fall when Lorenzo, to the admiring amazement of Italy, went in person to Naples, and somehow managed to negotiate a peace, which was signed in 1480. Florence, of course, had to pay a price, losing some of her territory, mainly to the advantage of Siena ; but Lorenzo's position was saved. The Pope was chagrined at the turn of events and disposed to carry on the conflict, but at this juncture a force of Turks captured Otranto and he had to give his attention to larger issues than the advancement of his kinsfolk.

Lorenzo's escape from ruin was followed at Florence by constitutional changes of an extremely complicated character. Broadly, it may be said that, while the old republican machinery, slightly remodelled, continued to give occupation and pleasure to those who were chosen to make its wheels go round, it was now supplemented by new administrative dynamos which, under the control of the Medici, supplied all the driving force of the State. Until his death in 1492, Lorenzo's hold on the government of Florence was never so much as threatened.

In the meantime Italian politics had been further compli- *Schemes of Ludovico Sforza in Milan* cated by occurrences in Milan and by the release of Venice from the burden imposed on her by the long war with the Turks. The regency of Bona of Savoy, mother of Gian Galeazzo Sforza, had been resented by the late Duke's brothers, whom she had exiled. When Ferrante of Naples was at war with Florence, he aided their schemes, with the result that the eldest, Ludovico called Il Moro, overthrew the existing government, secured a complete ascendancy over his nephew, had him proclaimed of age, and, in fact if not in name, governed for him. For some time he remained friendly with Ferrante, and the young Duke was married to the King's granddaughter. Ludovico ruled Milan firmly but with moderation, and was not unpopular. Nevertheless, he was obviously cast for the part of wicked uncle, and indeed the inevitable suspicions were warranted by his intentions. But he knew well that the King of Naples would attack him if any misfortune befell Gian Galeazzo, whose young duchess, Isabella, actually complained to her parents of the disrespect which was shown by Ludovico towards her and her husband. Thus the friendship between Ludovico and Ferrante began to cool rapidly.

The situation was fraught with peril for Italy. And, to *New war provoked by Venice, 1482* make things worse, the government of Venice, its self-respect and reputation much impaired by the outcome of the Turkish war, looked for compensation near home. In alliance with Sixtus IV, it attacked the Este family, which ruled Ferrara, and in 1482 seized Rovigo and other places. To frustrate this act of brigandage—for it deserves no better name—the old league of Milan, Florence, and Naples was revived. In the interests of Italy as a whole, this was an excellent thing. Its immediate effect, too, was good; for Neapolitan troops having invaded the Papal States and gone to the rescue of Ferrara, Pope Sixtus immediately threw Venice over, so that she was constrained to make peace. But here appeared the influence of the ambitions of Ludovico Sforza, who, not wishing to weaken the chief rival of Naples, allowed Venice to escape with very favourable terms, including the retention of Rovigo. Naturally, the triple alliance had no health in it thereafter.

Ferrante of Naples now had a great many enemies. For the hostility felt towards him by Milan, Venice, and the Papacy he was in no wise to blame. But it was his increasing caprice and cruelty that provoked the rising of Neapolitan nobles which broke out in 1485. The rebels were encouraged by Pope Innocent VIII and the Venetians, and they promised René, Duke of Lorraine, their support if he would go to Naples in pursuance of the Angevin title to the crown. Florence and Milan let it be known that they would oppose René, who did nothing; and the movement failed. Ferrante, however, had been seriously scared: he agreed to restore the old tribute due from Naples to the Papacy—it had been remitted by Sixtus IV —and to grant an amnesty to the insurgents. The latter undertaking he broke, and rebel leaders who returned to the country were put to death. A number, however, had discreetly remained in exile.

*Rising in Naples, 1485*

In 1492 came the death of Lorenzo the Magnificent. He had recovered for Florence most of what she had lost in 1480, and at his death his reputation stood very high both at home and abroad. To the end, though with ever-increasing difficulty, he had managed to avert an open breach between Milan and Naples. But his son Piero, who was generally regarded as the inevitable heir to his power, was a foolish young man. He abandoned the pretences whereby even Lorenzo had somewhat disguised the nature of his influence, and annoyed all classes in Florence by his arrogance and ostentation. What was still more fatal in its effects, he gave up the mediating rôle of Lorenzo and was soon manifestly hand-in-glove with Ferrante. Ludovico Sforza, still awaiting his opportunity, saw with consternation the rise of a new obstacle to the attainment of his ambitions. Naples alone he might perhaps have defied; but Naples and Florence together would certainly overpower him.

*Lorenzo succeeded by Piero de' Medici, 1492*

Such was the political situation when in 1493 the exiled Neapolitan nobles resolved to strike a new blow. They consulted the friendly Venetian government, and accepted the

*Charles VIII of France invited to Italy, 1493*

advice to call in Charles VIII of France, inheritor of the Angevin claim to Naples. Ludovico Sforza, hearing what was afoot, sent to France an embassy in support of their invitation, calculating that even if Ferrante were not overthrown, he would for long have no leisure to interfere in Milan. Of course, neither Ludovico nor the Venetians realized what they were doing. Foreigners, especially Frenchmen, had often been summoned to Italy before. It was only some fifty years since a Spaniard had ousted the head of a French dynasty from Naples : why should the rest of Italy be shocked if a French king drove out the Spaniard's son? Besides, most expeditions from abroad had accomplished little, even those which had been organized and backed by the French Crown. After all, Ferrante of Naples was strong, he was allied with Florence and with the new Pope, Alexander VI; even if worsted he would probably offer such resistance that the French would have no energy left to molest anyone else. Clearly, Ludovico did not expect them to support the Orléans claim to Milan. Venice perhaps thought and hoped that they would, and trusted that she might exact a good price from one side or the other for her support. She proved more far-seeing than Ludovico ; but neither anticipated the turn which events actually took. To do so would have required superhuman prescience.

Some authorities for chapter xix :—
i. Original sources—
   Aeneas Sylvius Piccolomini : *Commentarii rerum memorabilium quae temporibus suis contigerunt*. (With continuation by Cardinal Ammannati.) Repeatedly published, and trans. into English by F. A. Gragg. (*Northampton, Mass. : Smith College Studies in History*, vol. xxii, nos. 1–2 ; vol. xxv, nos. 1–4 [1939–40].)
   Beccadelli, Antonio, called Panormita : *De dictis et factis Alphonsi regis Aragonum libri 4*. Repeatedly published, though not since the eighteenth century.
   Bisticci, Vespasiano da : *Vite di uomini illustri del secolo xv*, ed. L. Frati, 3 vols., Bologna, 1892–3. English translation by W. G. and Emily Waters, London, 1926.
   Bracciolini, Poggio : *Historia Florentina*, in Muratori, *Scriptores rerum Italicarum*, vol. xx, Milan, 1731.
   Bruni, Leonardo, called Aretino : *Historiarum Florentini populi libri xii*, in *Script. rer. Ital.*, new edition, vol. xix, pt. 3, Città di Castello, 1914 ; *Rerum in Italia suo tempore gestarum commentarius*, ed. Carmine Di Pierro, in *Script. rer. Ital.*, new edition, vol. xix, pt. 3, 1914.
   Burchardus, Joannes : *Liber notarum*, in *Script. rer. Ital.*, new edition, vol. xxxii, pt. 1, Città di Castello, 1906. Also ed. L. Thusasne, Paris, 1883.

Infessura, Stefano: *Diario della Città di Roma*, ed. O. Tommasini, Rome, 1890.
Jacobus Volaterranus: *Diarium Romanum*, in *Script rer. Ital.*, new edition, vol. xxiii, pt. 3, Città di Castello, 1904.
Machiavelli, Niccolo: *Istorie Florentine*. Many editions. English trans. Everyman's Library, London, 1909. *Libro del Principe*. Many times printed and often translated into English.
Sigismondo dei Conti da Foligno: *Historia suorum temporum*, 2 vols., Rome, 1883.

ii. Modern works—

*Cambridge Medieval History*, vol. vii, chaps. i, ii ; vol. viii, chaps. v, vi.
Ady, Cecilia M.: *History of Milan under the Sforza*, London, 1908.
Ady, Cecilia M.: *The Bentivoglio of Bologna: a study in despotism*, Oxford, 1937.
Armstrong, E.: *Lorenzo de' Medici* (Heroes of the Nations), New York, 1896.
Horsburgh, E. L. S.: *Lorenzo the Magnificent and Florence in her Golden Age*, London, 1908.
Hutton, E.: *Sigismondo Pandolfo Malatesta, Lord of Rimini*, London, 1906.
Mesquita, D. M. Bueno de: *Giangaleazzo Visconti, Duke of Milan (1351–1402). A study in the political career of an Italian despot.*
Renaudet: *Laurent le Magnifique* (Hommes d'Etat, ii, ed. A. B. Duff and F. Galy, Paris, 1936).
Temple-Leader, J. T., and Marcotti, G.: *Giovanni Acuto (Sir John Hawkwood)*, Florence, 1889. Trans. by Leader Scott, London, 1889.
Young, G. F.: *The Medici*, London, 1909.

CHAPTER XX

# THE PAPACY AND THE CHURCH IN THE LATTER PART OF THE FIFTEENTH CENTURY

WHEN surveying the history of the several countries of continental Europe during the latter half of the fifteenth century, we have from time to time had occasion to touch upon ecclesiastical affairs. But such hasty glances at the relations between the temporal and spiritual authorities or the attitude of the laity towards the clergy give one a very defective notion of the general condition of the Church; and this, in view of the sequel, is a topic of particular interest and importance to the student of the period.

The responsibility for the failure of the Conciliar Movement lay mainly, as we saw, with the Papacy. To accomplish many of the reforms which the conciliar party most urgently demanded it would have been necessary for the Papacy to surrender profitable rights which it had long enjoyed. Thus to the Roman *curia* reform and revolution became synonymous. From the end of the Council of Basel to the beginning of the Reformation nine Popes occupied the Holy See. They were of very various characters, attainments, and ambitions. None showed any zeal for reform, only one any consciousness of its desirability.

*Prospects of reform*

The advocates of constitutional government for the Church had been effectively worsted. There was still talk of summoning a new General Council : men with a grievance against the Papacy would still appeal to " a future Council " and contend that it was superior to a Pope. But in the latter half of the century there was never any likelihood that a Council would meet, nor was much heard of plans for curtailing the Pope's authority. Yet the desire for reform was on the whole as strong as before, and if for a time it was less vocal, that was probably because it was now felt more keenly by the laity than by the clergy. This situation was full of peril for the established authorities. They had won a great victory and believed it to have been decisive. The discontent being in great measure inarticulate, its extent and depth were under-estimated.

*Religious state of Europe in the latter part of fifteenth century*

There has been much inconclusive controversy about the condition of the Church in the half-century after the Council of Basel. Much trouble might have been saved if the contestants had always made clear what they meant by the word " church." Defenders of the old order have pointed out evidences of religious zeal and devotion in the Europe of those days. The Church still had her saints, and the bellicose fervour of Capistrano, who helped to hurl back the Turk from the walls of Belgrade, contrasts effectively with the relentless asceticism of Francis de Paul, who comforted the death-bed of Louis XI of France. The " Observant " Friars, who strove to revive the spirit and principles of St. Francis of Assisi, did something to restore the sadly impaired prestige of the Mendicant Orders. The Brethren of the Common Life, founded late in the fourteenth century by Gerhard Groot of Deventer in the Netherlands, were at the height of their influence and usefulness; their schools were to be found all over northern Germany, and they were training some of the most distinguished scholars of the German Renaissance. Pulpit eloquence was more popular than ever before; an evangelist, especially if he were not above a little sensationalism, could generally attract large and impressionable crowds. Religious revivals were as frequent as in modern America, and their effects no less lasting. Manuals of devotion, translations of Scripture, the legends of the saints, annotated texts of the Church's services, were apparently in much demand, to judge from the numbers of them that were produced by the novel printing-presses. Many of the laity were liberal as well as pious. If the endowment of monasteries was rare, a great deal of money was bestowed on the foundation or maintenance of schools. Gilds for religious and charitable purposes were exceedingly numerous; they endowed chantries, supported hospitals, gave alms, sometimes restored, enlarged, or even built churches. More questionable if equally well-established practices held their position in popular esteem. There was still great resort of pilgrims to famous shrines. Relics continued to be eagerly and credulously collected. The market for indulgences was as good as ever. Only one notable means of grace had lost its appeal. It was impossible to arouse any widespread enthusiasm for a crusade, even when such an undertaking seemed necessary to secure Christendom from ruin. Still, it is probably true that at the end of the fifteenth century there was rather more genuine concern for religion among the people of Europe than there had been a hundred years before.

It must not be inferred, however, that the Church had recovered that hold over men's minds which she had possessed in the twelfth and thirteenth centuries. There is nothing in the evidence regarding the religious state of Europe from 1450 to 1500 which lends colour to the view that the Protestant Reformation was the work of a few self-seekers and fanatics, who, with the support of certain greedy potentates, succeeded, partly by cajolery, partly by force, in imposing their opinions on large numbers of reluctant victims. So far from the existence of religious fervour proving that no change was desired, it was this very thing that rendered the success of the Reformation possible. A society which cared nothing for religion would have shrugged its shoulders at the appeal of a Luther or a Calvin. It must not be supposed, however, that devotion to spiritual things was common, or that, where it existed, it was usually deep.

A great deal of contemporary piety was merely conventional; much was indistinguishable from superstition. We have seen something of the spiritual life of Louis XI. Philip the Good, for all his treacherous dealings, his goodly company of bastards, his greed, ruthlessness, and wastefulness, passed for a most religious man, spending much of his time in church at prayer, and performing wonderful feats of fasting. The *condottiere* Montesecco, suborned by the kinsmen of Pope Sixtus IV to murder the Medici brothers, refused to commit the crime in a church. Pilgrimages were notoriously occasions for great licence. Regular attendance at church was compatible with gross irreverence during the services. The cult of the saints was so misunderstood and abused that some of the most thoughtful of the clergy, following in this the views of the great Gerson, encouraged their flocks to transfer their devotion to the angels, who, being less clearly individualized, were not so likely to become the subjects of silly and baseless legends. As for indulgences, while the official teaching of the Church still insisted that they remitted nothing but the temporal punishment for sin and while this doctrine was clearly stated in many popular handbooks of devotion, there is no doubt that the vast majority of the laity of western Europe thought that they were a means of purchasing forgiveness and that many of the clergy suffered them to remain under this delusion.

It is, furthermore, beyond question that there was a general hatred and contempt of the clergy. The revivalist preachers of the time could always win the interest and sympathy of their audiences by denouncing their fellow-ecclesiastics. And, without going beyond Catholic and contemporary testimony, there is ample evidence that popular feeling was in this respect well grounded. The evils that had flourished at the beginning of the century and had been denounced by such men as Nicolas de Clémanges, Dietrich of Niem, and the spokesmen of the reform party at Pisa and Constance were, taken in the gross, as potent as ever. And there was this difference in the situation: in 1400 men were eagerly planning and expecting reform; in 1500 the need of it was equally felt, but it had been attempted and failed. There were thus countless people ready to respond to the trumpet of rebellion when in the fullness of time it should be sounded.

*Policy of Nicolas V, 1447-55*

When the Council of Basel, or Lausanne, came to its inglorious end, the Pope was the recently-elected Nicolas V. It was naturally his desire that the victory which he had completed should be turned to the best advantage of the Papacy. He must, of course, evade the fulfilment of the promise to summon a new General Council. This presented no great difficulty, as neither the King of the Romans nor the King of France was eager to have one, while the reform party in the Church was discredited and disheartened. Politically, it was the desire of Nicolas to maintain peace. He upheld papal power in Italy, and strengthened his hold on the States of the Church. But he showed no great aptitude for diplomacy, and his efforts to reconcile Frederick III and the German princes were futile. Towards Bohemia he was unyielding, but there he was confronted by a spirit as stubborn as his own, and he found in the regent George of Podiebrad a politician who in cunning was actually a match for the papal envoy, Aeneas Sylvius. It was not, however, on such matters that the heart of Nicolas was really set. He was a scholar, a bibliophile, and a patron of learning. The Italian Renaissance was nearing its flood. The country swarmed with Humanists. Enthusiasm for classical antiquity was growing fast, and the moral and intellectual licence of the scholars and artists was causing grave concern among the more conservative. But though his mind might be utterly worldly, and his innermost convictions far more pagan than Christian, the Humanist scholar was seldom disposed to fall out with the authorities of the Church. From the Humanists of that day, Nicolas recognized, the Papacy itself had little to fear; the Conciliar Movement had derived none of its force from them. Still, the growth of a secular temper among scholars manifestly carried with it a certain danger to the Church. It would be well to obviate all risk. Why should not the friendliness of the Humanists towards the Papacy be active as well as passive? The Holy See might become the patron and protector of the Revival of Art and Learning: Rome might supplant Florence as the centre of the new enlightenment.

In trying to identify the Papacy with the Italian Renaissance, Nicolas was but following the traditions of his office. The dialectic of Abelard, regarded as subversive of the faith in his day, had afterwards been turned to the vindication of official orthodoxy. St. Francis had for some time been under suspicion of heresy; so had St. Thomas Aquinas; both had become conspicuous pillars of that edifice which was surmounted by the Papacy. There seemed to Nicolas no reason why the learning, acumen, and wit of a Poggio or a Valla should not be turned to the greater glory of the Roman Church. There were already Humanists in the papal service; Nicolas's patronage attracted many more to Rome, where not a few received posts in the *curia*, and others made a living by executing literary commissions for the Pope. Rome resounded with their verbose orations and their scurrilous quarrels. Nicolas permitted them great freedom and indeed licence. The foul-mouthed Poggio retained his favour even after he had published his *Facetiae*, a collection of the jokes exchanged between him and his colleagues in the papal Chancery. Nor did the Pope appear shocked by the notorious controversy between Poggio and Valla, although the methods and language used were considered unwarrantable by many of their fellows: indeed, it was to Nicolas that Valla addressed one of his most vituperative contributions to the brawl. It seems never to have occurred to the Pope that, even if he succeeded in harnessing the Renaissance, it might disregard the rein and run away, dragging the Papacy at its heels.

Nicolas patronized art as generously as letters. It was his wish to make Rome the most beautiful and magnificent of cities. The amount of building accomplished during his eight years' pontificate is amazing. He repaired the city walls and improved the defences of the castle of St. Angelo. Several churches were restored under his direction. The rebuilding of St. Peter's was begun. He added much to the Vatican, where he started the building of the library, of which he may fairly be called the founder. What astonished contemporaries was his interest in detail: everything built at his instance was decorated and furnished with the most scrupulous judgment, so that Nicolas had to surround himself not only with architects but also with painters and expert craftsmen of every kind. He had enlightened views on town-planning, and had he lived long would perhaps have transformed large areas of the city. What he did deserves admiration; but it is possibly just as well that his schemes were never fulfilled, for like many scholars of the time, he combined a theoretical enthusiasm for antiquity with a practical contempt for its productions, and many relics of ancient Rome—the Colosseum among them—were used as quarries for his new buildings. While it was of course in Rome that the traces of the Pope's architectural interests were most evident, he was responsible for much work—military, domestic, and religious—throughout the States of the Church.

The plans of Nicolas were on the whole proceeding to his satisfaction when there came the news of the fall of Constantinople. The Pope was not specially to blame; indeed he had sent a squadron of galleys to the aid of the threatened city. But he had hoped that his pontificate would go down to posterity as one of the most glorious, and now, he believed, men would remember him as the Pope in whose day the infidel captured New Rome. He proclaimed a crusade, and did what he could to stimulate the warlike ardour of the princes of Europe. They replied with mere words: and indeed it is probable that the heart of Nicolas himself was not in the business. But he saw that his policy for the exaltation of the Papacy to the leadership of art and letters must perforce be abandoned. To spend money on such things now would scandalize Christendom. It was doubtless the frustration of his hopes no less than the shock caused by the catastrophe itself that destroyed the Pope's health. He sank gradually into his grave, dying early in 1455. On his death-bed he gave the bystanders a review of his achievements and an apologia for what he had spent on them.

The successor of Nicolas was Cardinal Alfonso Borgia, who took the name of Calixtus III. A Spaniard by birth, he was now seventy-seven years old, and owed his election to the fact that the electors, unable to reach an agreement, compromised by choosing a man who could hardly occupy the Holy See for long. Historians have dwelt complacently on the purity of this aged man's private life; but he seems to have had a full share of the headstrong cantankerousness and self-satisfied unscrupulousness that so often accompany old age. His mind was set on two things—the organization of a Crusade and the advancement of his nephews. It cannot indeed be said that he was hostile to the plans of Nicolas V; he was simply not interested in them. The splendour of the papal court departed; there were no more contracts for architects and decorators, no more pleasant tasks for men of letters. Some of the buildings restored by Nicolas are said to have been despoiled of their fittings and ornaments, and some of the books in the Vatican library stripped of their bindings. There is no doubt that the Pope's zeal for a crusade was genuine. In 1456 a naval squadron under Cardinal Scarampi was sent to cruise in Greek waters, in order to frighten the Turks and hearten the Christians. It merely served to put the former on their guard and fill the latter with false hopes. Short-sighted self-interest was doubtless the main cause of the failure of the sovereigns of Europe to respond to the Pope's exhortations; but they were also affected by doubts as to his sincerity. It is not astonishing that many believed his crusading fervour to be a cloak for his family ambitions. Nepotism had often discredited previous popes; but none had practised it so shamelessly as Calixtus. One of his first acts was to raise to the Cardinalate two of his nephews, young men in their twenties, one of whom was afterwards to become the Vicar of Christ under the name of Alexander VI. Another nephew was subsequently made Prefect of the City of Rome and Duke of Spoleto, while in 1458, when King Alfonso of Naples died, Calixtus claimed that the kingdom had escheated to the Papacy and named this nephew Vicar of Benevento and Terracina. Rome was entirely under the power of the Pope's young kinsmen, who stuck at nothing to increase their influence and fill their pockets. Few popes have been less mourned than Calixtus when in 1458 he died.

*Pius II, 1458-64*

His successor stands in the sharpest contrast to the fond and foolish old man. Aeneas Sylvius Piccolomini, called Pius II, is assuredly unsurpassed among the popes for calculating and profitable knavery. No rat ever timed his departure from a doomed ship more nicely. He sailed to fortune in the Council of Basel, and abandoned it at the right moment. Then he transferred his services to Frederick III. Soon, as we have seen, he ingratiated himself with the Papacy, and for some years, while nominally remaining in the German king's service, he lent himself increasingly to the purposes of the Holy See. It had cost him much intrigue and self-abasement to secure the Cardinalate. Nobody trusted and few liked him, and it was only owing to the marvellous subtlety he employed in the very Conclave that he was chosen as Pope.

It may at least be said for Pius II that during his pontificate the Papacy was concerned with large issues. In the forefront of the Pope's policy was the organization of a crusade. One of his first acts was to summon the kings and *The Congress* princes of Europe to a congress at Mantua, where plans for *of Mantua,* the expedition might be settled. Pius was there on the *1459* appointed day, but not one single potentate or plenipotentiary was present to meet him. Very slowly ambassadors drifted in, until most European states were represented. But some of the envoys were men of small account, unworthy to speak for powerful rulers on what was meant to be a great occasion.

Others were not empowered to do anything, but were sent merely to listen, ask questions, and report to their masters. Some had evidently come to transact business which had nothing to do with the crusade. The situation gave welcome opportunity for displays of eloquence by the Pope and many others. There was general agreement that Turks were bad. The envoys were willing to consider ways and means of fighting them. But when it was suggested that any particular country should provide a certain number of men or ships, or contribute a certain sum of money, there was always a good reason why the proposal could not be accepted. The French and the Germans, from whom Pius had expected much, were notably reluctant to commit themselves to anything. In the end the Pope had to content himself with declaring war—quite superfluously—against the Turks, with promising indulgences to all Christians who took part in it or contributed to it, and with imposing taxes for its promotion on both clergy and laity. He then, in January 1460, dissolved the Congress, hoping for the best.

It is likely that Pius II was glad to escape from the Congress so lightly. During its course there had been one or two disquieting episodes. The French, who objected to the Pope's support of King Ferrante of Naples, had assumed a very independent tone. The German reform party was represented, and its leading spokesman, the jurist Gregory Heimburg—an old enemy of Aeneas Sylvius—was utterly distrustful of the Pope and largely responsible for the refusal of the Germans to commit themselves. Further, Sigismund of Habsburg, who had quarrelled bitterly with Cardinal Nicolas of Cusa over the latter's rights as Bishop of Brixen, visited Mantua at the invitation of the Pope, who wished to mediate. His lands having been put under an interdict, he had appealed to a future Council: what perhaps troubled Pius yet more, Gregory Heimburg, speaking on Sigismund's behalf, alluded to his early friendship with Aeneas Sylvius and to the uncommonly frank love-letters which the latter had penned for him. Pius never lived down his past indiscretions—Heimburg indeed took care that they should not be forgotten—and as a rule he was sensible enough to ignore references to them. But it would never do to pass over Sigismund's appeal to a Council. Just before the Congress

*Opposition to the Pope*

**The constitution *Execrabilis*, Jan. 18, 1460**

ended Pius accordingly published the constitution *Execrabilis* —the second famous papal decree to begin with that word —in which he denounces every appeal to a future Council as "an execrable abuse," lacking in all validity, and declares all concerned in making it to be *ipso facto* excommunicate. Thus did the Papacy, through the mouth of one who had defended in writing the deposition of Eugenius IV by the Council of Basel, flatly repudiate the basic principle of the Conciliar Movement. It is true that the bull did not stop the practice which it condemned; but that Pius ventured to make such a pronouncement was a measure of the security which the Papacy now enjoyed.

**Maintenance of papal claims by Pius**

The bull *Execrabilis* was not the Pope's only stroke against the meagre results of the reform movement. In 1461, as we have seen in another connexion, he induced Louis XI to withdraw the Pragmatic Sanction of Bourges, though this victory was short-lived and in any case more apparent than real. In relation to Bohemia, after waiting to see whether George of Podiebrad would come to heel of his own accord, he abandoned all pretence of conciliating the Utraquists, and in 1462 explicitly annulled the famous Compacts. Podiebrad's defiance of the Pope was probably unexpected, but even if foreseen it would hardly have deterred him from acting as he did. It was clear to all that Pius was determined to uphold the uttermost tittle of the papal claims. Any doubt on the matter was dispelled by a bull which he issued in 1463 when giving judgment on a dispute between the Bishop of Liége and his subjects, who had justified their procedure in the case from opinions stated by the Pope in an early phase of his career. Pius declares that he has maintained many views which he now repudiates. If, he says, his writings contain anything contrary to the supremacy of the Holy See over the whole Church, let it be rejected. "Believe the old man rather than the youth; do not value the layman more highly than the Pope; reject Aeneas, receive Pius." Then, lest anyone should say that the change in his views was merely a consequence of his election as Pope, he gives an apologetic account of his intellectual development, showing how the more he learned, the more he came to see the strength of the case for the Papacy. The document has a most ingenuous air, but is a little too plausible to be convincing. At all events, the Pope's contemporaries did not believe in him.

The diplomacy of Pius made itself felt in almost every part of Europe. Often it had the sole object of promoting the material interests of the Papacy. In Italy, without involving himself deeply in the conflict, he aided Ferrante of Naples to defeat John of Calabria; he overthrew Gismondo Malatesta, the brilliant, learned, sceptical tyrant of Rimini; he put down one of the recurrent republican outbreaks in Rome; and he contrived, without imitating the extravagant nepotism of Calixtus III, to make good provision for some of his kinsfolk. His interferences in other countries did not seem to be actuated by any motives more lofty than those which had long swayed the Papacy. The lukewarmness of the response to his crusading schemes was doubtless due in great measure to mere selfishness, but it is partly to be explained by the usual belief that the Pope was using the Holy War as a cloak for his own private ambitions, some imaginative cynics actually saying that he hoped to become Emperor of Constantinople himself.

*Diplomacy of Pius*

It was gradually borne in on Pius that his crusading zeal was generally questioned. "If we plan a Congress," he lamented, "our experience at Mantua shows it to be futile. If we despatch legates, they are mocked. If we tax the clergy, they appeal to a future Council. If we offer indulgences, we are called avaricious. . . . The worst construction is put on all our doings." So in 1462 he announced that he would head the Crusade himself. The Duke of Burgundy had promised to go if any other prince would; let him then accompany Pius. Venice would surely provide shipping. If only France could be induced to participate, there would be no need of further delay. But, though the Pope set about promoting his plan with the greatest energy, he fared no better than before. Of the states beyond the Alps only Burgundy would make any definite promises, and those were not very generous, while several Italian states did not conceal their coldness towards the whole project. But in September 1463 Pius announced his determination to set out against the Turks, and commanded the Cardinals to accompany him. "We do not go to fight, but we will imitate Moses, who

*The Pope's crusade and death, Aug. 1464*

prayed on the mountain while Israel fought Amalek. We will stand on the prow of our ship, or on the top of a hill, and with the Holy Sacrament before us, will pray Jesus Christ to grant safety and victory to our soldiers in the battle." The crusade was now vehemently preached throughout western and central Europe. But the response was still lamentably small. Pius did indeed succeed in making an alliance with Venice and Hungary, the three parties pledging themselves to continue the fight against the Turk for three years; but this was a commonplace political arrangement based on obvious self-interest, and no token of crusading fervour. Early in 1464, when the preparations were lagging badly, the Pope received a terrible blow from the Duke of Burgundy, who had apparently connived with Louis XI to concoct a plausible excuse for breaking his promises. Nevertheless, Pius, though in wretched health, left Rome in June, and made his way by easy stages to Ancona, where he and a number of crusaders were to embark. The Venetian ships for their transport had not arrived. The Pope, his strength failing rapidly, waited nearly a month, while the troops, contemptibly few at the beginning, steadily deserted. At last the Venetian fleet sailed into the harbour. The Pope was carried to the window of his bedchamber to see the spectacle, but two days later he died.

*Character and attainments of Pius II*   Modern historians have treated the death of Pius II as one of the most moving incidents of History. Contemporaries were much less affected. To the last very few of them believed that Pius was in earnest about the crusade. And in truth he had only himself to blame for the universal doubts of his sincerity. Even if we admit that he had been genuinely convinced of the falsity of his early opinions, it is evident that throughout his pontificate he was much given to posing and self-advertisement. He liked to display his piety in elaborate and slightly vulgar ceremonial; and he professed an affection for the simple charms of rural life, indulging his taste in ways that remind one of the member of the luxurious Country Club roughing it in the American woods. He seems while Pope to have refrained from the grosser sins of the flesh; but his record handicapped him sadly when he was called upon to correct scandals in the Cardinals' College, and an extant rebuke which he once administered to Rodrigo

Borgia for shameless debauchery is a classic example of how to condone with faint blame.

Nevertheless, while Pius was not an admirable man, he was an extremely interesting one. Few men of the Middle Ages stand before us so completely self-revealed. For, clever politician as he was, it was his literary work that gave him distinction. He was in the forefront among contemporaries as poet, letter-writer, novelist, memoir-writer, and historian. He is still read for what he wrote, not merely for how he wrote it. He was, for that matter, not highly esteemed by the leading Humanists of his time. His style, they said, had been damaged by his long sojourn beyond the Alps, and was not purely classical. That was enough to damn him in their eyes, but the criticism troubled Pius but little. To him the matter was always as important as the form; he sometimes voiced in stinging terms his contempt for the empty verbiage which, if only it was Ciceronian, satisfied contemporary taste. Contrary to expectation, he did not renew the policy of Nicolas V; and the men of letters, disappointed of their hopes, vented their chagrin by belittling the Pope's abilities. Pius, it is true, was not wholly free from some of the vices which he condemned in others. His writings usually have more in them than those of his contemporaries, but they are extremely wordy. His speeches, of which he delivered an incredible number, likewise seem intolerably verbose to modern taste; but he prided himself on their terseness, they were highly admired by diplomatists, and if professional rhetoricians criticized them adversely, it was because Pius would treat the Latin language as if it still had some vitality and had not stopped short in the cultivated court of the Emperor Trajan. As a judge of art he was far more open-minded than the average scholar of the day, with his unmitigated reverence for classical antiquity. Pius could even admire Gothic architecture; he prized contemporary work with excellent discrimination. He is not, however, remembered as a great builder, for his most pretentious architectural projects were concerned with his birthplace, Corsignano, which he renamed Pienza, making it an episcopal see, and endowing it with the public buildings which an important city was expected to possess. Geographical and economic forces have frustrated the

Pope's pious designs, and the place has remained a mere village.

*Paul II, 1464-71*

Pius commands respect as a man of letters and patron of art, as a politician he was no worse than most of his rivals, as a pope he was perhaps the last man of the time who should have been chosen. But he had at least upheld the *plenitudo potestatis*, and made his power felt all over Europe. His successor, Paul II, a Venetian who had been made a cardinal by his uncle, Eugenius IV, was morally a better man than Pius and the only pope of the latter part of the century to show any concern for the reform of abuses. Thus he refrained from granting benefices in expectancy, sold indulgences very sparingly, and abolished the College of Abbreviators, who constituted a large part of the staff of the papal Chancery, on the ground that it was unnecessary. But he enunciated no great principles, and set up no machinery for the enforcement of a reform policy, so that his successor was able to revert to the old ways and restore the old arrangements without causing any upheaval. And by flatly repudiating the promises which, in common with his fellow-cardinals, he had made in the Conclave in view of the possibility of his election, he flaunted in the most cynical manner the doctrine that papal power could be restricted by no promise, however solemn.

Paul II was a kindly and peace-loving man. He suppressed disorder in the States of the Church, gave the city of Rome a revised code of by-laws, and delighted to please the populace with pageantry and festivity. In Italian politics he was not grasping, and he abandoned an attempt to annex Rimini on perceiving that he could only do so by engaging in a war which would involve nearly all Italy. Beyond the Alps Paul's diplomacy was much less insistent than that of Pius II; he took, however, a very high line with George of Podiebrad, refused to negotiate with him, and eventually proclaimed his deposition as a heretic. When in 1468 Frederick III visited Rome—the last time a Holy Roman Emperor ever did so—the Pope treated him with a contemptuous condescension which anyone else would have found intolerable. Paul was acting a rehearsed part, and his Master of Ceremonies was ordered to record all that was done. "The power of the Pope," that functionary says in the course of his account, " was formerly what princes permitted; but now it is different—a trifling boon from the Pope, a mere act of courtesy, is very highly valued."

Paul II has incurred much odium because he fell foul of the Humanists. He was no enemy of the Renaissance; indeed, he amassed a magnificent collection of objects of art, which was really the leading interest in his life. But he viewed with concern some of the tendencies of the scholars of the time, and was especially scandalized by the scoffs at Christianity and by the pagan beliefs and ceremonies which were the vogue among the members of the Roman Academy, the president of which was the celebrated Humanist, Pomponius Laetus. Paul ascribed to the Humanists much greater sincerity and resolution than they possessed. He arrested Pomponius, the equally renowned Platina, and a number of lesser fry. A very short experience of prison reduced them to abject contrition, and after the Pope deemed them to have been sufficiently humiliated, they were released. The Academy was suppressed, though it was revived by Paul's successor. The Pope's conduct was ill-advised. The Italian Humanists knew on which side their bread was buttered, and however sacrilegiously they might prate among themselves, they would never have revolted against the Church. Paul's victims took a literary revenge, representing him as a cruel tyrant and barbarous obscurantist, and their account of him enjoyed a long currency.

At his death in 1471 Paul II might have claimed that he left the Papacy no more deeply involved in scandal than he had found it. His omissions in this respect were amply supplied by his successor. Sixtus IV, who was Pope for the long term of thirteen years, was a peasant by birth and a Franciscan friar by profession. He had a high reputation for his clean life and his theological learning. There has never been a more striking example of the effects of elevation to the Holy See.

At the very beginning of his rule, he revived the project of a crusade, tried to stir to action the princes of Europe, and despatched a naval squadron to harry the Turkish coasts. But the response of the princes was even less encouraging than it had been in the days of Pius II, and the Pope's galleys were too few to win any but trivial successes.

So after a year or two Sixtus relegated his spiritual functions to the background. Now and again he assumed the Pope, but generally he was just an Italian prince, bent on increasing his political influence and territorial possessions by any means that promised good fortune.

The pontificate of Sixtus IV thus belongs to the political history of Italy rather than to the history of the Church, and the little that need be said about his wars and diplomacy in a book of this scope may be found in another chapter. What scandalized contemporaries most in Sixtus IV was his nepotism. His kinsfolk were apparently inexhaustible, like his liberality towards them. Within a few weeks of his election, two nephews, both under thirty, had been made cardinals, and a third, also a young man, Prefect of Rome. The most notorious of this trio was Piero Riario, a Franciscan friar like his uncle, and responsible in great measure, through his intrigues with the cardinals, for the result of the Conclave. His excesses killed him in 1474 at the age of twenty-eight; but in the meantime Sixtus had permitted him to enjoy unbridled power, and he had amazed even contemporary Italy with his acquisitiveness, ostentation, extravagance, and profligacy. The first place in the Pope's affections was taken by Girolamo Riario, Piero's brother, a layman, for whom Sixtus secured the hand of a bastard daughter of Galeazzo Maria Sforza. He was as big a knave as Piero, but more discreet, and after directing papal policy for ten years, outlived his uncle. Piero and Girolamo cared nothing for appearances or conventions, and the Papacy ceased to give its misdoings that cloak of respectability that had hitherto usually shrouded them. It took very little of Sixtus IV to impair gravely the prestige of the Holy See. In 1450 there had been a "jubilee" for which immense multitudes had journeyed to Rome; but at the next one, held in 1475, the visitors were very few. We have seen, further, how Sixtus was an accomplice in the Pazzi conspiracy against the Medici, a scheme which he knew could not succeed without assassination. After the plot failed, he strove to punish the people of Florence for punishing the murderers. His curses were answered by some plain speaking, much of it from clergy, which in itself shows how low in public esteem the Holy See had fallen. The longer Sixtus lived, the worse he became. One of his last exploits was to secure the surrender of a stronghold of his enemies the Colonna family by promising to restore to them the captain's brother, whom he had taken prisoner. He restored him dead.

Now and then Sixtus bethought him of the religious aspect of his authority. It was he who authorized the establishment of the Spanish Inquisition. He was a great patron of both the Franciscans and the Dominicans, whose privileges he confirmed and enlarged. He retained his interest in theology and was a strong advocate of the doctrine of the Immaculate Conception of the Virgin, though he formally declared that it was a question on which Catholic Christians might differ. But he was quite out of touch with the religious feeling of transalpine Europe, as is shown by the fact that he was seriously perturbed by the vagaries of the Archbishop of the Craina, who, having grievances against the Pope, went to Basel and summoned a General Council. The man was doubtless tainted in his wits, and people treated him as a joke; but Sixtus took him seriously and his perturbation was one of the causes which led him to withdraw from his war with Ferrara in 1482. *Religious interests of Sixtus*

The reputation of Sixtus has escaped more lightly than it deserves, for he was a lavish patron of Humanists, architects, and painters. By rebuilding a considerable part of Rome, he rendered a service to public health and public order. His artistic taste, however, was not good, and the buildings which he caused to be erected or restored—the best known being the Sistine Chapel—rarely exhibit much architectural distinction. The painters he employed were on the whole better than his architects, but he lacked a capacity for just discrimination between them, and it may be on this account that the most gifted seldom produced their best work in his service. *Sixtus as patron of the arts*

On the Italians of his own time, immersed as they were in the petty politics of their country, Sixtus made a deep impression. Even to Machiavelli it seemed as if he had raised papal power to a pitch never before attained. And many modern historians, while of course not sharing such a view, have been so far influenced by contemporary judgment as to believe that the pontificate of Sixtus marks a turning-point in papal history. Creighton, in his *History of the Papacy*, *Significance of the pontificate of Sixtus* actually speaks of him as "the beginner of the secularization of the Papacy." Such an estimate betrays a misunderstanding not merely of Sixtus himself but also of the whole trend of the history of the medieval Church. There was nothing original in either the policy or the methods of Sixtus. His concentration on secular interests was unusually intense, but not without precedent. Nepotism was an old evil, and some of his predecessors had practised it very nearly if not quite as shamelessly as he. There had been no lack of profligacy at the papal court in times past, even though it had not paraded itself so openly. Under the rule of Sixtus the Papacy merely took a big step in a descent that had begun long before. His pontificate is important in that at a time when the Papacy had lately emerged from a crisis, when its reputation was still under a cloud, when men throughout Europe were wondering how it would use its regained authority, Sixtus made it obvious to all that the Papacy had learned nothing from its trials and that for the good estate of the Catholic Church it cared not a whit.

Innocent VIII, 1484-92

The relation of the Papacy to the Church was not much affected by the next Pope, Cardinal Cibo, a Genoese, who styled himself Innocent VIII. His chief title to renown is that he was the first pope who openly acknowledged his children. Their precise number is uncertain; but it is pleasing to be assured that at least two, though illegitimate, were begotten before their father took orders. Innocent was a good-natured weak man. On the Church at large he left singularly little impress. In Italian politics he usually strove for peace; but he can hardly be said to have had any definite views of his own, being influenced at first by Cardinal Rovere, the late Pope's nephew, and later by Lorenzo de' Medici. He was a feeble ruler; Rome in his time was full of brawling and robbery, the nobles waged their inveterate feuds, and the Cardinals with their retinues contributed their share of bloodshed. The papal *curia* became more corrupt and costly than ever, for in order to raise ready money Innocent created a vast number of new posts and put them up for sale. Though no scholar or artist, he was quite friendly towards the Renaissance, and Humanists and architects still found plenty of scope in Rome. Innocent died in 1492; the best that can be said for him is that a worse came in his place.

## FROM BAD TO WORSE AT ROME

The entire pontificate of Alexander VI must be left to another volume. A review of it would merely confirm the impression produced by the popes we have been discussing. The Papacy was strong enough to prevent the Church from reforming itself. And it had no intention of reforming the Church. At the same time, it had forfeited much of the veneration which, even at the height of the Conciliar Movement, it had commanded all over Catholic Europe. People in the more remote countries might almost forget its existence. Elsewhere events were forcing the idea of revolt before the minds of earnest men. It must be remembered that while constitutional reform had failed, the fifteenth century furnished an example of successful rebellion. Both Sixtus IV and Innocent VIII had virtually abandoned the attempt to suppress the Bohemian Utraquists, and their King Ladislas, though himself a sound Catholic, owed his throne to them. To later Protestants the difference between Romanists and Utraquists seemed so trivial that the continued existence of the latter lost its significance in their eyes. Yet in principle Utraquism was just as much a defiance of Rome as Lutheranism or Calvinism was destined to be. It is amazing that with this successful revolt confronting them, the Popes should by their policy have encouraged their critics to imitate the Bohemians.

*Position of the Papacy at the end of fifteenth century*

Some authorities for chapter xx :—
i. Original sources—
  The *Commentarii* of Aeneas Sylvius and Ammannati (see under chap. xix); Raynaldus, *Annales*, vols. xxix and xxx (see under chap. v); also the works of Burchard, Infessura, Sigismondo dei Conti, Vespasiano da Bisticci, and Jacobus Volaterranus, noted under chap. xix.
  Manetti, Gianozzo : *Vita Nicolai V*, in Muratori, *Script. rerum Ital.*, vol. iii, pt. 2, Milan, 1734.
  Platina, B. : *Liber de vita Christi ac omnium pontificum*, ed. G. Gaida, in *Script. rerum Ital.*, new edition, vol. iii, pt. 1, Città di Castella, 1913–23.
  *Vite di Paolo II di Gaspare da Verona e Michele Canensis*, ed. G. Zippel, in *Script. rerum Ital.*, new edition, vol. iii, pt. 16, Città di Castella, 1904–11.
ii. Modern works—
  Creighton, *History of the Papacy*, vols. iii and iv; Flick, *Decline of the Medieval Church*, vol. ii; Seppelt, *Das Papsttum im Spätmittelalter und in der Zeit der Renaissance*; Pastor, *History of the Popes*, vols. ii–v. (See under chapter v.)
  Ady, Cecilia M. : *Pius II*, London, 1913.
  Gregorovius, F. : *Geschichte der Stadt Rom im Mittelalter*, 5th ed., vols. vi and vii, Stuttgart and Berlin, 1908.
  Voigt, G. : *Ænea Silvio de' Piccolomini als Papst Pius der Zweite, und sein Zeitalter*, Berlin, 1856–63.

## CHAPTER XXI

## THE CLASSICAL RENAISSANCE, AND ITS RELATION TO THOUGHT, LETTERS, AND ART IN THE FIFTEENTH CENTURY

*Traditional view of "the Renaissance"*

IT has been customary for historians to speak of "the Renaissance" as one of the great landmarks in the career of mankind. And, in view of the accredited conception of human history, the estimate was justified. For History fell into three clear-cut divisions. There was Ancient History, concerned with the fortunes of Greece from Homer to Alexander the Great and of Rome from Romulus to Marcus Aurelius or thereabouts, and thus dealing with communities which attained great material well-being, technical dexterity, intellectual power, and artistic taste. Then, with the decline of Rome, History entered its second phase—the Middle or Dark Ages, which lasted upwards of a thousand years. The regions comprised in the western half of the Roman Empire were submerged in barbarism. It was, in the words of a modern oracle, " a glacial age of the spirit." Its literature was dismissed as "monkish," its art as "Gothic," its thought, we were told, culminated in the man whose name gave us the word "dunce." Even after the Romantic Movement of the early nineteenth century had revived a sympathetic interest in the Middle Ages, they were admired because they were romantic, picturesque, or quaint. It was characteristic that medieval architecture was for long most highly appreciated when it was ruined. Even the great scholars who wrote on medieval history in the latter half of the nineteenth century, though they attributed many merits to medieval culture, usually assumed the existence of a great gulf between the Middle Ages and what were called Modern Times—the third Age of History.

There was a general agreement that what at length lightened the darkness of error and superstition in which Europe had been wandering was the Renaissance, the re-birth of learning and art, moribund if not dead since the barbarians had overwhelmed Rome. Ancient literature, especially that of Greece, was revealed to minds weary of the tyranny of monks and schoolmen. The result was miraculous. "Men opened their eyes and saw." And, looking at the world freely and directly, not through stained-glass windows, they saw that it was good. Scrutinizing the features and forms of their fellows, they found them worthy of admiration as creatures of flesh and blood, and not merely edifying as immortal souls destined probably for damnation. Their minds and imaginations emancipated, they turned from the trivialities of scholastic disputation to the great problems of life. Traditions, legends, superstitions crashed headlong. Beauty once more awoke. Literature recovered her form and comeliness. Grace and dignity unseen since the age of Pericles sprang into being under paint-brush and chisel. Man strode forth with head erect, ready not merely to endure but to master his fate. It was an inexhaustible theme, and much fine writing was provoked by it.

Here and there a voice protested that the darkness of medieval times was less intense, and the succeeding radiance less pure, than commonly depicted. A few remonstrances—from the pre-Raphaelite school, for instance—went further, actually denouncing the effects of the Renaissance as mainly evil, and bewailing the ruin of medieval art and the disruption of medieval society. But as the pre-Raphaelites and their kin were profoundly ignorant of the Middle Ages, they were easily refuted. The beliefs summarized above continued to be maintained by the most weighty authorities. The writer was brought up to accept them as beyond serious question.

Such views are still to be heard and read. Nevertheless, a distinguished American historian was able in 1929 to assert that they were now held only "by mechanical creatures of habit, by those who stopped thinking and reading twenty or thirty years ago, and who refuse to give up any catchword or prejudice that was instilled into their minds in childhood." Whatever we may think of this severe judgment, it is undeniable that within the last quarter of a century research into the Middle Ages and the times immediately following has fundamentally changed the old conception of the development of modern culture. It has become evident, nay

*Medieval culture in the light of modern research*

obvious, that there was no suspension of intellectual life in medieval Europe. If there was a Revival of Learning, it occurred about the year A.D. 1000, since when human knowledge has never ceased to advance. It cannot even be said that the Humanists of the fourteenth and fifteenth centuries revived the study of the classics. Scholars had been nourished on the classics for centuries. Neither can it be maintained that the distinguishing feature of the Humanists was their acquaintance with Greek thought. In the first place, the classical writer most studied in the Middle Ages was a Greek, Aristotle, and though nearly all medieval students perforce read him in translation, the defects of the versions at their service were far less grave than most historians have asserted. Further, the early Humanists knew little or no Greek; indeed, even among the Italians passable Greek scholars were rare until late in the fifteenth century. It has often been alleged that what differentiated the Schoolman from the Humanist was the former's subservience to authority. But in this respect there was little to choose between the two. The Humanist usually kept the peace with the Church, and for the Schoolman's Aristotle he substituted other classical divinities, notably Cicero.

These considerations would not justify a denial that there was a very real difference between the Schoolman and the Italian Humanist of the fifteenth century. But it was a difference of standpoint rather than a difference in learning or originality. It has been judiciously pointed out that all extant manuscripts of the classics, apart from a few fragments of papyrus, are medieval. That is to say, the works they enshrine were known somewhere at some time during the Middle Ages. And actually the medieval scholars of western Europe were acquainted with most of the Latin authors familiar to us. In regard to the Greeks, their position was less fortunate, for the Greek dramatists, poets, and historians were hardly known at all, even in translation. Through becoming acquainted with them, the Humanists gained a great advantage, which few of them turned to the best account. It was not, however, in the Humanist's knowledge of the classics, but in his treatment of them that the difference between him and the Schoolman lies. The medieval scholar had read them for moral edification, or for the philosophical and scientific instruction which they were believed to supply; the Humanist read them for the light which they shed upon mankind and because of the beauty of their literary art. There had, it is true, been a Humanist school in the twelfth century, with its centre at Chartres, but its life had been short, and in the later enthusiasm of the Italian scholars for the classics as literature and as a revelation of man, there was a re-birth of something that had flourished in Ancient Times, but had scarcely existed in the Middle Ages.

*The Italian Humanists of the fifteenth century*

At all events, it was with manifestly genuine zeal that the fifteenth-century scholars of Italy studied the writings of Greek and Roman antiquity. Every sentence, every phrase, every word, underwent meticulous scrutiny. Petrarch, who died just before the beginning of the time covered by this volume, has often been counted the first of the Humanists. But it was not long before he was far surpassed in depth of learning and elegance of style. Among his earlier successors, whose careers lie mainly in the first half of the fifteenth century, special notice may be given to Leonardo Bruni, Poggio Bracciolini, and Lorenzo Valla. The scholars of their generation were largely occupied with the discovery and collection of manuscripts, particularly of the works of authors who had long been neglected. All the while, however, a knowledge of Greek was steadily, if slowly, spreading. From the first years of the fifteenth century there was no lack of teachers of Greek in Italy. The contact of the West with Greek thought and culture became still closer during the negotiations for ecclesiastical union which culminated in the Council of Florence. Long before the fall of Constantinople every Italian scholar who wanted to learn Greek had ample opportunity of doing so, and there were in Italy countless manuscripts of the Greek classics. Yet modern historians, even though they betray a knowledge of these things, still repeat the myth that "the Renaissance" was caused by the capture of Constantinople and the imaginary stampede of learned men that followed.

*Knowledge of Greek*

In the second part of the century the Humanists applied themselves more thoroughly to the analysis and annotation of the literature at their disposal. Of course one may not draw a hard and fast line between the two phases of the Humanist movement; some long-lived scholars, such as the renowned Filelfo, belonged to both. Among the greater names of the second half of the century are Pomponius Laetus, Platina, and Politian. It must be understood that the strength of Humanism did not lie in the Universities, and that few of the great classical scholars of the century could have gained their renown, or indeed lived at all, but for the assistance of princely or ecclesiastical patrons. Among these the successive heads of the Medici family were pre-eminent. Alfonso of Naples was also a liberal friend of learning and art. Among the popes, as we have seen, the Humanists owed much to Nicolas V and Sixtus IV. And one might fill a page with the names of lesser princes and nobles who, whether from taste or from ostentation, patronized the " new learning." With such encouragement, the Humanist scholars were full of confidence in themselves. They wrote a good deal—grammars, commentaries, handbooks on rhetoric, a few histories (whether of ancient times or their own), imaginary dialogues, and controversial pamphlets. They emitted an immense torrent of talk in lectures and orations. They discerned and sometimes applied certain of the principles of historical criticism: perhaps, indeed, it was the earlier phase of Humanism, when the weight of erudition was less oppressive, that was most favourable to the rise of a critical spirit: at all events, it was Lorenzo Valla who performed the most notable feats of iconoclasm, demonstrating in 1440 that the document called the Donation of Constantine was a forgery and arguing also that the Apostles' Creed was not composed by the Apostles. Such achievements were naturally rare, and to most Humanists the paths of Higher Criticism seemed a little too dangerous. But in amending the texts of the classics, many of which had become grievously corrupt, they did very useful work. Further, their ability to read Aristotle in the original gave them a better comprehension of his philosophy than had been usual among medieval scholars. And a knowledge of Plato, whose works had for centuries been only in small part available and whose doctrines had seldom aroused much interest, was now widespread among the scholars of Italy. It must be admitted that the Humanists did not always discriminate intelligently between the teachings of Plato himself and the travesty of them known as

*Achievements of the Humanists*

neo-Platonism; but what were supposed to be Plato's doctrines became for a time the fashionable philosophy and furnished the Humanists with a useful weapon in their war against scholasticism.

Nevertheless, the fruit of all this learning and activity is woefully lacking in savour and nourishment. Not one of these fifteenth-century Humanists, so brilliant in their own eyes, produced a work which posterity has ranked among the masterpieces of literature. No one reads their writings now save a few historians who use them as sources just as they use the "monkish" chroniclers whom the Humanists so wittily decried. And of the fifteenth-century scholars, the one most prized as an historical authority is probably Aeneas Sylvius, whom his contemporaries deemed secondrate. Such of the speeches of the time as have been reported seem to modern taste intolerably windy. The polemics of the Humanists usually turned on trivialities, not infrequently personal. They may have understood ancient philosophy, but none was capable of making any advance upon it. The few who grasped the principles of historical criticism applied them timorously. And though Valla's exposure of the Donation of Constantine was the most convincing of the century, it should not be forgotten that his conclusions had been anticipated by Nicolas of Cusa—an amphibious scholar, partly Humanist, partly Schoolman—and that they were reached a few years later, quite independently, by the English bishop Reginald Pecock, who had been educated entirely in the atmosphere of the "old learning." The main cause of the barrenness of the Humanists was probably their lack of sincerity. Valla might question the authenticity of the Apostles' Creed, but when his doubts involved him in trouble with ecclesiastical authority he pretended that his argument had been only an academic exercise. Pomponius Laetus and Platina, whose tongues spared neither God nor man while the skies were clear, ate their words greedily as soon as Paul II clapped them in prison. And all the while these men and countless other scholars were conforming outwardly to a religion which everyone knew they derided. But nobody was quite certain which was a pose —the conformity or the derision.

If the Italian Humanists as a class were astonishingly

sterile, in some respects they did positive harm. For a while —though not until after the end of the fifteenth century— they and their followers beyond the Alps dictated the opinions of educated Europe. They spread the contempt of their pedantic minds for the culture and art of the Middle Ages, and the distorted view of History thus created is only now being corrected. They destroyed the ascendancy of the scholastic philosophy and the dialectical method of education in the universities, replacing them by that regiment of the classics under the monstrous tyranny of which the youth of Europe suffered for centuries and in some places suffers still. And, paradoxical though it seems, in their exaltation of the Latin classics the Humanists ruined Latin as a living language. For medieval Latin, largely because it differed considerably from classical Latin, was an excellent medium of both written and oral expression. Having a much richer vocabulary, it could give voice to a much wider range of ideas than the Latin of the Augustan age. For the clergy and the educated laity it was an established vehicle of communication all over central and western Europe. Then came the Humanists damning it as barbarous because it was not identical with the Latin used by Cicero 1,500 years before. The Latin of Cicero came to be accepted as the only Latin a scholar might use. It was a speech quite inadequate to express many ideas familiar to the man of the sixteenth century. Indeed, it had never been spoken by anybody, even in Cicero's time, except in set orations. For a while it was used for works of erudition and academic discourses; but its employment for such purposes steadily declined, since a language forbidden to develop inevitably becomes ever more lifeless as time goes on. So bemused have later generations been by the self-praise of the Humanists that they have commonly lauded them for their overthrow of what has been foolishly called "monkish" Latin. How much the advance of knowledge has been retarded through the consequent necessity of spending time and energy on the study of foreign tongues it is impossible to compute.

*Humanism outside Italy*

This chapter has hitherto treated the Humanists as if they were exclusively Italians. So indeed they nearly all were during the years with which this volume is concerned. Though the Latin classics had been studied with increasing zest in France throughout the century, Greek was not taught in Paris until 1476; and the French literary movement, vigorous though it was, had different roots and a different spirit from those of the so-called classical Renaissance. Only in the ninth decade of the century was it possible to learn Greek in England, and English letters were but feebly affected by Humanism until about the same time. Into Germany, it is true, the influence of the Italian scholars penetrated somewhat sooner. As yet, however, their spirit seldom appeared there undiluted. This was largely because the great nursery of German classical scholars was the school of Deventer, the most notable of the numerous schools founded by the Brethren of the Common Life. Thus most of the earlier German Humanists were clergy, and they were usually versed and interested in theology as well as letters. They advocated the reform of educational method, preferring the reading of classical texts to the logic-chopping long in favour. But the unreasoning contempt of the Italians for everything later than the second century A.D. was not shared by the Germans. In their theology they were mostly conservative, though anxious for the remedy of ecclesiastical abuses. The nearest German approach to the Italian type was perhaps Rudolf Agricola (1442–85), who studied in Italy and acquired there the literary polish and empty verbosity then characteristic of that country's scholars. The man who did most to establish a thorough classical curriculum in German schools was Alexander Hegius (1433–98), the head of Deventer. But he used to declare that "all learning is harmful which is gained at the expense of piety," a dictum which reveals how wide a gulf separated him from such men as Poggio or Platina.

At the death of the Emperor Frederick III, however, the most brilliant phase of German Humanism was just opening, and in the next twenty-five years its temper became far more radical. To pursue it further, however, would mean trespassing on another's territory.

The term Renaissance, as we have seen, gives a very misleading notion of the development of learning in the fourteenth and fifteenth centuries. Nor does it serve much better to indicate the character of contemporary art. It is, in fact, only to Italian architecture that it can be justly applied. In

*Renaissance architecture*

architecture there was undoubtedly a classical revival, with very lamentable results. It is true that Gothic architecture had never flourished in Italy; and it is hard to say whether the early architects of the so-called Renaissance were continuing the Romanesque tradition or drawing inspiration from ancient Rome. And it was some time after Italian architects had unquestionably begun to imitate classical models that they became utterly subservient to classical authority. Further, there is no denying that the Italian architects of the later Middle Ages produced some magnificent work. Genius always manifests itself, however much it may be trammelled by pedantic principles; and such men as Brunelleschi and Alberti impressed on all their buildings the stamp of the true and original artist. But their successors —with but a handful of exceptions like Bramante, Giulio Romano, and the eccentric Michael Angelo—were dull. Their works are the productions not of artists but of scholars. Domestic architecture, it is true, suffered less than ecclesiastical; indeed, it derived some benefits from the Renaissance, though these were rather utilitarian than æsthetic. But the final result of the architectural Renaissance was the stifling of originality. Architects acquired the habit of conforming to recognized "styles," and they did not escape from it until the Americans began to build skyscrapers.

*Brunelleschi (1377–1446) and Alberti (1404–47)*

*The Renaissance and vernacular literature*

There is no need to add much about the "classical revival." It is often stated that it encouraged a growth of vernacular literature in several European countries By discrediting the expressive and adaptable Latin which had been in current use, it probably did something to promote such a movement. But its influence in this respect was indirect and slow. Dante, who belongs essentially to the Middle Ages, wrote his greatest work in Italian; Petrarch, often praised as the first Humanist, forsook Italian for Latin. Vernacular writings in fifteenth-century Italy were usually trivial and ephemeral, for the literary leaders of the day disdained to write in anything but Latin. It was only towards the end of the century that, thanks largely to the encouragement and example of Lorenzo de' Medici, there were renewed tokens of a widespread interest in Italian as a means of literary expression, Pulci (1431–87) and Boiardo (1434–94) confirming what Dante and Boccaccio had proved long before—that it was an admirable tongue for poets. Machiavelli and Guicciardini were soon to illustrate its merits in prose. But their work belongs to the sixteenth century; and in France, England, and Germany, all through the fifteenth, the use of the vernacular for literary composition was spreading apace, though the impact of Italian Humanism was hardly felt in these lands until the century was far advanced.

This development of vernacular literature shows that the peoples of Europe were naturally and spontaneously outgrowing the ways of thought and action characteristic of the Middle Ages. There was no need for them to resort to the classics for incentives. They might and did learn much through the more intense and intelligent study of Roman and Greek literature which the Humanists introduced. But it is plain that many causes besides the so-called rediscovery of the Ancient World were at work to produce the great advances in thought and art which distinguished the fifteenth century. For, whatever we may call it, the epoch was one of widespread and rapid progress. *Evolution of thought and art in fifteenth-century Europe*

Take, for instance, the arts of sculpture and painting. The period covered by this book has justly been accepted as one of the most glorious in their history. But the sculptors and painters of those days have been sadly maligned by many of their professed admirers, who have written as though all their inspiration had been drawn from the ancient Greeks and Romans. The Humanists, to do them justice, knew better, their general neglect of contemporary artists being due to the belief that these men showed insufficient regard for antique authority.

It is of course false to say that the art of sculpture had been moribund during the Middle Ages. The famous Italian sculptors of the early fifteenth century—Ghiberti, Donatello, Luca della Robbia—learned much from the study of classical examples, they owed more to the promptings of their native genius, but they were also the heirs of a long and splendid tradition. It has often been said that the Italian sculptors of the period departed from medieval practice by treating secular as well as sacred subjects, by producing works significant in themselves and not merely accessory to architecture, and by following nature instead of arbitrary conventions. *Sculpture in the fifteenth century*

They were thus, it is urged, able to render due honour to the beauty of the human body, which medieval man is alleged to have despised. It is true that nearly, though not quite all, medieval sculpture was attached to or placed in a building, usually a sacred building. But it is a delusion to suppose that all the carving in a medieval church was necessarily concerned with religious subjects. On the other hand, the nooks and corners of a cathedral, the capitals of piers, the *misericordiæ* and canopies of choir-stalls, the jambs and tympana of doorways, pinnacles, corbels, water-spouts, provided excellent accommodation for representations of mere nature, of the comic, the grotesque, the horrible, the obscene, the devilish. It is also essential to grasp that in northern Europe a re-birth of sculpture, like the re-birth of learning, had taken place in the eleventh century. It occurred in France, whence the revival soon spread to other countries. The art progressed rapidly until the thirteenth century, after which it somewhat fell away, though remaining at a high level. All western, central, and southern Europe was influenced by it. Even in Italy, always slow to accept foreign teaching or example, its effects may be traced; the great sculptors Niccolo and Giovanni Pisano, and even Giotto, owed something to it. In the last years of the fourteenth century, and for long afterwards, the sculpture of northern Europe was dominated by the so-called Burgundian school, of which the most renowned masters were Jean de Marville and Claus Sluter; its works are notable for admirable composition and an astonishing vitality, though marred at times by a heaviness verging on grossness. Donatello himself did not scorn to learn from the Burgundians, who alone prove that there were in the last medieval century men capable of producing great sculpture by merely carrying on the tradition in which they were reared.

In architecture, where antique models were abundant, the achievements of the Renaissance were disappointing. In sculpture, where antique models (though available) were less readily accessible and not as numerous as they are to-day, it did far better. In painting, where antique models were altogether lacking, it reached its greatest heights.

Most extant examples of medieval painting are concerned with religious subjects. It must be remembered, however, that mural paintings in ecclesiastical buildings and pictures belonging to churches have had a better chance of survival than other products of the painter's art. And as a matter of fact we may often read in medieval records of frescoes and easel pictures which adorned secular buildings, and have disappeared. Nevertheless, we still possess a great many delightful miniatures illustrating secular books; nor must it be forgotten that, just as worldly topics appear in the carvings of churches, so do they figure in the pictures in religious books. It was, for example, common for books of devotion to contain calendars illustrated with miniatures of an entirely worldly character. Thus when Italian painters of the fifteenth century handled themes from classical mythology, they were not doing anything revolutionary; and, for that matter, all through this century, to say nothing of the next, religious subjects commanded most of their attention. Doubtless the growing interest in classical literature and the growing knowledge of Ancient Times had its effect on the spirit of their work. But the painting of the fourteenth and fifteenth centuries was essentially a development, though extraordinarily rapid and far-spreading, of what had gone before. That there was no need of classical influence to stimulate pictorial art is shown by the Flemish school of the early fifteenth century, with its leaders the brothers Hubert and Jan van Eyck and Roger van der Weyden, and by the French school of a somewhat later date, headed by Jean Fouquet. Fouquet, it is true, was acquainted with contemporary Italian work and slightly affected by it. But both he and the earlier Flemings are essentially medieval in method and spirit; and they display a mastery of their craft and a freedom of resource which was hardly excelled even in contemporary Italy. Nevertheless, while these northern schools are of the highest interest as showing what could come out of an environment that was in all important respects medieval, it is true that the greatest painting of our period was Italian. *Fifteenth-century painters*

*The Flemish and French schools*

The fifteenth-century Italian artists, sculptors as well as painters, merit the most comprehensive admiration. Many of them were men of the most charming simplicity and the most scrupulous uprightness. As artists, regarded collectively they are unsurpassed for enthusiasm, sincerity, power, and versatility. They stand in refreshing contrast *Pre-eminence of the Italian painters* to the scholars of the time, with their verbosity, conceit, and pedantry. One can judge them aright only by looking at their work. To read about them is worth little. No good purpose would be served by giving a long list of their names.

*Masaccio (? 1402–29)* After the achievements of Giotto, early in the fourteenth century, Italian painting made little advance until the short but dazzling career of Tommaso, called Masaccio, a very close observer and faithful follower of nature, who, though he died at twenty-eight, inaugurated a series of great masters which far outlasted the century.

Historians and art critics are wont to distinguish between various local " schools " of Italian painters. The grounds for the accepted grouping are not always very clear, and some artists refuse to be captured and labelled. Such a one, for instance, is Fra Angelico (1387–1455), a manifest survival from a fast vanishing age, much admired by those who are touched by the rather insipid devoutness which is one of his main characteristics. Still, as the fashionable classification is commonly followed in picture-galleries, it would perhaps be captious to disregard it.

*The Florentine school* Masaccio was a Florentine, and of all the schools that of Florence was the most distinct and distinguished. It was remarkable for austerity, reserve, regard for form, and yet for its devotion to nature and freedom from convention. Its greatest figures were Fra Filippo Lippi (1406–69), that ill-regulated genius, the first man to use his models' faces for the sacred characters he painted and obviously ill at ease in handling the religious subjects he was required to treat. Among his numerous pupils were Filippino Lippi (1457–1504), generally and, it seems, rightly believed to be his son, a painter conspicuous for charm and grace, and also Botticelli, admired by contemporaries, overshadowed by successors, and now exalted very high, perhaps too high—an artist tender rather than strong, and, though the first man to make extensive use of classical themes, open to the charge of extravagant religious emotionalism. Another eminent Florentine was Ghirlandajo (1449–94), very notable for his command over the technical resources of his art, but lacking insight and inspiration, and, in fact, a little dull. Fra Bartolommeo, a great colourist, who must also be termed a Florentine, illustrates the defects of this grouping into schools, for he was a disciple of Savonarola and extremely devout, his morality so dominating his art that nude humanity shocked him.

There is usually said to have been a Siennese school, which is not very clearly differentiated; it was notable for strong religious sentiment, not to say sentimentality. Its influence merged with that of Florence to produce what is called the Umbrian school, whose most illustrious master was Perugino (1446–1524), who had "a body belonging to the Renaissance containing a soul belonging to the Middle Ages." His technique was of a very high standard; his work is marked by religious devotion of a rather inert type. Mention may be made of a Ferrarese and Bolognese school, whose leading representatives were Costa (1460–1536) and Francia (1450–1518), a very pious painter, much affected by Perugino; and the critics talk of a Lombard school, centred at Milan, though it hardly had a clear existence before the sixteenth century.

*The Umbrian and other schools*

The north-east of Italy produced some of the finest work of our period. The Paduan school was more influenced by the study of the classics than any other, a characteristic which it owed largely to Francesco Squarcione (1394–1474), no great painter, but a most inspiring teacher and an enthusiastic admirer of ancient sculpture. His influence is very evident in the statuesque work of Mantegna (1431–1506), a master of composition and of light and shade, whose pictures, if rather stiff, are of remarkable dignity.

*The Paduan school*

The Venetian school is in many ways very different from any other. It shows no deep religious feeling and no particular interest in the classics. It has been argued that the Venetians were hard-headed business men, who did not pretend to be artistic, but knew what they liked—namely, the pleasant things of life, in as rich profusion as possible, with of course "the best of everything." From the beginning, therefore, Venetian painting was inclined to be exuberant, and more remarkable for colour than for form. The influence of the gorgeous East is manifest here, as it had been all through Venetian history. The earliest masters who truly represent the Venetian school were the Vivarini family of Murano, a Venetian dependency. They painted whatever in the natural world appealed to their love of colour. Of their successors before the end of the century, the Bellinis

*The Venetian school*

32

—Jacopo (1400–64), Gentile (1426–1507), and Giovanni (1428–1516)—are the most worthy to be remembered. The best of them was Giovanni, a splendid colourist, whose landscape backgrounds are particularly famous. But the greatest of the Venetian masters were to come later.

The highest peak of Italian painting was reached in the early years of the following century. In the year 1500 that prodigy of versatility, Leonardo da Vinci (1452–1519), scholar, painter, sculptor, architect, scientist, mechanic, engineer, was already renowned. Michael Angelo (1474–1564) and Raphael (1483–1520) were just rising to fame. Andrea del Sarto (1486–1531) and Correggio (1494–1534) were growing up.

*Original genius of the Italian artists*

There has never been a more astonishing outburst of creative originality than appeared among the Italian artists of the fifteenth century and the years immediately following. Its real nature has been obscured by the obsession which ascribed it all to the alleged re-birth of the classics and denied that anything good could evolve from the Middle Ages. It is true that the painters were increasingly disposed to select their themes from classical mythology. It is true that in their drawing many of them were much influenced by the study of classical sculpture. But their art had its roots in the earlier Middle Ages, they went to nature far more than to the classics for their inspiration, and what made them so magnificently great was not the teaching or example of the ancient Romans, or even of the ancient Greeks, but their own inborn genius.

*Narrow influence of the Humanists and the artists*

The merits of the artists and the influence of the Humanist scholars must be acknowledged. But one must beware of exaggerating the practical results of their work. It is undeniable that very few people knew or cared anything about the sayings or doings of the Humanists. Even the educated classes were less influenced than one might think. The old learning was entrenched in the universities, and it took a long time to oust it. The Italian universities themselves devoted far more attention to law than to literature in the fifteenth century. The influence of the artists, many may urge, was wider. It may be true that the artistic taste of ordinary people was better in the Middle Ages than it is now. Perhaps, too, those are right who contend that the Italians have a unique capacity for the just appreciation of art, though, apart from the period which we are now considering, there is not much in history to lend colour to such a view. It is not incredible, furthermore, that in certain Italian cities, notably Florence, there was an amazingly widespread interest in art of every form during the fifteenth century. But, when every permissible concession has been made, the plain fact remains that the masterpieces of Renaissance sculpture can have been seen by few, those of Renaissance painting by fewer. And in those days, unless you actually saw them, you could not tell what they were like. North of the Alps of course the influence of both Humanists and artists was much less than it was in Italy. It is, in short, vain to pretend that the revival of the study of classical literature or the exuberant fruitfulness of Renaissance art had much to do with the rapid spread of the teachings of the ecclesiastical reformers of the next century.

Some authorities for chapters xxi and xxii :—
> *Cambridge Medieval History*, vol. vii, chap. xxv ; vol. viii, chaps. xxiv, xxv, with bibliographies, Cambridge, 1932 and 1936.
> *Cambridge Modern History*, vol. i, chaps. i, xvi, xvii, xviii, with bibliographies, Cambridge, 1903.
> Schirmer, W. F. : *Der englische Frühhumanismus*, Leipzig, 1931.

1. Learning and Art—
> Beccadelli, Antonio (called Panormita) : *Epistolarum libri œii*, ed. L. Mehus, Florence, 1741.
> Bruni, Leonardo (called Aretino) : *Epistolarum libri viii*, ed. L. Mehus, 2 vols., Florence, 1741.
> Bracciolini, Poggio : *Epistolae*, ed. T. Tonelli, 3 vols., Florence, 1832-61.
> *Angelo Polizianos Tagebuch* (1471-9), ed. Wesseleski, Jena, 1929.
> *The treatise of Lorenzo Valla on the Donation of Constantine*. Trans. C. B. Coleman, New Haven, 1922.
> Vasari, G. : *Le Vite de' più eccelenti pittori, scultori e architettori*. Many editions in both Italian and English.

These works will give some idea of the standpoint of the fifteenth-century humanists and artists. For what may be called the traditional view of the Renaissance, the following books may be consulted :
> Burckhardt, J. : *The Civilization of the Renaissance in Italy*. Trans. from the 15th German edition by S. G. C. Middlemore, London, 1878.
> Symonds, J. A. : *The Renaissance in Italy*, 7 vols., London, 1875-86 ; *A Short History of the Renaissance in Italy* (abridgment of the last-named work by A. Pearson), London, 1893.
> Voigt, G. : *Die Wiederbelebung des classischen Alterthums*, 2 vols., Berlin, 3rd ed., Berlin, 1893.

The contrasting attitude of recent historians is exemplified in the articles by E. F. Jacob and A. S. Turberville in *History*, 1931-2.

Mention may also be made of W. Shepherd : *Life of Poggio Bracciolini* (Liverpool, 1802) ; E. Walser : *Poggius Florentinus' Leben und Werke*,

(Leipzig, 1914); Wolff, M. von : *Lorenzo Valla, sein Leben und seine Werke* (Leipzig, 1893), and *Leben und Werke des Antonio Beccadelli genannt Panormita* (Leipzig, 1894). Many of the works enumerated under chaps. xix and xx of course shed much light on the history of the Renaissance.

ii. Geographical Discovery—

Baker, J. N. L. : *A History of Geographical Discovery and Exploration*, new edition, London, 1937.

Beazley, C. R. : *Prince Henry the Navigator* (Heroes of the Nations), New York, 1890 ; *The Dawn of Modern Geography*, 3 vols., London, 1897–1906.

Margry, P. : *La conquête et les conquérants des Iles Canaries*, Paris, 1896.

Markham, Sir C. R. : *Life of Christopher Columbus*, London, 1892.

Major, R. H. : *Life of Prince Henry of Portugal*, London, 1868.

Newton, A. P. : *The Great Age of Discovery*, London, 1932.

Prestage, E. : *The Portuguese Pioneers*, London, 1933.

*Select documents illustrating the 4 voyages of Columbus*, trans. and ed. C. Jane, 2 vols., 1930–3.

Vignaud, H. : *Histoire critique de la grande entreprise de Christophe Colomb*, Paris, 1911. (Most important.)

Williamson, J. A. : *The Voyages of John and Sebastian Cabot*, London, 1937.

Young, A. B. Filson : *Christopher Columbus and the New World of his discovery*, 3rd ed., London, 1911.

Recent works which deal with the beginnings of printing are J. C. Oswald : *A History of Printing* (New York, 1928), and G. P. Winship : *Gutenberg to Plantin* (Cambridge, 1926).

CHAPTER XXII

## SCIENCE, DISCOVERY, AND INVENTION IN THE FIFTEENTH CENTURY

IN the fifteenth century men's minds were unquestionably in a restless state. There was a feeling of change in the air. Old ideas were ceasing to satisfy. The extravagances of the Humanists were a symptom rather than a cause of this condition of affairs. One must not suppose that it was due, as in our own time, to scientific discovery, in the usual sense of the term. The intellectual movement of the fifteenth century caused little advance in science. Not indeed that science stood still; it progressed somewhat, but not noticeably faster than it had done since the revival of learning in the eleventh century. The notion that Nicolas of Cusa, who in any case was not a typical Humanist, discarded the geocentric theory of the universe and believed that the earth moved round the sun, has recently been shown to be a delusion; while the celebrated German mathematician, Johann Müller, called Regiomontanus, often praised as having revolutionized the study of mathematics and rendered possible the discovery of America, is now seen to have been only a distinguished member of a long series of mathematicians. Copernicus, it must be remembered, though born in the fifteenth century, did not announce his startling theories until shortly before his death in 1543, and they had small influence on European thought until the seventeenth century. Throughout the sixteenth, the old authorities were revered, the old beliefs accepted, the old deductive methods followed. The practice of alchemy, astrology, and sorcery in all its branches was never more widespread. It was only in the seventeenth century that there came that revolt against the authority of the ancients which was a condition precedent of any substantial scientific progress.

Nevertheless, valuable contributions to science were made in the fifteenth century through the remarkable achievements

**Medieval exploration**

of the explorers, even though they were rarely if ever actuated by any scientific interest. A great deal of exploration had of course been accomplished by Europeans during the previous centuries of the Middle Ages. For the most part travellers had turned their attention to the East and had journeyed by land. Some of them were astonishingly successful. It has been said that "the thirteenth century knew China better than we knew it in the middle of the nineteenth century." The incentive of these extensive travels was partly commercial, partly religious, and it would be hard to say whether spices or souls proved the stronger stimulus to enterprise. Maritime exploration, however, lacked encouragement. Ships were small, aids to navigation inadequate. The Mediterranean peoples, who were the most inclined towards travel, used the galley, unsuited for oceanic voyages. The maritime nations of the west and north had enough to occupy their energies without hazarding their lives and fortunes on the Atlantic.

In the fourteenth century, however, conditions altered. Political changes in the Far East, the rise of the Ottoman Turks nearer at hand, rendered more precarious the supply of those Oriental luxuries which had become almost necessary to western Europe. Merchants began to consider means of circumventing their difficulties. It was not merely a question of finding a new way of journeying eastward to India and the lands beyond. Every educated man and able seaman knew that the world was round; Marco Polo had greatly over-estimated the length of the land journey from Europe to China and Japan; and already there had been speculation as to the possibility of reaching those parts by sailing westward. But it was probably Africa which principally interested the fourteenth-century explorers. There was a good deal of southward travel in that continent by land or river. Missionaries went far up the Nile; the Sahara was crossed and the Niger reached. There were also attempts to solve the mysteries of Africa by maritime enterprise. Genoese sailors tried, though in vain, to circumnavigate it. The coast of the Sahara was known to be singularly forbidding; but at least since the time of Edrisi, the Arab geographer of the twelfth century, men had been aware that beyond there lay a fertile littoral, watered by a great river—the Senegal. It was supposed that this river rose in east Africa, not far from the source of the Nile, and that Christian Abyssinia could be reached by ascending it. Here, then, were prospects not only of great wealth, but also of inflicting a blow on Islam by outflanking the long line of Mohammedan peoples along the southern shores of the Mediterranean, and precluding their southward expansion.

In this quickening oceanic enterprise the lead at first was taken by Italians, especially by the Genoese. Information as to their early doings is scanty and obscure ; but it is evident that their predominance soon began to be challenged by the Portuguese. The first substantial achievements of these maritime explorers were not performed on the African mainland, but among the Atlantic islands. By the middle of the fourteenth century the Canaries had been repeatedly visited, and both the Portuguese and the Castilians had acquired claims to their possession. Mariners of unknown nationality had called at Madeira. The Azores, 750 miles from the mainland of Europe, had also been discovered, though when and by whom we do not know. No attempt, however, had been made to colonize any of these islands. What principally attracted adventurers westward and southward was the possibility of a lucrative traffic in slaves. Hitherto the African slave trade had been mainly in the hands of Moslems, who shipped their wares from north Africa across the Mediterranean and found a good market for them in the Spanish peninsula and even in southern France. How far along the African coast their Christian competitors had been enticed it is impossible to say. The famous Florentine map known as the Laurentian Portolan, which was drawn in 1351, shows Africa shaped very much as it actually is ; but one cannot say how much the cartographer was relying on ascertained fact and how much on brilliant guesswork.

In the second half of the fourteenth century oceanic voyages were few. The disturbance of economic and social life occasioned by recurrent visitations of the Black Death was partly responsible for this ; but it so happened that the peoples most interested in maritime enterprise had much of their attention absorbed by domestic dissension or conflicts with one another. In 1402, however, the Frenchmen Jean de Bethencourt and Gadifer de la Salle (an

*Expedition of Bethencourt and La Salle to the Canaries, 1402*

honoured name in the history of geography) inaugurated a new phase of exploring activity. They selected a definite objective, the Canary Islands, and sailed thither, as they themselves said, to explore, to conquer, and to convert. They soon found, however, that the conquest of the whole group was beyond their unaided powers. Having received fair treatment when calling at a Castilian port, they decided to appeal to Castile, and leaving La Salle to hold what had been won, Bethencourt sailed thither. Henry III of Castile accepted his offer of homage for the archipelago, and

*The Canaries under the sovereignty of Castile*

invested him with very great authority there. A hard-headed, bargain-driving Norman, Bethencourt took all grants and favours for himself, the unfortunate La Salle being disgracefully ignored. Despite trouble with the natives and mutiny among his followers, La Salle, during his colleague's absence, had explored most of the westerly islands of the Canary group, virtually completed the conquest of Lanzarote, and extracted from the native king of the island and his subjects a profession of Christianity. On Bethencourt's tardy return in 1404, he nevertheless showed himself indifferent to La Salle's claims on his generosity, and the two naturally fell out. Each went to Spain to urge his rights; but Bethencourt had sedulously ingratiated himself at the Castilian court; and La Salle could get no satisfaction. He went back to France, and vanished from the story.

Bethencourt's later career, one is glad to find, was not prosperous. He had trouble with members of his original expedition, who resented his treatment of La Salle. He conquered the island of Fuerteventura, but though he got fresh settlers from France, he failed to subjugate the rest of the group. His followers became obsessed with the belief that quick and easy wealth was to be gained by slave-trading. Bethencourt had to humour them, and even sanctioned a raid on the mainland, which, though falling short of expectations, yielded considerable profits. He organized the administration of the two islands in which his authority was effective, and in 1405 went once more to Spain for men and supplies. He managed to secure the appointment of a bishop for his colonists and converts: but he could not get the material help he needed, financial misfortunes befell him, he went home, and never visited the Canaries again. He probably died in 1425.

Though Bethencourt's undertaking was only in part successful, it is of great historical importance. It was the first serious effort for centuries at European colonization in uncivilized regions outside Europe itself. It turned the mind of Castile towards the advantages of maritime exploration. And Bethencourt's doings caused much concern to the Portuguese, and were undoubtedly a stimulus of that amazing enterprise which they again began to display immediately afterwards.

Bethencourt's brother, to whom the explorer bequeathed his rights in the Canaries, never derived any advantage from them. Before leaving the islands, Bethencourt had placed his nephew Maciot in charge of their administration. This young man intrigued with France for the transfer of his allegiance to the French Crown. Being discovered and threatened with punishment, he ceded the islands (which were not his) to the Castilian admiral sent to chastise him; he then fled and sold them to Prince Henry the Navigator of Portugal. The prince was encouraged to revive the dormant Portuguese claim to the Canaries, but two expeditions which he organized to enforce it ended in failure. The claims of the Castilian admiral passed from hand to hand in a bewildering way, until about the middle of the century they were owned by Diego de Herrera, who, with the acquiescence of the Castilian Crown—which had apparently ceased to care about the Canaries—succeeded in establishing his authority in the islands which Bethencourt had subjugated. He held his ground against renewed Portuguese attacks; but when Ferdinand and Isabella were secure on their thrones, they bethought themselves of the Canaries, welcomed complaints against Herrera's rule, and constrained him to accept an offer whereby he was to abandon all claim whatsoever to the three islands of Grand Canary, Palma, and Teneriffe in return for confirmation of his authority, under the lordship of Spain, over the other islands.

Ferdinand and Isabella at once undertook the conquest of their share. Portugal again offered armed opposition; but in the general pacification of 1479 between the two countries it was agreed that Spain should have the Canaries, while Portugal should enjoy exclusive rights of conquest and trade on the mainland of Africa, from Morocco to Guinea, and in the Azores, Madeira, and the Cape Verde Islands.

*Vicissitudes of the Canaries*

**Conquest of the Canaries completed, 1496**

Ferdinand and Isabella found their task by no means easy. The details of its accomplishment are strikingly like those which marked the conquest of the still unknown Mexico and Peru. One observes the same ruthless treachery both towards the natives and among the conquerors. A particularly valiant resistance was offered by the inhabitants of Grand Canary, who were not constrained to surrender until 1483. They had to accept Christianity, but were otherwise treated with leniency. Palma and Teneriffe also gave great trouble. Eventually Alfonso de Lugo, a typical *conquistador*, reduced Palma in 1492. Two years later, however, he was beaten by the people of Teneriffe and driven out of that island, which only succumbed to a renewed invasion in 1496. The three conquered islands were incorporated in the kingdom of Castile; but the Herrera family held the rest of the group until the end of the eighteenth century. The subsequent lot of the natives is a subject that lies outside the scope of this survey.

The value of the Canaries was not properly realized by the Spaniards when they were acquired. It might have been suggested by the fact that in 1492 Columbus touched at Grand Canary, took in provisions, and carried out important repairs. Had the island not been in Spanish hands, it is extremely likely that his voyage would have failed. The islands speedily proved a most valuable stepping-stone between Spain and her American Empire.

It cannot be denied, however, that the part taken by Spaniards in medieval exploration was a humble one. Aragon had a long seaboard, and her mariners, especially the Catalans, were very active and skilful, but her attention was naturally turned towards the east. Castile had no lack of coast or seaports, but during most of the later Middle Ages she was in a state of internal disturbance and she still had a Moslem enemy at her gates. Portugal, facing west, with a long coast-line in proportion to her area, had a much stronger motive to attempt overseas discovery.

Though, as we have seen, Portuguese sailors had been to the Canaries and had probably shared in the discovery of Madeira and the Azores, Portugal had no overseas possessions at the end of the fourteenth century. The capture of Ceuta, however, excited great enthusiasm and a desire for further conquest in Africa. Prince Henry, the third son of King John I, Master of the Military Order of Christ, had already begun to encourage exploration, and soon his energy was almost wholly absorbed in the promotion of Portuguese expansion overseas.

*The Portuguese explorations*

To understand the course of discovery in the fifteenth century, it must be understood that the mariner's compass had long been known and was now widely used. Some had viewed it askance as savouring of magic, but this prejudice was almost extinct. The astrolabe, too, was familiar. There were maps which purported to show the Atlantic coasts of Europe and Africa, together with such islands as had been discovered, but they were of little practical aid to navigation. Clocks, though invented some time before, were as yet too inaccurate to be of service in taking observations; they slowed down gradually from the moment they were wound up, and it took very little disturbance to stop them at any moment. The Middle Ages had invented the rudder, but ocean-going ships were still very clumsy. Those used by Europeans had only one mast and being wholly square-rigged could hardly sail into the wind at all. The marvel is that the mariners of the time could achieve so much.

*Difficulties of oceanic navigation*

Though Prince Henry is commonly styled "the Navigator," he rarely left land himself. He spent most of his time at Sagres, now Cape St. Vincent, where he built a palace which contained a primitive observatory. He seems to have been genuinely interested in mathematics and what passed then for astronomy, but there has been much exaggeration in the tales of his collecting scientists from all parts of Europe and establishing a school of navigation. Word went round among seafaring men and others of an adventurous turn that remunerative employment might be obtained from this Portuguese prince. Men of very various nationalities thus made voyages under his patronage, which meant that he supplied much of the necessary capital and drew a proportionate share of the profits.

*Prince Henry the Navigator*

Geographical discoveries no doubt interested and pleased the Prince, especially when they were made in his service. But it is probable that his main object was gain—for himself naturally—but still more for his country. It was to be achieved through traffic in tropical products, but especially

*His motives*

through the slave trade. Striking testimony as to the outlook and aims of the Portuguese explorers and their patrons is afforded by the enthusiasm which greeted the first lucrative capture of slaves by one of the Prince's expeditions and the increase of maritime activity which ensued. It was of course hoped also that new lands would be conquered for Portugal and the Order of Christ and that many heathen would consequently become Christians. The belief that the Moslems of north Africa might be hemmed in provided a further incentive, but it is only late in the Prince's life that there are traces of a serious expectation that the southern extremity of Africa might be doubled and a new route to India thus become available.

*Achievements of Portuguese seamen*

The Canaries having been seized by Castile, it was natural that the Portuguese should make sure of Madeira and the Azores, long known but never occupied, and indeed unvisited for many years. In 1419 and 1420 the Madeira group of islands was annexed, and in the following years, thanks largely to Prince Henry's assistance, colonized. In the fourth decade of the century the settlement of the Azores was begun. Meanwhile, progress was being made with what was accounted a more important task—the establishment of commercial relations with the fertile regions of the west African littoral. How ill-equipped and timid were the navigators of the time is shown by the failure of several expeditions to double Cape Bojador, thus far the southward limit of Portuguese travel. The feat, however, was accomplished in 1434, and two years later Affonso Gonçalves Baldaya reached Rio de Oro. Hitherto the financial results of the undertakings promoted by Prince Henry had been disappointing, but in 1441 an expedition which got to Cape Blanco brought back a profitable cargo of natives. This marks the beginning of the Portuguese slave trade as a source of wealth. Large ventures were now fitted out, not with the object of going anywhere new, but simply to seize slaves in regions that were soon familiar. Nevertheless, there were still sailors who, whether from greed or from curiosity, braved the unknown. In 1445 the Senegal river was at last reached. In the following year

*Cape Verde reached, 1446*

Diniz Diaz made the most westerly promontory of Africa, which he called Cape Verde, and another adventurer, going farther, reached Guinea, where he found genuine negroes, much more powerful than the natives to the north and manifestly worth more in the European market. The evidence concerning the events of the next few years is confusing. For some time, it seems, little progress was made. In 1460, however, the Cape Verde Islands were discovered. But of this achievement Prince Henry can hardly have heard, for in that year he died.

The maritime activity of the Portuguese scarcely slackened, for now it could pay for itself. Affonso " the African," though an imprudent ruler in some respects, strove to advance Portuguese commerce, and on the island of Arguin he repaired and strengthened a fort, originally built at the instance of Prince Henry, which served as a depot for the West African trade. And in 1471 further notable exploits were performed; for Fernando Po sailed to the very end of the Gulf of Guinea, while other pilots discovered the islands of San Thomé and Annabon, and thus crossed the Equator. *The Equator crossed, 1471*

Under John II maritime enterprise was yet more generously promoted. It was in his time that the great stronghold of San Jorge de Mina was founded on the Gold Coast. In 1484 Diego Cam reached the mouth of the Congo, while two years later Bartholomew Diaz rounded the Cape of Good Hope, and sailed far enough beyond to satisfy himself that the southernmost limit of Africa had been reached. But traditional ideas were still strong in Portugal, and men did not allow these southern voyages to absorb all their interest. About this time Portuguese expeditions were striving to reach Abyssinia from the Red Sea and from the Senegal, and there was actually one seeking the north-east passage to China. *The Cape of Good Hope rounded by Diaz, 1486*

The discovery of America, which followed so soon, had consequences so stupendous that one is apt to undervalue the work of the Portuguese along the west coast of Africa. To the men of that age, however, their discoveries seemed marvellous, and the ,sensation caused by the exploits of Columbus was hardly greater. His great feat, indeed, excited contemporaries less than one might think, since for some time afterwards men did not realize that a new world had been found, and recognition of the fact came so gradually as to cause comparatively little shock. Let it be remembered *Significance of the Portuguese discoveries* that the vaguest notions prevailed as to the size, shape, climate, and physical characteristics of Africa; for if some cartographers had made wonderfully accurate guesses, these had met with no wider acceptance than conjectures which were grossly incorrect. The Portuguese voyages settled many geographical controversies, and they brought to the knowledge of Europe races of men, species of beasts, natural products in profusion, meteorological phenomena, constellations, which had been previously unknown or told of only by fleeting rumour. The effect on the minds of contemporaries is eloquently described in a letter addressed to King John II by the Humanist Politian, who, notwithstanding his devotion to the Ancients, hoped to be entrusted with the task of recording the feats of the Argonauts of his own day.

It will have been noticed that the southward advance of the Portuguese became increasingly rapid during the latter half of the fifteenth century. It was partly that men became accustomed to the idea of venturing into the unknown. But both the exploits just recounted and the still more astonishing feats to be performed in the last decade of the century are in part to be explained by recent improvements in the rig of ships. Most of the vessels that now sailed the Atlantic had two and some had three masts. They were consequently capable of manœuvres utterly beyond the capacity of the craft of fifty years before. One could now make some headway with a contrary wind, especially in those ships that were fitted with a bowsprit. The successes of Diaz, Columbus, and Vasco da Gama are not therefore to be wholly attributed to their superior daring and skill; they were far better equipped than their predecessors of the days of Prince Henry.

**Career of Christopher Columbus**

Before Columbus first appeared in Portugal, probably in 1476, the sailors of that country were familiar with the theory that China might be reached by sailing west and also knew many stories about unexplored lands far beyond the Azores. There was thus no disposition to dismiss Columbus out of hand, especially since he was an experienced mariner, who had been to Madeira in one direction and Iceland in the other. The last years of the reign of Affonso the African were not however propitious for speculative sailors. But when John II had succeeded to the throne, Columbus put forward detailed proposals for a voyage of discovery, which were submitted to the judgment of experts. That his plans were rejected is not astonishing when we consider what the Portuguese were doing and on the point of achieving : why spend money on a problematical quest when success was certain elsewhere ? In 1484, therefore, Columbus, having sent his brother Bartholomew to urge his views in France and England, betook himself to Castile. The Count of Medina Celi befriended him and gave him an introduction at court, where he appeared in 1485. The King and Queen having heard him, his claims and requests were referred to a committee. When its tardy report was presented in 1490, it was adverse to Columbus, who resolved to try his luck in France. On the way he called at the monastery of La Rabida near Palos. There Juan Perez, a former confessor of Queen Isabella, became greatly interested in his opinions and projects, and it was through the influence of Perez that he was recalled and summoned before the two sovereigns near Granada in the summer of 1491. Columbus' statement of his case now made a deep impression, but his demands, both for aid and for reward if successful, were so extravagant that in January 1492 he was again dismissed. He departed northward, to all seeming no better off than when he had first arrived in Castile some seven years before. But already pressure was being brought to bear on the Queen by some who believed that Columbus was offering Spain an opportunity which it would be madness to reject. Before he had gone ten miles, Columbus was overtaken by a royal messenger. Negotiations were resumed, and in April an agreement was at last reached. He was to be viceroy and to have the hereditary title of admiral in the lands which he should discover, and if he contributed one-eighth of the cost of the expedition, he was to receive a like proportion of the profits. Though Isabella authorized the recall of Columbus, it was apparently from the revenues of Aragon that most of the money for his enterprise was drawn. At all events, the old view that Ferdinand was positively opposed to the undertaking must be discarded.

The preparations were taken in hand vigorously, but it would probably have been impossible to enlist a sufficient number of recruits but for the assistance of Martin Pinzon, a very famous pilot, who had long been interested in Columbus' projects. It was largely owing to him that the expedition was able to sail from Palos on August 8. Columbus had three caravels and some 120 men. The *Santa Maria* was much the biggest of his ships and the only one that was decked. Most of the sailors were Andalusians. It has been pointed out that there was no priest in the whole company. After a quick passage Columbus made Grand Canary on August 9, and there he remained for repairs until September 6. Then the little squadron had five weeks at sea. The crews became frightened, and disaffection bordering on mutiny was shown. But on October 12 Watling's Island in the Bahamas was sighted and the whole direction of human history altered. Columbus of course did not know what he had done. He had sailed unexpectedly far without making land, and he concluded that he must have missed the new land that he had expected to find or else that it did not exist. He therefore believed that he had reached the Orient.

[Marginal note: Discovery of America, Oct. 12, 1492]

It is too often forgotten that Columbus' first voyage did not end here. He was not satisfied with Watling's Island, which was soon found to be but a poor place. On October 28 he made the north coast of Cuba. He landed, and despatched two of his men to the court of the Great Khan. Thence he sailed to Haiti, which he called Española because it looked like Spain, though Pinzon believed it to be the Cipango of the Far East. Here the *Santa Maria* was wrecked. Columbus left forty men in a fort, promising to return for them as soon as he could, and having tried to make friends with the natives he sailed for home on January 4, 1493. It was barely a year since he had been dismissed from the Spanish court, his life apparently a hopeless failure.

[Marginal note: Return of Columbus to Spain, May 1493]

On the homeward voyage Columbus called at the Azores, where he was for a time in danger of being arrested. He landed at Lisbon, where the Portuguese were manifestly very jealous, though after some hesitation they let him go. He was at Palos again on May 15. Ferdinand and Isabella forthwith applied to the Pope for the recognition of Spain's right to the new discoveries.

Here Columbus may fittingly be left, happy amid the applause which his achievements aroused. With his later discoveries and disappointments we cannot concern ourselves. He was not a great man. Seldom have such pregnant achievements been accomplished by anyone with so unimpressive a personality.

To round off the story of fifteenth-century exploration one should glance at the doings of Vasco da Gama and the Cabots, though before they performed their greatest feats Columbus had completed his second voyage, with its ill-fortune and disillusionment. The reply of the Portuguese to Spain's success was Vasco's expedition in 1497. He had with him four fine ships, and was furnished with every known aid to navigation. After making the Cape Verde Islands he stood out to sea and did not sight land for three months. He rounded the Cape in November and in March 1498 was at Mozambique. Thence he sailed to Mombasa and across the Indian Ocean to Calicut. He was back at Lisbon in September 1499 with two ships and one-third of his men. He had performed a very great feat of seamanship, demanding more skill, if not more courage, than that of Columbus. *Vasco da Gama*

Already another notable enterprise had been carried out by the Cabots. It ought to be more generally remembered that as early as 1480 an expedition had sailed westward from Bristol to seek new lands across the Atlantic. It failed, but further voyages to the same end were promoted by the enthusiasm of John Cabot, a Venetian citizen of Genoese birth, who, after vainly trying his luck in Spain and Portugal, settled in England. It was not until 1496, however, that he and his four sons, sailing under royal authority, landed in North America, though whether in Labrador, Newfoundland, Cape Breton Island, or somewhere farther south remains uncertain. They came back with wild reports of the value of their discovery, which they believed to belong to the dominions of the Great Khan. Strange to say, their fish stories had the most truth in them. Henceforth the Grand Banks and the adjacent waters were a great resort for the fishermen of western Europe, whose rulers thus had less need to conciliate the Scandinavian powers and the Hanseatic League. Cabot's next voyage was less encouraging. For that reason and others, little more exploration was attempted by the English for a long time, and trade in North American waters fell almost exclusively into the hands of the Portuguese and the French. *The Cabots*

The full effects of all these discoveries were of course not

*Historical importance of the discoveries*

discernible until long after the end of the fifteenth century, if indeed they are discernible yet. But on the minds of the people of Europe they immediately began to have an influence far greater than that exerted by any revival of learning or development of art. Only a few were affected by the changes in education, or saw the masterpieces of contemporary sculptors and painters. But besides scholars and politicians, all business men, everybody with the least smattering of learning, and a great many more—every one for instance who dwelt in a seaport or knew a sailor—would hear of the marvels brought to light through the voyagers. The mind of Europe was violently jolted. No one could guess what might next be discovered. People became accustomed to believe the incredible. The plain man knew nothing of what it feels like to look into Homer for the first time, or to become aware of a new planet; but he could share the wild surmise of stout Cortes.

And the explorers had done more than open new paths for trade and disturb the mind of Europe. The fifteenth century was a critical time in the history of the secular conflict between East and West. For long the initiative had been held by the East. Europe had been at bay, desperately warding off the onrush of foes that threatened her very vitals. The Franks had checked the Arabs in the West, and the Spaniards had made a successful if limited counter-attack. An ambitious sortie—the Crusades—had held off the Turkish menace for over two centuries. Meanwhile, however, the Tatar onrush of the thirteenth century had nearly shattered the flank of the Christian defence; and scarcely had that peril been averted when the Ottoman Turks began that relentless offensive which we have summarily traced elsewhere. Where would their advance be stayed? In the year 1500 men had no reason to believe that it was nearing its limit. Venice had been worsted. Even Italy had been invaded, and that the attack had failed was due rather to the domestic discords of the Moslems than to the military prowess of the Christians. The victory of the Spaniards in Granada was very small compensation for the losses of Christendom in the East. A glance at a map of the then known world will show that in the fifteenth century the area held by Christianity and western culture was small and shrinking.

# EFFECTS OF THE DISCOVERIES

Then, long before Canning, the explorers called a New World into existence to redress the balance of the Old. The Portuguese laid open three-quarters of a continent to Christian enterprise, and furthermore outflanked the Moslem position. The relations between Western Europe and the Turkish Empire were at once fundamentally altered. Next, with the discovery of America, an enormous new area was made available for European settlement. At the worst, if the Turks could not be stayed, it might afford a haven of refuge to those inhabitants of western Europe who, like Aeneas and his followers, preferred risks and hardships in the west to an ignominious life amid the ruins of all they valued. And in any event it offered Europeans an opportunity which, albeit tardily, they have seized. Consider how much of the earth's surface belonged to European civilization in the fifteenth century, and compare it with the domain of European civilization now. Very little of the Old World has transferred its cultural allegiance. That the relative strength of western civilization has so greatly increased is due almost entirely to its spread into the new lands opened before it by the fifteenth-century explorers.

The effect of the discoveries and of the new opinions that were being propagated would have been felt far less quickly and powerfully had it not been for the invention of printing. It may be an exaggeration to say that it is the most momentous invention in the history of the world, but it is certainly the most momentous since that of writing, and of more fundamental consequence than any of the countless inventions of the last two centuries, however much they may have transformed the conditions of life.

*Invention of printing*

It is of course true that the art of printing with movable types was known in China in the eleventh century. But there, owing to the nature of the Chinese alphabet, it proved to be of little practical use. In any case, it did not spread westward. The Europeans invented printing independently.

It is most astonishing that the invention of printing was so long delayed. Dies, stamps, and seals had been employed for thousands of years. Wood-blocks were used in the Far East in the eighth century A.D. and became common there later. But when, in the fourteenth century, they appear in Europe, they, too, seem to have been the outcome of European inventiveness. Late in the same century, block-books began to be made, each page being printed from a single block. They were of necessity short, and the pictures were commonly more important than the text. Prints from blocks were produced by rubbing, not by means of a press; the ink employed was thin and sickly-looking; and altogether a block-book, however interesting historically, is seldom at all attractive in appearance. It is clear that this use of wood-blocks was unlikely to lead far. To make a block of a page of written matter cost far more time and trouble than to copy it by hand. The method, therefore, could be used only for short announcements, exhortations, or pamphlets, of which it could be confidently predicted that a large number of copies would be required.

It was therefore only with the invention of separate types for each letter, types which could be employed over and over again, that printing became a valuable substitute for writing by hand. It is not known where, when, or by whom printing in this sense was first done. On all these questions there has been angry controversy. The issue has been confused by patriotism, positive and negative, some writers being anxious to advance the honour of their own country, others seeking to discredit the claims of a traditional enemy. Forgery has been employed to substantiate the theories of disputants. In the present state of knowledge, an open-minded agnosticism seems the most prudent attitude.

One may venture to say, however, that it seems on the whole likely that the first real printing was done in Holland in the second quarter of the fifteenth century. That Laurens Janszoon Coster of Haarlem, who died in 1440, was the inventor is attested by no better authority than a posthumous work of one Hadrianus Junius, who died in 1575. It is in any case certain that if the practice of printing was known in the Low Countries before 1450, it was afterwards discontinued there, for when, in the last years of his life, Duke Philip the Good wished to have a book printed, he was obliged to have recourse to Cologne. The specimens of early printed books which apparently come from the Netherlands are indeed very crude. It seems likely that for that reason the new art failed to commend itself and proved unremunerative. One can readily think of modern inventions which had a vogue as novelties and then fell into temporary disfavour because of technical defects which were afterwards overcome.

The man who first made typography both an art and an industry was John Gutenberg. He stands to printing as George Stephenson stands to steam locomotion. So much seems certain, yet his career is very mysterious. Nothing printed during his lifetime bears his name as printer or gives any information about him in that capacity. He was probably born in 1898 in Strasbourg, and he died in 1468 in Mainz. It appears that as early as 1438 he was actively interested in printing. But the first piece of typography which can be attributed to him is an indulgence (commonly known as the 31-line indulgence) which was issued in 1454. There are also ascribed to Gutenberg's press a number of Bibles, grammars, and an encyclopædia of theology called the *Catholicon*. Particularly famous among his productions are two magnificent Bibles—the " 36-Line Bible " and the " 42-Line " or " Mazarin " Bible. Which was printed first is disputed, but each is a very fine example of typographical art. Once books of this kind could be produced, the triumph of the new invention was assured. *John Gutenberg, 1898 ?–1468*

Years before Gutenberg's death, however, his fame had been overshadowed by that of Fust and Schoeffer. Fust was a goldsmith who had for some time been in partnership with Gutenberg. Each accused the other of breaking his contract, and in 1455 a lawsuit gave Fust possession of Gutenberg's plant. Fust then went into partnership with Schoeffer, who is said to have formerly been Gutenberg's principal workman. The two co-operated until Fust's death in 1466, and are believed to have printed 115 books. Later the business was carried on by Schoeffer alone. He was a very great printer : indeed, modern experts have gone so far as to say that by him typography was " brought to perfection." He made a number of technical improvements in his art : he was, for instance, the first to print in colours, to use lead spacing between the lines, to cast Greek types. Type-founding in general was immensely advanced by him. Mainz was his business centre ; but he had branches in other towns, and he became the publisher of other men's productions as well as his own. *Development of printing in Germany*

Once the work of the Mainz printers had revealed the

advantages of the new art, it spread with astonishing rapidity. Its adoption was of course opposed by the very numerous people interested, directly or indirectly, in the copying and sale of manuscripts. It is nevertheless a mistake to imagine that the Church in general or the monks in particular were hostile towards the new invention.

It is questionable whether Bamberg or Strasbourg was the second city of Germany to possess a printing-press. Both were important centres of typography in the seventh decade of the century. Augsburg was another place where printing of very high quality was done before 1470, and its output of books soon became very great. By the end of the century the leading centre of the industry was probably Nürnberg, the scene from 1471 to 1513 of the labours of Anthony Koberger, who has been called "the first Captain of the Printing Industry." He eventually possessed, it is said, twenty-four presses and employed a hundred journeymen. He produced mainly religious books and editions of the classics, though perhaps his most famous publication was the so-called Nuremberg Chronicle—entitled by him the *Liber Chronicarum*, a compilation which appeared in 1493. Koberger had agents all over Europe, and was constantly seeking manuscripts which might be profitably reproduced. Cologne was another early centre of printing, and one particularly interesting to Englishmen, for it was Cologne's first printer, Ulrich Zell, a very prolific but not a very good worker, who taught the art to William Caxton. Many other German cities had printing-presses by the end of the century.

*Printing in Italy*

The priority of Germany in the invention of printing was generally acknowledged at the time, and in other countries typography was often referred to as "the German Art." But it was soon practised elsewhere. It spread first to Italy, where the earliest printers were Germans. The first Italian press was set up in 1464 at Subiaco, under the patronage of the great Benedictine monastery there; by the end of the century seventy-three Italian towns had presses, and there were thirty-eight printers in Rome alone. But the great centre of the art was Venice, long famous for its manufacture of paper and as a market for manuscripts. It has been computed that by the year 1500 there were a hundred separate printing works in Venice. The quality as well as the quantity of their output was indeed amazing. The industry had been started in Venice by Germans, but the greatest among the early printers of the republic was Nicolas Jenson, a Frenchman. Italians soon began to produce very good work, and all previous printers of Venice were surpassed by the great Aldus Manutius, whose magnificent achievements as a printer of classical, especially Greek, texts belong mainly to the sixteenth century.

There is a well-known story that in 1458 Charles VII of France, having heard of the new art, sent Nicolas Jenson, then a master of the Paris Mint, to learn its secrets at Mainz. If the tale is true, the King must have been disappointed, for whatever discoveries Jenson made were not turned to account in France. There great hostility was for long shown towards printing, especially by the booksellers of Paris, whose enmity drove Fust away when in 1468 he tried to sell printed Bibles in the city. But printing was viewed with friendly interest by Louis XI and the Sorbonne ; and in 1470, thanks to the encouragement of John Heynlin, the German prior of the celebrated college, and William Fichet, its librarian, three skilled Germans set up printing-presses within its walls. Before long they had independent establishments, and shortly afterwards French printers began to compete with them. Paris soon had numerous presses, though for a short time before the end of the century Lyons was the chief centre of French printing. *Printing in other countries*

Typography was introduced into Spain, perhaps as early as 1468, certainly by 1475. Several cities had presses before the century closed. Here, as usual, the art was first practised by Germans, but natives soon took it up.

The Netherlands, after the lapse mentioned above, witnessed a great development of the new industry. Of the numerous places where it was conducted, special reference may be made to Bruges, since it was there that Caxton worked under Colard Mansion and produced the first books printed in English—the *Recuyell of the Historyes of Troye* and *The Game and Playe of the Chesse.* Very shortly after their publication, Caxton went to England, where in 1476 he set up his renowned press at Westminster.

In considering the early diffusion of printing, one must not forget that in the years under review there were many *Itinerant printers* wandering printers, each with his portable press. Such men went from place to place looking for commissions from rich patrons of learning or religious corporations. When given a job, the printer lodged in the most convenient village, unless he was so lucky as to be given quarters in a castle or a monastery. Thus if one finds some obscure village named as the place where a book was published, one may not infer that it possessed a permanent printing-office. Travelling typographers were very active in Germany, France, and Spain, until the activity of the presses in the towns destroyed the demand for their services.

*Various types in use* Early printed books closely resembled manuscripts in appearance. The handwriting of the time was copied by the type-founders. This was unfortunate, because the script in vogue in fifteenth-century Germany was neither clear nor beautiful—much inferior to that employed two hundred years before. From it, however, was derived " Gothic " type—sometimes called Black Letter—which was customarily used in Germany until recent times and is not yet ousted, despite its manifest defects. But when German printers went to Italy, they found that the fashionable script there was one which the Humanists had derived from what is styled the " Carolingian minuscule," the hand used by the best scribes in the age of Charles the Great and his earlier successors and thus exemplified in many of the manuscripts of the classics which the Humanists had unearthed or collected. Consequently, the Gothic type used in the first books printed in Italy was disliked, and the German printers invented a new type, copied from the script favoured by the Humanists. Thus was created " Roman " type, which before long was adopted in France and Spain, eventually drove " Blackletter " out of England, and is used in this book. Italic type was first employed by Aldus Manutius.

The art of typography developed with amazing rapidity. Before the end of the century it had produced some of its most magnificent achievements. But it was the number, not the artistic merits of its products, that made it a revolutionary force in history. There is no need to insist on its effects on the dissemination of knowledge; indeed their very familiarity creates a danger that they may be under-estimated. What is more likely to be overlooked is that it now first became possible for the text of a book to be preserved from progressive corruption and for a large number of people to possess accurate texts of the same work. In education, lower and higher, reading by the pupil now had an unprecedented importance; listening and disputing, for good or evil, held a much humbler place than heretofore. It was a change advocated by the Humanists, but printing would have brought it to pass without them. And this is a reminder that many ill-considered statements have been made concerning the relation of printing and Humanism. Typography undoubtedly facilitated the spread of the so-called " New Learning " and later of Protestant opinion; but it was equally at the service of conservative propaganda. Printers were no more inclined towards heterodoxy than other men, and there was no ecclesiastical animosity against their craft. The early products of the presses were for the most part either religious books or famous works of the " Old Learning." We have seen that Gutenberg's best known productions were religious. The first book printed by Fust and Schoeffer was a Psalter, the first by Schoeffer alone was the *Summa* of Thomas Aquinas. The earliest product of the printing-press in Italy was the time-honoured Latin grammar ascribed to Donatus. Caxton's first work as a printer was done on an edition of Bartholomew the Englishman's *De proprietatibus rerum*, a well-known encyclopædia of the thirteenth century. Mentelin, one of the earliest and greatest printers of Strasbourg, limited himself almost exclusively to theological works, on the ground that they paid best. One of his undertakings was the *Speculum*, the huge encyclopædia of Vincent of Beauvais, which he published in eight folio volumes. The productions of the great Koberger were mostly works of conservative theology. Missals and other books of devotion appeared in great numbers; and new editions of the Canon Law were likewise common. Besides Donatus, the most familiar school-books and university textbooks, on which the youth of the Middle Ages had been nourished for centuries, were freely printed. Along with these, especially in Italy, there appeared numerous editions of the classics. The fact is that in the controversies of the fifteenth century, and the still more bitter ones of the sixteenth, the part of the new invention was strictly neutral. At the same time, it is true that the quick dissemination and the easy exchange of ideas facilitate the introduction of novel opinions and render it harder for conservative forces to check the flow of subversive thought. Thus the greatest medieval gift to human civilization was destined to hasten the downfall of medieval culture.

# GENEALOGIES

## THE HOUSE OF ANJOU

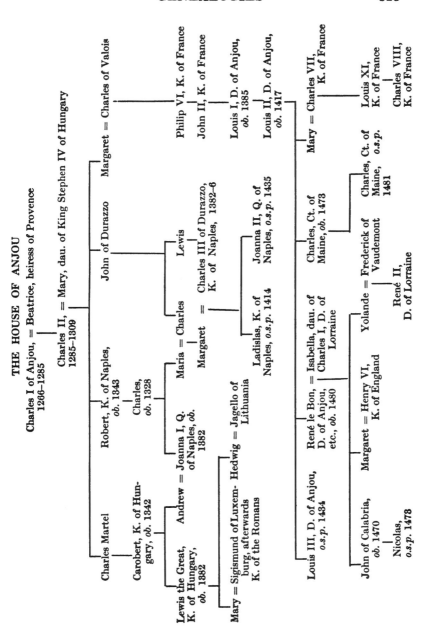

## THE HOUSE OF HABSBURG

Albert, D. of Austria, *ob.* 1358.

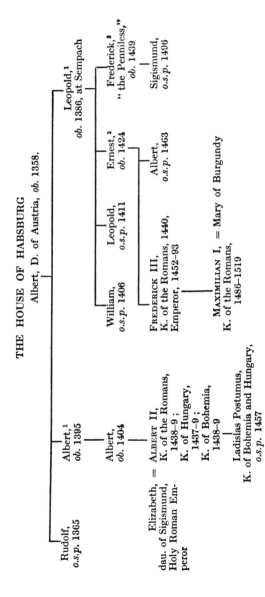

[1] On the death of Rudolf in 1365 the Habsburg Lands were divided between his surviving brothers, Albert receiving Austria, Leopold all the rest.
[2] After various arrangements among the sons of Leopold, Styria, Carinthia, and Carniola were held by Ernest, Tyrol and the Habsburg lands in Swabia by Frederick.
[3] This was the Frederick of Habsburg who figured so prominently at the time of the Council of Constance.

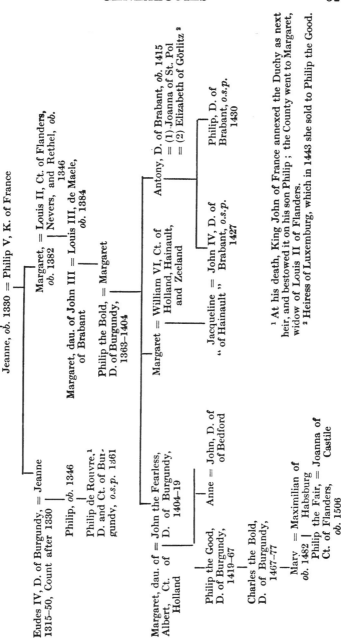

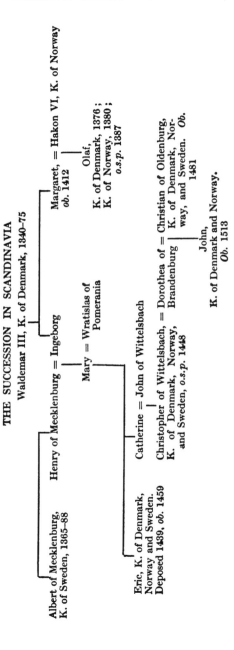

# GENEALOGIES 529

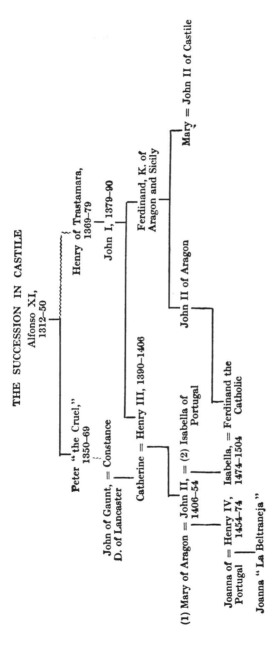

THE SUCCESSION IN CASTILE

# EUROPE FROM 1378 TO 1494

## THE ROYAL HOUSE OF ARAGON

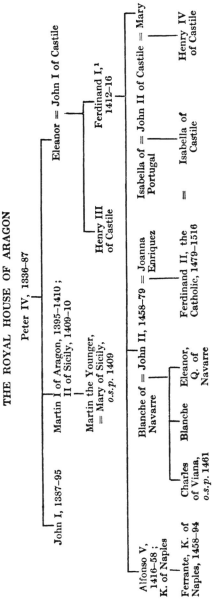

[1] He was elected King of both Aragon and Sicily, which were thenceforward united.

# INDEX

## A

Aachen, 99, 114, 161.
Aargau, 337.
Adamites, 224.
Adrianople, 429, 437, 441.
Affonso V, the African, King of Portugal, 394, 400, 511.
Africa, discoveries in, 504, 510, 511, 512, 515.
Agincourt, battle of, 44 sq.
Agricola, Rudolf, 493.
*Aides*, 11, 13, 14, 18, 27, 28, 86, 137.
Ailly, Peter d', Cardinal, 127, 133, 136, 143, 174, 180.
Albania, 436, 440, 441, 444.
Albert Achilles, *see* Brandenburg.
Albert II, King of the Romans (Albert I of Austria), 231, 314, 414, 418.
— of Mecklenburg, King of Sweden, 352, 396 sq.
Alberti, Leone Battista, 494.
Albizzi, the, 452, 457.
Albret, Charles d', Constable of France, 45.
Alcantara, Military Order of, 382.
Aleman, Louis d', Cardinal, 201, 204, 205.
Alençon, 48, 57.
— John I, Count, afterwards Duke of, 32, 45.
— John II, Duke of, 45, 75, 80, 84, 85, 94, 245, 247, 251.
Alexander V (Peter Philarghi), Pope, 152, 176, 217.
— VI (Rodrigo Borgia), Pope, 396, 423, 465, 474, 485.
Alfonso V, King of Aragon (Alfonso I of Naples), 391, 456, 457, 459, 490.
— of Castile, son of John II, 385, 386, 393.
Aljubarotta, battle of, 379, 399.
Alsace, 281, 282, 285, 286, 288, 324, 362.
Altmark, 329.
Amboise, 261.
America, discovery of, 511.
Amiens, 23, 250, 252.
Anagni, 125.
Ancenis, treaty of, 248.

Ancona, 177, 456, 478.
Andrea del Sarto, 500.
Angers, 140, 242.
Angora, battle of, 433.
Anjou, 41, 42, 56, 57, 80, 250, 258.
— Louis I, Duke of, 10, 19, 127 sq.
— Louis II, Duke of, 23, 26, 30, 128, 142, 153, 154.
— Louis III, Duke of, 456.
— René "the Good," Duke of, 87, 95, 257 sq., 277, 305 sq., 393, 457.
— Yolande of Aragon, Duchess of (wife of Louis II), 63, 92.
— Yolande of (daughter of René the Good), 258, 285.
— duchy of, 41, 42, 56, 57, 80, 258.
Annabon, 511.
Anne of Beaujeu, 262 sqq.
— of Bohemia, Queen of England, 24, 105, 214.
— of Brittany, Queen of France, 266, 268.
Ansbach, 326.
Antwerp, 355.
Appenzell, 336.
Apulia, 128.
Aquitaine, 24, 33, 34, 41, 42, 60, 65, 81, 83, 87, 90, 91, 93, 126, 249, 251, 267, 394.
Aragon, kingdom of, 127, 136, 147, 181, 205, 378, 386 sqq., 406.
Arbedo, battle of, 337.
Architecture, 3 sq., 451, 493 sq.
Argentan, 48.
Argos, 444.
Arguin, 511.
Arles, kingdom of, 100.
Armagnac, Bernard VII, Count of, 32, 46, 47, 49, 50, 179, 453.
— Jacques d', Duke of Nemours, 245, 247, 253.
— John IV, Count of, 85, 93, 189.
— John V, Count of, 93, 245, 247, 250, 251.
Armagnacs, the, 32, 33, 34, 36, 38, 42, 43, 52, 53, 317, 338.
Arras, 38, 40, 94, 255, 256.
— treaty of (1435), 81, 245, 274; (1482), 256.
Artevelde, Philip van, 14, 15.

Artois, 44, 63, 82, 85, 249, 255, 256, 269, 274.
Aschaffenburg, 318.
Asti, 128.
Athens, 444.
— duchy of, 443.
Augsburg, 348, 520.
Aussig, battle of, 165, 232.
Austria, 103, 271, 315, 316, 319, 323, 424.
— Albert III, Duke of, 103.
— See Albert II, King of the Romans, and Habsburg.
Auvergne, 80, 84.
Auxerre, 33, 82.
Avesnes, 255.
Avignon, 17, 25, 26, 109, 123, 125, 127, 129, 134, 135, 136, 138, 139, 140, 154, 194, 201, 212, 453.
Aviz, Military Order of, 399.
Azores, the, 505, 507, 510, 514.

B

Baden, 117.
Bahamas, the, 396, 514.
Bajazet I, Sultan, 430, 431, 432.
— II, Sultan, 422, 441, 444.
Baldaya, Affonzo Gonçalves, 510.
Balearic Isles, the, 389.
Balue, John, Cardinal, 249, 261.
Bamberg, 520.
Bar, duchy of, 258.
— Edward, Duke of, 45.
Barbara of Cilly, Empress, 169, 418.
Barbiano, Alberigo da, 127.
Barcelona, 388 sq., 393.
— treaty of, 269.
Barnet, battle of, 250.
Basel, 106, 191, 286.
— Council of, 81, 96, 168, 191, 192 sqq., 314, 317, 476.
Baudricourt, Robert de, 72.
Baugé, battle of, 57.
Bavaria, 102, 106, 286, 325, 327, 328, 334.
— Lewis, Duke of (brother of Queen Isabel), 36.
— Lewis IX, Duke of, 361.
— Stephen, Duke of, 21, 113.
Bayeux, 48.
Bayonne, 90.
Bayreuth, 326.
Beaufort, family of, 87, 89.
— Henry, Bishop of Winchester, afterwards Cardinal, 67, 76, 81, 166, 184, 233.
— See Somerset.
Beaufort-en-Valée, 57.
Beaugency, 58, 75.
Beaujeu, Peter, Lord of, 258, 261, 262.
Beaujolais, 258, 298.

Beauvais, 50, 76, 251.
— Pierre Cauchon, Bishop of, 78.
Bedford, John, Duke of, 59, 67, 74, 75, 76, 77, 80, 81, 191, 192; his policy as Regent of France, 50 sqq., 93; his victory at Verneuil, 66.
Belgrade, 421, 434, 440.
Bellini family, 499 sq.
Beltran de la Cueva, 385, 394.
Benedict XIII (Peter de Luna), Pope, his election, 135; his disputes with France, 25 sq., 135 sqq., 145 sq.; his negotiations with Gregory XII, 143 sqq.; deserted by cardinals, 147; holds Council at Perpignan, 147, 148; proceedings against him at Pisa, 151 sq.; at Constance, 178, 183; his negotiations with Sigismund, 178, 178 sq.; after the Council of Constance, 67, 189, 191.
Bergen, 357, 376.
Berlin, 328.
Berne, 282, 289.
Berry, John, Duke of, 10, 13, 14, 19, 20, 22, 23, 24, 29, 30, 32, 46, 137, 141, 306.
— Charles, Duke of, afterwards successively Duke of Normandy and of Guienne, 245, 246, 247 sqq.
Bethencourt, 44.
— Jean de, 505 sqq.
Beverhoutsveld, battle of, 15.
Béziers, 13.
Bingen, 164.
Blanche of Navarre, Queen of Aragon, 392.
Blanco, Cape, 510.
Bogomile heresy, the, 441.
Bohemia, 2, 5, 102, 105, 108, 110, 111, 113, 117, 126, 158, 163 sqq., 198, 208 sqq., 314, 315, 322, 324, 341, 403, 410, 415, 418 sqq., 422, 423 sq., 470.
Böhm, Hans, 361.
Boiardo, Matthew, 494.
Bologna, 150, 153, 154, 171, 194, 454.
Bona of Savoy, 463.
Boniface IX (Piero Tomacelli), Pope, 22, 23, 112, 114, 115, 128, 131, 189 sqq., 153.
Bordeaux, 90, 91, 251, 297, 311.
Bordelais, the, 90, 91.
Bornholm, 352.
Bosnia, 412, 422, 430, 432, 433, 437, 441.
Botticelli, 498.
Boucicaut, Geoffrey de, 138.
— Jean le Maingre de, Marshal of France, 27, 45, 145, 304, 432.

# INDEX

Bourbon, Charles, Duke of, 84, 85.
— John I, Duke of, 45.
— John II, Duke of, 245, 247, 253, 262.
— Louis, Duke of, 10, 27, 28, 82, 245, 247, 253, 262.
Bourbourg, 17.
Bourges, 33, 64, 300.
— Pragmatic Sanction of, 86, 96, 204, 243, 310.
Brabant, 272.
— Antony, Duke of, 45, 150, 272.
— John, Duke of, 59, 67, 272.
Braccio da Montone, 456.
Bramante, Donato, 494.
Brandenburg, 101, 102, 104, 110, 157, 158, 163, 325, 326, 327, 331, 334, 350.
— Albert Achilles, Elector of, 319, 322, 326, 328.
— Frederick I of Hohenzollern, Elector of, 112, 113, 157, 163, 165, 167, 168, 234, 314.
— John Cicero, Elector of, 321.
Brankovic, George, 434.
Breisach, 287.
Brescia, 115.
Breslau, 226.
Brest, 25.
Brethren of the Common Life, 313, 468, 493.
Brézé, Pierre de, 92, 94, 242, 302.
Brittany, 80, 248, 251, 256, 266, 267, 293, 297.
— Francis II, Duke of, 243 sq., 246, 247, 248, 249, 250, 252, 256, 266.
— John V, Duke of, 20, 23, 25, 82, 43, 49, 60, 63, 84, 85.
Bruges, 15, 276, 355, 388.
Brunelleschi, Filippo, 494.
Bruni, Leonardo, 489.
Brunkebjerg, battle of, 375.
Brunswick, 104, 117, 328, 329.
— Frederick, Duke of, 113.
— Otto of, 128.
Brussels, 275.
Buchan, John Stewart, Earl of, 57.
Bulgaria, 430, 435.
Bureau, Gaspard, 3, 89, 90, 307.
— Jean, 3, 89, 90, 92, 307.
— de la Rivière, 22.
Burgundian party, the, 32, 33, 34, 86, 38, 46, 48 sqq., 56, 58, 59, 61, 74, 78.
— School of sculpture, 496.
Burgundy, county of (Franche-Comté), 49, 254, 256, 269, 272, 274, 280, 288, 290.
— duchy of, 254, 256, 271.
— House of, 2, 3, 7, 256, 271, 319, 341, 477.

Burgundy, Charles the Bold, Duke of, as Count of Charolais, 244 sqq.; in the War of the Public Weal, 245 sq.; his further relations with Louis XI, 247 sqq., 281; his character, 278; his political aims, 278; suppresses Liége and Dinant, 279; rebellions of his subjects, 279 sq., 286, 287; nature of his government, 280 sq.; his dealings with Sigismund of Habsburg, 281 sq., 286 sq.; annexes Guelders, 283; his conference with Frederick III, 283 sqq.; his relations with Lorraine, 285, 288, 290; his increasing troubles, 286, 287; besieges Neuss, 287 sq.; at war with the Swiss, 288; his disasters and death, 288 sqq.
— John the Fearless, Duke of, marries, 20; at Nicopolis, 431; his rivalry with Louis of Orléans, 28 sqq.; his murder of Louis and its sequel, 30 sqq., 179; calls in the English, 33; in control of the government, 33 sqq.; driven from Paris, 88; treats with Henry V of England, 40, 47, 51; fails to resist English, 43; wages civil war, 46, 48; allies with Sigismund, 47; allies with Queen Isabel, 48; seizes Paris and controls French government, 49 sq.; negotiates with Armagnacs, 33, 49, 51; murdered, 52, 55; his relations with the Church, 142, 150; his domestic policy, 272.
— Mary of, daughter of Charles the Bold, 250, 253, 254, 255, 256, 282, 284, 316.
— Philip the Bold, Duke of, 10, 15, 17, 19, 20, 21, 22, 24, 25, 26, 28, 134, 139, 141, 271 sq.
— Philip the Good, Duke of, allies with the English, 52 sqq.; relieves Cosne, 58; his strained relations with the English, 59, 67, 74, 79 sq.; renews alliance, 76; besieges Compiègne, 77; signs Treaty of Arras, 81, 274; relations with Charles VII, 63, 85, 94 sq.; relations with Louis XI, 94, 240, 243 sq.; his territorial acquisitions, 272 sq., 276 sq.; his character, 274 sq.; his government, 274, 275; rebellions against him, 276, 277; his unrealized ambitions, 277.

Byzantine Empire, the, 200, 202 sqq., 427 sqq., 430, 432, 433, 434, 436, 437 sqq., 451.

C

Cabochians, the, 35 sq.
Cabot, John, 515.
Caen, 48, 55, 56, 80, 90, 311.
Cagliari, 27.
Calabria, John of, *see* Lorraine.
Calais, 25, 29, 43, 46, 47, 57, 83, 252.
Calatrava, Military Order of, 382.
Calicut, 515.
Calixtus III (Alfonso Borgia), Pope, 96, 473 sq.
Cam, Diego, 511.
Canary Isles, 379, 396, 505 sqq., 514.
Canterbury, Treaty of, 47, 162, 180.
Cape of Good Hope, 511.
Cape Verde Islands, 507, 510.
Capistrano, 440.
Carinthia, 103, 315, 319, 361.
Carmagnola, Francesco, 337, 455.
Carniola, 103, 315.
Carrara, Francesco, 453.
Casimir III, King of Poland, 404.
— IV, King of Poland, 415 sqq., 422 sq., 424.
Caslav, diet at, 229.
Castile, 2, 4, 20, 112, 130, 257, 379, 393, 513; its attitude in the Great Schism, 127, 130, 136, 138, 140, 147, 178 sq., 181, 182 sq.; its constitution, 379 sqq.; its society, 381 sqq.; political conditions, 383 sqq.; its union with Aragon, 393 sqq.; under Ferdinand and Isabella, 394 sqq.; acquires the Canaries, 506 sqq.
Castillon, battle of, 91.
Castriota, George, *see* Scanderbeg.
Catalonia, 257, 386, 387 sqq., 392, 393.
Catherine of France, Queen of England, 39, 40, 51, 53.
Cauchon, Pierre, Bishop of Beauvais, 78, 96.
Caux, 83, 251.
Caxton, William, 520, 521.
Cerdagne, 257, 269, 393.
Cerigo, 443.
Cesarini, Julian, Cardinal, 168, 192, 193, 195, 201, 202, 234, 435, 436.
Ceuta, 399, 508.
Chalcidice, 428.
*Chambre des Comptes*, 29, 37, 60, 64.
Champagne, 52, 53, 60, 61, 75, 76, 80, 249, 263, 299, 300.
Charles IV, Emperor, 99, 105, 106, 210, 364.
— V, King of France, 5, 10, 18, 21, 27, 127, 293.

Charles VI, King of France, his uncles, 10 sq.; suppresses rebellions, 13 sq., 16; his Flemish campaigns, 15, 17; his marriage, 20 sq., 47; his coup d'état, 21; failure of his government, 21 sqq.; his insanity, 23 sq., 27; his entente with England, 25; his attitude towards the Great Schism, 26; his relations to French parties, 31, 33, 38, 50; meets Henry V, 51; accepts Treaty of Troyes, 53; under Henry's regency, 54 sq.; dies, 59.
— VII, King of France, as Dauphin, 47, 51, 52, 55, 58; his character, 63; his helplessness, 63 sqq.; his relations with Joan of Arc, 72 sq., 75, 77, 78, 79, 96; crowned, 76; fails to use his opportunities, 76 sq., 80, 84; accepts Treaty of Arras, 81 sq.; treatment of Paris, 83; suppresses rebellions, 84 sq., 93 sq.; his methods of government, 86, 92 sq.; his standing army, 88 sq.; his mistresses, 92; his relations with the Dauphin, 94; his relations with Philip the Good, 94 sq.; his foreign policy, 95; his ecclesiastical policy, 95 sq.; dies, 97.
— VIII, King of France, as Dauphin, 253, 254, 257, 261; under the guardianship of the Beaujeus, 261 sqq.; his relations with Brittany, 268; his marriage, 268 sq.; prepares an expedition to Italy, 269, 465.
— of Durazzo, King of Naples, 128, 411.
— of Viana, 392.
Charolais, Charles the Bold, Count of, *see* Burgundy.
Chartrain, the, 60.
Chartres, 32, 57, 80, 489.
Chastel, Tanguy du, 63.
Chastellain, George, 281, 303, 304.
Cherbourg, 49, 90.
Chinon, 72.
Chioggia, 452.
Chios, island of, 302, 445.
Christ, Military Order of, 509, 510.
Christian I, King of Denmark, Norway, and Sweden, 873.
Christopher of Wittelsbach, King of Denmark, Norway, and Sweden, 372 sq.
Cilly, Barbara of, Empress, 169, 418.
— Ulrich III, Count of, 421.

# INDEX

Cividale, Council of, 153.
Clarence, George, Duke of, 250.
— Thomas, Duke of, 52, 56.
Clement VII (Robert of Geneva), Pope, 15, 16, 17, 19, 22, 23, 25, 109, 126 sqq., 130, 182, 184.
— VIII, anti-pope, 189.
Cleves, 184, 334.
— Adolf, Duke of, 320.
Clisson, Olivier de, 20, 23.
Coeur, Jacques, 92, 298, 300 sqq., 307.
Cologne, 114, 356, 518, 520.
— Dietrich von Mörs, Archbishop of, 317, 320.
— Frederick of Saarwerden, Archbishop of, 111, 112, 115, 117, 118, 157.
— Rupert, Archbishop of, 287.
Colonna family, the, 483.
Columbus, Bartholomew, 513.
— Christopher, 396, 400, 508, 511, 512 sqq.
Commynes, Philippe de, 242, 246, 248, 254, 258.
Compacts of Prague, the, 238, 239, 419, 420, 423.
*Compagnies d'ordonnance*, 88.
Compiègne, 56, 58, 77.
Constance, Council of, 6, 150, 161, 171 sqq., 194, 195, 219 sqq., 470.
Constantine XI, Byzantine Emperor, 437 sqq.
Constantinople, 202, 402, 425, 427, 429, 430, 431, 432, 434, 436 sqq., 444, 472.
— Joseph, Patriarch of, 203.
Copenhagen, 353.
Copernicus, 503.
Corfu, 443.
Cornelius, Bastard of Burgundy, 276.
Correggio, 500.
Corsica, 390, 391.
Cortes of Aragon, the, 386 sq., 389, 391.
— of Castile, the, 4, 379 sqq., 383, 385, 398.
— of Catalonia, 388, 391.
— of Portugal, 398, 400.
— of Valencia, 389, 391.
Cortona, 454.
Corvinus, John, 424.
— Matthias, King of Hungary, 322, 323, 418, 420, 421, 441.
Cosne, 58.
Cossa, Cardinal Baldassare, *see* John XXIII, Pope.
Costa, Lorenzo, 499.
Coster, Laurens Janszoon, 518.
Cotentin, the, 49, 90.
Couette, Thomas, 313.

Council, the Royal (French), 22, 35, 87, 92, 259, 264, 265, 266.
Courtecuisse, Jean, 146.
Cracow, 404, 415.
— Zbigniev, Bishop of, 410.
Craina (part of the coast of Dalmatia), Andreas, Archbishop of the, 483.
Cramaud, Simon de, Patriarch of Alexandria, 150.
Craon, Pierre de, 23.
Cravant, battle of, 65.
Crete, 443.
Croatia, 412.
Crusades, 7, 16 sq., 20, 27, 130, 163, 165, 167 sq., 193, 223, 226, 233, 234 sq., 284, 399, 427, 431, 435, 440, 467, 473, 474 sq., 477 sq., 481.
Cuba, 514.
Cyprus, 27, 444.
Czechs, the, *see* Bohemia.

## D

Daim, Olivier de, Count of Meulan, 262.
Dalecarlia, 374.
Dalmatia, 161, 411, 414, 447, 454.
Dammartin, Antoine de Chabannes, Count of, 242, 258.
Damme, 17, 19.
Danzig, 353, 374, 408, 418.
Dauphiné, 84, 93, 94, 243.
Denmark, 5, 6, 342, 349, 352, 353, 354, 368 sqq.
Despenser, Henry, Bishop of Norwich, 16–17, 130.
Deutschbrod, 230.
Deventer, 468, 493.
Diaz, Bartholomew, 511, 512.
— Diniz, 511, 512.
Dieppe, 83.
Diet, the German, 100, 101, 111, 118, 163, 165, 166, 169, 314, 315, 316, 318, 320.
Dietrich of Niem, 470.
Dijon, 254, 275, 309.
Dinant, 279.
Dobrzyn, 408.
Döffingen, battle of, 108.
Domrémy, 71.
Donatello, 495, 496.
Doriole, Pierre, 258.
Doyat, Jean de, 262.
Dreux, 58.
Dunkirk, 17.
Dunois, Bastard of Orleans, 67, 73, 90, 92, 245, 302.
Durazzo, 442, 444.
Dushan, Stephen, 429.

## E

Écorcheurs, the, 80, 85, 95, 338.
Edward, King of Portugal, 399.
Edward IV, King of England, 244, 250, 252 sq., 256, 356, 393.
Eger, Convention of, 197, 235.
Elba, 27.
Eleanor of Navarre, 393.
Electors, the German, 100, 102, 105, 109, 111, 112 sq., 157 sq., 162, 163, 164 sq., 195, 204, 284 sq., 314 sq., 316, 317, 320 sq., 323, 327.
Elizabeth of Poland, sister of Casimir III, 404.
— Queen of Hungary and Poland, 411, 412.
— wife of Albert II, King of the Romans, 314, 315.
El-Mahadia, 27.
Eltham, treaty of, 33.
Emden, 353.
Engelbrektsson, Engelbrekt, 372.
England, *see under* Richard II, Henry IV, and other English kings.
Épinal, 95.
Eric of Pomerania, King of Denmark, Norway, and Sweden, 370 sqq.
Ermeland, 418.
Estates of Alsace, 286.
— of Burgundy, 290.
— of Flanders, 280, 290.
— German, *see* Landtage.
Estates-General of France, the, 4, 11, 12, 84 sqq., 54 sq., 86, 247, 258, 259, 263 sqq., 301.
Estates, Provincial, of France, 12, 13, 55, 62, 65, 86, 259, 290, 301.
Este family, the, 463.
Étaples, treaty of, 269.
Eu, Charles, Count of, 45.
Eugenius IV (Gabriel Condolmaro), Pope, 96, 168 ; elected, 192 sq. ; defied by Council of Basel, 193 sqq. ; defeated by Council, 197 ; again at strife with the Council, 199 sqq. ; negotiates with the Eastern Church, 200, 202 sqq. ; deposed by Council of Basel, 204 sq. ; makes agreement with Frederick III, 316 sq. ; outwits the German Electors, 317 sq.
Évreux, 49, 87.

## F

Falaise, 48.
Falsterbo, 354.
Fastolf, Sir John, 73, 75, 76.
Fécamp, 83.

Felix V, anti-pope (Amadeus, Duke of Savoy), 205 sq., 317.
Ferdinand I, King of Aragon, 178, 179, 384, 391.
— II, King of Aragon, 257, 384, 393 sqq., 507, 513, 514.
— the Handsome, King of Portugal, 398.
Fernando Po, 511.
Ferrante, King of Naples, 392, 460, 462, 475, 477.
Ferrara, 202, 436, 463, 483.
Ferrer, Saint Vincent, 313.
Ferrette, county of, 282.
Filelfo, Francesco, 490.
Fillastre, William, Cardinal, 174, 180.
Flanders, 11, 14 sqq., 24, 25, 26, 31, 38, 41, 63, 85, 126, 249, 255, 274, 280, 282, 290, 293, 296, 298.
Florence, 115, 131, 141, 149, 153, 168, 171, 200, 447, 449, 452 sqq., 457 sq., 460 sqq., 482, 501.
— Council of, 203 sq., 436, 489.
Florentine school of painting, 498 sq.
Foix, Jean de Grailly, Count of, 65, 178, 179.
— Gaston IV, Count of, 245, 393.
Fondi, 126.
Forchheim, 112.
Forez, 308.
Formigny, battle of, 90
Fortebraccio, Niccolo, 197.
Foscari, Francesco, 455, 459.
*Fouages*, 11, 12, 13, 14.
Fougères, 89.
Fouquet, Jean, 497.
Fra Angelico, 498.
Fra Bartolommeo, 498.
Franche Comté, *see* Burgundy, county of.
Francia, Francesco, 499.
Francis de Paul, 261, 468.
Franconia, 108, 234, 320, 326, 334, 361.
Frankfort, 106, 111, 112, 114, 118, 157, 165, 166.
Frederick III, Emperor, 95, 206, 332, 417, 419 ; relations with Burgundy, 277, 283 sqq. ; his election, 315 ; character and policy, 315 sq. ; relations with the Papacy, 316 sqq., 331, 470, 480 ; crowned Emperor, 319 ; troubles with his subjects, 321 sqq., 361, 420 ; defeated by Matthias Corvinus, 323 ; his death, 324.
Free Archers, the, 89, 256, 260.
Freiburg (Switzerland), 336.
Friuli, 454.
Fugger family, the, 348.
Fust, John, 519, 521, 523.

# INDEX

## G

Gabelle, the, 11, 242, 276.
Gaeta, 153.
Gallipoli, 428, 429, 432.
Gascony, see Aquitaine.
Gaucourt, Raoul, lord of, 43.
Gaveren, battle of, 276.
Genoa, 26, 95, 111, 130, 144, 304, 428, 437, 438, 444, 445, 452, 454, 460, 505.
George Brankovic, despot of Serbia, 434, 435, 436, 440.
— of Podiebrad, King of Bohemia, 321 sqq., 415, 419, 471, 476, 480.
Gerson, John, 133, 140, 179, 190, 221, 469.
Ghent, 11, 14 sqq., 276, 279 sq.
Ghiberti, 495.
Ghirlandajo, Domenico, 498.
Giac, Pierre de, 64.
Gibraltar, 395.
Giengen, battle of, 322.
Gilds, 3, 7; of Paris, 16, 35 sq.; craft, 297 sq., 346, 347, 348, 452; religious, 468.
Giotto, 496, 498.
Giulio Romano, 494.
Giustiniani, John, 438, 439.
Glarus, 336.
Glendower, Owen, 29.
Gloucester, Humphrey, Duke of, 49, 59, 67, 83, 89, 272.
Golden Bull, the, 99, 326.
Golden Fleece, Order of the, 283.
Görlitz, duchy of, 102.
— Elizabeth of, 277.
Gothland, 352.
Granada, 378, 395 sq., 513.
Granson, battle of, 288 sq.
Greece, 428, 434, 436.
Greek Church, the, 191, 200 sq., 202 sqq., 209, 211, 402, 403, 406, 409, 416, 436, 437, 439.
Gregory XI (Pierre Roger), Pope, 125
— XII (Angelo Correr), Pope, 118, 143 sqq., 173, 174 sqq., 177, 216.
Guelders, Adolf, of, 283.
— Arnold, Duke of, 283.
— William, Duke of, 21, 28.
Guienne, see Aquitaine.
Guinea, 507, 510.
Guinegate, battle of, 255.
Guise, 56, 58.
Gutenberg, John, 519.

## H

Habsburg, House of, 101, 103, 116, 117, 314 sqq., 331, 332, 335.
— See also Albert II, Austria, Frederick III and Maximilian.

Habsburg, Albert of (brother of Frederick III), 315, 323.
— Frederick "the Penniless" of, Count of Tyrol, 161, 162, 175, 180, 315, 337.
— Leopold the elder of, 103, 107, 336.
— Leopold the Younger of, 115
— Sigismund of, Count of Tyrol, 254, 281 sq., 286, 315, 324, 337, 348, 475.
— William of, 405.
Hagenbach, Peter of, 283, 286, 287.
— Stephen of, 287, 288.
Hague, The, 275.
Hainault, 20, 67, 103, 254, 255, 272, 274.
— Jacqueline of, see Holland.
Haiti, 514.
Hakon VI, King of Norway, 369.
Halle, 329.
Hamburg, 353.
Hanseatic League, the, 3, 8, 104, 328, 329, 349 sqq., 366, 368, 407.
Harancourt, Guillaume de, Bishop of Verdun, 249.
Harcourt, Jacques d', 56, 57, 58.
Harfleur, 42 sq., 46, 83.
Hawkwood, John, 447, 449, 453.
Hegius, Alexander, 493.
Heimburg, Gregory, 475.
Henry III, King of Castile, 140, 379, 384, 506.
— IV, King of Castile, 384, 385, 393.
— IV, King of England, 33.
— V, King of England, 7, 33, 67, 89; claims the French throne, 39; negotiates with French, 39 sqq., 50, 51, 53, 59; invades France, 42; takes Harfleur, 43; fights at Agincourt, 44 sqq.; allies with Sigismund, 47, 162; conquers Normandy, 48 sqq., 52, 55 sq.; signs Treaty of Troyes, 53; marries, 53; as regent of France, 54 sqq., 60, 93; visits England, 56; renews offensive in France, 57 sqq.; dies, 58 sq.; influences Council of Constance, 184.
— VI, King of England, 59, 60, 79, 87, 89, 91, 250.
— VII, King of England, 268, 269.
— of Trastamara, King of Portugal, 379.
— the Navigator, Prince, 399, 507, 509 sqq.
Herrera, Diego de, 507, 508.
Herrings, battle of the, 73.
Herzegovina, the, 441.
Hesse, 112, 117, 325.
Heynlin, John, 521.

Hildesheim, 329, 345.
Hohenzollern, family of, 321, 326, 328, 334, 350.
— Frederick of, *see* Brandenburg.
Holland, 20, 101, 103, 272, 274, 518.
— Albert of Wittelsbach, Count of, 20, 103, 272.
— Jacqueline, Countess of, 47, 59, 67, 272.
— William of Ostrevant, Count of, 20, 47, 150, 272.
Holstein, 342, 358, 371 sqq.
— Adolf, Count of, 371, 373.
— Gerhard, Count of, 871.
Horodlo, Union of, 409, 423.
Humanists, the, 451, 471, 479, 481, 484, 488 sq., 500, 503, 523.
Hungary, 5, 6, 7, 108, 110, 117, 126, 161, 163, 231, 233, 314, 319, 324, 402, 403, 411 sqq., 420, 421 sqq., 433, 434, 435 sq., 437, 440, 441, 478.
Hunyadi, John, 415, 419, 421, 435 sq., 440.
Hus, John, 42, 161, 191, 211; early life, 213 sq.; as a preacher, 214, 216; his relation to Wycliffe, 214 sqq.; in conflict with the ecclesiastical authorities, 216 sqq.; at Constance, 173, 219 sqq.; his death, 177, 221 sq.
Hussites, the, 76, 163, 165, 167 sq., 192, 193, 197, 198, 199, 222 sqq., 320, 344, 403, 410, 420.

I

Iglau, 199.
Ile de France, 60, 76, 87, 263.
Ingeborg of Denmark, 369, 370.
Innocent VII (Cosimo Migliorati), Pope, 141 sq., 216.
— VIII (Giovanni Battista Cibo), Pope, 464, 484.
Inquisition, the Spanish, 397, 483.
Isabel of Bavaria, Queen of France, 21, 28, 29, 36, 47, 48, 50, 51, 52.
— Queen of England, 24, 25, 28.
Isabella of Portugal, Queen of Castile, 385.
— " the Catholic," Queen of Castile, 257, 884, 885, 886, 393 sqq., 507 sq., 513, 514.
— of Naples, 463.
Ivan III, Grand-duke of Muscovy, 354, 424.

J

Jacqueline of Hainault, *see* Holland.
Jadwiga, Queen of Poland, 405 sq., 410.

Jagello, Grand-duke of Lithuania, *see* Ladislas II, King of Poland.
Jakobek of Mies, 223.
James III, King of Scotland, 376.
Janissaries, the, 431, 432, 439.
Janow, Matthias of, 211, 215.
Jargeau, 75.
Jenson, Nicolas, 521.
Jerome of Prague, 178, 218, 223.
Jews, the, 12, 107, 362, 364, 383, 384, 387, 389, 397, 423.
Joan of Arc, 6, 69, 71 sqq., 96.
Joanna of Castile, " La Beltraneja," 385, 894.
— Enriquez, Queen of John II of Aragon, 392.
— I, Queen of Naples, 19, 128.
— II, Queen of Naples, 391, 456 sq.
— of Portugal, Queen of Henry IV of Castile, 385.
John Albert, King of Poland, 423.
— V, Byzantine Emperor, 429.
— VIII, Byzantine Emperor, 200, 203 sq., 436.
— Dauphin, 47.
— I, King of Aragon, 390
— II, King of Aragon, 251, 257, 392 sq., 395, 460.
— I, King of Castile, 130, 140, 379, 383, 398.
— II, King of Castile, 384, 391.
— King of Denmark, Norway and Sweden, 375.
— I, " the Great," King of Portugal, 898 sq., 400.
— II, King of Portugal, 400, 511, 512.
— of Falkenberg, 180, 186.
— of Gaunt, Duke of Lancaster, 20, 130, 379.
— of Luxemburg, Duke of Görlitz,102.
— XXIII (Baldassare Cossa), Pope, 149, 153, 171, 172 sqq., 188 sq., 217.
Jost, Margrave of Moravia, 102, 109, 116, 117, 157 sq.
Jouvenel des Ursins, Jean, 22, 302, 303, 307.

K

Kalmar, Union of, 5, 6, 352, 370 sq., 873, 375.
Kempten, abbey of, 362.
Kieff, Isidore, Archbishop of, 204.
Knutsson, Karl, 372, 373 sq.
Koberger, Anthony, 520, 522.
Königsberg, 353.
Korybut, Prince, *see* Lithuania.
Koszyce, Pact of, 404.
Knights of St. John (Hospitallers), 483, 445.
Kossovo, battles of, 430, 436.

# INDEX

Kremsier, Milic of, 211, 212.
Kroja, 442.
Kulm, 418.
Kunovica, battle of, 435.
Kuttenberg, 229 sq.
Kyriel, Sir Thomas, 90.

## L

La Brossinière, battle of, 65.
La Charité, 58, 77.
Ladislas Postumus, King of Bohemia and Hungary, 315, 322, 414, 415, 418 sq., 421.
— II, King of Bohemia (Ladislas VII, King of Hungary), 322, 324, 418, 420 sq., 422, 423, 424.
— King of Naples, 128, 131, 132, 139, 144, 145, 146, 149, 153, 154, 155, 161, 171, 218, 412, 413, 414, 454, 456.
— II (Jagello), King of Poland, 230, 405, 406, 408 sqq.
— III, King of Poland (Ladislas V, King of Hungary), 410 sq., 414 sq., 435 sq.
— Corvinus, 421.
La Hire (Étienne de Vignolles), 85.
Lalaing, Jacques de, 276, 304.
Landais, Peter, 266.
Landes, the, 90.
*Landtage* in Germany, 101, 325, 333, 334.
Languedoc, 13, 14, 22, 34, 49, 65, 86, 93, 298, 301.
Languedoil, 12, 34, 54, 86.
— Estates-General of, 86.
La Réole, 87.
La Rochelle, 54, 299.
La Salle, Gadifer de, 505 sq.
La Trémoille, George, Lord of, 64, 75, 80, 84, 300.
— Louis, Lord of, 267.
Lausanne, 206.
Lazar, Prince of Serbia, 430.
Lazarevic, Stephen, 431, 434.
Le Crotoy, 56, 58, 83.
Leghorn, 146, 454.
Leipzig, 217.
Le Mans, 24, 69, 89.
Leonardo da Vinci, 500.
Leonor Telles de Menezes, Queen of Portugal, 398.
Lepanto, 443.
Lermite, Tristan, 242.
Lewis II, King of Hungary and Poland, 404.
Lewis III, Elector Palatine, 114, 157, 162, 164, 173.
Liége, 245, 247, 248 sq., 277, 279 sqq., 248, 476.

Liége, John of Bavaria, Bishop of, 82
— Louis of Bourbon, Bishop of, 248, 276.
Lille, 15, 275.
Limburg, 272.
Lipan, battle of, 198, 237.
Lippi, Fra Filippo, 498.
— Filippino, 498.
Lisbon, 398, 514.
Lithuania, 403, 405 sq., 408, 409 sq., 415 sqq., 418, 423, 425.
— Grand-dukes of : Alexander, 423 ; Sigismund Korybut, 230, 232, 233, 409 sq. ; Swidrigiello, 409 ; Witold, 229, 230 sq., 408 sq.
Lizard, League of the, 416, 417.
Loches, 94.
Lodi, Peace of, 459.
Lorraine, duchy of, 71, 95, 252, 253, 258, 284, 288, 290 sq.
— John of Calabria, Duke of, 245, 246, 257, 258, 393, 460, 477.
— Nicolas, Duke of, 258, 285.
— René II, Duke of, 254, 267, 285, 288, 290, 464.
Louis, Dauphin, son of Charles VI, 31, 33, 36, 88, 46.
— XI, King of France, 7 ; as Dauphin, 84, 85, 93, 94, 95, 338 ; his character, 240 sq. ; relations with his ministers, 242, 249, 258 ; his domestic policy, 242 sq., 258 sqq. ; relations with the French nobility, 243 sqq., 249, 250 sq., 252, 253, 256 ; dealings with Charles the Bold, 244 sqq., 277 sqq., 254, 277, 278, 279, 281, 285, 286, 287, 288, 290, 291 ; dealings with Maximilian of Austria, 254 sq. ; relations with the Swiss, 253, 254, 260, 286, 288, 338 ; his foreign policy, 244, 249 sq., 252, 254, 256 sq. ; relations with René of Anjou, 257 sq. ; his death, 260 sq.
— de Maele, Count of Flanders, etc., 14 sq., 17, 272.
Louvet, Jean, 63.
Louviers, 49.
Lower Union, the, 286, 290.
Lübeck, 350, 351, 356.
Luca della Robbia, 495.
Lucca, 130, 145, 168, 457.
Lucerne, 336.
Luna, Alvaro de, 384 sq.
Lusatia, 102, 420, 422.
Luxemburg, duchy of, 28, 110, 277.
— House of, 28, 101 sq., 105, 116, 208, 210.
— Jacquetta of, Duchess of Bedford, 80.

## 540 EUROPE FROM 1378 TO 1494

Luxemburg, John of, 77.
— Wenzel, Duke of, 102.
— *See also* Jost; Sigismund; Wenzel, King of the Romans.
Lyons, 14, 35, 206, 297, 299, 300, 521.

## M

Mâcon, 82.
Madeira, 505, 507, 510.
Magdeburg, 103, 328, 331.
*Maillotins*, the, 12.
Maine, 41, 42, 56, 57, 65, 67, 80, 87, 89.
— Charles, Count of, 258.
Mainz, city of, 106, 519.
— province of, 102, 209.
— diet of (1439), 204.
— Adolf of Nassau, Archbishop of, 322.
— Berthold of Henneberg, Archbishop of, 323.
— Diether von Isenburg, Archbishop of, 322.
— John of Nassau, Archbishop of, 111, 112, 113, 117, 118, 157, 162.
Malaga, 395.
Malatesta family, the, 147.
— Carlo, Lord of Rimini, 149, 150, 153, 155, 173, 177.
— Gismondo, 477.
Malesset, Guy de, Cardinal, 150.
Mansion, Colard, 521.
Mantegna, 409.
Mantes, 51.
Mantua, Congress of, 474 sq.
Manuel II, Byzantine Emperor, 430, 432, 433, 434.
Manutius, Aldus, 521, 522.
Marbach, league of, 117.
Margaret of Anjou, Queen of England, 87, 250.
— of Austria, 256, 269.
— of Flanders, Duchess of Burgundy, 272.
— Queen of Denmark, Norway, and Sweden, 352, 369 sqq.
— Queen of Scotland, 376.
— of York, Duchess of Burgundy, 248, 253, 281.
Maria of Aragon, Queen of Castile, 385.
— Queen of Sicily, 390.
Marienburg, 409, 417, 418.
Maritza, battle of the, 430.
*Marmousets*, the, 22, 24.
Marseilles, 144, 301.
Martin I, King of Aragon (Martin II of Sicily), 138, 152, 390 sq.
— I, King of Sicily, 390 sq.
— V (Otto Colonna), Pope, 67, 81, 162, 167, 185; policy of, 188 sqq., 223, 233, 234, 456.

Marville, Jean de, 496.
Mary, Queen of Hungary, 405, 411, 412, 413.
Masaccio, 498.
Maximilian I, King of the Romans, 254, 255, 266, 282, 283, 316, 328 sqq., 334, 354, 424.
Meaux, 58, 86, 303.
Mecklenburg, 104, 329, 352.
— Henry of, 369.
Medici family, the, 457, 458, 460, 490
— Cosimo de', 457 sq., 459, 460.
— Giovanni de', 457.
— Giuliano de', 462.
— Lorenzo de', 458, 461, 462 sq., 464, 484, 494.
— Piero I de', 460 sq.
— Piero II de', 464.
— Salvestro de', 452.
Meissen, 104, 165.
Melun, 54.
Memel, 405, 407.
Mentelin, John, 523.
Meulan, 51, 53.
Michael Angelo, 494, 500.
Mies, 233.
Milan, 110, 113, 114, 205, 337, 447, 452, 453, 455, 457, 460, 461, 462, 463 sq., 465, 599.
— *See also* Sforza and Visconti.
Mohammed I, Sultan, 433 sq., 443.
— II, Sultan, 3, 436 sqq., 443, 444.
Moldavia, 416, 422.
Molinella, battle of, 448.
Mombasa, 515.
Monaco, 27.
Monemvasia, 445.
Montargis, 69.
Montdidier, 82, 250.
Montenegro, 441.
Montereau-faut-Yonne, 52, 54, 82, 84.
Montlhéry, 246.
Montpellier, 11, 301.
Mont St. Michel, 52.
Moors, the, 378, 382, 383, 384, 389, 395 sq., 399.
Morat, battle of, 289.
Moravia, 102, 208, 222, 231, 232, 237, 238, 420, 421, 422.
Moravian Church, the, 419.
Morea, the, 428, 436, 443, 444.
Morocco, 507.
Mortagne, 48.
Moscow, 354, 406.
Mozambique, 515.
Mülhausen, 282, 286, 337.
Müller, Johann Regiomontanus, 503.
Murad I, Sultan, 429, 430.
— II, Sultan, 434 sqq.
Muscovy, Grand-duchy of, 354, 406, 418, 424.

# INDEX

## N

Näfels, battle of, 336.
Namur, 274.
Nancy, 72, 253, 288, 290 sq.
Naples, kingdom of, 19, 23, 26, 87, 95, 128, 129, 131, 147, 258, 391, 411, 442, 447, 451, 453, 456 sq., 460, 461, 462, 463, 464, 465.
Narbonne, capitulation of, 178, 181.
Navarre, 126, 178, 179, 257, 378, 392, 395.
— Blanche of, Queen of Aragon, 392.
Naxos, 445.
Negropont, 444.
Nemours, Jacques d'Armagnac, Duke of, 245, 247, 253.
Nesle-en-Vermandois, 251.
Neumark, 102.
Neuss, 287 sq.
Nevers, 81, 272.
Nicaea, Bessarion, Archbishop of, 204.
Nice, 173, 177.
Nicolas V (Thomas of Sarzana), Pope, 206, 318, 321, 470, 490.
— de Clémanges, 470.
— of Cusa, Cardinal, 475, 491, 503.
Nicopolis, battle of, 27, 28, 110, 304, 418, 431.
Nimwegen, 283.
Nish, 433, 435.
Nocera, 129, 130.
Normandy, 13, 28, 33, 38, 41, 42, 48 ; Estates of, 57, 59, 76, 81, 87, 246, 247, 259 ; English conquest of, 48, 49, 50 sq., 52 ; English rule in, 55 sq., 60, 61, 62, 80, 83 ; French recovery of, 87, 90, 301 sq.
Norway, 5, 368 sqq.
Novgorod, 354, 355, 425.
Nürnberg, 165, 166, 316, 317, 320, 328, 345, 367.

## O

Oberlahnstein, 113.
Olaf VI, King of Denmark and Norway, 352, 369.
Olmedo, battle of, 386.
Olmütz, Treaty of, 422, 424.
Orkhan, Sultan, 429.
Orkney Island, 376.
Orléans, 69, 73 sqq., 140.
— Charles, Duke of, 28, 32, 36, 40, 45, 84, 87, 95, 305, 458.
— Louis I, Duke of (brother of Charles VI), 21, 22, 23, 24, 26, 27 sqq., 111, 117, 128, 136, 137, 139, 140, 143, 411, 435.
— Louis II, Duke of, 261, 262, 266, 267.
Otranto, 444, 462.
Oxford, Bohemians at, 214.

## P

Padua, 115, 454, 499.
Palos, 514.
Papal States, the, 26, 128, 129, 131, 144, 147, 153, 155, 188, 447, 456, 470, 480.
Paris, 10, 11 sq., 28, 29, 30, 31, 82, 33, 84, 85, 46, 48, 52, 53, 77, 137, 142, 143, 144, 240, 246, 521 ; risings in, 12 sq., 16, 35 sq., 37 sq., 49 ; captured by the Burgundians, 49 sq. ; under Henry V, 54 sq. ; captured for Charles VII, 82 sq.
— Parlement of, 22, 35, 37, 38, 55, 60, 64, 93, 94, 142, 249, 251, 253, 254, 259, 260, 262.
— University of, 10, 81, 84, 35, 86 ; denounces Joan of Arc, 79 ; attitude of, towards Great Schism, 25, 112, 127, 132 sqq., 135, 138, 140, 142, 145, 150, 155.
Parlement of Paris, see Paris.
Parlements, provincial, 93, 251.
Parliament, the English, 19, 41, 56, 67, 82, 131, 325, 380.
Passau, 331.
Patay, battle of, 76.
Paul II (Pietro Barbo), Pope, 420, 480 sq., 491.
Pavia, 186, 190, 452.
Payne, Peter, 325.
Pazzi family, the, 462.
Peñiscola, 178.
Perez, Juan, 513.
Péronne, 44, 82, 248, 279.
Perpignan, 147, 148, 178.
Perugia, 130, 132, 454.
Perugino, 499.
Peter IV, King of Aragon, 390.
— the Cruel, King of Castile, 379.
Petit, John, 31, 134, 142, 179, 186.
Petrarch, 494.
Philip the Fair, Count of Flanders, 256, 324.
— of Mézières, 10.
Picardy, 28, 33, 56, 60, 76, 250, 252, 255, 256, 267.
Picquigny, treaty of, 252.
Pillenreuth, battle of, 320.
Pilsen, 236.
Pinzon, Martin, 513, 514.
Pisa, 146, 454.
— Council of, 118, 147, 148 sqq., 454.
Pisano, Giovanni, 496.
— Niccolo, 496.
Pius II (Aeneas Sylvius Piccolomini), Pope, 96, 317, 322, 420, 442, 471, 474 sqq., 491.
Platina, 481, 490, 491.
Plessis-les-Tours, 240, 261.

Podiebrad, *see* George.
Podolia, 415.
Poggio Bracciolini, 471, 489.
Poitiers, 20, 64, 72.
Poitou, 42, 64, 84.
Poland, the Poles, 5, 6, 149, 163, 180, 186, 190, 234, 341, 353, 402, 403, 404 sqq., 414 sqq., 420, 422 sq., 424.
Politian, 490, 512.
Pomerania, 104, 325.
Pomerellia, 408.
Pomponius, 481, 490, 491.
Pont de l'Arche, 49.
Ponthieu, 42, 82.
Pontoise, 38, 52, 83, 87.
Portugal, 5, 7, 127, 131, 149, 181, 378, 394, 398 sqq., 505, 507, 508 sqq.
Pot, Philippe, 264.
Pouilly, Treaty of, 51.
Pragmatic Sanction of Bourges, 86, 96, 204, 264.
Pragmatic Sanction of St. Louis, 96.
Prague, 210, 212, 214, 217, 218 sq., 225, 226 sq., 231, 232, 233, 237, 239, 419, 423.
— Compacts of, 238, 239, 419, 420, 423, 476.
— the Four Articles of, 226, 227, 229, 230, 233, 234, 235, 236, 237, 238.
— University of, 210, 212, 213 sqq., 216 sq., 218, 226.
— Zbynek of Hasenburg, Archbishop of, 216, 218.
*Praguerie*, the, 84.
Pressburg, 234.
— Treaty of, 424.
Printing, invention of, 517 sqq.
Procop the Great, 167, 192, 197, 232 sqq., 404.
Provence, 26, 138, 154, 258.
Prussia, 103, 353, 403, 406 sqq., 416 sqq.
Pteleon, 444.
Puck, battle of, 418.
Pulci, 494.

R

Rais, Gilles de, 80, 312 sq.
Raphael, 500.
Ravenna, 456.
Reichstag, the, *see* Diet, the German.
Renaissance, the Italian, 1, 4, 8, 342, 367, 401, 471 sq., 481, 486 sqq.
Rense, 113.
Rheims, 11, 21, 34, 75, 76, 111, 136, 242, 261.
— Renaud de Chartres, Archbishop of, 75.
Riario family, the, 481 sq.
Ricci, the, 452.

Richard II, King of England, 10, 17, 21, 23, 24 sq., 105, 130, 136.
— III, King of England, 267.
Richemont, Arthur, Count of, afterwards Duke of Brittany, 45, 63, 80, 81, 83, 84, 92.
Rieux, Marshal, 267.
Rimini, 149, 154, 477, 480.
Rio de Oro, 510.
Ripaille, 205.
Rocca Secca, battle of, 154.
Rokycana, John, 233, 235, 419.
Rolin, Nicolas, 307.
Romagna, the, 456.
Roman Academy, the, 481.
Rome, 23, 125, 127, 129, 130, 132, 136, 139, 141, 144, 146, 149, 153, 154, 155, 168, 171, 188, 192, 193, 200, 204, 318, 451, 456, 471, 472, 480, 483, 484.
— *See also under* individual popes.
Roosebeke, battle of, 15.
Rostock, 329, 353.
Rouen, 12, 13, 16, 35, 43, 49; siege of, 50 sq., 55, 56, 60, 78 sq., 80, 81, 90, 302.
— Jean de la Rochetaillée, Archbishop of, 191.
Roussillon, 147, 257, 269, 393.
Rovigo, 463, 464.
Roye, 82.
Rumelia, 428.
Rupert, King of the Romans, Elector Palatine, 2, 102, 110, 111, 112, 113 sqq., 140, 148, 150, 154, 157, 447, 454.
Russia, 354, 358, 402, 406, 424 sq.

S

Saaz (Zatec), 229.
Sablé, Treaty of, 268.
Sagres (Cape St. Vincent), 509.
Saintrailles, Poton de, 85.
Salisbury, Robert Hallam, Bishop of, 184.
— Thomas Montagu, Earl of, 55, 57, 65, 69, 73.
Salonica, 428, 429, 434.
Salzburg, 331, 332, 361.
— Piligrim, Archbishop of, 107.
Samogitia, 408, 409.
Sandwich, 92.
San Jorge de Mina, 511.
San Thomé, 511.
Santiago, Military Order of, 382, 384.
Sardinia, 27, 390, 391.
Savona, 144.
Savoy, Amadeus VI, Count of, 429.
— Amadeus VIII, Count, afterwards Duke of, 150, 205.

# INDEX 543

Savoy, Amadeus IX, Duke of, 256.
— Charlotte of, Queen of France, 94.
— Yolande, Duchess of, 251, 256, 288, 290.
Saxe-Wittenberg, duchy of, 102, 165.
Saxony, Frederick I of Meissen, Elector of, 165, 232, 234.
— Frederick II, Elector of, 234, 315, 321.
— Rudolf III, Elector of, 102, 109, 112, 113, 157.
— William of (brother of the Elector Frederick II), 277.
Scala, Antonio della, 453.
Scales, Edward Woodville, Lord, 268.
— Thomas, Lord, 73.
Scanderbeg, 435, 436, 441 sq., 444.
Scania, 354.
Scarampi, Cardinal, 473.
Schaffhausen, 175, 336.
Schism, the Great, 22, 25, 105, 111, 112, 118, 120 sqq., 171 sqq., 309, 330, 391, 411.
Schoeffer, Peter, 519, 523.
Scotland, the Scots, 6, 54, 57, 65, 66, 126, 135, 147, 179, 368.
Sées, 48.
Segovia, 386.
Semendria, 434.
Sempach, battle of, 336.
Senegal, river, 504, 510.
Senlis, Treaties of, 253, 269.
Sens, 54.
Serbia, 429 sq., 431, 432, 433, 434, 435, 436, 440, 441.
Sforza, Attendolo, 456.
— Francesco, Duke of Milan, 197, 246, 455 sq., 458 sqq., 462.
— Galeazzo Maria, Duke of Milan, 290.
— Gian Galeazzo, Duke of Milan, 462, 463.
— Ludovico (Il Moro), 463 sq., 465.
Shetland Islands, 376.
Sicily, 23, 87, 154, 390, 391, 392, 460.
Siena, 145, 147, 153, 168, 190, 454, 462.
Sigismund, Emperor, 2, 81, 82, 102, 110 ; character of, 99, 158 sqq. ; his relations with King Wenzel, 108, 109, 110, 113, 114, 116 sqq., 158, 160, 223 ; secures the Hungarian crown, 108, 405, 411 sq. ; policy of, as King of Hungary, 409, 412 sqq. ; fights the Turks, 110, 167, 414, 431 ; attitude towards the Great Schism, 139 sq., 148, 154, 161 sq., 171, 177, 178 ; elected King of the Romans, 157 sq. ; his relations with Ger-

Sigismund, Emperor (contd.)—
many, 160 sq., 162 sqq., 167, 169, 365 ; at war with Venice, 161, 414, 447 ; his relations with Hus, 219, 220, 222 ; at the Council of Constance, 173 sq., 177, 181 sq., 183, 184 ; succeeds to the Bohemian crown, 163, 225, 227 ; fights the Hussites, 163, 167 sqq., 226 sq., 229, 234 ; crowned Emperor, 168, 447 ; his dealings with Eugenius IV, 168 ; attitude towards the Council of Basel, 168, 192, 196, 199 ; reconciled with the Hussites, 199, 237, 238 sq. ; accepted as King of Bohemia, 239 ; dies, 169.
— of Habsburg, Count of Tyrol, see Habsburg.
Silesia, 102, 233, 420, 422.
Sixtus IV (Francesco of Savona), Pope, 261, 331, 461, 463, 464, 481 sqq., 490.
Skanör, 354.
Slesvig, 342, 371, 373 sq., 376.
Sluter, Claus, 496.
Smyrna, 433.
Soest, 320.
Sofia, 440.
Soissons, 38.
Solothurn, 336.
Somerset, Edmund Beaufort, Duke of, 90.
— John Beaufort, Earl and Duke of, 57, 87.
Somme river, 44, 56, 82, 245, 249, 252.
— towns of, 245, 247.
Sophia, Queen of Bohemia, 216, 217, 223, 225.
Sorel, Agnes, 92, 94, 302.
Speyer, 103, 331.
Squarcione, Francesco, 499.
St. Amand, 82.
St. Aubin-du-Cormier, battle of, 268.
St. Denis, 33, 38, 77, 83.
St. Gall, abbey of, 336.
St. George, Company of, 127.
— Society of, 106 sq.
St. Jakob, battle of, 338.
St. Malo, 268.
St. Maur-les-Fossés, Treaty of, 246.
St. Omer, Treaty of, 282, 286 sq.
St. Pol, Louis of Luxemburg, Count of, 253.
St. Quentin, 44, 250.
Stans, Compact of, 337.
Stitny, Thomas of, 211, 212 sq.
Stockholm, 352, 370, 373.
Stralsund, Treaty of, 369.
Strasbourg, 103, 106, 180, 520.

Sture, Sten, Regent of Sweden, 375.
Styria, 103, 315, 361.
Subiaco, 520.
Suffolk, William de la Pole, Earl and Duke of, 73, 87, 89.
Swabia, 103, 107, 108, 281, 324.
Swabian League : (i), 106, 107, 108 ; (ii), 324, 349, 362.
Sweden, 5, 6, 352, 358, 368 sqq.
Swiss Confederation, the Swiss, 107, 282 ; Habsburgs defeated by, 336, 337 ; character of the Confederation, 335, 336 sq. ; its expansion, 336, 337 sq. ; Swiss relations with France, 95, 253, 254, 260, 262, 268, 286, 338 ; Swiss breach with Burgundy, 285, 286 ; Swiss defeat Charles the Bold, 288 sqq., 338 ; their military methods, 338 sq.
Sylvius, Aeneas, *see* Pius II, Pope.

T

Taborites, the, 224, 225, 226, 227, 230, 232, 235, 237.
Tachau, 233.
Talbot, John, Earl of Shrewsbury, 69, 73, 75, 76, 87, 91.
Tamerlane (Timur), 379, 432.
Tangier, 399, 400.
Tannenberg, battle of, 408, 416.
Tatars, the, 402, 424, 425, 433.
Tauss, 168, 193, 235.
Teutonic Order, the, 103, 163, 180, 342, 352, 353, 403, 404, 406 sqq., 410, 416 sqq., 422.
Tewkesbury, battle of, 250.
Thérouanne, David, Bishop of (also Bishop of Utrecht), 276.
Thorn, Peace of : (1411), 409 ; (1466), 418.
Thurgau, 337.
Timur, *see* Tamerlane.
Toggenburg Succession, War of the, 338.
Toplica, battle of the, 430.
Tordesillas, Treaty of, 396.
Toros de Guisando, Treaty of, 386, 394.
Toul, 95, 284.
Toulouse, 93, 140.
Touques, 48.
Touraine, 41, 42, 240.
— Louis, Duke of, *see* Orléans.
Tournai, 18, 75, 82.
Tours, 47, 48, 65, 86, 244, 247, 250, 258, 259.
Trent, 115, 162, 180.
Treviso, 453.
Trier, 284 sq.

Trier, Jacob of Sirk, Archbishop of, 317, 321.
— Werner of Falkenstein, Archbishop of, 111, 112, 157.
Trondhjem, 373.
Troyes, 48.
— Treaty of, 53, 54, 55, 56, 60, 81, 299.
*Tuchins*, the, 14.
Tunis, 27.
Turks, the, 5, 200, 314, 473, 475, 478, 504 ; conquer the Balkan peninsula, 428 sqq., 432, 433 sq., 440 sq., 443 sq. ; at war with Hungary, 412, 414, 421, 422, 431, 484 sqq., 440, 441 ; defeated by Timur, 432 sq. ; capture Constantinople, 436 sqq. ; checked by Scanderbeg, 441 sq. ; at war with Venice, 442 sqq. ; invade German territory, 319, 324, 361 ; invade Italy, 444.
Tver, 425.
Tvrtko, King of Bosnia, 430.
Tyrol, 103, 104, 162, 281, 324.
— Counts of, *see under* Habsburg.

U

Ulman, Hans, 362.
Ulrich of Rosenberg, 419.
Unity of the Brethren, 419, 420.
Upsala, John Oxenstierna, Archbishop of, 374.
— University of, 375.
Urban VI (Bartholomew Prignano), Pope, 16, 109, 125 sqq.
Uri, 337.
Utraquists or Calixtines, 224, 226, 229, 230, 233, 236, 237, 238, 419, 423, 476, 485.
Utrecht, 276, 284.

V

Valais, 336.
Valencia, 386, 389.
Valla, Lorenzo, 471, 472, 489.
Valladolid, 394.
Val Leventina, 337.
Van der Weyden, Roger, 497.
Van Eyck brothers, 497.
Vannes, 267.
Varna, battle of, 415, 435 sq.
Vasco da Gama, 512, 515.
Vatican, the, 472.
Vaucouleurs, 72.
*Vehmgericht*, the, 362 sqq.
Velay, 308.
Vendôme, Louis, Count of, 45.
Venice, 115, 144, 148, 153, 347, 447, 449, 499 sq., 520 sq. ; at war with

# INDEX

Venice (*contd.*)—
  Sigismund, 161, 168, 414; her Eastern possessions, 428, 443 sq., 445; at war with the Turks, 433, 437, 440, 442 sqq., 463, 478; her Italian policy, 452, 453, 454 sq., 459, 461, 462, 463, 464 sq.
Verdun, 95, 284.
Verneuil, battle of, 66.
Vernon, 51.
Verona, 453.
Vicenza, 453.
Victualling Brothers, the, 352.
Vienna, 317, 323, 424, 425.
— Concordat of, 318.
Villandrando, Rodrigo de, 80, 85.
Villon, François, 309.
Visconti, Bernabo, Lord of Milan, 452.
— Bianca, 458.
— Filippo Maria, Duke of Milan, 65, 161, 168, 190, 197, 454, 455, 456, 457, 458.
— Galeazzo, Lord of Milan, 452.
— Gian Galeazzo, Duke of Milan, 22, 110, 111, 114, 115, 116, 128, 452, 453 sq.
— Valentina, Duchess of Touraine and Orléans, 22, 31, 32, 128, 453, 458.
— Virida, daughter of Bernabo, 459.
Vivarini family, the, 499.
Volhynia, 415.

## W

Waldemar III, King of Denmark, 369.
Waldenses, the, 209.
Waldhausen, Conrad of, 211.
Waldshut, 282.
Wallachia, 430, 433, 444.
— Mircea, Prince of, 431, 432.
— Vlad II, Prince of, 435.
Wandomme, the Bastard of, 77.
Warwick, Richard Beauchamp, Earl of, 67, 83.
— Richard Neville, Earl of, 250, 356.

Wassili IV, Grand-duke of Muscovy, 354.
Welf family, 109, 112, 325.
Wenzel, King of the Romans, 100, 102, 118, 136, 214, 453; character of, 105 sq.; his relations with Germany, 105 sqq., 110 sq., 157 sq., 364; his dealings with Sigismund, 108, 109, 110, 113, 116, 117, 157 sq., 411; deposed by the German Electors, 112 sqq.; as King of Bohemia, 105 sq., 110, 111, 113, 117, 216 sq.; relations with Hus and the Hussites, 217 sqq., 223, 225; dies, 163, 225.
Westphalia, 320, 363 sqq.
Wettin family, 104, 112, 165, 320, 321, 325, 327, 329, 331.
— *See also* Meissen and Saxony.
Wiener Neustadt, 321.
Winkelried, Arnold, 336.
Wisby, 352.
Witold, *see* Lithuania.
Wittelsbach family, 20, 28, 102, 103 sq., 107, 112, 320, 321 sq., 372.
Wordingborg, peace of, 353.
Würtemberg, 104, 326.
— Eberhard, Count of, 324.
— Ulrich, Count of, 106, 117.
Wycliffe, John, 155, 191, 214, 215.

## Y

York, Edward, Duke of, 39.
— Edward of Langley, Duke of, 398.
— Richard, Duke of, 83.
Ypres, 15, 17.

## Z

Zara, 161.
Zatec (Saaz), 229.
Zeeland, 20, 103, 272, 274.
Zell, Ulrich, 520.
Zizka, John, 163, 192, 225 sqq., 404.
Zürich, 338.